HARNESSING AUTOCAD®

Thomas A. Stellman
G. V. Krishnan
and
Robert A. Rhea

 Delmar Publishers Inc.

NOTICE TO THE READER

Publisher does not warrant or guarantee any of the products described herein or perform any independent analysis in connection with any of the product information contained herein. Publisher does not assume, and expressly disclaims, any obligation to obtain and include information other than that provided to it by the manufacturer.

The reader is expressly warned to consider and adopt all safety precautions that might be indicated by the activities described herein and to avoid all potential hazards. By following the instructions contained herein, the reader willingly assumes all risks in connection with such instructions.

The publisher makes no representations or warranties of any kind, including but not limited to, the warranties of fitness for particular purpose or merchantability, nor are any such representations implied with respect to the material set forth herein, and the publisher takes no responsibility with respect to such material. The publisher shall not be liable for any special, consequential or exemplary damages resulting, in whole or in part, from the readers' use of, or reliance upon, this material.

Cover design and illustration by Michael Speke.

Delmar Staff:
   Associate Editor: Kevin Johnson
   Developmental Editor: Mary Beth Ray
   Project Editor: Judith Boyd Nelson
   Production Supervisor: Wendy Troeger
   Senior Design Supervisor: Susan C. Mathews

Trademarks
AutoCAD® is registered in the U.S. Patent and Trademark Office by Autodesk, Inc.
AutoLISP® is registered in the U.S. Patent and Trademark Office by Autodesk, Inc.

Chapter opener art for Chapters 1, 15, 16, and 17 courtesy of Autodesk, Inc.
Chapter opener art for Chapter 5 courtesy of CalComp Inc.
Chapter opener art for Chapter 14 courtesy of Summagraphics Corporation.

For information, address Delmar Publishers, Inc.
2 Computer Drive West, Box 15-015
Albany, NY 12212-9985

Copyright © 1992 by Delmar Publishers Inc.

Printed in the United States of America
Published simultaneously in Canada
by Nelson Canada
a division of The Thomson Corporation

10 9 8 7 6 5 4 3 2 1

Library of Congress Cataloging-in-Publication Data

Stellman, Thomas A.
       Harnessing AutoCAD / Thomas A. Stellman, G.V. Krishnan, and Robert
   Rhea.
            p. cm.
       Includes index.
       ISBN 0-8273-4685-9 (text). -- ISBN 0-8273-4686-7 (IG)
       1. Computer graphics. 2. AutoCAD (Computer program).
   I. Krishnan, G. V.   II. Rhea, Robert A.   III. Title.
T385.S75   1992
620'.0042'02855369—dc20   91-44931
                                                            CIP

CONTENTS

Chapter 9   Utility Commands 529

Display Option 542
ON Option 542
OFF Option 542
Reset Option 542
AUDIT COMMAND 542

Chapter 10   Special Features—Slides and Scripts 543

MSLIDE—MAKING A SLIDE 543
SLIDE LIBRARIES 544
VSLIDE—VIEWING A SLIDE 545
SCRIPT 546
The Script Text 546
Scripts with the ACAD.EXE Initiation 546
Spaces and End-of-Lines in Script Files 547
Changing Block Definitions with a Script File 547
Scripts from within the Editor 551
Utility Commands for Script 551
Delay Subcommand 551
Resume Subcommand 551
GRAPHSCR and TEXTSCR Subcommands 551
RSCRIPT Subcommand 552

Chapter 11   Isometric Drawing 553

DRAWING TOOLS 556
ISOMETRIC CIRCLES 558
ISOMETRIC TEXT 558
ISOMETRIC DIMENSIONING 558
PROJECT EXERCISE — CREATING THE PROJECT DRAWING 560
LAB EXERCISES 11-1 THROUGH 11-7 571

Chapter 12   AutoCAD 3D 585

WHAT IS 3D? 585
VIEWING 586
VPOINT Command 586
Rotate Option 588
Using Icons 588
DVIEW Command 589
CAmera Option 591
TArget Option 593
Distance Option 595
Off Option 595
POints Option 596
PAn Option 596

Appendix A Hardware and Software Introduction 829

Appendix B DOS and File Handling 839

PREFACE

Writing a book on AutoCAD® is much like reigning in a team of wild horses, with each new release unleashing greater design and graphics power. *Harnessing AutoCAD®* is a book written to give you skills to reign in and channel this seemingly boundless program so that AutoCAD® is working for you.

We have created a comprehensive book providing information, references, instructions and exercises for persons of varied skill levels, disciplines, and requirements for applying this powerful design/drafting software. The book opens with an overview of all aspects of AutoCAD® so that the student can get a good feeling of how CAD works. Students immediately gain a broad range of knowledge of the elementary CAD concepts necessary to complete a simple drawing. We do not believe the student should be asked to wade through all components of every command or concept the first time that command or concept is introduced. Therefore, we have set up the early chapters so that fundamentals are covered and practiced extensively to better prepare the students for the more advanced topics covered later in the book. For example, basic skills and knowledge about LAYERS and DIMENSIONING are within the capabilities of a novice AutoCAD® user, but the newcomer need not be burdened with everything there is to know about these features on the first drawing. Likewise, DRAW and EDIT features like LINE, MOVE, and COPY should be applied to a completed drawing before tackling commands such as PLINE (Polyline) and ARRAY.

Harnessing AutoCAD® is intended to be both a classroom text and a desk reference with tabs for easy access to particular chapters. Highlights of the book include:

- the new release of AME 2.0
- presentation of AutoCAD® for WINDOWS Extension
- all features of AutoCAD® Release 11 covered in detail, including:
  - DRAW, EDIT, DIMENSIONING, BLOCKS, LAYERS, DISPLAY, DRAWING SETUP, and UTILITIES
  - Plotting
  - Attributes and data extraction
  - Customizing menus
  - Hatch patterns
  - Shapes and fonts
  - AutoLISP programming
  - and external references

All commands are accompanied by examples. Ample exercises are designed to give readers the chance to test their level of skill and understanding. In addition, appendices are included that cover such subjects as the disk operating system (DOS), hardware (that part of the computer station you can put your hands on), and other valuable tables of information for ready reference. A sequence suitable

for learning, ample exercises and examples, and thorough coverage of the AutoCAD®
program should make *Harnessing AutoCAD®* a must for multiple courses in
AutoCAD®, as well as self-learners, everyday operators on the job, and aspiring
customizers.

ABOUT THE AUTHORS

Thomas A. Stellman received a B.A. degree in architecture from Rice University and has over 20 years of experience in the architecture, engineering, and construction industry. He has taught at the college level for over ten years and has been teaching courses in AutoCAD since the introduction of version 1.4 in 1984. He is the author of *Practical AutoLISP* (Delmar Publishers, 1990), and conducts seminars covering both introduction to AutoLISP and advanced AutoLISP. In addition, he develops and markets third-party software for AutoCAD. He is currently a CADD consultant, AutoLISP programmer, and project coordinator for Testenger, Inc. in Port Lavaca, Texas.

G. V. Krishnan is director of the Applied Business and Technology Center, University of Houston—Downtown, an authorized AutoCAD Training Center and Autodesk Multimedia Training Center. He has used AutoCAD since the introduction of version 1.4 and writes about AutoCAD from the standpoint of a user, instructor, and general CADD consultant to area industries. He has taught for the last seven years courses ranging from basic to advanced levels of AutoCAD, including customizing, 3D AutoCAD, solid modeling, and AutoLISP programming.

Robert Rhea is an associate professor in the Engineering Technology Department at the University of Houston—Downtown. He is the coordinator of the Process and Piping Design program, the only four-year B.S. degree in Piping offered in the United States. He is a co-author of *Using Intergraph MicroStation, PC* (Delmar Publishers, 1990) and has taught AutoCAD in professional development programs and regular CAD courses at the college level for six years.

Contributions by David G. Wilson to the AutoCAD for Windows chapter (Chapter 17) are acknowledged and appreciated.

CHAPTER
1   Overview

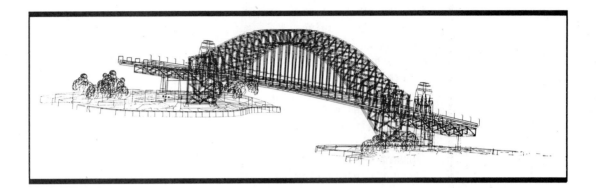

The beginning of this chapter describes how to get into the AutoCAD Editor to create and save a drawing file on the computer. If you need to set up the AutoCAD program on the computer and you are not familiar with computer operating systems (files, drives, directories, operating system commands, etc.) you may wish to review the Appendix on Disk Operating System (DOS), refer to the Installation & Performance Guide that comes with the program, and/or consult the dealer from whom you purchased AutoCAD. Once the computer is set up (which may be the case if you are using this book in the classroom), you will have at your disposal a powerful design/drafting tool that continues to grow in power with each new release.

The balance of this chapter is a brief overview of the basic concepts, commands, and skills which can help you use AutoCAD to its fullest. Some of the concepts involve general drafting principles. These concepts, while not specifically tied to a particular command, are the "tools of the trade" for all drafters and designers and the backbone of a Computer-Aided Drafting and Design (CAD) program. Detailed explanations and examples are provided for the concepts and commands throughout the chapters that follow.

Commands are divided into related categories as much as possible by AutoCAD. For example, DRAW is not a command, but a category of commands used for creating primary entities such as lines, circles, arcs, text (lettering), and other useful objects that are visible on the screen. Other categories include EDIT, DISPLAY, and another group listed under SETTINGS for controlling the electronic drawing environment. The commands under SETTINGS are also referred to as "Tools," "Drawing Aids," and "Utility Commands" throughout the book. Learning the program can progress at a better pace if the concepts and commands are mentally grouped into their proper categories. This not only helps you find them when you need them, but also helps you grasp the fundamentals of computer-aided drafting more quickly.

```
        A U T O C A D (R)
Copyright (c) 1982-91  Autodesk, Inc.  All Rights Reserved.
Release R11 c2 (4/5/91) 386 DOS Extender
Serial Number:  117-10024292




Main Menu

  0.  Exit AutoCAD
  1.  Begin a NEW drawing
  2.  Edit an EXISTING drawing
  3.  Plot a drawing
  4.  Printer Plot a drawing

  5.  Configure AutoCAD
  6.  File Utilities
  7.  Compile shape/font description file
  8.  Convert old drawing file
  9.  Recover damaged drawing

Enter selection:
```

Figure 1-1 The Main Menu

MAIN MENU

Design/drafting is what AutoCAD (and this book) is all about. So, how do you get into the Drawing Editor? If you (or the person who has set up the computer for AutoCAD) has not provided a menu in DOS to call up the AutoCAD program, then you should first log onto the drive/directory (using DOS) that the AutoCAD program files are on. Then you can type in ACAD. This causes the ACAD.EXE program file to activate AutoCAD. This, in turn, will cause AutoCAD's Main Menu to be displayed on your screen (see Figure 1-1). Several tasks (other than drawing) are possible to initiate from the Main Menu. For now, however, we will be concerned primarily with those that you would use to create a new drawing or edit an existing one.

CAUTION!
Unless certain DOS paths and system configurations are properly set up, you should not initiate the AutoCAD program from a directory other than the one that the AutoCAD files are in.

The Main Menu offers you 10 options. The beginner to AutoCAD is concerned only with Tasks 0, 1, and 2. To start a new drawing, select Task 1. To edit an existing drawing, select Task 2. To exit the AutoCAD program, select Task 0. Tasks 3 and above will be covered in later chapters.

Pressing the numeral **1** causes **1** to be displayed after the "Enter Selection" prompt. Do not confuse the lowercase letter "l" with the numeral **1**. You are also cautioned

```
         A U T O C A D (R)
Copyright (c) 1982-91  Autodesk, Inc.  All Rights Reserved.
Release R11 c2 (4/5/91) 386 DOS Extender
Serial Number:  117-10024292




Main Menu

   0.  Exit AutoCAD
   1.  Begin a NEW drawing
   2.  Edit an EXISTING drawing
   3.  Plot a drawing
   4.  Printer Plot a drawing

   5.  Configure AutoCAD
   6.  File Utilities
   7.  Compile shape/font description file
   8.  Convert old drawing file
   9.  Recover damaged drawing

Enter selection: 1

Enter NAME of drawing:
```

Figure 1-2 Selecting a Task from the Main Menu

to distinguish between the numeral **0** and the upper case letter O. By the way, just entering the **1** will do nothing but display the **1** where the cursor had been. So you will quickly see the need to press the RETURN key (⏎) in order to enter the typed-in response. Some programs will respond automatically to certain one-character entries, but not in this case. This **1**, like most AutoCAD responses, is not "self-entering." Figure 1-2 shows the response when Task 1 has been selected by typing in the numeral **1** and pressing ⏎.

FILENAMES

When AutoCAD prompts for a name of a drawing, you must follow certain rules. The name you enter will be the name of a file in which information about the drawing is stored. It must satisfy the requirements for filenames as specified by the particular operating system your computer uses. DOS and UNIX are the two most common operating systems.

Filenames in DOS

In PC-DOS (TM) and MS-DOS (TM) each drawing is a file with a "file specification." The file specification, or filespec as it is called, is the full name of the file. A filename has two parts. To distinguish the two, we will coin a new name for the first part and call it the keyname. The second part is called the extension or the file type. For example, in the filename PLAN.DWG, "PLAN" is the keyname and ".DWG" is the extension. The keyname is the group of characters (with a limit of eight) that precede the extension. The keyname and extension are separated by a period with the extension limited to three characters. Keynames may be made up of combinations of uppercase or lowercase letters, numbers, the underscore (_), the hyphen (-), and the dollar sign ($). DOS converts all of the characters to uppercase. No blank spaces are allowed in the keyname. It has to be one word.

Valid examples are as follow:

    Pipeplan
    lab1
    abc-xyz
    $floor12
    PART_NO3

Examples of improper keynames are as follows:

    *special   asterisk not a valid character

    nametoolong   name too long; more than eight characters

When AutoCAD prompts for a drawing name, just type in the keyname and AutoCAD will automatically assume the extension .DWG. In other programs, you have the freedom to select any valid characters as an extension (three or less), but in AutoCAD, drawings must have the extension of .DWG. When exiting AutoCAD, the extension of .DWG will automatically be appended to the name used at the start of the session.

In the following example, you wish to name your drawing PLOTPLAN. The prompt and response will appear as follow:

                Enter NAME of drawing: **plotplan**

AutoCAD will open a drawing file whose filespec is PLOTPLAN.DWG. Again, just type in the keyname and AutoCAD will automatically assume the extension .DWG.

As you progress through the lessons, take note of how various functions ask for names of files. If AutoCAD performs the file processing, it will usually add the proper extension. If you use DOS, you should include the extension.

THE PATH

If you wish to create a new drawing or edit a drawing that is on a drive and/or directory other than the current drive/directory, then you must furnish what is called the path to the drawing file as part of the file specification that you enter. Specifying a path requires only that you use the correct pathfinder symbols, the slash (/ or \) and/or the colon (:). Slashes enclose the name of the directory where the drawing is (or will be) located. The drive whose name is a letter (usually A through E) is identified as such by a colon, which will immediately follow it.

Examples of path/keyname combinations are as follow:

a:plan   in working directory on drive A
b:/jones/elev   elev is in /jones directory on drive B
\houses\smith   in /houses directory
ACME\doors   in working directory's ACME subdirectory
../PENNCAD/valves   in parent directory's PENNCAD subdirectory

> **NOTE:** When naming a drawing file in response to Task 1, you may use either forward or backward slashes to specify the path to a directory. AutoCAD will accept either, unlike specifying directory paths while at the operating system's prompt.

If you wish to work on the drawing called PLOTPLAN in a directory called HOUSE, and a subdirectory of ACAD, the prompt and response will be:

Enter NAME of drawing: **c:\house\acad\plotplan**

For a detailed explanation about DOS, see Appendix B.

DRAWING EDITOR

Once you respond with the proper drawing name for Task 1 (Begin a NEW drawing), the Main Menu is replaced with the Drawing Editor. Figure 1-3 shows the Drawing Editor.

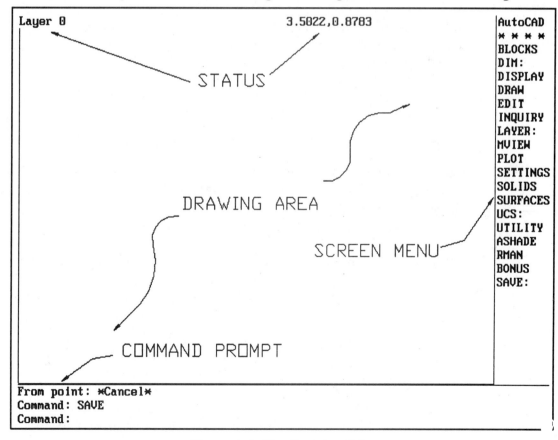

Figure 1-3 The Drawing Editor

The Drawing Editor Screen consists of four parts.

1. **Drawing Area**-The drawing area is where AutoCAD places the entities you draw. In this area AutoCAD will display the cursor, indicating your current working point. As you move your pointing device (usually a mouse or puck) around on a digitizing tablet, mouse pad, or other suitable surface, the cursor will mimic your movements on the screen. It may be in the form of cross-hairs when you are being prompted to select a point. It changes to a small pick box when you are required to select an object on the screen. AutoCAD uses combinations of cross-hairs, boxes, dashed rectangles, and arrows under various situations so you can quickly see what type of selection or pick mode to use.

2. **Status Line**-The status line at the top of the screen displays important information about the current layer, the status of various modes, and the cursor's coordinates.

3. **Screen Menu**-The screen menu on the right side of the screen provides one way to enter AutoCAD commands and selected responses to some prompts. By moving the cross-hairs into the screen menu area and pressing the pick button on your pointing device, you can initiate commands instead of having to type them in on the keyboard. Since only few commands or items can be displayed on the screen menu, AutoCAD contains a heirarchy of menus and submenus beneath the ones initially displayed. See Appendix D for the hierarchy of the screen menu layout.

4. **Command Prompt**-When you see "Command:" displayed in the bottom prompt area, it signals that AutoCAD is ready to accept a command. Once you have entered a command name or selected a command from one of the menu devices, the Prompt Area will continue to inform you of the type of response(s) that you must furnish until the command is either completed or terminated. For example, if you pick the LINE command, the prompt will display "From point:" and after selecting a starting point by appropriate means, you will see "To point:" asking for the end point of the line.

Each command has its own series of prompts. The prompts that appear when using a particular command in one situation may differ from the prompts or sequence of prompts when used in another situation. You will become familiar with the prompts as you learn to use each command.

When you type the command name or give any other response by typing from the keyboard, make sure to press ⏎. The ⏎ sends the input to the program for processing. For example, if you type in **LINE** you must press the spacebar or ⏎ in order for AutoCAD to start the line drawing part of the program. If you type in **LIN** and press the spacebar or ⏎, you will get an error message, unless someone has customized the program and created a command alias or command named "LIN". Likewise, typing in **LINEZ** and pressing the spacebar or ⏎ is not a standard AutoCAD command.

The spacebar has the same function as ⏎ except when you are typing in strings of words, letters, or numbers in response to the TEXT command.

Overview

You can press the spacebar or ↵ at the "Command:" prompt to repeat the previous command. When repeated in this manner, a few commands skip some of their normal prompts and assume default settings.

Terminating a Command

There are three ways by which you can terminate a command.

1. Complete the command sequence and return to the "Command:" prompt.

2. Use ⟨Ctrl⟩ + ⟨C⟩ (cancel) to terminate the command before it is completed.

3. Invoke another command from one of the menus that automatically cancels any command in progress.

INPUT METHODS

There are several ways to input an AutoCAD command.

Keyboard

To enter a command from the keyboard, simply type the command name at the "Command:" prompt and then press ↵ or the spacebar (↵ and the spacebar are interchangeable except when entering text).

Screen Menu

As explained earlier, the screen menu provides one way to enter AutoCAD commands. Moving the pointing device to the right will cause the cursor to move into the screen menu area. Moving the cursor up and down in the menu area will cause selectable items to be highlighted. When the desired one is highlighted, you may choose that item by pressing the designated pick button on the pointing device. If the item is a command, it will either be put into action or the menu area will be changed to a list of actions which are options of that command. The screen menu is made of menus and submenus. At the top of every screen menu is the word "AutoCAD." When selected, it will return you to what is called the root menu. The root menu is the one that is displayed when you first call up a drawing. It lists the main classifications of commands or functions available.

At the bottom of every menu are the _ _LAST_ _, DRAW, and EDIT items. The DRAW and EDIT items will cause the list of Entity Draw commands and list of editing commands, respectively, to appear in the screen menu areas when selected. The _ _LAST_ _ item, when selected, will return the previous menu to the screen. It was the menu from which you gained access to the current one.

A menu item whose name is all uppercase and does not end with a colon (example: DRAW) displays a submenu when selected. A menu item whose name ends with a colon (example: LINE:) not only displays a submenu, but cancels execution of any

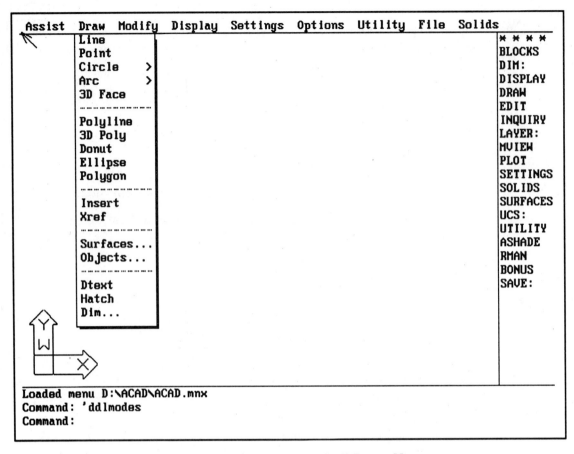

Figure 1-4 Example of a Pull-Down Menu

command in progress and invokes the named command. Subcommands and options are lowercase or a mixture of uppercase and lowercase, and work properly only when picked in appropriate sequence responses. See Appendix D for the hierarchy of the screen menu.

Pull-Down Menus

In a manner similar to the way the right side screen menu is used, you may select items from menu bars that drop down from the top of the screen. When you move the cursor to the top (status area) of the screen, the headings of the pull-down menus will appear. Selecting one of these headings will pop that menu bar onto the screen (see Figure 1-4). Selecting from the list is a simple matter of moving the cursor down until the desired item is highlighted and then pressing the designated pick button on the pointing device. See Appendix D for hierarchy of the pull-down menus.

Icon Menus and Dialogue Boxes

Some commands offer icon menus (pictures on the screen) so items can be selected by pictures rather than words (see Figure 1-5). Other commands provide dialogue boxes that cover the screen with lists and descriptions of options, long rectangles for receiving your input data and, in general, a more convenient and more user-friendly method of communicating with the AutoCAD program for that particular command (see Figure 1-6).

Overview

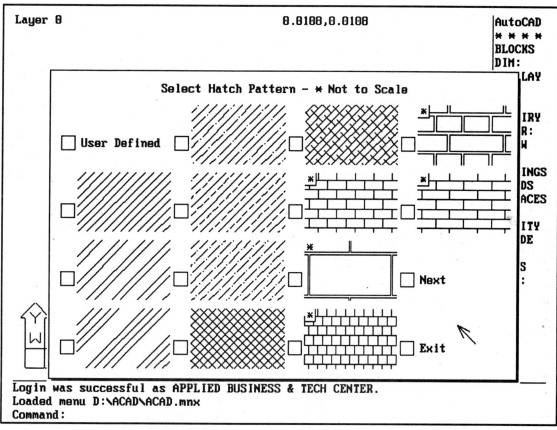

Figure 1-5 Example of an Icon Menu

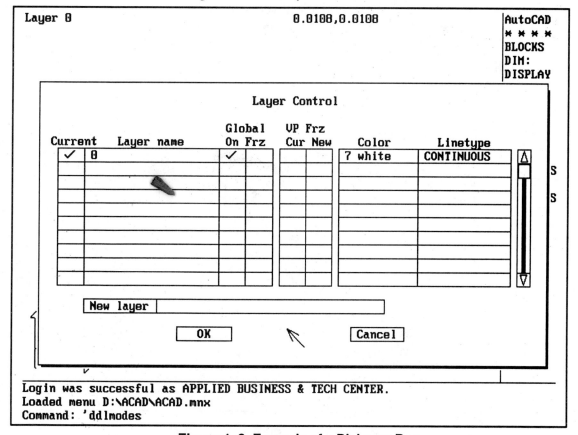

Figure 1-6 Example of a Dialogue Box

Digitizing Tablet

AutoCAD supports various accessory devices for interacting with the Drawing Editor. After the mouse, the digitizing tablet is the most common. It combines the screen cursor control of a mouse with its own printed menu areas for selecting items. See Appendix D for the layout of the tablet menu. The most significant feature of tablet menu selection is comparable to the icon menus in that you can select from pictures in addition to words. Another powerful feature of the tablet (not related to entering commands) is that it allows you to lay a map or other picture on the tablet and trace over it with the puck (the specific pointing device for a digitizing tablet), thereby transferring the object entities to the drawing.

GETTING HELP

When you are in the Drawing Editor, AutoCAD provides a simple help facility to explain the available commands and what they do. The HELP command provides a limited amount of on-line assistance within AutoCAD. When an invalid command is entered, AutoCAD prints a message to remind you of the availability of the help facility.

Whenever you need help, at the "Command:" prompt type **help** or **?** and press the spacebar or ⏎ and AutoCAD will respond with the following prompt:

Command name (RETURN for list):

You have two choices. If you enter a command, you will receive help for that specific command. If you press ⏎, you will see a series of screen displays similar to the one shown in Figure 1-7. These displays contain a list of AutoCAD commands for which help is available.

```
     AutoCAD Command List   (' = transparent command)

   APERTURE     CHANGE       DIVIDE       EXTEND       ISOPLANE
   ARC          CHPROP       DONUT        FILES        LAYER
   AREA         CIRCLE       DOUGHNUT     FILL         LIMITS
   ARRAY        COLOR        DRAGMODE     FILLET       LINE
   ATTDEF       COPY         DTEXT        FILMROLL     LINETYPE
   ATTDISP      DBLIST       DVIEW        'GRAPHSCR    LIST
   ATTEDIT      DDATTE       DXBIN        GRID         LOAD
   ATTEXT       DDEDIT       DXFIN        HANDLES      LTSCALE
   AUDIT        'DDEMODES    DXFOUT       HATCH        MEASURE
   AXIS         'DDLMODES    EDGESURF     'HELP / '?   MENU
   BASE         'DDRMODES    ELEV         HIDE         MINSERT
   BLIPMODE     DDUCS        ELLIPSE      ID           MIRROR
   BLOCK        DELAY        END          IGESIN       MOVE
   BREAK        DIM/DIM1     ERASE        IGESOUT      MSLIDE
   CHAMFER      DIST         EXPLODE      INSERT       MSPACE

   Press RETURN for further help.
```

Figure 1-7 The HELP Menu

The HELP command is one that can be used while you are in the middle of another command. This is referred to as being used transparently. To use a command transparently (if it is one of those that can be used that way), simply prefix the command name with an apostrophe. For example, to use HELP transparently type **'help** or **'?** in response to any prompt that is not asking for a text string. AutoCAD displays help for the current command. Often the help is general in nature, but sometimes it is specific to the command's current prompt.

On single-screen systems, HELP flips to the text screen, so you probably will need to press the flip screen (F1) key to switch back to the graphics screen.

EXITING AUTOCAD DRAWING EDITOR

Getting out of the AutoCAD Drawing Editor is as easy as getting into it. Either of two options, END or QUIT, will return to AutoCAD's Main Menu.

The END command saves your drawing and returns you to the Main Menu. AutoCAD maintains a backup copy of your drawing while you are editing it. When you end the drawing for the first time, it will create a drawing file with an extension .DWG. When you subsequently edit the drawing and use the END command, the updated drawing becomes the .DWG file, the old copy of the drawing becomes the new .BAK file, and any previous .BAK file will be deleted.

The QUIT command does not save your work; it simply exits directly from the Drawing Editor back to the Main Menu. When you select the QUIT command, AutoCAD will respond with the following prompt:

Really want to discard all changes to drawing?

You must answer **yes** or **y** to actually discard the session and AutoCAD will take you back to the Main Menu. The .DWG file as well as .BAK file are unchanged.

It is recommended that you save your changes periodically without exiting the Drawing Editor, thereby protecting your work from possible power failures, editing errors, and other disasters. This can be done with the SAVE command. Additional information about this, and the END and QUIT commands is provided in Chapter 2.

PROTOTYPE DRAWINGS

Just as the board drafter starts a drawing in an environment, the blank screen (electronic drawing) of the AutoCAD Drawing Editor has an environment. Placing a blank sheet on the drafting board limits the area in which you can draw. Likewise, there are limits set in your electronic drawing, but less restrictive because you can change the electronic sheet size any time during the drawing process. The drawing instrument in your hand, combined with your dexterity, determine the type of line you can put on the paper. Likewise, linetypes in an AutoCAD drawing determine whether lines are Continuous or Dashed. The Colors feature in AutoCAD can be used in conjunction with plotting parameters to determine line widths through pen assignments. The board drafter's scale corresponds to a system variable called LUNITS in the AutoCAD drawing (the setting of the linear units corresponds to the value assigned to the system variable UNITS). Just as the board drafter picks up the architectural scale, you can set the UNITS to architectural. UNITS is another property of the drawing environment.

System Variables

The electronic drawing sheet that you start with when you "Begin a NEW drawing" has many properties associated with it. The above mentioned LIMITS, LINETYPES, and UNITS are just a few of the AutoCAD commands that affect one of the 100 or so environmental properties that can be either used as they come off the shelf or, if not acceptable, changed to suit your drawing. In order to create a drawing, it is not necessary to learn the names of the system variables that store environmental settings. Their settings will be automatically changed during an editing session as you use the AutoCAD commands that affect individual system variables. The important thing to note is that they do exist and are set to some value that affects the drawing environment. In addition to the system variables being affected automatically as you draw by the various AutoCAD commands, you can change their settings directly by using the SETVAR command or typing the system variable at the "Command:" prompt.

ACAD.DWG

The ACAD.DWG (drawing) file will be referred to occasionally throughout the text. The ACAD.DWG file is a drawing data file with preset system variables settings describing the environment of a drawing before you add objects to it. It is like a blank sheet of vellum, drawing instrument, scale, and drafting machine that the board drafter starts out with. The blank sheet has properties such as size, thickness, and type of material. You are considered to have started a drawing by just positioning it on the board. In a similar manner, when you invoke the AutoCAD Editor, your beginning drawing environment copies all of the settings of the ACAD.DWG file. The ACAD.DWG file in this situation is known as the prototype drawing. Unless an AutoCAD installation configuration is changed, the ACAD.DWG file will be the default prototype drawing. The ACAD.DWG file comes with the program.

While it is possible, it is not advisable to add entities to the ACAD.DWG file such as a border, title block, and resident symbols called BLOCKs. There are methods that are more preferable to create prototype drawings than to add entities to the ACAD.DWG file. It might be useful, however, to change the environment of the ACAD.DWG file by altering the settings of some of its system variables to better suit your drawing needs. One example is the UNITS variable. The ACAD.DWG file comes off the shelf with the drawing UNITS set to decimal. You may wish to have your drawings start out with the UNITS set to architectural. You may also wish to have a different area of "the world" displayed than the area that first appears in the off-the-shelf ACAD.DWG. The start-up display area can be changed by changing the LIMITS settings of the ACAD.DWG file. Once the desired changes have been made to the ACAD.DWG environment settings, you may then use the END or SAVE command to affix the settings.

There are several ways to have your drawing start up with the environment variables different than those in the ACAD.DWG file.

1. The original ACAD.DWG environment settings were set up according to certain defaults. Such things as the settings of the linear and angular units and the area that displays on the screen when you ZOOM All are a few of the enivronmental settings. When you change the ACAD.DWG settings and do not configure another prototype drawing, your start-up settings will conform to the latest ACAD.DWG environment settings. However, you may revert to the original defaults by entering the new drawing name followed by an equal sign as follows:

Enter NAME of drawing: **name-of-drawing=**

2. During the configuration procedure you may specify a prototype drawing other than the ACAD.DWG file. When responding with a drawing keyname, it will start out with the same settings as the prototype, for example:

Enter NAME of drawing: **name-of-drawing**

However, the prototype drawing must be accessible or an error message will be displayed.

3. If you wish to have the new drawing be identical to some drawing other than the ACAD.DWG or other configured prototype drawing, the procedure is to respond with the new drawing name followed by an equal sign and the name of that other drawing, for example:

Enter NAME of drawing: **name-of-drawing=name-of-other-drawing**

COORDINATE SYSTEMS

In accordance with the convention of the Cartesian coordinate system, horizontal distances increase in the positive X direction toward the right and vertical distances increase in the positive Y direction upward. Distances perpendicular to the XY plane that you are viewing increase toward you in the positive Z direction. This set of axes defines the World Coordinate System, abbreviated as the WCS.

The significance of the WCS is that it is always in your drawing; it cannot be altered. An infinite number of other coordinate systems can be established relative to it. These others are called user coordinate systems (UCS) and can be created with the UCS command. Even though the WCS is fixed, you can view it from any angle, side, or rotation without changing to another coordinate system.

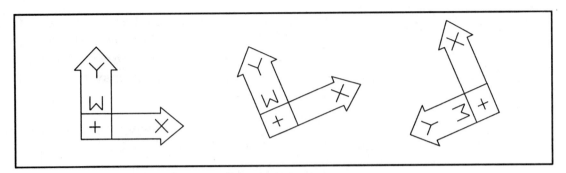

Figure 1-8 Examples of Coordinate System Icons

AutoCAD provides what is called a coordinate system icon to help keep your bearings among different coordinate systems in a drawing. The icon will show you the orientation of your current UCS by indicating the positive directions of the X and Y axes. Figure 1-8 shows some examples of coordinate system icons.

Computer-aided drafting permits you to always draw an object at its true size and then make the border, title block, and other nonobject associated features fit the object. The completed combination is reduced (or increased) to fit the plotted sheet size you require when you plot.

A more complicated condition is when you wish to draw objects at different scales on the same drawing. This can be handled easily by one of several methods with the more advanced commands provided in AutoCAD.

Drawing a schematic that is not to scale is one situation where the graphics and computing power is hardly used to its potential. But even though the symbols and distances between them have no relationship to any real-life dimensions, the sheet size, text size, line widths and other visible characteristics of the drawing must be considered in order to give your schematic the readability you desire. Some planning, including sizing, needs to be applied to all drawings.

When AutoCAD prompts for a location of a point, you can use one of several point entry techniques available, which include absolute rectangular coordinates, relative rectangular coordinates, relative polar coordinates, spherical coordinates and cylindrical coordinates.

The rectangular coordinates method is based on specifying a point location by giving its distances from two intersecting perpendicular axes in two-dimensional (2D) or from three intersecting perpendicular planes for three-dimensional (3D) points. Each point distance is measured along the X axis (horizontal), Y axis (vertical), and Z axis, toward or away from the viewer. The intersection of the axes, called the origin (X,Y,Z=0,0,0) divides the coordinates into four quadrants for 2D or eight sections for 3D (see Figure 1-9).

Absolute Rectangular Coordinates

Points are located by absolute rectangular coordinates in relation to the origin. You can specify in reference to the WCS origin or UCS origin. In AutoCAD, by default the origin (0,0) is located at the lower left corner of the drawing as shown in Figure

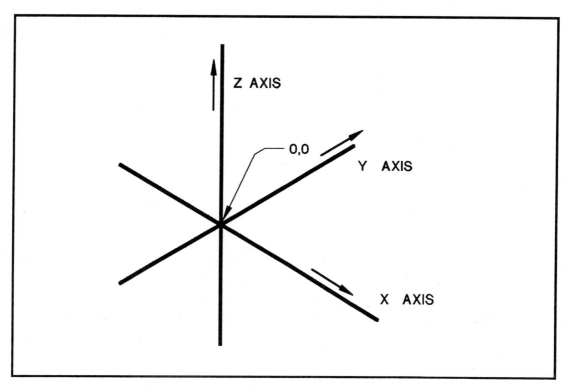

Figure 1-9 Specifying Rectangular Coordinates Using the Intersections of the X, Y, and Z Axes

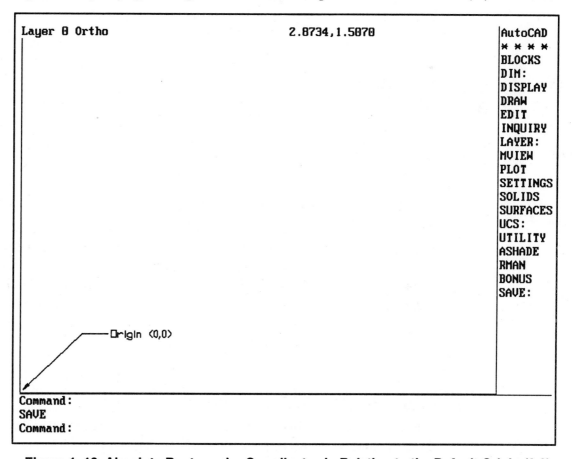

Figure 1-10 Absolute Rectangular Coordinates in Relation to the Default Origin (0,0)

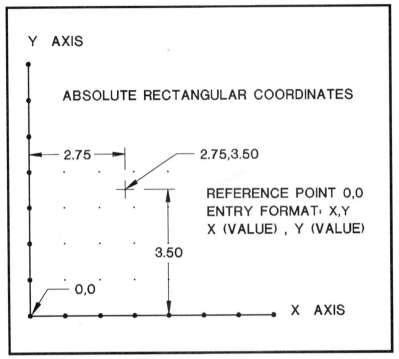

Figure 1-11 Specifying Absolute Rectangular Coordinates

1-10. As mentioned earlier, the horizontal distance increases in the positive **X** direction from origin, and the vertical distance increases in the positive **Y** direction from origin. You can specify a point by typing its X,Y,Z in decimal, fractional, or scientific notation separated by commas. For example, to specify the point with an X coordinate of 2.75, and Y coordinate of 3.5 (see Figure 1-11) you would enter:

2.75,3.5

Relative Rectangular Coordinates

Points are located by relative rectangular coordinates in relation to the previous position or point, rather than the origin. This is like specifying a point as an offset from the last point you entered. In AutoCAD, whenever you specify relative coordinates, the @ (at symbol) must precede your entry. This symbol is selected by holding the SHIFT key and pressing the **2** key at the top of the keyboard simultaneously. For example, if the last point specified was 3,4 then, entering:

@5,2

is equivalent to specifying the absolute coordinates 3+5,4+2, or, 8,6 (see Figure 1-12). If you want to draw an entity from the previous data point, simply enter @ for the relative specification. It specifies a zero offset from the last point. For example, if the last point you entered was 6,7 entering just @ specifies 6,7 point again.

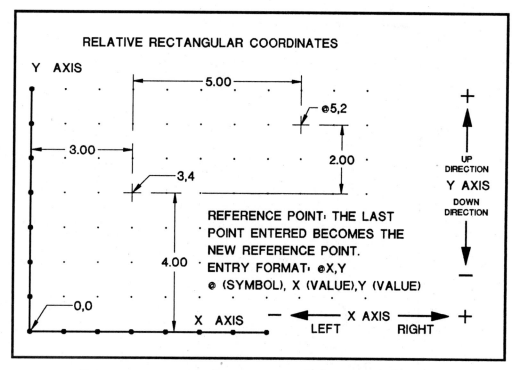

Figure 1-12 Specifying Relative Rectangular Coordinates

Relative Polar Coordinates

Polar coordinates are based on a distance from a fixed point at a given angle. In AutoCAD, a polar coordinate point is determined by distance and angle measured from the previous point. In AutoCAD, by default the angle is measured in the counterclockwise direction. It is important to remember that points located using polar coordinates are always positioned relative to the previous point and not the origin (0,0). You can specify a point by entering its distance from the previous point and its angle in the XY plane, separated by < (not a comma). This symbol is selected by holding the SHIFT key and pressing the "," key at the bottom of the keyboard simultaneously. For example, to specify a point at a distance of 7 drawing units from the previous point at an angle of 75 degrees relative to the positive X axis (see Figure 1-13) you would enter:

@7<75

> **NOTE:** Whenever you enter relative coordinates, make sure to precede them with the @ symbol.

If you are working with UCS and would like to enter points in reference to WCS, enter coordinates preceded by an * (asterisk). For example, to specify the point with an X coordinate of 3.5, and Y coordinate of 2.57 in reference to WCS, regardless of the current UCS, you would enter:

*3.5,2.57

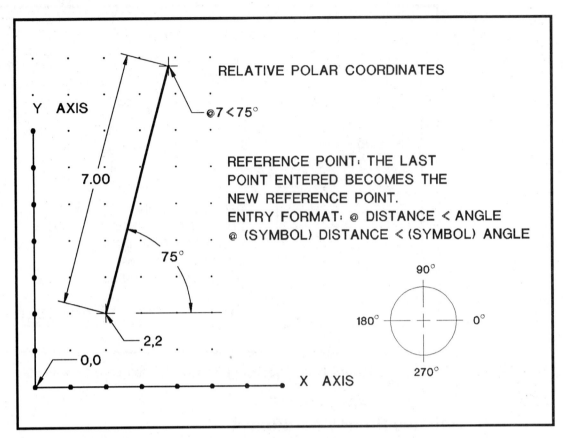

Figure 1-13 Specifying Relative Polar Coordinates

In the case of relative coordinates, the * (asterisk) will be preceded by @ symbol. For example:

@*4,5

It represents as offset 4,5 from the previous point in relation to WCS.

LAB EXERCISES

In exercises 1-1 through 1-5, write down the coordinates necessary to draw the figures. See Figure 1-14 for an example of how this is done.

Overview

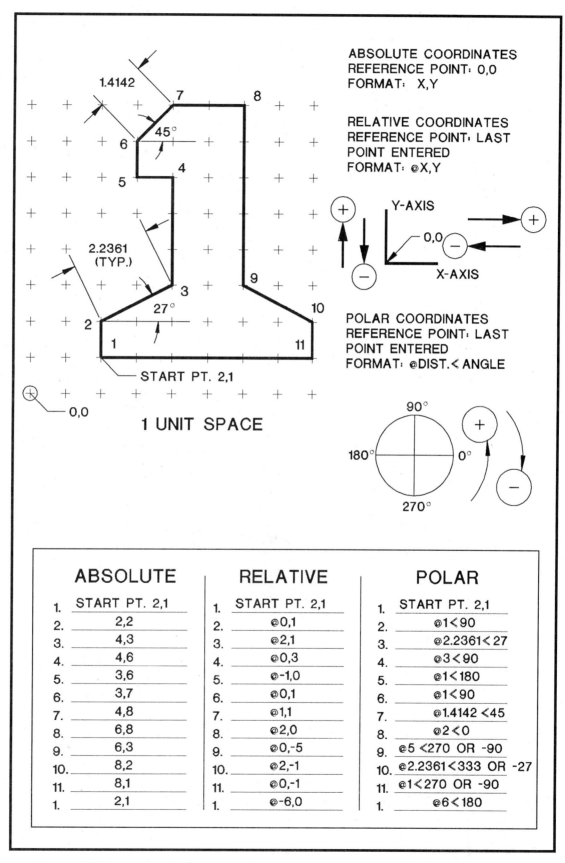

Figure 1–14 Review of Absolute, Relative, and Polar Coordinates

Lab Exercise 1-1

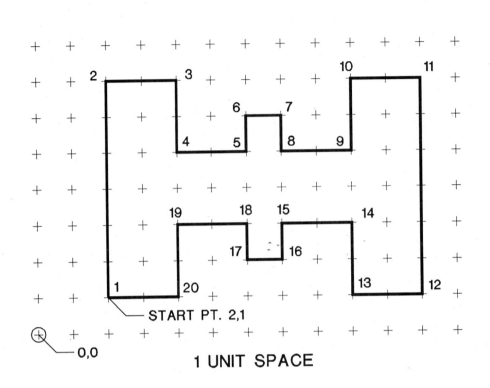

1 UNIT SPACE

ABSOLUTE COORDINATE EXERCISE
FORMAT IS X,Y (X COORDINATE),(Y COORDINATE)
REFERENCE POINT IS 0,0

ENTER THE COORDINATES NECESSARY TO DRAW THE FIGURE

1. START POINT IS 2,1
2. _____
3. _____
4. _____
5. _____
6. _____
7. _____
8. _____
9. _____
10. _____

11. _____
12. _____
13. _____
14. _____
15. _____
16. _____
17. _____
18. _____
19. _____
20. _____ BACK TO 1. _____

FILL IN THE COORDINATES BEFORE STARTING THE DRAWING

Overview

Lab Exercise 1-2

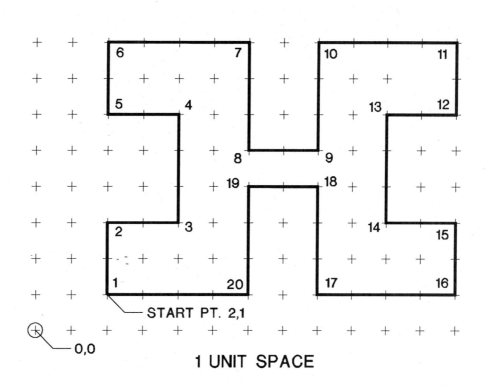

START PT. 2,1

0,0

1 UNIT SPACE

RELATIVE COORDINATE EXERCISE
FORMAT IS @X,Y
X= (DIST. + OR – ALONG THE X AXIS)
Y= (DIST. + OR – ALONG THE Y AXIS)
REFERENCE POINT IS THE LAST POINT ENTERED

ENTER THE COORDINATES NECESSARY TO DRAW THE FIGURE

START POINT IS 2,1

1. _____
2. _____
3. _____
4. _____
5. _____
6. _____
7. _____
8. _____
9. _____
10. _____

11. _____
12. _____
13. _____
14. _____
15. _____
16. _____
17. _____
18. _____
19. _____
20. _____ BACK TO 1. _____

FILL IN THE COORDINATES BEFORE STARTING THE DRAWING

Lab Exercise 1-3

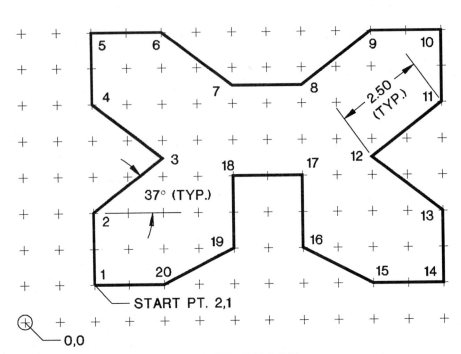

1 UNIT SPACE

POLAR COORDINATE EXERCISE
FORMAT IS @ DISTANCE < ANGLE
REFERENCE POINT IS THE LAST POINT ENTERED

ENTER THE COORDINATES NECESSARY TO DRAW THE FIGURE

1. START POINT IS 2,1 _____
2. _____
3. _____
4. _____
5. _____
6. _____
7. _____
8. _____
9. _____
10. _____

11. _____
12. _____
13. _____
14. _____
15. _____
16. _____
17. _____
18. _____
19. _____
20. _____ BACK TO 1. _____

FILL IN THE COORDINATES BEFORE STARTING THE DRAWING

Lab Exercise 1–4

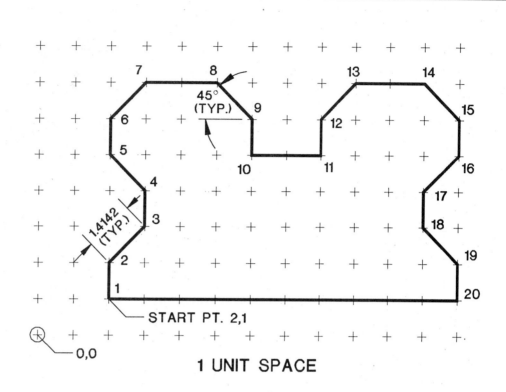

1 UNIT SPACE

USE ABSOLUTE, RELATIVE, OR POLAR COORDINATES
TO COMPLETE THIS EXERCISE

ENTER THE COORDINATES NECESSARY TO DRAW THE FIGURE

1. START POINT IS 2,1   11. _____

2. _____   12. _____

3. _____   13. _____

4. _____   14. _____

5. _____   15. _____

6. _____   16. _____

7. _____   17. _____

8. _____   18. _____

9. _____   19. _____

10. _____   20. _____ BACK TO 1. _____

FILL IN THE COORDINATES BEFORE STARTING THE DRAWING

Lab Exercise 1-5

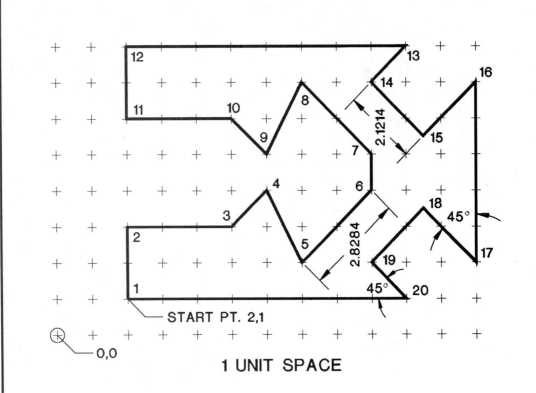

1 UNIT SPACE

USE ABSOLUTE, RELATIVE, OR POLAR COORDINATES
TO COMPLETE THIS EXERCISE

ENTER THE COORDINATES NECESSARY TO DRAW THE FIGURE

1. START POINT 2,1 _____
2. _____
3. _____
4. _____
5. _____
6. _____
7. _____
8. _____
9. _____
10. _____

11. _____
12. _____
13. _____
14. _____
15. _____
16. _____
17. _____
18. _____
19. _____
20. _____ BACK TO 1. _____

FILL IN THE COORDINATES BEFORE STARTING THE DRAWING

DRAWING ENVIRONMENTS

In AutoCAD Release 11, you have the option to work on your drawing in two different environments, Model Space or Paper Space. Most of the drafting and design work will be done in Model Space. You will use Paper Space to arrange, annotate, and plot various views of your model. While Model Space is a 3D environment, Paper Space is a 2D environment for arranging views of your model. Prior to Release 11, the drawings were created entirely in the Model Space. The system variable TILEMODE toggles back and forth between the Model and Paper Space. See Chapter 8 for additional information.

DRAWING SETUP

A unit can correspond to whatever form of measurement your drawing requires. It can be inches, feet, millimeters, or whatever units you require. This allows you to draw with real world values and eliminates the possibility of scaling errors. Once the drawing is complete you may plot it at whatever scale you like. As mentioned earlier, drawing in real world is an advantage of AutoCAD that some overlook. If a drawing is done with this principle, you can plot it at several different scales, which eliminates the need for separate drawings at different scales.

AutoCAD allows you to choose from several formats for the display and entry of the coordinates and distances. For example, you can choose feet and fractional inches for architectural drafting; other options include scientific notation and engineering formats. Similarly, you can select the format used for display and entry of angles. Degrees in decimal form are the most common choice, however, you might also select gradient, radians, degrees/minutes/seconds, or surveyor's units.

AutoCAD assumes that you are drawing in a rectangular area. The drawing limits are the borders of this rectangle, with lower left and upper right corners expressed in X and Y coordinates. You may select whatever limits make sense for your drawing. For example, if you are drawing a printed circuit board that is 6 inches high by 8 inches wide, you can choose a drawing unit to be in inches and place the lower left corner of the board on the coordinate (2,2). You can then set your drawing limits at the lower left corner of the rectangle to 0,0 and upper right corner of the rectangle to 10,8.

If your drawing grows beyond your original plans or the drawing limits become too restrictive, you can easily change the drawing limits.

Just as the drawing limits specify the potential size of your drawing, the drawing extents specify the smallest rectangular area being used by objects (drawing entities) in the drawing at the present time.

For additional information on LIMITS and UNITS commands, see Chapter 2.

DRAWING AIDS

AutoCAD provides six different tools to make your drafting and design easier. The tools include GRID, SNAP, ORTHO, COORDINATES DISPLAY, OSNAP, and XYZ

FILTERS. The following are brief explanations of these tools; a more detailed explanation is provided in Chapters 2, 3, and 4.

The GRID command displays a reference Grid of dots with any desired spacing. This feature helps you to get a sense of the sizes of drawing entities and their relationships. You can turn the Grid display on and off at will, and change the dot spacing easily. The Grid is not considered part of the drawing; it is for visual reference only and is never plotted. The function key F7 or (Ctrl) + (G) toggles the display of the Grid on and off.

If the points you wish to specify coincide with points on a uniformly spaced Grid, then the SNAP mechanism can help you enter points by locking into the rectangular Grid. Using Snap mode, you can enter points quickly, letting AutoCAD ensure that they line up precisely. You can set the Snap spacing the same as Grid spacing or to some increment in between Grid points. A change in the Snap value only affects the coordinates of points you subsequently enter. Entities already in the drawing retain their coordinates, even if they do not line up the new Snap value. You can even set up a Snap grid in which the points are in arrays that are parallel to the three axes of an isometric Grid. The function key F9 or (Ctrl) + (B) toggles the Snap lock on and off.

The ORTHO setting, when turned on, limits your pointer movement to right angles from the last point. This means you can use the Ortho mode if you want the new point to be displaced from the base point along an orthogonal line (horizontal or vertical); Ortho mode restricts the rubberband line and the new point accordingly. It also forces lines to be parallel to one of the three isometric axes (depending on the current Isoplane) when the snap style has been set to Isometric. The function key F8 or (Ctrl) + (O) toggles the Ortho mode on and off.

The Coordinates Display is a report in the status area at the top of the screen. It has three settings. On most systems the function key F6 toggles between the three settings. The three settings are as follow:

1. This setting causes the display to report the location of the cursor when the prompt is in the "Command:" status or when you are being prompted for the first point selection of a command. It then changes to a relative polar mode when you are prompted for a second point that could be specified relative to the first point. In this case the report is in the form of the direction/distance. The direction is given in terms of the current angular units setting and the distance in terms of the current linear units setting.

2. This setting is similar to the previous one, except that the display for the second location in given in terms of its coordinates, rather than relative to the first point.

3. This setting is used to save either the location in the display at the time you toggle to this setting or the last point entered. It does not change dynamically with the movement of the cursor and will not change until you select a new point.

Osnap (Object Snap) refers to the feature in AutoCAD that permits you to specify some point on an existing entity. You can place the cursor on that entity near the location of the specified point and be assured that particular point will be the one chosen in response to a prompt requiring a point as a response. The key word above is near. For example, draw a line starting at point 0,0 for a distance of 3 units and at an angle of 30 degrees. If you wish to continue (drawing another line) using the endpoint of the line just drawn as the starting point of the next line, AutoCAD allows automatic line-line continuation by just picking the endpoint only of that next line. If you wish to use the endpoint of that first line for some other purpose, the center of a circle for instance, without using Osnap, you would have to stop and calculate its coordinates. You could do so and arrive at the point where the X coordinate is 2.598076211 and Y coordinate is 1.500000000. Then you would have to read your calculator, key-in the numbers, and hope that you did not make a mistake in the reading, typing in, or method of calculation. Also, you are limiting yourself to the accuracy of the number of significant figures on your calculator. In most cases, eight places are accurate enough. By using the Osnap mode called ENDPOINT while AutoCAD is asking for a point, you can put the cursor near the end of the line, press the pick button, and have that endpoint used as the response to the prompt. Also, the accuracy will be approximately 14 significant figures.

Other Osnap modes include CENTER, INSERTION POINT, INTERSECTION, MIDPOINT, NEAR, NODE, PERPENDICULAR, QUADRANT, and TANGENT. You may not have to make your drawing as accurate as AutoCAD permits, but if the precision is there, why not use it? In most cases it is quicker and easier to use Osnap mode with all of its accuracy than to not use it. For example, if you wish to start a line at the center of a circle, trying to place the cursor at the center of the circle on the screen is not as easy as picking somewhere on the circle itself after invoking the Osnap mode called CENTER. The Osnap menu is displayed by selecting the assist menu on the pull-down menu or selecting the '* * * *' on the screen menu.

The XYZ FILTERS feature allows you to specify a point by specifying separate coordinates (2D and 3D) or combinations of coordinates (3D) in separate steps. Specifying the coordinates can combine keyboard and pointing methods. It is especially useful in combination with the Osnap mode, by which you can specify a point on an existing object and then have the XYZ Filter feature extract the desired coordinates (X, Y, and/or Z) for use in the point for which you are being prompted. A detailed explanation of all the drawing aids are provided in Chapters 2 through 4.

DRAW COMMANDS

AutoCAD gives you an ample variety of drawing elements (called entities). It also provides you with many ways to generate each entity in your drawing. You will learn about the properties of these entities as you progress in this text. It is important to keep in mind that the examples in this text of how to generate the various lines, circles, arcs, and other entities are not always the only methods available. You are invited, even challenged, to find other more expedient methods to perform tasks demonstrated in the lessons. You can also progress at a better rate if you make an effort to learn as much as possible as soon as possible about the descriptive properties of the individual entities. When you become familiar with how the CAD program creates, manipulates, and stores the data that describes the entities, you are then able to create drawings more effectively.

You can add text to a drawing by means of the TEXT and DTEXT commands. TEXT entities can be drawn with a variety of character patterns or fonts, and can be stretched, compressed, obliqued, mirrored, or drawn in a vertical column by applying a style to the font. AutoCAD comes with various types of fonts. For the list of fonts available see Appendix J. Each text string can be rotated and justified to fit your requirements. Text can be of any size (height and width). DTEXT allows you to see the text on the screen as you enter it and also allows you to enter multiple lines of text in one command.

You can create filled areas with the SOLID command, filled lines (having width) with the TRACE command, or filled and/or tapered line-arc combinations with the PLINE (for polyline) command. TRACE command is easier to learn before advancing to polyline.

Hatch patterns for filling areas can be drawn with the HATCH command. The patterns are made from combinations of continuous and/or broken and dotted lines. Lines within one family of the pattern are similar and parallel to each other, and may be combined with families of lines going in another direction. You should note that the area selected to be filled must be a closed area, that is, the lines and/or arcs that define it must meet at all endpoints; otherwise, the results will be unpredictable. AutoCAD also comes with various types of hatch patterns. For the list of available patterns see Appendix I. Many other hatch patterns are available from third-party vendors. You can also create your own hatch patterns.

See Table 1-1 for a brief description of the DRAW commands available in AutoCAD. A detailed explanation of all the Entity Draw commands are provided in Chapters 2 through 6.

EDIT COMMANDS

To edit an entity is to make a change to one of its existing characteristics. There are several options open to a user among the EDIT commands offered by AutoCAD.

When an EDIT command is activated, the first step is to select the entity that you wish to edit. In other words, you have to show AutoCAD which entity you want to edit. To identify an entity, the user will move the screen cross-hair to touch the desired entity and press the appropriate pick button. When this is done, the entity will be highlighted to indicate that this is the one chosen.

Table 1-1 The DRAW Commands

ENTITY TYPE	DESCRIPTION
LINES	Drawn with 2D or 3D coordinates with various linetypes.
ARCS & CIRCLES	Drawn using several methods with various linetypes.
POINTS	Drawn with either 2D or 3D coordinates, appear as dots, squares, circles, Xs, or any combination of these.
TEXT	Can appear in a variety of fonts, sizes, and orientations.
TRACES	2D, solid-filled lines of any user-specified width.
SOLIDS	2D, solid-filled triangular or quadrilateral objects.
BLOCKS	Compound entities formed from groups of other entities.
ATTRIBUTES	Attach constant or variable text information to each instance of a block.
DIMENSIONS	Compound entities containing all the lines, arcs, arrows, and text comprising a dimension annotation.
POLYLINES	2D connected line and arc segments, with optional linetypes, widths, and tapers.
HATCH	Block patterns, either system-generated or user-created, that fill horizontally or vertically in a specified drawing area. One or more sets of parallel lines (continuous or broken lines) with spaces, arrangements, and angles designed to fill a space with a specific pattern.
3D POLYLINES	3D entities composed of straight-line segments.
3DFACES	3D triangular or quadrilateral plane sections.

The editing facilities of AutoCAD make it easy to correct or revise a drawing. Often, the experienced CAD operator will create an entity in anticipation of using a particular editing command. For instance, if you wish to draw two parallel lines of equal length, you can draw one line and then use the OFFSET command to create the second line. And, if you wish to create an array of radial lines similar to spokes on a wheel, you only need to draw one line, then you can generate the other spokes with the one editing command called ARRAY. Some editing functions are specific to certain entities. See Table 1-2 for a brief description of the EDIT commands available in AutoCAD. A detailed explanation of all the EDIT commands are provided in Chapters 2 through 6.

DISPLAYING AND VIEWING THE DRAWING

AutoCAD offers many ways for you to display or view your drawing while it is in progress and after it is completed. You can magnify or shrink the visual image of the drawing on the screen. This can be accomplished with the help of the ZOOM command which allows you to adjust the size of your viewing area. You can tell AutoCAD how large or small an area of the world you wish to have displayed on your screen. This operates similar to a zoom lens on a camera (without the perspective effect).

Table 1-2 The EDIT Commands

ENTITY TYPE	DESCRIPTION
ERASE/OOPS	Used to remove unwanted objects and retrieve objects accidently removed.
FILLET	Used for connecting lines, arcs, or circles by means of a smoothly fitted arc of a specified radius.
CHAMFER	Used for trimming two intersecting lines a specified distance from the intersection and connects the trimmed ends with a new line segment.
TRIM	Used on some objects so they end precisely at a cutting edge or edges defined by one or more other objects.
BREAK	Used to remove a part of a line, trace, circle, arc, or 2D polyline.
OFFSET	Used for constructing an entity parallel to another entity at either a specified distance or through a specified point.
DIVIDE/MEASURE	Used to divide an entity into several equal-length parts or at intervals of specified distance by placing markers.
MOVE	Move one or more entities from their present location to a new one without changing their orientation or size.
COPY	Copies of the selected objects at the specified displacement without changing their orientation or size, leaving the originals intact.
ROTATE	Used to change the orientation of existing entities by rotating them about a specified base point.
MIRROR	Used to make mirror images of existing objects, either deleting or retaining the original objects.
SCALE	Used to change the size of existing entities, larger or smaller.
EXTEND	Used to lengthen existing objects so they end precisely at boundary edges defined by other objects.
STRETCH	Used to move a selected portion of a drawing, preserving connectives to parts of the drawing left in place.
ARRAY	Used to make multiple copies of selected objects in a rectangular or circular (polar) pattern; each resulting object can be manipulated independently.
CHANGE	Used to change the properties (layer, color, thickness, etc.) of existing objects or modify objects by trimming or extending their ends or cutting sections.
EXPLODE	Used for replacing block reference or associative dimension with copies of the simple entities. Also forms simple lines and arcs from 2D and 3D polylines.
PEDIT	Used for editing 2D and 3D entities.
UNDO/REDO	UNDO is used for backing up step-by-step to any earlier point in an editing session. REDO will undo the UNDO.

The PAN command allows you to move across the drawing in any direction. Panning also allows you to view a different portion of the drawing without changing its magnification.

AutoCAD lets you divide your display into several smaller displays or windows called viewports. Each viewport may be different, perhaps with a closer view, or a view from a different angle, or of a different area of the drawing. Panning and zooming can be performed in each viewport independently. You can have 16 viewports at any time, but only one can be active at any time. You can draw entities from one viewport to another by activating the viewport as you go along.

For a detailed explanation of the DISPLAY commands, refer to Chapters 2, 4, and 8.

LAYER STRUCTURE

AutoCAD offers a means of grouping entities in a drawing in a manner similar to the manual drafter drawing groups of objects on separate transparent sheets superimposed in a single stack. You can assign various portions or groups of entities of your drawing to different layers, and define as many layers as you like. Layering allows you to view and plot related aspects of a drawing separately or in any combination. There is only one current layer. The current layer could be compared to the manual drafter's top sheet on the stack of transparencies. A color and a linetype are associated with each layer, and you can elect to use these instead of specifying individually each entity's color and linetype. You can turn off a specific layer if you do not want to see it on the screen or be plotted and freeze selected layers which will be excluded when the drawing is regenerated and plotted. Whenever you like, you can thaw a frozen layer. For a detailed explanation of layers, see Chapter 2.

BLOCKS AND ATTRIBUTES

The term block seems to have its origin in word processing software. By marking the beginning and end of one or more characters or words, they become a block that can be edited as a single grouping. For example, if you had a paragraph you wanted to move to another place in the text, the word processor's MOVE command could be applied to the whole group. Other commands can be used to copy and delete the entire group.

AutoCAD provides a similar but more powerful feature by means of the BLOCK command. It permits you to group entities under a user-determined name and gives you the ability to perform certain editing commands on the group as though they were a single entity.

With the WBLOCK command you can save a block or an entire drawing to a file as a mini-drawing for insertion later or insertion into another drawing. WBLOCK causes blocks to take with them the layer, linetype, system variable settings, and other environmental characteristics of the parent drawing.

When you insert a block, you can specify a scale factor or separate X and Y scale factors (making ellipses out of circles and rectangles out of squares). You can also specify a rotation angle.

Blocks can contain other blocks, called nested blocks. They (or parts of them) can be created on the default layer (∅) and then when inserted those parts will shift to the current layer, while parts created on layers other than zero stay on their respective layers.

Using the BLOCK command can conserve computer memory and reduce the size of the drawing data file. Blocks can improve drafting and design speed and reduce burden on the designer to create symbols each time they are needed.

You can attach constant or variable text information to any instance of a block. This text information is referred to as attributes.

For a detailed explanation of blocks and attributes, see Chapter 6.

EXTERNAL REFERENCE DRAWING

With Release 11, AutoCAD supports a feature that lets you display or view the contents of unlimited numbers of drawing files while working in your current drawing file. This function can be accomplished using an external reference file. When a drawing is externally referenced, the user can view and snap to the referenced drawing from the current drawing. If necessary, you can move, copy, rotate, or scale a reference file by using the regular AutoCAD EDIT commands. You can also control the visibility, color, and linetype of the layers belonging to an external drawing file. All the manipulations performed on an external reference file will not affect the original drawing file because a reference file is only an image that has been scaled or rotated.

When you attach a drawing file as an external reference file, it is permanently attached until it is detached or bounded to the current drawing. When you load your drawing into the drawing editor, AutoCAD automatically reloads each external reference drawing file; thus, each external drawing file reflects the latest state of the referenced drawing file. If necessary, you can make an external reference file a permanent part of your current drawing. This is similar to inserting a drawing with the INSERT command. You can also make dependent symbols such as layers, linetypes, text style, and/or dimension style as part of the current drawing file. For a detailed explanation of the external reference file, see Chapter 7.

INQUIRY COMMANDS

AutoCAD provides commands that will print, in the prompt area or on the text screen, various information about entities in the drawing. They can be found in the Inquiry Menu and are briefly described below.

The LIST command prints entity data such as endpoints and length of a line or an arc, center and radius of a circle or an arc, significant angles associated with certain entities, or angles of rotation at which they might be drawn. Data concerning entities selected will include the properties that are stored about those entities in the drawing data file.

The DBLIST command prints lists of data about all of the entities in the drawing. It can take a long time to scroll through all the data in a large drawing. DBLIST can, like other commands, be terminated by cancelling with ⌨Ctrl + ⌨C.

The ID command prints out the coordinates of a point selected on the screen either by picking with the pointing device or Osnapping to it using a selected Osnap mode point on an entity on the screen.

The DIST command prints out the distance, in the current units, between two points either selected on the screen or keyed in from the keyboard.

The AREA command prints out the area and perimeter of an enclosed shape selected on the screen by either entering a series of points defining the shape or selecting a closed entity such as a polygon, circle, or closed polyline.

For a detailed explanation of the Inquiry commands, see Chapter 3.

DIMENSIONING

AutoCAD provides a comprehensive set of commands and system variable settings for putting dimensions on your drawing. A great variety of discipline-related conventions are accommodated. Once the variables are set, you can simply pick two points on an object and one point to establish the location of the dimension line and AutoCAD does the rest. It will automatically provide the gap between the object and the extension line that you specified when you set the appropriate variable. Other variables set how far the extension lines extend past the dimension line, the size of arrows, and height of text. You can also change or override some of the variable settings in the middle of putting in a dimension. Other variables and their effects on the dimensions in your drawings will be introduced throughout the text as they apply to different drafting and design disciplines.

PLOTTING

Hardcopy refers usually to something you can hold in your hand and read or view such as a letter printed out by a printer or a drawing plotted on a sheet of vellum, mylar, or other medium.

The three primary objectives of the computer-designer/drafter when producing a CAD drawing are:

1. To view objects on the screen,
2. to plot the drawing, and
3. to use the data generated for analysis and design.

Of these three, plotting (producing a hard copy) is the most common application of a computer-generated drawing. If this is your objective, you should keep the desired plotted sheet in mind when you create a drawing. And, in light of this, you must be aware of the relationship between the plot and the display. In order to plot a drawing, or part of a drawing, the view to be plotted must be a potential display. The PLOT command is available while you are in the Drawing Editor or from the Main Menu. Once invoked, you will be prompted to specify the view you wish to plot. So, when you create a drawing in anticipation of making a plot from it, be sure that the desired view is one that can be displayed on the screen also.

Other options allow rotating the whole drawing (but not any object by itself within the drawing) from the plot command. That configuration (changing an individual object) on your display is not possible without going into the Drawing Editor to make those changes.

Plotting can be done on a pen plotter, electrostatic plotter, or a printer with graphics capability at various scale factors. You can also instruct AutoCAD to write the plot output in a disk file (for later transmission to a plotter). See Chapter 5 for a detailed explanation of the PLOT command.

SPECIAL FEATURES

Following are some of the special features of AutoCAD.

Slides

The current display can be saved as a slide that can be recalled quickly to be displayed again. AutoCAD slides are recognized by many desktop publishing programs, so you can use slides to incorporate your drawings in other applications. You can also group slides into a slide library, and write a script file to display them in a slide show.

Drawing Interchange Capability

AutoCAD can write drawing information in a format easily processed by user-written programs. Translations between AutoCAD and other CAD systems data base formats, and special-purpose analysis and modification of AutoCAD drawings can be accomplished by means of this mechanism. Interchange files can also be read and written in Data Exchange Format (DXF) and Initial Graphics Exchange Standard (IGES) formats.

Entity Handles

You can choose to have AutoCAD assign each entity a handle. An entity handle is a unique, permanent identifier that is saved with the entity in a drawing file. Handles can be used to link the AutoCAD drawing file to external data bases.

AutoLISP

AutoCAD provides an embedded programming language with which you can use expressions and variables, define your own functions and commands, and perform calculations. These can be done from the keyboard or saved for later use by writing them in American Standard Code for Information Interchange (ASCII) format in a file with the extension of .LSP. You can also customize the .MNU file which controls how the various menu (screen, mouse buttons, etc.) devices respond to input. With AutoLISP it is possible to develop third-party software for enhancing the off-the-shelf AutoCAD program.

ADS

The AutoCAD Development System (ADS) provides a variation of the open architecture available with AutoLISP described above, except it is in a C-language environment. Whether you choose AutoLISP or ADS depends upon your particular needs relative to the strengths of the two approaches.

AME

The AutoCAD Advanced Modeling Extension (AME) allows you to create 3D objects for solid modeling and analysis. Solids can be built from basic shapes such as box, cube, cylinder, torus, sphere, wedge, and cone. You can define an object's physical and material properties, thus allowing analysis of the object. You can easily edit the shape of the solid object to create several different designs. Several commands are provided to extract 2D geometric shapes from the 3D solid model.

For an additional explanation of special features, see Chapters 10, 13, and 16.

WARNINGS

Following are the warnings that are to be kept in mind while working in AutoCAD. These things can get you into trouble if you are not careful.

UNDO Command

When AutoCAD introduced the UNDO command it unleashed a potential "drawing eater" if indiscriminately turned loose. The UNDO command undoes the previous operation that AutoCAD has performed. You can undo the UNDO with the REDO command one time only! If you UNDO two things in a row, then the REDO command can only be used to restore the undoing of the last UNDO, not the one prior to it. Imagine this, you have made an error by copying a selected group of entities to the wrong location, perhaps on top of another group of entities. It would take quite a long time to select and erase each entity from the copied group. UNDO does it with a single command entry. You invoke the UNDO command and before using another command you glance away from the screen and inadvertantly lay a book (or your elbow) on the spacebar long enough to hear the "beeeeeeeeeeep" from the keyboard telling you that the last command (UNDO) has been going wild in your drawing, that is, if there is any drawing left. There are occasions when you might wish to invoke multiple UNDOs. Just remember, you can only REDO the last UNDO.

COLOR and LINETYPE Commands

Color usage is twofold, one is for visually distinguishing entities on the screen, the other is for communicating to the plotter what pen to use (permitting different plotted colors and line widths). An early (and still the most common) means to achieve different colors is to assign colors to layers and draw entities that need to be a particular color on a layer having that color. Recent versions of AutoCAD permit you to also use the COLOR command to assign individual entities different colors on the same layer. Unless you have a very specific reason to do so, this usage along with different layer colors can cause confusion as the drawing becomes more complex. Therefore, you are advised to **not** use the COLOR command indiscriminately. While the COLOR command is easy to use, it is not the best way to achieve the two primary purposes of using colors in all but the most advanced applications.

Linetypes (center, hidden, dotted, etc.) are likewise achieved through both the layer assignments and using the LINETYPE command. Like the COLOR command, you are advised **not** to attempt to achieve different linetypes by using the LAYER and LINETYPE commands.

The BLOCK command combines a group of selected entities into a unit that acts like a single entity when operated upon by various entity editing commands (like MOVE and COPY). If the individual entities that make up a block have been assigned various colors/linetypes by the two methods mentioned above, and then the block has been placed on a particular layer with its assigned color/linetype, you can (or maybe you can not) imagine the resulting misinterpretations that might occur.

MENU Command

Normally, beginning AutoCAD users do not need the MENU command. It calls up special program files that cause AutoCAD commands to be accessible on various devices such as the side screen menu, the pull-down screen menus, the tablet menu, and the mouse/puck buttons menu. The ACAD.MNX is compiled (what AutoCAD does to make it more efficient) from a file called ACAD.MNU. This program file is automatically called into operation whenever you call up a new drawing or an existing drawing that was previously saved while the ACAD MENU was in effect. For beginning students, the ACAD MENU offers as complete an access to the AutoCAD drafting features as you could need. Custom (third-party) programs designed for use with AutoCAD often come with a menu (filename.MNX) that can be called into use when necessary. Therefore, unless you know what a particular menu file is for, know its filename, and have a need for it, you should forego using the MENU command.

LOAD Command

The term load shows up in several places. It is the name of a command that causes certain SHAPE files to become available for use. It is normally for advanced usage with symbols that you (or third parties) can create using the SHAPE command. Emphasis will be placed using blocks rather than shapes in this textbook because of their more universal usage. Another use of load will be explained in the LINETYPE command. The use of (load "filename") in AutoLISP is covered in *Practical AutoLISP,* a text/reference book for custom AutoLISP programmers.

Running Osnap

There are two ways to work with the powerful Osnap feature that causes AutoCAD to Snap to a specified endpoint, midpoint, center, etc. on existing entities. One way is to enter an Osnap mode while being prompted to select a point; i.e., starting point of a line, location of text, etc. This method does not require using the word OSNAP in the process. Another method is to invoke the Osnap mode and then specify the particular mode(s) that you wish to have used automatically for all subsequent point selections. This is referred to as the running Osnap. You should learn early the difference between a one-time Osnap mode usage and the running Osnap usage. Once invoked, the running Osnap mode is there whether you want it or not. You must take action to disable it, either for one particular point selection or for all following selections. The concepts of this feature and its importance to accurate drafting dictate that you study and practice deliberately until you are confident and comfortable using it.

ZOOM All—Object Too Small

The All option to the ZOOM command causes the screen to display the area that you have set up as your electronic drawing sheet known as the limits. It will cause the display to also include any objects that have been drawn outside the limits. Normally, this is not a problem as long as you can see the area defined by the limits on the screen and at the same time see any object(s) located outside the limits. If you inadvertantly cause an entity to be drawn an extreme distance outside the limits and then use the ZOOM command's All option, that distance might reduce the limits and the objects to such a small size that they will be difficult to spot. It might even appear that there is nothing is on the screen. This can happen if you mistakenly key in a coordinate or distance; e.g., 1.23456 as 123456, leaving out the decimal point. As you can see, the omission of a decimal point can cause an error factor in the magnitude of 100000 to 1. So do not panic if everything seems to disappear from view during the ZOOM All. Use the F1 key to flip to the text screen if necessary and review the previous sequences and values to find a clue. Other tactics can be employed. You can use ZOOM .8X to increase the area you are viewing so that the errant entity will show up inside the viewing area instead of on one edge. Or you can use the UNDO command to get back to a point before the mistake was made.

ZOOM All may also display an expanded area caused by a entity drawn outside the limits and placed on a layer that is currently turned off. Solutions to these problems will become clearer as you progress through the chapters.

This chapter is designed to give you a quick overview of the AutoCAD program. For a detailed explanation of all the AutoCAD commands, refer to the corresponding chapters.

CHAPTER

2

Fundamentals I

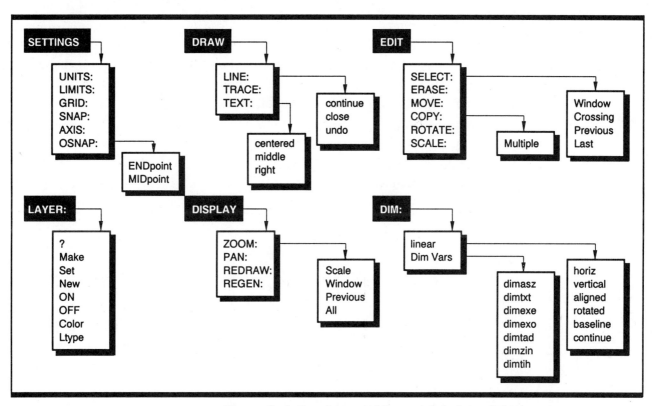

Figure 2-1 Fundamental Commands Introduced

This chapter introduces some of the basic commands and concepts in AutoCAD that can be used to complete a seemingly simple drawing. The project drawing used in this chapter is relatively uncomplicated, but for the newcomer to AutoCAD it presents ample challenge. It has fundamental problems that are "grist for the mill" for lessons in drawing setup, creating and editing entities, and putting in text and dimensioning. Lessons in setting up the drawing environment entail how to accommodate the type of drawing being done and how to anticipate the final plotted sheet (hard copy). The basic entities that will be introduced are LINE, TRACE, TEXT, and LINEAR DIMENSIONING. These can be created by using certain commands from the DRAW and DIM: menu(s). Also introduced are editing features that can be used to make creation of the final drawing quicker, easier, and more accurate. See Figure 2-1 for the commands and options that are covered in this chapter. When you learn how to get to and use commands, how to find your way around the screen, and how AutoCAD makes use of coordinate geometry, you can apply these skills to the chapters containing more advanced drawings and projects.

DRAWING SETTINGS

UNITS Command

In conventional drafting, the drawing is normally done to a certain scale such as 1/4" = 1'-0" or 1" = 1'-0". But in AutoCAD, you draw full scale. All lines, circles, and other entities are drawn and measured as full size. For example, if a part is 150 ft long, it is drawn 150 ft actual size. When you are ready to plot, the drawing is scaled to fit a given sheet size.

Whenever you start a new drawing in AutoCAD, you should invoke the UNITS command first. The UNITS command is used to set the display format measurement and precision of your drawing units. When you begin a new drawing, the default display format measurement and precision are governed by the prototype drawing. You can change them as often as you wish while drawing. The UNITS command allows you to change any one or all of the following:

    Unit display format
    Unit display precision
    Angle display format
    Angle display precision
    Angle direction

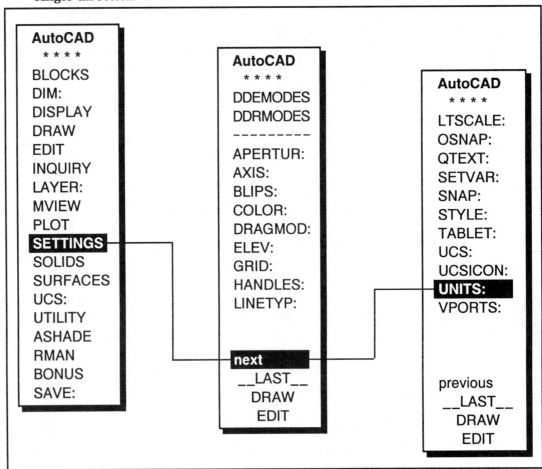

Figure 2-2 The UNITS Command

The UNITS command is invoked from the Screen Root Menu Settings (see Figure 2-2), or at the "Command:" prompt type in **UNITS** and press ⏎.

Command: **units**

When you invoke the UNITS command your screen flips to text mode (unless you are operating at a dual-monitor station). Remember, you flip (toggle) back and forth between the text screen and graphics screen by pressing the F1 key. The text screen will display the following:

Report formats:	(Examples)
1. Scientific	1.55E+01
2. Decimal	15.50
3. Engineering	1'-3.50"
4. Architectural	1'-3 1/2"
5. Fractional	15 1/2
Enter choice, 1 to 5 <default>:	

Choose the report format you prefer. To illustrate the various report formats, the menu shows how a distance of 15.5 drawing units would be displayed in each format. The current format will have its corresponding number displayed where <default> is shown. The prototype default is 2 (Decimal).

The Engineering and Architectural report formats produce feet and inches displays. These formats assume each drawing unit represents one inch. The other formats make no such assumptions, and can be used to represent whatever real-world units you like.

Once you have selected the report format, AutoCAD asks for the precision. If you select 1, 2, or 3 the following prompt appears:

Number of digits to right of decimal point (0 to 8) <default>:

and for 4 or 5, the following prompt is displayed:

Denominator of smallest fraction to display
(1, 2, 4, 8, 16, 32, or 64) <default>:

Drawing a 150-ft long object might, however, differ depending on the units mode chosen. For example, if you use the Decimal unit and decide that one unit equals one foot, then the 150-ft long object will be 150 units long. If you decide that one unit equals one inch, then the 150-ft long object will be drawn 1800 units (150 × 12) long. In Architectural and Engineering unit modes, the unit automatically equals one inch. You may then give the length of the 150-ft long object as 150' or 1800" or simply 1800.

Fundamentals I

After you have selected the report format and precision, AutoCAD prompts you for an angle format:

Systems of angle measure:	(Examples)
1. Decimal degrees	45.0000
2. Degrees/minutes/seconds	45d0'0"
3. Grads	50.0000g
4. Radians	0.7854r
5. Surveyor's units	N45d0'0"E
Enter choice, 1 to 5 <default>:	

The menu illustrates the various formats by showing how an angle of 45 degrees would be displayed in each format.

Angle Display Precision After specifying the angle format AutoCAD will prompt you for the precision with which angles should be displayed. The prompt is:

Number of fractional places for display of angles (0 to 8) <default>:

You can specify a precision of up to eight places. If you are working with degrees/minutes/seconds, the number you enter determines the accuracy of the minutes and seconds. If you specify 0, for example, only degrees are displayed; if you specify 1 or 2, minutes also are displayed; 3 or 4 display degrees, minutes, and seconds; and 5 to 8 will display additional fractional seconds (one to four decimal places).

Next, AutoCAD prompts you for the direction for angle 0. The following prompt will appear:

Direction for angle 0:			
East	3 o'clock	=	0
North	12 o'clock	=	90
West	9 o'clock	=	180
South	6 o'clock	=	270
Enter direction for angle 0 <current>:			

AutoCAD, by its default settings, assumes that 0 degrees is to the right (East, or 3 o'clock) (see Figure 2-3), and that angles increase in the counterclockwise direction. You can change measuring angles starting with any direction by supplying

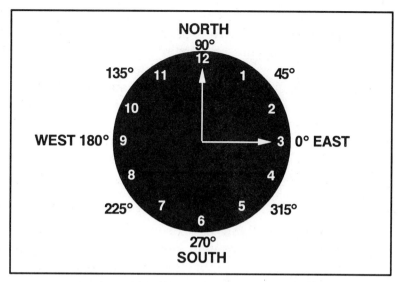

Figure 2-3 Specifying an Angle Direction

the starting direction to this prompt. Note that you always respond to this prompt with an angle specified in the default mode. For example, if you want to make North (12 o'clock) as 0 degrees, then to the prompt type **90** and press ⏎. You can also show AutoCAD the direction you want for angle 0 by specifying two points.

The final prompt controls the direction in which the angles are measured, clockwise or counterclockwise. The prompt follows:

Do you want angles measured clockwise? <n>:

If you accept the default, the angles will be measured in the counterclockwise direction (see Figure 2-4), or if you answer with **y** or **yes**, AutoCAD will measure angles in the clockwise direction.

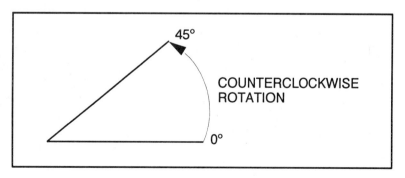

Figure 2-4 Accepting the Counterclockwise Angle Default

NOTE: When AutoCAD prompts you for a distance, displacement, spacing, or coordinates you can always reply with numbers in integer, decimal, scientific, or fractional format. If Engineering or Architectural report format is in effect, you can also input feet, inches, or a combination of feet and inches. However, feet-and-inches input format differs slightly from the report format because it cannot contain a blank. For example, a distance of 75.5 inches can be entered in the feet/inches/fractions format as 6'3-1/2". Notre the absence of spaces and the hyphen in the unconventional location between the inches and the fraction. Normally, it will be displayed in the status area as 6'-3 1/2. If you wish, you can use the SETVAR command to set the UNITMODE system variable to 1 (default UNITMODE system variable is 0) to display feet-and-inches output in the accepted format. For example, if you set UNITMODE to 1, AutoCAD displays the fractional value of 45 1/4 as you enter it: 45-1/4. The feet input should be followed by an apostrophe (') and inches with a trailing double quote ("). When Engineering or Architectural report format is in effect, the drawing unit equals one inch, so you can omit the trailing double quote (") if you like. When you enter feet-and-inches values combined, the inches values should immediately follow the apostrophe, without an intervening space. Distance input does not permit spaces because the spacebar is the same as ⏎.

LIMITS Command

The LIMITS command allows you to place an imaginary rectangular drawing sheet in the CAD drawing space. But, unlike the limitations of the drawing sheet of the board drafter, you can move or enlarge the CAD electronic sheet (the limits) after you have started your drawing. Other than possibly changing the area of the screen, the LIMITS command does not affect the current display on the screen. The defined area determined by the limits governs the portion of the drawing indicated by the visible Grid (see GRID command on p. 73). Limits are also factors that determine how much of the drawing is displayed by the ZOOM All (see ZOOM All on p. 37).

As described in Chapter 1, when you start a new drawing, the default area that is displayed on your screen is determined by the default setting of the limits. The default limits form a rectangle whose lower left corner is at coordinate 0,0 and upper right corner is 12,9. It should be re-emphasized that the default linear units are decimals and can be inches, meters, miles, millimeters, or whatever you decide. These conditions are contingent upon the ACAD.DWG file (the drawing whose properties the new drawings assume) not being altered. Novices are advised to **not** alter ACAD.DWG.

The limits are expressed as a pair of 2D points in the WCS, a lower left and an upper right limit. For example, to set limits for an A-size sheet, set lower left as 0,0 and upper right as 11,8.5 or 12,9; for a B-size sheet set lower left as 0,0 and upper right as 17,11 or 18,12. Most architectural floor plans are drawn at a scale of 1/4" = 1'-0". To set limits to plot on a C-size (22" x 17") paper at 1/4" = 1'-0", the limits are set lower left as 0,0 and upper right as 88',68' (4 x 22, 4 x 17).

The LIMITS command is invoked from the Screen Root Menu Settings (see Figure 2-5), pull-down menu Utility (see Figure 2-6) or, at the "Command:" prompt, type in **LIMITS** and press ⏎.

> Command: **limits**
> ON/OFF/<lower left corner> <default>:

You can accept the default by pressing ⏎ or you can enter a new value for the lower left corner and press ⏎. The response you give for the lower left corner gives the location of the lower left corner of the imaginary rectangular drawing sheet. Then AutoCAD prompts:

> Upper right corner <default>:

You can accept the default by pressing ⏎ or you can enter a new value. The response you give for the upper right corner gives the location of the upper right corner of the imaginary rectangular drawing sheet.

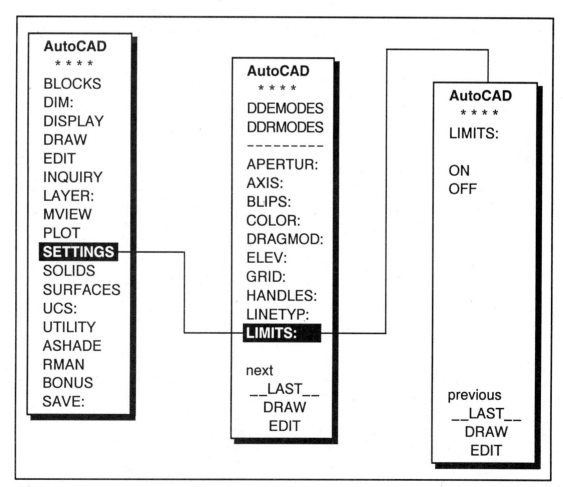

Figure 2-5 The LIMITS Command Invoked from the Screen Root Menu Settings

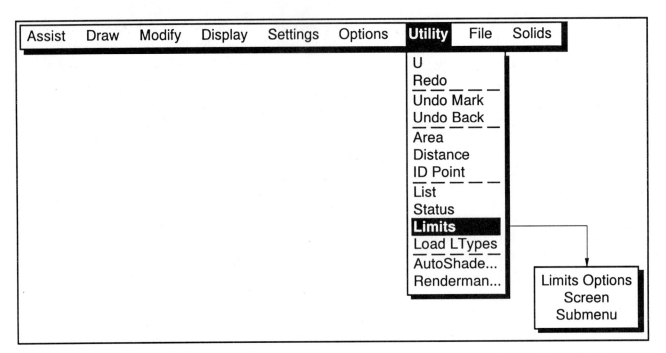

Figure 2-6 The LIMITS Command Invoked from the Pull-Down Menu Utility

There are two additional options available for the LIMITS command. When AutoCAD prompts for the lower left corner, you can respond to the ON or OFF options. The ON/OFF options set whether or not you can specify a point outside the limits when prompted to do so. When you select the ON option, then limits checking is on and you cannot start or end an entity outside the limits, nor can you specify displacement points required by the MOVE or COPY commands outside the limits. You can, however, specify two points (center and point on circle) that draw a circle, part of which might be outside the limits. The limits check is simply an aid to help you avoid drawing off the imaginary rectangular drawing sheet. Leaving the limits checking ON is a sort of safety net to keep you from inadvertantly specifying a point outside the limits. This can also be a hindrance if you need to specify such a point.

When you select the OFF option (default), AutoCAD disables limits checking, allowing you to draw the entities and specify points outside the limits.

Whenever you change the limits, you will not see any change on the screen unless you use the All option of the ZOOM command. ZOOM All lets you see entire newly set limits on the screen. For example, if your current limits are 12 by 9 (lower left corner 0,0 and upper right corner 12,9) and you change the limits to 42 by 36 (lower left corner 0,0 and upper right corner 42,36), you will still see the 12 by 9 area. You can draw the entities anywhere on the limits 42 by 36 area, but you will see on the screen the entities that are drawn only in the 12 by 9 area. To see the entire limits, execute the ZOOM command using the All option.

The ZOOM command is invoked from the DISPLAY menu or at the "Command:" prompt, type in **ZOOM** and press ⏎. AutoCAD displays the following prompt line:

Command: **zoom**
All/Center/Dynamic/Extents/Left/Previous/Vmax/Window/<Scale(X/XP)>:

Type **A** or **ALL** and press ⏎. (For a detailed explanation of the ZOOM command see p. 101). You will see on the screen the entire limits or current extents (whichever is greater). If the drawing extends outside the drawing limits or entities are drawn outside the limits, ZOOM All will include all entities in their entirety.

Whenever you change the limits, you should always invoke ZOOM All to see on the screen the entire limits or current extents.

For example, the following command sequence shows steps to change limits for an existing drawing (see Figures 2-7a and 2-7b).

Command: **limits**
ON/OFF/<lower left corner><-10'-0",-10'-0">: ⏎
Upper right corner <50'-0",35'-0">: 100',70'
Command: **zoom**
All/Center/Dynamic/Extents/Left/Previous/Vmax/Window/<Scale(X/XP)>:**all**

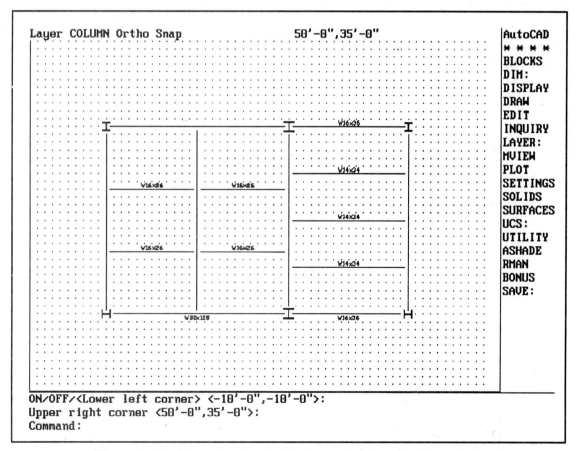

Figure 2-7a Changing the Limits for an Existing Drawing (Before)

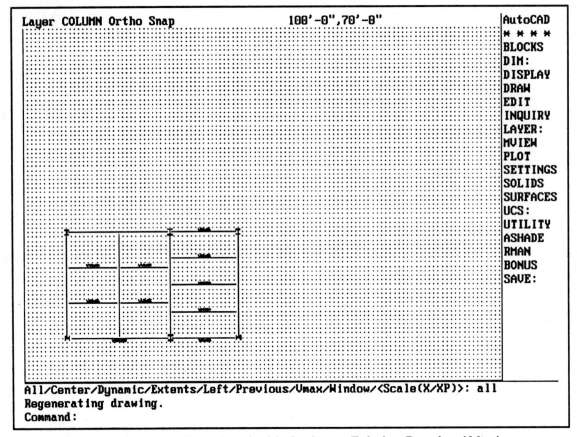

Figure 2-7b Changing the Limits for an Existing Drawing (After)

DRAW COMMANDS

LINE Command

The primary drawing entity is the line. A series of connected straight line segments can be drawn by invoking the LINE command and then selecting the proper sequence of endpoints. AutoCAD will connect the points with a series of lines. The LINE command is one of the few AutoCAD commands that automatically repeats in this fashion. It uses the ending point of one line as the starting point of the next, continuing to prompt you for each subsequent ending point. In order to terminate this continuing feature you must give a null response (press ⏎). Even though a series of lines is drawn using a single LINE command, each line is a separate entity as though it had been drawn with a separate LINE command.

You can specify the endpoints using either 2D (x,y) or 3D (x,y,z) coordinates, or a combination of the two. If you enter 2D coordinates, AutoCAD uses the current elevation as the Z element of the point (zero is the default). This chapter is concerned only with 2D points whose elevation is zero. 3D concepts and nonzero elevations are covered in later chapters.

Invoke the LINE command from the Screen Root Menu Draw (see Figure 2-8), pull-down menu Draw (see Figure 2-9), or at the "Command:" prompt, you can type in **LINE** and press ⏎.

> Command: **line**
> From point:

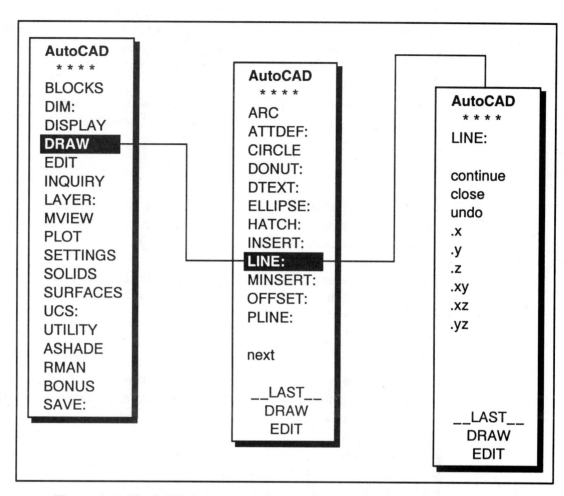

Figure 2–8 The LINE Command Invoked from the Screen Root Menu Draw

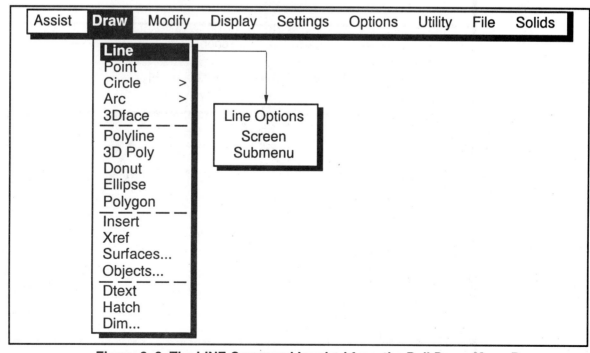

Figure 2–9 The LINE Command Invoked from the Pull-Down Menu Draw

Where to Start? The first point of the first entity in a drawing normally establishes where all of the points of other entities must be placed. It is like the cornerstone of a building. Careful thought should go into locating the first point.

You can specify the starting point of the line by absolute coordinates or by using your pointing device (mouse or puck). Then AutoCAD prompts:

    To point:

Where to From Here? In addition to the first point being the cornerstone, the direction of the first entity is also critical to where all other points of other entities are located with respect to each other.

You can specify the end of the line by absolute coordinates, relative coordinates, or by using your pointing device to specify the end of the line on the screen. Again, AutoCAD will repeat the prompt:

    To point:

You can enter a series of connected lines. To save time, the LINE command remains active and asks for a new "To point:" after each point you specify. When you have finished entering a connected series of lines, give a null reply (press ⏎) to terminate the LINE command.

For example, the following command sequence shows placement of connected lines as shown in Figure 2-10 by absolute coordinates (see Figure 2-11):

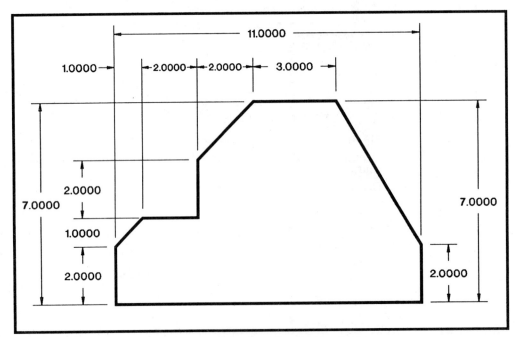

Figure 2-10 Placing Connected Lines

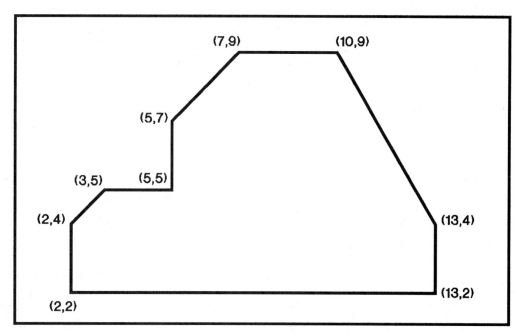

Figure 2–11 Placing Connected Lines Using Absolute Coordinates

Command: **line**
From point: **2,2**
To point: **2,4**
To point: **3,5**
To point: **5,5**
To point: **5,7**
To point: **7,9**
To point: **10,9**
To point: **13,4**
To point: **13,2**
To point: **2,2**
To point: ⏎
Command:

The following command sequence shows placement of connected lines as shown in Figure 2–10 by relative rectangular coordinates (see Figure 2–12):

Command: **line**
From point: **2,2**
To point: **@0,2**
To point: **@1,1**
To point: **@2,0**
To point: **@0,2**
To point: **@2,2**
To point: **@3,0**
To point: **@3,-5**
To point: **@0,-2**
To point: **2,2**
To point: ⏎
Command:

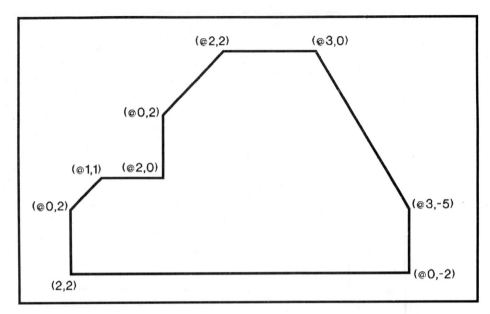

Figure 2-12 Placing Connected Lines Using Relative Rectangular Coordinates

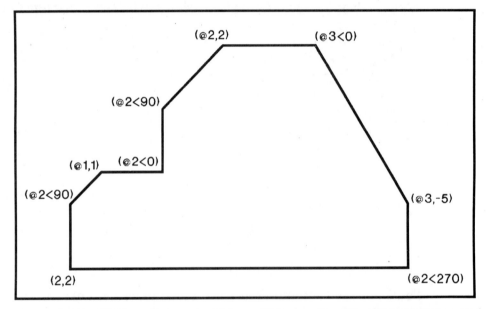

Figure 2-13 Placing Connected Lines Using a Combination of Polar and Rectangular Coordinates

The following command sequence shows placement of connected lines as shown in Figure 2-10 by using a combination of polar and rectangular coordinates (see Figure 2-13).

Command: **line**
From point: **2,2**
To point: **@0<90**
To point: **@1,1**
To point: **@2<0**
To point: **@0<90**
To point: **@2,2**
To point: **@3<0**

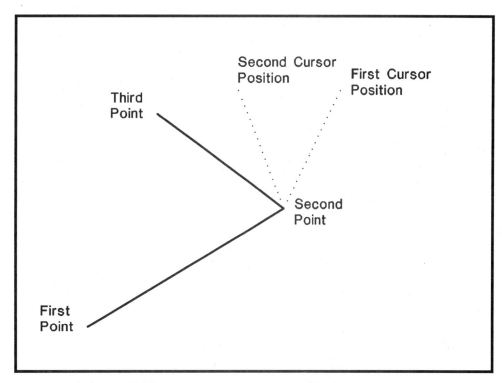

Figure 2-14 Placing Points with the Cursor Rather than with Coordinates

To point: **@3,-5**
To point: **@0<270**
To point: **2,2**
To point: ⏎
Command:

If you are placing points with a cursor instead of providing coordinates, a rubberband line is displayed between the starting point and the cross-hairs. This helps you see where the resulting line will go. In Figure 2-14 the dotted lines represent previous cursor positions.

Most of the AutoCAD commands have a variety of options. For the LINE command there are three options available: Continue, Close and Undo.

Continue Option When you invoke the LINE command and respond to the "From point:" prompt with a null response or select the option Continue, AutoCAD automatically sets the start of the line to the end of the most recently drawn line or arc. This provides a simple method for constructing a tangentially connected line in an arc-line continuation.

The subsequent prompt sequence depends on whether a line or arc was more recently drawn. If the line is more recent, the starting point of the new line will be set as the ending point of that most recent line, and the "To point:" prompt will appear as usual. If an arc is more recent, its end defines the starting point and the direction of the new line. AutoCAD prompts for:

Length of the line:

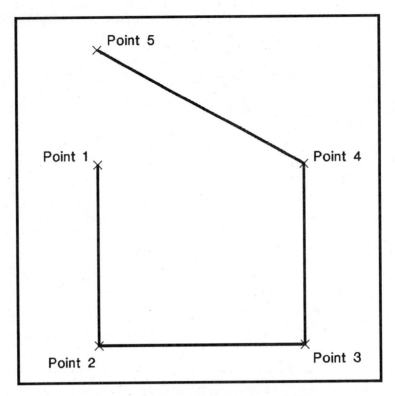

Figure 2-15 Using the Continue Option

Specify the length of the line to be drawn, and then AutoCAD continues with the normal "To point:" prompt.

The following command sequence shows an example using the Continue option (see Figure 2-15).

```
Command: line
From point: pick point 1
To point: pick point 2
To point: pick point 3
To point: ↵
Command: to continue line from the point 3, pick
          Continue option under the LINE command
From point: AutoCAD automatically picks the last
          point of the previous line
To point: pick point 4
To point: pick point 5
To point: ↵
Command:
```

Close Option If the sequence of lines you are drawing forms a closed polygon, then you can use the Close option to join the last and first point automatically. AutoCAD

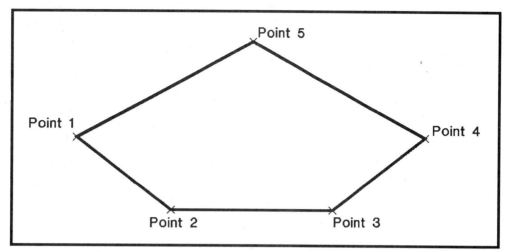

Figure 2-16 Using the Close Option

draws the final line segment if you respond to the "To point:" prompt with a **C** or **close** and press ⏎ or select the Close option from the menu. AutoCAD performs two steps when you select the Close option. The first step closes the polygon and the second step terminates the LINE command (equivalent to a null response) and brings you back to the "Command:" prompt.

The following command sequence shows an example of using the Close option (see Figure 2-16).

> Command: **line**
> From point: *pick point 1*
> To point: *pick point 2*
> To point: *pick point 3*
> To point: *pick point 4*
> To point: *pick point 5*
> To point: **C**
> Command:

Undo Option When drawing a series of connected lines, you may wish to erase the most recent entity and continue from the end of the previous entity. You can do so by staying in the LINE command without exiting by using the Undo option. Whenever you wish to erase the most recent entity, at the "To point:" prompt, enter **U** or **undo** and press ⏎ or you can select the Undo option from the menu. If necessary, you can enter multiple Us or repeat the Undo option from the menu, and it will erase the most recent entity one at a time. Once you are out of the LINE command, it is too late to use the Undo option of the LINE command to erase the most recent entity.

The following command sequence shows an example using the Undo option (see Figure 2-17).

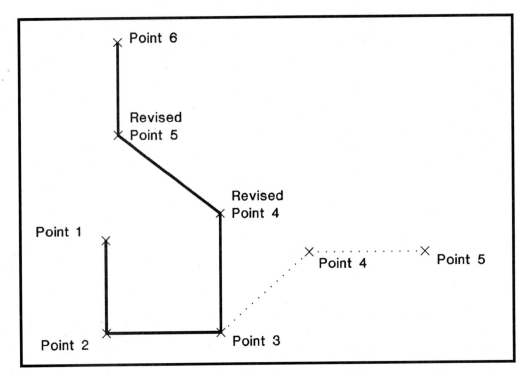

Figure 2-17 Using the Undo Option

Command: **line**
From point: *pick point 1*
To point: *pick point 2*
To point: *pick point 3*
To point: *pick point 4*
To point: *pick point 5*
To point: **U**
To point: **U**
To point: *pick revised point 4*
To point: *pick revised point 5*
To point: *pick point 6*
To point: ⏎
Command:

TRACE Command

When it is necessary to draw thick lines, the TRACE command may be used instead of the LINE command. Traces are entered just like lines except that the line width is set first. To specify the width, you can type a distance or select two points and let AutoCAD use the measured distance between them. When you draw using the TRACE command, the previous TRACE segment is not drawn until the next endpoint is specified.

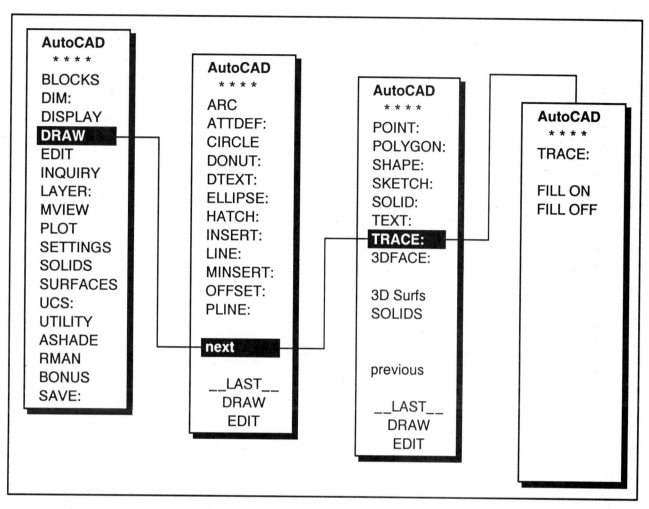

Figure 2-18 The TRACE Command Invoked from the Screen Root Menu Draw

Invoke the TRACE command from the Screen Root Menu Draw (see Figure 2-18) or, at the "Command:" prompt, you can type in **TRACE** and press ⏎.

Command: **trace**
Trace width <default>:

For example, the following command sequence shows placement of connected lines using the TRACE command (see Figure 2-19).

Command: **trace**
Trace width <default>: **.05**
From point: *pick point 1*
To point: *pick point 2*
To point: *pick point 3*
To point: *pick point 4*
To point: ⏎
Command:

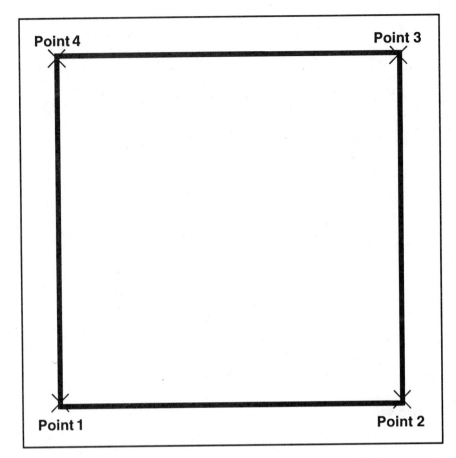

Figure 2-19 Placing Connected Lines Using the TRACE Command

UTILITY COMMANDS

SAVE Command

While working in the Drawing Editor, you should save your drawing once every 10 to 15 minutes without exiting the drawing. By saving your work periodically, you are protecting your work from possible power failures, editing errors, and other disasters. This can be accomplished by the SAVE command. Save as often as you can afford to lose your work.

The SAVE command is invoked from the Side Root Menu (see Figure 2-20), pull-down menu File (see Figure 2-21), or at the "Command:" prompt, type in **SAVE** and press ⏎.

    Command: **save**

A dialogue box will appear and the cursor changes to an arrow pointing up and to the left as shown in Figure 2-22. You can click to the ⟨ ᴏᴄ ⟩ button to save the drawing to the current drawing file. If you save a drawing that already exists, a dialogue box will appear with the following message:

Figure 2–20 The SAVE Command Invoked from the Side Root Menu

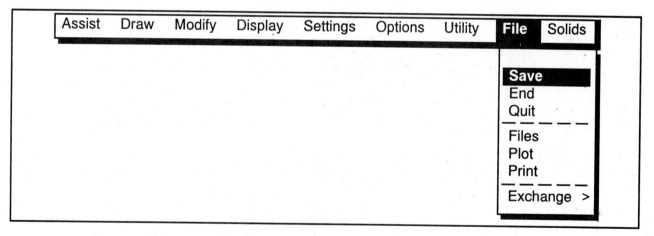

Figure 2–21 The SAVE Command Invoked from the Pull-Down Menu File

The specified file already exists.
Do you want to replace it?

You can click ⟨ OK ⟩ to replace, or click ⟨Cancel⟩ to go back to the previous dialogue box.

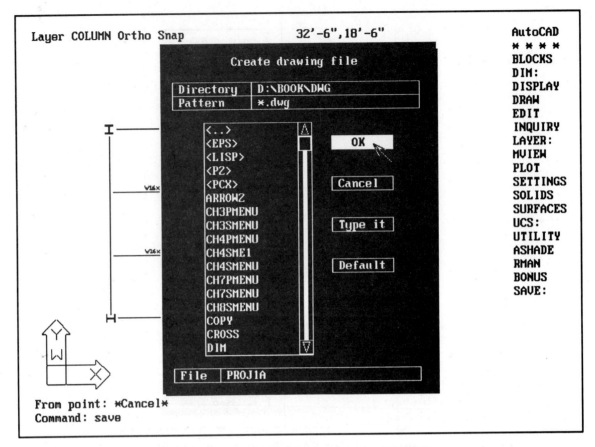

Figure 2-22 The Dialogue Box for the SAVE Command

Instead of saving the drawing in the default drawing name, you can click `Type It` to save the drawing with a different output filename. AutoCAD will prompt for the new filename and you can type a new name or press ⏎ to take the default name.

If you decide not to save the drawing, click `Cancel` in the dialogue box and AutoCAD will take you back to the "Command:" prompt.

Whenever you save the drawing, AutoCAD writes the drawing in its current state to the disk.

END Command

The END command will save your drawing, and at the same time, exit the Drawing Editor to return to the Main Menu.

The END command is invoked from the Side Root Menu (see Figure 2-23), pull-down menu File (see Figure 2-24), or at the "Command:" prompt, type in **END** and press ⏎.

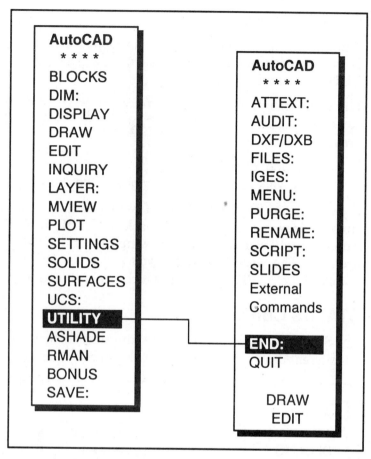

Figure 2–23 The END Command Invoked from the Side Root Menu

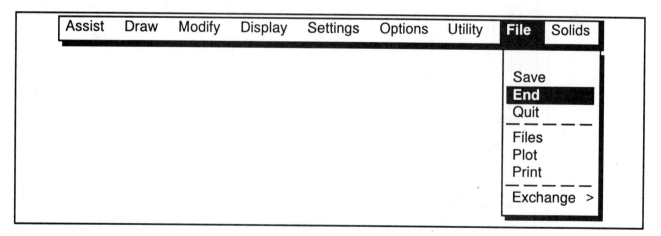

Figure 2–24 The END Command Invoked from the Pull-Down Menu File

Command: **end**

When you issue the END command, AutoCAD automatically saves the drawing to the given drawing filename and appends the file extension .DWG. The old version, if present, is saved as a backup, with the file extension .BAK.

QUIT Command

The QUIT command will allow you to exit the Drawing Editor without saving the drawing since the last time you saved the drawing. Think twice before issuing the QUIT command.

The QUIT command is invoked from the Side Root Menu (see Figure 2-25), pull-down menu File (see Figure 2-26), or at the "Command:" prompt, type in **QUIT** and press ⏎.

> Command: **quit**
> Really want to discard all changes to the drawing?

If you respond **Y** or **Yes**, AutoCAD will quit the Drawing Editor without saving the current drawing, and take you back to the Main Menu. If you respond **N** or **No**, AutoCAD will remain in the Drawing Editor and take you back to the "Command:" prompt. The work is saved if you enter the QUIT command immediately after entering the SAVE command, which is similar to using the END command.

STATUS Command

The STATUS command will report information about your current settings of some of the current drawing parameters such as Grid spacing, Snap spacing, limits, etc.

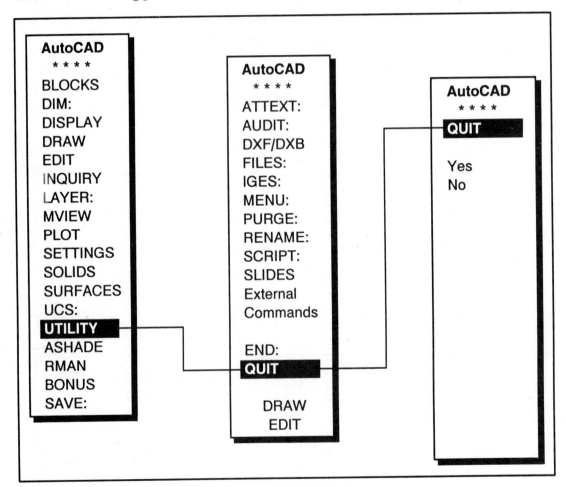

Figure 2-25 The QUIT Command Invoked from the Side Root Menu

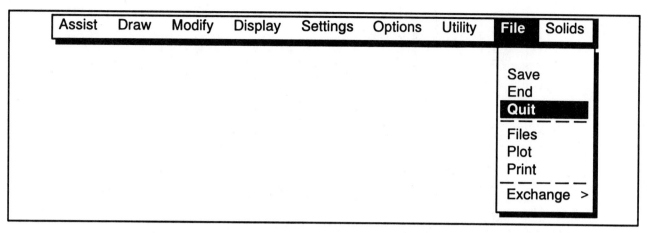

Figure 2-26 The QUIT Command Invoked from the Pull-Down Menu File

The STATUS command is invoked from the Side Root Menu Inquiry (see Figure 2-27), or at the "Command:" prompt, type in **STATUS** and press ⏎.

Command: **status**

AutoCAD will provide the information shown in Figure 2-28.

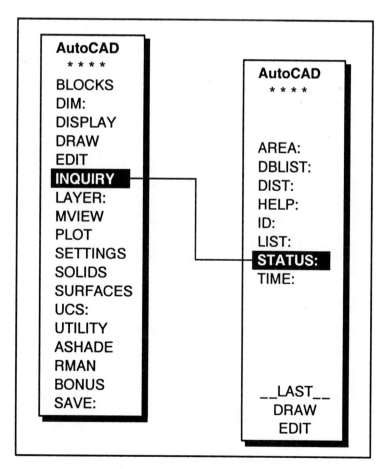

Figure 2-27 The STATUS Command Invoked from the Side Root Menu Inquiry

```
221 entities in C:\DWG\PROJ1A
Model space limits are X:   -10'-0"   Y:   -10'-0"   (Off)
                       X:    50'-0"   Y:    35'-0"
Model space uses       X:    -8'-0"   Y:    -8'-0"
                       X:    48'-0"   Y:    33'-0"
Display shows          X:   -10'-0"   Y:   -10'-0"
                       X: 52'-1 9/16"  Y:    35'-0"
Insertion base is      X:     0'-0"   Y:     0'-0"   Z:     0'-0"
Snap resolution is     X:     0'-6"   Y:     0'-6"
Grid spacing is        X:     1'-0"   Y:     1'-0"

Current space:      Model space
Current layer:      COLUMN
Current color:      BYLAYER -- 1 (red)
Current linetype:   BYLAYER -- CONTINUOUS
Current elevation:     0'-0"  thickness:     0'-0"
Axis off  Fill on  Grid off  Ortho on  Qtext off  Snap on  Tablet off
Object snap modes:   None

Free disk: 1589248 bytes
```

Figure 2-28 The STATUS Screen

All coordinates and distances are displayed in the format specified by the most recent UNITS command format control. The OFF option in the LIMITS command menu refers to limit checking explained in the previous section. The free disk amount refers to the amount of memory left on the drive that contains the drawing file. If the disk space is dangerously low, AutoCAD automatically ends the drawing session by saving your drawing on the drive that contains the drawing file. In addition, the STATUS command provides the information about the tools that are on or off, such as Ortho, Snap, and Coords.

LAB EXERCISES

In exercises 2-1 through 2-3, use absolute, relative, and polar coordinates in any combination to draw the figures.

Set limits   lower left: 0,0
              upper right: 12,9

NOTE: When you change the limits do not forget to ZOOM All. Do not add the dimensions.

Lab Exercise 2-1

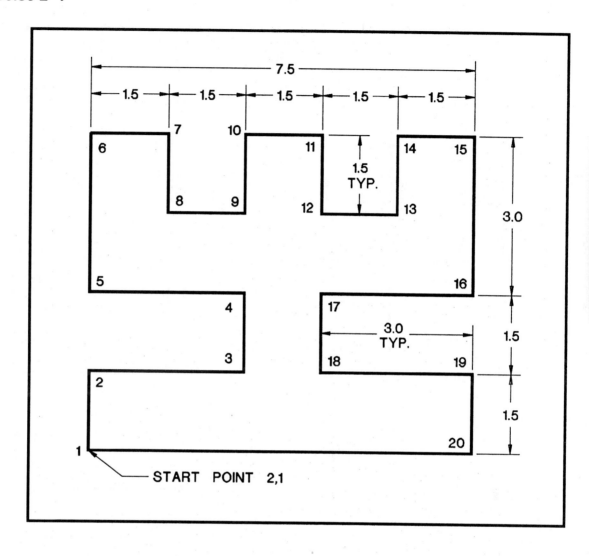

Lab Exercise 2-2

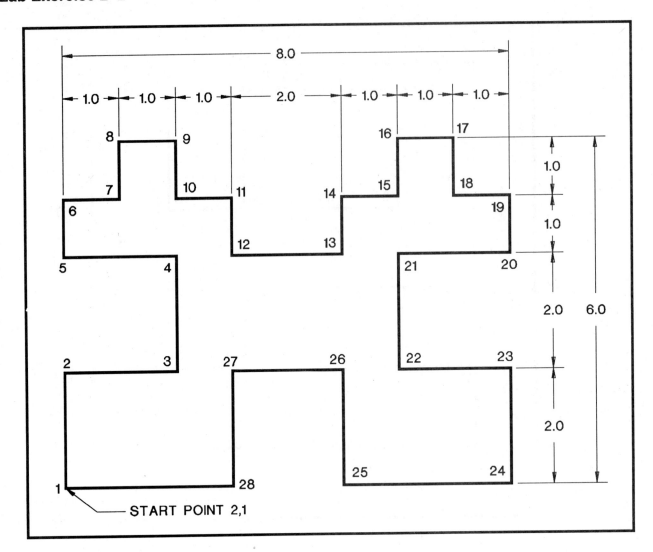

Lab Exercise 2-3

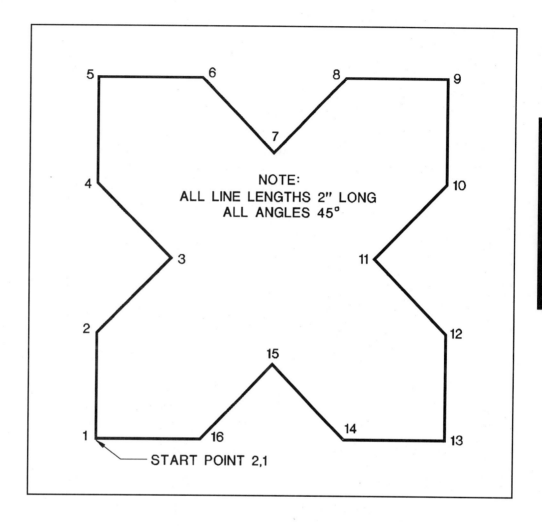

NOTE:
ALL LINE LENGTHS 2" LONG
ALL ANGLES 45°

START POINT 2,1

LAB EXERCISES

In exercises 2–4 through 2-8, use absolute, relative, and polar coordinates in any combination to draw the figures.

Set limits   lower left: 0,0
             upper right: 17,11

Hint: It is much easier to do these exercises if you write down the coordinate entries before you enter them on the computer. If you make a mistake simply enter a **U** and a ⏎. Then enter the coordinate value again.

Lab Exercise 2–4

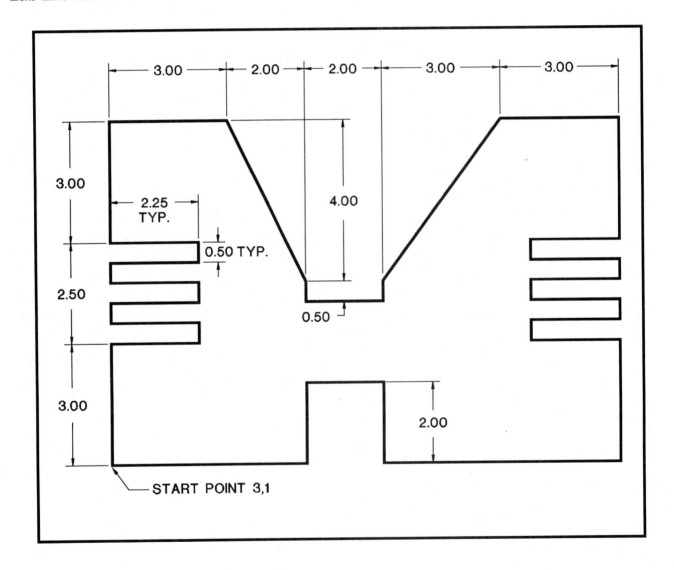

Lab Exercise 2-5

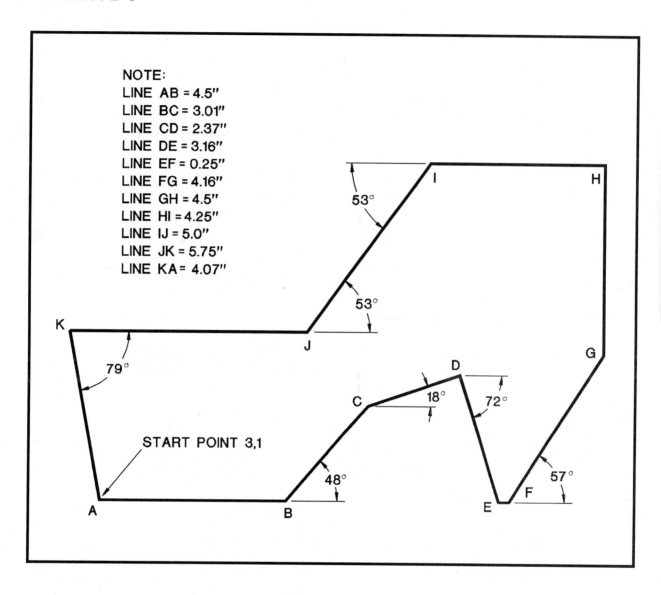

NOTE:
LINE AB = 4.5"
LINE BC = 3.01"
LINE CD = 2.37"
LINE DE = 3.16"
LINE EF = 0.25"
LINE FG = 4.16"
LINE GH = 4.5"
LINE HI = 4.25"
LINE IJ = 5.0"
LINE JK = 5.75"
LINE KA = 4.07"

START POINT 3,1

Lab Exercise 2-6

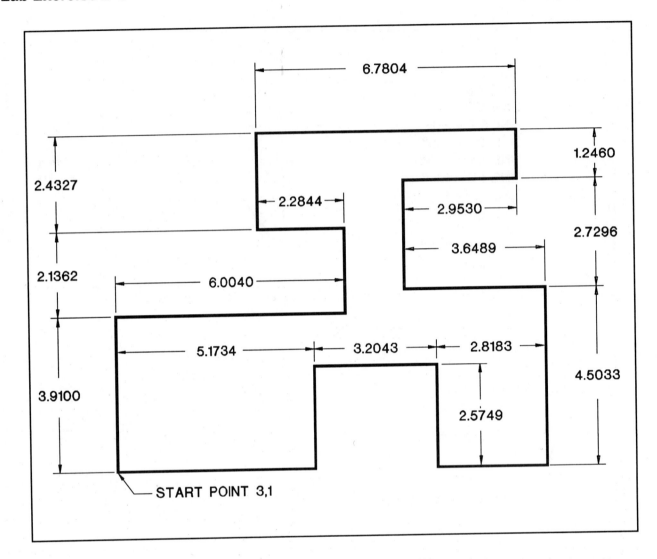

Lab Exercise 2-7

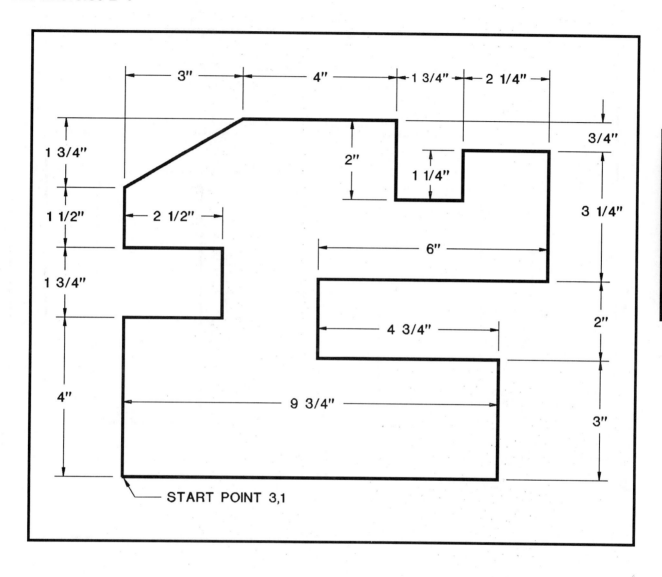

START POINT 3,1

Lab Exercise 2-8

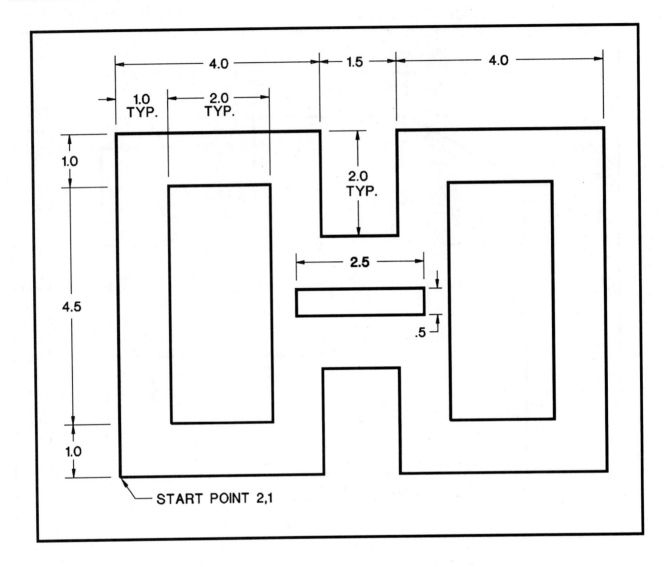

START POINT 2,1

DRAWING TOOLS

The following drawing tools assist you in drawing rapidly while ensuring the highest degree of precision.

GRID Command

The GRID command displays a reference Grid of dots with any desired spacing. AutoCAD creates a Grid that is similar to a sheet of graph paper. You can turn the Grid display on and off at will, and you can change the dot spacing. The Grid is just a drawing tool, not part of the drawing; it is for visual reference only and is never plotted. While in the WCS the Grid fills the area defined by the limits.

The Grid has several uses within the Drawing Editor. First, it shows the extent of your drawing size. For example, if you set your limits to 42 x 36 units and Grid spacing is set for .5 units, then you will have 84 x 72 dots in the X and Y directions respectively. This will give you a better sense of the drawing's size than if it were on a blank background.

Second, using the Grid with the SNAP command (discussed in the next section) is helpful when you create a design in terms of evenly spaced units. For example, if your design is .5 units and multiples, then you can set Grid spacing as .5 and complete the drawing easily. You could check your drawing visually by comparing the locations of the Grid dots and the cross-hairs. Figure 2-29 shows a drawing with a Grid spacing of .5 units with limits set to 0,0 and 17,11.

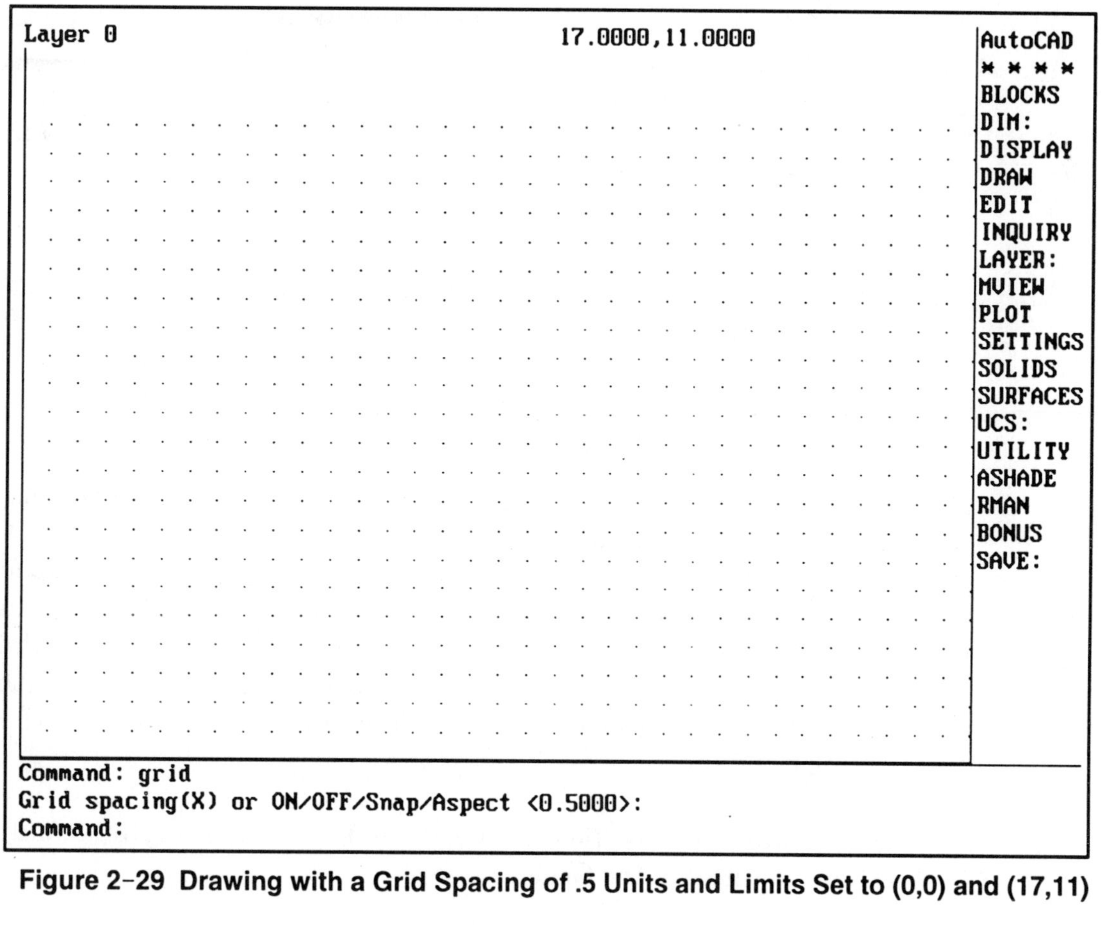

Figure 2-29 Drawing with a Grid Spacing of .5 Units and Limits Set to (0,0) and (17,11)

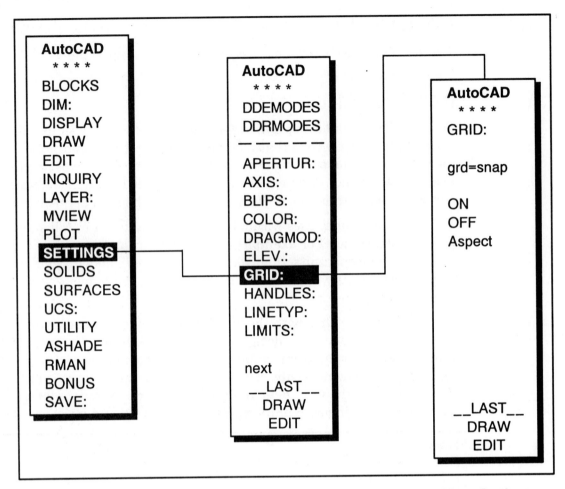

Figure 2-30 The GRID Command Invoked from the Screen Root Menu Settings

The GRID command is invoked from the Screen Root Menu Settings (see Figure 2-30), or at the "Command:" prompt you can type in **GRID** and press the spacebar or ⏎.

Command: **grid**
Grid Spacing (X) or ON/OFF/Snap/Aspect <default>:

You can accept the default by pressing the spacebar or ⏎ or you may enter a new value representing a new Grid spacing and press the spacebar or ⏎. The Grid is turned on automatically when you either accept the default Grid spacing or enter a new Grid spacing value. It is often useful to set the Grid spacing equal to the Snap resolution or a multiple of it. To specify the Grid spacing as a multiple of the Snap value, enter **X** after the value. For example, to set up the Grid value three times the current Snap value (Snap=0.5 units), enter **3X** for the prompt, which is the same as setting to 1.5 units.

ON Option The ON option has the same effect as accepting the default Grid-spacing value and turns on the Grid.

OFF Option The OFF option turns off the Grid. Also, you can toggle the Grid on and off with the function key F7 or with the ⟨Ctrl⟩ + ⟨G⟩ key combination.

Snap Option The Snap option provides a simple means of locking the Grid spacing to the current Snap resolution.

Aspect Option The Aspect option will allow you to set different X and Y values for the Grid. When you select the Aspect option, AutoCAD prompts for the X and Y values. This is handy if you are dealing with modules of unequal dimensions. For example, suppose you want a horizontal Grid spacing of 1 and vertical spacing of .5. Enter the following:

```
Command: grid
Grid spacing (X) or ON/OFF/Snap/Aspect <0>: A
Horizontal spacing (X)<0>: 1
Vertical spacing (Y)<0>: .5
```

The Aspect option provides the Grid dot spacing as shown in Figure 2-31.

If the spacing of the visible Grid is set too small, AutoCAD displays the following message and does not show the dots on the screen:

```
Grid too dense to display
```

To display the Grid, issue another GRID command and specify a larger spacing.

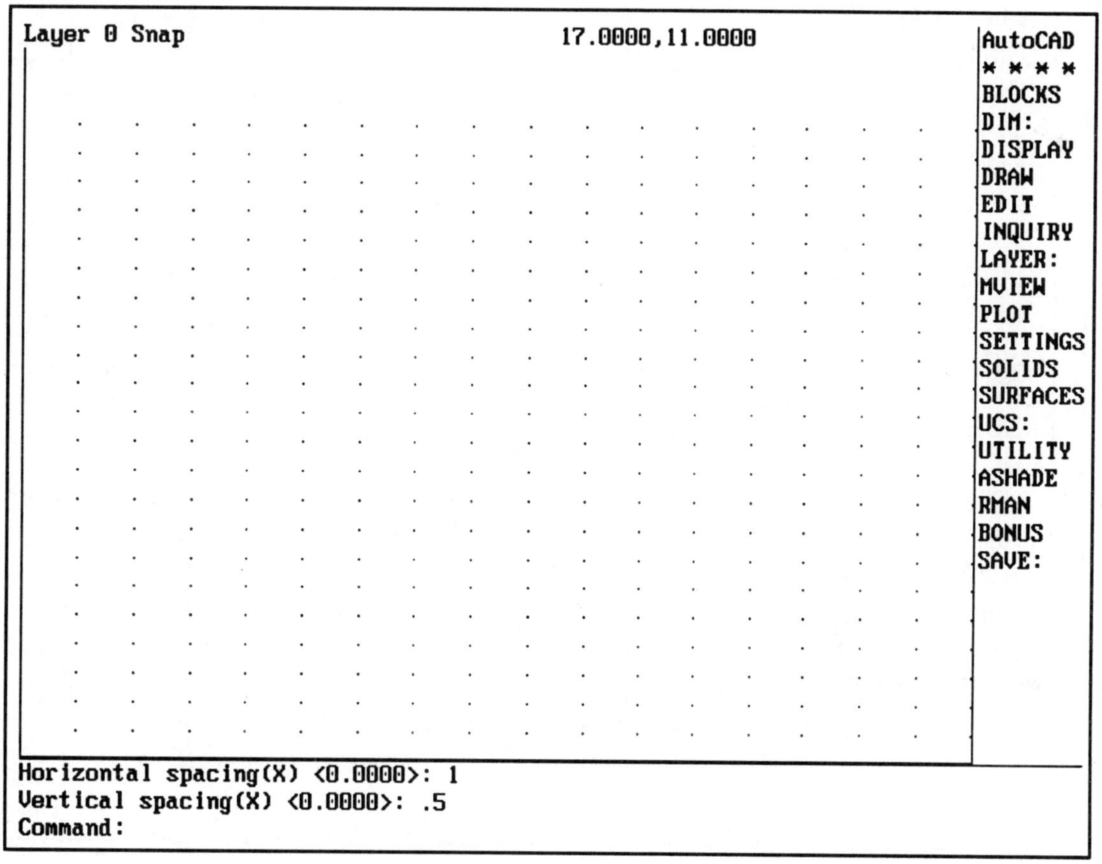

Figure 2-31 Using the Aspect Option of the GRID Command

SNAP Command

The SNAP command provides an invisible reference Grid and when turned on, causes the cursor to lock in to the nearest point on the specified Grid. Using the SNAP command, you can enter points quickly, letting AutoCAD ensure that they are placed precisely. You can always override the Snap spacing by entering absolute or relative coordinate points from the keyboard, or by simply turning off the Snap mode. When the Snap mode is turned off, it has no effect on the cursor. When it is turned on, you cannot pick a point with the pointing device that is not on one of the specified snap locations. Snap and Grid can be used together.

The SNAP command is invoked from the Screen Root Menu Settings (see Figure 2-32), or at the "Command:" prompt, type **SNAP** and press ⏎.

> Command: **snap**
> Snap spacing or ON/OFF/Aspect/Rotate/Style <default>:

You can accept the default by pressing ⏎ or you can enter a new value representing a new Snap spacing and press ⏎. The Grid is turned on automatically when you

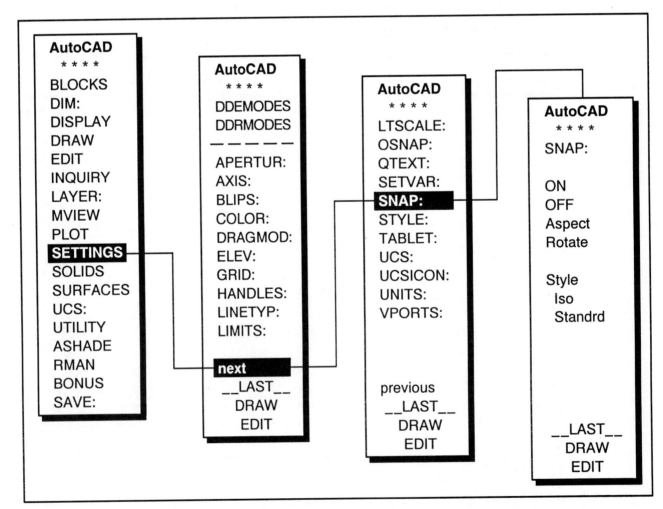

Figure 2-32 The SNAP Command Invoked from the Screen Root Menu Settings

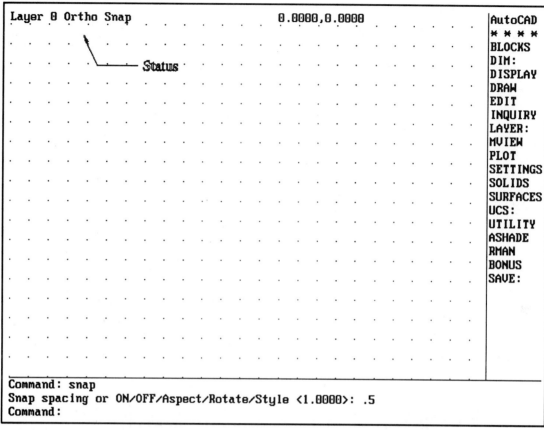

```
Layer 0 Ortho Snap                    0.0000,0.0000          AutoCAD
                                                             * * * *
                                                             BLOCKS
                   Status                                    DIM:
                                                             DISPLAY
                                                             DRAW
                                                             EDIT
                                                             INQUIRY
                                                             LAYER:
                                                             MVIEW
                                                             PLOT
                                                             SETTINGS
                                                             SOLIDS
                                                             SURFACES
                                                             UCS:
                                                             UTILITY
                                                             ASHADE
                                                             RMAN
                                                             BONUS
                                                             SAVE:




Command: snap
Snap spacing or ON/OFF/Aspect/Rotate/Style <1.0000>: .5
Command:
```

Figure 2-33 Turning the Snap Command ON or OFF

either accept the default Snap spacing or enter a new Snap spacing value. It is often useful to set the Grid spacing equal to the Snap resolution or a multiple of it. When the Snap mode is on, the word **SNAP** appears in the status line at the top of your screen (see Figure 2-33).

ON Option The ON option has the same effect as accepting the default Snap spacing value and turns on the Snap.

OFF Option The OFF option turns off the Snap. Also you can toggle Snap on and off with function key F9 or with the (Ctrl) + (B) key combination.

Aspect Option The Aspect option is the same as in Grid, allows you to set X and Y spacings to different values.

Rotate Option The Rotate option allows you to rotate at any angle both the visible Grid and the invisible Snap grid. First, AutoCAD prompts you for a base point (the point around which the Grid will be rotated) and then prompts for the angle of rotation. The sequence of prompts is as follows:

Command: **snap**
Snap spacing or ON/OFF/Aspect/Rotate/Style <current>: **r**
Base point <0,0>: *select or specify new origin*
Rotation angle <0>: *specify new angle of rotation*

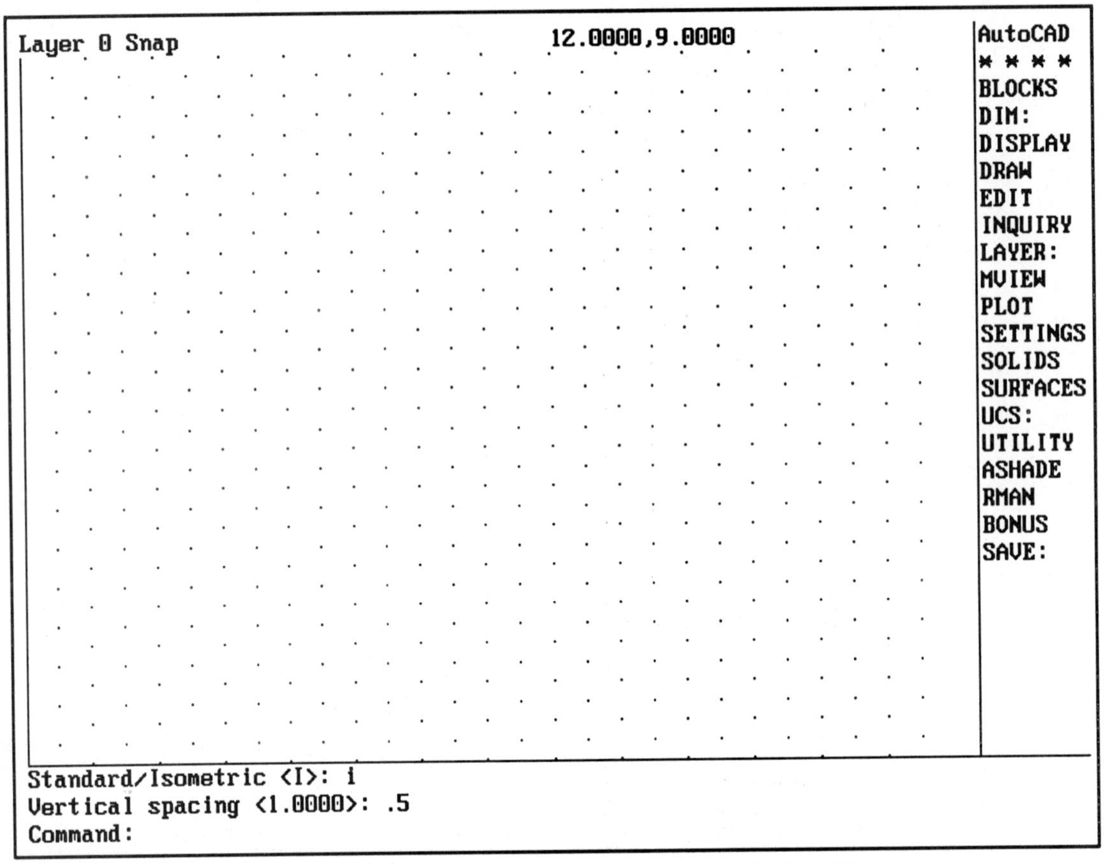

```
Layer 0 Snap                              12.0000,9.0000            AutoCAD
                                                                    * * * *
                                                                    BLOCKS
                                                                    DIM:
                                                                    DISPLAY
                                                                    DRAW
                                                                    EDIT
                                                                    INQUIRY
                                                                    LAYER:
                                                                    MVIEW
                                                                    PLOT
                                                                    SETTINGS
                                                                    SOLIDS
                                                                    SURFACES
                                                                    UCS:
                                                                    UTILITY
                                                                    ASHADE
                                                                    RMAN
                                                                    BONUS
                                                                    SAVE:




Standard/Isometric <I>: i
Vertical spacing <1.0000>: .5
Command:
```

Figure 2-34 Setting the Snap for Isometric Drafting

Style Option The Style option permits you to select one of the two available formats, Standard and Isometric. Standard refers to the normal rectangular type of Grid (default) and Isometric refers to a Grid designed for Isometric drafting purposes (see Figure 2-34).

ORTHO Command

The ORTHO command lets you draw lines parallel to the X and Y axes orthogonal and are therefore perpendicular to each other. This mode is helpful when you need to draw lines that are horizontal or vertical. It also forces lines to be parallel to one of the three isometric axes when the Snap style has been set to Isometric.

At the "Command:" prompt, type in **ORTHO** and press ⏎.

> Command: **ortho**
> Ortho On/Off:

The ORTHO command has only two options, ON and OFF. The ON option will turn the Ortho mode on, and the OFF option will turn the Ortho mode off. When it is on, the word **ORTHO** appears in the status line at the top of the screen (see Figure 2-35). Also, you can toggle Ortho on and off with function key F8 or (Ctrl) + (O) key combination (Ctrl + letter O, not Ctrl + number 0).

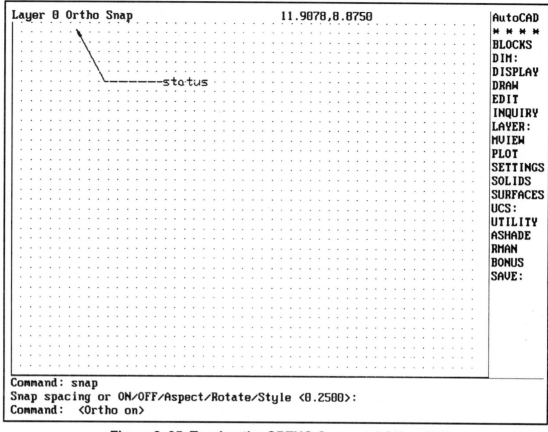

Figure 2-35 Turning the ORTHO Command ON or OFF

When Ortho mode is active, you can draw linear and specify displacements only in the horizontal or vertical directions, regardless of the cursor's on-screen position. The direction in which you draw is determined by the change in the X value of the cursor movement compared to the change in the cursor's distance to the Y Axis. AutoCAD will allow you to draw horizontally, if the distance in X is greater than the distance in Y; conversely, if the change in Y is greater than X, then it will allow you to draw vertically.

AXIS Command

The AXIS command places tickmarks along the bottom and right side of the display screen as shown in Figure 2-36. The axes are useful in determining distances when preparing a drawing layout.

The AXIS command is invoked from the Screen Root Menu Settings (see Figure 2-37), or at the "Command:" prompt, type in **AXIS** and press the spacebar or ⏎.

> Command: **axis**
> Tick spacing (X) or ON/OFF/Snap/Aspect <default>:

You can accept the default by pressing ⏎ or you can enter a new value representing a new tick spacing and press the spacebar or ⏎. The Axis is turned on

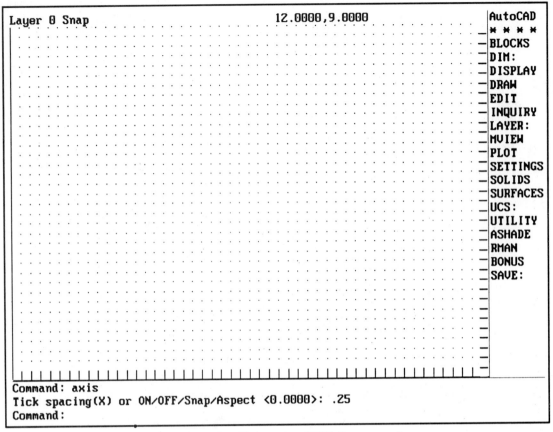

Figure 2-36 Using the AXIS Command

automatically when you either accept the default Axis spacing or enter a new tick spacing value. It is often useful to set the Axis spacing equal to the Snap resolution or a multiple of it. You can enter an X after the number to set the tick spacing to a multiple of the Snap resolution.

ON Option The ON option has the same effect as accepting the default tick spacing value and turns on the Axis.

OFF Option The OFF option turns off the Axis.

Aspect Option The Aspect option is the same as in Grid and Snap and allows you to set horizontal and vertical spacings to different values.

Using the Pull-Down Menu to Set the Drawing Tools

The AutoCAD drawing tools can be set or changed using the pull-down menu dialogue box. Select the Settings menu from the pull-down bar and in turn pick **Drawing Tools...** (see Figure 2-38). A dialogue box then appears on the screen (see Figure 2-39). Or, at the "Command:" prompt, type in **DDRMODES** and press the spacebar or ↵; the drawing aids dialogue box will be displayed.

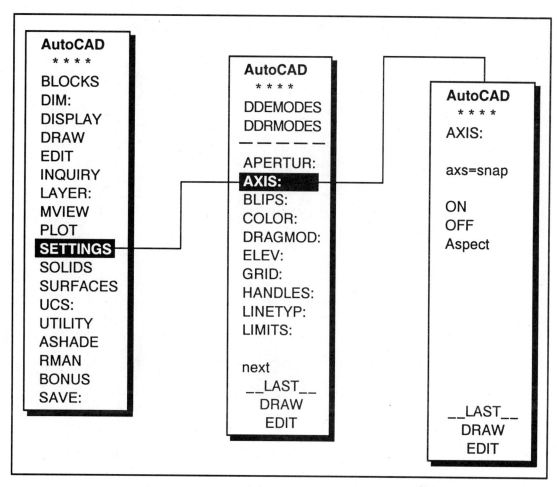

Figure 2-37 The AXIS Command Invoked from the Screen Root Menu Settings

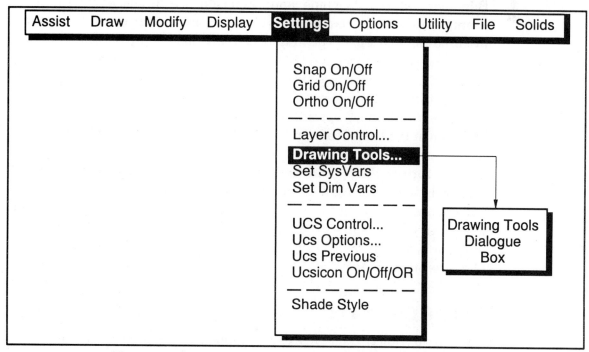

Figure 2-38 Setting the Drawing Tools Using the Pull-Down Menu

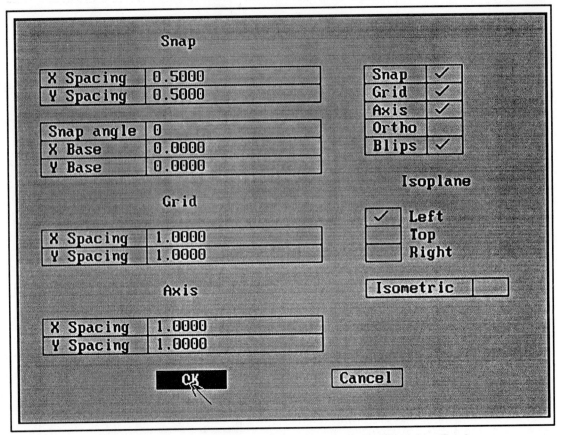

Figure 2-39 The Dialogue Box for Setting the Drawing Tools

Use the dialogue box to change or set the Snap, Grid, Axis, Ortho, Isoplane, and Blipmode values. Isoplane and Blipmode are discussed in Chapter 11. For example, to set the Snap mode to .5, move the cursor arrow to the Snap spacing input box and pick it. Type in the desired value and press ⏎. The input box also extends its own Cancel and OK action buttons. When satisfied, you can pick OK, or pick Cancel to change your mind. Selecting OK automatically sets the X and Y spacing to the same values. To set the Y spacing to a different value, move the cursor arrow to the Y spacing input box. Type the required value. Set the Grid and Axis in the same manner.

You can turn on Snap, Grid, and Axis by moving the cursor arrow to the appropriate box in the upper right corner of the dialogue box. Pick each item; if it is on, it will change to off or vice versa. A check in the box next to the name indicates it is on. When you are satisfied with your entries, pick the OK box at the bottom of the dialogue box. Figure 2-39 shows Grid at 1, Snap .5, and Axis at 1 with Snap, Grid, and Axis on, and Ortho off.

OSNAP Command

The Osnap (Object Snap) feature lets you specify points on existing entities in the drawing. For example, if you need to draw a line from an endpoint of an existing

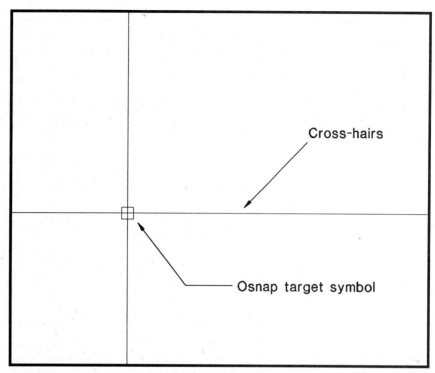

Figure 2-40 Screen Showing the Cross-hairs and Target Symbol in the Osnap Mode

line then you can use the Osnap mode called ENDpoint. This facility is similar to the basic SNAP command, which locks to invisible reference Grid points.

Osnap modes can be invoked while executing an AutoCAD command which requests a point, like LINE, CIRCLE, MOVE, COPY, etc. The Osnap modes may be typed at the prompt line, selected from the Assist pull-down menu or from the screen menu "* * * *." Each Osnap mode has a specific application. When typed at the prompt line, only the first three letters are required. Whenever you are in an Osnap mode, a target symbol is added to the screen cross-hairs to indicate the area within which AutoCAD will search for Osnap candidates (see Figure 2-40). Following are the Osnap modes available in AutoCAD:

CENter	Snaps to the center of an arc or circle
ENDpoint	Snaps to the closest endpoint of a line or arc
INSert	Snaps to the insertion point on a block, shape, or text entity
INTersection	Snaps to the intersection of two entities
MIDpoint	Snaps to the midpoint of an arc or line
NEArest	Snaps to a point on an object nearest to the cross-hairs
NODe	Snaps to a point entity; drawn with the POINT command
PERpend	Creates a perpendicular line from one point to a line, arc, or circle
QUAdrant	Snaps to the closest quadrant point of an arc or circle
QUICK	Allows Osnap to find the quickest selection for the specified OSNAP mode that is selected immediately after QUICK
TANgent	Forms a line tangent to a picked arc or circle
NONE	Turns running Osnap off

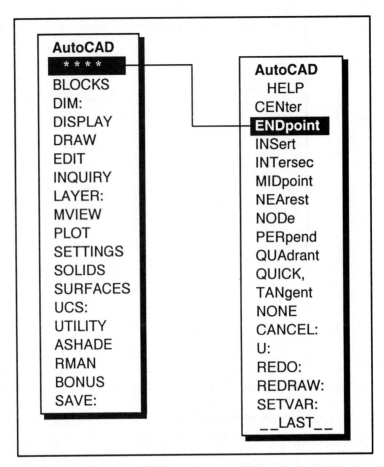

Figure 2-41 Invoking the Osnap ENDpoint Option from the Pull-Down Menu Assist

In this section, Osnap modes ENDpoint and MIDpoint are explained. The remaining modes are explained in later chapters.

OSNAP ENDpoint Option To specify a point on the endpoint of an existing line or arc, use the ENDpoint option. Make sure you are in the appropriate AutoCAD command, and invoke Assist from the pull-down menu or "* * * *" from the screen menu and select the ENDpoint option (see Figure 2-41). For example, to connect a line to the endpoint of an existing line as shown in Figure 2-42, the following command sequence is used:

Command: **line**
From point: **endpoint of** *move the aperture cursor near the end of Line A and pick*
To point: *pick a point*
To point: ⏎

OSNAP MIDpoint Option To connect a line or arc, or to place a center point of a circle, arc, or ellipse on the midpoint of an existing line or arc, use the MIDpoint Osnap. Make sure you are in the appropriate AutoCAD command, and invoke Assist from the pull-down menu or "* * * *" from the screen menu and select the MIDpoint option (see Figure 2-43). For example, to connect a line to the midpoint of an existing line as shown in Figure 2-44, the following command sequence is used:

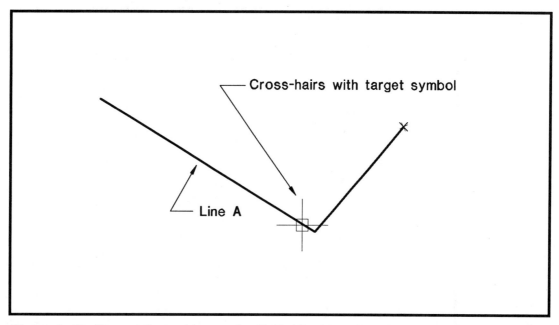

Figure 2-42 Connecting a Line to the Endpoint of an Existing Line Using the Osnap ENDpoint Option

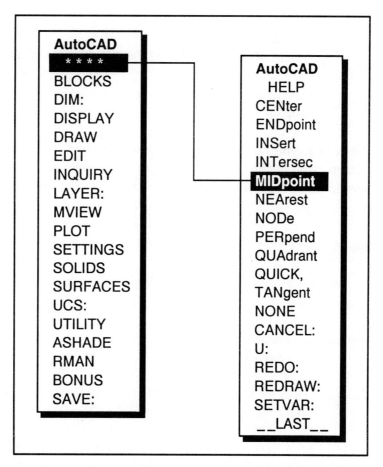

Figure 2-43 Invoking the Osnap MIDpoint Option from the Pull-Down Menu Assist

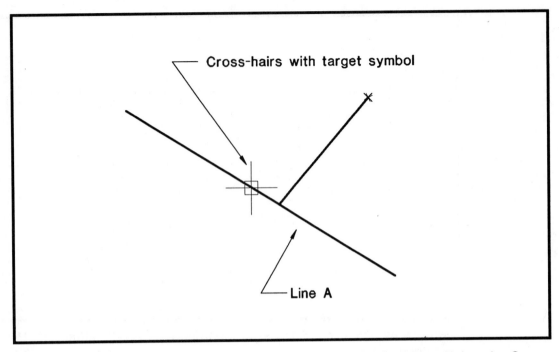

Figure 2-44 Connecting a Line to the Midpoint of an Existing Line Using the Osnap MIDpoint Option

Command: **line**
From point: **Midpoint of** *move the aperture cursor to anywhere on the Line A and pick*
To point: *pick a point*
To point: ⏎

Normally, you should not allow the pick box to cover more than one entity (or intersection in the case of the intersection mode). Otherwise, there is a chance the wrong point may be used.

LAB EXERCISE

In exercise 2-9, use absolute, relative, and polar coordinates in any combination to draw the figure.

Set limits   lower left: 0,0
              upper right: 17,11

Set Grid to .5 and Snap to .25

Lab Exercise 2-9

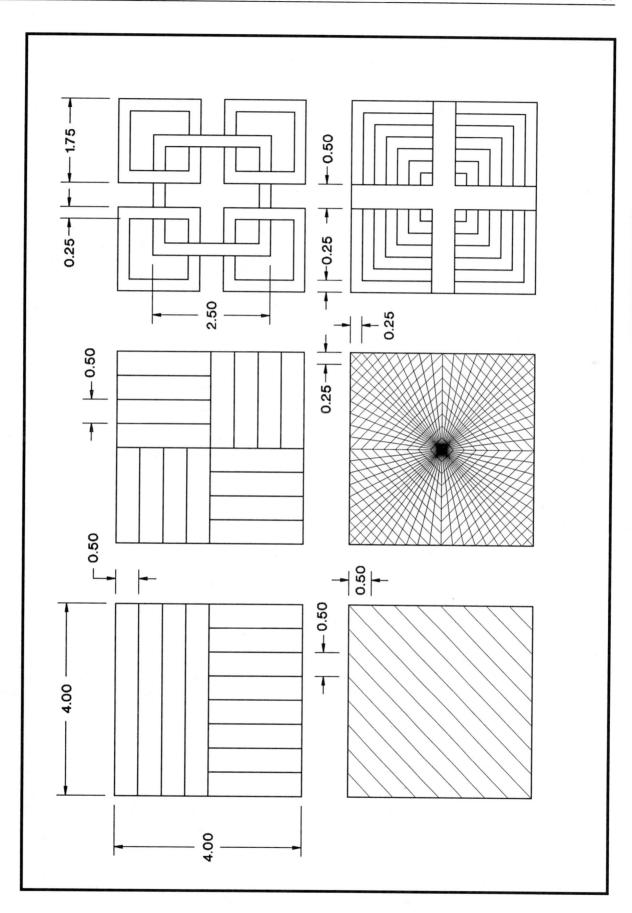

Fundamentals I

LAYER COMMAND

AutoCAD offers a means of grouping entities on layers in a manner similar to the manual drafter drawing groups of objects on separate transparent sheets superimposed in a single stack. Under these conditions, the manual drafter would be able to draw on the top sheet only. Likewise, in AutoCAD you can only draw on the current layer. However, AutoCAD permits you to transfer selected entities from one layer to another with commands called CHANGE and CHPROP. Let's see the manual drafter try that.

A common application of the layer feature is in using one layer for construction (layout) lines. You can create geometric constructions with fundamental entities such as lines, circles, and arcs. These will generate intersections, endpoints, centers, points of tangency, midpoints, and other useful data that might take the manual drafter considerable time to calculate on a calculator or hand-measure on the board. From these you can create other entities using intersections or other data generated from the layout. Then the layout layer can be turned off (making it no longer visible). It is not lost, but can be recalled (turned on) for viewing later as required.

The same drawing limits, coordinate system, and zoom factors apply to all layers in a drawing. There is no limit to the number of layers in a drawing, nor is the number of entities per layer restricted in any way.

To draw an entity on a particular layer, first make sure that layer is set as "current layer." There is one and only one current layer. Whatever you draw will be placed on the current layer. The current layer could be compared to the manual drafter's top sheet on the stack of transparencies. The significance of the current layer is that when an entity is first created it is drawn on the current layer. In order to draw an entity on a particular layer, first that layer must have been created, and if it is not the current layer you must make it the current layer.

You can always move, copy, or rotate any entity whether it is on the current layer or not. When you copy an entity that is not on the current layer, the copy will be placed on the layer that the original entity is on. This is also true with the mirror or an array of an entity or group of entities.

A layer can be visible (on) or invisible (off). Only visible layers are displayed or plotted. Invisible layers are still part of the drawing, they just are not displayed or plotted. You can turn layers on and off at will, in any combination. It is possible to turn off the current layer. If this happens and you draw an entity, it will not appear on the screen. It will be placed on the current layer and will appear on the screen when that layer is turned on (provided you are viewing the area in which the entity was drawn). This is not a common occurrence, but it can cause concern to both the novice and even the more experienced operator who has not faced the problem before. Do not turn off the current layer; the results can be very confusing. When the system variable TILEMODE is off, you can make specified layers visible only in certain viewports. For additional information see Chapter 8.

Each layer in a drawing has an associated name, color, and linetype. The name of a layer may be up to 31 characters long. It may contain letters, digits, and the special

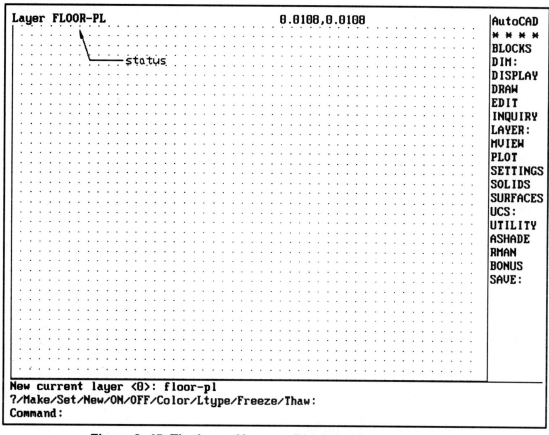

Figure 2-45 The Layer Name as Displayed in the Status Line

characters dollar ($), hyphen (-), and underscore (_), but no blank spaces. The name has to be one word. All layer names are converted to uppercase. Always give descriptive names appropriate to your application, such as floor-plan, plumbing, etc. The first eight characters of the current layer's name are displayed in the status line (See Figure 2-45). You can change the name of a layer any time you wish, and you can delete unused layers. These functions are handled by the RENAME and PURGE commands. They are described in Chapter 9.

Any number of layers in a drawing can have the same color. You can assign a layer any one color from available 256 colors between 0 and 255. If your graphics monitor is only capable of monochrome output, all color numbers will produce the same visual effect. Color numbers are useful even here, because can be assigned to a different pen on a pen plotter to plot in different line weights and colors. This works even for single-pen plotters; you can ask AutoCAD to pause for pen changes.

A linetype is a repeating pattern of dashes, dots, and blank spaces. The assigned linetype is used to draw all the entities that use lines, circles, and arcs on the layer. The following are some of the linetypes that are provided in the AutoCAD in a library file called ACAD.LIN:

Border	Dashdot	Dot
Center	Dashed	Hidden
Continuous	Divide	Phantom

See Appendix K for examples of each of these linetypes. Linetypes are another means of conveying visual information. You can assign a specific linetype to any number of layers. In some drafting disciplines, conventions have been established giving specific meanings to particular dash-dot patterns. If a line is too short to hold even one dash-dot sequence, AutoCAD draws a continuous line between the endpoints. When you are working on large size drawings, you may not see the gap between dash-dot patterns in a linetype, unless the scaling for the linetype is set for a large value. This can be done by the LTSCALE command. This command is discussed in more detail later on in this chapter.

Every drawing will have a layer called layer 0 (zero). By default, layer 0 is assigned color white and linetype continuous and is turned on. Layer 0 can not be renamed nor can be deleted. If you need additional layers, you have to create them and assign specific names. For each one by default, the new layer will be assigned color white and linetype continuous. If necessary, you can always reassign the color and linetype of the new layer.

The LAYER command has many different options. The LAYER command is invoked from Screen Root Menu Layer (see Figure 2–46) or at the "Command:" prompt, type in **LAYER** and press the spacebar or ⏎.

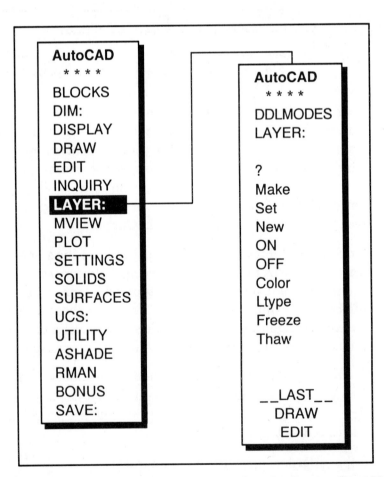

Figure 2–46 Invoking the LAYER Command Using the Screen Root Menu Layer

```
Command: layer
?/Make/Set/New/ON/OFF/Color/Ltype/Freeze/Thaw: ?

Layer name(s) to list <*>:

        Layer name        State         Color         Linetype
  ------------------   ---------   -------------   -------------
  0                       On         7 (white)     CONTINUOUS
  DIM                     On         3 (green)     CONTINUOUS
  HIDDEN                  On         2 (yellow)    HIDDEN
  LAYOUT                  On         4 (cyan)      CONTINUOUS
  OBJECT                  On         5 (blue)      CONTINUOUS

  SECTION                 On         9             CONTINUOUS
  TEXT                    On         1 (red)       CONTINUOUS

  Current layer: OBJECT

  ?/Make/Set/New/ON/OFF/Color/Ltype/Freeze/Thaw:
```

Figure 2-47 Using the LAYER ? Option to Show Currently Defined Layer Names

Command: **layer**
?/Make/Set/New/ON/OFF/Color/LType/Freeze/Thaw:

? Option

The ? option produces a list of the currently defined layers, showing their names, on/off states, color, and linetypes. When you select this option, AutoCAD will prompt:

Layer name(s) to list <*>:

You can enter a list of layer names, using wild cards if you wish, or press the spacebar or ⏎ to accept the default to list all layer names. See Figure 2-47 for a list of layers.

Make Option

The Make option effectively does three different things. When this option is invoked, AutoCAD prompts you for a layer name. Once you enter a name, Make does the following:

1. Searches for the layer to determine whether it exists.
2. If the layer does not exist, creates it and gives it the default color and linetype.
3. Sets the newly made layer to be the current layer.

When you select this option, AutoCAD will prompt:

New current Layer <default>:

If the layer you selected exists and is presently turned off, AutoCAD turns it on automatically, using the color and linetype previously assigned to that layer and makes it the current layer.

Set Option

The Set option tells AutoCAD on which layer you want to draw. When you select this option, AutoCAD prompts:

Current Layer <default>:

Enter the layer's name (it must be an existing layer) and press the spacebar or ⏎. This layer becomes the current layer. The first eight characters of the layer name are placed on the status line.

New Option

The New option allows you to create new layers. When you select this option, AutoCAD prompts:

New Layer name(s):

You can enter more than one name at a time by separating the names with a comma. It you need to separate characters in the name, use the underscore (_) instead of pressing the spacebar (in AutoCAD pressing the spacebar is the same as pressing ⏎). Each layer thus created is automatically turned on, and is assigned color white and linetype continuous.

OFF Option

The OFF option allows you to turn off selected layers. When you select this option, AutoCAD prompts:

Layer name(s) to turn off:

The list should contain only existing layer names, and it may include wild card characters. When you turn off a layer, the entities will not be displayed on the graphics monitor and they are not plotted. The entities still exist in the drawing; they are just invisible. They are still calculated during the regeneration of the drawing, even though they are not visible.

ON Option

The ON option allows you to turn on layers that have been turned off. When you select this option, AutoCAD prompts:

Layer name(s) to turn on:

This list should contain only existing layer names, and it may include wild-card characters. Each designated layer is turned on using the color and linetype previously associated with it. Turning a layer on does not cause it to be the current layer.

Color Option

The Color option allows you to change the color associated with that specific layer. When you select this option, first AutoCAD prompts:

> Color:

Respond with one of the standard color names or with a legal color number between 0 and 255. After you specify the color, AutoCAD prompts:

> Layer name(s) to color n <default>:

This prompt will actually have the code number of the color selected in place of the "n" shown above.

Reply with the names of existing layers separated by commas and it may include wild-card characters. The specified layers are given the color you designated and are then automatically turned on if they are off. If you would prefer to assign the color but turn the layers off, precede the color with a minus sign (-).

Linetype Option

The Linetype option allows you to change the linetype associated with a specific layer. When you select this option, first AutoCAD prompts:

> Linetype (or ?) <continuous>:

Reply with the name of an existing defined linetype. AutoCAD then asks for a list of layer names to which the linetype should be applied. For example, if you had replied to the first prompt with the linetype named HIDDEN, the next prompt would be:

> Layer names(s) for linetype hidden <default>:

Reply with the names of existing layers separated by commas and it may include wild-card characters.

Freeze and Thaw Options

Many draftsmen and designers have used a nonprint blue pencil to layout some reference or construction lines on their drawings. In AutoCAD the same thing can be accomplished by using the LAYER command to freeze certain layers. The layers that are frozen will not be visible on the display nor will they be plotted out on the finished drawing. In this respect Freeze is similar to OFF. However, layers that are simply turned off still go through a screen regeneration each time the system regenerates your drawing. Later, if you want to see the frozen layer, you simply Thaw it and automatic regeneration of the screen takes place. The reference or construction lines will be visible once more to be used until they are frozen again.

CAUTION!

Turning layers on and off is extremely useful. However, like many other advanced features, you must consider the effects when editing. If objects on layers that are turned on are associated with objects on layers that are turned off, and you wish to move them, those that are on the *OFF* layer will not be affected by the editing command unless the association between them is that they are in the same block.

Whenever you give a null response to the LAYER command, it takes you back to the "Command:" prompt.

Modifying Layers Using the Pull-Down Menu

New layers can also be added and existing layer properties changed with the pull-down menu. Select Settings from the pull-down menu bar and select Layer Control... from the menu (see Figure 2–48). You can also type at the "Command:" prompt **DDLMODES** and press the spacebar or ⏎. A dialogue box is then displayed (see Figure 2–49).

The dialogue box for Modifying Layers has eight columns titled Current, Layer name, Globally On and Frozen, Viewport Frozen Current and New, Color, and Linetype. The Current, Globally On and Frozen, Viewport Frozen Current and New

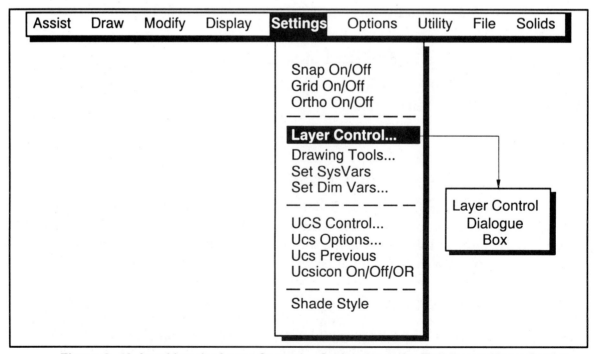

Figure 2–48 Invoking the Layer Control... Option from the Pull-Down Menu Settings

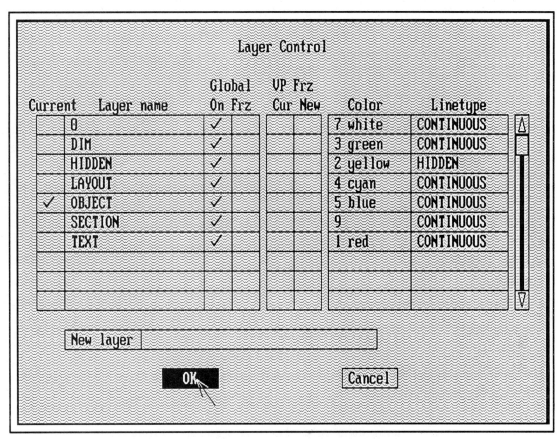

Current	Layer name	Global On	Frz	VP Frz Cur	New	Color	Linetype
	0	✓				7 white	CONTINUOUS
	DIM	✓				3 green	CONTINUOUS
	HIDDEN	✓				2 yellow	HIDDEN
	LAYOUT	✓				4 cyan	CONTINUOUS
✓	OBJECT	✓				5 blue	CONTINUOUS
	SECTION	✓				9	CONTINUOUS
	TEXT	✓				1 red	CONTINUOUS

New layer

OK   Cancel

Figure 2–49 The Dialogue Box for Modifying Layers

have check boxes. Pick a box to change the status of any layer. For example, move the cursor to the Current column and pick the layer that you want to draw on (current).

Add A New Layer

To add a layer, move the cursor arrow to the New Layer input box. When the box highlights, type the new layer name and press ⏎, or accept the name by picking OK or pick Cancel if you change your mind (see Figure 2-50). If you pick OK or press ⏎, the typed name fills a blank box in the layer name column. By default, new layers are assigned a white color and continuous linetype.

Layer Name Change

If necessary, you can change a layer name. To do so, move the cursor arrow to the layer name input box. When the box highlights, type the desired layer name. Pick the OK box or pick Cancel when finished (see Figure 2-51).

Change Layer Color

A layer's color may be changed at any time. Move the cursor arrow in the dialogue box and pick the check box of the intended color. Suppose you want to change the

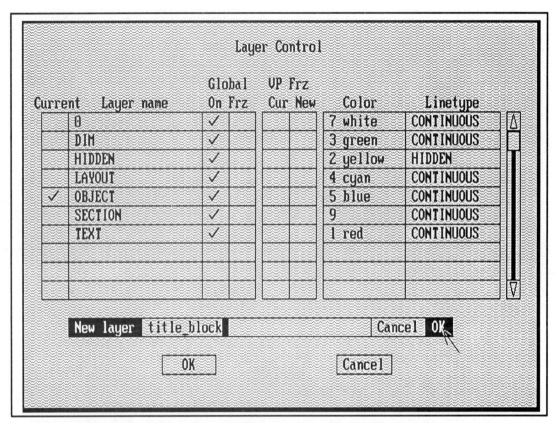

Figure 2-50 Adding or Cancelling a New Layer Using the Dialogue Box

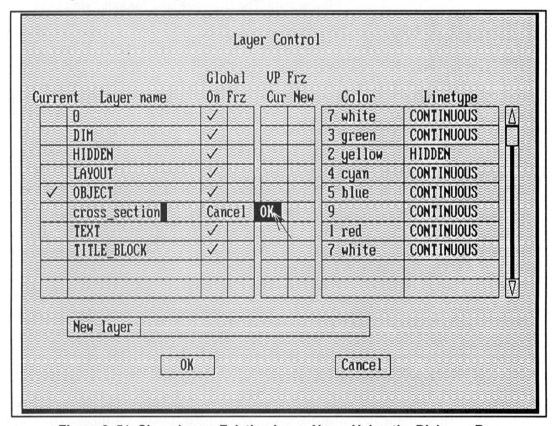

Figure 2-51 Changing an Existing Layer Name Using the Dialogue Box

white color of Dim Layer to red. Pick "white" and an expanded Select Color dialogue box appears. The box displays the available colors. The current color is indicated by a check mark. Move the cursor arrow to the check box of the desired color and pick it. Notice that the color code at the bottom of the dialogue box reflects the current color. Pick the ⬚ ∝ ⬚ box when finished.

Change Layer Linetype

To change layer linetype using the pull-down menu, pick the linetype box next to the layer you want to change. AutoCAD then displays the Select Linetype expanded dialogue box. Pick the linetype for that layer (see Figure 2-52). Pick ⬚ ∝ ⬚ for return to the Modify Layer dialogue box.

The dialogue box displays information on 10 layers. You can scroll through the list with the help of the scroll bar on the right hand side. By moving the arrow cursor to a section or position of the scroll bar and picking it, you shift the viewing area to another part of the list. Every section or position of the scroll bar moves the viewing area.

After making all the necessary layer changes and additions, to return to the drawing, pick the ⬚ ∝ ⬚ box. If you change your mind about the changes to the layer and are not interested in saving the new settings, then pick ⬚ Cancel ⬚ to return to the drawing.

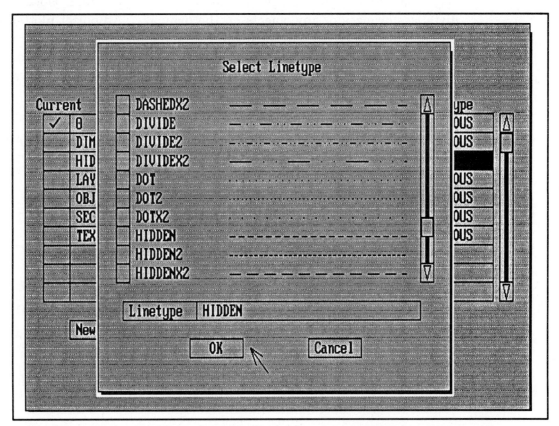

Figure 2-52 Changing an Existing Layer Linetype Using the Dialogue Box

LTSCALE Command

Before using linetypes, the effect of the linetype scale (set by the LTSCALE command) should be understood. The definition of a linetype tells AutoCAD how many units long to make dashes and spaces between dashes and dots. As long as the LTSCALE is set to 1.0 the displayed lengths of dashes and spaces will coincide with the definition. The sequence of prompts is as follows:

Command: **ltscale**
New scale factor <default>: *a positive integer or decimal, not a fraction*

Changing the linetype scale affects all linetypes in the drawing. If you want dashes which have been defined as .5 units long in the DASHED linetype to be displayed as 10 units long you can set the LTSCALE to 20. This also makes the dashes that were defined as 1.25 units long in the CENTER linetype display as 25 units long and the short dashes (defined as .25 units long) display as 5 units long. Note that the 1.25-unit long dash in the CENTER linetype is 2.5 times longer than the 0.5-unit long dash in the DASHED linetype. This ratio will always remain the same, no matter what the setting of the LTSCALE. So if you wish to have some other ratio of dash and space lengths between different linetypes, you will have to change the definition of one of the linetypes.

Remember that linetypes are for visual effect. The actual length of dashes and spaces are bound more to how they should look on the final plotted sheet than to distances or sizes of any objects on the drawing. An object plotted full size can probably use an LTSCALE setting of 1.0. A 50'-long object plotted on an 18" x 24" sheet might be plotted at a 1/4" = 1'-0" scale factor. This would equate to 1=48. An LTSCALE setting of 48 would make dashes and spaces plot to the same lengths as the full-size plot with a setting of 1.0.

LAB EXERCISES

In exercises 2-10 and 2-11, use absolute, relative, and polar coordinates in any combination to draw the figure with dimensioning.

Set limits   lower left: 0,0
                upper right: 150',130'

Set units to Architectural

Set LTSCALE = 48

Set text height = 6" to 2'-0" as needed

Lab Exercise 2–10

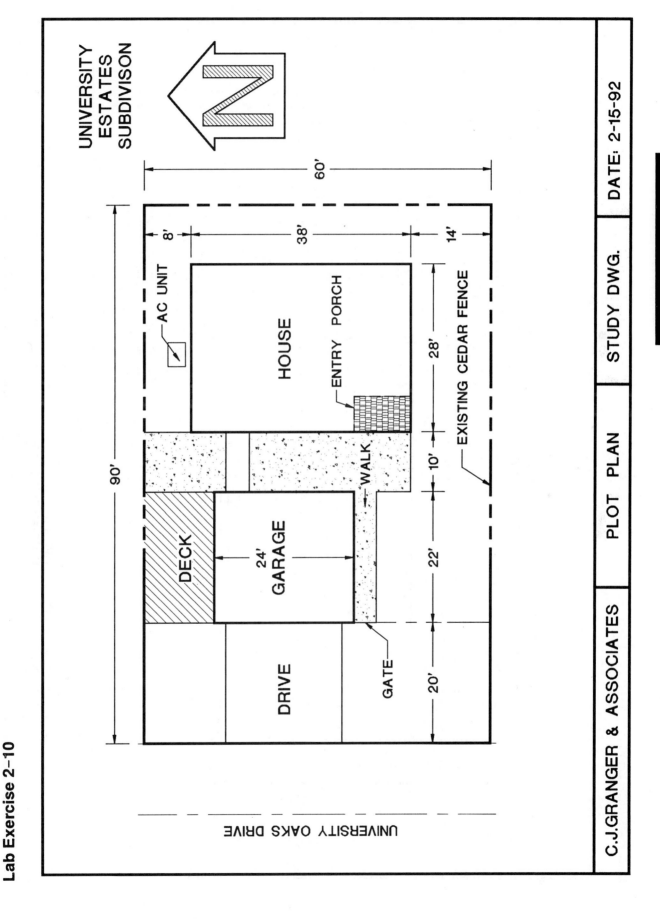

UNIVERSITY ESTATES SUBDIVISON

N

60'

8'

38'

14'

AC UNIT

HOUSE

ENTRY PORCH

28'

90'

WALK

10'

EXISTING CEDAR FENCE

DECK

24' GARAGE

22'

GATE

DRIVE

20'

UNIVERSITY OAKS DRIVE

C.J.GRANGER & ASSOCIATES | PLOT PLAN | STUDY DWG. | DATE: 2-15-92

Fundamentals I

Lab Exercise 2-11

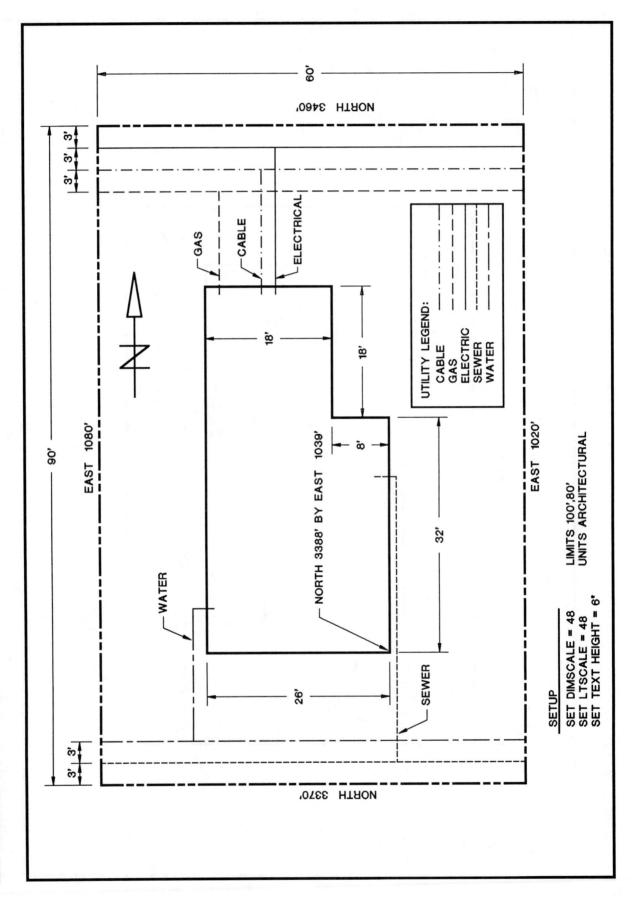

DISPLAY COMMANDS

There are many ways to view a drawing in AutoCAD. These viewing options vary from on-screen viewing to hard copy plots. The hard copy options are discussed in Chapter 5. Using the display commands, you can select the portion of the drawing to be displayed, establish 3D perspective views and much more. By letting you see your drawing in different ways, AutoCAD gives you the means to draw faster, more easily, and more accurately.

The commands that are explained in this section are like utility commands. They make your job easier and help you to draw more accurately.

ZOOM Command

The ZOOM command acts like a zoom lens on a camera. You can increase or decrease the viewing area, although the actual size of objects remains constant. As you increase the visible size of objects, you view a smaller area of the drawing in greater detail. As you decrease the visible size of objects, you view a larger area. This ability provides the means for accuracy and detail.

The ZOOM command has many options. The ZOOM command is invoked from the Screen Root Menu Display (see Figure 2-53), or at the "Command:" prompt, type in **ZOOM** and press ↵.

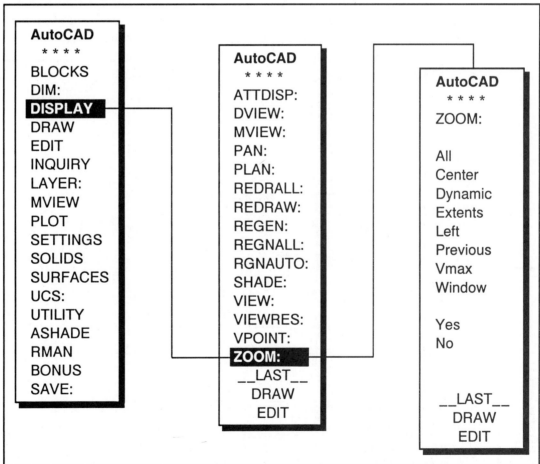

Figure 2-53 Invoking the ZOOM Command from the Screen Root Menu Display

Command: **zoom**
All/Center/Dynamic/Extents/Left/Previous/Vmax/Window/<Scale(X/XP)>:

Scale Option The Scale option is the default option and lets you enter a display scale (or magnification) factor. The scale factor when entered as a number (must be a value not expressed in units of measure) is applied to the area covered by the limits. For instance, if you enter a scale of 3, each object appears three times as large as it does in the full view. A scale factor of 1, displays the entire drawing (the full view), which is defined by the established limits. If you enter a value less than 1, AutoCAD decreases the magnification about the full view. For instance, if you enter a scale of .5, each object appears half the size as it does in the full view and the viewing area will have horizontal and vertical dimensions twice those of the limits area. When you use this option, the object in the center of the screen remains centered. See Figures 2-54a and 2-54b for the difference between the full view and after .5 zoom.

If you enter a number followed by X, the scale is determined relative to the current view. For instance, entering 2X causes each object to be displayed 2 times its current size on the screen.

The XP option under scale factor is explained in Chapter 8 as it is related to Paper and Model Space units.

All Option The All option lets you see the entire drawing. In a plan view, it zooms to the drawing's limits or current extents, whichever is larger. If the drawing extends

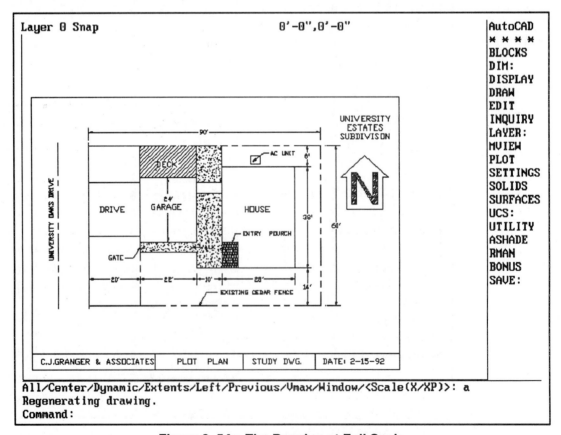

Figure 2-54a The Drawing at Full Scale

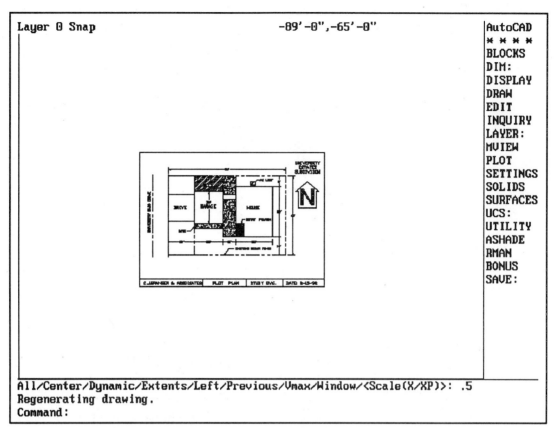

Figure 2-54b The Drawing After a .5 Zoom

outside the drawing limits, the display does as well, showing all entities in their entirety.

Extents Option The Extents option lets you see your entire drawing on-screen. It uses only the drawing extents, not its limits, and results in the largest possible display of all the entities. See Figures 2-55a and 2-55b, which illustrate the difference between the options All and Extents.

Previous Option The Previous option displays the last displayed view. While editing or creating a drawing, you may want to zoom into a small area, back out to view the larger area, and then zoom into another small area. To do this, AutoCAD saves the current view whenever it is being changed by any of the zoom options, or by any of the other display commands. So, you can return to the previous view by entering the Previous option, which can restore the previous 10 views.

Window Option The Window option lets you specify an area of the drawing you wish to see by placing two opposite corner points of a rectangular window. The center of the area selected becomes the new display center, and the area inside the window is enlarged to fill the display as completely as possible.

```
Command: zoom
All/Center/Dynamic/Extents/Left/Previous/Vmax/Window/<Scale(X/XP)>:
First corner: pick a point
Other corner: pick a point
```

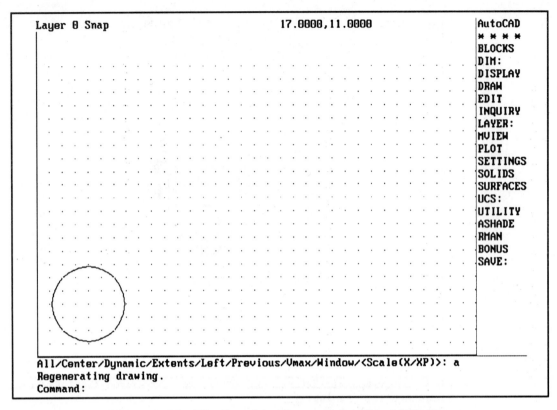

Figure 2-55a The Drawing Shown Using the All Option

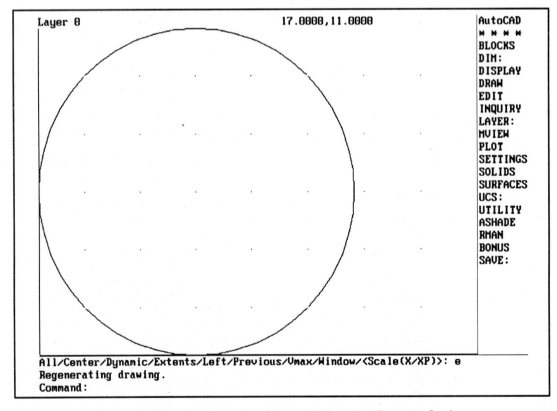

Figure 2-55b The Drawing Shown Using the Extents Option

You can enter two opposite corner points to specify an area by coordinates or with the pointing device (see Figures 2-56a and 2-56b).

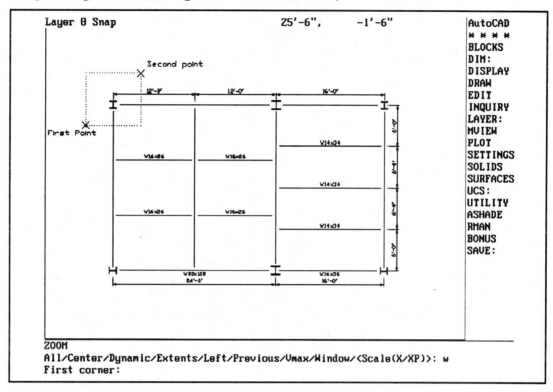

Figure 2-56a Specifying a Window Area (Before)

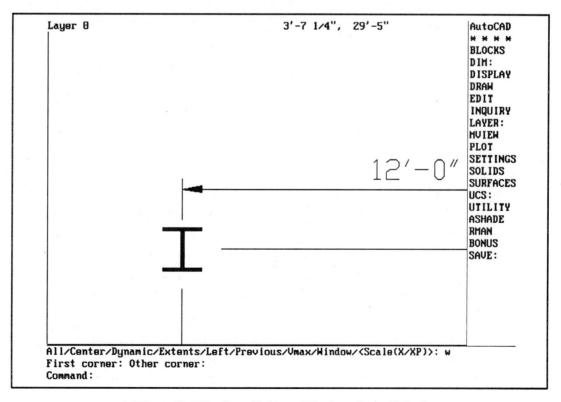

Figure 2-56b Specifying a Window Area (After)

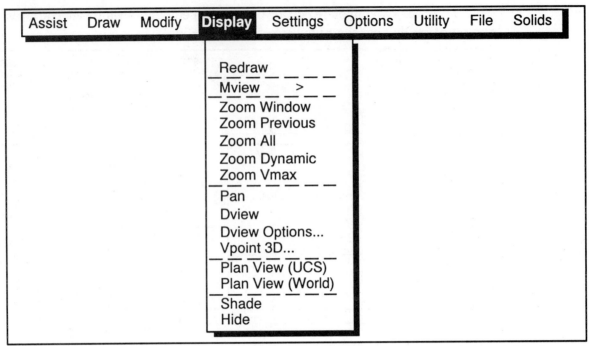

Figure 2-57 Invoking the ZOOM Command from the Pull-Down Menu Display

Pull-Down Display Menu

Often-used display commands can be accessed from the pull-down menu. Invoke the display from the pull-down bar and four options of the ZOOM command are available, such as Zoom Window, Zoom Previous, Zoom Dynamic, and Zoom All (see Figure 2-57). The pull-menu options are quicker to perform compared to screen menu.

For example, to invoke the ZOOM command with the Window option, select Display and Zoom Window from the pull-down menu, rather than DISPLAY, ZOOM and Window from the screen menu, or AutoCAD, Display, Zoom, and Window if the root menu is not the current one.

The Center, Dynamic, Left, and Vmax options are explained in Chapter 4.

PAN Command

The PAN command lets you view a different portion of the drawing in the current view, without changing the magnification. You can move your viewing area to see details that are currently off-screen. Imagine that you are looking at your drawing through the display window and that you can slide the drawing left, right, up, and down without moving the window.

The PAN command is invoked from the Screen Root Menu Display (see Figure 2-58), pull-down menu Display (see Figure 2-59) or, at the "Command:" prompt, type in **PAN** and press the spacebar or ↵.

        Command: **pan**
        Displacement:

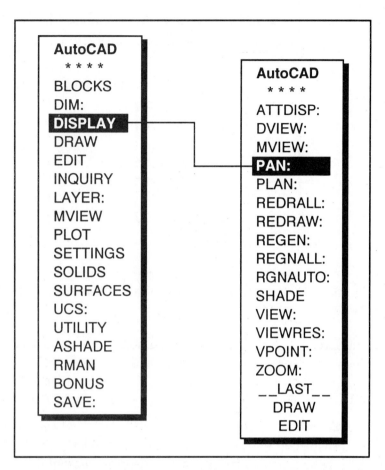

Figure 2–58 Invoking the PAN Command Using the Screen Root Menu Display

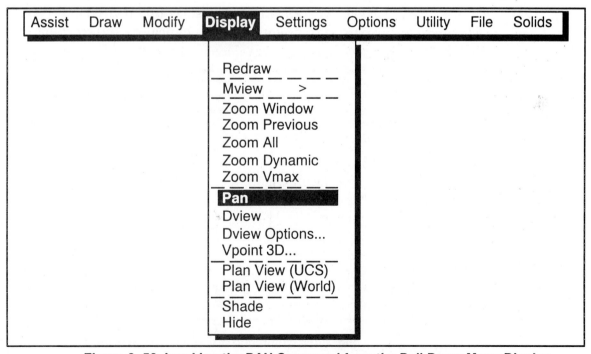

Figure 2–59 Invoking the PAN Command from the Pull-Down Menu Display

Fundamentals I

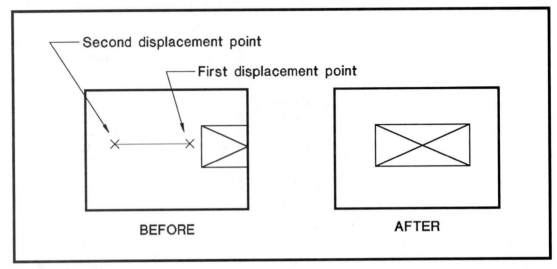

Figure 2-60 Using the PAN Command to Move the Drawing by Specifying Two Data Displacement Points

You must tell AutoCAD what direction to move the drawing, and how far to move it. You can designate two points, in which case AutoCAD computes the displacement from the first point to the second. For example, the following command sequence will move the drawing by placing two data points as shown in Figure 2-60.

Command: **pan**
Displacement: *pick first displacement point*
Second point: *pick second displacement point*

AutoCAD calculates the distance and direction between the two points and pans the drawing accordingly. You can enter a single coordinate pair indicating the relative displacement of the drawing with respect to the screen. If you give a null response to the second point prompt, you are indicating the coordinates provided

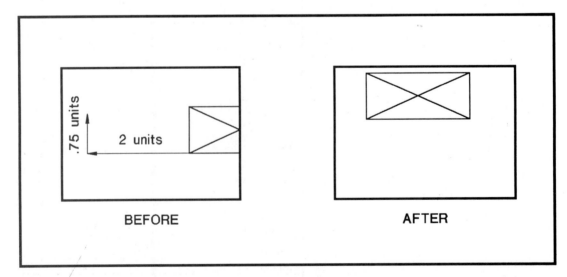

Figure 2-61 Using the PAN Command to Move the Drawing by Specifying Two Coordinates

are the displacement of the drawing with respect to the origin. If you provide the coordinates for the second point instead of giving a null response, then AutoCAD will compute the displacement from the first point to the second. For instance, the following command sequence will move the drawing by 2 units to the left and .75 units up as shown in Figure 2-61.

Command: **pan**
Displacement: **-2,.75**
Second point: ⊐

REDRAW Command

The REDRAW command tells the computer to redraw the on-screen image. You can use this command whenever you see an imcomplete image of your drawing or if the drawing seems to contain garbage that was not there before. Also, use the REDRAW command to remove the blip marks on the screen. If you draw two lines in the same place and erase one of the lines, it appear as if both the lines are erased. By issuing the REDRAW command the second line will reappear. This is considered as a screen refresh as opposed to a data base regeneration.

The REDRAW command does not have any options. The REDRAW command is invoked from the Screen Root Menu Display (see Figure 2-62), pull-down menu

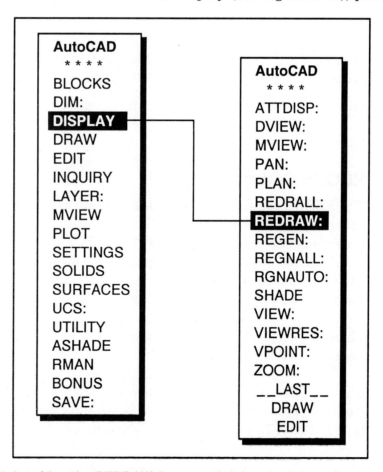

Figure 2-62 Invoking the REDRAW Command Using the Screen Root Menu Display

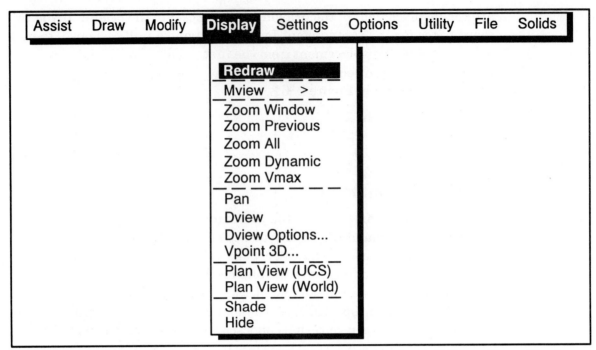

| Assist | Draw | Modify | **Display** | Settings | Options | Utility | File | Solids |

Redraw
Mview   >
Zoom Window
Zoom Previous
Zoom All
Zoom Dynamic
Zoom Vmax
Pan
Dview
Dview Options...
Vpoint 3D...
Plan View (UCS)
Plan View (World)
Shade
Hide

Figure 2–63 Invoking the REDRAW Command from the Pull-Down Menu Display

Display (see Figure 2–63), or at the "Command:" prompt type in **REDRAW** and press ⏎.

    Command: **redraw**
    Command:

REGEN Command

The REGEN command is used to regenerate the drawing's data on the screen. In general, you should use the REGEN command if the image presented by REDRAW does not correctly reflect your drawing. REGEN goes through the drawing's entire data base and projects the most up-to-date information on the screen; this command will give you the most accurate image possible. Because of the manner in which it functions, a REGEN takes significantly longer than a REDRAW.

There are certain AutoCAD commands where REGEN takes place automatically unless REGENAUTO is turned off.

The REGEN command does not have any options. The REGEN command is invoked from the Screen Root Menu Display (see Figure 2–64) or at the "Command:" prompt type in **REGEN** and press the spacebar or ⏎.

    Command: **regen**
    Command:

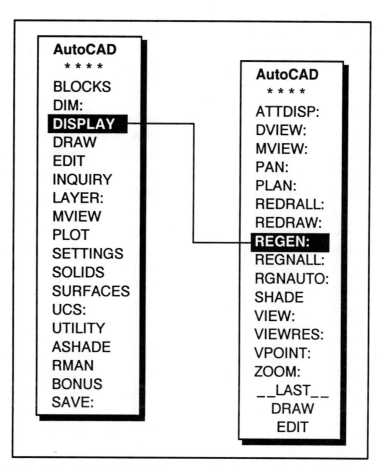

Figure 2-64 Invoking the REGEN Command from the Screen Root Menu Display

Transparent Commands

You can use the ZOOM, PAN, and REDRAW commands transparently. In other words you can use these commands while working in another AutoCAD command. To do this, enter apostrophe with the command name, for instance, **'ZOOM**, **'PAN**, and **'REDRAW** at any prompt that is not asking for a text string.

> **NOTE:** Options that cause a regeneration, such as ZOOM All, cannot be performed transparently.

OBJECT SELECTION

Many AutoCAD editing commands asks you to select one or more objects for manipulation. Whenever you select the object, AutoCAD highlights the selected object to help you. The selected objects for the manipulation are called the selection set. There are several different ways of selecting the objects for manipulation. The selection methods include Window, Crossing, Last, Previous, Add, Remove, Box, and Undo.

Most of the editing commands require a selection set, for which AutoCAD prompts:

Select objects:

AutoCAD replaces the screen cross-hairs with a small box called the object selection target. Using this target box you can select individual objects for manipulation. Using your pointing device (or the keyboard's cursor keys), position the target box so it touches only the desired object or a visible portion of it. The object selection target helps you point to the object without having to be very precise. Every time you select an object, the "Select objects:" prompt reappears. To indicate your acceptance of the selection set, give a NULL reply to the "Select objects:" prompt.

Window Option The Window option in the selection of the objects for manipulation allows you to designate all the objects contained completely in a rectangular area, or dynamically manipulated window. AutoCAD prompts you for two diagonally opposite corner points describing the rectangle:

First corner:
Other corner:

If there is an object that is partially inside the rectangular area, then that object will not be included in the selection set. You can select only objects currently visible on the screen. To select a partially visible object, you must include all its visible parts within the window. See Figure 2–65, in which only the lines will be included, not the circle, as a portion of the circle is outside the rectangular area.

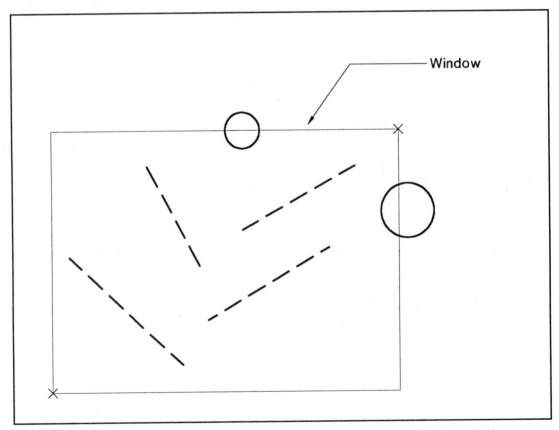

Figure 2–65 Selecting a Partially Visible Object Using the Window Option

CHAPTER 2: FUNDAMENTALS I • 113

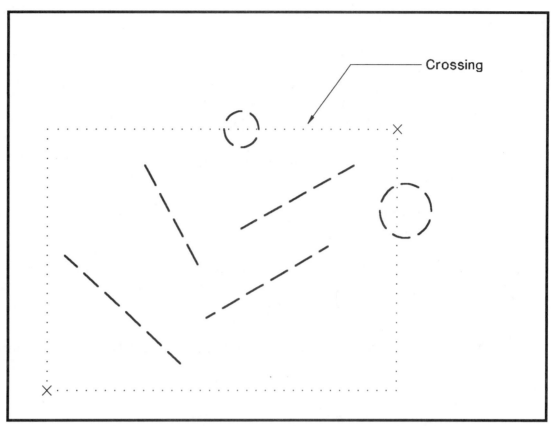

Figure 2-66 Selecting Objects Using the Crossing Option

Crossing Option The Crossing option is similar to the Window option, but selects all objects within or crossing the window boundary. If there is an object that is partially inside the rectangular area, then the whole object is included in the selection set. Crossing displays a dashed box to differentiate it from a window selection box. See Figure 2-66 in which all the lines and circles will be included although part of the circle is outside the rectangle.

Previous Option The Previous option enables you to perform several editing operations on the same group of objects. AutoCAD remembers the most recent selection set and allows you to reselect it with the Previous option. For instance, if you have just moved several objects and now wish to copy them somewhere else, you can issue the COPY command and respond to the "Select objects:" prompt with **p** to select the same objects again.

There is even a command called SELECT that does nothing but create a selection set; you can then use the Previous option to refer to this set in subsequent commands.

Last Option The Last option is an easy way to select the most recently created object currently visible. Only one object is designated, no matter how often you use the Last option when constructing a particular selection set.

Box, Add, Remove, and Undo options are explained in Chapter 4.

EDIT COMMANDS

ERASE Command

AutoCAD not only allows you to draw entities easily, but also allows easy editing of the objects you have drawn. Of the many editing commands available, the ERASE command probably will be the one you use most often. Everyone makes mistakes, but in AutoCAD it is easier to erase them. Or, if you are through with an entity that you have created for construction of other entities, you may wish to erase it.

The ERASE command lets you specify entities that you want removed from the drawing.

Invoke the ERASE command from the Screen Root Menu Edit (see Figure 2-67), pull-down menu Modify (see Figure 2-68), or at the "Command:" prompt, type in **ERASE** and press the spacebar or ⏎.

Command: **erase**
Select objects: *select objects to be erased and then press the spacebar or* ⏎

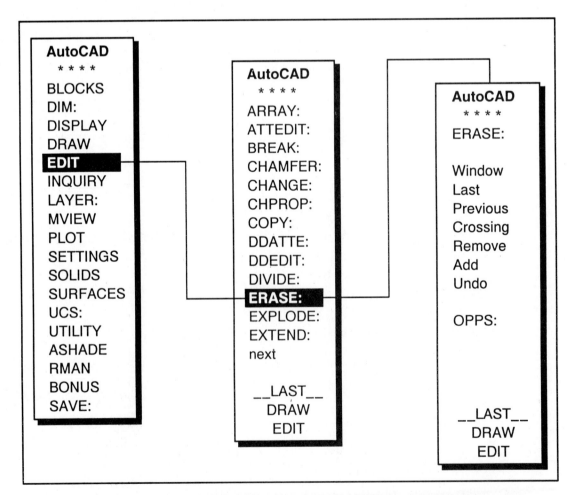

Figure 2-67 Invoking the ERASE Command from the Screen Root Menu Edit

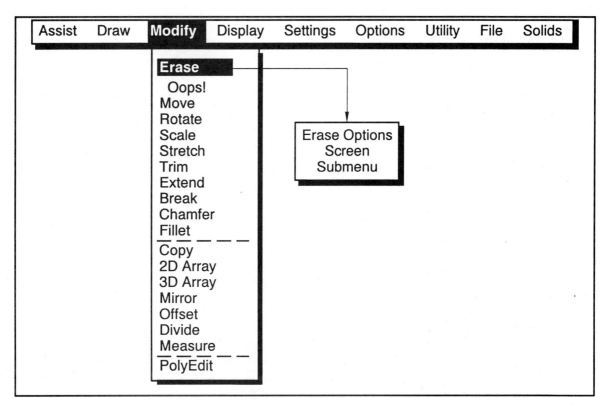

Figure 2-68 Invoking the ERASE Command from the Pull-Down Menu Modify

You can use one or more object selection methods. After selecting the object(s), press ⏎ (null response) in response to the next "Select objects:" prompt to complete the ERASE command. All the objects that were selected will disappear.

The following command sequence shows an example of erasing individual objects as shown Figure 2-69.

> Command: **erase**
> Select objects: *pick line 2 (the line is highlighted)* 1 selected, 1 found
> Select objects: *pick line 4* 1 selected, 1 found
> Select objects: ⏎
> Command:

The following command sequence shows an example of erasing a group of objects as shown in Figure 2-70 by the Window option:

> Command: **erase**
> Select objects: *pick window option from the screen menu or type W and press*
> ⏎
> First corner: *pick point 1*
> Other corner: *pick point 2* 4 found
> Select objects: ⏎
> Command:

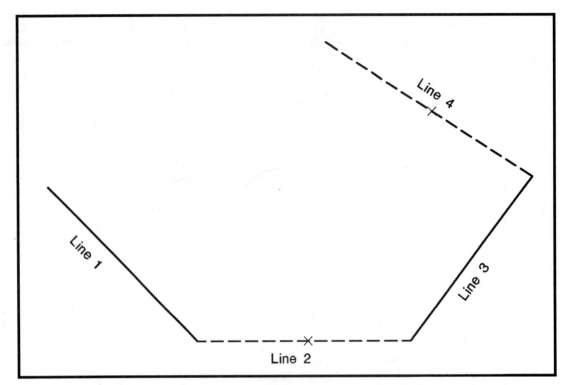

Figure 2-69 Using the ERASE Command to Erase Individual Objects

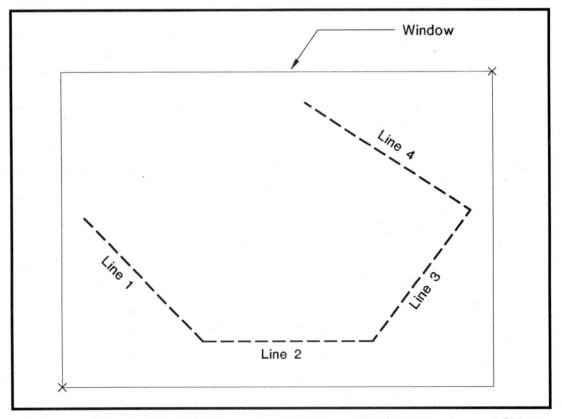

Figure 2-70 Using the Window Option of the ERASE Command to Erase a Group of Objects

OOPS Command

The OOPS command restores entities that have been unintentionally erased. Whenever the ERASE command is used, the last group of entities erased is remembered. The OOPS command will help you to restore the entities and can be used at any time. It only restores the entities erased by the most recent ERASE command. See Chapter 4 on the UNDO command, if you need to step back further than one ERASE command.

The OOPS command is invoked from the pull-down menu Modify (see Figure 2–71), or at the "Command:" prompt, type in **OOPS** and press the spacebar or ⏎. There are no options available for the OOPS command.

> Command: **oops**
> Command:

The following example shows the command sequence for using the OOPS command in conjunction with the ERASE command:

> Command: **erase**
> Select objects: **window**
> First corner: *select a point*
> Other corner: *select a point*
> Select objects: ⏎
> Command: **oops** *(will restore the erased objects)*

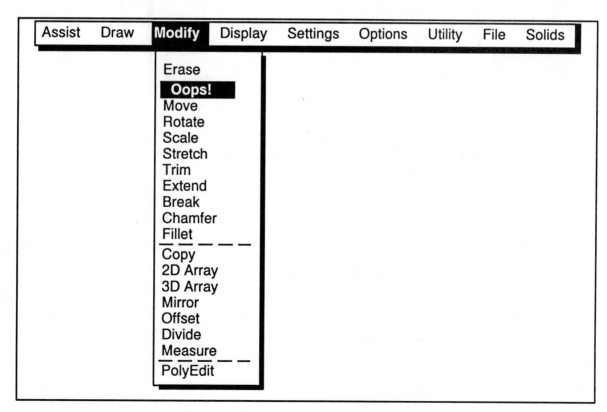

Figure 2–71 Invoking the OOPS Command from the Pull-Down Menu Modify

MOVE Command

The MOVE command lets you move one or more objects from their present location to a new one without changing orientation or size. After you define the selection-set of objects to be moved, AutoCAD prompts for "Base point or displacement:". Here, you should provide the move-from point or displacement vector to indicate how far the objects are to be moved, and in what direction. Then AutoCAD prompts for "Second point of displacement:". Here, you should provide the move-to point or give a null response if the first point provided is a displacement vector.

The MOVE command is invoked from the Screen Root Menu Edit (see Figure 2–72), pull-down menu Modify (see Figure 2–73), or at the "Command:" prompt, type in **MOVE** and press the spacebar or ⏎.

Command: **move**
Select objects: *show what to move and then give a null response*
Base point or displacement: *first point or x,y,z point*
Second point of displacement: *second point or null response*

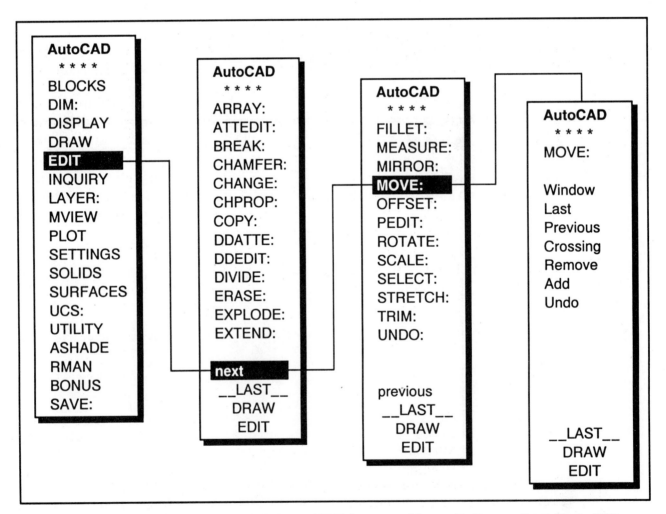

Figure 2–72 Invoking the MOVE Command from the Screen Root Menu Edit

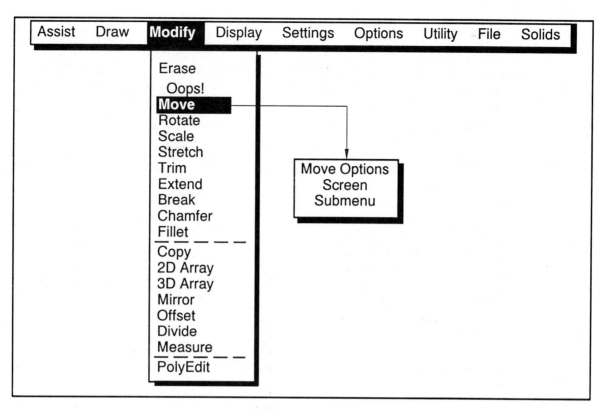

Figure 2-73 Invoking the MOVE Command from the Pull-Down Menu Modify

For instance, to specify a displacement using the keyboard, enter **0,0,0** in response to the first point and when AutoCAD prompts for a second point, enter **X,Y,** and **Z** displacement amounts as if they were absolute X,Y,Z coordinates. Alternatively, you can enter the displacement amount in response to the first prompt and give a null response to the second prompt. Or, you can use your pointing device to specify a displacement by picking a "from point" and a "to point." AutoCAD assists you in visualizing the displacement by drawing a rubberband line from the first point as you move the cross-hairs to the second point.

The following command sequence shows an example of moving a group of objects selected by the Window option, as shown in Figure 2-74, by vector displacement:

Command: **move**
Select objects: *pick Window option from the screen menu or type* **W** *and press*
⏎
First corner: *pick point 1*
Other corner: *pick point 2*
Select objects: ⏎
Base point or displacement: **7,1**
Second point of displacement: ⏎

The following command sequence shows an example of moving a group of objects selected by the Window option, as shown in Figure 2-75, by specifying or picking two data points:

Command: **move**
Select objects: *pick Window option from the screen menu or type* **W** *and press*
⏎
First corner: *pick point 1*
Other corner: *pick point 2*
Select objects: ⏎
Base point or displacement: *pick base point*
Second point of displacement: *pick second point*

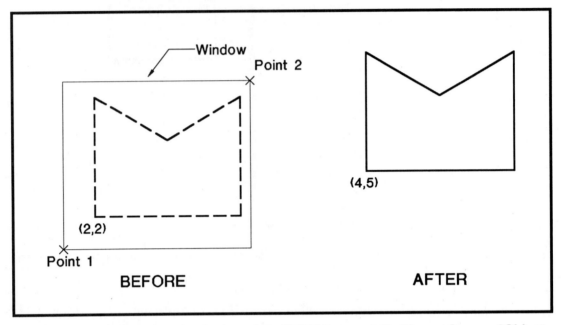

Figure 2-74 Using the Window Option of the MOVE Command to Move a Group of Objects by Vector Displacement

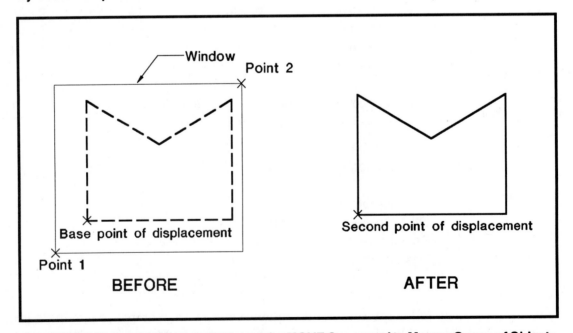

Figure 2-75 Using the Window Option of the MOVE Command to Move a Group of Objects by Specifying Two Data Points

COPY Command

The COPY command is similar to the MOVE command, but it places copies of the selected objects at the specified displacement, leaving the original objects intact. The copies are oriented and scaled the same as the original. If necessary, you also can make multiple copies of selected objects. Each resulting copy is completely independent of the original and can be edited and manipulated like any other simple entity.

The COPY command is invoked from the Screen Root Menu Edit (see Figure 2-76), pull-down menu Modify (see Figure 2-77), or at the "Command:" prompt, type in **COPY** and press the spacebar or ⏎.

> Command: **copy**
> Select objects: *show what to copy and then give a null response*
> <Base point or displacement>/Multiple: *first point or x,y,z point*
> Second point of displacement: *second point or null response*

If you specify or pick two data points, AutoCAD computes the displacement and copies the object(s). If you provide a null response to the second point of displacement

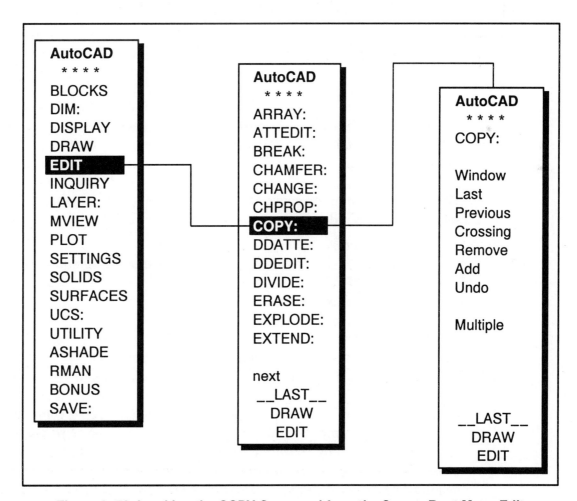

Figure 2-76 Invoking the COPY Command from the Screen Root Menu Edit

Fundamentals I

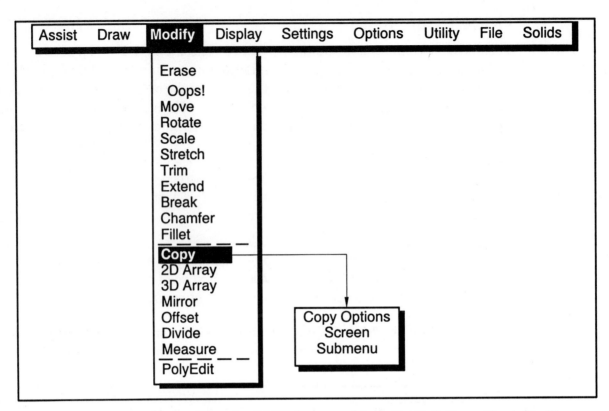

Figure 2-77 Invoking the COPY Command from the Pull-Down Menu Modify

AutoCAD considers the point provided as the second point of displacement vector with the origin (0,0,0) as the first point, indicating how far to copy the objects and in what direction.

The following command sequence shows an example of copying a group of objects selected by the Window option, as shown in Figure 2-78, by placing two data points:

    Command: **copy**
    Select objects: *select Window option from the screen menu or type* **W** *and*
        press ⏎
    First corner: *pick point 1*
    Other corner: *pick point 2*
    Select objects: ⏎
    <Base point or displacement)/Multiple: *pick base point*
    Second point of displacement: *pick second point*

Multiple Copies To make multiple copies using one COPY command, respond to the base point prompt by entering **m** for multiple. The base point prompt then reappears followed by repeated second point prompts, and a copy of the selected objects is made at each displacement you enter. Each displacement is relative to the original base point. When you have made all the copies you need, give a null response to the second point prompt.

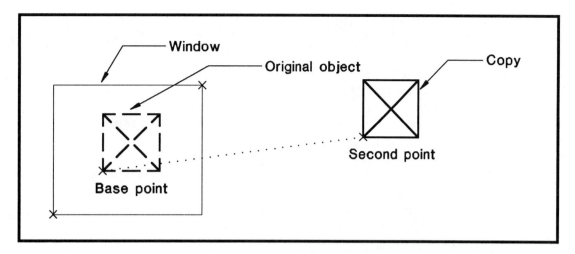

Figure 2-78 Using the Window Option of the COPY Command to Copy a Group of Objects by Specifying Two Data Points

The following command sequence shows an example of placing multiple copies of a group of objects selected by the Window option, as shown in Figure 2-79.

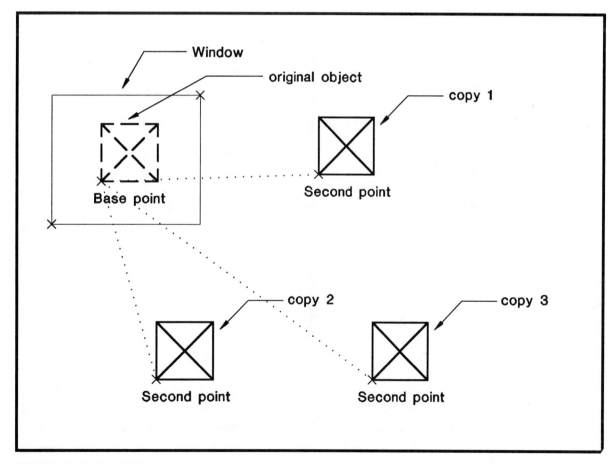

Figure 2-79 Using the Window Option of the COPY Command to Make Multiple Copies of a Group of Objects

Command: **copy**
Select objects: *select Window option from the screen menu or type* **W** *and
    press* ⏎
First corner: *pick point 1*
Other corner: *pick point 2*
Select objects: ⏎
<Base point or displacement)/Multiple: *pick Multiple option from the screen
    menu or type* **M** *and null option*
Multiple base point: *pick point 1*
Second point of displacement: *pick second point for copy 1*
Second point of displacement: *pick second point for copy 2*
Second point of displacement: *pick second point for copy 3*
Second point of displacement: ⏎
Command:

ROTATE Command

The ROTATE command changes the orientation of existing entities by rotating
them about a specified point, labeled as the base point. Design changes often

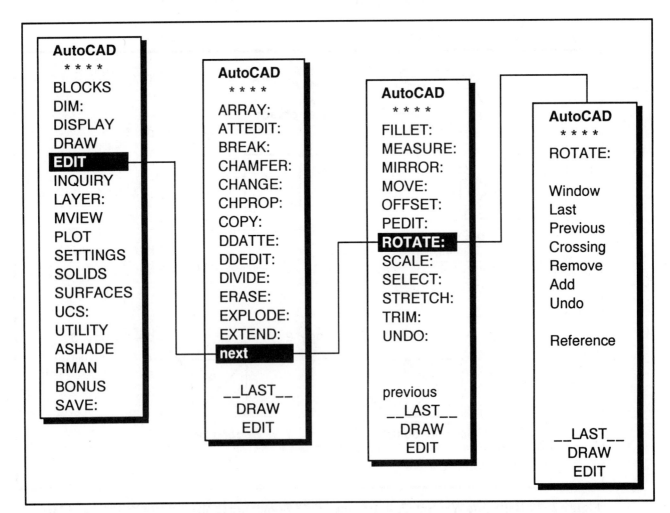

Figure 2-80 Invoking the ROTATE Command from the Screen Root Menu Edit

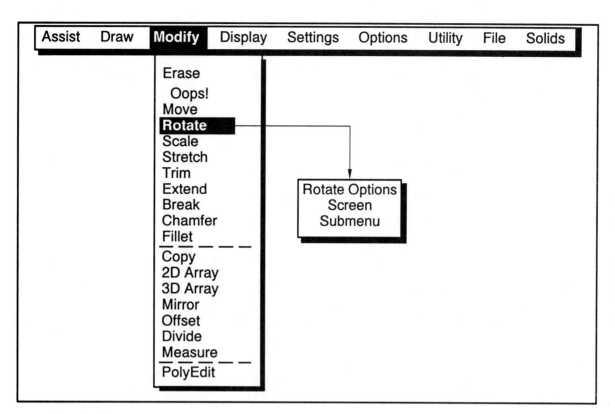

Figure 2-81 Invoking the ROTATE Command from the Pull-Down Menu Modify

require that an object, feature, or view be rotated. By default, a positive angle rotates the object in counterclockwise direction, and a negative angle rotates in clockwise direction.

The ROTATE command is invoked from Screen Root Menu Edit (see Figure 2-80), pull-down menu Modify (see Figure 2-81), or at the "Command:" prompt, type in **ROTATE** and press ⏎.

Command: **rotate**
Select objects: *show what to rotate and then give a null response*
Base point: *pick a point about which object(s) will be rotated*
<Rotation angle>/Reference: *type a positive or negative rotation angle or pick a point on screen*

The base point can be anywhere in the drawing. If a portion of a selected object lies on the base point, that portion remains on the base point as the object's orientation changes.

The following command sequence shows an example of rotating a group of objects selected by the Window option, as shown in Figure 2-82.

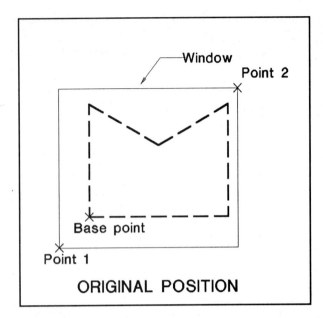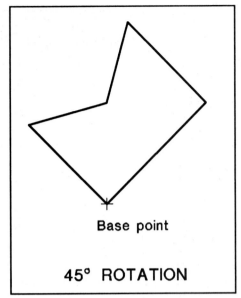

Figure 2-82 Using the Window Option of the ROTATE Command to Rotate a Group of Objects

Command: **rotate**
Select objects: *pick Window option from the screen menu or type* **W** *and press* ⏎
First corner: *pick point 1*
Other corner: *pick point 2*
Select objects: ⏎
Base point: *pick base point*
<Rotation angle>/Reference: **45**
Command:

Reference ANGLE Option If an object has to be rotated in reference to current orientation, you can use the Reference option to do the same. Specify the current orientation as reference angle or show AutoCAD the angle by pointing to the two endpoints of a line to be rotated and specify the desired new rotation. AutoCAD will automatically calculate the rotation angle and rotate the object appropriately. This method of rotation is very useful when you want to straighten an object or align it with other features in a drawing.

The following command sequence shows an example of rotating a group of objects selected by the Window option in reference to current orientation, as shown in Figure 2-83.

Command: **rotate**
Select objects: *pick Window option from the screen menu or type* **W** *and press* ⏎
First corner: *pick point 1*
Other corner: *pick point 2*
Select objects: ⏎

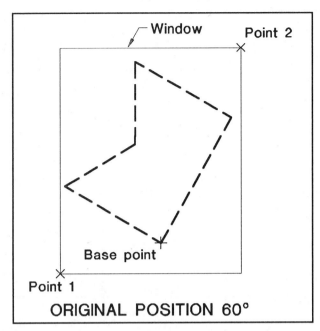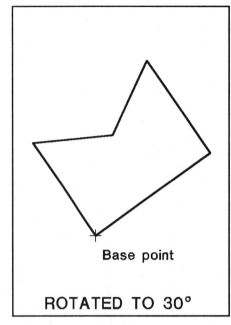

Figure 2–83 Using the Window Option of the ROTATE Command to Rotate a Group of Objects in Reference to Current Orientation

Base point: *pick base point*
<Rotation angle>/Reference: **R**
Reference angle: **60**
New angle: **35**
Command:

SCALE Command

The SCALE command lets you change the size of existing entities or the complete drawing. Objects can be made larger or smaller. The same scale factor is applied to X and Y dimensions. To enlarge an object, enter a scale factor greater than 1. For instance, a scale factor of 3 would make the selected objects 3 times larger. To shrink an object, use a scale factor between 0 and 1. Do not give a negative scale factor. For instance, a scale factor of 0.75 would shrink the selected objects to three-quarter their current size.

The SCALE command is invoked from Screen Root Menu Edit (see Figure 2–84), pull-down menu Modify (see Figure 2–85), or at the "Command:" prompt, type in **SCALE** and press ⏎.

Command: **scale**
Select objects: *show what to scale and then give a null response*
Base point: *pick a point on or near the object or enter coordinates*
<Scale factor>/Reference: *type a scale factor*

The base point can be anywhere in the drawing. If a portion of a selected object lies on the base point, that portion remains on the base point as the object's size changes.

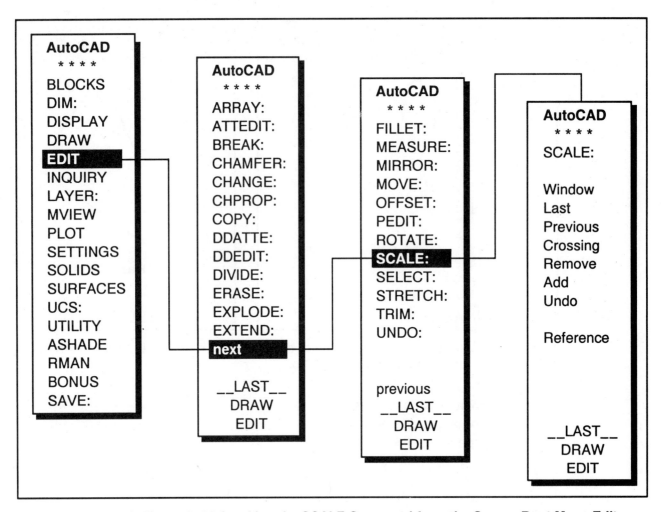

Figure 2-84 Invoking the SCALE Command from the Screen Root Menu Edit

The following command sequence shows an example of using the SCALE command to enlarge a group of objects selected by the Window option, as shown in Figure 2-86.

Command: **scale**
Select objects: *pick Window option from the screen menu or type* **W** *and press*
 ↵
First corner: *pick point 1*
Other corner: *pick point 2*
Select objects: ↵
Base point: *pick base point*
<Scale Factor>/Reference: **3**
Command:

Reference SCALE Option If an object has to be scaled in reference to a current dimension, you can use the Reference option to do the same. Specify the current dimension as reference length or show AutoCAD the reference length by pointing to the two endpoints of a line to be scaled and specify the desired new length. AutoCAD

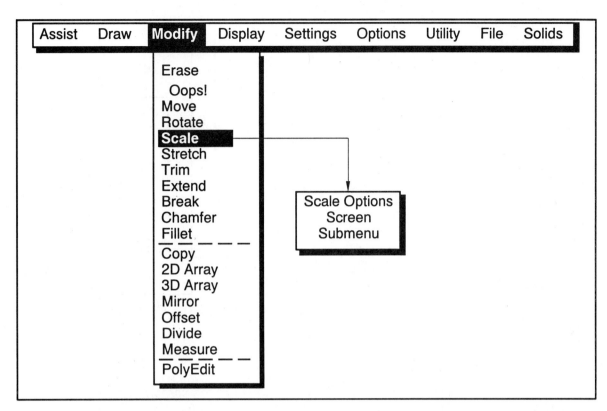

Figure 2–85 Invoking the SCALE Command from the Pull-Down Menu Modify

will automatically calculate the scale factor and enlarge or shrink the object appropriately.

The following command sequence shows an example of using the SCALE command to enlarge a group of objects selected by the Window option in reference to a current dimension, as shown in Figure 2–87.

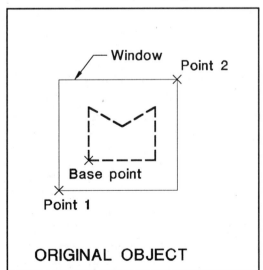

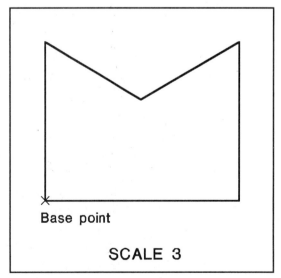

Figure 2–86 Using the Window Option of the SCALE Command to Enlarge a Group of Objects

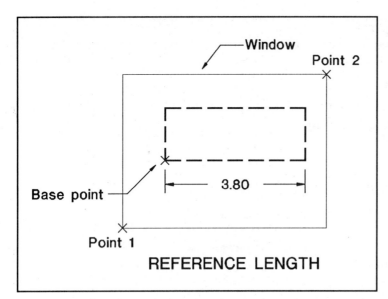 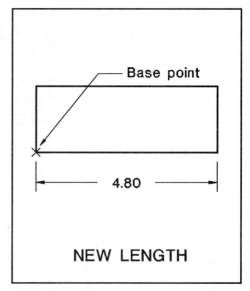

Figure 2-87 Using the Window Option of the SCALE Command to Enlarge a Group of Objects in Reference to a Current Dimension

Command: **scale**
Select objects: *pick Window option from the screen menu or type* **W** *and press*
⌐⌐
First corner: *pick point 1*
Other corner: *pick point 2*
Select objects: ⌐⌐
Base point: *pick base point*
<Scale Factor>/Reference: **R**
Reference length: **3.8**
New length: **4.8**
Command:

TEXT Command

Any experienced manual drafter will appreciate the many benefits associated with the TEXT command. Whether you are using freehand, template, or Leroy lettering, the process of placing the extensive notes associated with many engineering drawings is a time consuming and tedious process.

Text is used to label the various components of your drawing and used in placing the necessary shop or field notes needed for fabrication and construction of your design. Because of the extensive use of text on engineering drawings the TEXT command is a very important AutoCAD command. Text placement is easily achieved with AutoCAD because of the many text parameters. This section is devoted to the use of text and the many ways it can be entered on your drawing. AutoCAD furnishes the designer with a large number of text patterns or text fonts. Text can be stretched, compressed, obliqued, mirrored, or drawn in a vertical column by applying a style to the font. Each string can be sized, rotated, and justified to meet your drawing needs. You should be aware that a text string, which means all the characters that comprise the string, will be considered as one entity.

The TEXT command is invoked from the Screen Root Menu Draw (see Figure 2–88), or at the "Command:" prompt, you can type in **TEXT** and press the spacebar or ⏎.

Command: **text**
Justify/Style/<Start point>:

Start Point Option This is the default option. It allows you to select a point on the screen where you want the text to begin. You can specify the starting point by absolute coordinates or by using your pointing device. This point by default indicates the lower left corner of the text. After you specify the starting point, AutoCAD prompts:

Height <default>:

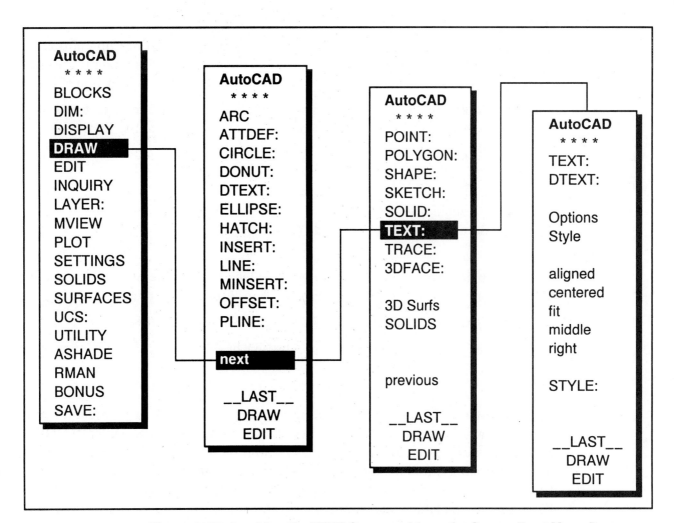

Figure 2–88 Invoking the TEXT Command from the Screen Root Menu Draw

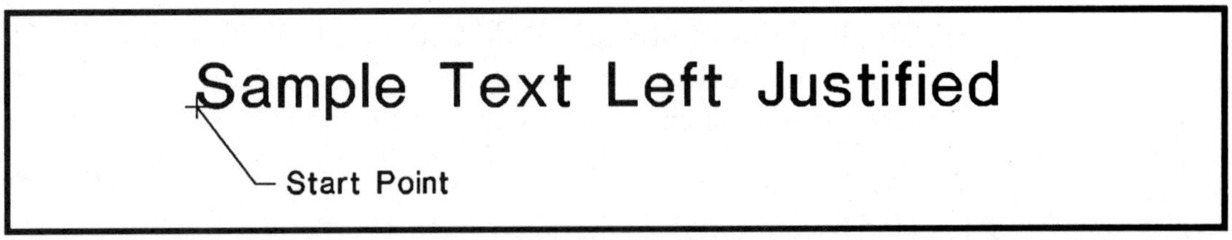

Figure 2-89 Using the TEXT Command to Place Text by Specifying a Starting Point (Left Justified)

This allows you to select the text height. You can accept the default text height by giving a null response, or typing in appropriate text height. Next, AutoCAD prompts:

Rotation angle <default>:

This allows you to place the text at any angle in reference to 0 degrees (default is 3 o'clock or east, measured in counterclockwise direction). The default value of the rotation angle is 0 degrees and the text is placed horizontally at the specified start point. The last prompt is:

Text:

Type the desired text and press ↵. If you need to place another line of text, go back to the TEXT command and give a null response to the "Start point:" prompt; automatically AutoCAD places the second line of text below the first line of text.

For example, the following command sequence shows placement of text as shown in Figure 2-89 by providing the starting point (left justified) of the text.

Command: **text**
Justify/Style/<Start point>: *pick point 1*
Height <.20>: **.25**
Rotation angle <0>: ↵
Text: **Sample Text Left Justified**

Justify Option This option allows you to place text in one of the 14 available alignment options. When you select this option, AutoCAD prompts:

Align/Fit/Center/Middle/Right/TL/TC/TR/ML/MC/MR/BL/BC/BR:

Type in the option you would like to place the text, or select the option from the screen menu.

Center Option The Center option allows you to select the center point for the base line of the text. Base line refers to the line along which the bases of the capital letters lie. Letters with descenders, such as g, q, or y, dip below the base line. After providing the center point, enter the text height and rotation angle.

For example, the following command sequence shows placement of text, as shown in Figure 2-90, by providing the center point (center justified) of the text.

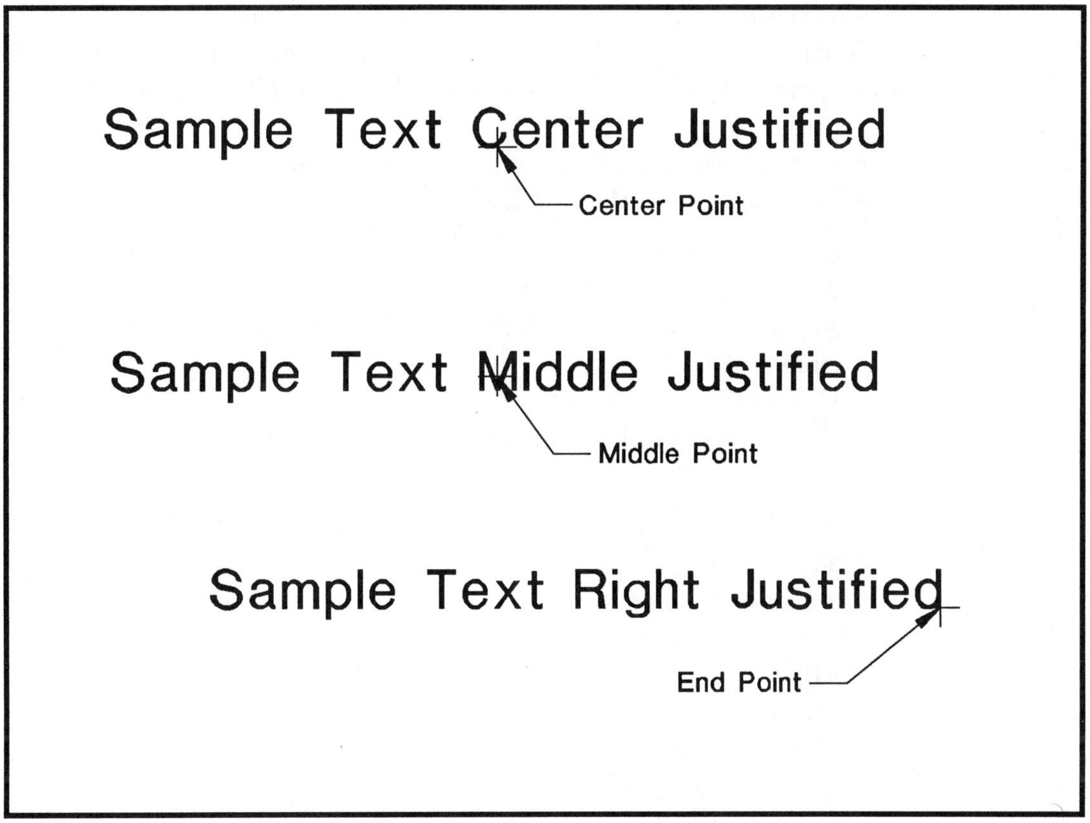

Figure 2-90 Using the TEXT Command to Place Text by Specifying a Center Point (Center Justified), a Middle Point (Middle Justified), and a Right Point (Right Justified)

```
Command: text
Justify/Style/<Start point>: j
Align/Fit/Center/Middle/Right/TL/TC/TR/ML/MC/MR/BL/BC/BR: center
Height <.20> .25
Rotation angle <0>: ⏎
Text: Sample Text Center Justified
```

Middle Option The Middle option allows you to center the text both horizontally and vertically at a given point. After providing the middle point, enter the text height and rotation angle.

For example, the following command sequence shows placement of text, as shown in Figure 2-90, by providing the middle point (middle justified) of the text.

```
Command: text
Justify/Style/<Start point>: j
Align/Fit/Center/Middle/Right/TL/TC/TR/ML/MC/MR/BL/BC/BR: middle
Height <.20> .25
Rotation angle <0>: ⏎
Text: Sample Text Middle Justified
```

Right Option The Right option allows you to place the text in reference to lower right corner (right justified). Here, the point you provide is where the text will end. After providing the point, enter the text height and rotation angle.

For example, the following command sequence shows placement of text, as shown in Figure 2-90, by right justified.

> Command: **text**
> Justify/Style/<Start point>: **j**
> Align/Fit/Center/Middle/Right/TL/TC/TR/ML/MC/MR/BL/BC/BR: **right**
> Height <.20> **.25**
> Rotation angle <0>: ⏎
> Text: **Sample Text Right Justified**

Other options are combinations of the above and are listed as follows:

> TL – top left
> TC – top center
> TR – top right
> ML – middle left
> MC – middle center
> MR – middle right
> BL – bottom left
> BC – bottom center
> BR – bottom right

Align Option The Align option allows you to place the text by designating the endpoints of the base line. AutoCAD computes the text height and orientation such that the text just fits between those two points. The overall character size adjusts in proportion to the height. The height and width of the character will be same.

For example, the following command sequence shows placement of text, as shown in Figure 2-91, using the Align option.

> Command: **text**
> Justify/Style/<Start point>: **j**
> Align/Fit/Center/Middle/Right/TL/TC/TR/ML/MC/MR/BL/BC/BR: **align**
> First text line point: *specify the first point*
> Second text line point: *specify the second point*
> Text: **Sample Text Aligned**

Fit Option The Fit option is similar to Align option, but in the case of Fit option AutoCAD uses the current text height and adjusts only the text's width, expanding or contracting it to fit between the points you specify.

For example, the following command sequence shows placement of text, as shown in Figure 2-91, using the Fit option.

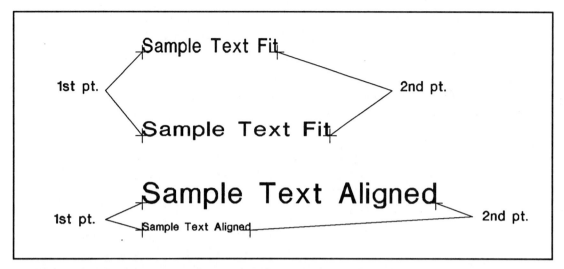

Figure 2-91 Using the Align and Fit Option of the TEXT Command to Place Text

Command: **text**
Justify/Style/<Start point>: **j**
Align/Fit/Center/Middle/Right/TL/TC/TR/ML/MC/MR/BL/BC/BR: **fit**
First text line point: *specify the first point*
Second text line point: *specify the second point*
Height <default): **0.25**
Text: **Sample Text Fit**

The Style option is explained in Chapter 4.

LAB EXERCISES

In exercises 2-12 and 2-13, draw the schematic diagram by using appropriate Grid and Snap.

Set limits   lower left: 0,0
              upper right: 17,11

Set Grid to .25 and Snap to .125

Set text height .125

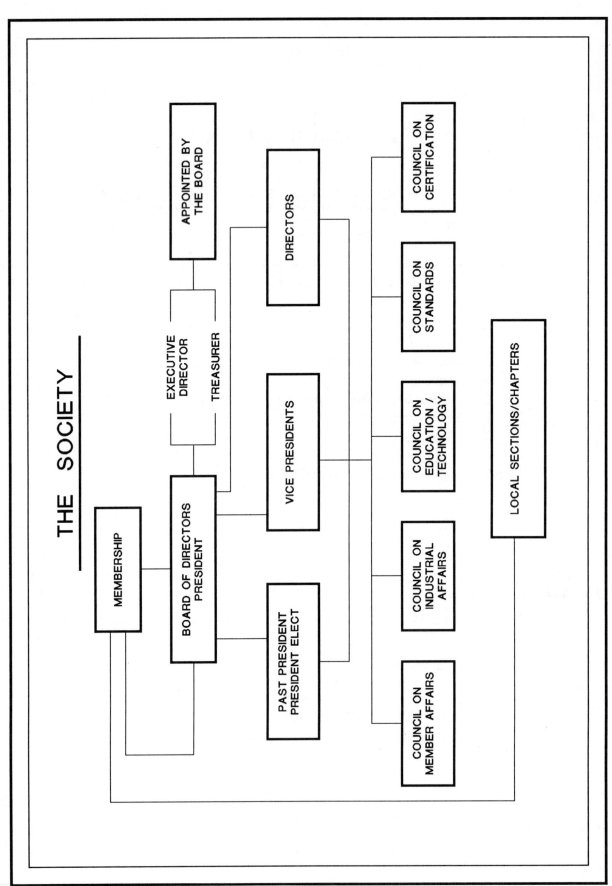

THE SOCIETY

MEMBERSHIP

BOARD OF DIRECTORS
PRESIDENT

EXECUTIVE DIRECTOR

TREASURER

APPOINTED BY THE BOARD

DIRECTORS

VICE PRESIDENTS

PAST PRESIDENT
PRESIDENT ELECT

COUNCIL ON MEMBER AFFAIRS

COUNCIL ON INDUSTRIAL AFFAIRS

COUNCIL ON EDUCATION / TECHNOLOGY

COUNCIL ON STANDARDS

COUNCIL ON CERTIFICATION

LOCAL SECTIONS/CHAPTERS

Lab Exercise 2-13

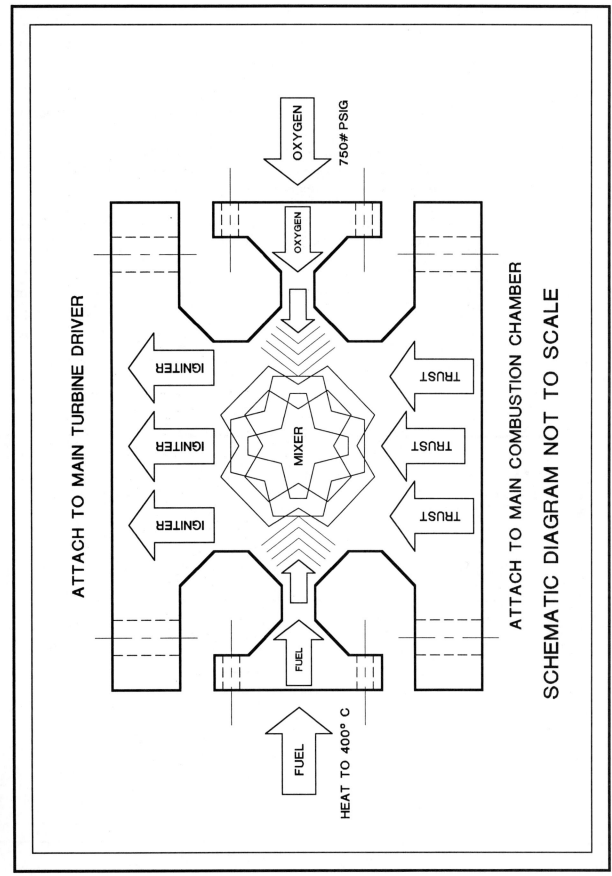

SCHEMATIC DIAGRAM NOT TO SCALE

DIMENSIONING

AutoCAD's dimensioning feature provides an excellent means of adding to your drawing such critical information as lengths, widths, angles, tolerances, and clearances.

Dimensioning of any drawing is typically the last step in the drawing process. This need not be any different in AutoCAD, but due to AutoCAD's unique drawing environment, dimensioning does not have to be the last step. If for some reason, you need to perform editing on the drawing, such as stretching or extending entities, the dimensions can be updated automatically.

AutoCAD provides a set of dimensioning variables that control the way AutoCAD draws dimensions. You can change their settings to meet the requirements of a particular dimensioning situation.

AutoCAD provides five basic types of dimensioning: Linear, Angular, Diameter, Radius, and Ordinate. Figure 2-92 shows examples of these five basic types of dimensioning.

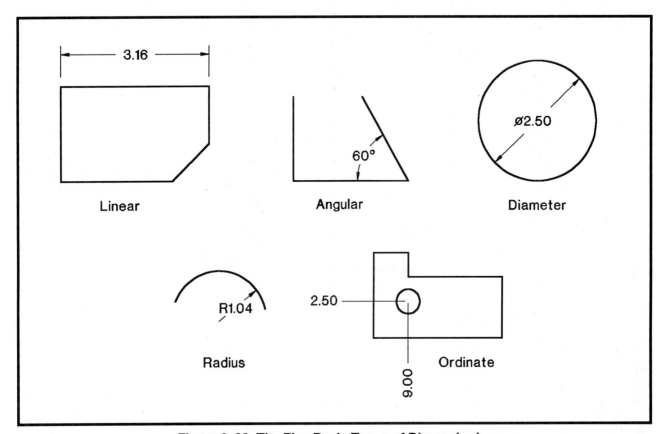

Figure 2-92 The Five Basic Types of Dimensioning

Dimensioning Terminology

Following are the terms commonly used in AutoCAD dimensioning.

Dimension Line This is a line with markers at each end (arrows, dots, ticks, etc). The dimensioning text is located along this line; you may place it above the line or in a break at the center of the dimension line. Usually, the dimension line is inside the measured area. If there is insufficient space, then AutoCAD places the dimensions with two short lines drawn outside the measured area with arrows pointing inward.

Arrows The arrows are placed on both ends of the dimension line. AutoCAD is very flexible in this area, allowing you to place arrows, tick marks, or an arbitrary symbol of your own design. You can also adjust the size of the symbol.

Extension Lines The extension lines (also called witness lines) are the ones that extend from the object to the dimension line. Extension lines are normally drawn perpendicular to the dimension line. If necessary, you can make them oblique by using the OBLIQUE command. Also, you can suppress one or both of the extension lines.

Dimension Text This is a text string that usually indicates the actual measurement. You can accept the default measurement computed automatically by AutoCAD by pressing ⏎, or change it by supplying your own text. If necessary, you can also suppress the text entirely by pressing the spacebar and then ⏎. This is useful when you wish to keep from having the dimension lines forced outside the extension lines.

The format of the default text is governed by the UNITS command and current text style. For example, you start a drawing using decimal units with 4 decimal places, and when you are ready to do dimensioning, you decide to do dimensoning with 2 decimal places. Before you start dimensioning, select the UNITS command and change the number of decimal places from 4 to 2. Automatically the dimensioning will be presented to 2 decimal places, even though the drawing was done with 4 decimal places. Whatever format is selected in the UNITS command, AutoCAD will draw dimensioning text in that format.

Figure 2–93 shows the different components of a typical dimensioning.

Leader The leader line is drawn from text to an object, as shown in Figure 2–94. For some dimensioning, the text may not fit next to the object it describes, hence, it is customary to place the text nearby and draw a leader.

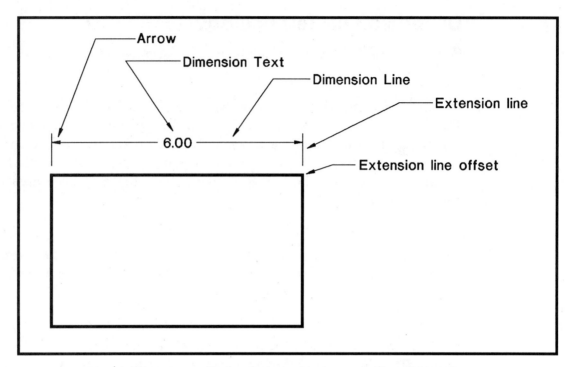

Figure 2-93 The Different Components of a Typical Dimensioning

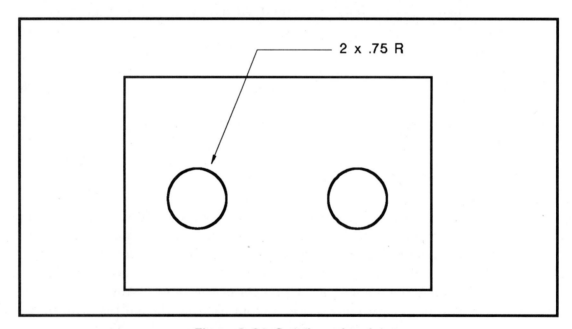

Figure 2-94 Creating a Leader

Types of Dimensions

There are essentially two types of dimensions in AutoCAD, associative and normal. With associative dimensioning, AutoCAD's default method of inserting a dimension, all the lines, arrows, arcs, and text items comprising a dimension are drawn as a single entity. Editing this type of entity is easier because the entire dimension acts as a single object. When you use editing commands to modify the object dimensioned, AutoCAD modifies the dimension text automatically to reflect the change. It also draws the dimension entity to its new location, size, and rotation. If you want to edit individual components of a dimension, you can use the EXPLODE command (see Chapter 6) to separate an associative dimension entity into its individual simpler entities.

In the normal method, the component entities that make up the dimension are drawn as separate entities. The dimension text is a text entity, the dimension lines are lines, etc. When you use editing commands to modify the object dimensioned, AutoCAD does not modify the dimension text automatically to reflect the change if the dimensioning is done by the normal method.

You can switch back and forth between associative and normal dimensioning with the help of the dimensioning variable DIMASO. If the DIMASO in on then associative dimensioning is enabled and normal disabled; if it is off then normal is enabled and associative disabled.

Dimensioning Commands

There are two ways to enter dimensioning commands at the "Command:" prompt, DIM and DIM1. When you enter DIM at the "Command:" prompt and press ⏎, it will take you into the dimensioning mode. In this mode, the normal set of AutoCAD commands is replaced by a special set of dimensioning commands. Also, the regular "Command:" prompt will be replaced by the "Dim:" prompt after each dimensioning command until you explicitly request it to return to the standard "Command:" prompt. To do this, issue the EXIT command or respond to the "Dim:" prompt with `Ctrl` + `C` one or more times. If you press ⏎ or the spacebar at the "Dim" prompt, the previous dimensioning command will be repeated. If you plan to execute several dimensioning commands, use the DIM command.

The DIM1 command allows you to execute one dimensioning command, and then returns to the "Command:" prompt. If you have to do just one dimension, then it is appropriate to use the DIM1 command.

The DIM command is invoked from the Screen Main Menu (see Figure 2-95) or you can type **DIM** or **DIM1** at the "Command:" prompt and the spacebar or ⏎.

The dimensioning commands can be grouped into seven categories:

Linear dimensioning
Angular dimensioning
Associative dimensioning
Radius dimensioning
Diameter dimensioning
Ordinate dimensioning
Dimensioning utility

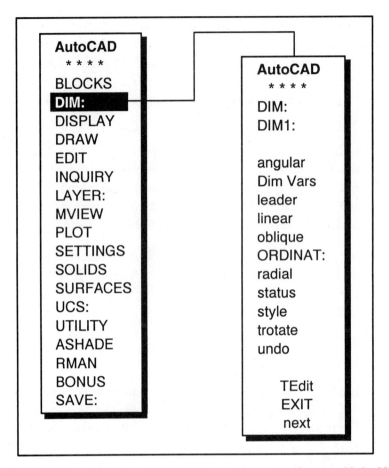

Figure 2-95 Invoking the DIM Command from the Screen Main Menu

The following section explains linear dimensioning. Other dimensioning commands are explained in the following chapters.

Linear Dimensioning Linear dimensioning is the basic type of dimensioning used by AutoCAD. It measures the straight-line distance from one point to another. AutoCAD provides four basic types of linear dimensioning options. They are as follow:

Horizontal
Vertical
Aligned
Rotate

The only difference between the four basic types is the angle at which the dimension line is drawn. All of these options share certain similarities, including some common prompts. Nothing is drawn until you have answered all the dimensioning prompts. The following section explains the four basic linear dimensioning options.

Horizontal Dimensioning The DIM command can be invoked from the Screen Root Menu and then you can invoke Linear to get into Horiz option (see Figure 2-96), or at the "Dim:" prompt you can also type **HOR** and press ⏎ to get into horizontal dimensioning. AutoCAD prompts:

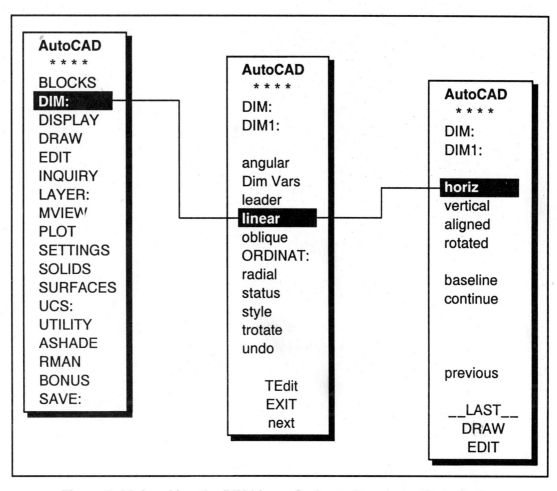

Figure 2-96 Invoking the DIM Linear Option to Reach the Horiz Option

Command: **dim**
DIM: **hor**
First extension line origin or ⏎ to select:

If you specify a point, AutoCAD uses it as the start point (origin) for the first extension line. This point can be the endpoint of a line, or intersection of a line, the center point of a circle, and even the insertion point of a text entity. You can select a point on the object itself. AutoCAD provides a gap between the object and the extension line that is equal to the value of the dimensioning variable DIMEXO, which you can change at any time.

After designating the start point (origin), then AutoCAD prompts:

Second extension line origin:

Designate the point at which the second extension line should start. Even though the first point may not be on the same horizontal line as the second, the distance used by the horizontal mode is the horizontal distance between the two points.

Instead of indicating the start point for the first extension line, you can give a null response, then AutoCAD prompts:

Select line, arc, or circle:

AutoCAD is asking you to select the entity you want to dimension. You must select the object by pointing to it; no other methods are permitted. This feature is handy to dimension a single entity, AutoCAD positions extension lines automatically. If you indicate a line or an arc, AutoCAD uses the endpoints for the first and second extension lines. If you indicate a circle, the endpoints of the diameter line are used.

After you have specified the extension line origins or selected an entity, AutoCAD prompts:

Dimension line location:

Specify a point where the dimension line is to be drawn. This places the line on which the dimension text is placed. If there is enough room between the extension lines, the dimension text will be centered in or on this line. However, if the dimension line, arrows, and text do not fit between the extension lines, they are drawn outside. The text will be placed near the second extension line. If the object selection is used to produce automatic extension lines, the second extension line is the one furthest from the point used to select the object.

Once you have given the location for the dimension line, then AutoCAD measures the appropriate distance and prompts:

Dimension text <length>:

A null response will cause AutoCAD to use the measured length as the dimension text. If necessary, you can override the calculated dimensioning text. You can supply the text by typing it in from the keyboard. By doing so you can also supply the prefix or suffix to the dimension text. AutoCAD automatically draws the required extension lines, dimension lines, arrowheads, and numerals. You can cause AutoCAD not to place the dimension text by pressing the spacebar and then ⏎ in response to the dimension text. This is useful if you wish to keep the text from forcing the dimension lines outside the extension lines. The desired text can then be drawn in by using the TEXT command.

The "Dim:" prompt is issued after each dimension is complete. You can continue additional horizontal dimensioning by pressing the spacebar or ⏎ and AutoCAD will cycle through the prompts for horizontal dimensioning.

The following command sequence shows an example of placing linear horizontal dimensions by providing two data points for the first and second line origins, respectively, as shown in Figure 2-97.

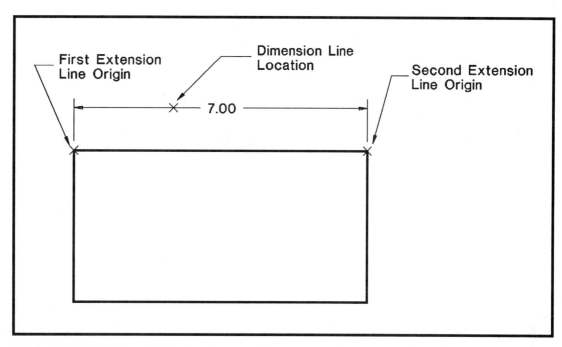

Figure 2-97 Placing Linear Horizontal Dimensions by Specifying the Origin of Two Data Points for the First and Second Line Origins

Command: **dim**
DIM: *pick linear from the screen menu*
DIM: *pick horiz from the screen menu*
First extension line origin or ⏎ to select: *pick the origin for the first extension line*
Second extension line origin: *pick the origin for the second extension line*
Dimension line location: *pick the location for the dimension line*
Dimension text <7.00>: ⏎
DIM:

The following command sequence shows an example of placing linear horizontal dimensions to a single entity, as shown in Figure 2-98.

Command: **dim**
DIM: *pick linear from the screen menu*
DIM: *pick horiz from the screen menu*
First extension line origin or ⏎ to select: ⏎
Select line, arc, or circle: *select the line*
Dimension line location: *pick the location for the dimension line*
Dimension text <7.00>: ⏎
DIM:

Vertical Dimensioning The DIM command can be invoked from the Screen Root Menu and then you can invoke Linear to get into Vertical option (see figure 2-99), or at the "Dim:" prompt, you can also type **VER** and press the spacebar or ⏎ to get into vertical dimensioning. AutoCAD prompts:

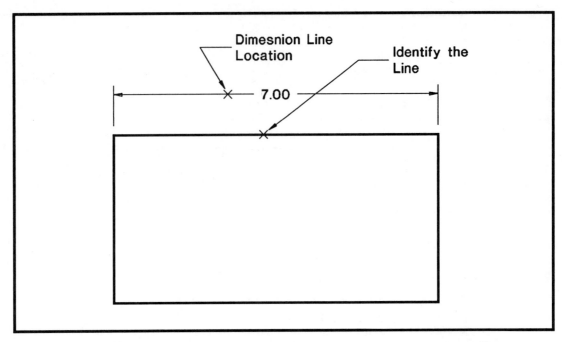

Figure 2-98 Placing Linear Horizontal Dimensions to a Single Entity

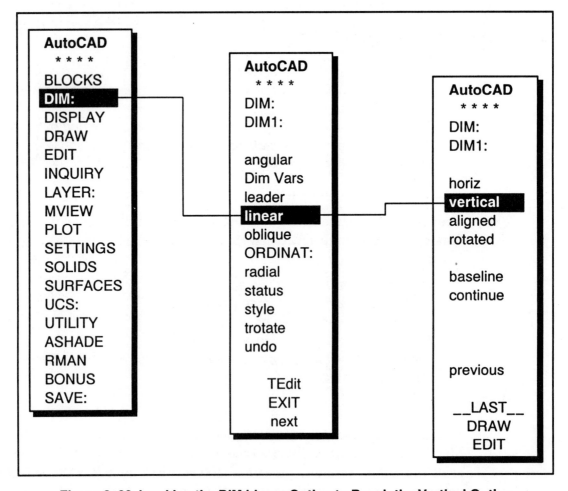

Figure 2-99 Invoking the DIM Linear Option to Reach the Vertical Option

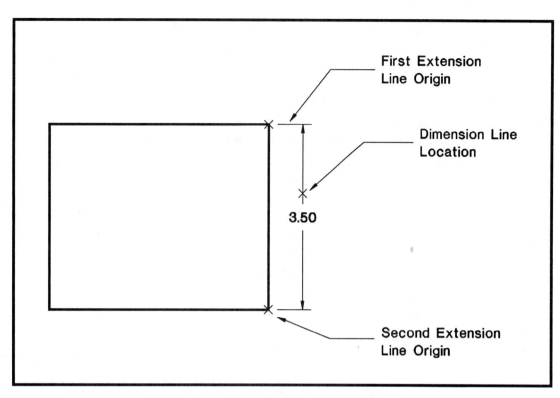

Figure 2-100 Placing Linear Vertical Dimensions by Specifying Two Data Points for the First and Second Line Origins

Command: **dim**
DIM: **ver**
First extension line origin or ⏎ to select: *pick the origin for the first extension line*
Second extension line origin: *pick the origin for the second extension line*
Dimension line location: *pick the location for the dimension line*
Dimension text <length>: ⏎
DIM:

The prompts are similar to the horizontal dimensioning as explained in the previous section, except the dimensioning is done in the vertical Axis. By default, AutoCAD draws the dimension text horizontally (zero degrees) even for vertical dimension lines. If you need to draw the dimension text at the same orientation as the dimension line, then you can set the dimension variable DIMTIH to do so.

The following command sequence shows an example of placing Linear Vertical dimensions by providing two data points for the first and second line origins, respectively, as shown in Figure 2-100.

Command: **dim**
DIM: *pick linear from the screen menu*
DIM: *pick vert from the screen menu*
First extension line origin or ⏎ to select: *pick the origin for the first extension line*

Second extension line origin: *pick the origin for the second extension line*
Dimension line location: *pick the location for the dimension line*
Dimension text <3.50>: ⏎
DIM:

Aligned Dimensioning When dimensioning a line drawn at an angle, it may be necessary to align the dimension line with the object line. For example, auxiliary views are normally placed at an angle. In order to properly dimension these features, the Aligned option can be used.

The DIM command can be invoked from the Screen Root Menu and then you can invoke Linear to get to the Aligned option (see Figure 2-101), or at the "Dim:" prompt you can also type **ALI** and press the spacebar or ⏎ to get into aligned dimensioning. AutoCAD prompts:

Command: **dim**
DIM: **ali**
First extension line origin: *pick the origin for the first extension line*
Second extension line origin: *pick the origin for the second extension line*

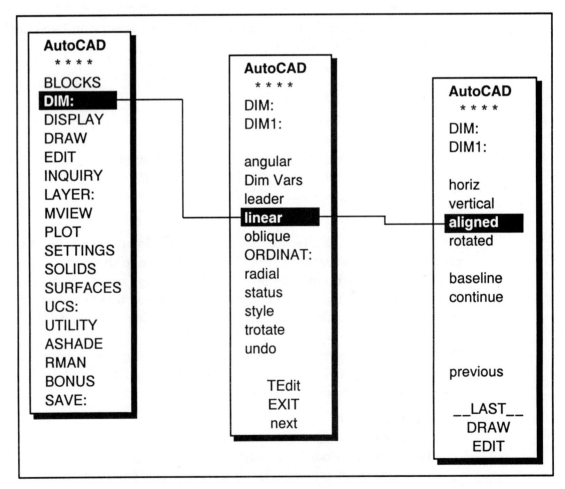

Figure 2-101 Invoking the DIM Linear Option to Reach the Aligned Option

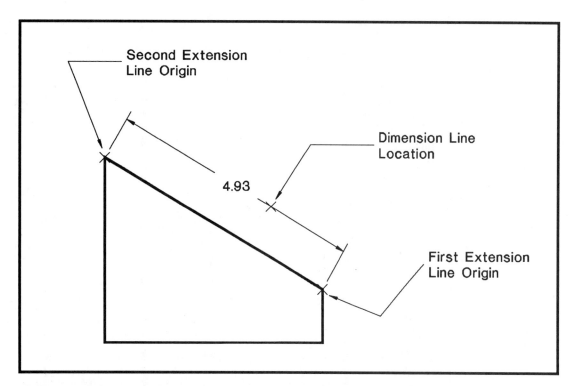

Figure 2-102 Placing Linear Aligned Dimensions by Specifying Two Data Points for the First and Second Line Origins

Dimension line location: *pick the location for the dimension line*
Dimension text <length>: ⏎
DIM:

The prompts are similar to the horizontal dimensioning as explained in the previous section, except the dimensioning is done at an angle.

The following command sequence shows an example of placing Linear Aligned dimensions by providing two data points for the first and second line origins, respectively, as shown in Figure 2-102.

Command: **dim**
DIM: *pick linear from the screen menu*
DIM: *pick rotated from the screen menu*
First extension line origin: *pick the origin for the first extension line*
Second extension line origin: *pick the origin for the second extension line*
Dimension line location: *pick the location for the dimension line*
Dimension text <4.93>: ⏎
DIM:

Rotated Dimensioning Rotated dimensioning is useful when you need to place the dimension at a specified angle that is not horizontal, vertical, or at the angle determined by the two points you select as in aligned dimensioning.

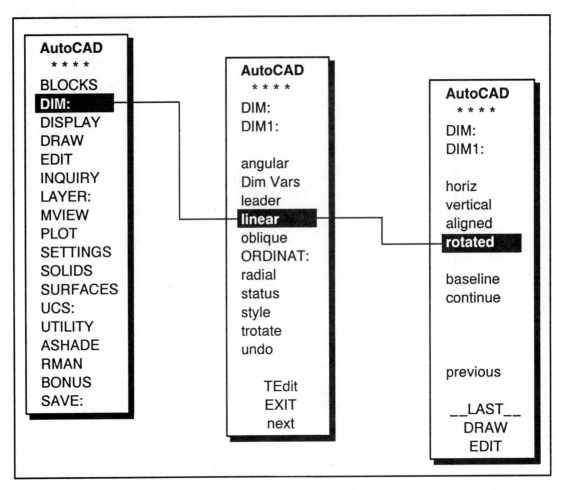

Figure 2-103 Invoking the DIM Linear Option to Reach the Rotated Option

The DIM command can be invoked from the Screen Root Menu and then you can invoke Linear to get to the Rotated option (see Figure 2-103), or at the "Dim:" prompt, you can also type **ROT** and press the spacebar or ⏎ to get into rotated dimensioning. AutoCAD prompts:

> Command: **dim**
> DIM: **rot**
> Dimension line angle <angle>: *type dimension line angle or pick two points on the drawing*
> First extension line origin: *pick the origin for the first extension line*
> Second extension line origin: *pick the origin for the second extension line*
> Dimension line location: *pick the location of the dimension line*
> Dimension text <length>: ⏎
> DIM:

The Rotated option is slightly different from the other dimensioning options. The first request is for a dimension line angle and the remaining prompts are similar to horizontal, vertical, and aligned. Unlike the Aligned option, the points selected do not have to be parallel to the direction of the dimensioned distance.

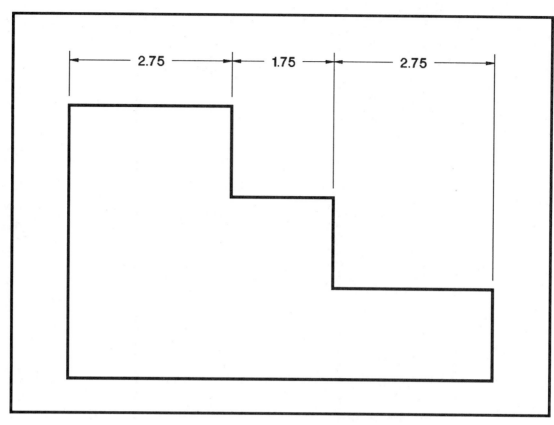

Figure 2-104 Using Chain Dimensioning

Continue (chain) Dimensioning Continue dimensioning, also called point-to-point, places dimensions in a line from one feature to the next. Chain dimensioning is sometimes used in mechanical and architectural drafting. See Figure 2-104 for an example of chain dimensioning. AutoCAD automatically spaces and places the extension lines, dimension lines, arrowheads, and numerals.

The DIM command can be invoked from the Screen Root Menu and then you can invoke Linear to get into the Continue option (see Figure 2-105), or at the "Dim:" prompt you can also type **CONT** and press the spacebar or ⏎ to get into continue dimensioning.

> Command: **dim**
> DIM: **cont**
> Second extension line origin or ⏎ to select: *pick the origin of the second extension line*

The above prompt will appear only if the previous dimension was a linear dimension. AutoCAD picks the second extension line origin of the previous dimension as the first extension line origin. If you give a null response to the above prompt, or if the previous dimension was not a linear dimension, AutoCAD prompts you to select a linear dimension to use as the basis for the next dimension:

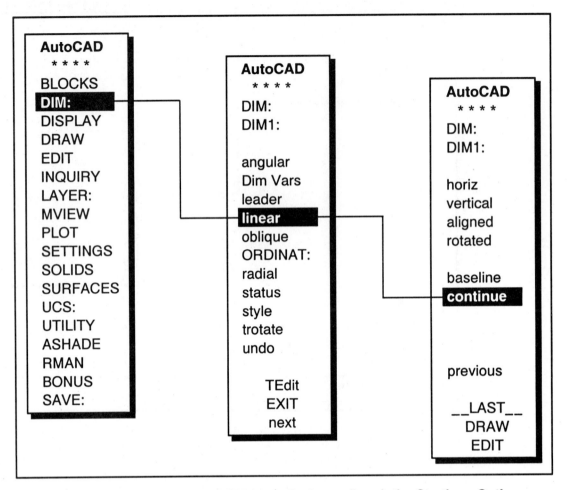

Figure 2–105 Invoking the DIM Linear Option to Reach the Continue Option

Select continued dimension: *pick a linear dimension line*

AutoCAD uses the selected dimension's second extension line origin as its first extension line origin and prompts:

Second extension line origin: *pick the origin of the second extension line*
Dimension text <length>: ⏎
DIM:

You can continue dimensioning by pressing the spacebar or ⏎ and AutoCAD will cycle through the prompts for continued dimensioning.

The following command sequence shows an example of placing continue (chain) dimensioning by using the Continue option, as shown in Figure 2–106.

Command: **dim**
DIM: *pick linear from the screen menu*
DIM: *pick horiz from the screen menu*
First extension line origin or ⏎ to select: *pick the origin for the first extension line*
Second extension line origin: *pick the origin for the second extension line*
Dimension line location: *pick the location for the dimension line*
Dimension text <1.80>: ⏎

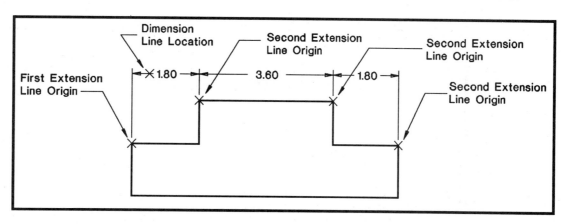

Figure 2-106 Placing Chain Dimensions Using the Continue Option

DIM: *pick continue from the screen menu*
Second extension line origin: *pick the origin of the second extension line*
Second extension line origin: *pick the origin of the second extension line*
Second extension line origin: ⏎
DIM:

The following command sequence shows an example of placing continue dimensioning by using the Continue option for an existing Linear Horizontal Dimension, as shown in Figure 2-107.

Command: **dim**
DIM: *pick linear from the screen menu*
DIM: *pick continue from the screen menu*
Select continued dimension: *pick the dimension line*
Second extension line origin: *pick the origin of the second extension line*
Second extension line origin: *pick the origin of the second extension line*
Second extension line origin: ⏎
DIM:

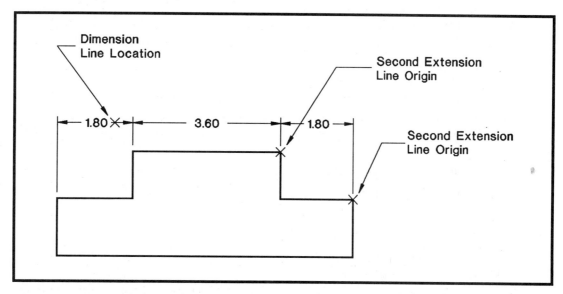

Figure 2-107 Placing Continue Dimensioning Using the Continue Option for an Existing Linear Horizontal Dimension

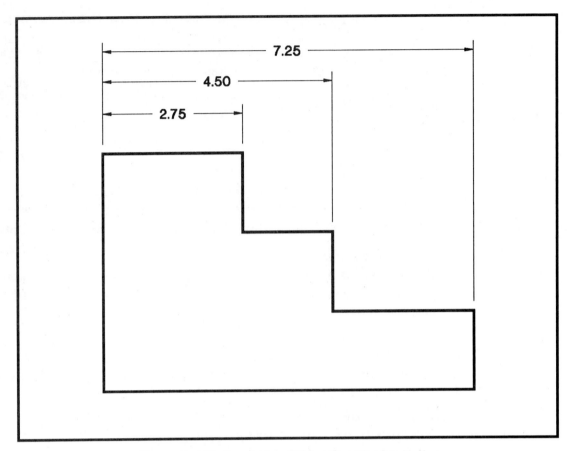

Figure 2-108 Example of Baseline Dimensioning

Baseline (datum) Dimensioning With baseline or datum dimensioning, all dimensions on an object originate from a common surface, center line, or centerplane. Baseline dimensioning is commonly used in mechanical drafting because all dimensions are independent, even though they are taken from a common datum. See Figure 2-108 for an example of baseline dimensioning.

AutoCAD has provided the Baseline option under dimensioning to perform datum dimensioning. AutoCAD automatically spaces and places the extension lines, dimension lines, arrowheads, and dimension text.

The DIM command can be invoked from the Screen Root Menu and then you can invoke Linear to get into the Baseline option (see Figure 2-109), or at the "Dim:" prompt you can type **BASE** and press the spacebar or ⏎ to get into baseline dimensioning. AutoCAD prompts:

Command: **dim**
DIM: **base**
Second extension line origin or RETURN to select: *pick the origin of the second extension line*

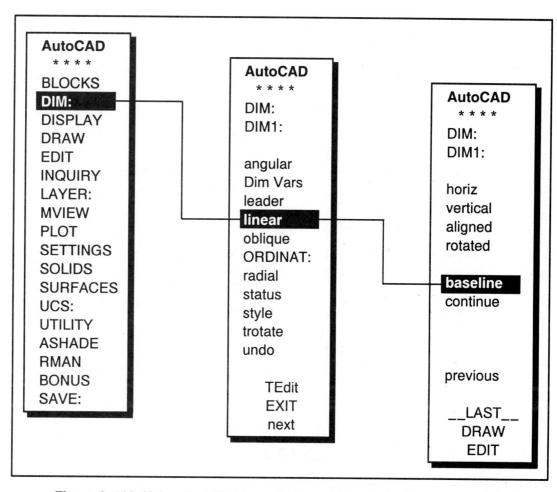

Figure 2-109 Using the DIM Linear Option to Reach the Baseline Option

The above prompt will appear only if the previous dimension was a linear dimension. AutoCAD picks the first extension line origin of the previous dimension as the origin of the baseline. If you give a null response to the above prompt, or if the previous dimension was not a linear dimension, AutoCAD prompts you to select a linear dimension to use as the basis for the next dimension:

> Select baseline dimension: *pick a linear dimension line*

When you select the base dimension by pointing, AutoCAD uses the extension line closest to the selection point as the origin for the first extension line and prompts:

> Second extension line origin: *pick the origin of the second extension line*
> Dimension text <length>: ⏎
> DIM:

You can continue additional dimensions by pressing the spacebar or ⏎ and AutoCAD will cycle through the prompts for baseline dimensioning.

The following command sequence shows an example of placing baseline dimensioning, as shown in Figure 2-110.

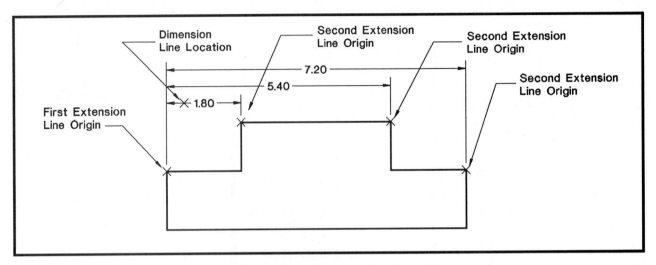

Figure 2-110 Example of Placing Baseline Dimensioning

Command: **dim**
DIM: *pick linear from the screen menu*
DIM: *pick horiz from the screen menu*
First extension line origin or ⏎ to select: *pick the origin for the first extension line*
Second extension line origin: *pick the origin for the second extension line*
Dimension line location: *pick the location for the dimension line*
Dimension text <1.80>: ⏎
DIM: *pick baseline from the screen menu*
Second extension line origin: *pick the origin of the second extension line*
Second extension line origin: *pick the origin of the second extension line*
Second extension line origin: ⏎
DIM:

The following command sequence shows an example of placing baseline dimensioning to an existing Linear Horizontal dimension, as shown in Figure 2-111.

Command: **dim**
DIM: *pick linear from the screen menu*
DIM: *pick baseline from the screen menu*
Select base dimension: *pick the dimension line*
Second extension line origin: *pick the origin of the second extension line*
Second extension line origin: *pick the origin of the second extension line*
Second extension line origin: ⏎
DIM:

Dimensioning Variables

As mentioned earlier, AutoCAD provides a set of dimensioning variables that control the way it draws dimensions. It allows you to change the appearance of dimensions. You can change the values of these variables at any time. All default values for dimensioning variables are set in the AutoCAD prototype drawing.

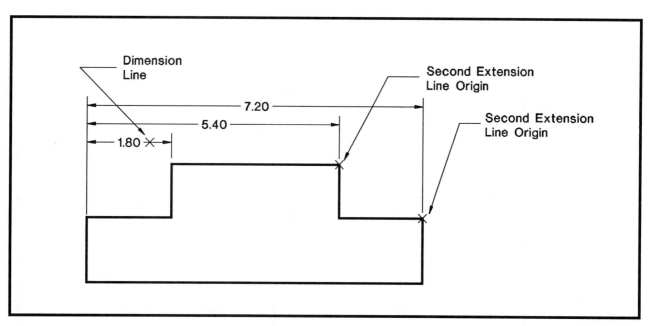

Figure 2-111 Example of Placing Baseline Dimensioning to an Existing Linear Horizontal Dimension

There are a total of 41 dimensioning variables, and they are listed in alphabetical order on the screen menu. The first three letters of each variable are "dim" and the remaining letters are a code abbreviating the purpose of each variable. These codes make it easier for you to remember the content of each variable.

To change a variable, invoke the DIM command from the Screen Root Menu and then you can invoke Dim Vars (see Figure 2-112). You will see the first of the three pages in the dimensioning variable menu. You can move from one page to another by invoking Next or Previous. Return to the DIM menu by invoking DIMMENU. To change a variable value, invoke the appropriate variable name. The default, or current value is shown in brackets. Keep this value by pressing ⏎ or type a new value and then press ⏎. The first and second page of the dimensioning variable menu has listing of 13 names each, and the third page has 15 names in alphabetical order.

In this chapter, DIMTXT, DIMASZ, DIMEXO, DIMEXE, DIMZIN, DIMTAD, and DIMTIH are the dimensioning variables introduced following the sequence in which you might use them. The remaining variables are explained in later chapters.

DIMTXT (TeXT size) Variable This variable specifies the text size used in dimensioning. The default text size is 0.18. Here is where some calculating will help. Because you are drawing to true size, when you plot to a reduced scale, objects such as dimension text are reduced in size as well. For example, plotting at a scale of 1/4"=1'0" means objects will be reduced to 1/48 of their true size. Therefore, if you want your text to be plotted at 1/8" height you draw it 48 times 1/8" or 48/8" or 6" high. So, you can set your dimension variable DIMTXT to a value of 6. Other variables such as DIMASZ, DIMEXE, and DIMEXO can be

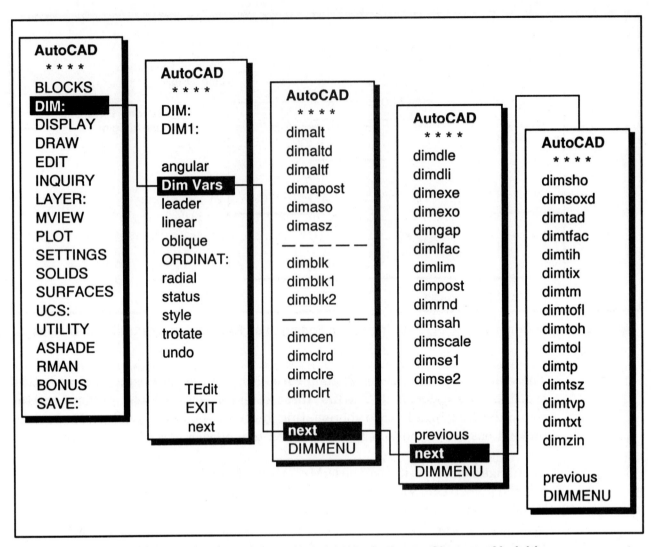

Figure 2-112 Invoking the DIM Dim Vars Option to Change a Variable

established the same way. The following command sequence shows an example of changing the text size from 0.18 to 0.25, as shown in Figure 2-113.

Command: **dim**
DIM: **dimtxt**
Current value <0.1800> New value: **.25**

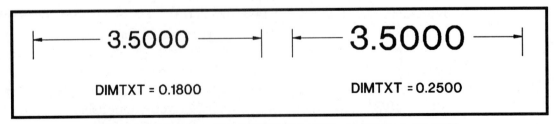

Figure 2-113 Using the DIMTXT Variable to Change Text Size

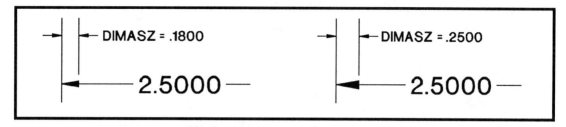

Figure 2-114 Using the DIMASZ Variable to Change Arrow Size

DIMASZ (Arrow SiZe) Variable This variable specifies the size of the arrows drawn at the ends of the dimension lines. The default arrow size is 0.18. The following command sequence shows an example of changing the arrow size from 0.18 to 0.25, as shown in Figure 2-114.

Command: **dim**
DIM: **dimasz**
Current value <0.1800> New value: **.25**

DIMEXO (EXtension line Offset) Variable This variable specifies the distance between the object and start of the extension line. Thus, you can select points on the object, and the extension line will be drawn by leaving the specified gap. The default gap is 0.0625. The following command sequence shows an example of changing the extension line offset from 0.0625 to 0.1250, as shown in Figure 2-115.

Command: **dim**
DIM: **dimexo**
Current value <0.1800> New value: **.25**

DIMEXE (EXtension line Extension) Variable This variable specifies how far the extension line should extend beyond the dimension line. The default distance is 0.1800. The following command sequence shows an example of changing the distance for the extension line beyond the dimension line from 0.1800 to 0.2250, as shown in Figure 2-116.

Command: **dim**
DIM: **dimexe**
Current value <0.1800> New value: **.2250**

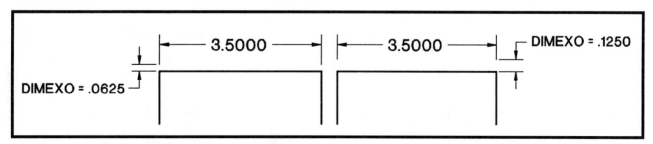

Figure 2-115 Using the DIMEXO Variable to Change Extension Line Offset

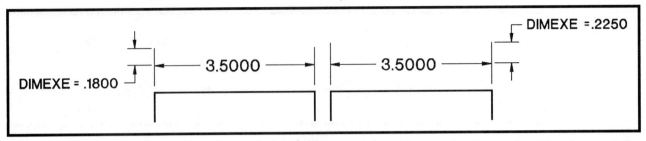

Figure 2–116 Using the DIMEXE Variable to Change the Distance for the Extension Line beyond the Dimension Line

DIMZIN (Zero INch dimensioning) Variable This variable is relevant only when architectural or fractional units are used. This variable lets you suppress the inches portion of a feet-and-inches dimension when the dimension includes 0 inches or the feet portion when the distance is less than one foot. The only valid responses to this variable are 0, 1, 2, or 3 and the default is 0. Table 2–1 below shows several examples of placing dimension text of 3/4", 3", 3', and 3'-0 3/4" by changing DIMZIN values from 0 to 3.

Table 2–1 Examples of Placing Dimension Text by Changing DIMZIN Variable Values

DIMZIN VALUE	EXAMPLES			
	3/4"	3"	3'	3' -0 3/4"
0	3/4"	3"	3'	3' -0 3/4"
1	0' -0 3/4"	0' -3"	3' -0"	3' -0 3/4"
2	0' -0 3/4"	0' -3"	3'	3' -0 3/4"
3	3/4"	3"	3' -0"	3' -0 3/4"

The following command sequence shows an example of changing the DIMZIN value from 0 to 1 and the result is shown in Figure 2–117.

    Command: **dim**
    DIM: **dimzin**
    Current value <0> New value: **1**

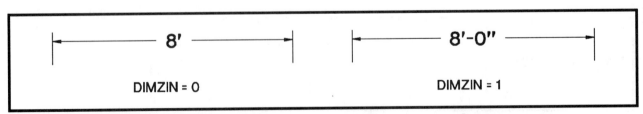

Figure 2–117 Using the DIMZIN Variable to Change Zero Inch Dimensioning

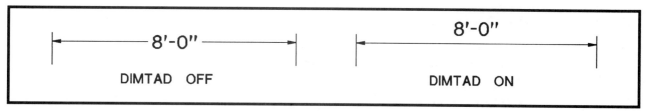

Figure 2-118 Using the DIMTAD Variable to Place Dimension Text in a Break in the Dimension Line or above the Dimension Line

DIMTAD (Text Above Dimension line) Variable This variable controls placement of the dimension text in a break in the dimension line or above the dimension line. In architectural drafting, the dimension text often appears above the dimension line. The valid responses for this variable are on and off. If the setting is off, the dimension text is placed in a break in the dimension line. If you change it to on, the dimension text will be placed above the dimension line. The following command sequence shows an example of changing the DIMTAD value from off to on and the result is shown in Figure 2-118.

Command: **dim**
DIM: **dimtad**
Current value <off> New value: **on**

DIMTIH (Text Inside Horizontal) Variable This variable controls orientation of the dimension text. The valid responses for this variable are on and off. If the setting is on, the dimension text is placed horizontally, even for the vertical dimensioning. If you change it to off, the dimension text will be aligned with the dimension line. The following command sequence shows an example of changing the DIMTIH value from on to off and the result is shown in Figure 2-119.

Command: **dim**
DIM: **dimtih**
Current value <on> New value: **off**

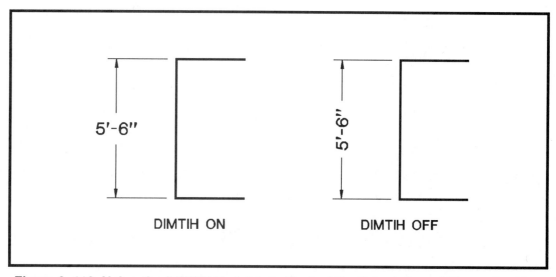

Figure 2-119 Using the DIMTIH Variable to Control the Orientation of Dimension Text

LAB EXERCISES

In exercises 2-14 through 2-16, follow the instructions given on the exercise sheet to create this series of prototype drawings.

Set Grid to .5 and Snap to .25

Set text height = .125

Limits for ProtoA
    lower left: 0,0
    upper right: 12,9

Limits for ProtoB
    lower left: 0,0
    upper right: 18,12

Limits for ProtoC
    lower left: 0,0
    upper right: 24,18

Lab Exercise 2-14

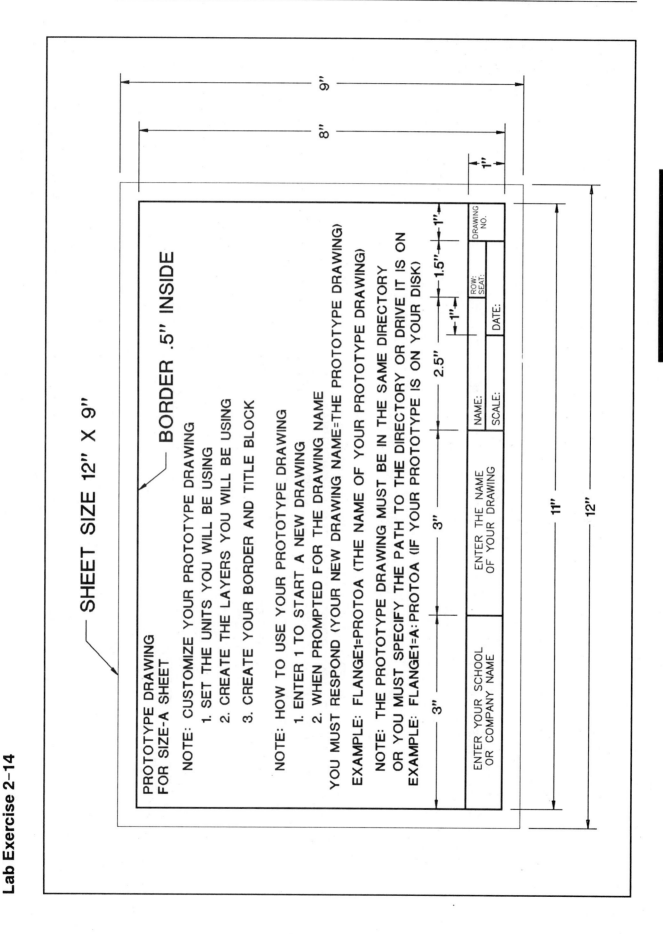

SHEET SIZE 12" X 9"

BORDER .5" INSIDE

PROTOTYPE DRAWING
FOR SIZE-A SHEET

NOTE: CUSTOMIZE YOUR PROTOTYPE DRAWING
1. SET THE UNITS YOU WILL BE USING
2. CREATE THE LAYERS YOU WILL BE USING
3. CREATE YOUR BORDER AND TITLE BLOCK

NOTE: HOW TO USE YOUR PROTOTYPE DRAWING
1. ENTER 1 TO START A NEW DRAWING
2. WHEN PROMPTED FOR THE DRAWING NAME
YOU MUST RESPOND (YOUR NEW DRAWING NAME=THE PROTOTYPE DRAWING)

EXAMPLE: FLANGE1=PROTOA (THE NAME OF YOUR PROTOTYPE DRAWING)

NOTE: THE PROTOTYPE DRAWING MUST BE IN THE SAME DIRECTORY
OR YOU MUST SPECIFY THE PATH TO THE DIRECTORY OR DRIVE IT IS ON

EXAMPLE: FLANGE1=A:PROTOA (IF YOUR PROTOTYPE IS ON YOUR DISK)

ENTER YOUR SCHOOL
OR COMPANY NAME

ENTER THE NAME
OF YOUR DRAWING

NAME:
SCALE:
ROW:
SEAT:
DATE:
DRAWING
NO.

9"
8"
1"
1"
1.5"
1"
2.5"
3"
3"
11"
12"

Lab Exercise 2–15

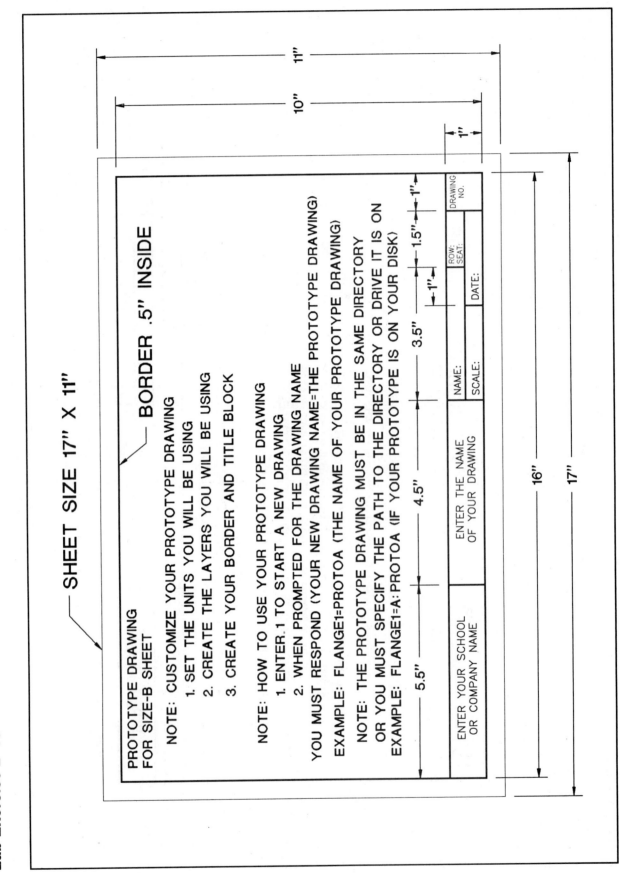

SHEET SIZE 17" X 11"

BORDER .5" INSIDE

PROTOTYPE DRAWING
FOR SIZE-B SHEET

NOTE: CUSTOMIZE YOUR PROTOTYPE DRAWING
1. SET THE UNITS YOU WILL BE USING
2. CREATE THE LAYERS YOU WILL BE USING
3. CREATE YOUR BORDER AND TITLE BLOCK

NOTE: HOW TO USE YOUR PROTOTYPE DRAWING
1. ENTER 1 TO START A NEW DRAWING
2. WHEN PROMPTED FOR THE DRAWING NAME
YOU MUST RESPOND (YOUR NEW DRAWING NAME=THE PROTOTYPE DRAWING)

EXAMPLE: FLANGE1=PROTOA (THE NAME OF YOUR PROTOTYPE DRAWING)

NOTE: THE PROTOTYPE DRAWING MUST BE IN THE SAME DIRECTORY
OR YOU MUST SPECIFY THE PATH TO THE DIRECTORY OR DRIVE IT IS ON
EXAMPLE: FLANGE1=A:PROTOA (IF YOUR PROTOTYPE IS ON YOUR DISK)

ENTER THE NAME
OF YOUR DRAWING

ENTER YOUR SCHOOL
OR COMPANY NAME

NAME:

SCALE:

ROW:
SEAT:

DATE:

DRAWING
NO.

11"

10"

1"

1"

1.5"

3.5"

1"

4.5"

5.5"

16"

17"

Lab Exercise 2-16

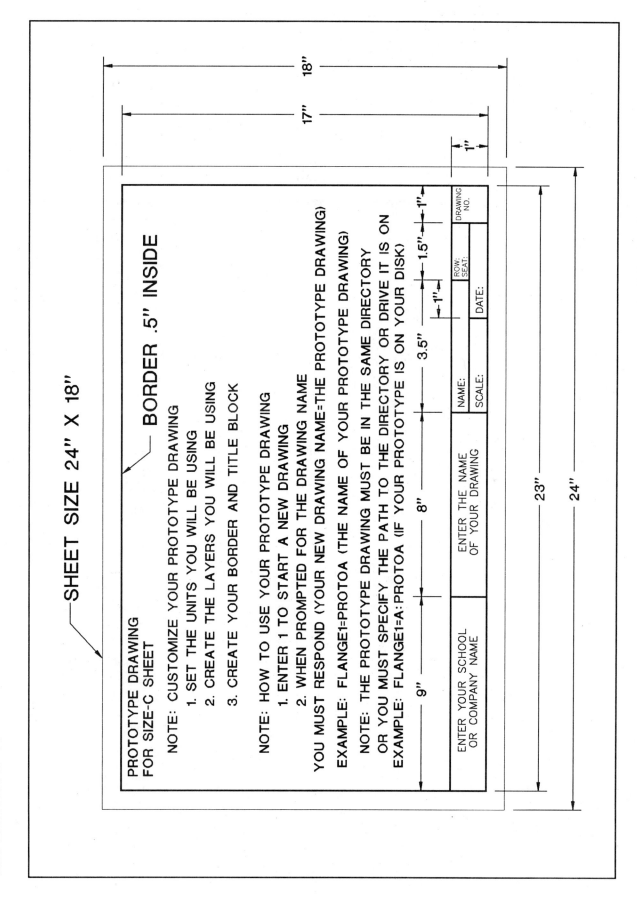

SHEET SIZE 24" X 18"

BORDER .5" INSIDE

PROTOTYPE DRAWING
FOR SIZE-C SHEET

NOTE: CUSTOMIZE YOUR PROTOTYPE DRAWING
1. SET THE UNITS YOU WILL BE USING
2. CREATE THE LAYERS YOU WILL BE USING
3. CREATE YOUR BORDER AND TITLE BLOCK

NOTE: HOW TO USE YOUR PROTOTYPE DRAWING
1. ENTER 1 TO START A NEW DRAWING
2. WHEN PROMPTED FOR THE DRAWING NAME
YOU MUST RESPOND (YOUR NEW DRAWING NAME=THE PROTOTYPE DRAWING)

EXAMPLE: FLANGE1=PROTOA (THE NAME OF YOUR PROTOTYPE DRAWING)

NOTE: THE PROTOTYPE DRAWING MUST BE IN THE SAME DIRECTORY
OR YOU MUST SPECIFY THE PATH TO THE DIRECTORY OR DRIVE IT IS ON
EXAMPLE: FLANGE1=A:PROTOA (IF YOUR PROTOTYPE IS ON YOUR DISK)

ENTER YOUR SCHOOL
OR COMPANY NAME

ENTER THE NAME
OF YOUR DRAWING

NAME:
SCALE:
ROW:
SEAT:
DATE:
DRAWING NO.

18"
17"
1"
1"
1.5"
1"
3.5"
8"
9"
23"
24"

LAB EXERCISES

In exercises 2-17 through 2-22, draw three views: top, front, and right side of the figure.

Use the appropriate size prototype title block.

> **NOTE:** When you start a new drawing make the name of the new drawing equal to the prototype drawing name.

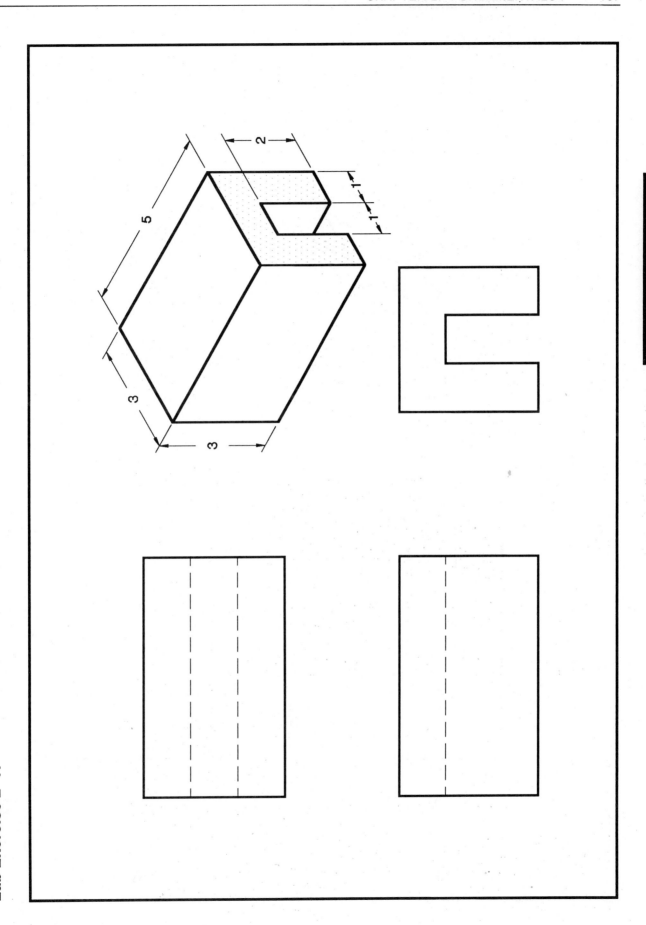

Lab Exercise 2-17

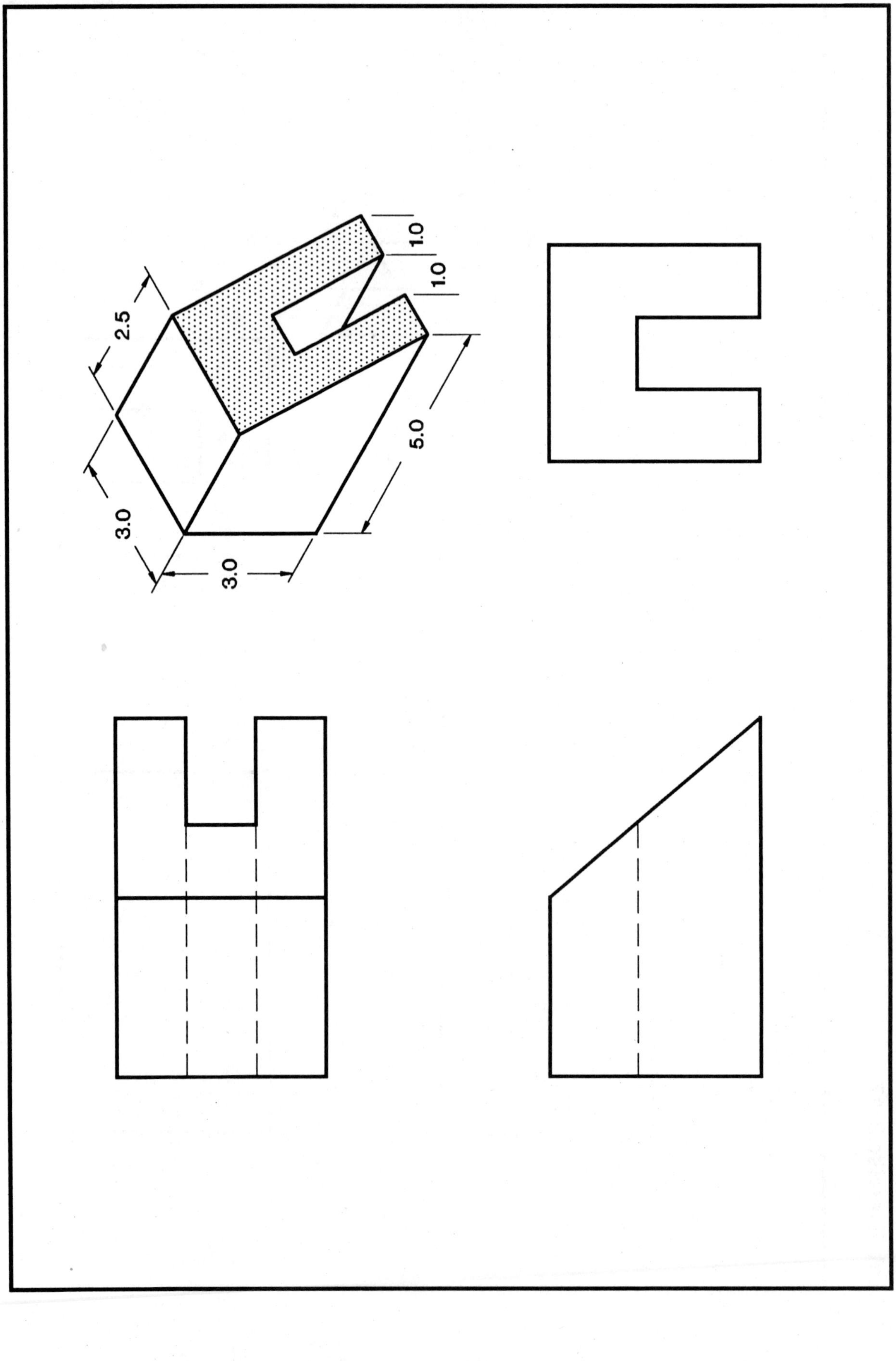

Lab Exercise 2–18

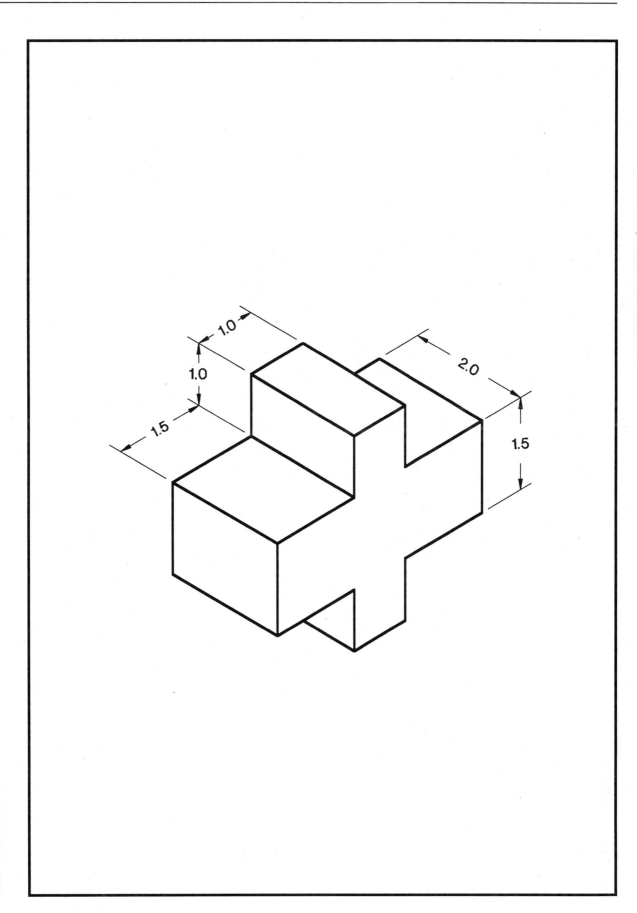

Lab Exercise 2–19

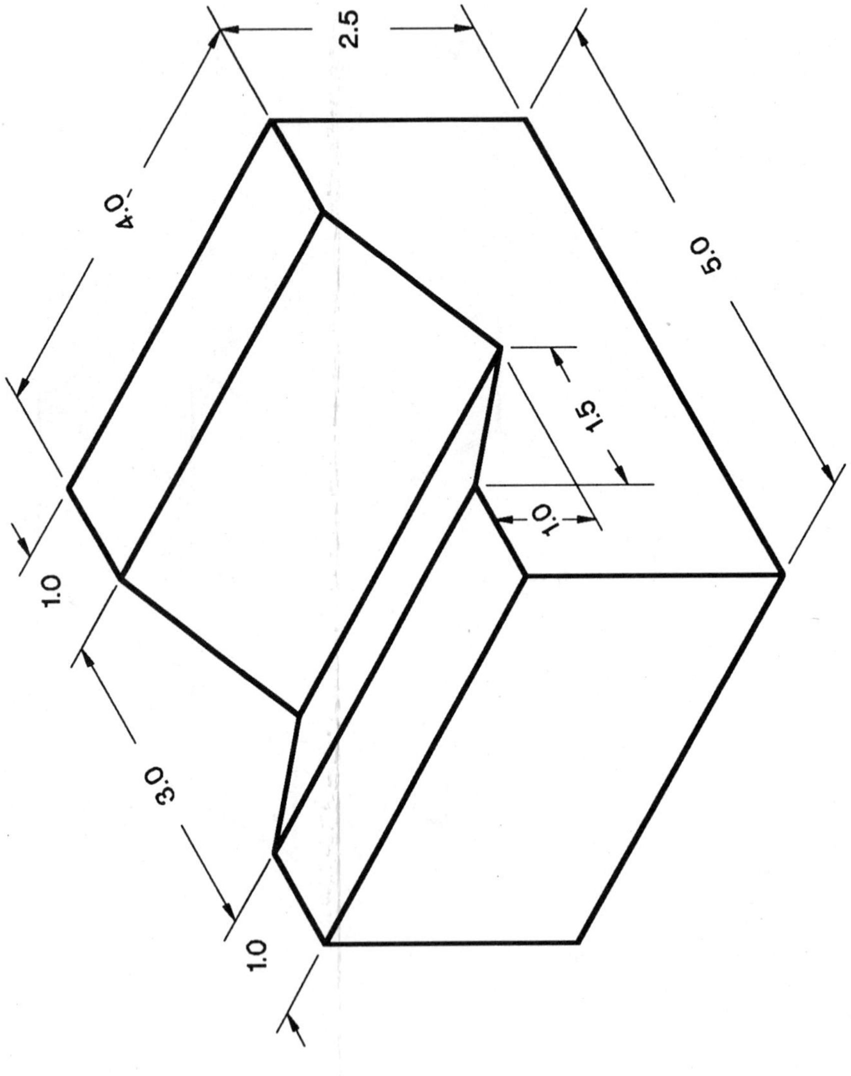

Lab Exercise 2–20

Fundamentals I

Lab Exercise 2-21

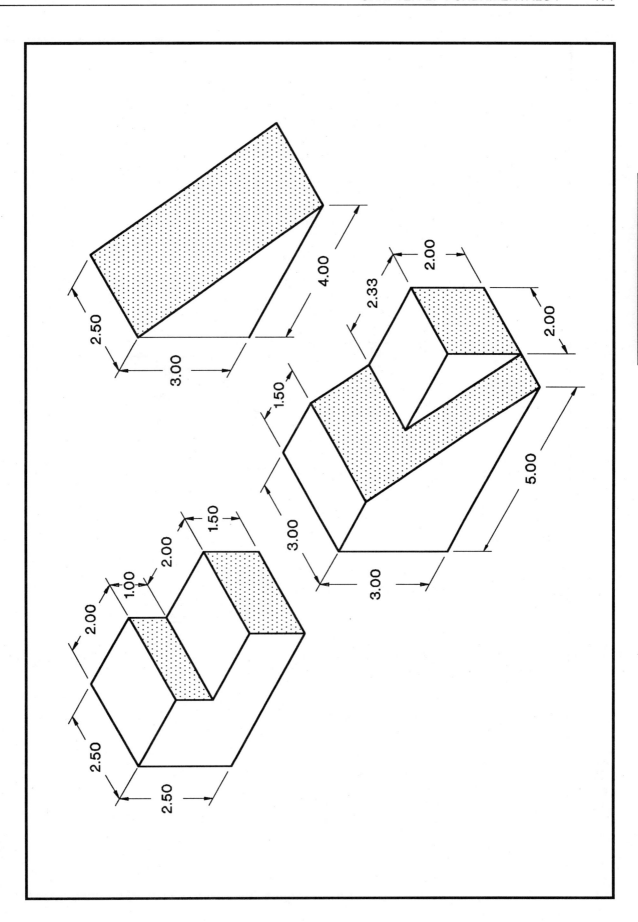

Lab Exercise 2-22

LAB EXERCISE

In exercise 2-23, draw the view shown, including dimensions.

Set units to architectural

Set limits   lower left: 0,0
                 upper right: 24,18

Set Grid to 2' and Snap to 1'

Lab Exercise 2-23

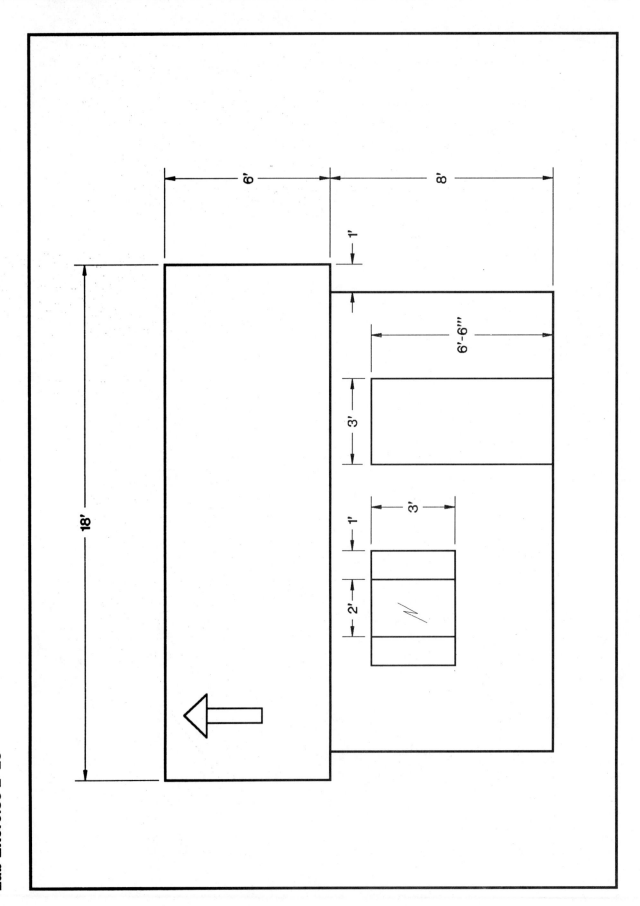

LAB EXERCISES

In exercises 2–24 and 2–25, draw the views shown, including dimensions.

Set units to architectural

Set limits   lower left: 0,0
                  upper right: 80',60'

Set Grid to 2' and Snap = 1'

Lab Exercise 2-24

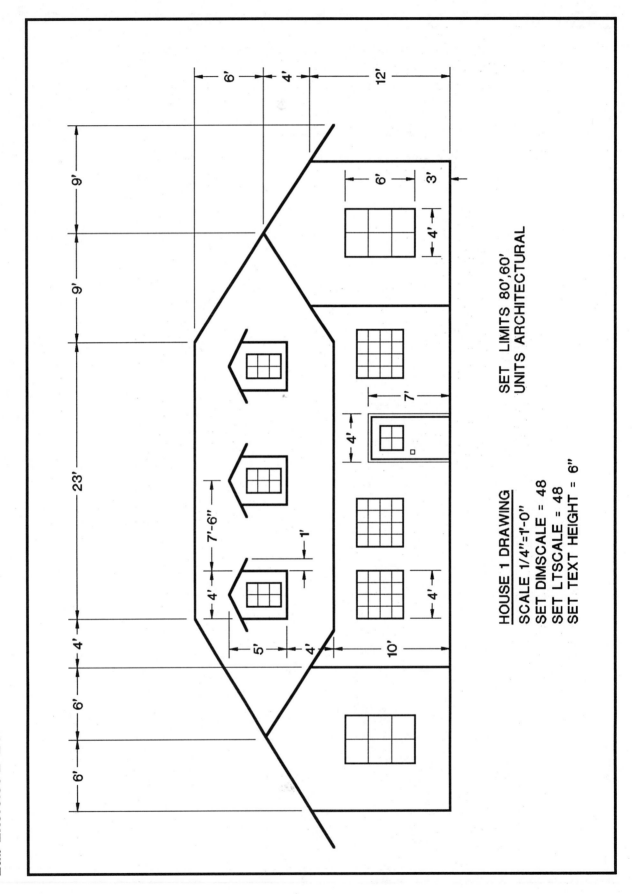

SET LIMITS 80',60'
UNITS ARCHITECTURAL

HOUSE 1 DRAWING
SCALE 1/4"=1'-0"
SET DIMSCALE = 48
SET LTSCALE = 48
SET TEXT HEIGHT = 6"

Lab Exercise 2-25

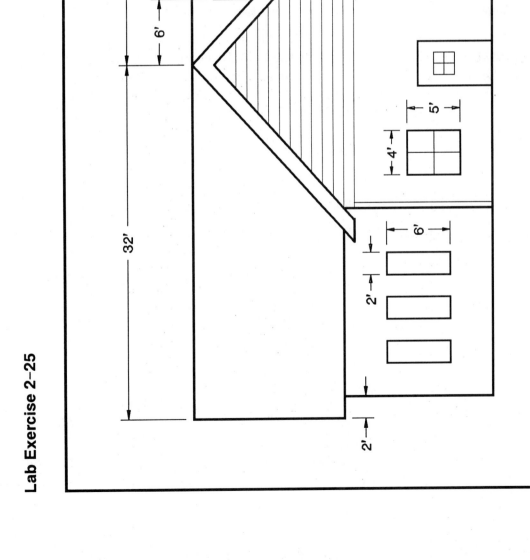

HOUSE 2 DRAWING
SCALE 1/4"=1'-0"
SET DIMSCALE = 48
SET LTSCALE = 48
SET TEXT HEIGHT = 6"

SET LIMITS 80',60'
UNITS ARCHITECTURAL

Chapter 2 Project Exercise

CREATING THE PROJECT DRAWING

The end of this chapter marks a milestone for the novice. The concepts introduced to this point have been organized to give you a foundation of CAD knowledge and skills upon which you can build advanced and more discipline-oriented expertise.

You can now apply these concepts to produce a complete drawing in step-by-step fashion, as shown in Figure 2–120. Fundamental concepts and skills that must be applied to this drawing project are as follow:

1. Drawing setup including UNITS, LIMITS, GRID, SNAP, and LAYERS.
2. Display commands ZOOM and PAN.
3. Draw commands LINE and TRACE.
4. Edit commands MOVE, COPY, and ERASE are also recommended.
5. Text input command.
6. Linear dimensioning commands and related dimension variables.

The object of this project is to set LIMITS corresponding to an 8 1/2" × 11" sheet (or 11 × 8.5 to be technically correct, placing the X dimension first) and permit drawing the 40' × 24' structural steel plan as shown in Figure 2–120, allowing room on the sheet for dimensioning and a border. The drawing will be done in Architectural units, and 3/16" = 1'-0" (or 1:64) scale will be appropriate for plotting on 8 1/2" × 11" sheet (8 1/2 × 64 = 45'-4" and 11 × 64 = 58'-8") and still leave adequate space around the plan for dimensions. It is often convenient, however, to have the coordinates of one corner of the object to be 0,0.

STEP 1:   Begin a NEW drawing called proj1.

STEP 2:   Set up the units and limits:

Command: **units**

Report formats:	(Examples)
1. Scientific	1.55E+01
2. Decimal	15.50
3. Engineering	1'-3.50"
4. Architectural	1'-3 1/2"
5. Fractional	15 1/2

Enter choice, 1 to 5 <default>: **4**
Denominator of smallest fraction to display (1, 2, 4, 8, 16, 32, or 64)
<16>: ⏎

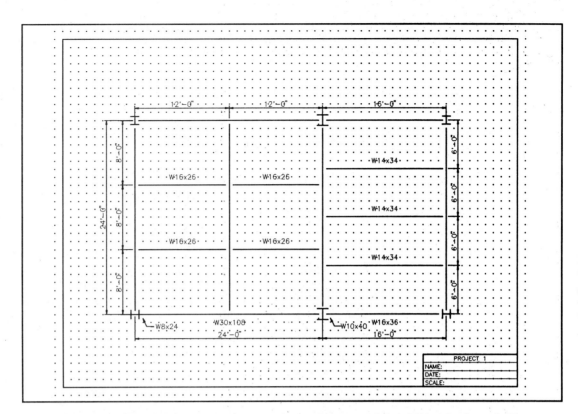

Figure 2-120 Completed Drawing of the Structural Steel Plan in AutoCAD

Systems of angle measure:	(Examples)
1. Decimal degrees	45.0000
2. Degrees/minutes/seconds	45d0'0"
3. Grads	50.0000g
4. Radians	0.7854r
5. Surveyor's units	N45d0'0"E

Enter choice, 1 to 5 <default>: **1**
Number of fractional places for display of angles (0 to 8) <default>: **0**

Direction for angle 0:

East	3 o'clock	=	0
North	12 o'clock	=	90
West	9 o'clock	=	180
South	6 o'clock	=	270

Enter direction for angle 0 <default>: **0**
Do you want angles measured clockwise? <default>: **N**
Command:**limits**
on/off/<Lower left corner> <default>: **-10',-10'**
Upper right corner <default>: **50',35'**
Command: **zoom**
All/Center/Dynamic/Extents/Left/Previous/Vmax/Window/Scale(x/
XP)>: **a**

STEP 3: Create layers layout, plan, column, dim, text, and border with appropriate colors and linetypes and set layer layout as the current layout as shown below:

Command: **layer**
?/Make/Set/New/ON/OFF/Color/Ltype/Freeze/Thaw: **n**
New layer name(s): **layout,plan,column,dim,text,border**
?/Make/Set/New/ON/OFF/Color/Ltype/Freeze/Thaw: **c**
Color: **blue**
Layer name(s) for color 5 (blue) <0>: **layout**
?/Make/Set/New/ON/OFF/Color/Ltype/Freeze/Thaw: **c**
Color: **green**
Layer name(s) for color 3 (green) <0>: **plan**
?/Make/Set/New/ON/OFF/Color/Ltype/Freeze/Thaw: **c**
Color: **red**
Layer name(s) for color 1 (red) <0>: **column**
?/Make/Set/New/ON/OFF/Color/Ltype/Freeze/Thaw: **c**
Color: **cyan**
Layer name(s) for color 4 (cyan) <0>: **dim**
?/Make/Set/New/ON/OFF/Color/Ltype/Freeze/Thaw: **c**
Color: **yellow**
Layer name(s) for color 2 (yellow) <0>: **text**
?/Make/Set/New/ON/OFF/Color/Ltype/Freeze/Thaw: **s**
New current layer <0>: **layout**
?/Make/Set/New/ON/OFF/Color/Ltype/Freeze/Thaw: ⏎

STEP 4: Set up the AutoCAD tools:

Command: **grid**
Grid spacing or ON/OFF/SNAP/Aspect <default>: **1'**

Command: **snap**
Snap spacing or ON/OFF/Aspect/Rotate/Style <default>: **6**

STEP 5: Create a layout of the lines where the beams will be drawn, as shown in Figure 2–121.

Command: **line**
From point: **0,0**
To point: **@40',0**
To point: **@0,24'**
To point: **@-40',0**
To point: **close**

Command: **line**
From point: **0,8'**
To point: **@24',0**
To point: ⏎
Command: **copy**
Select objects: *select line 1 as shown in Figure 2–122*
Select objects: ⏎
<Base point or displacement>/Multiple: **0,0**
Second point of displacement: **@0,8'**

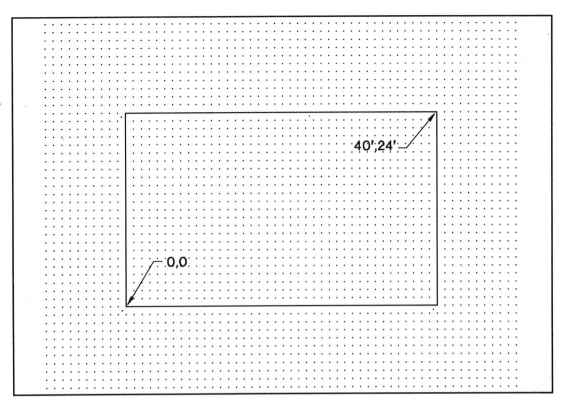

Figure 2-121 Creating a Layout of the Lines Where the Beams Will Be Drawn

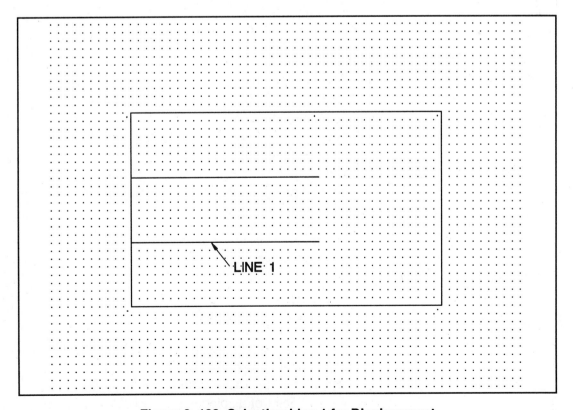

Figure 2-122 Selecting Line 1 for Displacement

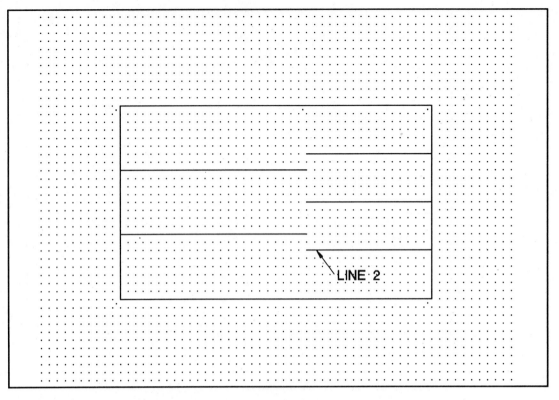

Figure 2-123 Selecting Line 2 for Displacement

Command: **line**
From point: **24',6'**
To point: **@16',0**
To point: ⏎

Command: **copy**
Select objects: *select line 2 as shown in Figure 2-123*
Select objects: ⏎
<Base point or displacement>/Multiple: **m**
Base point: **0,0**
Second point of displacement: **@0,6'**
Second point of displacement: **@0,12'**
Second point of displacement: ⏎

Command: **line**
From point: **12',0**
To point: **@0,24'**
To point: ⏎

Command: **copy**
Select objects: *select line 3 as shown in Figure 2-124*
Select objects: ⏎
<Base point or displacement>/Multiple: **0,0**
Second point of displacement: **@12',0**

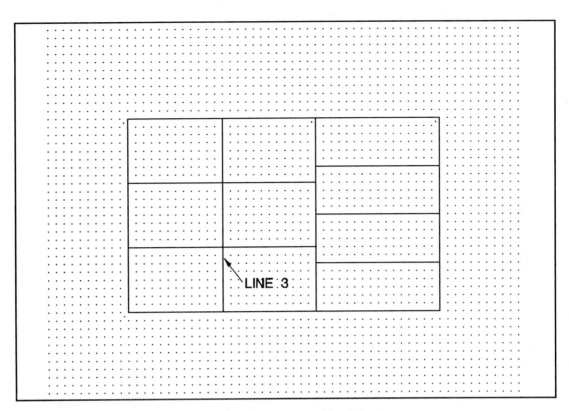

Figure 2-124 Selecting Line 3 for Displacement

STEP 6: Set column as the current layer:

Command: **layer**
?/Make/Set/New/ON/OFF/Color/Ltype/Freeze/Thaw: **s**
New current layer <0>: **column**
?/Make/Set/New/ON/OFF/Color/Ltype/Freeze/Thaw: ⏎

STEP 7: Create a 12" × 12" column using the TRACE command by Snapping to the invisible dots:

Command: **zoom**
All/Center/Dynamic/Extents/Left/Previous/Vmax/Window/<Scale (X/XP)>: **window**
First corner: *select point 1 as shown in Figure 2-125*
Other corner: *select point 2 as shown in Figure 2-125*

Command:**trace**
Trace width <default>: **1**
From point: *select point 1 as shown in Figure 2-126*
To point: *select point 2 as shown in Figure 2-126*
To point: ⏎
Command:**trace**
Trace width <default>: **1**
From point: *select point 3 as shown in Figure 2-126*
To point: *select point 4 as shown in Figure 2-126*
To point: ⏎
Command:**trace**
Trace width <default>: **1**

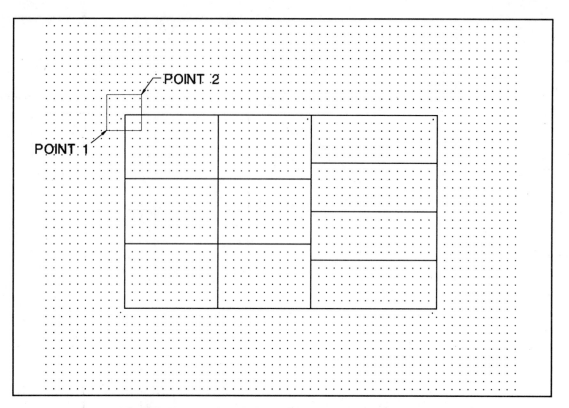

Figure 2-125 Using ZOOM Window to Select Point 1 and Point 2

From point: *select point 5 as shown in Figure 2-126*
To point: *select point 6 as shown in Figure 2-126*
To point: ⏎

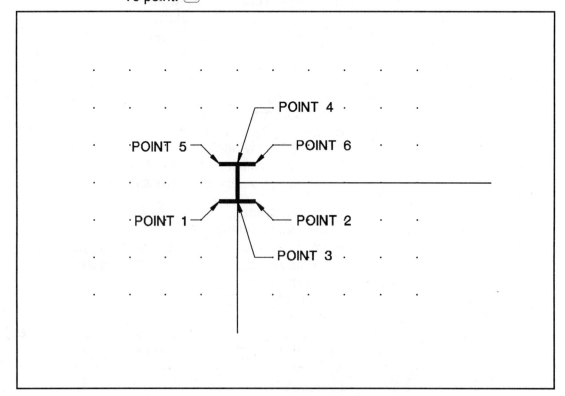

Figure 2-126 Creating a 12" × 12" Column Using the TRACE Command

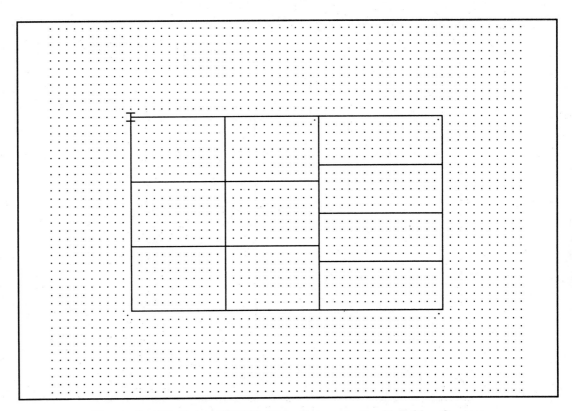

Figure 2-127 Using ZOOM All to Return to the Full-Size Screen

> Command: **zoom**
> All/Center/Dynamic/Extents/Left/Previous/Vmax/Window/<Scale
>   (X/XP) >:**a** (See Figure 2-127.)

STEP 8: Make multiple copies of the 12" × 12" columns, as shown in Figure 2-128:

> Command: **copy**
> Select objects: **window**
> First corner: *select point 1 as shown in Figure 2-128*
> Other corner: *select point 2 as shown in Figure 2-128*
> Select obejcts: ⏎
> <Base point or displacement>/Multiple: **m**
> Base point: **0,0**
> Second point of displacement: **@24',0**
> Second point of displacement: **@40',0**
> Second point of displacement: **@0,-24'**
> Second point of displacement: ⏎

STEP 9: Increase the size of the column 12" × 12" to 16" × 16" using the SCALE command as shown in Figure 2-129:

> Command: **scale**
> Select objects: **window**
> First corner: *select point 1 as shown in Figure 2-129*
> Other corner: *select point 2 as shown in Figure 2-129*

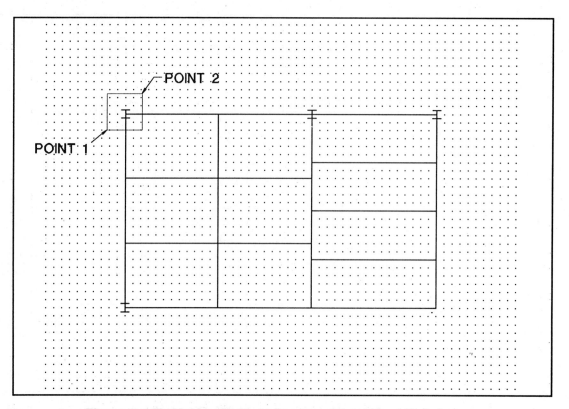

Figure 2-128 Making Multiple Copies of the 12" × 12" Columns

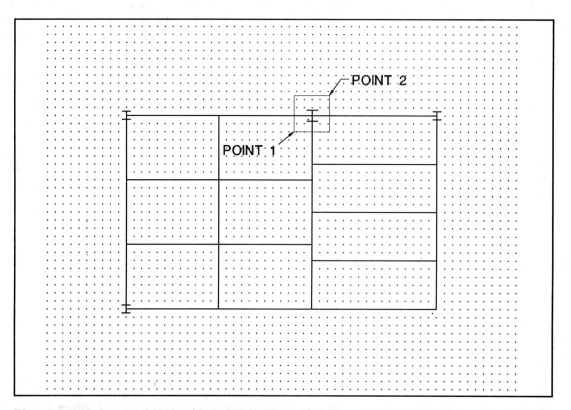

Figure 2-129 Increasing the Size of the 12" × 12" Column to 16" × 16" Using the SCALE Command

Select objects: ⏎
Base point: *select base point in the middle of the column*
<Scale factor>/Reference: **r**
Reference length <default>: **12**
New length: **16**

STEP 10: Make copy of the 16" × 16" column:

Command: **copy**
Select objects: **window**
First corner: *select point 1 as shown in Figure 2-130*
Other corner: *select point 2 as shown in Figure 2-130*
Select objects: ⏎
<Base point or displacement>/Multiple: **0,0**
Second point of displacement: **@0,-24'**

STEP 11: Rotate the column by 90 degrees:

Command: **rotate**
Select objects: **window**
First corner: *select point 1 as shown in Figure 2-131*
Other corner: *select point 2 as shown in Figure 2-131*
Select objects: ⏎
Base point: **0,0**
<Rotation angle>/Reference: **90**

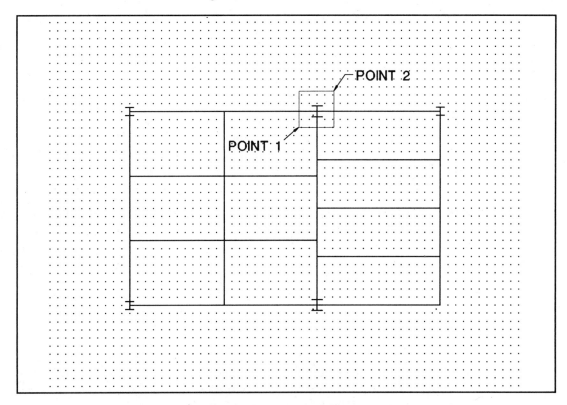

Figure 2-130 Making a Copy of the 16" × 16" Column

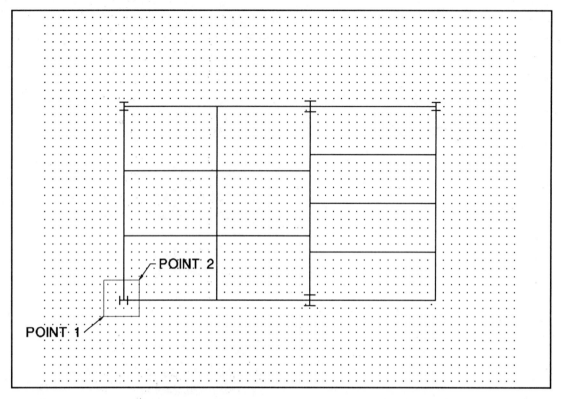

Figure 2–131 Rotating the Column by 90 Degrees

STEP 12: Make a copy of the 12" x 12" rotated column:

> Command: **copy**
> Select objects: **window**
> First corner: *select point 1 as shown in Figure 2–132*
> Other corner: *select point 2 as shown in Figure 2–132*
> Select objects: ⏎
> <Base point or displacement>/Multiple: **0,0**
> Second point of displacement: **@40',0**

STEP 13: Set plan as the current layer:

> Command: **layer**
> ?/Make/Set/New/ON/OFF/Color/Ltype/Freeze/Thaw: **s**
> New current layer <0>: **plan**
> ?/Make/Set/New/ON/OFF/Color/Ltype/Freeze/Thaw: ⏎

STEP 14: Draw lines over the layout lines to show the location of the beams by leaving a 6" gap between the columns and beams by Snapping to the invisible dots, as shown in Figure 2–133. (Make sure GRID and SNAP are turned ON.)

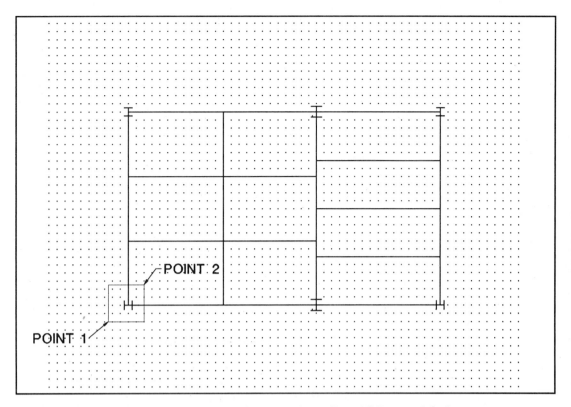

Figure 2-132 Making a Copy of the 12" × 12" Rotated Column

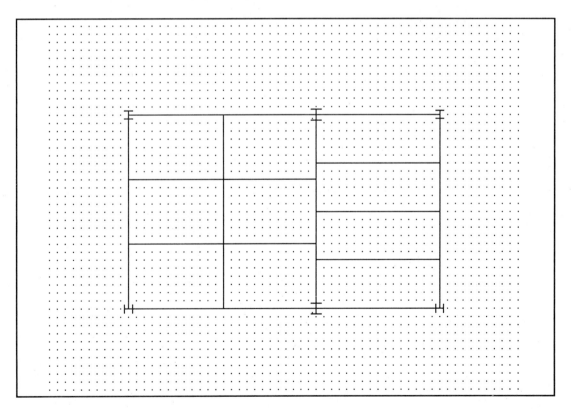

Figure 2-133 Drawing Lines over the Layout Lines to Show the Location of the Beams

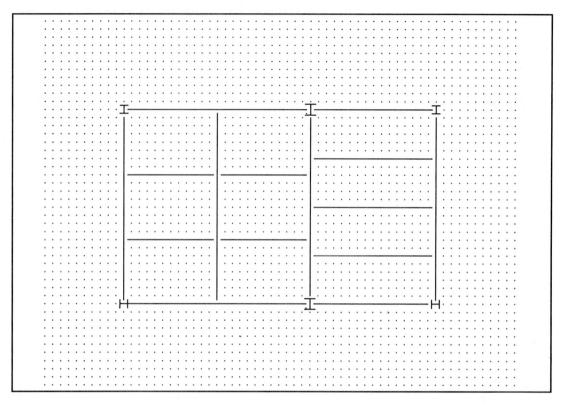

Figure 2–134 Turning the Layer Off and Setting Text as the Current Layer

STEP 15: Turn layer layout off and set text as the current layer, as shown in Figure 2–134:

> Command: **layer**
> ?/Make/Set/New/ON/OFF/Color/Ltype/Freeze/Thaw: **off**
> Layer name(s) to turn off: **layout**
> ?/Make/Set/New/ON/OFF/Color/Ltype/Freeze/Thaw: **s**
> New current layer <0>: **text**
> ?/Make/Set/New/ON/OFF/Color/Ltype/Freeze/Thaw: ⏎

STEP 16: Place appropriate text as indicated below:

> Command: **text**
> Justify/Style/<Start point>: **m**
> Middle point: **6',17'**
> Height <default>: **6**
> Rotation angle <0>: ⏎
> Text: **W16x26**

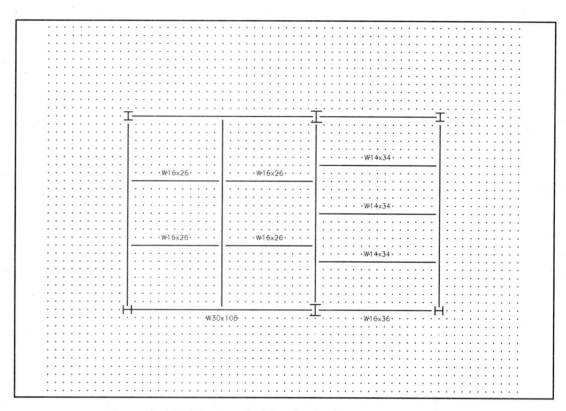

Figure 2–135 Placing the Text in the Appropriate Columns

Command: **text**
Justify/Style/<Start point>: **m**
Middle point: **32',19'**
Height <default>: **6**
Rotation angle <0>: ⏎
Text: **W14x34**

Command: **text**
Justify/Style/<Start point>: **m**
Middle point: **12',-1'**
Height <default>: **6**
Rotation angle <0>: ⏎
Text: **W30x108**

Command: **text**
Justify/Style/<Start point>: **m**
Middle point: **32',-1'**
Height <default>: **6**
Rotation angle <0>: ⏎
Text: **W16x36**

Command: **copy**
Select objects: *select the text W16x26*
Select objects: ⏎
<Base point or displacement>/Multiple: **m**
Base point: **0,0**
Second point of displacement: **@12',0**
Second point of displacement: **@0,-8'**
Second point of displacement: **@12',-8'**
Second point of displacement: ⏎

Command: **copy**
Select objects: *select the text W14x34*
Select objects: ⏎
<Base point or displacement>/Multiple: **m**
Base point: **0,0**
Second point of displacement: **@0,-6'**
Second point of displacement: **@0,-12'**
Second point of displacement: ⏎

The drawing should now look like Figure 2–135.

STEP 17: Set dim as the current layer.

Command: **layer**
?/Make/Set/New/ON/OFF/Color/Ltype/Freeze/Thaw: **s**
New current layer <text>: **dim**
?/Make/Set/New/ON/OFF/Color/Ltype/Freeze/Thaw: ⏎

STEP 18: Set up the necessary dimensioning variables, as shown below, before starting the dimensioning:

Command: **dim**
DIM: **dimexe**
Current value <default>: New value: **3**
DIM: **dimexo**
Current value <default>: New value: **3**
DIM: **dimasz**
Current value <default>: New value: **6**
DIM: **dimzin**
Current value <default>: New value: **1**
DIM: **dimtih**
Current value <default>: New value: **off**
DIM: **dimtad**
Current value <default>: New value: **on**
DIM: **dimtxt**
Current value <default>: New value: **6**

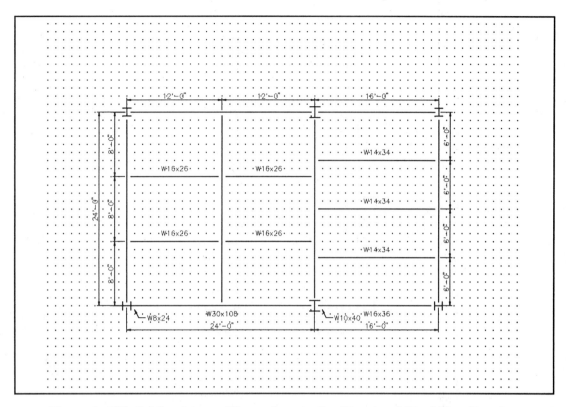

Figure 2–136 Adding Linear Dimensions to the Structural Steel Plan Drawing

STEP 19: Add dimensions using the linear dimensioning options, as shown in Figure 2–136.

STEP 20: Set the border as the current layer:

> Command: **layer**
> ?/Make/Set/New/ON/OFF/Color/Ltype/Freeze/Thaw: **s**
> New current layer <0>: **border**
> ?/Make/Set/New/ON/OFF/Color/Ltype/Freeze/Thaw: ⏎

STEP 21: Draw a border and create a title block, as shown in Figure 2–137.

STEP 22: End the drawing:

> Command: **end**

Fundamentals I

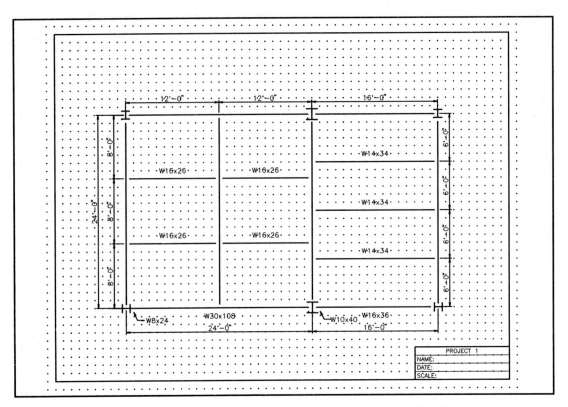

Figure 2-137 Drawing a Border to Create a Title Block

CHAPTER
3
Fundamentals II

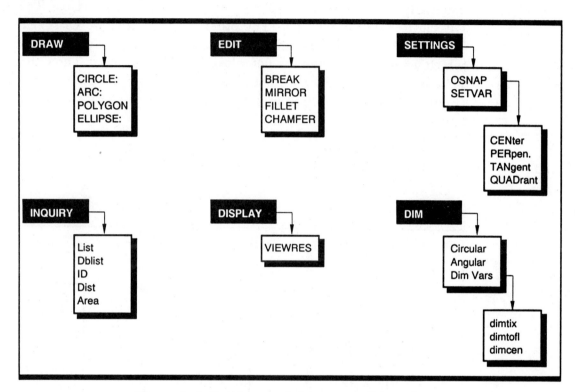

Figure 3-1 Fundamental Commands II Introduced

Along with the POINT and the LINE, the CIRCLE and the ARC round out (excuse the pun) the fundamental entities of coordinate geometry used in AutoCAD. This chapter introduces the many methods available in AutoCAD to draw circles and arcs. The project exercise drawing includes some of the drafting problems encountered when drawing circles and arcs.

Also introduced in this chapter are features for dimensioning RADII, DIAMETERS, and ANGLES in addition to commands like POLYGON, MIRROR, LIST, AREA, ID, DIST, and OSNAP.

See Figure 3-1 for a list of commands and options covered in this chapter.

DRAW COMMANDS

In this chapter, four additional DRAW commands are explained—the CIRCLE, ARC, POLYGON, and ELLIPSE commands—in addition to the commands explained in Chapter 2.

CIRCLE Command

The CIRCLE command offers five methods for drawing circles. The default is the CENTER-RADIUS method. The other methods include CENTER-DIAMETER, TWO-POINT, THREE-POINT, and Tangent, Tangent, Radius (TTR) methods (for which you must override the default on the first prompt). The CIRCLE command is invoked from the Screen Root Menu Draw (Figure 3-2), pull-down menu Draw (Figure 3-3), or at the "Command:" prompt, type in **CIRCLE** and press ⏎ or the spacebar.

Command: **circle**
3P/2P/TTR/<Center point>:

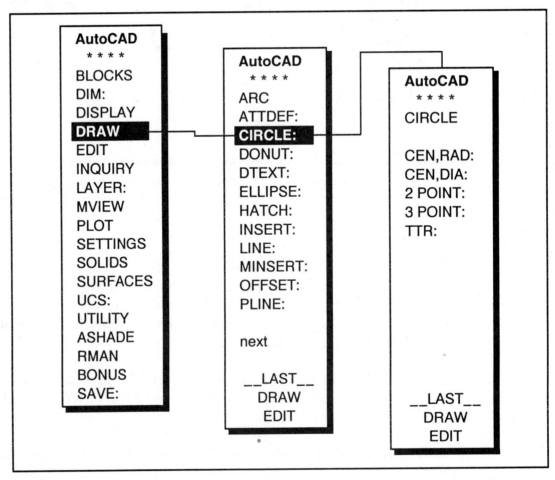

Figure 3-2 The CIRCLE Command Invoked from the Screen Root Menu Draw

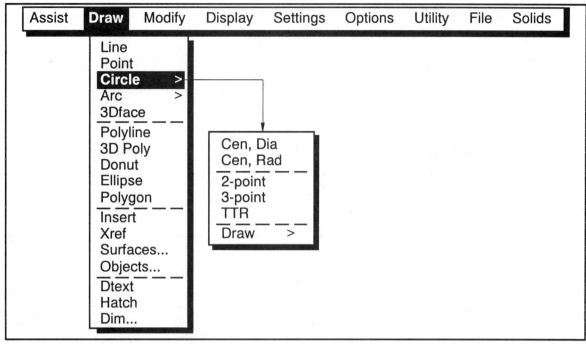

Figure 3-3 The CIRCLE Command Invoked from the Pull-Down Menu Draw

Center-Radius Option This is the default option of the CIRCLE command and the following command sequence shows an example (see Figure 3-4).

> Command: **circle**
> 3P/2P/TTR/<Center point>: **2,2**
> Diameter/<Radius>: **1**

The same circle can be generated as follows (see Figure 3-5):

> Command: **circle**
> 3P/2P/TTR/<Center point>: **2,2**
> Diameter/<Radius>: **3,2**

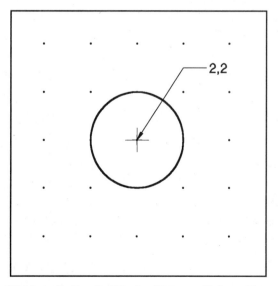

Figure 3-4 A Circle Drawn Using the Default Option

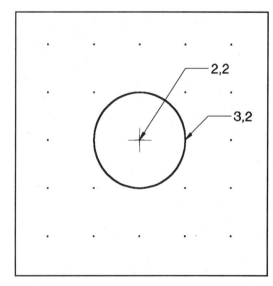

Figure 3-5 A Circle Drawn Using the Center-Radius Option

In the last example, AutoCAD used the distance between the center point and the second point given for the radius of the circle.

Center-Diameter Option (Overriding the Second Prompt) The CENTER-DIAMETER method of drawing a circle begins in the same way as the CENTER-RADIUS method, by specifying the center of the circle. The sequence to draw the previous circle is as follows:

Command: **circle**
3P/2P/TTR/<Center point>: **2,2**
Diameter/<Radius>: **d**
Diameter: **2**

> *NOTE:* The **d** response allows you to override the Radius default, or you can select the option from the menu.

The same circle can be generated as follows (see Figure 3–6):

Command: **circle**
3P/2P/TTR/<Center point>: **2,2**
Diameter/<Radius>: **d**
Diameter: **4,2**

> *NOTE:* Specifying a point causes AutoCAD to use the distance to it (the point specified) from the previously selected center as the value for the diameter of the circle to be drawn.

Three-Point Circle Option (Overriding the First Prompt) If you wish to draw a circle by specifying three known points on the circle, the following command sequence shows an example (see Figure 3–7).

Command: **circle**
3P/2P/TTR/<Center point>: **3P**
First point: **2,1**
Second point: **3,2**
Third point: **2,3**

> *NOTE:* The **3P** response allows you to override the Center Point default, or you can select the option from the menu.

Two-Point Circle Option If you wish to draw a circle by specifying the two endpoints of one of its diameters, the following command sequence shows an example (see Figure 3–8).

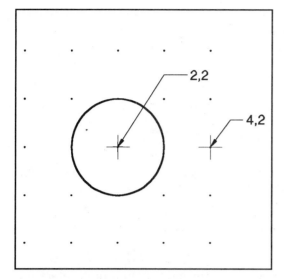

Figure 3-6   A Circle Drawn Using the Center-Diameter Option

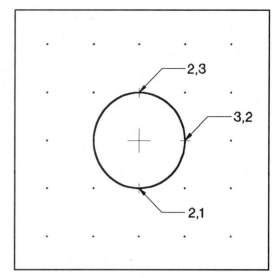

Figure 3-7   A Circle Drawn Using the Three-Point Option

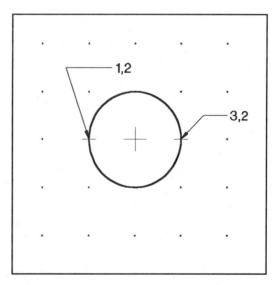

Figure 3-8 A Circle Drawn Using the Two-Point Option

Command: **circle**
3P/2P/TTR/<Center point>: **2P**
First point on diameter: **1,2**
Second point on diameter: **3,2**

NOTE: The **2P** response allows you to override the Center Point default, or you can select the option from the menu.

Tangent, Tangent, Radius (TTR) Option The TTR option allows you to draw a circle by selecting two objects (lines, arcs, or other circles to which the circle will be tangent) and specifying a radius. The following sequence of prompts will appear:

Command: **circle**
3P/2P/TTR/<Center point>: **TTR**
Enter Tangent spec: *select first line, arc, or circle*
Enter second Tangent spec: *select other line, arc, or circle*
Radius: *enter a value*

For specifying the "tangent-to" objects, it normally does not matter where on the objects you make your selection. However, if more than one circle can be drawn to the specifications given, AutoCAD will draw the one whose tangent point is nearest to the selection made.

Circles with OSNAP-TAN If you use the Three-Point method of drawing a circle, you can use the OSNAP mode of TANGENT for any of the point selections (see Figure 3-9). At any or all of the prompts for a point, you can invoke the TAN mode and then select a line, arc, or other circle. If a circle exists that satisfies the tangent point, AutoCAD will construct that circle so it will be tangent to the object(s) selected.

The Uppercase Rule Note in the 2P option that the P is uppercase. When an option is shown in the prompt, you must enter all uppercase initial letters. The P

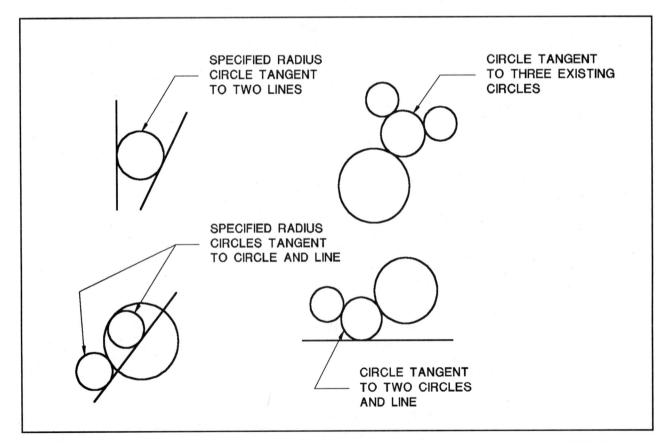

Figure 3-9 A Circle Drawn Using the Three-Point Method with the OSNAP-TANGENT Mode

is uppercase and has no lowercase letters preceding it. Therefore, it (the P) must be included.

ARC Command

The ARC command offers eight combinations to draw an arc. Methods 8, 9, and 10 are just rearrangements of methods 2, 3, and 4, respectively. They are as follows:

1. Three point (3-point)
2. Start, center, end (S,C,E)
3. Start, center, included angle (S,C,A)
4. Start, center, length of chord (S,C,L)
5. Start, end, included angle (S,E,A)
6. Start, end, radius (S,E,R)
7. Start, end, starting direction (S,E,D)
8. Center, start, end (C,S,E)
9. Center, start, included angle (C,S,A)
10. Center, start, length of the chord (C,S,L)
11. Continuation from line or arc (CONTIN)

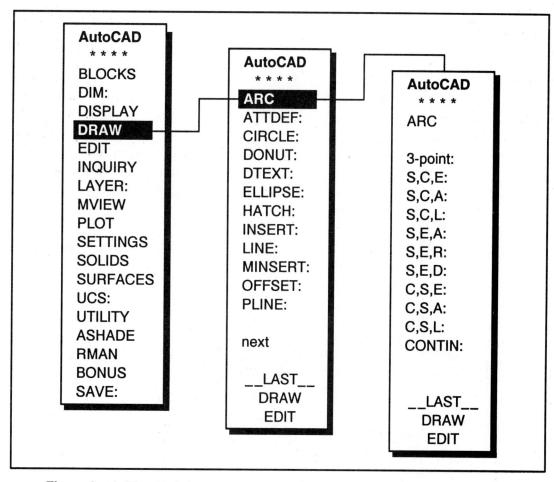

Figure 3-10 The ARC Command Invoked from the Screen Root Menu Draw

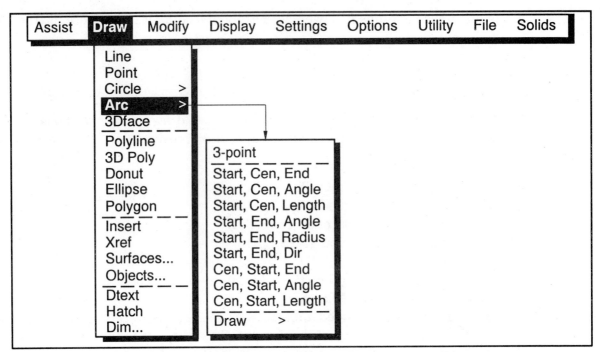

Figure 3-11 The ARC Command Invoked from the Pull-Down Menu Draw

The ARC command is invoked from the Screen Root Menu Draw (Figure 3-10), pull-down menu Draw (Figure 3-11), or at the "Command:" prompt, type in **ARC** and press ⏎ or the spacebar.

```
Command: arc
Center/<Start point>:
```

Once the command is invoked, you can use the default Three-Point method or you may override an option being prompted for by entering the initial letter of the override specification such as A for included Angle, C for Center, D for starting Direction, E for Endpoint, L for Length of chord, or R for Radius. Or, you can select any of the options from the screen or pull-down menu.

Three-Point Arc Option (3-point) This is the default option of the ARC command and the following command sequence shows an example (see Figure 3-12).

```
Command: arc
Center/<Start point>: 1,2
Center/End/<Second point>: 2,1
Endpoint: 3,2
```

Start, Center, End Option (S,C,E) In this option, instead of "Second point," AutoCAD prompts for "Center" point of the arc. The following command sequence shows an example (see Figure 3-13).

```
Command: arc
Center/<Start point>: 1,2
Center/End/<Second point>: c
Center: 2,2
Angle/Length of chord/<Endpoint>: 2,3
```

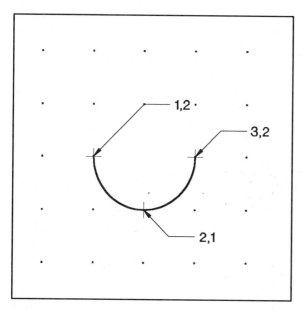

Figure 3-12 An Arc Drawn Using the Default Option

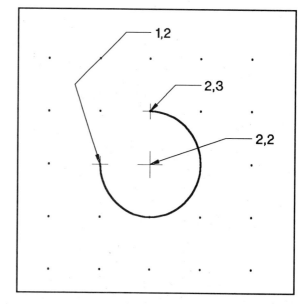

Figure 3-13 An Arc Drawn Using the Start, Center, End (S,C,E) Option

Arcs drawn by this method are always drawn counterclockwise from the starting point. The radius is determined by the distance between the center and the starting point. Therefore, the point specified in response to "Endpoint" only needs to be on the same radial line of the desired endpoint. For example, specifying the point 2,2.5 or 2,4 will cause the same arc to be drawn.

An alternative sequence to the same method is to specify the center point first, as follows (see Figure 3-14):

> Command: **arc**
> Center/<Start point>: **c**
> Center: **2,2**
> Start point: **1,2**
> Angle/Length of chord/<Endpoint>: **2,3**

Start, Center, Included Angle Option (S,C,A) This method draws an arc similar to the start, center, end method, but places the endpoint on a radial line that is the specified angle from the line between the center and the start point. The angle will be counterclockwise if positive and clockwise if negative. The following command sequence shows an example (see Figure 3-15).

> Command: **arc**
> Center/<Start point>: **1,2**
> Center/<Endpoint>: **c**
> Center: **2,2**
> Angle/Length of chord/<Endpoint>: **a**
> Included angle: **270**

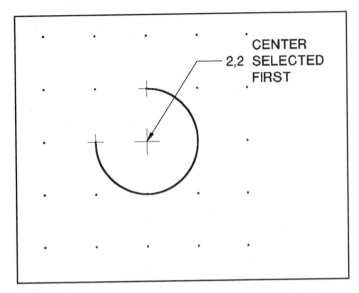

Figure 3-14 An Arc Drawn by Specifying the Center Point First

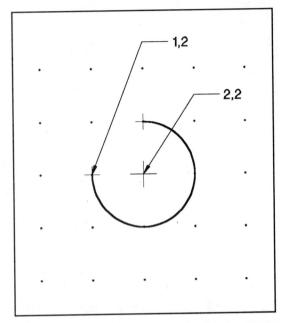

Figure 3-15 An Arc Drawn Using the Start, Center, Included Angle (S,C,A) Option

> ***NOTE:*** If a point directly below the specified center were selected in the example above in response to the "Included angle:" prompt, AutoCAD would read the angle (270 degrees) of the line (from zero) as the included angle for the arc. In Figure 3-15, the point selected in response to the "Included angle:" prompt causes AutoCAD to read the angle between the line it establishes from the center and the zero direction (east in the default coordinate system). It does not measure the angle between the line the point establishes from the center and the line established from the center to the start point.

Start, Center, Length of Chord Option (S,C,L) This method uses the specified chord length as the straight line distance from the start point to the endpoint. With any chord length (less than the diameter length) there are four possible arcs that can be drawn, a major arc in either direction and a minor arc in either direction. Therefore, all arcs drawn by this method will be counterclockwise from the start point. A positive value for the length of chord will cause AutoCAD to draw the minor arc; a negative value will result in the major arc.

The following command sequence shows an example of drawing a minor arc, as shown in Figure 3-16.

    Command: **arc**
    Center/<Start point>: **1,2**
    Center/<Endpoint>: **c**
    Center: **2,2**

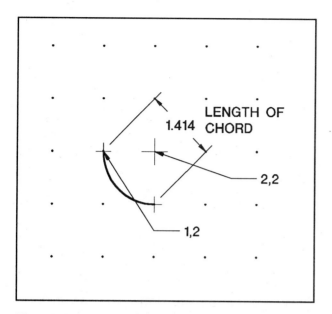

Figure 3–16 An Arc Drawn Using the Start, Center, Length of Chord (S,C,L) Option (Minor)

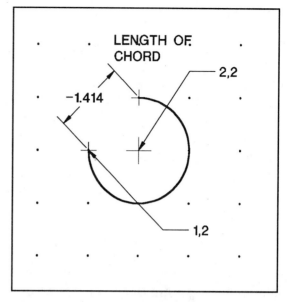

Figure 3–17 An Arc Drawn Using the Start, Center, Length of Chord (S,C,L) Option (Major)

Angle/Length of chord/<Endpoint>: **l** *letter l, not number 1*
Length of chord: **1.414**

The following command sequence shows an example of drawing a major arc, as shown in Figure 3–17.

Command: **arc**
Center/<Start point>: **1,2**
Center/<Endpoint>: **c**
Center: **2,2**
Angle/Length of chord/<Endpoint>: **l** *letter l, not number 1*
Length of chord: **-1.414**

Start, End, Included Angle Option (S,E,A) This method draws an arc similar to the start, end, included angle method. It also places the endpoint on a radial line that is the specified angle from the line between the center and the start point. The angle will be counterclockwise if positive and clockwise if negative. The arc shown in Figure 3–18 will be drawn using the following sequence:

Command: **arc**
Center/<Start point>: **3,2**
Center/End/<Second point>: **e**
End point: **2,3**
Angle/Length of chord/<Endpoint>: **a**
Included angle: **90**

The arc shown in Figure 3–19 will be drawn with a negative angle using the following sequence:

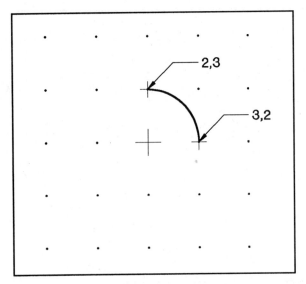

Figure 3-18 An Arc Drawn Counterclockwise Using the Start, End, Included Angle (S,E,A) Option

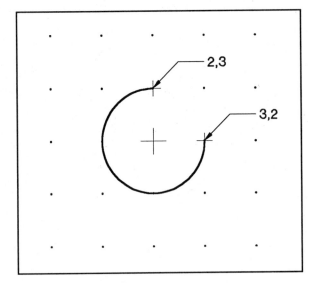

Figure 3-19 An Arc Drawn Clockwise Using the Start, End, Included Angle (S,E,A) Option

Command: **arc**
Center/<Start point>: **3,2**
Center/End/<Second point>: **e**
End point: **2,3**
Angle/Length of chord/<Endpoint>: **a**
Included angle: **-270**

Start, End, Radius Option (S,E,R) This method allows you to specify a radius after selecting the two endpoints of the arc. As with the chord length method, there are four possible arcs that can be drawn, a major arc in either direction and a minor arc in either direction. Therefore, all arcs drawn by this method will be counterclockwise from the start point. A positive value for the radius will cause AutoCAD to draw the minor arc; a negative value will result in the major arc.

The following command sequence shows an example of drawing a minor arc, as shown in Figure 3-20.

Command: **arc**
Center/<Start point>: **1,2**
Center/End/<Second point>: **e**
Endpoint: **2,3**
Angle/Direction/Radius/<Center point>: **r**
Radius: **-1**

The following command sequence shows an example of drawing a major arc, as shown in Figure 3-21.

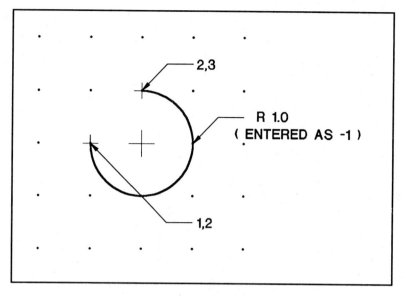

Figure 3-20 An Arc Drawn Using the Start, End, Radius (S,E,R) Option (Minor)

Command: **arc**
Center/<Start point>: **2,3**
Center/End/<Second point>: **e**
Endpoint: **1,2**
Angle/Direction/Radius/<Center point>: **r**
Radius: **1**

Start, End, Starting Direction Option (S,E,D) This method allows you to draw an arc between two selected points by specifying a direction in which the arc

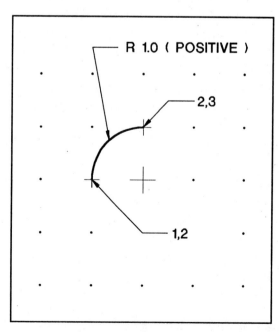

Figure 3-21 An Arc Drawn Using the Start, End, Radius (S,E,R) Option (Major)

will start from the selected start point. The direction can either be keyed in or you may select a point on the screen with your pointing device. If you select a point on the screen, AutoCAD will use the angle from the start point to the selected point as the starting direction. The arc shown in Figure 3-22 will be drawn using the following sequence:

```
Command: arc
Center/<Start point>: 3,2
Center/End/<Second point>: e
Endpoint: 2,3
Angle/Direction/Radius/<Center point>: d
Direction from start point: 90
```

Center, Start, End Option (C,S,E) This method is similar to the second option start, center, end (S,C,E), except in this option the beginning point will be the center point of the arc rather than the start point.

Center, Start, Included Angle Option (C,S,A) This method is similar to the third option start, center, included angle (S,C,A), except in this option the beginning point will be the center point of the arc rather than the start point.

Center, Start, Length of Chord Option (C,S,L) This method is similar to the fourth option start, center, length of the chord (S,C,L), except in this option the beginning point will be the center point of the arc rather than the start point.

Line-Arc and Arc-Arc Continuation Option You can use an automatic start point, endpoint, starting direction method to draw an arc by pressing ⏎ as a response to the first prompt of the ARC command. After pressing ⏎, the only other input is to select or specify the endpoint of the arc you wish to draw. AutoCAD uses the endpoint of the previous line or arc (whichever was drawn last) as the start point of the arc you are drawing. It then uses the ending direction of that last drawn entity as the starting direction of the arc. Examples are shown in the following sequences and figures.

The start point of the existing arc is 2,1 and the endpoint is 3,2 with a radius of 1. This makes the ending direction of the existing arc 90 degrees, as shown in Figure 3-23.

The following command sequence will draw an arc, as shown in Figure 3-24 (arc-arc continuation).

```
Command: arc
Center/<Start point>: ⏎
Endpoint: 2,3
```

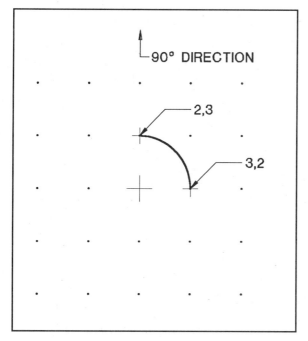

Figure 3-22 An Arc Drawn Using the Start, End, Starting Direction (S,E,D) Option

Figure 3-23 An Arc Drawn Using Start Point (2,1), Endpoint (3,2), and a Radius of 1

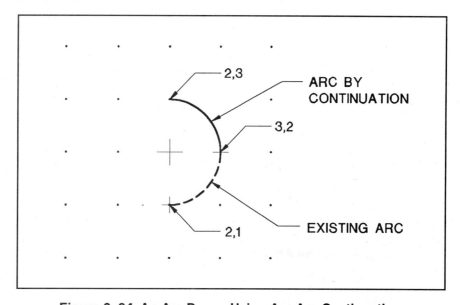

Figure 3-24 An Arc Drawn Using Arc-Arc Continuation

The arc, as shown in Figure 3-23, is drawn clockwise instead, with its start point at 3,2 to an endpoint of 2,1 (see Figure 3-25).

The following command sequence will draw the automatic start point, endpoint, starting direction arc, as shown in Figure 3-26.

Command: **arc**
Center/<Start point>: ⏎
Endpoint: **2,3**

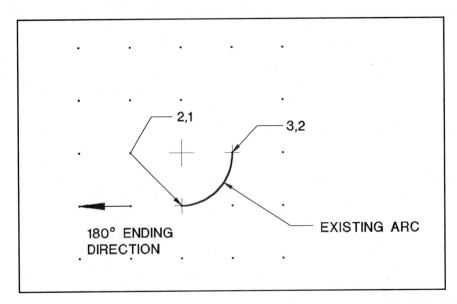

Figure 3-25 An Arc Drawn Clockwise with Start Point (3,2) and Endpoint (2,1)

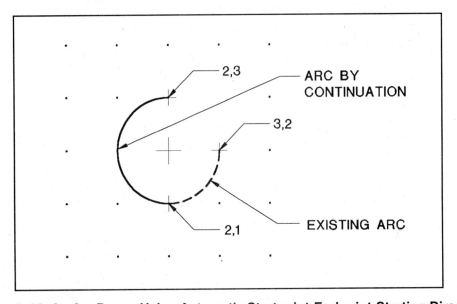

Figure 3-26 An Arc Drawn Using Automatic Startpoint-Endpoint-Starting Direction

In the last case, the direction used was 180 degrees. The same arc would have been drawn if the last "line-or-arc" drawn was a line starting at 4,1 and ending at 2,1.

> **NOTE:** This method uses the last drawn of either an arc or a line. If you draw an arc, then draw a line, then draw a circle, and then use this continuation method, AutoCAD will use the line as the basis for the start point and direction. That is because the line was the last of the "line-or-arc" base entity.

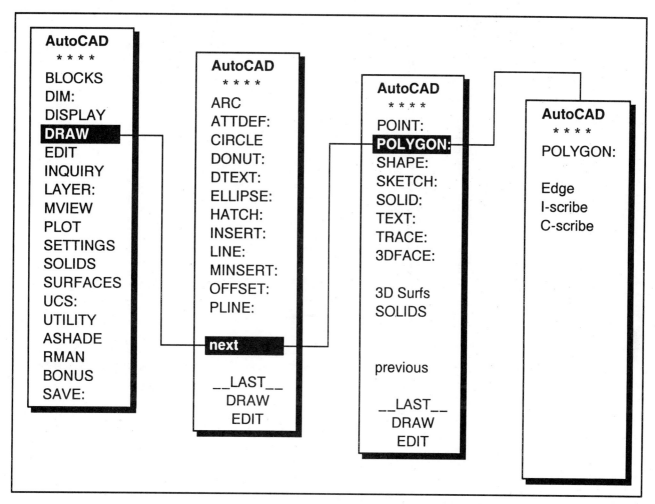

Figure 3-27 The POLYGON Command Invoked from the Screen Root Menu Draw

POLYGON Command

You can draw regular (all edges are equal length) 2D polygons with the POLY-GON command. The maximum number of sides is 1024. There are three primary ways to use the POLYGON command. The POLYGON command is invoked from the Screen Root Menu Draw (Figure 3-27), pull-down menu Draw (Figure 3-28), or at the "Command:" prompt, type in **POLYGON** and press ⏎ or the spacebar.

Command: **polygon**
Number of sides:

Polygon Inscribed in Circle Option After specifying the number of sides and center of the polygon, this option allows you to specify the distance from the center to a vertex between edges. This defines the radius of a circle in which the polygon is inscribed (see Figure 3-29).

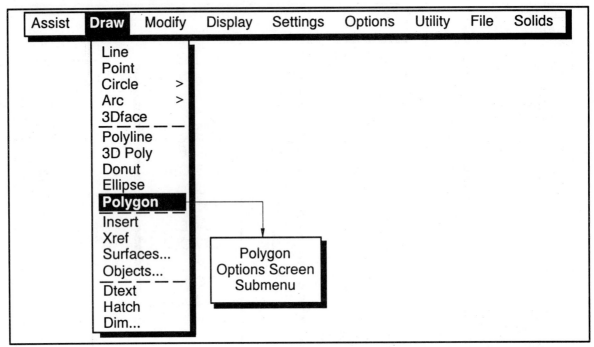

Figure 3-28 The POLYGON Command Invoked from the Pull-Down Menu Draw

For instance, the following command sequence shows steps in drawing a six-sided polygon (see Figure 3-30).

Command: **polygon**
Number of sides: **6**
Edge/<Center of polygon>: **3,3**
Inscribed in circle/Circumscribed about circle (I/C): **i**
Radius of circle: **2**

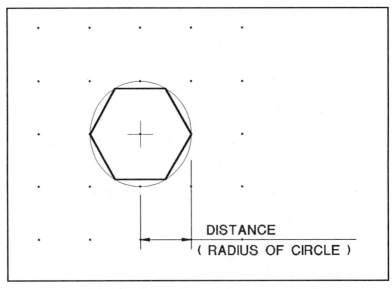

Figure 3-29 A Polygon Drawn Using the Inscribed in Circle Option

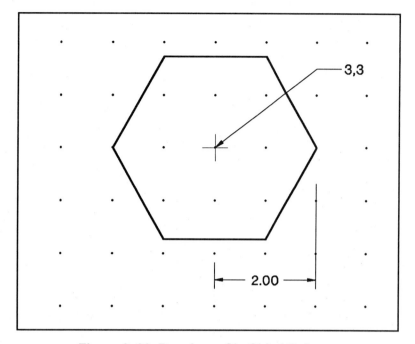

Figure 3-30 Drawing a Six-Sided Polygon

This method draws a polygon with six sides, centered at 3,3, whose edge vertices are 2 units from the center of the polygon. Specifying the radius with a keyed-in value causes the direction of the bottom edge to be aligned with the zero rotation angle of the current coordinate system.

Another option for specifying the radius is to specify the coordinates, use relative coordinates, or select a point on the screen as follows:

    Command: **polygon**
    Number of sides: **8**
    Edge/<Center of polygon>: **3,3**
    Inscribed in circle/Circumscribed about circle (I/C): **i**
    Radius of circle: **@2<90** *(or @0,2 or 3,5)*

This method of selecting the point of one of the vertices causes the angle of rotation of the polygon to conform to the angle necessary to have a vertex at the selected point.

Polygon Circumscribed About a Circle Option This option allows you to specify the distance from the center to the midpoint (shortest or perpendicular distance) of one of the edges, as shown in Figure 3-31. This defines the radius of a circle about which the polygon is circumscribed.

An example of the circumscribed method, as shown in Figure 3-32, is as follows:

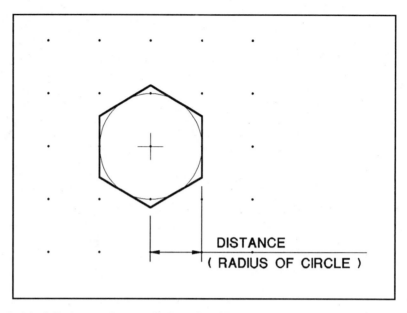

Figure 3-31 A Polygon Drawn Using the Circumscribed about a Circle Option

Command: **polygon**
Number of sides: **6**
Edge/<Center of polygon>: **3,3**
Inscribed in circle/Circumscribed about circle (I/C): **c**
Radius of circle: **2**

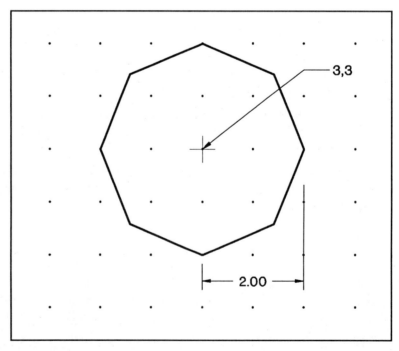

Figure 3-32 A Polygon Drawn Using the Circumscribed about a Circle Option by Specifying a Radius of 2

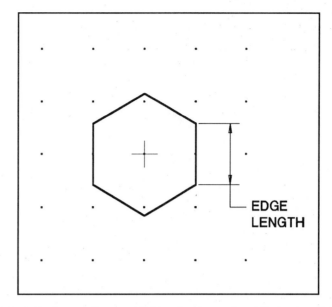

Figure 3-33 A Polygon Drawn Using the Length of Polygon Edge Option

Another option to specifying the radius is to specify the coordinates, use relative coordinates, or select a point on the screen as follows:

Command: **polygon**
Number of sides: **6**
Edge/<Center of polygon>: **3,3**
Inscribed in circle/Circumscribed about circle (I/C): **c**
Radius of circle: **5,3** *(or @2<0 or @2,0)*

This method of selecting one of the edge midpoints causes the angle of rotation of the polygon to conform to the angle necessary to have an edge midpoint at the selected point.

Length of Polygon Edge Option This option allows you to specify the length of one of the edges, as shown in Figure 3-33.

An example of the edge-length method, as shown in Figure 3-34, is as follows:

Command: **polygon**
Number of sides: **7**
Edge/<Center of polygon>: **e**
First endpoint of edge: **1,1**
Second endpoint of edge: **3,1**

About the ELLIPSE Command

AutoCAD provides several convenient methods of drawing ellipses. The ELLIPSE command should be used with certain precautions. The more you know about the geometry of an ellipse and how AutoCAD draws one the better you will be able to apply the ELLIPSE command.

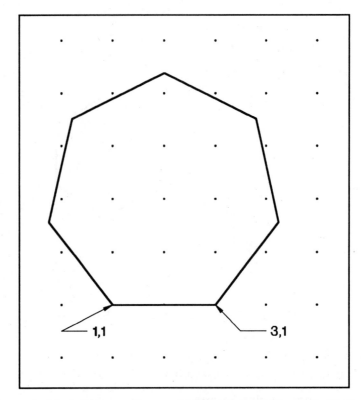

Figure 3-34 A Polygon Drawn Using the Edge-Length Method

Ellipses the Old Way Earlier releases of AutoCAD used a special method of inserting a circle with different X and Y scale factors in order to draw the true representation of an ellipse. You can still apply this method once you become familiar with the concept of UNIT BLOCKS (described in Chapter 6). For example, you can draw a circle one unit in diameter, store it by using the BLOCK command, and later use the INSERT command to generate an ellipse (from the circle) by using the appropriate X and Y scale factors when inserting. This old method has built-in problems, however, which will be noted at this time for future reference.

Warnings about Blocks

Nonbreakable You will discover that you can draw entities such as lines, circles, and arcs and then use the edit command called BREAK to remove parts of these entities, either from one end (except for circles, of course) or from the middle. However, when any entity is made part of a block, you cannot use the BREAK command to remove parts of it. Therefore, partial ellipses are not possible to obtain by using the BREAK command on a circle that has been made into a Block and inserted as an ellipse.

Arcs into Partial Ellipses It is also difficult to draw an arc and make it into a block in anticipation of inserting it with the X and Y scale factors necessary to arrive at the desired partial ellipse.

If any arc or circle that resides within an inserted block crosses another entity such as a line, arc, or circle, you can use the Osnap mode of INTERSECTION to select the point where they intersect. You can also use the OSNAP modes NEAR, PERPENDICULAR, and TANGENT to Snap to a point on such arcs or circles in blocks. However, if the block has been inserted with different X and Y scale factors, the above four (NEA, INT, PER, and TAN) OSNAP modes cannot be used on circles or arcs in blocks.

Again, this applies to the old method of creating ellipses from inserted blocks. You can, however, OSNAP to the center or quadrant of circles and arcs and to the endpoint of arcs in blocks whether they are inserted with equal or unequal X and Y scale factors.

Warnings about the Ellipse Command

Before learning the different methods of using the ELLIPSE command, you should be aware of the type of entity (or entities) that are being generated when you use the command.

Polyline Arcs (or Polyarcs) Later chapters will introduce the PLINE command. It is used to generate a polyline, which is a combination of lines and/or arcs. Polyline segments are joined together (end-to-end) as you draw them. They are treated as one entity instead of several when you select a polyline for editing by an entity editing command. When you use the ELLIPSE command, it creates the ellipse from 16 arcs joined together into a single polyline. Therefore, if you wish to move the ellipse, you can touch it anywhere with the cursor and move the 16 arcs as a single entity.

OSNAP INT and CEN Because the ellipse created with the ELLIPSE command is a series of joined arcs, each vertex can be considered an intersection by the OSNAP mode called INTERSECTION. If there is a line crossing the ellipse, and you wish to select that intersection by using the OSNAP mode, you should be careful that the correct intersection is used and not one of the vertices where two of the 16 arcs connect. Also, if you need to select the center of the ellipse created with the ELLIPSE command, the OSNAP mode called CENTER will not operate in the same way as it would on a circle or on an ellipse created by inserting a block (made from a circle). The OSNAP feature will select the center of one of the arcs used to generate the ellipse.

ELLIPSE Command

The ELLIPSE command is invoked from the Screen Root Menu Draw (Figure 3–35), pull-down menu Draw (Figure 3–36), or at the "Command:" prompt type in **ELLIPSE** and press ⏎ or the spacebar.

Command: **ellipse**
<Axis endpoint 1>/Center:

Fundamentals II

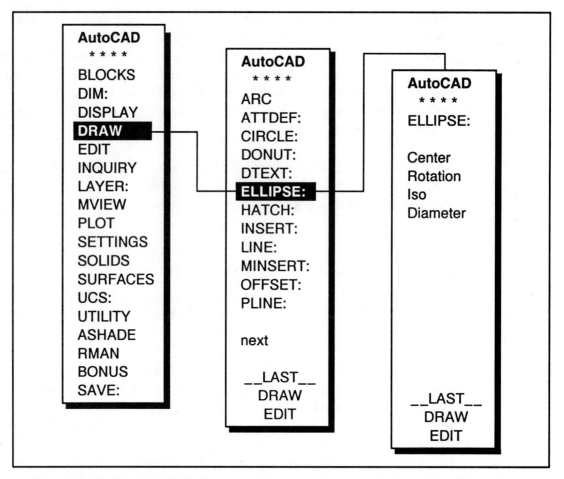

Figure 3-35 The ELLIPSE Command Invoked from the Screen Root Menu Draw

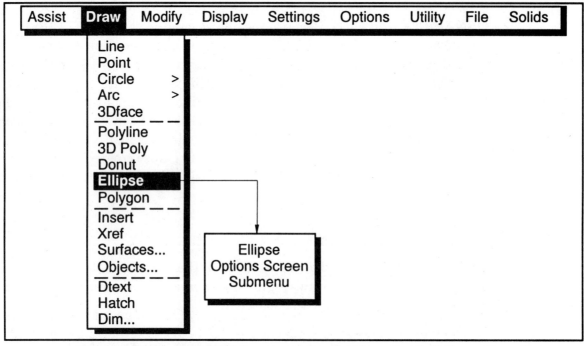

Figure 3-36 The ELLIPSE Command Invoked from the Pull-Down Menu Draw

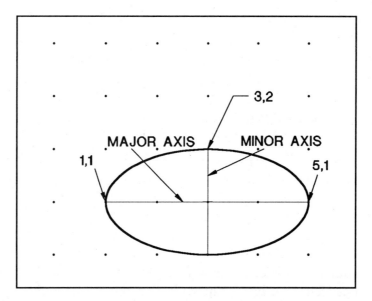

Figure 3-37 An Ellipse Drawn Using the Axis and Eccentricity Option

Axis and Eccentricity Option The default method (if you are not in the isometric Snap mode) is to select the endpoints of one Axis, and then select one endpoint of the other Axis. The prompts are as follow:

Command: **ellipse**
<Axis endpoint 1>/Center: **1,1**
Axis endpoint 2: **5,1**
<Other Axis distance>/Rotation: **3,2**

The above responses will generate an ellipse whose major Axis is 4 units long and horizontal and whose minor Axis is 2 units long and vertical, as shown in Figure 3-37.

An ellipse of similar proportions whose long Axis is vertical can be generated using the following sequences:

Command: **ellipse**
<Axis endpoint 1>/Center: **2,1**
Axis endpoint 2: **4,1**
<Other Axis distance>/Rotation: **3,3**

or

Command: **ellipse**
<Axis endpoint 1>/Center: **3,-1**
Axis endpoint 2: **3,3**
<Other Axis distance>/Rotation: **2**

Note that the last response was a distance. This will be interpreted by AutoCAD as the distance from the center of the ellipse to the second Axis endpoint (or half the length of the second Axis).

Center Option This method allows you to specify the center point of the ellipse and one endpoint of the major and minor Axis. The prompts are as follow:

Command: **ellipse**
<Axis endpoint 1>/Center: **c**
Center point: **3,1**
Axis endpoint 2: **1,1**
<Other Axis distance>/Rotation: **3,2**

The above responses will generate an ellipse similar to previous example with the major Axis 4 units long and horizontal and minor Axis 2 units long and vertical.

Rotation Angle Option You can specify eccentricity by giving the rotation angle (or the angle about which a circle would be rotated to project an ellipse). Another way to describe this method is that the angle of rotation specified is the angle that your line of sight makes with the plane in which the circle that you are viewing lies. This method is shown in the following sequence:

Command: **ellipse**
<Axis endpoint 1>/Center: **3,-1**
Axis endpoint 2: **3,3**
<Other Axis distance>/Rotation: **r**
Rotation around major Axis: *rotation angle*

See Figure 3-38 for examples of ellipses with various rotation angles.

Center and Axis Option Another option of the ELLIPSE command is to specify the center of the ellipse, an endpoint of one Axis and the length of the other Axis (either by selecting a point or specifying a half-distance for the second Axis). This method is shown in the following sequence:

Command: **ellipse**
<Axis endpoint 1>/Center: **c**
Center of ellipse: *select the center of the ellipse*

The next prompts should be responded to in the same manner as the Axis and Eccentricity method.

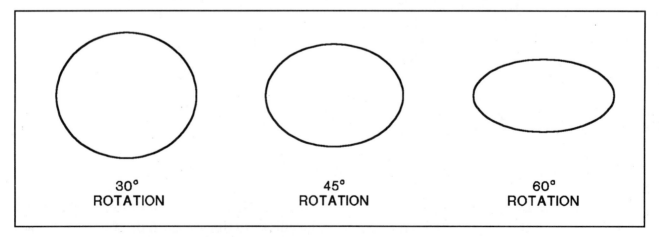

Figure 3-38 An Ellipse Drawn Using Various Rotation Angles

Axis endpoint:
<Other Axis distance>/Rotation:

Isometric Circles (or Isocircles) Option The isometric planes by definition (iso meaning same and metric meaning measure) are all being viewed at the same angle of rotation (see Figure 3-39). That angle is approximately 54.73561031 degrees. Therefore, AutoCAD uses this angle of rotation automatically for ellipses drawn in the Isocircle mode. It can also be shown that a circle of 1 unit in diameter that is being viewed in an isometric plane will project a short Axis dimension of 0.8164965809 units. However, lines in isometric that are 1 unit in length and parallel to one of the three main axes also project to 0.8164965809 units long. Therefore, you automatically increase the entire projection by a fudge factor of 1.224744871 (the reciprocal of 0.8164965809) in order to use true dimensioning along the isometric axes. This means that circles of 1 unit long will be measured along one of their isometric diameters rather than their long Axis. This facilitates using true lengths as the lengths of distances projected from lines parallel to one of the isometric axes.

The Isometric Circle method becomes one of the options of the ELLIPSE command when you are in the isometric Snap mode as follows:

Command: **ellipse**
<Axis endpoint 1>/Center/Isocircle: **i**
Center of circle: *select the center of the isometric circle*
<Circle radius>/Diameter: *enter the radius or override with d*

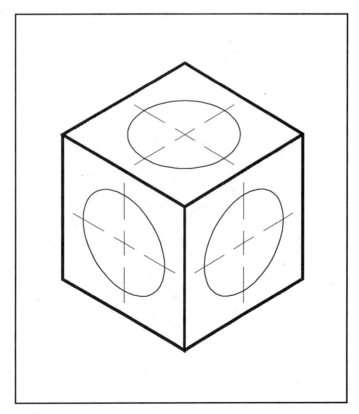

Figure 3-39 An Ellipse Drawn Using the Isocircles Option

If you **override** the last prompt default by typing **d**, the following prompt will appear:

Circle diameter: *enter the desired diameter*

> **NOTE:** The Iso and Diameter options will work only when you are in the isometric Snap mode.

LAB EXERCISES

Lab Exercise 3-1

Lay out the gasket shown in exercise 3-1. Use the CIRCLE and ARC commands. Do not dimension.

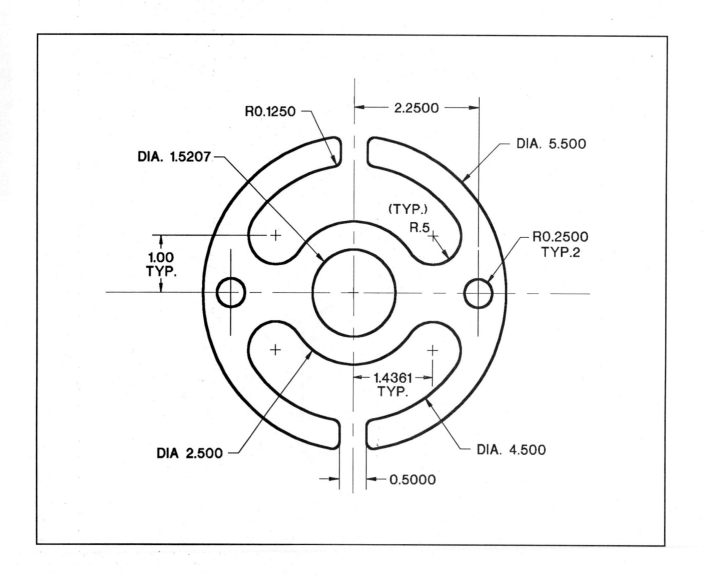

Lab Exercise 3-2

Lay out the figure in exercise 3-2 on a B-size sheet or make EX 3-2=PROTO-B or the name of your prototype B-size drawing (created as an exercise in Chapter 2). If the prototypes are on your floppy disk in A: drive you must indicate by naming the current drawing EX 3-2 =A:PROTO-B. Use your prototype drawings as much as possible as this will save you from having to reproduce the title block each time. Show all dimensions and callouts.

Set DIMTXT=.125
Set text height=.125

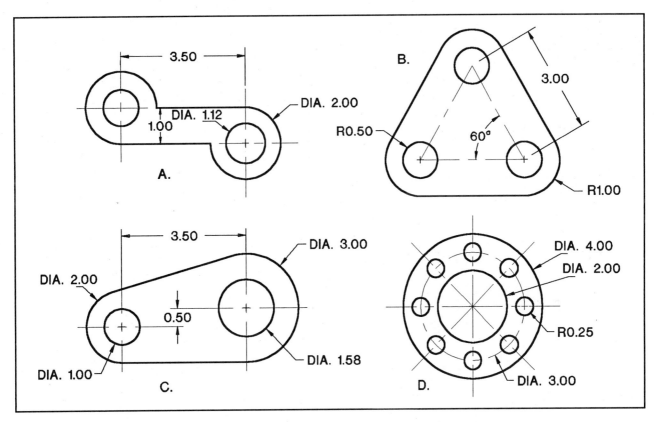

Lab Exercise 3-3

Lay out the gasket in exercise 3-3 on a B-size sheet or PROTO-B drawing. Use the CIRCLE and ARC commands. Show all dimensions and callouts.

Set DIMTXT =.125

Set text height=.125

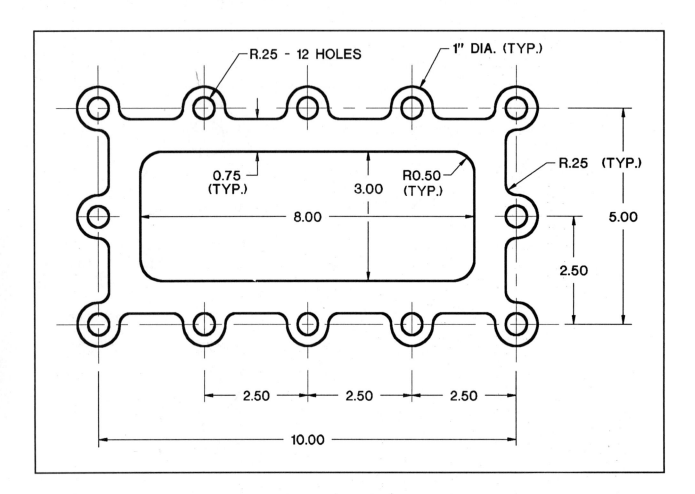

EDIT COMMANDS

In this chapter, four additional EDIT commands are explained, the BREAK, MIRROR, FILLET, and CHAMFER commands, in addition to the commands explained in Chapter 2.

BREAK Command

The BREAK command is used to remove parts of entities from the drawing. The BREAK command can be used on lines, arcs, circles, traces, and 2D polylines.

The BREAK command removes the part of an object between two selected points or from a selected point to an end beyond which a second point is selected.

The BREAK command can be used on only one object at a time. There are two different procedures for using the BREAK command. One is to select an object by pointing to it and have AutoCAD use that point (by which the object was selected) as the first point for breaking. The other procedure is to select an object by the Window, Crossing, or Last option and then select the first break point. Or, if you wish to use the pointing method of selecting the object but have for the first break point one other than that used to select the object, then you may respond to the second prompt with **f**. Then AutoCAD will prompt you for first and second point, respectively.

Object selection can be done by any normal method. If the method used includes more than one object in the selection set, AutoCAD will use the last entity. If the entity to be used is not eligible for use with the BREAK command, you will be prompted to select another object.

The BREAK command is invoked from the Screen Root Menu Edit (Figure 3-40), pull-down menu Modify (Figure 3-41), or at the "Command:" prompt, type in **BREAK** and press ⏎ or the spacebar. The sequence of prompts is as follows:

> Command: **break**
> Select object: *make selection by Window or Crossing*
> Enter first point: *select first point of deletion*
> Enter second point: *select second point of deletion or past end to be removed*

If the selection was by pointing and you wish to have a different point as the first break point, the sequence will be as follows:

> Command: **break**
> Select object: *point to object*
> Enter second point (or F for first point): **f**
> Enter first point: *select first point*
> Enter second point: *select second point*

If the second point is not on the object, AutoCAD will use a point nearest the one selected.

An object can be broken into two parts without removing any of the object by selecting the same point for first and second points as follows:

Fundamentals II

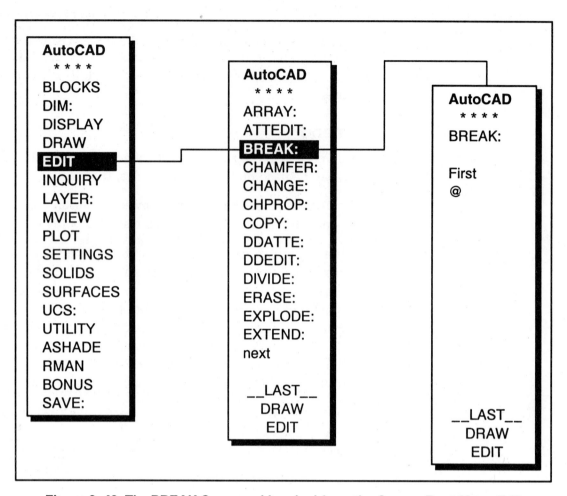

Figure 3-40 The BREAK Command Invoked from the Screen Root Menu Edit

Command: **break**
Select object: *select first point*
Select second point (or F for first point): **@**

As mentioned earlier, the @ symbol means last point.

A line, trace, or arc will have the part between the two selected points removed or will be divided into two parts where the two points coincide or will have one end removed in the direction where the second point is beyond that end.

A circle will have that part removed between the two selected points that is counterclockwise from the first to the second point.

A closed 2D polyline will have that part removed between two selected points in the direction of the first to the last vertex. If one of the break points is the first vertex, one open polyline will result. Otherwise, there will be two polylines, from the first vertex and from the closing vertex to the break points, respectively.

2D polylines and traces with width will result in square ends at the break points.

The BREAK command cannot be applied to viewport entity borders.

See Figure 3-42 for examples of the BREAK command.

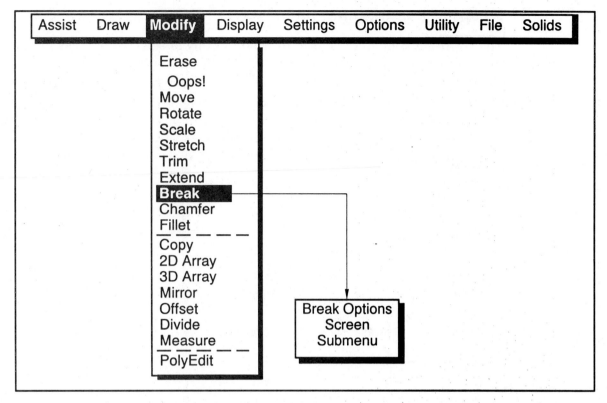

Figure 3-41 The BREAK Command Invoked from the Pull-Down Menu Modify

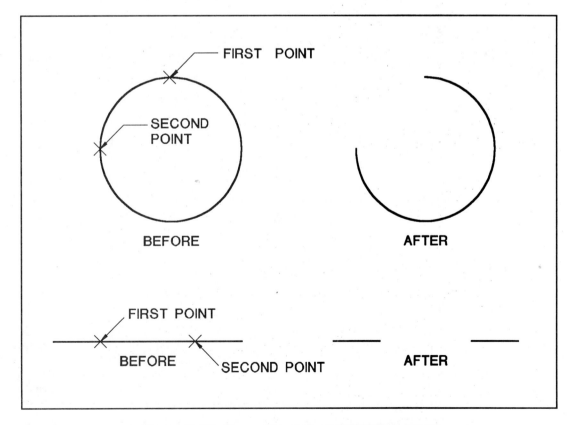

Figure 3-42 Examples of the BREAK Command

MIRROR Command

The MIRROR command is used to create a copy of selected entities in reverse, or mirrored about a specified line. One of the options includes mirroring the selected entities and then deciding whether to have them (the ones originally selected) deleted from the drawing or retain them, making the new ones reflected copies of the old. Another available option is to have the nontext items mirrored, and the text moved to mirrored locations. In this case they individually retain their original orientation for readability purposes in their new locations.

The MIRROR command is invoked from the Screen Root Menu Edit (Figure 3–43), pull-down menu Modify (Figure 3–44), or at the "Command:" prompt type in **MIRROR** and press ◡.

Command: **mirror**
Select objects: *select the objects*
First point of mirror line: *select point*
Second point: *select point*
Delete old objects? <N>: *select y or n*

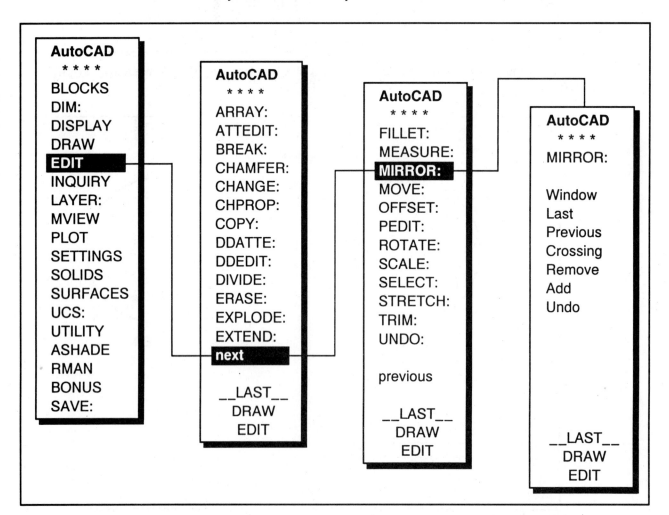

Figure 3–43 The MIRROR Command Invoked from the Screen Root Menu Edit

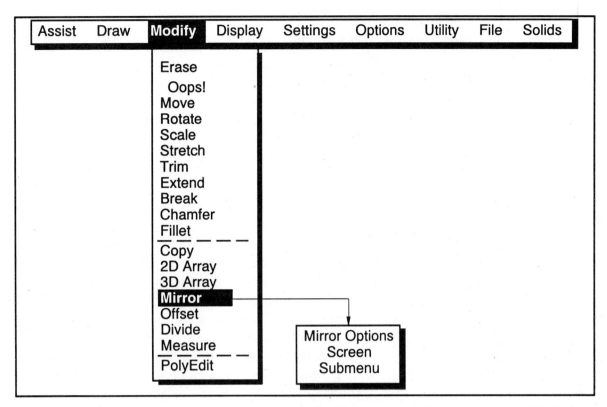

Figure 3-44 The MIRROR Command Invoked from the Pull-Down Menu Modify

The first and second points (which must not be the same) define a line about which the selected objects will be mirrored. You can place the mirror line at any angle.

The following command sequence shows an example of mirroring a group of objects selected by the Window option, as shown in Figure 3-45:

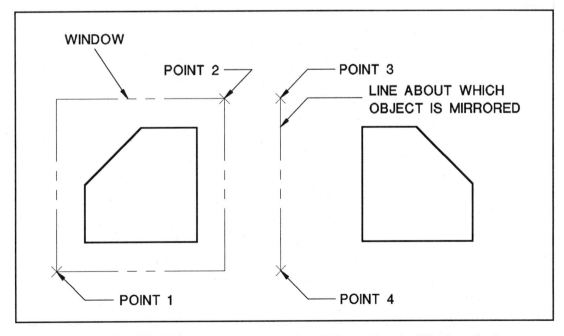

Figure 3-45 Mirroring a Group of Objects Selected by the Window Option

Fundamentals II

Command: **mirror**
Select objects: *select Window option from the screen menu or type* **w** *and*
     press ⏎
First corner: *pick point 1*
Second corner: *pick point 2*
Select objects: ⏎
First point of mirror line: *pick point 3*
Second point: *pick point 4*
Delete old objects?<N>: ⏎

The locations of mirrored text will be mirrored relative to other objects within the selected group. But the text will or will not retain its original orientation depending upon the setting of the system variable called MIRRTEXT. If the value of the setting is 1, then text items in the selected group will have their orientations reversed along with their locations within the group. That is, if their characters were normal and they read left-to-right in the original group, in the mirrored copy they will read right-to-left and the characters will be backwards. If the value of the MIRRTEXT system variable is set to 0 (zero), then the text strings in the group will have their locations reversed within the copied group, but the individual text strings would retain their left-to-right, normal character appearance in the copy if that is the way they were in the original group. The MIRRTEXT system variable, like other system variables, can be changed by the SETVAR command or typing **MIRRTEXT** at the "Command:" prompt (Release 11) as follows:

Command: **setvar**
Variable name or ?: **mirrtext**
New Value for MIRRTEXT <1>: **0**

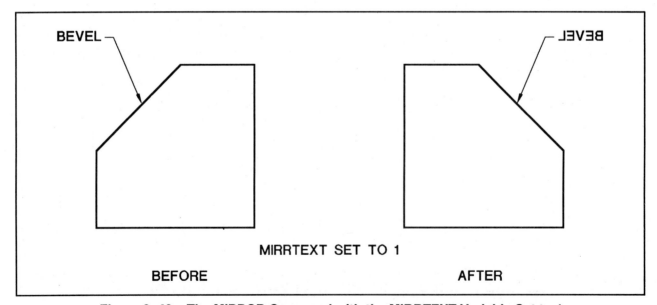

Figure 3-46a The MIRROR Command with the MIRRTEXT Variable Set to 1

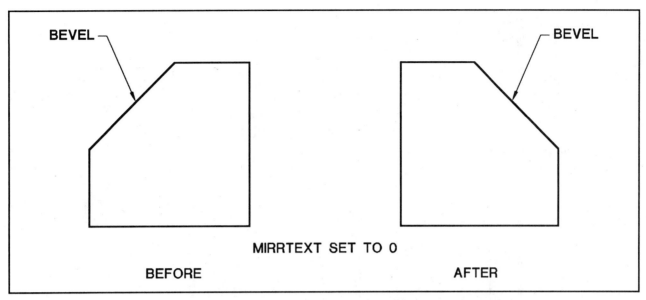

Figure 3-46b The MIRROR Command with the MIRRTEXT Variable Set to 0

The above setting will cause text that is in the group selected to be mirrored to retain the same orientation as in the original group.

Figures 3-46a and 3-46b show the result of the MIRROR command when the MIRRTEXT variable is set to 1 and 0, respectively.

FILLET Command

The FILLET command joins two lines, arcs, or circles with an arc of a specified radius. In the process of drawing the fillet, AutoCAD cleans up any resulting corners so they end on the new arc. The FILLET command is invoked from the Screen Root Menu Edit (Figure 3-47), pull-down menu Modify (Figure 3-48), or at the "Command:" prompt type in **FILLET** and press ⏎ or the spacebar.

> Command: **fillet**
> Polyline/Radius/<Select two objects>:

By default, AutoCAD prompts to select two objects in order to draw a rounded corner to the default radius. If necessary, you can change the radius by selecting the Radius option as shown below:

> Command: **fillet**
> Polyline/Radius/<Select two objects>: **r** *or select radius from the menu*
> Enter fillet radius <current>: *enter value*

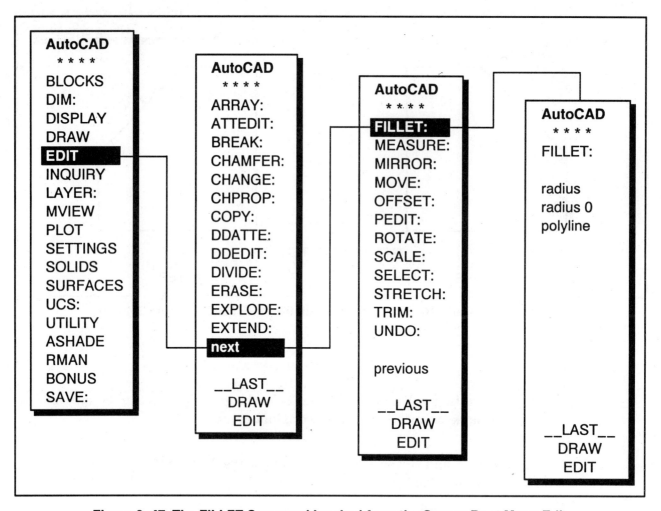

Figure 3-47 The FILLET Command Invoked from the Screen Root Menu Edit

The following sequence will draw a fillet with a radius of .25, as shown in Figure 3-49.

Command: **fillet**
Polyline/Radius/<Select two objects>: **r**
Enter fillet radius <current>: **0.25**
Command: ⏎ *to cause command repetition*
Polyline/Radius/<Select two objects>: *select two objects*

The following sequence will draw a fillet with a 0 radius, as shown in Figure 3-50.

Command: **fillet**
Polyline/Radius/<Select two objects>: **r**
Enter fillet radius <current>: **0**
Command: ⏎ *to cause command repetition*
Polyline/Radius/<Select two objects>: *select two objects*

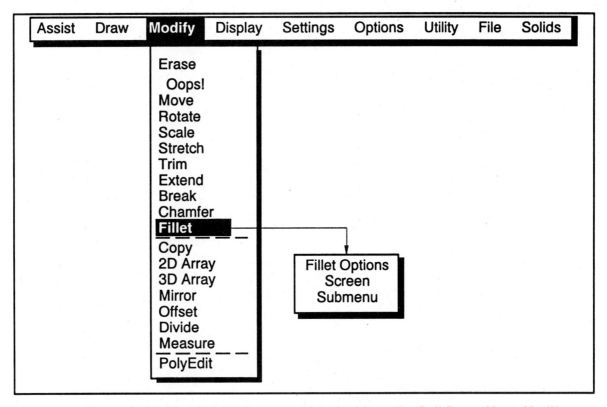

Figure 3-48 The FILLET Command Invoked from the Pull-Down Menu Modify

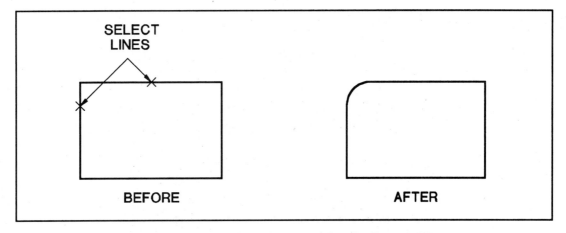

Figure 3-49 A Fillet Drawn with a Radius of .25

Polyline Option Fillets may be drawn at all vertices of the same radius in one step to a polyline by selecting the Polyline option.

The following sequence will draw a fillet with a radius of .50 to a polyline, as shown in Figure 3-51.

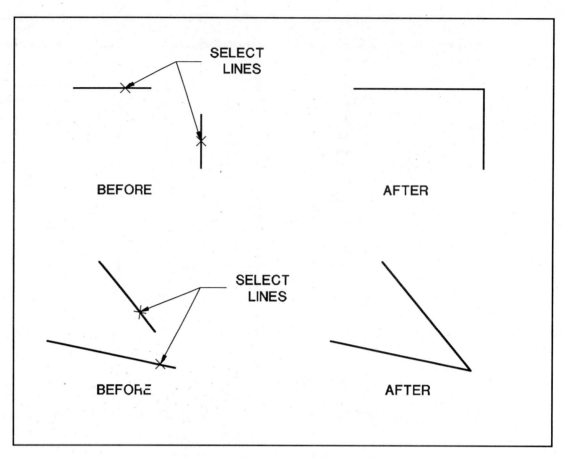

Figure 3-50 A Fillet Drawn with a Radius of 0

Command: **fillet**
Polyline/Radius/<Select two objects>: **r**
Enter fillet radius <current>: **0.50**
Command: ⏎ *to cause command repetition*
Polyline/Radius/<Select two objects>: **p**
Select polyline: *select polyline*

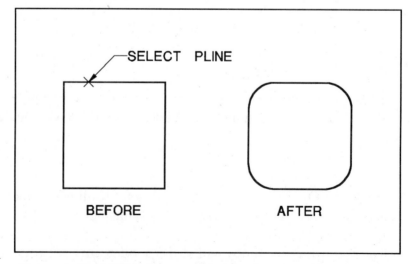

Figure 3-51 A Fillet Drawn with a Radius of .50 to a Polyline

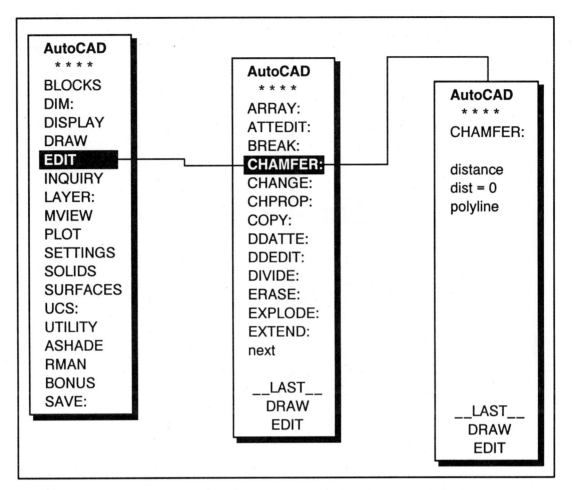

Figure 3-52 The CHAMFER Command Invoked from the Screen Root Menu Edit

CHAMFER Command

The CHAMFER command operates very similar to the FILLET command. This command allows you to draw angled corners on the drawing. The size of the chamfer is determined by its distance from the corner. If it is to be a 45-degree chamfer, the two distances will be the same. The CHAMFER command is invoked from the Screen Root Menu Modify (Figure 3-52), pull-down menu Modify (Figure 3-53), or at the "Command:" prompt type in **CHAMFER** and press ◡ or the spacebar.

    Command: **chamfer**
    Polyline/Distance/<Select first lines>:

By default, AutoCAD prompts you to identify two entities to draw the chamfer. The angled corner will be drawn to the default distances from the corner. To override the default distances, select the Distance option or enter **d** at the prompt, and specify the first and second chamfer distances as follows:

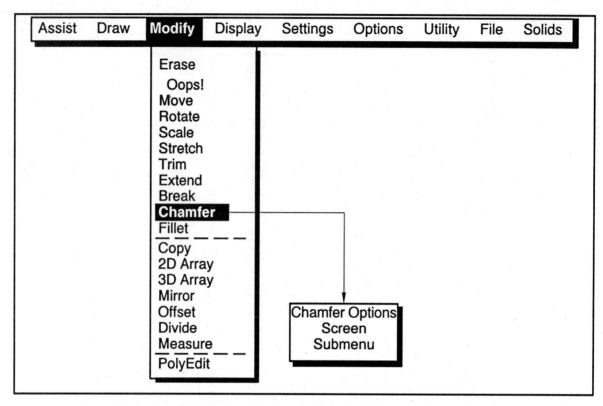

Figure 3-53 The CHAMFER Command Invoked from the Pull-Down Menu Modify

Command: **chamfer**
Polyline/Distance/<Select first lines>: **d**
Enter first chamfer distance <current>: *specify a chamfer distance*
Enter second chamfer distance <current>: *press* ⏎ *to accept the default or type in a new distance*

After you specify the new chamfer distances, they remain in effect for subsequent chamfers until changed.

The following sequence will draw a chamfer with chamfer distances of .5 and 1 as shown in Figure 3-54.

Command: **chamfer**
Polyline/Distance/<Select first lines>: **d**
Enter first chamfer distance <current>: **.5**
Enter second chamfer distance <current>: **1**
Command: ⏎ *to cause command repetition*
Polyline/Distance/<Select first lines>: *pick the first line*
Select second line: *pick the second line*

Polyline Option   A chamfer may be drawn at all vertices of a polyline by selecting the Polyline option.

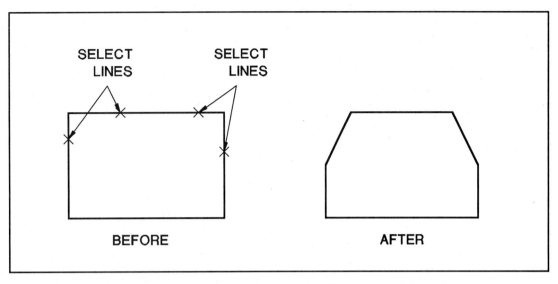

Figure 3–54 A Chamfer Drawn with Distances of .5 and 1

The following sequence will draw a chamfer to a polyline with both distances of .5 from the corners, as shown in Figure 3–55.

Command: **chamfer**
Polyline/Distance/<Select first lines>: **d**
Enter first chamfer distance <current>: **.5**
Enter second chamfer distance <.5>: ⏎
Command: ⏎ *to cause command repetition*
Polyline/Distance/<Select first lines>: **p**
Select polyline: *pick the polyline*

> **Note:** Chamfer set at zero distance operates the same way the FILLET command operates set at zero radius.

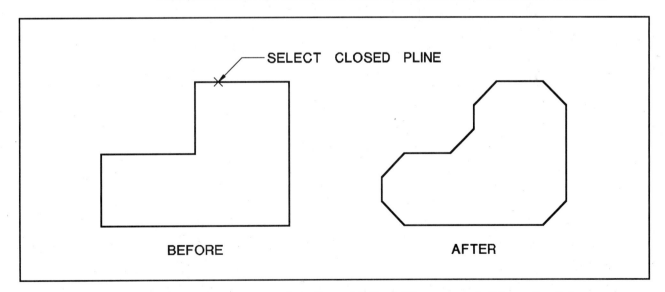

Figure 3–55 A Chamfer Drawn to a Polyline with Both Distances of .5 from the Corners

LAB EXERCISES

Lab Exercise 3-4

Lay out the figure using the CIRCLE command as shown in exercise 3-4. Use the TTR option to lay out the 4 inch and 8 inch radius. Then use the TRIM or BREAK command to remove parts of the circles that are not needed.

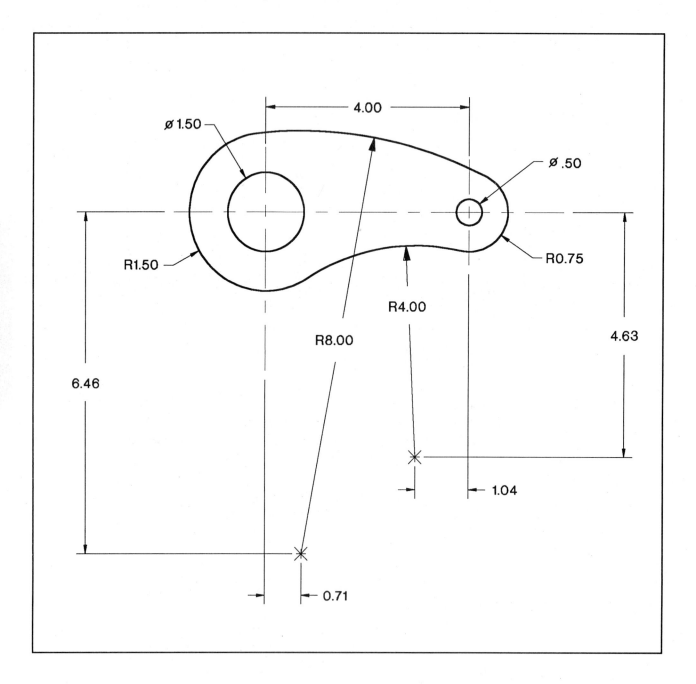

Lab Exercise 3-5

For exercise 3-5, lay out the center lines first. Next, place larger circles and use the INTERSECTION OSNAP mode to place smaller circles at the intersection of the center lines.

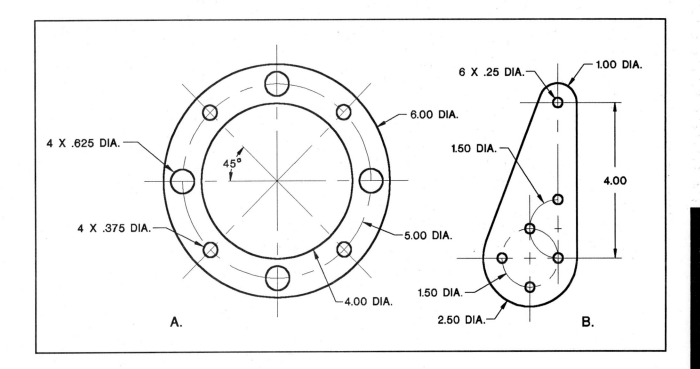

Lab Exercise 3-6

For exercise 3-6, lay out the gasket according to the given dimensions. Show all dimensions on the finished drawing.

Set DIMTXT=.125
Set text height=.125

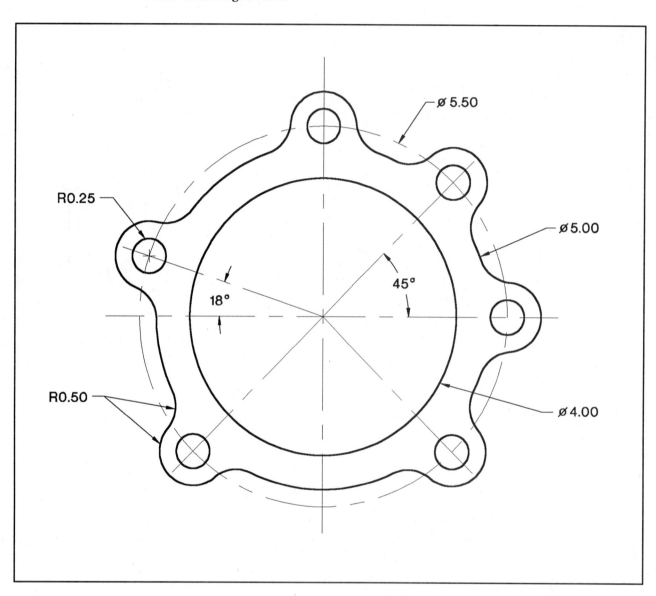

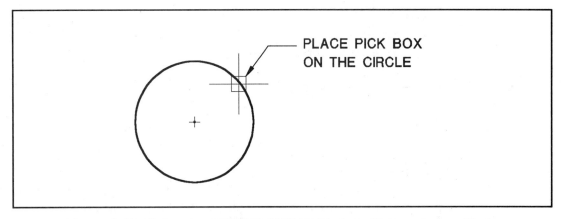

Figure 3-56 Using the CENTER OSNAP Mode to Pick an Arc or Circle

OBJECT SNAP — CIRCULAR APPLICATIONS

In this chapter, four OSNAP modes are explained, the CENTER, QUADRANT, and TANGENT modes (which are exclusive to circles and arcs) and the PERPEN-DICULAR mode as it pertains to circular applications.

CENTER Mode

The CENTER OSNAP mode causes AutoCAD to use the coordinates of the center of the selected circle or arc when prompted for a point. It is important to note that when being applied, part of the circle or arc must be in the aperture pick box in order to work, as shown in Figure 3-56.

Selecting where the cursor is in Figure 3-57 for both point specifications in the following sequence will result in the line shown in Figure 3-57.

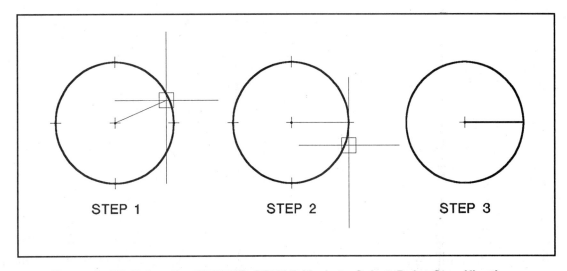

Figure 3-57 Using the CENTER OSNAP Mode to Select Point Specifications

Command: **line**
From point: **cen**
　　of *select point on circle*
To point: **qua**
　　of *select same point*

QUADRANT Mode

The QUADRANT OSNAP mode allows you to select a point that is located at one of the quadrant points of a circle or arc. The quadrant points are located 0 deg, 90 deg, 180 deg, and 270 deg from the center of the circle or arc, as shown in Figure 3-58. The quadrant points are determined by the 0 deg direction of the current coordinate system.

In Figure 3-59 a line can be drawn to a quadrant as follows:

Command: **line**
From point: *select A*
To point: **qua**
　　of *select A1*

A line can also be drawn to a quadrant as follows (see Figure 3-60):

Command: **line**
From point: *select A*
To point: **qua**
　　of *select A2*

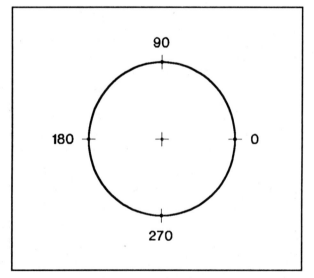

Figure 3-58 The QUADRANT OSNAP Mode Quadrant Points

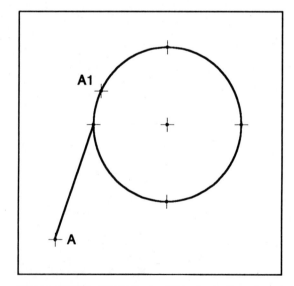

Figure 3-59 Drawing a Line to a Quadrant — Method #1

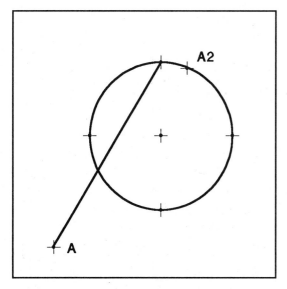

Figure 3-60 Drawing a Line to a Quadrant — Method #2

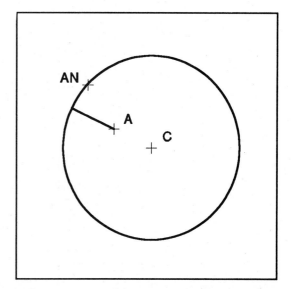

Figure 3-61 Using the PERPENDICULAR OSNAP Mode to Specify the Endpoint of a Line Perpendicular to a Circle from Inside a Circle (Near Side)

> *NOTE:* Special precautions should be taken when attempting to select circles or arcs in Blocks or Ellipses that are rotated at an angle that is not a multiple of 90 deg. When a circle or an arc in a block is rotated, the point that the QUADRANT OSNAP mode specifies also rotates. But when a circle/arc not in a block is rotated, the QUADRANT OSNAP points stay at the 0, 90, 180, 270 points.

PERPENDICULAR Mode

The PERPENDICULAR OSNAP mode can be used to specify the endpoint of a line, not only perpendicular to another line, but perpendicular to a circle or an arc, as shown in Figure 3-61. The following sequences show examples of how you can draw lines using the PERPENDICULAR OSNAP mode.

From inside the circle:

    Command: **line**
    From point: *select A*
    To point: **per**
        to *select near side point AN*

    Command: **line**
    From point: *select point A*
    To point: **per**
        to *select far side point AF, as shown in Figure 3-62*

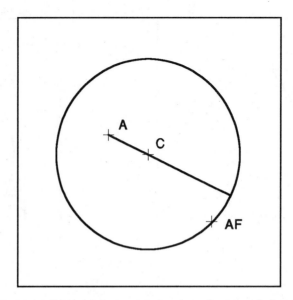

Figure 3-62 Using the PERPENDICULAR OSNAP Mode to Specify the Endpoint of a Line Perpendicular to a Circle from inside a Circle (Far Side)

From outside the circle:

Command: **line**
From point: *select point B*
To point: **per**
     to *select near side point BN, as shown in Figure 3-63*

Command: **line**
From point: *select point B*
To point: **per**
     to *select far side point BF, as shown in Figure 3-64*

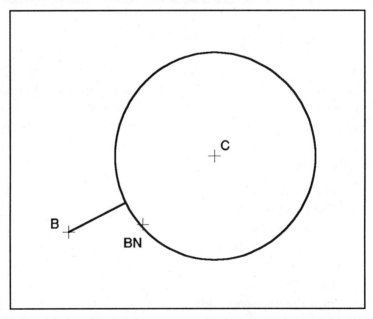

Figure 3-63 Using the PERPENDICULAR OSNAP Mode to Specify the Endpoint of a Line Perpendicular to a Circle from outside a Circle (Near Side)

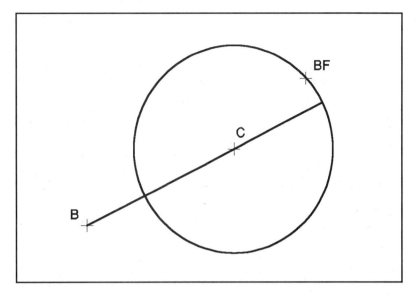

Figure 3-64 Using the PERPENDICULAR OSNAP Mode to Specify the Endpoint of a Line Perpendicular to a Circle from outside a Circle (Far Side)

Using arcs in the PERPENDICULAR OSNAP mode works in a manner similar to using circles. When drawing a line perpendicular to another line, the point that AutoCAD establishes can be off the line selected (in response to the "perpendicular to" prompt) and the new line will still be drawn to that point (see Figure 3-65).

In Figure 3-65 lines from both A and B can be drawn perpendicular to line L.

Unlike drawing perpendicular to a line, when you select an arc as the object to which the new line will be perpendicular, the point established must be on the arc (see Figure 3-66).

In Figure 3-66 a line can be drawn perpendicular to arc from A, but not from B.

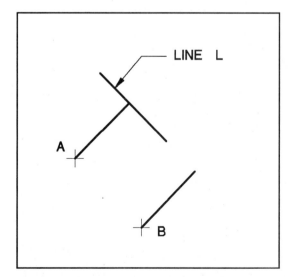

Figure 3-65 Using the PERPENDICULAR OSNAP Mode to Draw a Line Perpendicular to Another Line on an Arc

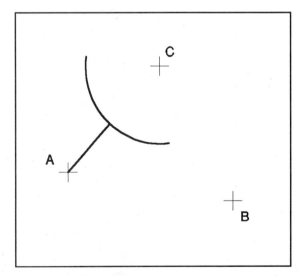

Figure 3-66 Using the PERPENDICULAR OSNAP Mode to Specify that a Line be Perpendicular to an Arc

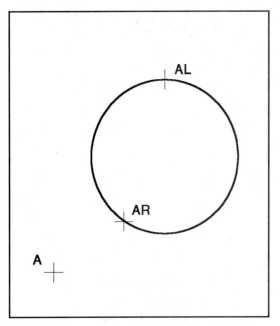

Figure 3-67 Using the TANGENT OSNAP Mode to Draw Lines to Two Points of Tangency on a Circle from Outside a Circle

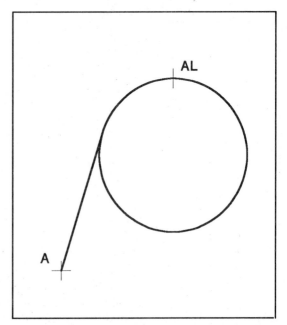

Figure 3-68 Using the TANGENT OSNAP Mode to Draw a Line from a Point outside a Circle Tangent to a Left Point on a Circle

TANGENT Mode

The TANGENT OSNAP mode was illustrated in the TTR option of the CIRCLE command. In this section, examples are provided to draw lines tangent to circles and arcs.

From a point A, outside of a circle, you can draw lines to two points of tangency on the circle, as shown in Figure 3-67.

The following command sequence will draw a line from point A tangent to a point on the circle, as shown in Figure 3-68.

> Command: **line**
> From point: *select point A*
> To point: **tan**
> to *select point AL toward left semicircle*

A line can also be drawn from point A tangent to a point on the circle, as shown in Figure 3-69.

> Command: **line**
> From point: *select point A*
> To point: **tan**
> to *select point AR toward right semicircle*

For the TANGENT OSNAP mode you can select an arc also. Like the PERPENDICULAR OSNAP mode, the tangent point must be on the arc selected (see Figure 3-70).

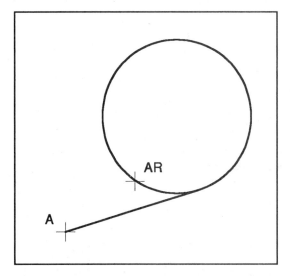

Figure 3-69 Using the TANGENT OSNAP Mode to Draw a Line from a Point Outside a Circle Tangent to a Right Point on a Circle

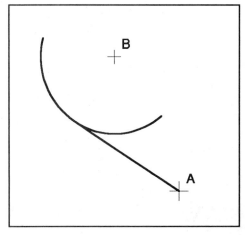

Figure 3-70 Using the TANGENT OSNAP Mode to Draw Lines of Tangency to a Point on an Arc

OSNAP COMMAND

The Object Snap (OSNAP) modes can be invoked in two ways. One is to respond to a prompt for a point with the name of the particular Object Snap mode desired. This is a one-time-only usage. The second method is to use the OSNAP command and respond with the name of a mode. This causes AutoCAD to always use the mode specified (running OSNAP) when you are requested to specify a point. This will be very helpful in dimensioning. You can specify more than one mode by separating the names with a comma as follows:

    Command: **osnap**
    Object snap modes: **mid,endp,cen**

Normally you would specify only one Object Snap mode for a running OSNAP. If you wish to override the running OSNAP mode with another mode or none at all, simply respond to the prompt for a point with the name of the other mode or with "NON" for no OSNAP mode.

One important difference between a one-time Object Snap and running OSNAP is that if during a one-time Object Snap you select a point on the screen where no valid point exists, AutoCAD will display an error message to select again. However, if the running OSNAP mode is on, you may select other points and have AutoCAD use them. For example, if CENTER mode is on and you select a point on, off, or near an entity that does not have a center, AutoCAD will still use the point selected.

Fundamentals II

> **NOTE:** If you have a running OSNAP mode in force, say end-point, and you respond to a prompt for a point with the coordinates of a point that, if selected with the cursor, would include an entity in the aperture box that has an endpoint, then AutoCAD will Snap to that endpoint. In this case it is wise to override the running OSNAP mode with "NON" before typing in the point coordinates.

SETVAR AND SYSTEM VARIABLES

The environmental state of the drawing is recorded in the drawing file in what are called the system variables. Such items as the LIMITS, CURRENT LAYER, UNITS settings, and the "Last Point" entered are just a few of the more than 120 system variables that are set to values that determine or are determined by conditions of the drawing environment. The SETVAR command may be used to read and change (if changeable) system variable settings as follows:

```
Command: setvar
Variable name or ?:
```

If you respond with ?, the following prompt will appear:

```
Variable(s) to list<*>:
```

Variable names can be specified, separated by commas, or you can use wild cards to have selected groups of system variables listed. In Release 11, the system variable can also be changed by typing the name of the variable at the "Command:" prompt.

Forms and Types of System Variables

Some system variables are "read only." This means that they cannot be changed directly by using the SETVAR command. For example, the system variable called CLAYER, which is "read only," when listed after the ? response, will display the name of the current layer. You can change it with the LAYER command only. But, you can change the status of the SNAP ON/OFF setting by properly applying the SETVAR command to the SNAPMODE system variable, which is not "read only."

Classification of System Variables

The system variables are classified by their type. The types are described below with the integers and points divided into two subtypes.

Integers (for switching) System variables that have limited nonnumerical settings can be switched by setting them to the appropriate integer value. For example, the SNAP can be either ON or OFF. The purpose of the SNAPMODE system variable is to turn the SNAP on or off by using the AutoCAD SETVAR command or the AutoLISP (setvar) function.

How the SNAP can be turned ON or OFF is demonstrated in the following example by changing the value of its system variable when its current value is set at "0", which is OFF.

```
Command: setvar
Variable name or ?: snapmode
New value for SNAPMODE (0): 1
```

The above sequence may seem rather unnecessary because the SNAP mode is so easily switched with a function key. Changing the SNAP with the SETVAR command is inconvenient, but performing the above does allow you to view the results immediately.

For any system variable whose status is associated with an integer, the method of changing the status is just like the above example. In the case of the SNAPMODE, "0" turns it OFF and "1" turns it ON. In a similar manner, the SNAPISOPAIR is switched from one isoplane to another by setting that system variable to one of three integers as follows: 0 is the left isoplane, 1 is the top, and 2 is the right isoplane.

It should be noted that the settings for the OSNAP system variable named OSMODE are members of the binomial sequence. The integers are 1, 2, 4,.....512, 1024. See Table 3-1 for the OSMODE system variable values. While the settings are switches, they are more than just ON and OFF. There may be several mode settings active at one time. It is important to note that the value of an integer (switching) has nothing to do with its numerical value.

Table 3-1 The OSMODE System Variables

The OSMODE system variable values are as follows:	
NONE	0
ENDPOINT	1
MIDPOINT	2
CENTER	4
NODE	8
QUADRANT	16
INTERSECTION	32
INSERT	64
PERPENDICULAR	128
TANGENT	256
NEAREST	512
QUICK	1024

Integers (for numerical value) System variables such as APERTURE and AUPREC are changed by using an integer whose value is applied numerically in some way to the setting, rather than just as a switch. For instance, the aperture (the target box that appears for selecting Osnap points) size is set in pixels (picture elements) according to the integer value entered in the SETVAR command. For example, setting the value of the APERTURE to 9 should render a target box that is three times larger than setting it to 3.

AUPREC is the variable that sets the precision of the ANGULAR units in decimal places. The value of the setting is the number of decimal places; therefore, is considered a numerical integer setting.

Point (x coordinate,y coordinate) LIMMIN, LIMMAX, and VIEWCTR are examples of system variables whose settings are points in the form of the X coordinate and Y coordinate.

Point (distance,distance) Some system variables whose type is point, are primarily for setting spaces rather than a particular point in the coordinate system. For instance, the SNAPUNIT system variable, though called a point type, uses its X and Y distances from (0,0) to establish the Snap X and Y resolution, respectively.

Real System variables that have a real number for a setting, such as the VIEWSIZE, are called REAL.

String These system variables at this time are read-only and therefore can only be read, not modified, by the SETVAR command. They are names like the CLAYER, for the current layer name and the DWGNAME for the drawing name.

INQUIRY COMMANDS

AutoCAD provides several commands that will display useful information about the entities in the drawing. These commands do not create anything, nor do they edit or have any effect on the drawing or entities therein. The only effect on the AutoCAD editor is that on the single screen systems, the screen switches to the text mode (not to be confused with the TEXT command) and the information requested by the particular INQUIRY command is then displayed on the screen. If you are new to AutoCAD it is helpful to know the FLIP SCREEN feature that will return you to the graphics screen so you can continue with your drawing. On most systems this is accomplished with the F1 function key. You can also change back and forth between graphic and text screens with the GRAPHSCR and TEXTSCR commands typed in at the "Command:" prompt, respectively.

INQUIRY commands include LIST, AREA, ID, DBLIST, and DIST. The INQUIRY commands are invoked from the Screen Root Menu Inquiry (Figure 3-71), or the pull-down menu Utility (Figure 3-72).

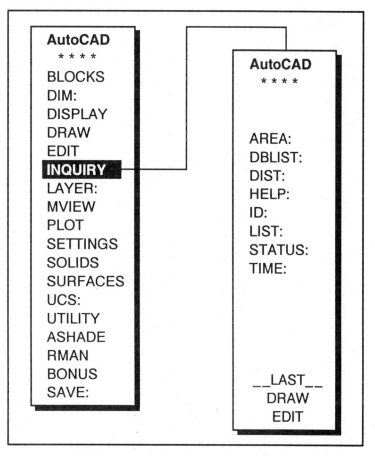

Figure 3-71 The INQUIRY Commands Invoked from the Screen Root Menu Inquiry

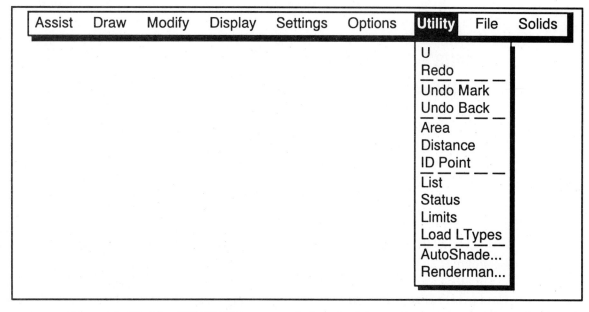

Figure 3-72 The INQUIRY Commands Invoked from the Pull-Down Menu Utility

LIST Command

The LIST command is used to obtain information about individual entities. It permits you to read on the screen information that is stored in the drawing data base by AutoCAD, such as coordinates of endpoints of lines and arcs, center points of circles and arcs, lengths of lines and arcs, directions of lines and starting directions of arcs, and the angle that they turn. The command sequence is as follows:

Command: **list**
Select objects: *select objects*

When you conclude the object selection process by pressing ⏎, the screen will flip to the text mode and begin displaying the list of data about each entity selected. If the report of all of the data more than fills the screen, then the data will scroll, normally too fast to read. You can press Ctrl + S to temporarily stop the scrolling in order to read the data and then press any key to cause scrolling to resume. Scrolling can be terminated by pressing Ctrl + C, terminating the LIST command also.

In addition to the data mentioned above, useful data include the following:

The location, layer, entity type, and space (Model or Paper) of any selected entity. Also, the color and linetype if not BYLAYER.

The distance in the main axes between endpoints of a line; i.e., the delta X, delta Y, and delta Z.

The area and circumference of a circle or the area of a closed polyline.

Insertion point, height, angle of rotation, style, font, obliquing angle, width factor, and actual string of a TEXT entity.

The entity handle is reported in hexadecimal if handles are enabled.

DBLIST Command

The DBLIST command prints lists of data about all of the entities in the drawing. It can take a long time to scroll through all the data in a large drawing. DBLIST can, like other commands, be terminated by cancelling with Ctrl + C. If necessary, you can also print it on a line printer by turning the printer echo on by pressing Ctrl + O (not zero).

AREA Command

The AREA command is used to report the area in square units of a selected closed geometric figure on the screen such as a circle, polygon, closed polyline, or a group of closed and end-connected entities. You may also specify a series of points which AutoCAD will consider a closed polygon and compute the area and report. The sequence of prompts is as follows:

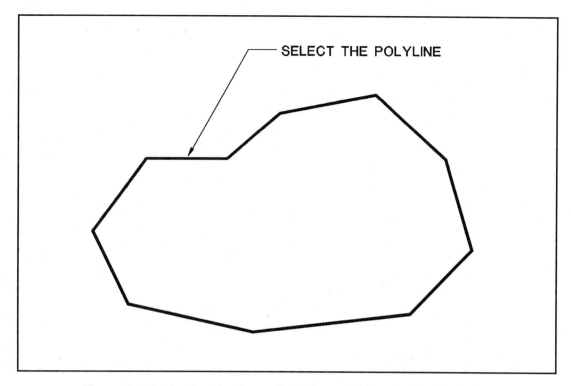

SELECT THE POLYLINE

Figure 3-73 Finding the Area of a Polygon Using the Entity Option

Command: **area**
<First point>/Entity/Add/Subtract:

The default option will allow you to calculate the area by picking the vertices of the entities. If you want to know the area of a specific entity like circle, polygon, or closed polyline, select the Entity option.

The following command sequence shows an example of finding the area of a polygon using the Entity option, as shown in Figure 3-73.

Command: **area**
<First point>/Entity/Add/Subtract: **e**
Select circle or polyline: *pick entity*
Area = 12.21   Perimeter = 13.79

The Add option allows you to add selected entities to form a total area and then you can use the Subtract option to remove selected entites from the running total.

The following example demonstrates the application of the Add and Subtract options. In the given example, the area is determined for the closed shape after subtracting the area of the four circles, as shown in Figure 3-74.

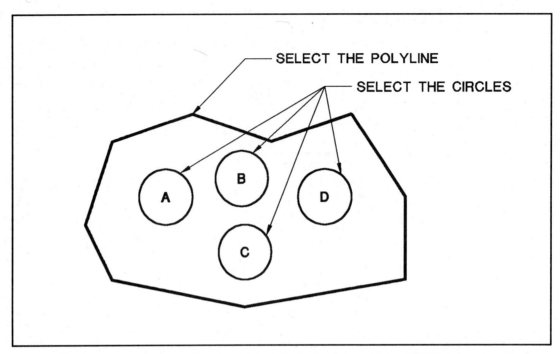

Figure 3-74 Using the Add and Subtract Options of the AREA Command

Command: **Area**
<First point>/Entity/Add/Subtract: **a**
<First point>/Entity/Subtract: **e**
(ADD mode) Select circle or polyline: *select polyline*
Area = 12.9096, Perimeter = 15.1486
Total area = 12.9096
(ADD mode) Select circle or polyline: ⏎
<First point>/Entity/Subtract: **s**
<First point>/Entity/Add: **e**
(SUBTRACT mode) Select circle or polyline: *select a circle*
Area = 0.7125, Circumference = 2.9992
Total area = 12.1971
(SUBTRACT mode) Select circle or polyline: *select second circle*
Area = 0.5452, Circumference = 2.6175
Total area = 11.6179
(SUBTRACT mode) Select circle or polyline: *select third circle*
Area = 0.7125, Circumference = 2.9922
Total area = 10.9394
(SUBTRACT mode) Select circle or polyline: *select fourth circle*
Area = 0.5452, Circumference = 2.6175
Total area = 10.3942
(SUBTRACT mode) Select circle or polyline: ⏎
<First point>/Entity/Add: ⏎
Command:

ID Command

The ID command is used to obtain the coordinates of a selected point. If you do not use an OSNAP mode to select a point that is not in the current construction plane, AutoCAD will assign the current elevation as the Z coordinate of the point selected. The sequence is as follows:

    Command: **id**
    Point: *select a point*

    X = *<X coordinate>*   Y = *<Y coordinate>*   Z = *<Z coordinate>*

If the BLIPMODE is ON, you can respond to the "Point:" prompt with the coordinates of a point and a blip will appear on the screen at that point, provided it is in the viewing area.

DIST Command

The DIST command prints out the distance, in the current units, between two points, either selected on the screen or keyed in from the keyboard. Included in the report are the horizontal and vertical distances (delta-X and delta-Y, respectively) between the points and the angles in and from the XY plane. The sequence is as follows:

    Command: **dist**
    First point: *select point*
    Second point: *select point*

The following information is reported:

    Distance = *<straight line distance is reported>*
    Angle in X-Y plane = *<angle is reported>*
    Angle from X-Y plane = *<angle is reported>*
    Delta X = *<horizontal distance is reported>*
    Delta Y = *<vertical distance is reported>*
    Delta Z = *<elevation distance is reported>*

WILD CARDS AND NAMED OBJECTS

AutoCAD provides a variety of wild cards for use in specifying selected groups of named objects when responding to prompts during commands that operate on those objects. By placing one or more of these wild cards in the string (your response) you can specify a group that includes (or excludes) all of the objects with certain combinations or patterns of characters.

The type of objects associated with a drawing that are referred to by name includes Blocks, Layers, Linetypes, Text styles, Dimension styles, Named User Coordinate Systems, Named views, Shapes and Named viewport configurations.

A list of wild cards and their use is shown below:

# (pound)	Matches any numeric digit
@ (at)	Matches any alpha character
. (period)	Matches any character except alphanumeric
* (asterisk)	Matches any string. It can be used anywhere in the search pattern; beginning, middle, or end of the string.
? (question mark)	Matches any single character
~ (tilde)	Matches anything but the pattern
[...]	Matches any one of characters enclosed
[~...]	Matches any character not enclosed
- (hyphen)	Specifies single character range
' (reverse quote)	Reads characters literally

The following table shows some examples of wild card patterns.

Pattern	Will match or included...	But not...
ABC	Only ABC	
~ABC	Anything but ABC	
?BC	ABC through ZBC	AB, BC, ABCD, XXBC
A?C	AAC through AZC	AC, ABCD, AXXC, ABCX
AB?	ABA through ABZ	AB, ABCE, XAB
A*	Anything starting with A	XAAA
A*C	Anything starting with A and ending with C	XA, ABCDE
*AB	Anything ending with AB	ABCX, ABX
AB	AB anywhere in string	AXXXB
~*AB*	All strings without AB	AB, ABX, XAB, XABX
[AB]C	AC or BC	ABC, XAC
[A-K]D	AD, BD, through KD	ABC, AKC, KD

CIRCULAR DIMENSIONING

Circular dimensioning includes three main AutoCAD dimensioning features: Angular, Diameter, and Radius. While linear dimensioning involves straight line distances, circular dimensions comprise the balance of the dimensioning spec-

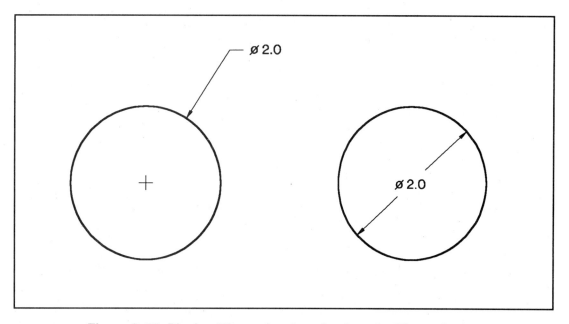

Figure 3-75 Placing Dimension Arcs for Angular Dimensioning

trum. Diameters and radii involve circles and arcs. Angles involve nonparallel lines. All three are aspects of circular measurements.

Features Common to Linear and Circular Dimensions

Items such as dimension lines, extension lines, arrows, dimension text, tolerances, limits, and alternate units are properties that are common to both linear and circular dimensioning. Some of the aspects of these terms that are particular to circular dimensioning are outlined in the following text and figures.

Dimension lines become dimension arcs for angular dimensions. The dimension arc will have as its center the intersection of the two lines whose angle (between the two) you are measuring. The location of the arc will be where you select, as shown in Figure 3-75.

In angular dimensioning, AutoCAD will provide radial extension lines if the location that you select for the dimension arc is beyond either or both of the lines selected for measuring the angle between, as shown in Figure 3-76. Diameter and radius dimensions do not add extension lines.

Dimension lines are straight for radius and diameter dimensions. The dimensions go toward or through the center of the circle or arc being dimensioned, as shown in Figure 3-77. The dimensions are also measured to a point or points on the circle or arc unless you select the diameter mode on an arc from a point where there is no part of the arc on the opposite end of the diameter beginning at the selected point. AutoCAD does not provide an extension arc in this case.

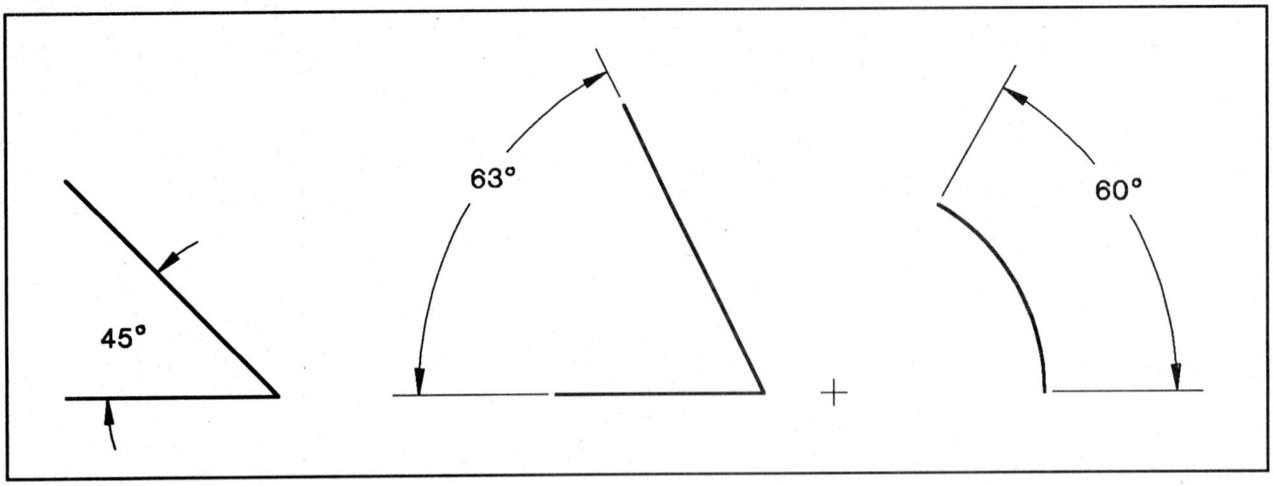

Figure 3-76 Example of Radial Extension Lines when Dimension Arcs Are Placed beyond Specified Angle Measurements

Dimension text for diameter and radius dimensions will be preceded by a diameter symbol (a circle with a diagonal line through it) or an R for radius. The UNITS command provides a special category for setting up the type of angular units you wish to have for the angle dimensioning text. See Chapter 2 for a detailed explanation of the UNITS command.

Angular Dimensioning

This feature provides commands to create dimensions of the angle between two nonparallel lines, using the conventions that conform to the dimension variable settings you have established. "Angle" is defined by *Webster's New Collegiate Dictionary* as "A measure of the amount of turning necessary to bring one line or plane into coincidence with or parallel to another." There are four methods by which you can use angular dimensioning: ARC, CIRCLE-POINT, TWO LINES, and THREE POINTS.

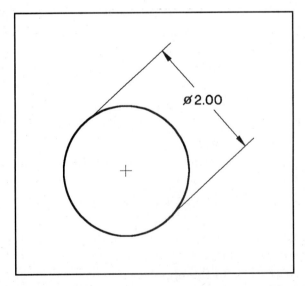

Figure 3-77 Placing Dimension Line for Diameter Dimensioning

The examples that follow are of sequences of command prompts (with responses) that will occur after you have initiated the DIM command. Remember, unless you are using the DIM1 command, you will not return to the "Command:" prompt until you use Ctrl + C, or the EXIT option when you are at the "Dim:" prompt. If you are in a subcommand prompt, such as "Select arc, circle, line, or RETURN:" requesting the first input for angular dimensioning, entering Ctrl + C will only return you to the "Dim:" prompt.

The DIM command can be invoked from the Screen Root Menu and then you can invoke Angular to get into the Angular command, or, at the "Dim:" prompt you can also type **ANG** and press ⏎ or spacebar to get into angular dimensioning.

> DIM: **ang**
> Select arc, circle, line or RETURN:

The method of angular dimensioning that AutoCAD utilizes depends on how you respond to the above prompt. If you select an arc, circle, or line then your method will be Arc, Circle-Point, or Two Lines, respectively. If you respond by pressing ⏎, then your method will be Three Points. The following sections describes these four methods.

Arc Method If you select an arc, AutoCAD uses the center of the arc as the vertex of the dimensioned angle and the endpoints of the arc as points on lines between which the angle will be measured, as shown in Figure 3-78. The sequence of prompts will be as follows:

> DIM: **ang**
> Select arc, circle, line or RETURN: *select an arc*
> Enter dimension line arc location: *select dimension arc location*

After this selection AutoCAD prompts for dimension text and text location (see Figure 3-79).

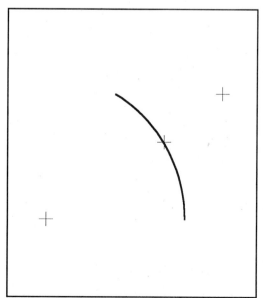

Figure 3-78 Using the ARC Method for Angular Dimensioning

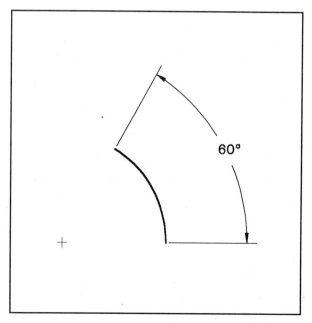

Figure 3-79 The Arc after Angular Dimensioning

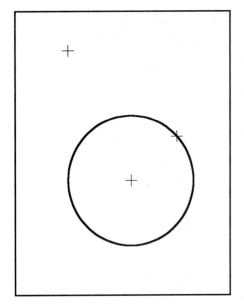

Figure 3-80 Using the Circle-Point Method for Angular Dimensioning

Figure 3-81 The Circle after Angular Dimensioning

Circle-Point Method If you select a circle at the first prompt, AutoCAD uses the center of the circle as the vertex of the dimensioned angle. The point where you select the circle snaps NEAREST to the circle and is used as a point on one line from which the dimensioned angle will be measured. You are then prompted for a second point which will be on the other angle-determining line. The second point does not have to be on the circle. It cannot, however, be the same point as the first selected, as shown in Figure 3-80. The sequence of prompts will be as follows:

> DIM: **ang**
> Select arc, circle, line or RETURN: *select a circle*
> Second angle endpoint: *select second point*
> Enter dimension line arc location: *select dimension arc location*

After this selection AutoCAD prompts for dimension text and text location (see Figure 3-81).

Two Lines Method If you select a line at the first prompt, AutoCAD prompts you for a second (nonparallel) line. AutoCAD then uses the point where the two lines intersect (or would intersect if one or both were infinite in length) as the vertex of the dimensioned angle, as shown in Figure 3-82.

> DIM: **ang**
> Select arc, circle, line or RETURN: *select a line*
> Second line: *select second line*
> Enter dimension line arc location: *select dimension arc location*

After this selection AutoCAD prompts for dimension text and text location.

The point you select to tell AutoCAD where to locate the dimension arc also indicates whether one angle or its supplement is dimensioned, as shown in Figure 3-83.

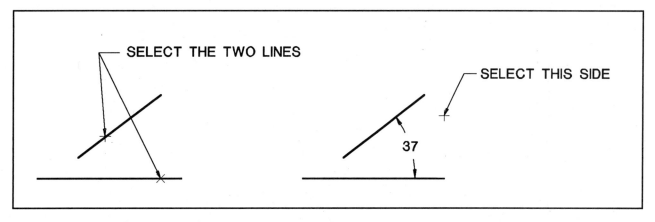

Figure 3-82 Using the Two Lines Method for Angular Dimensioning

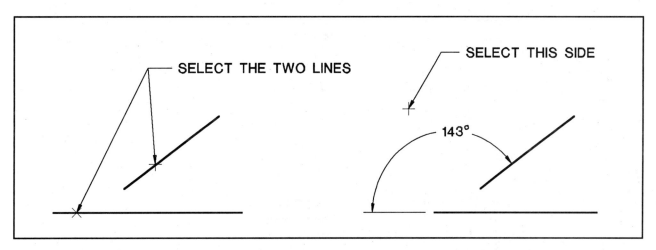

Figure 3-83 Specifying the Location of the Dimension Arc Using the Two Lines Method for Angular Dimensioning

Three Points Method If you respond to the first prompt by pressing ⏎, AutoCAD will utilize the Three Point angular dimensioning method, as shown in Figure 3-84, and prompt you as follows:

DIM: **ang**
Select arc, circle, line or RETURN: ⏎
Angle Vertex: *select point*
First angle endpoint: *select point*
Second angle endpoint: *select point*

After this selection AutoCAD prompts for dimension text and text location.

In all of the above cases, extension lines will be added where necessary, and the dimension arc will be forced outside the extension lines if it cannot be fitted inside along with the text. The dimension text prompt will be displayed as follows:

Dimension text <measured angle>:

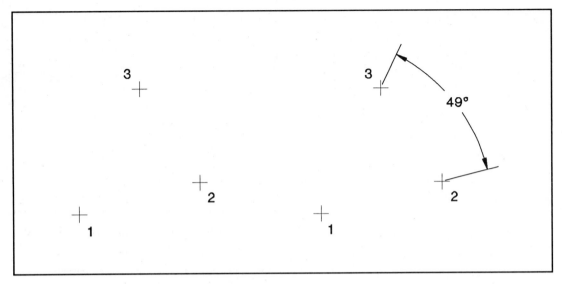

Figure 3-84 Using the THREE POINTS Method for Angular Dimensioning

You can default to the displayed text in the brackets by pressing ⏎, or you can add a prefix and/or suffix, or you can override the text entirely as in linear dimensioning.

Following the "Dimension text:" prompt you will be prompted for the text location as follows:

Enter text location:

Pressing ⏎ will cause the text to be located in a break at the midpoint of the dimension arc. Entering a point causes the text to be located at that point, breaking the dimension arc only if necessary to clear the text.

Diameter Dimensioning

This feature provides commands to create diameter dimensions for arcs and circles. The type of dimensions that AutoCAD utilizes depends upon the settings of the DIMTIX and DIMTOFL dimension variables, shown in Table 3-2.

The leader in diameter dimensioning is drawn in accordance with certain user screen picks and dimension variable settings. When the leader is drawn outside the circle, it will be on a radial line that starts at the point on the circle nearest to where the user selects the circle to be dimensioned. The leader length will be determined by picking a point with the cursor. The length will be equal to the distance from the cursor location to a line tangent to the circle at the point where the circle was first selected. If the leader radial direction is more that 15 degrees from horizontal, AutoCAD will add a horizontal segment pointing toward the text that is equal to the length of an arrow as determined by the dimension variable DIMASZ, as shown in Figure 3-85.

Table 3-2 The Settings of the DIMTIX and DIMTOFL Dimension Variables for Diameter Dimensioning

METHOD		EXAMPLE	DIMTIX	DIMTOFL	DIMCEN
NO.1	A	⌀ TEXT	OFF	OFF	POSITIVE (NONZERO)
	B	⌀ TEXT	OFF	OFF	NEGATIVE (NONZERO)
	C	⌀ TEXT	OFF	OFF	ZERO
NO.2		⌀ TEXT	OFF	ON	NO EFFECT
NO.3		⌀ TEXT	ON	ON	NO EFFECT

Setting the variables DIMTOFL and DIMTIX to OFF causes AutoCAD to omit the dimension line within the circle. A radial leader will be placed outside the circle along with the dimension text. With this method (no dimension line inside circle), there are three conditions that can be established concerning cross marks at the center of the circle. The condition used depends on the value to which the dimension variable DIMCEN is set. The conditions are as follows:

Method 1-A If DIMCEN is set to a positive nonzero value, AutoCAD draws cross marks at the center of the circle, the lengths of which are equal to twice the value set.

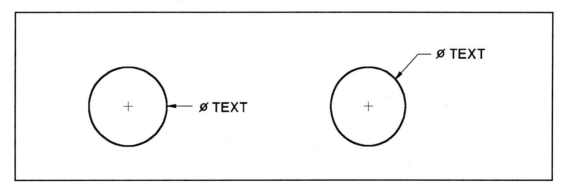

Figure 3-85 The Dimension Variable DIMASZ with Respect to Text Placement

Method 1-B If DIMCEN is set to a negative nonzero value, AutoCAD draws two center lines (horizontal and vertical) crossing at the center of the circle. The absolute value of the setting is equal to half the length of the center marks. It is equal to how far the ends of the center lines extend outside of the circle and the size of the gaps at the ends of the center marks.

Method 1-C If DIMCEN is set to zero then no cross marks are drawn.

Setting the variable DIMTOFL to ON and DIMTIX to OFF causes AutoCAD to add the dimension line within the circle. The leader and dimension text outside the circle follow the rules of Method No. 1-C above. The arrow on the leader is omitted. In this case, center marks are ignored.

Setting the variable DIMTIX to ON causes AutoCAD to place the dimension line and dimension text inside the circle, breaking the line for the text if the text will fit. If the text will not fit, AutoCAD reverts to Method No. 1-A or No. 1-C above, depending on the setting of the variable DIMTOFL, and prompts for a leader length.

The sequence of prompts will be as follows for the example shown in Figure 3-86 when DIMCEN is set to ∅ and DIMTOFL and DIMTIF are set to OFF.

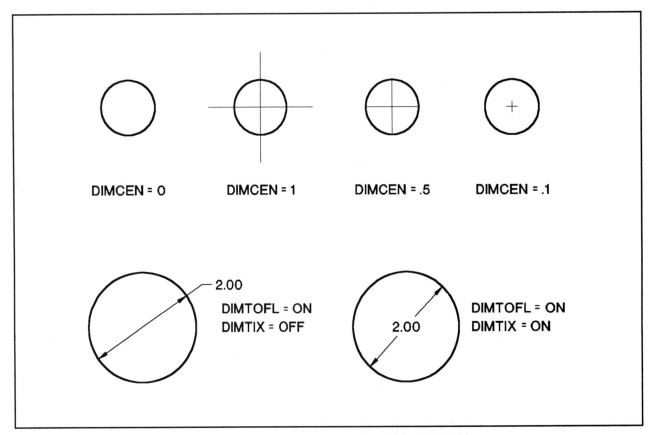

Figure 3-86 The Dimension Variable DIMCEN

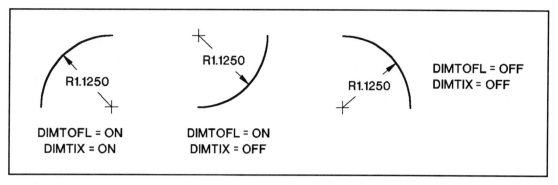

Figure 3-87 The Dimension Variable DIMCEN with Respect to Radius Dimensioning

Command: **dim**
DIM: **diameter**
Select arc or circle: *select circle where you wish arrow to be placed*
Dimension text <2.00>: ⏎
Enter leader length for text: ⏎
DIM:

Radius Dimensioning

This feature provides commands to create radius dimensions for arcs and circles. The type of dimensions that AutoCAD utilizes depends upon the settings of the DIMTIX and DIMTOFL dimension variables. It is very similar to diameter dimensioning, except dimension lines inside the arc or circle are only from the center to the selected point of the arc or circle and there is no arrow at the center. Center marks are similarly drawn (or not drawn) according to the settings of the dimension variable DIMCEN (see Figure 3-87).

Dimension text for radius dimensioning is preceded by the letter R. As in other dimension text, you can use the default text by pressing ⏎, or add a prefix and/or suffix, or override the text by keying in the desired text in response to the "Dimension text:" prompt.

The radius dimension leader can be forced to the inside of the arc or circle by responding with a negative length to the "Enter leader length for text:" prompt, or selecting a point inside the arc or circle.

See Appendix C for alphabetical list of dimensioning variables with a brief description.

LAB EXERCISES

Lab Exercise 3-7

Using the LINE, CIRCLE, and ARC commands draw the figures shown in exercise 3-7.

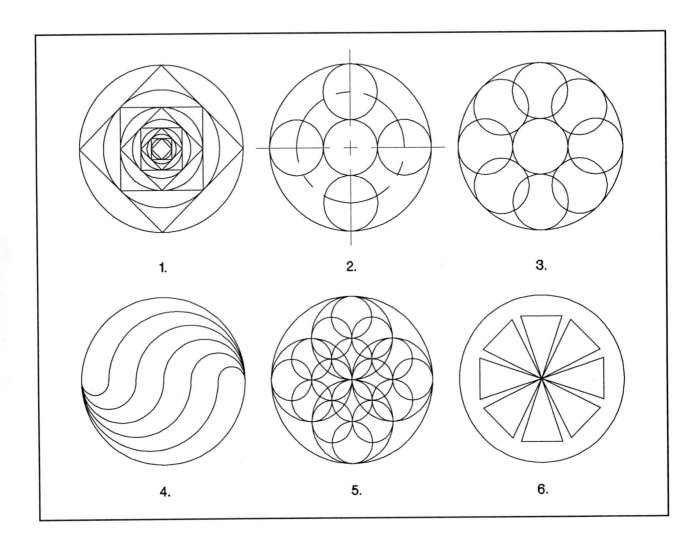

1. 2. 3.

4. 5. 6.

Lab Exercise 3-8

For exercise 3-8, lay out the crane pully plate using the LINE, CIRCLE, and ARC commands. Use a C-size sheet or PROTO-C drawing created in the exercises in Chapter 2. Show all dimensions and callouts.

Set DIMTXT=.125
Set text height=.125

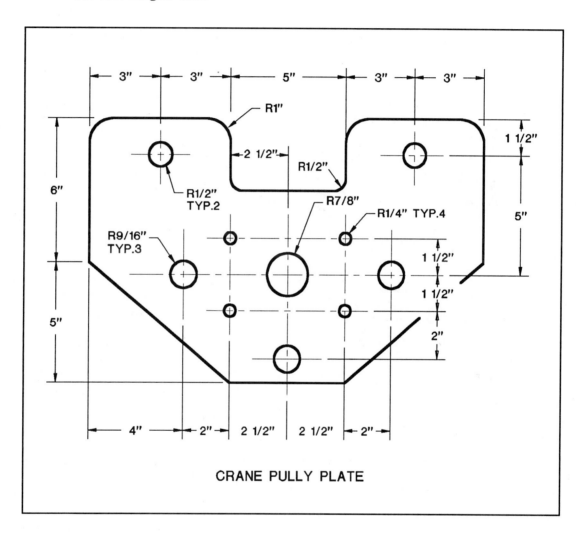

CRANE PULLY PLATE

Lab Exercise 3-9

For exercise 3-9, lay out the figure using the LINE, CIRCLE, and ARC commands. Use a C-size sheet or PROTO-C drawing. Show all dimensions and callouts.

Set DIMTXT=.125
Set text height=.125

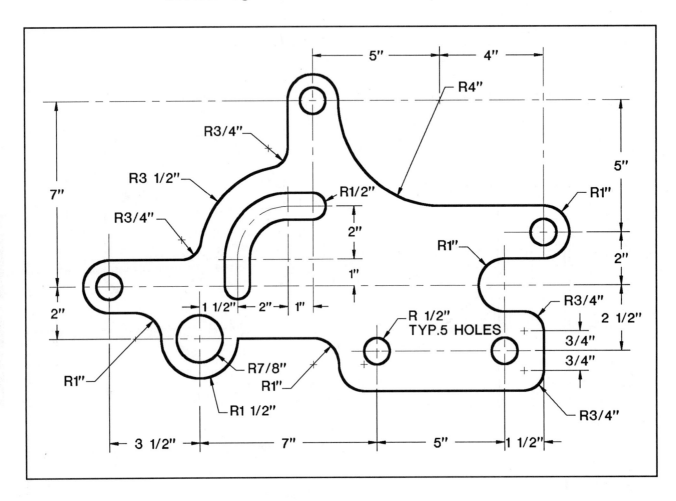

Lab Exercise 3-10

For exercise 3-10, lay out the wiring diagram on a C-size sheet or PROTO-C drawing. Set text height to .125. This text size is standard industry height. Do not be concerned if you cannot read this size of text zoomed out all the way. When the drawing is plotted out at full scale .125 text height is easy to read.

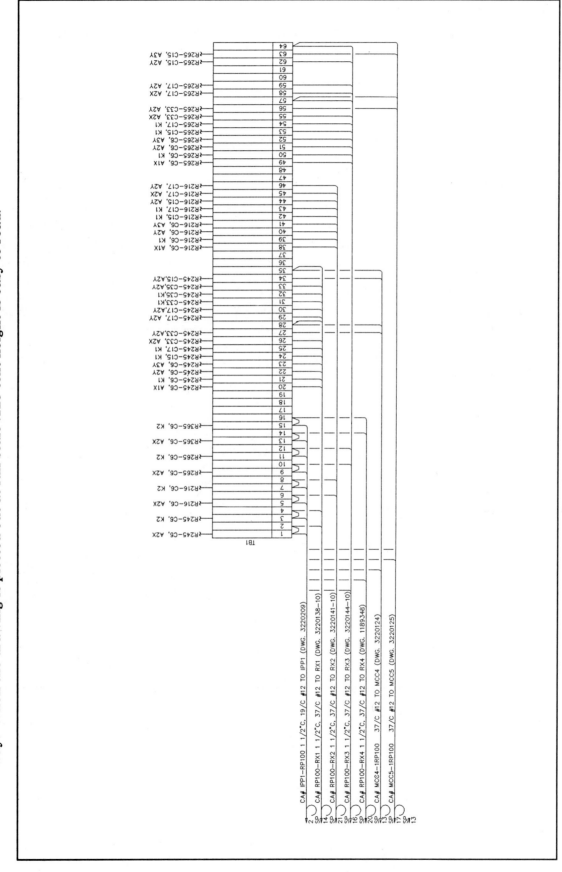

Lab Exercise 3–11

For exercise 3–11, lay out the top and front views of the pipe clamp. Show all dimensions. Use a C-size sheet or PROTO-C drawing.

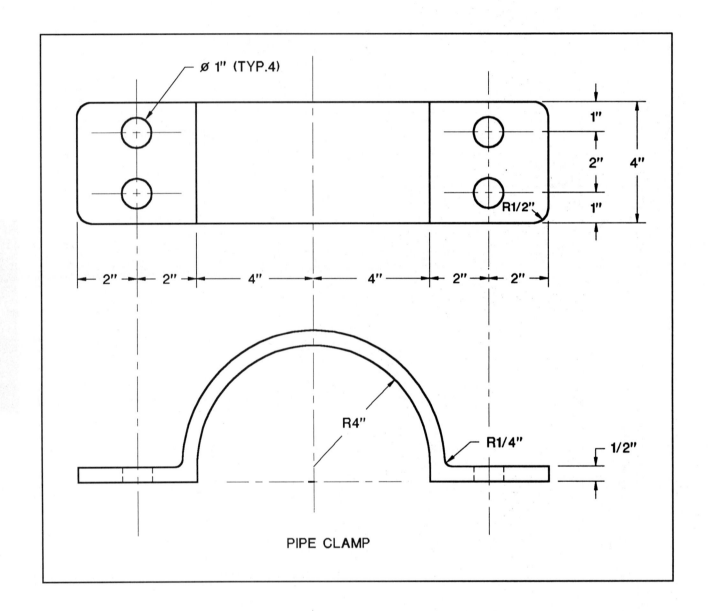

PIPE CLAMP

Lab Exercise 3-12

For exercise 3-12, lay out the top and front views of the beam clamp. Show all dimensions and callouts. Use a C-size sheet or PROTO-C drawing.

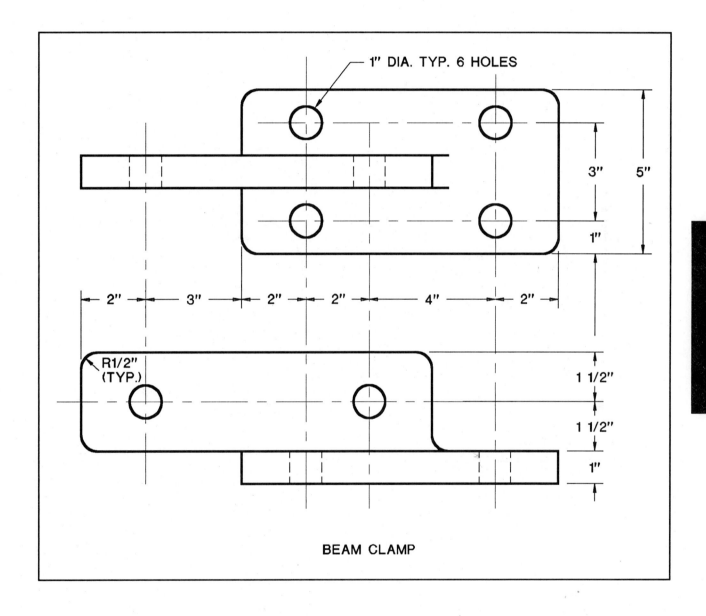

BEAM CLAMP

Lab Exercise 3-13

For exercise 3-13, lay out the figure using the CIRCLE, ARC, POLYGON, and
ELLIPSE commands. Use a B-size sheet or PROTO-B drawing. Show all dimensions and callouts.

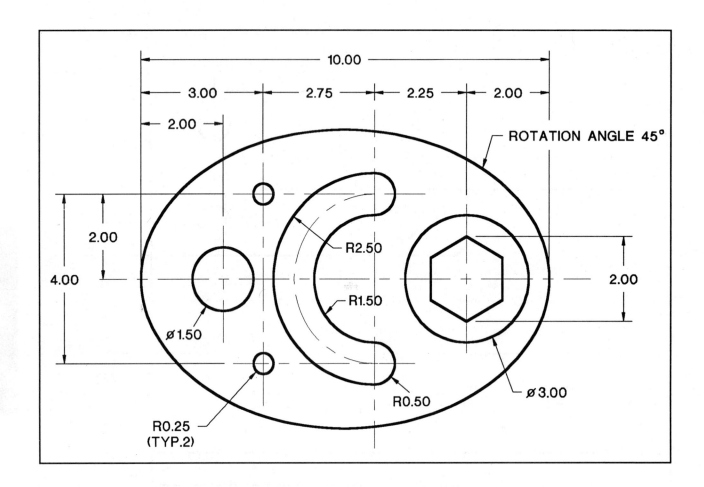

Lab Exercise 3-14

For exercise 3-14, lay out figures using the LINE, CIRCLE, and ARC commands. Use a C-size sheet or PROTO-C drawing.

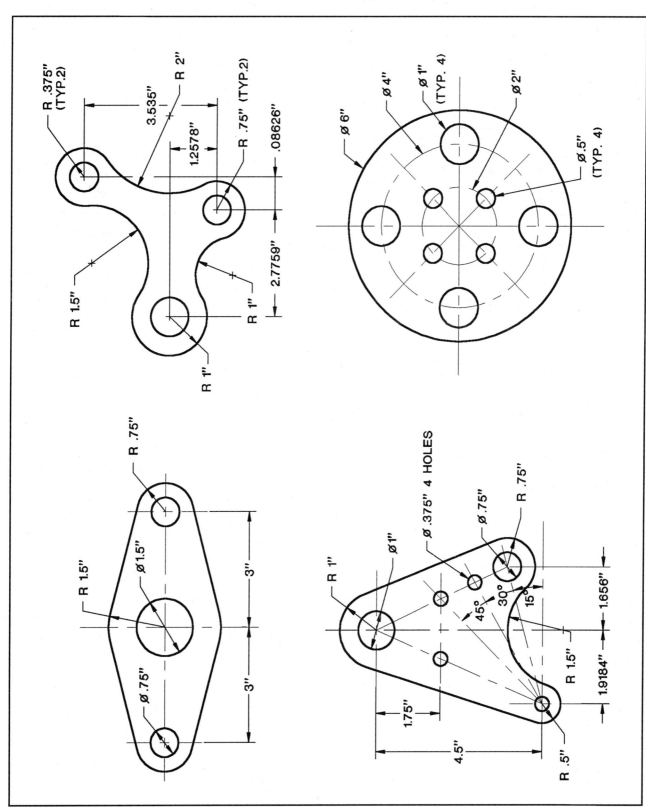

Lab Exercise 3-15

For exercise 3-15, lay out the top, front, and right side views. Show all dimensions and callouts. Use a B-size sheet or PROTO-B drawing.

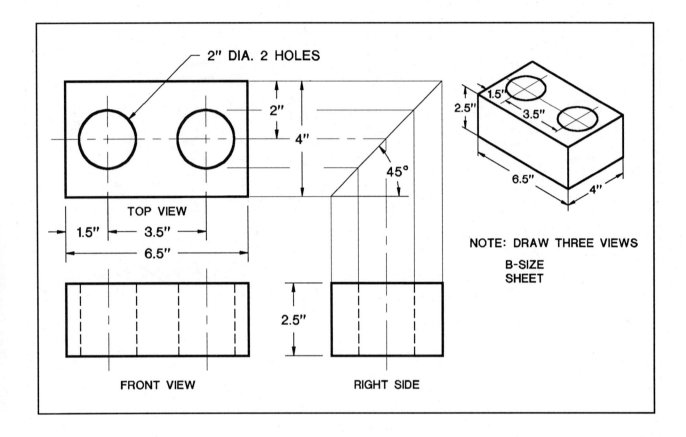

2" DIA. 2 HOLES

2"

4"

45°

TOP VIEW

1.5"   3.5"

6.5"

FRONT VIEW

2.5"

RIGHT SIDE

1.5"

2.5"

3.5"

6.5"

4"

NOTE: DRAW THREE VIEWS

B-SIZE
SHEET

Lab Exercise 3-16

For exercise 3-16, lay out the top and front views. Use an A-size sheet or PROTO-A drawing. Show all dimensions and callouts.

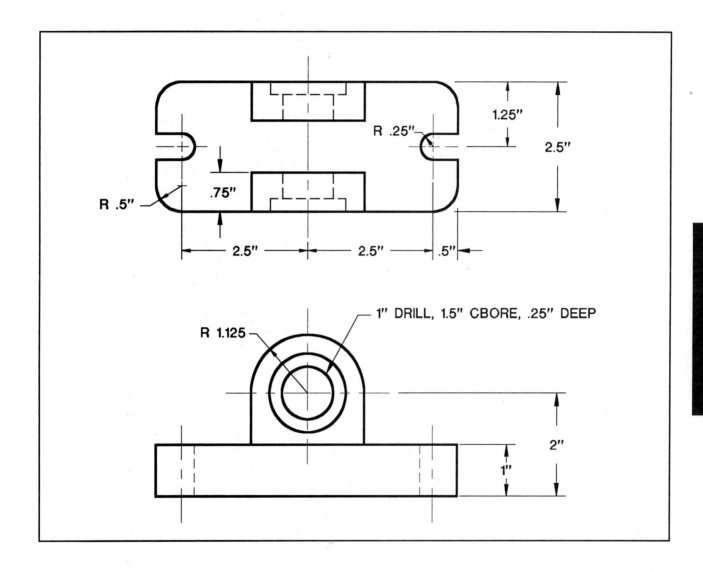

Fundamentals II

Lab Exercise 3-17

For exercise 3-17, lay out the top and front views. Use a B-size sheet or PROTO-B drawing. Show all dimensions and callouts.

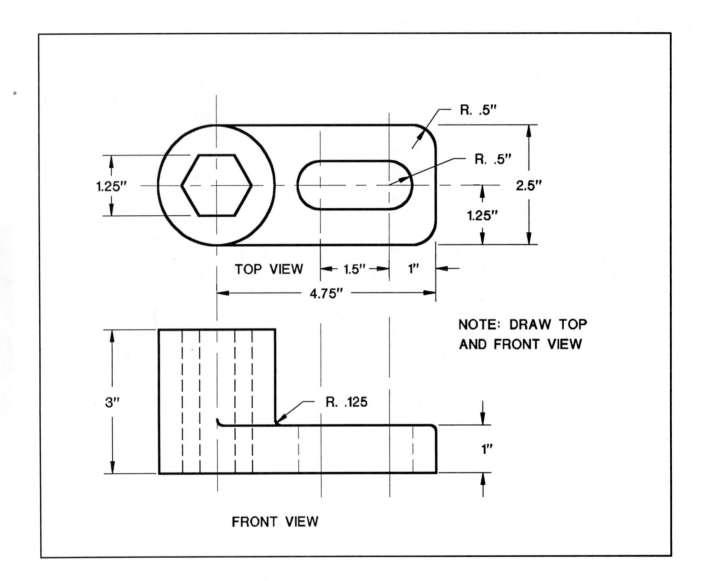

Lab Exercise 3-18

For exercise 3-18, lay out the front and right side views. Use a B-size sheet or PROTO-B drawing. Show all dimensions and callouts.

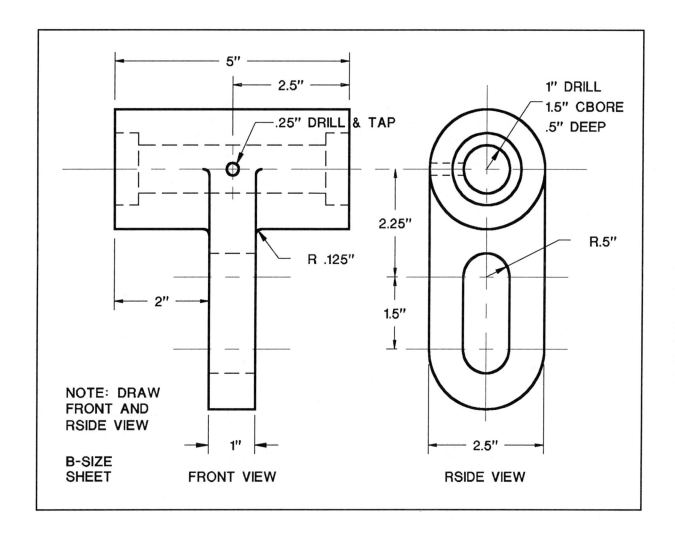

Lab Exercise 3-19

For exercise 3-19, lay out top, front, right side, and auxiliary views. Use a B-size sheet or PROTO-B drawing. Show all dimensions and callouts.

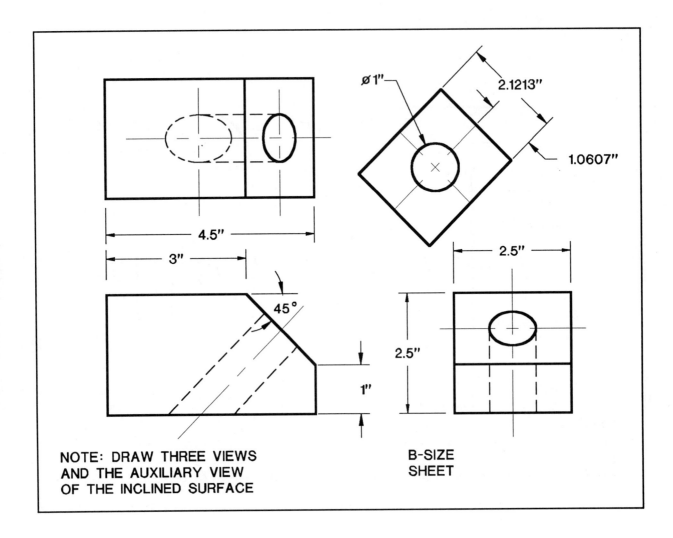

NOTE: DRAW THREE VIEWS
AND THE AUXILIARY VIEW
OF THE INCLINED SURFACE

B-SIZE
SHEET

Lab Exercise 3-20

For exercise 3-20, lay out top, front, and auxiliary views. Use a C-size sheet or PROTO-C drawing. Show all dimensions and callouts.

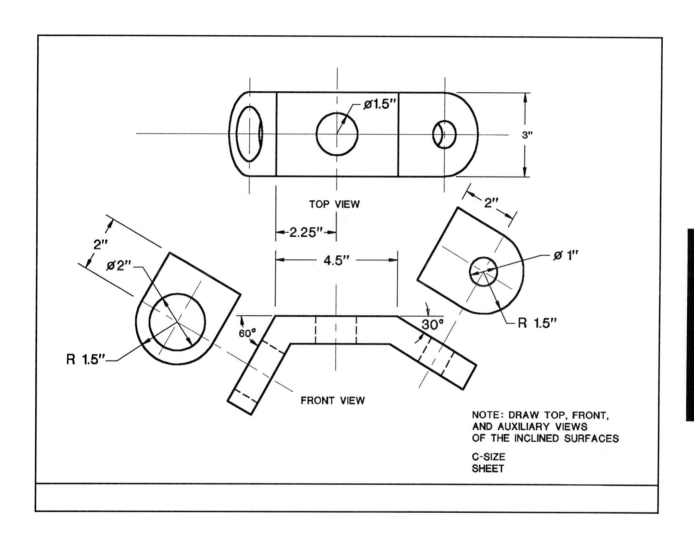

Lab Exercise 3-21

For exercise 3-21, lay out top, front, and auxiliary views. Use a C-size sheet or PROTO-C drawing. Show all dimensions and callouts.

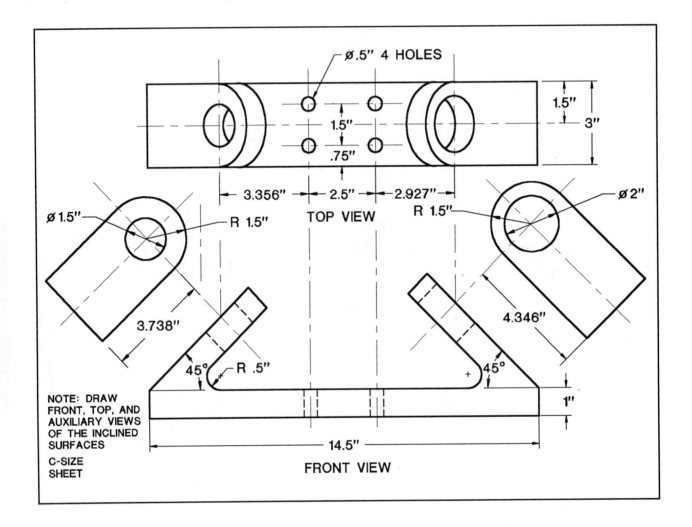

Ø.5" 4 HOLES

1.5"

3"

1.5"

.75"

3.356"   2.5"   2.927"

Ø 1.5"   R 1.5"   TOP VIEW   R 1.5"   Ø 2"

3.738"

4.346"

45°   R .5"   45°

NOTE: DRAW FRONT, TOP, AND AUXILIARY VIEWS OF THE INCLINED SURFACES

1"

14.5"

C-SIZE SHEET

FRONT VIEW

Lab Exercise 3-22

For exercise 3-22, lay out top and front views. Use a B-size sheet or PROTO-B drawing. Use baseline dimensions. Show all dimensions and callouts.

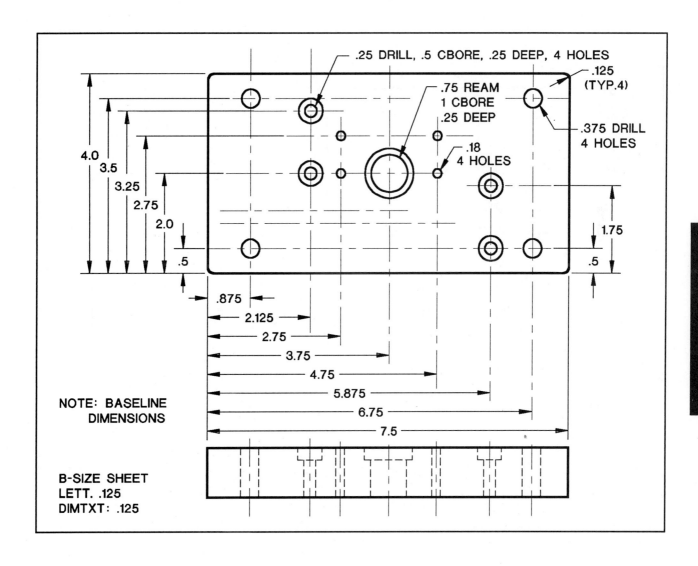

NOTE: BASELINE
DIMENSIONS

B-SIZE SHEET
LETT. .125
DIMTXT: .125

Fundamentals II

Lab Exercise 3-23

For exercise 3-23, lay out figure on a B-size sheet. Show all dimensions and callouts.

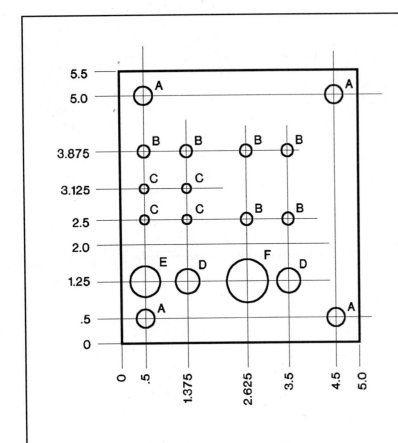

HOLE	
SIZE (SYMBOL)	DIAMETER
A	.375
B	.25
C	.1875
D	.5
E	.625
F	.875

ORDINATE DIMENSIONING

Chapter 3 Project Exercise

CREATING THE PROJECT DRAWING

Skills required to set up the project for this chapter were explained in Chapter 1 and Chapter 2. These included LINE, CIRCLE, and ARC commands in addition to the EDIT commands such as MOVE, COPY, ERASE, ROTATE, BREAK, and MIRROR. The utility commands include UNITS, LIMITS, LAYER, GRID, SNAP, and ZOOM, in addition to linear and angular dimensioning and some of the OSNAP modes.

The object of this project is to set up an 18" × 12" sheet for drawing the object, shown in Figure 3-88, at full scale with the origin (0,0) located at a point on the object convenient for dimensioning.

STEP 1   Begin a NEW drawing called proj2.

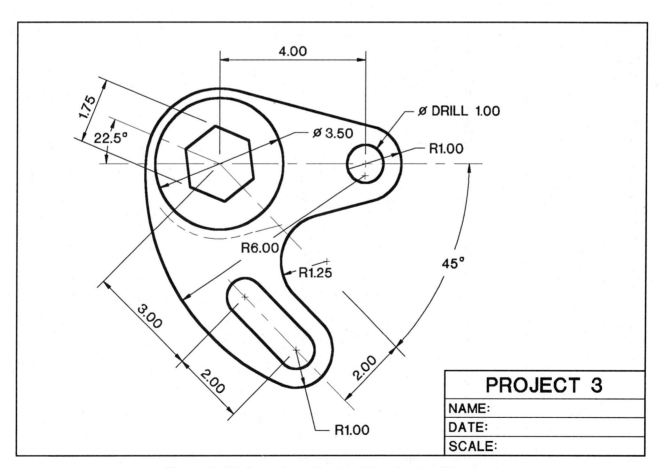

Figure 3-88 Completed Project Drawing for Chapter 3

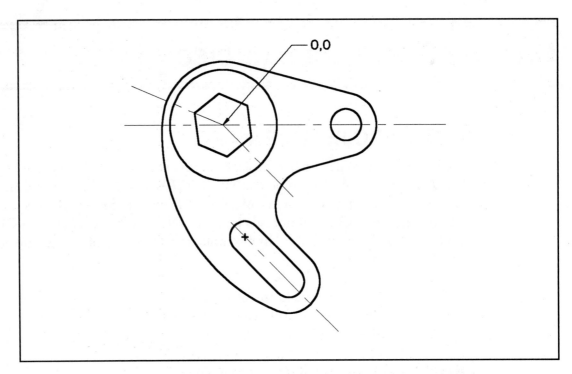

Figure 3-89 Establishing the Center of the Polygon (0,0)

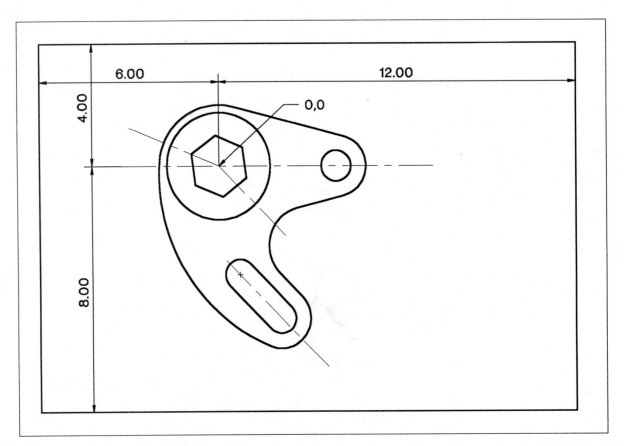

Figure 3-90 Establishing the Center of the Polygon (0,0) to Allow Room about the Object for Dimensioning

STEP 2   SET UP

The machine part will be plotted full scale on an 18" x 12" drawing sheet. It is good practice to establish the origin at a point on the object from which most dimensions will be given. In the case of the LEVER to be drawn, the center of the POLYGON will be the origin (0,0), as shown in Figure 3-89.

The location of the origin (0,0) on the drawing sheet will be established to allow room around the object for dimensioning and notes, as shown in Figure 3-90.

Placing the origin at the upper left third of the drawing sheet (as it appears to be on the object itself) is a reasonable start of the sheet layout (see Figure 3-91). Note that in CAD you can change the limits and origin location within the limits any time during the drawing process.

Set up the UNITS to decimal with 2 decimal places.

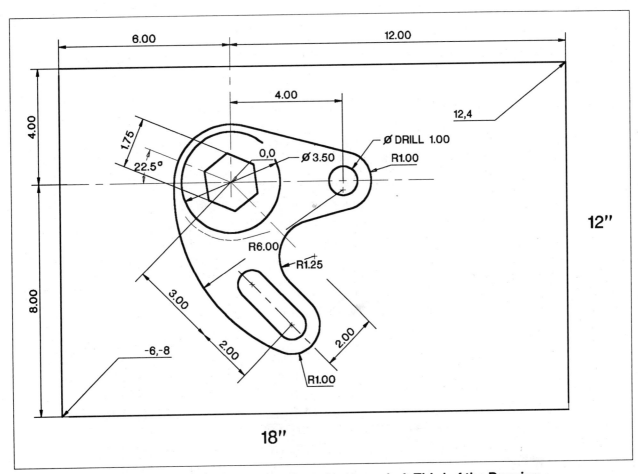

Figure 3-91 Placing the Origin at the Upper Left Third of the Drawing

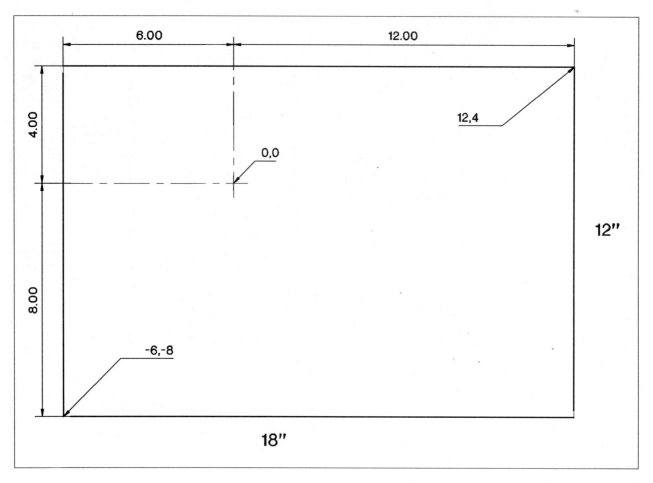

Figure 3-92 Placing the Origin Using Specified Limits

In order to place the origin, as shown in Figure 3-92 set up the LIMITS as shown below:

Command: **limits**
ON/OFF/<lower left corner> <0,0>: **-6,-8**
Upper right corner <12,9>: **12,4**
Command: **zoom**
All/Center/Dynamic/Extents/Left/Previous/Vmax/Window/<Scale(X/XP)>: **a**

STEP 3 Create the following layers with appropriate colors and linetypes as shown below:

LAYOUT1	GREEN	CONTINUOUS
LAYOUT2	BLUE	CONTINUOUS
OBJECT	RED	CONTINUOUS
CENTER	YELLOW	CENTER
PHANTOM	WHITE	PHANTOM
DIM	CYAN	CONTINUOUS

Set layer LAYOUT1 as the current layer, as shown in Figure 3-93.

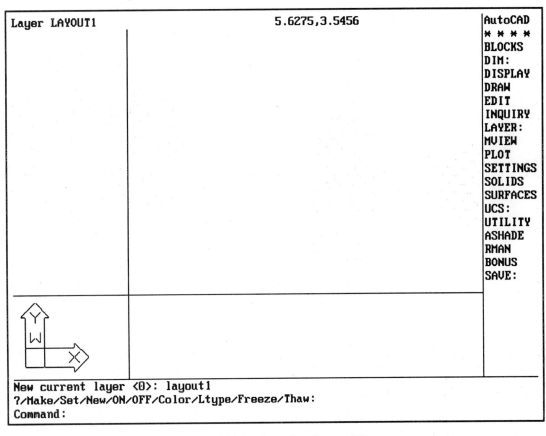

```
Layer LAYOUT1                        5.6275,3.5456              AutoCAD
                                                               * * * *
                                                               BLOCKS
                                                               DIM:
                                                               DISPLAY
                                                               DRAW
                                                               EDIT
                                                               INQUIRY
                                                               LAYER:
                                                               MVIEW
                                                               PLOT
                                                               SETTINGS
                                                               SOLIDS
                                                               SURFACES
                                                               UCS:
                                                               UTILITY
                                                               ASHADE
                                                               RMAN
                                                               BONUS
                                                               SAVE:


New current layer <0>: layout1
?/Make/Set/New/ON/OFF/Color/Ltype/Freeze/Thaw:
Command:
```

Figure 3-93 Setting the Current Layer

STEP 4 Set GRID and SNAP to 0.5.

STEP 5 Begin the layout of the drawing by drawing two circles as shown below:

> Command: **circle**
> 3P/2P/TTR/<Center point>: **0,0**
> Diameter/<Radius>: **2**
> Command: ⏎
> 3P/2P/TTR/<Center point>: **4,0**
> Diameter/<Radius>: **1**

STEP 6 Next you will draw the slot. It is offset 2" from a line rotated at 45 degrees clockwise, as shown in Figure 3-94. The centers on each end of the slot are 3" and 5" (along the offset line) from the origin. The SNAP Rotate command will assist in this layout:

> Command: **snap**
> Snap spacing or ON/OFF/Aspect/Rotate/Style <1.0>: **r**
> Base point <0,0>: ⏎
> Rotation angle <0>: **45**

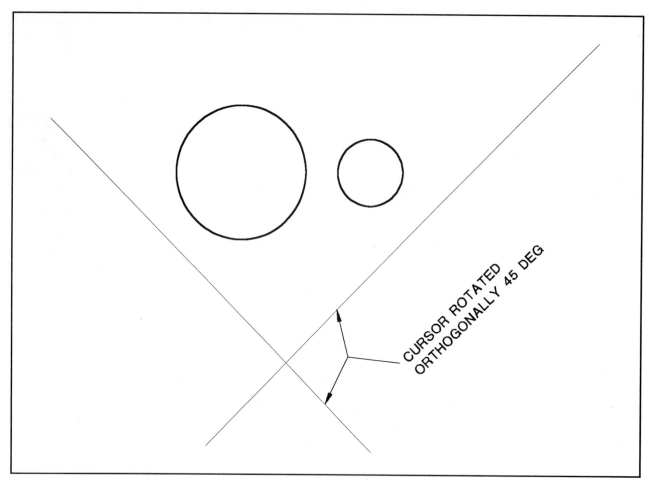

Figure 3-94 Drawing Two Circles with the Cursor Rotated Orthogonally 45 Degrees

Turn the Ortho mode to ON.

Command: **line**
From point: **0,0** *(See Figure 3-95.)*
To point: **@2<225** *(See Figure 3-96.)*
To point: **@3<315** *(See Figure 3-97.)*
To point: **@2<315**
To point: ⏎
Command:

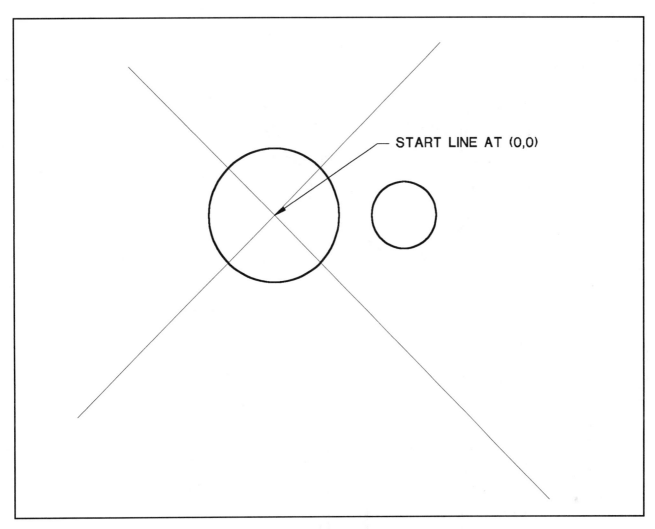

Figure 3-95 Placing the Start Point as (0,0)

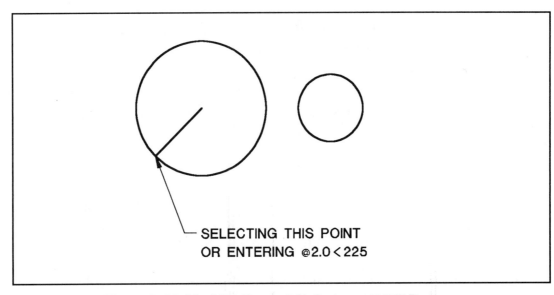

Figure 3-96 The Line Drawn 2 Units Long at 225 Degrees

Fundamentals II

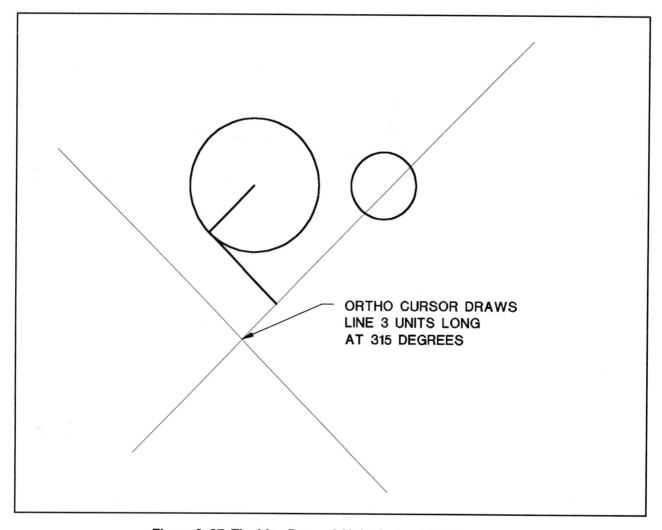

ORTHO CURSOR DRAWS
LINE 3 UNITS LONG
AT 315 DEGREES

Figure 3-97 The Line Drawn 3 Units Long at 315 Degrees

Rotate the SNAP to 0 degrees as shown in Figure 3-98 using the prompt sequence below:

Command: **snap**
Snap spacing or ON/OFF/Aspect/Rotate/Style <1.0>: **r**
Base point <0,0>: ⏎ *you wish to rotate about the origin*
Rotation angle <45>: **0**

Turn SNAP to OFF.

The result of the above layout procedure is one method of locating points whose distances can be established easily along some orthogonally rotated coordinate system.

STEP 7   The layout of the slotted arm, as shown in Figure 3-99, is drawn as follows:

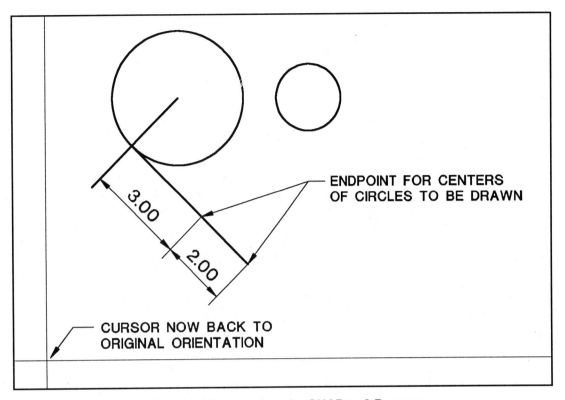

Figure 3-98 Rotating the SNAP to 0 Degrees

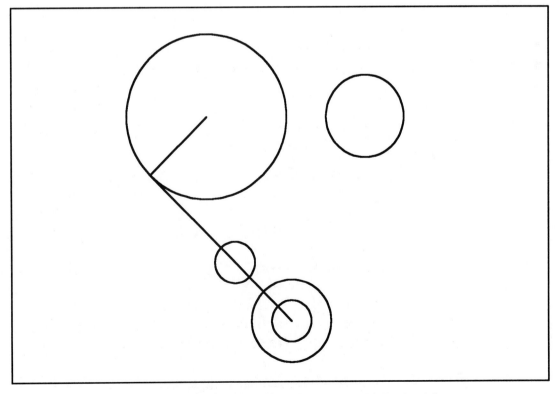

Figure 3-99 Establishing the Layout of the Slotted Arm

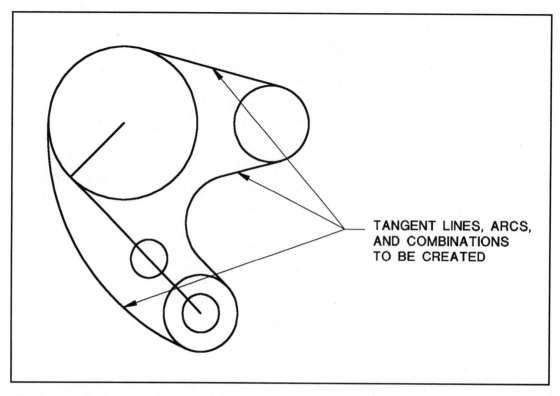

Figure 3-100 The Construction Lines and Circles for Drawing the Basis of the Outline of the Object

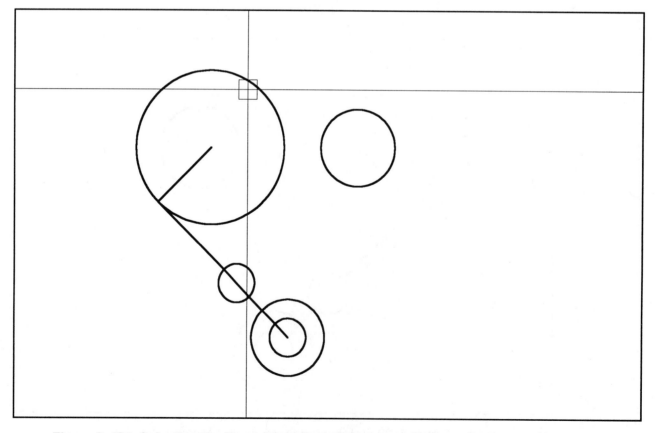

Figure 3-101 Selecting the Upper Right Part of the Large Circle to Create a Tangent Line

Command: **circle**
3P/2P/TTR/<Center point>: **endp**
of *(select intermediate endpoint between last two lines)*
Diameter/<Radius>: **.5**
Command: ⏎
3P/2P/TTR/<Center point>: **endp**
of *(select extreme endpoint of slot center line)*
Diameter/<Radius>: **.5**
Command: ⏎
3P/2P/TTR/<Center point>: **endp**
of *(select extreme endpoint again)*
Diameter/<Radius>: **1**

The construction lines (and circles) in Figure 3–99 are the basis for drawing the rest of the outline of the object which includes the lines, arcs, and combinations of line and arc segments shown in Figure 3–100.

STEP 8 The following sequence will allow you to draw the outline of the object which includes lines, arcs, and combinations of line and arc segments.

Command: **line**
From point: **tan**
to *(select upper right part of large circle), as shown in Figure 3–101*
To point: **tan**
to *(select upper part of small circle), as shown in Figure 3–102*
To point: ⏎ *(See Figure 3–103)*
Command:

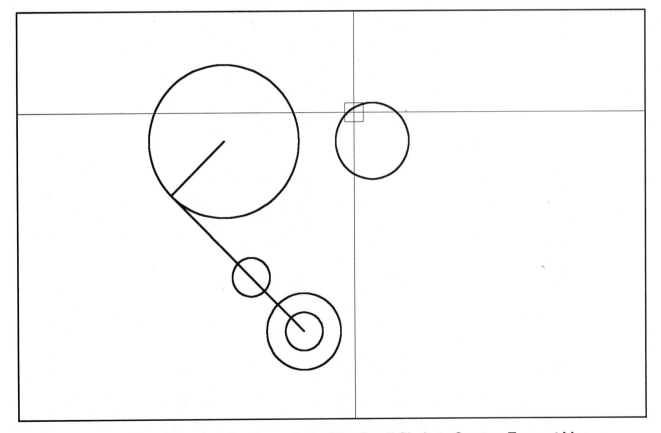

Figure 3–102 Selecting the Upper Part of the Small Circle to Create a Tangent Line

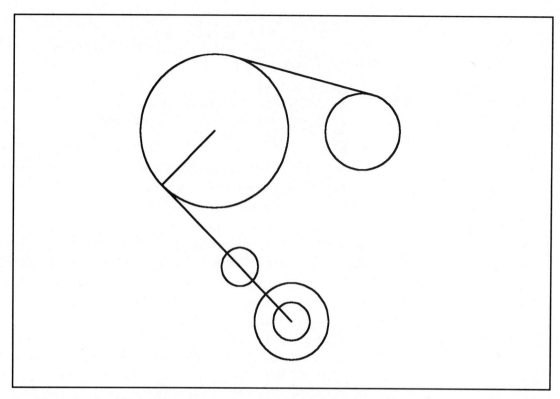

Figure 3-103 The Object with Two Lines Tangent to the Large and Small Circles

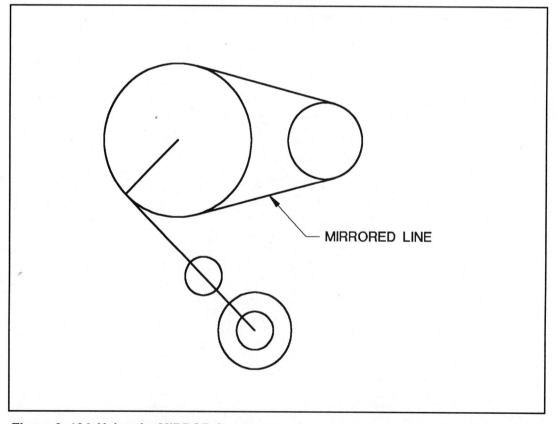

MIRRORED LINE

Figure 3-104 Using the MIRROR Command to Create a Construction Line that is Below and Tangent to the Same Two Circles

To create the construction line that is below and tangent to the same two circles in Figure 3-104, one method is to use the MIRROR command as follows:

Command: **mirror**
Select objects: *select last line created*
Select objects: ⏎
First point of mirror line: **0,0** *any point with y coordinate=0*
Second point: **4,0** *any other point with y coordinate=0*
Delete old objects? <N>: ⏎

Using the center line of the slot and copying it to one edge of the 1" radius circle helps generate the smaller (1.25 radius) tangent arc, as shown in Figures 3-105 and 3-106.

Command: **copy**
Select objects: *select slot center line*
Select objects: ⏎
<Base point or displacement>/Multiple: *select slot center line*
Second point of displacement: **@1<45**

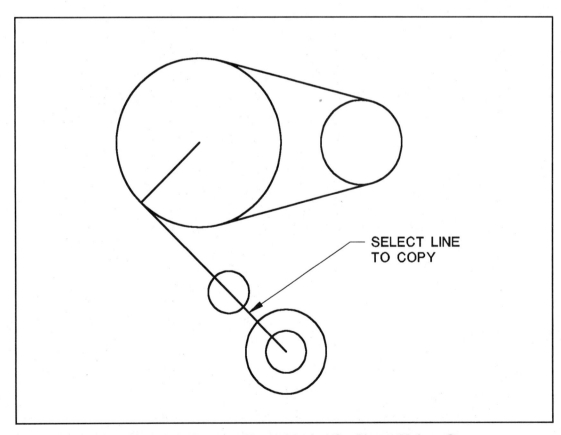

Figure 3-105 Using the Center Line of the Slot to Make a Copy

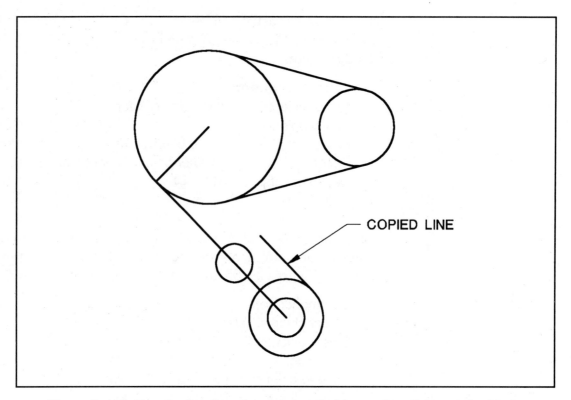

Figure 3-106 Result after Copying the Center Line to One Edge of the Circle

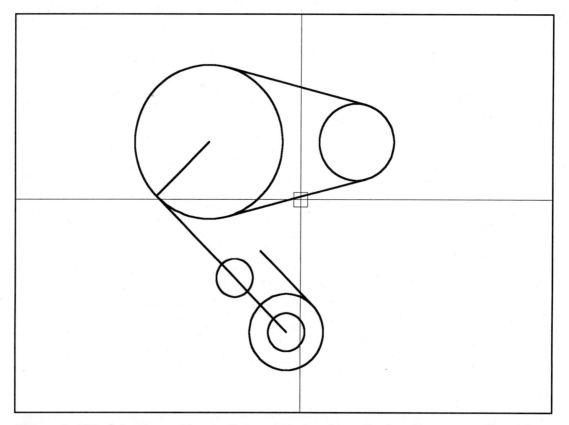

Figure 3-107 Selecting a Line to Draw a Circle with a Radius Tangent to Two Lines Using the TTR Option

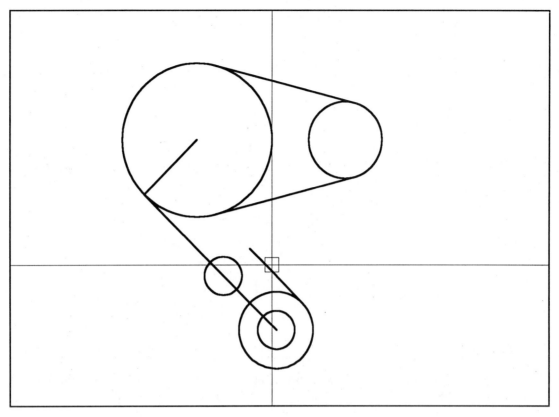

Figure 3-108 Selecting the Second Line to Draw a Circle with the TTR Option

Draw a circle with a radius 1.25 inches tangent to two lines using the TTR option, as shown in the following prompt sequence:

> Command: **circle**
> 3P/2P/TTR/<Center point>: **t** *for the TTR option*
> Enter Tangent spec: *identify line, as shown in Figure 3-107*
> Enter second Tangent spec: *identify line as shown in Figure 3-108*
> Radius: **1.25** *(See Figure 3-109.)*

Draw another circle with a radius 6 inches tangent to two circles using the TTR option, as shown in the following prompt sequence:

> Command: **circle**
> 3P/2P/TTR/<Center point>: **t**
> Enter Tangent spec: *identify circle, as shown in Figure 3-110*
> Enter second Tangent spec: *identify circle, as shown in Figure 3-111*
> Radius: **6** *(See Figure 3-112.)*

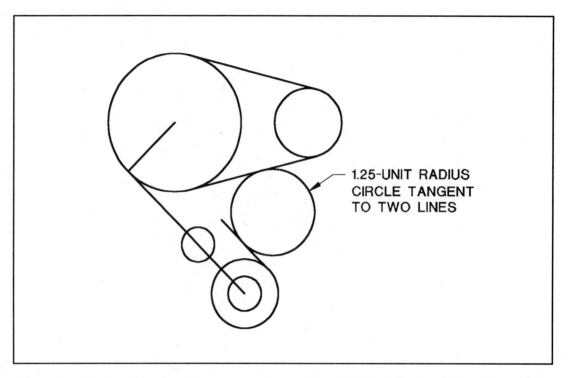

Figure 3-109 The Drawing After Generation with a 1.25-Unit Radius Circle Tangent to Two Lines

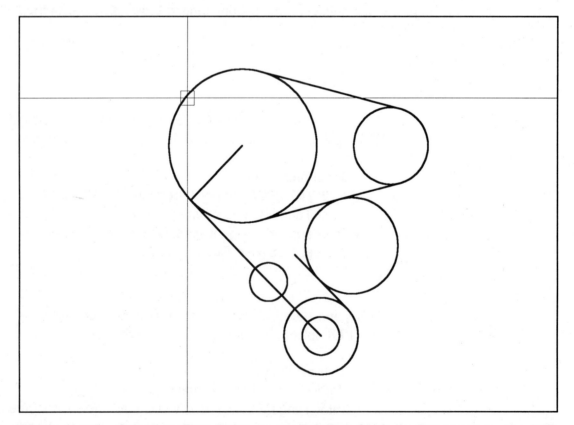

Figure 3-110   Selecting First Point on an Existing Circle in Response to the TTR Option

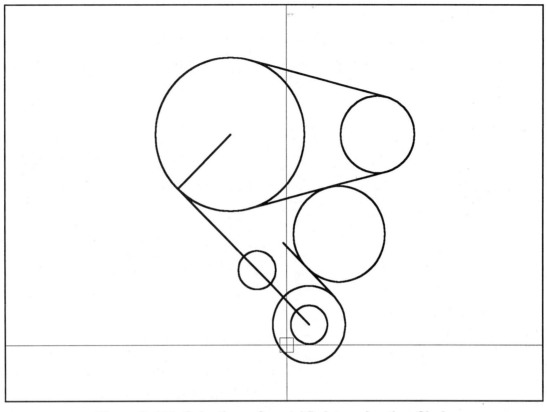

Figure 3-111 Selecting a Second Point on Another Circle

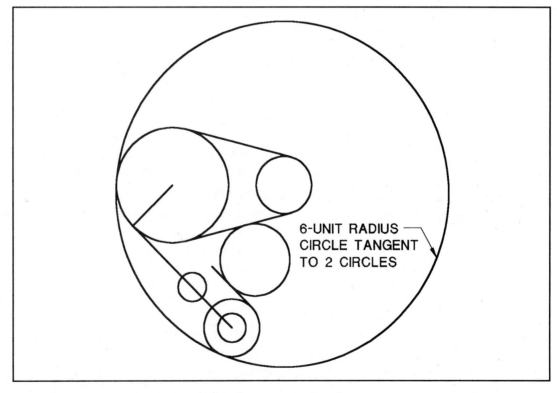

Figure 3-112 The Drawing After Generation with a 6-Unit Radius Circle Tangent to Two Circles

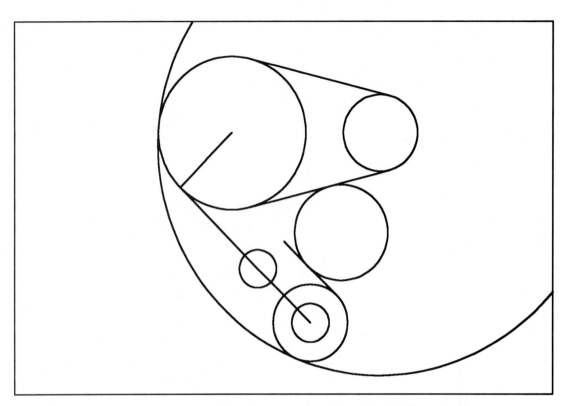

Figure 3-113 The Construction Elements in Place

The construction elements are now in place, as shown in **Figure 3-113**.

> ***NOTE:*** It appears that the correct arcs could be established from the tangent circles that have been generated during the previous sequences. The procedure would call for breaking the 6" radius circle at the points of tangency to the two smaller circles. However, you should note that the method the computer uses to generate circles may make it difficult to OSNAP to that point using the INTERSECTION mode. Therefore, trying to use the BREAK command in this manner is not recommended. But, you can specify an exact endpoint by the following sequences.

STEP 8   Set layer LAYOUT2 to be the current layer.
Draw construction lines to establish arcs and arc-lines.

> Command: **line**
> From point: **cen**
> of *(select the 2"-radius circle), as shown in Figure 3-114*
>
> To point: **per**
> to *(select the 6"-radius circle), as shown in Figure 3-115*
> To point: ↵ *(See Figure 3-116.)*
> Command:

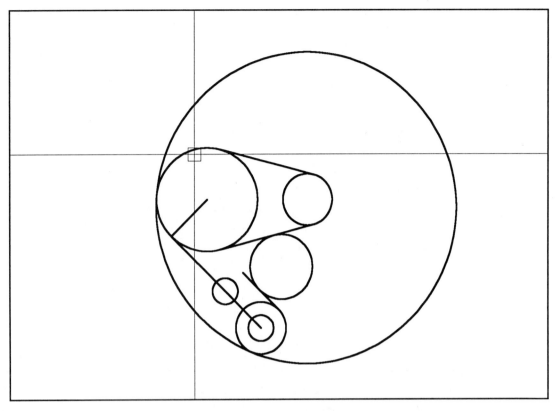

Figure 3-114 Selecting the 2"-Radius Circle to Draw a Line from the Center Point

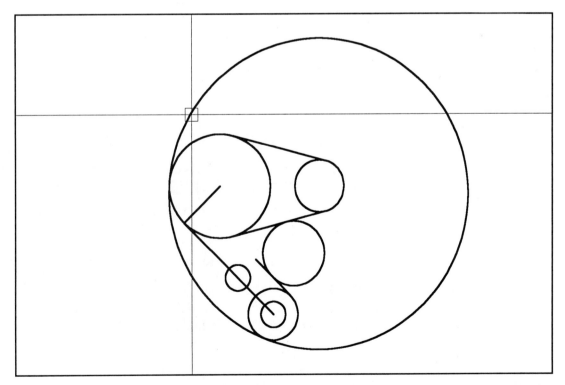

Figure 3-115 Selecting the 6"-Radius Circle to Draw the Line Perpendicular to the Circle

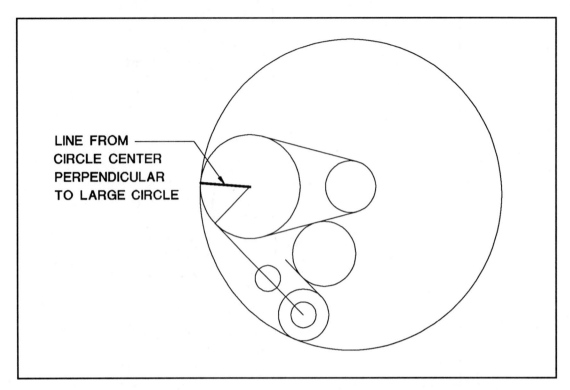

Figure 3-116 A Line Drawn from the Center of the 2" Circle Perpendicular to a Large Circle

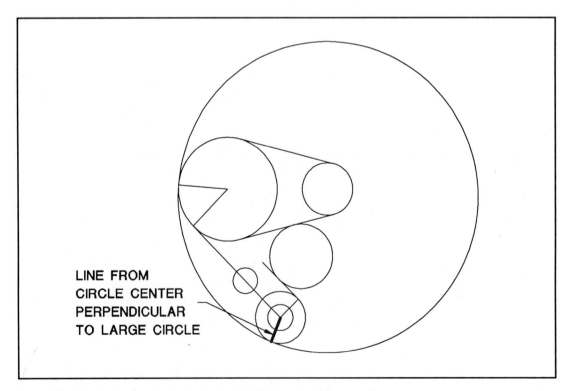

Figure 3-117 The Drawing After Selecting a Line from a Circle Center and Perpendicular to a Large Circle to Generate a Line at a 1"-Radius Circle

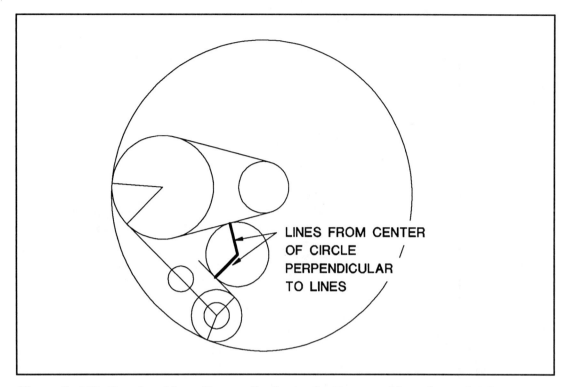

LINES FROM CENTER
OF CIRCLE
PERPENDICULAR
TO LINES

Figure 3-118 Drawing Lines Perpendicular to the Tangent Lines from the Center of a Circle

The same procedure can be used to establish a line at the 1"-radius circle. Also, a line must be drawn from the center of the circle perpendicular to the 45-degree line on the edge of the circle, as shown in Figure 3-117.

Then lines from the center of the 1.25"-radius circle can be drawn perpendicular to the tanget lines, as shown in Figure 3-118.

Similarly, three additional center perpendicular lines should be drawn, as shown in Figure 3-119.

The eight center perpendicular lines provide the end points necessary to draw the complete outline of the object. It is convenient to have only the eight lines visible on the screen and one method is to turn all layers OFF except LAYOUT2, the current one.

STEP 9   When you turn off layer LAYOUT1 and set the layer OBJECT as your current layer, your drawing should look like the figure shown in Figure 3-120.

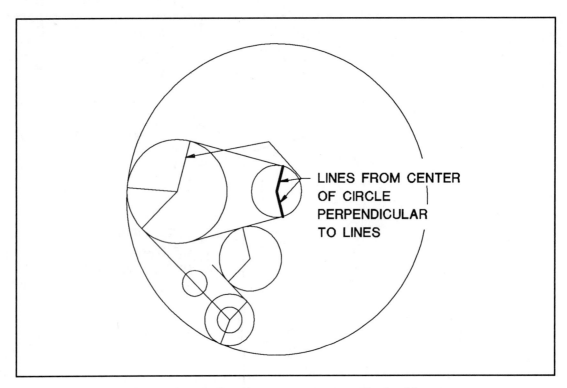

Figure 3-119 Drawing center perpendicular Lines

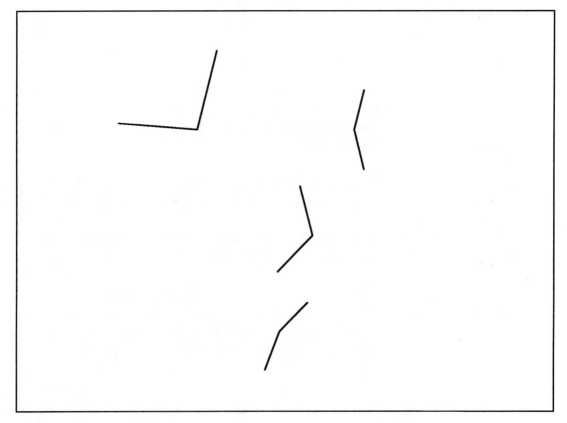

Figure 3-120 Setting the Layer OBJECT as your Current Layer and Turning Other Layers Off

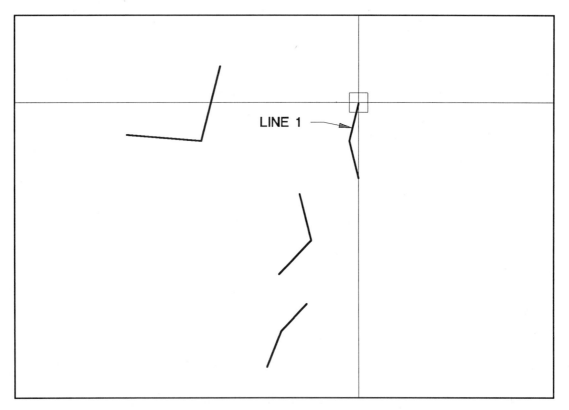

Figure 3-121 Drawing the Outline Using the LINE Command and Selecting Line 1

STEP 10   Set the running OSNAP command to ENDP as shown below, which is very convenient to Snap to the endpoints of the objects.

> Command: **osnap**
> Object Snap modes: **endp**
> Command:

Draw the outline by Snapping to the objects by using LINE and ARC commands.

> Command: **line**
> From point: *select line 1, as shown in Figure 3-121*
> To point: *select line 2, as shown in Figure 3-122*
> To point: ⏎ *(See Figure 3-123).*
> Command:

Draw an arc by utilizing the line-arc continuation feature.

> Command:**arc**
> Center/<Start point>: ⏎
> Endpoint: *select line 3, as shown in Figure 3-124*

Th arc will be drawn as shown in Figure 3-125.

> Command:

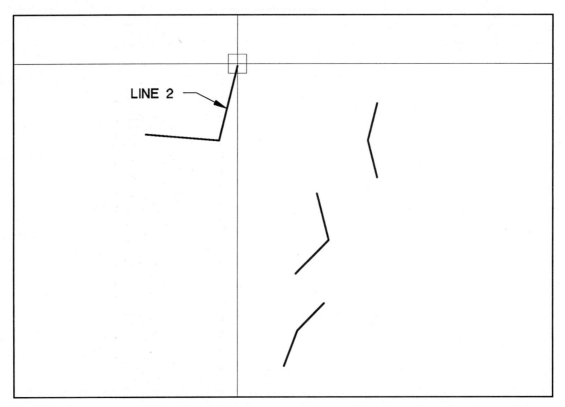

Figure 3-122 Drawing the Outline Using the LINE Command and Selecting Line 2

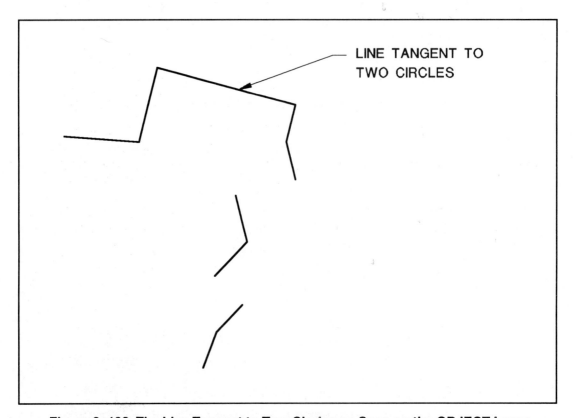

Figure 3-123 The Line Tangent to Two Circles as Seen on the OBJECT Layer

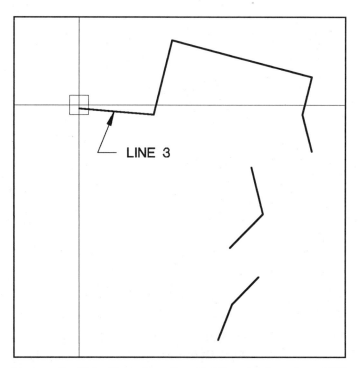

Figure 3-124 Drawing the Outline Using the ARC Command and Selecting Line 3

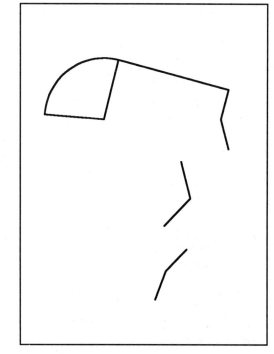

Figure 3-125 The Arc as Seen on the OBJECT Layer

Pressing ⏎ recalls the ARC command. Pressing it a second time invokes the arc-arc continuation (see Figures 3-126 and 3-127).

      Endpoint: *select line 4*
      Command:

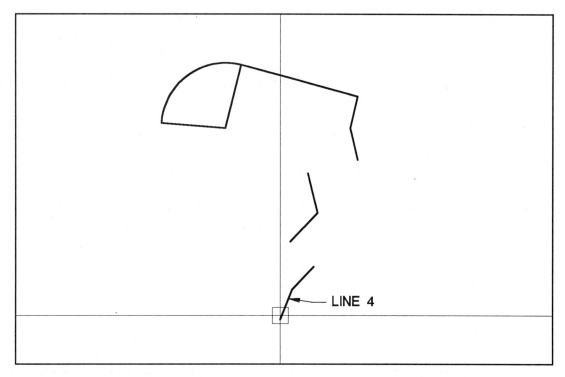

Figure 3-126 Drawing the Outline Using the ARC Command and Selecting Line 4

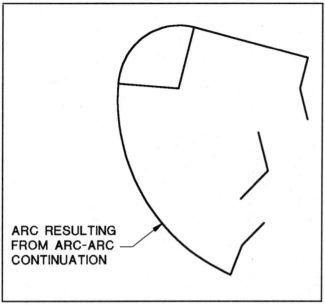

Figure 3-127 The Arc Resulting from the Application of an Arc-Arc Continuation

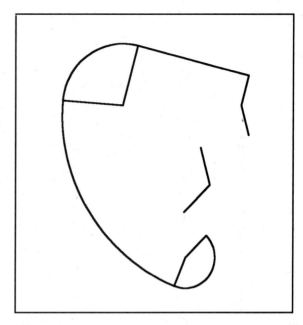

Figure 3-128 Drawing Resulting from the Application of another Arc-Arc Continuation

Draw another arc-arc continuation and your drawing should look like the drawing shown in Figure 3-128.

Draw another arc-line continuation and your drawing should look like the drawing shown in Figure 3-129.

The next arc-line-arc segments can be drawn using the same procedures, resulting as shown in Figure 3-130.

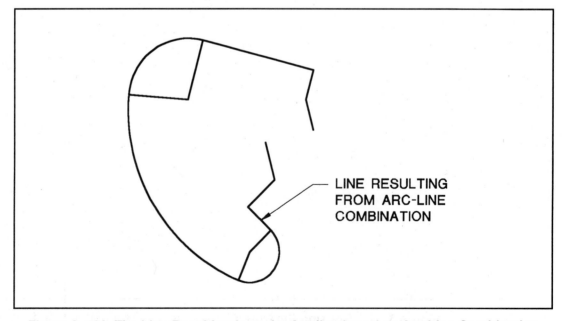

Figure 3-129 The Line Resulting from the Application of an Arc-Line Combination

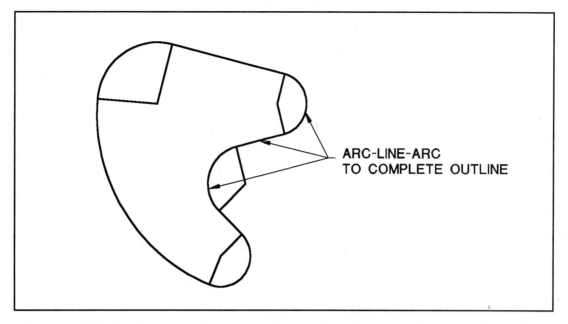

Figure 3-130 The Drawing After Application of Arc-Line-Arc to Complete the Outline

STEP 10 Turn off layer LAYOUT2 to display the outline only, as shown in Figure 3-131.

STEP 11 To complete the drawing, you need to use the construction lines drawn on layer LAYOUT1. So, turn on layer LAYOUT1 (see Figure 3-132).

STEP 12 Draw two parallel lines to the slot center line, as shown in Figure 3-133, by using the OFFSET command as shown below:

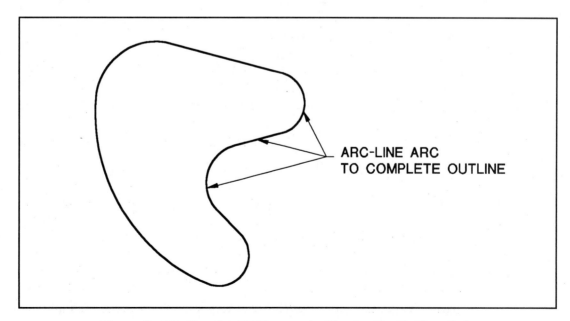

Figure 3-131 Turning Off Layers to Display the Outline Only

Fundamentals II

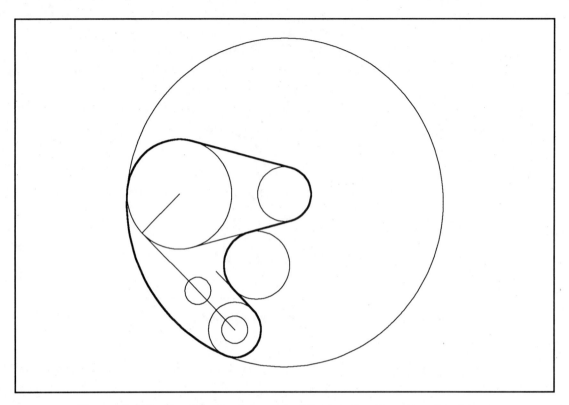

Figure 3-132 Turning On Layers to Display the Construction Lines

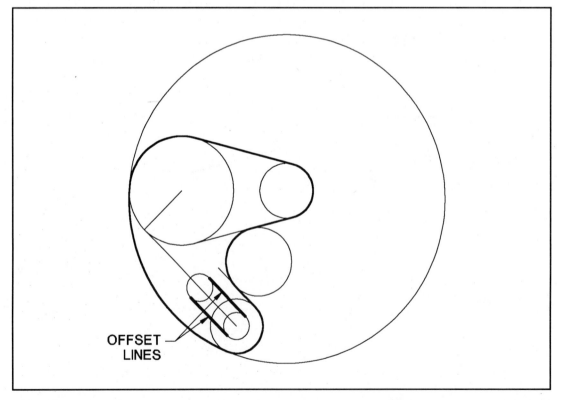

Figure 3-133 Drawing Two Parallel Lines to the Slot Center Line Using the OFFSET Command

Command: **offset**
Offset distance or Through <Through>: **.5**
Select object to offset: *select the center line*
Side to offset: *select a point on right side of center line*
Select object to offset: *select the center line*
Side to offset: *select a point on left side of center line*
Select object to offset: ⏎
Command:

The offset lines will be placed on layer LAYOUT1 and by using the CHPROP command we can move it to layer OBJECT as shown below:

Command: **chprop**
Select object: *select two new lines*
Select object: ⏎
Change what property (Color/LAyer/Ltype/Thickness)?: **la**
New layer <layout1): **object**
Change what property (Color/LAyer/Ltype/Thickness)?: ⏎
Command:

STEP 14 Draw the arcs at the ends of the slots by using the ARC command, as shown in Figure 3-134, using the following prompt sequence:

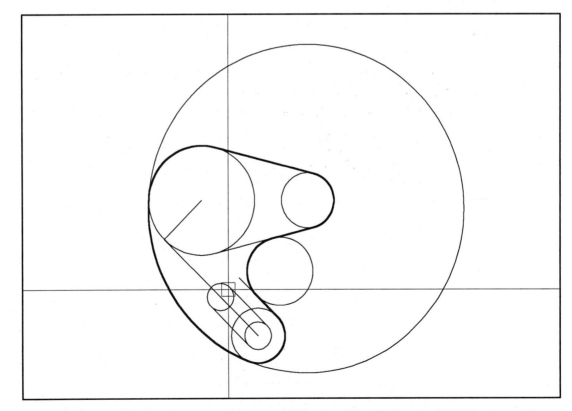

Figure 3-134 Drawing Arcs at the Ends of the Slot Using the ARC Command

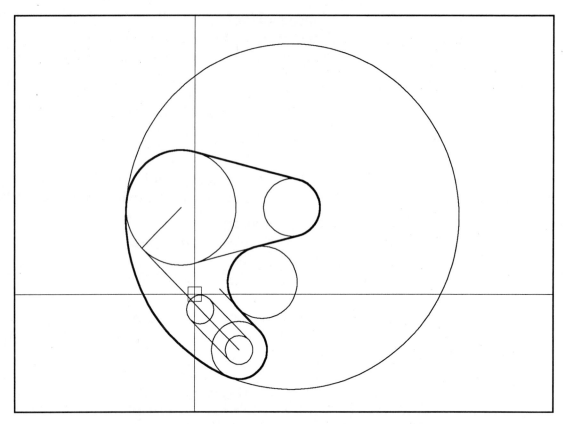

Figure 3-135 Selecting the Center Point of the Circle

```
Command: arc
Center/<Start point>: endp
of (select line)
Center/End/<Second point>: c
Center: cen
of (select circle), as shown in Figure 3-135
Angle/Length of chord/<Endpoint>: endp
of (select other line)
```

Repeating the above steps on the other end of the slot results in an arc drawn to the ends of the slot, as shown in Figure 3-136.

STEP 15 Before turning off the construction layer LAYOUT1, a minor reference line-arc combination should be drawn.

```
Command: line
From point: near
to (select line as shown in Figure 3-137)
To point: endp
of (select where line is tangent to 2"-radius circle), as shown in
    Figure 3-138
To point: ⏎
Command:
```

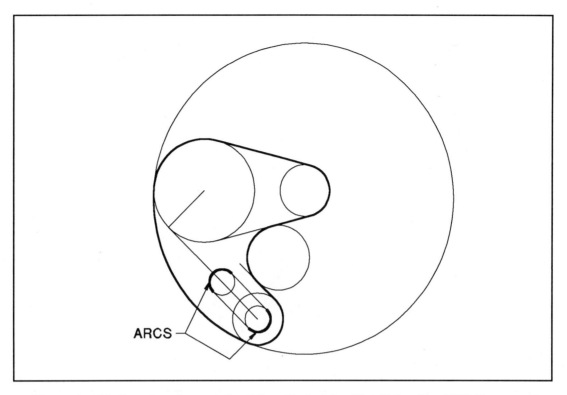

Figure 3-136 Drawing Arcs at the Other End of the Slot Using the ARC Command

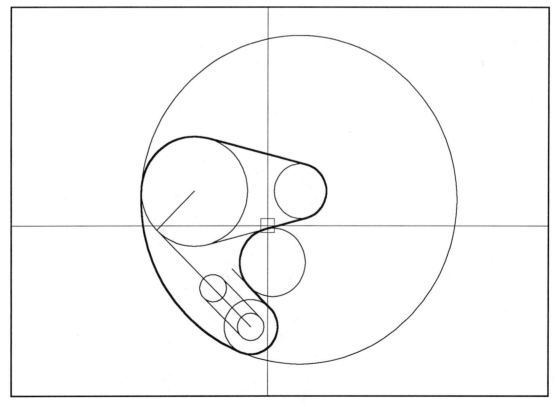

Figure 3-137 Selecting a Line-Arc Combination before Turning Off the Construction Layer

Fundamentals II

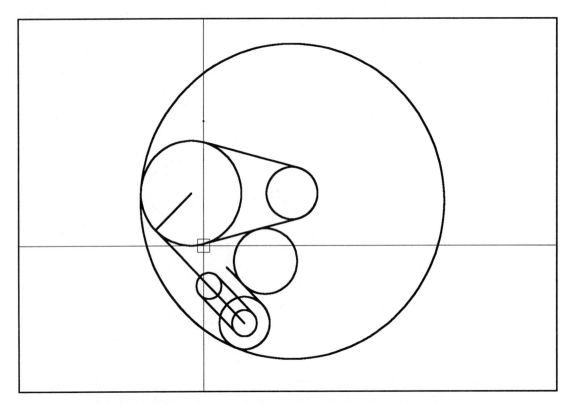

Figure 3-138 Selecting Where the Line is Tangent to a 2"-Radius Circle

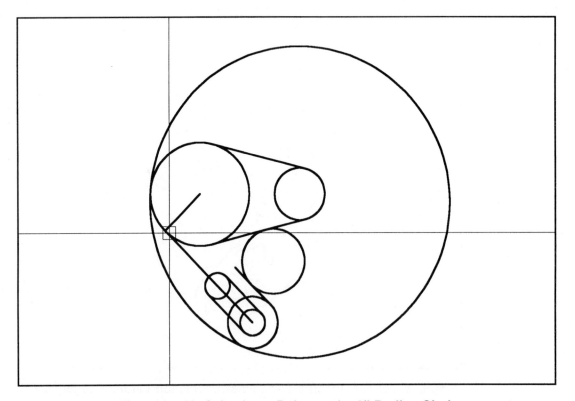

Figure 3-139 Selecting a Point on the 2"-Radius Circle

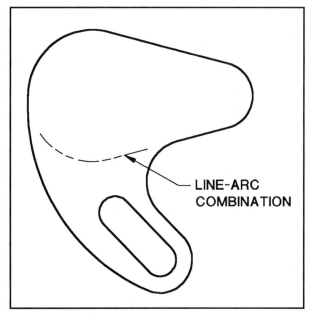

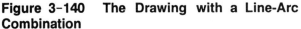

LINE-ARC
COMBINATION

**Figure 3-140 The Drawing with a Line-Arc
Combination**

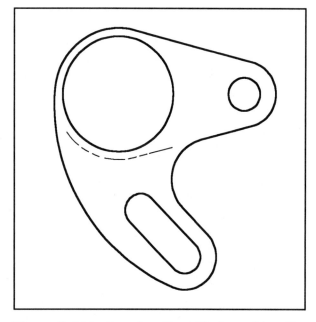

**Figure 3-141 Drawing Two Circles with a Ra-
dius of 1.75 and 0.5**

Command: **arc**
Center/<Start point>: ⏎
End point: **near**
to *(select point on 2"-radius circle as shown in Figure 3-139)*

STEP 16   By using the CHPROP command, move the two objects drawn in STEP 15 to layer PHANTOM.

STEP 17   Turn off layer LAYOUT1 and your drawing should look like the drawing shown in Figure 3-140.

STEP 18   Draw two circles, as shown in Figure 3-141, with a radius of 1.75 and 0.5, respectively.

Command: **circle**
3P/2P/TTR/<Center point>: **0,0**
Diameter/<Radius>: **1.75**
Command: **circle**
3P/2P/TTR/<Center point>: **4,0**
Diameter/<Radius>: **.5**
Command:

Draw a polygon, as shown in Figure 3-142, using the following prompt sequence:

Command: **polygon**
Number of sides: **6**
Edge/<Center of polygon>: **0,0**
Inscribed in circle/Circumscribed about circle(I/C): **c**
Radius of circle: **@.875<67.5**

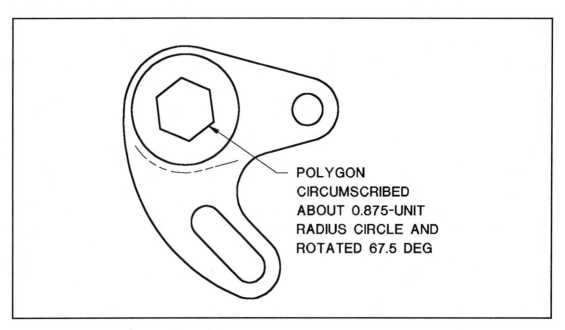

POLYGON
CIRCUMSCRIBED
ABOUT 0.875-UNIT
RADIUS CIRCLE AND
ROTATED 67.5 DEG

Figure 3-142 Drawing a Polygon Circumscribed about a 0.875-Unit Radius Circle and Rotated 67.5 Degrees

The last entry specified the radius distance (0.875) and the midpoint of one of the edges, thereby establishing the angle of rotation.

The object is complete along with one reference line/arc.

STEP 18 Set layer CENTER as the current layer.

The following is the command sequence to draw the center lines for the circles, as shown in Figure 3-143.

```
Command: line
From point: -3.75,0
To point: 7.25,0
To point: ⏎
Command: ⏎
From point: 0,0
To point: @7.25<315
To point: ⏎
Command: copy
Select object: l for last object drawn
Select object: ⏎
<Base point on displacement>/Multiple: select a point on the object
Second point of displacement: @2<225
Command:
```

The last line can be broken where required with the BREAK command.

STEP 19 Set layer DIM as the current layer.

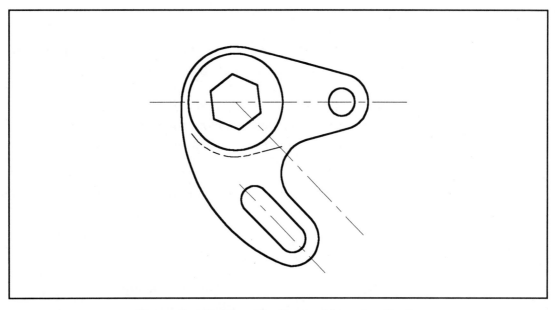

Figure 3-143 Drawing Center Lines for Circles

STEP 20   Set the following dimensioning variables:

Command: **dim**
DIM: **dimtad**
Current value <Off> New value: **on**
DIM: **dimtih**
Current value <On> New value: **off**

Dimension the drawing as shown in Figure 3-144.

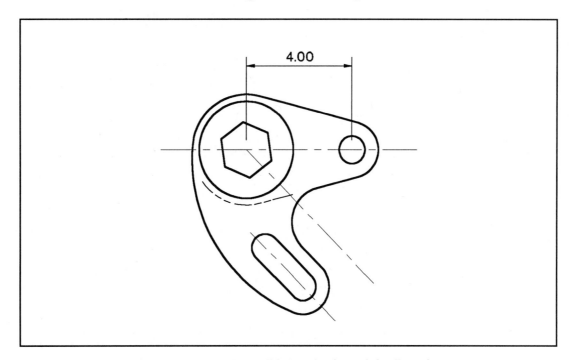

Figure 3-144 Linear Dimensioning of the Drawing

DIM: *select LINEAR*
DIM: **horiz**
First extension line origin or RETURN to select: **cen**
of *(select large circle whose center is 0,0)*
Second extension line origin: **cen**
of *(select smaller circle whose center is 4,0)*
Dimension line location: *select point above object*
Dimension text <4.00>: ⏎
DIM:

Placing a linear dimension at a rotated angle, as shown in Figure 3-145.

Dim: **rotated**
Dimension line angle <0>: **315**

In response to the "Dimension line angle:" prompt, you can also specify the angle by selecting two points.

First extension line origin or RETURN to select: *select center of circle or 0,0*
Second extension line origin: **cen**
of *(select the arc at the upper end of the slot)*
Dimension line location: *select a point to locate dimension line*
Dimension text <3.00>: ⏎

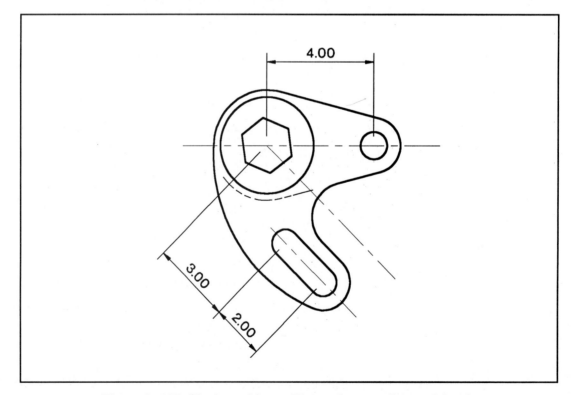

Figure 3-145 Placing a Linear Dimension at a Rotated Angle

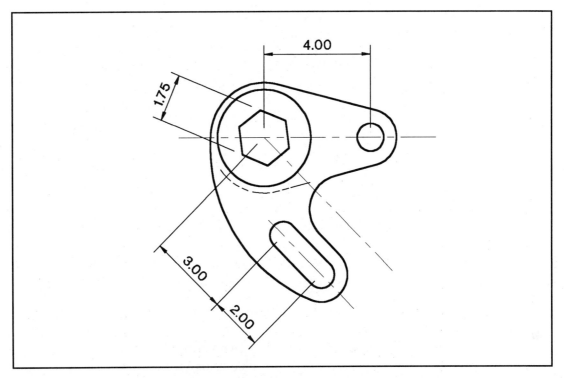

Figure 3-146 Using Rotated Linear Dimensioning to Dimension the End of the Polygon

Use the Continue option to continue the linear dimension.

> DIM: **continue**
> Second extension line origin or RETURN to select: **cen**
>   of *(select the arc at the lower end of the slot)*
> Dimension text <2.00>: ⏎
> DIM:

The end of the polygon can be dimensioned, as shown in Figure 3-146, by continuing with the rotated linear dimensioning mode as follows:

> DIM: **rotate**
> Dimension line angle <0>: **endp**
> of *(select an endpoint near polygon vertex)*
> Second point: **endp**
> of *(select other endpoint near polygon vertex)*

The above two points determine the angle of rotation. They are selected again as extension line origins as follows:

> First extension line origin or RETURN to select: **endp**
> of *(select first point again)*
> Second extension line origin: **endp**
> of *(select second point again)*
> Dimension line location: *select location for dimension line*
> Dimension text <1.75>: ⏎

Set the following dimensioning variables as shown below before continuing the dimensioning:

DIM: **dimse1**
Current value <Off> New value: **on**
DIM: **dimse2**
Current value <Off> New value: **on**

Place another linear rotated dimension between the center of the polygon and the center line of the slot as shown in Figure 3–147 by using the following prompt sequence:

DIM: **rotate**
Dimension line angle <0>: **near**
to *(select the center line of the slot)*
Second point: **per**
to *(select other center line going through center of polygon)*

In order to establish the rotated dimension angle to be perpendicular to the center lines chosen above, the NEAR-PERPENDICULAR sequence is used. The two points determine the angle of rotation. They are selected again as extension line origins. But, you may now use a NEAR-NEAR sequence as follows:

First extension line origin or RETURN to select: **near**
to *(select first point again)*
Second extension line origin: **near**

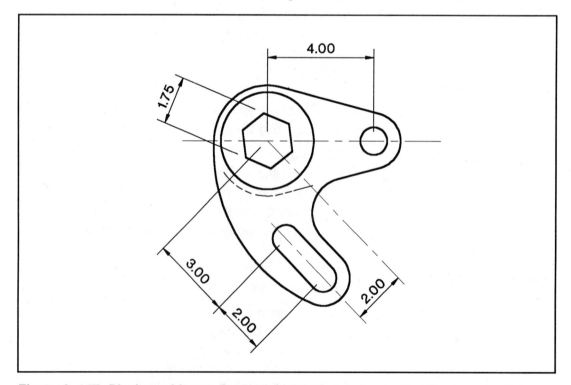

Figure 3–147 Placing a Linear Rotated Dimension between the Center of a Polygon and the Center Line of the Slot

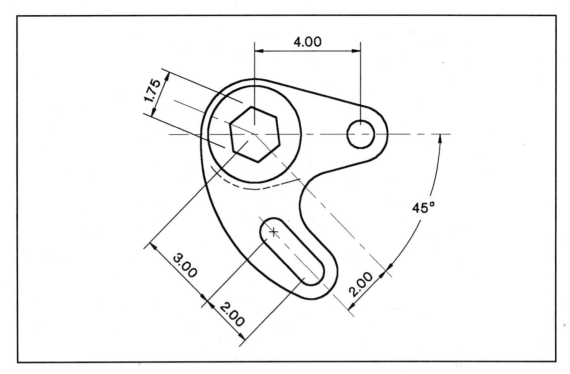

Figure 3-148 Placing an Angular Dimension on the Drawing

to *(select second point again)*
Dimension line location: *select location for dimension line*
Dimension text <2.00>: ⏎

Place an angular dimension, as shown in Figure 3-148, using the following prompt sequence:

DIM: **ang**
Select first line: *select a 45-deg line through the center of the polygon*
Second line: *select a horizontal line through the center of the polygon*
Enter dimension line arc location: **int**
of *(select where arrow of last dimension touches line)*
Dimension text <45>: ⏎
Enter text location: ⏎

Set the following dimensioning variables as shown below before continuing the dimensioning:

DIM: **dimtix**
Current value <On> New value: **off**
DIM: **dimtofl**
Current value <On> New value: **off**
DIM: **dimcen**
Current value <0.09> New value: **0**
DIM: **dimtad**
Current value <On> New value: **off**

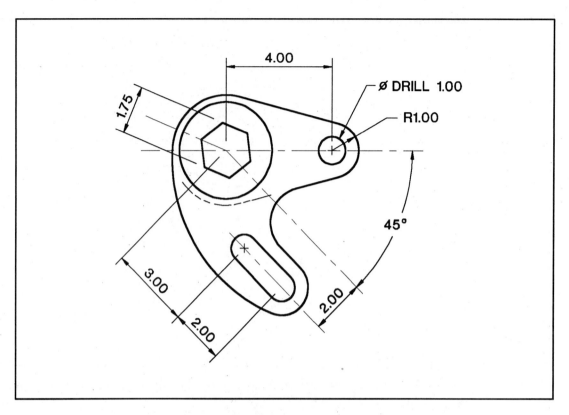

Figure 3–149 Overriding a Prompt to Place Text

Place the necessary radius and diameter dimensioning for circles and arc.

> DIM: **radius**
> Select arc or circle: *select arc at upper right of object*

Note that the point on the arc that you select will determine where the arrow will be.

> Dimension text <1.00>: ⏎
> Enter leader length for text: *select a point on screen*
> DIM: **diameter**
> Select arc or circle: *select circle at upper right of object*

The point selection applies in the same manner as with the radius dimensioning above. Also, in order to include the "DRILL" in the text, as shown in Figure 3–149, you will have to override the "Dimension text:" prompt as follows.

> Dimension text <1.00>: **%%cDRILL 1.00**
> Enter leader length for text: *select a point on screen*

The same sequence for radius dimensioning can be followed to dimension the arc at the lower end of the object near the end of the slot resulting in the object as shown in Figure 3–150.

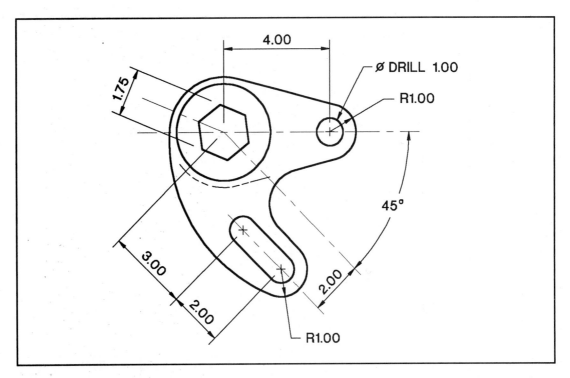

Figure 3-150 Using Radius Dimensioning to Dimension an Arc at the Lower End of an Object Near the End of the Slot

Dimension the remaining parts of the drawing. The completed drawing should look like the drawing shown in Figure 3-151.

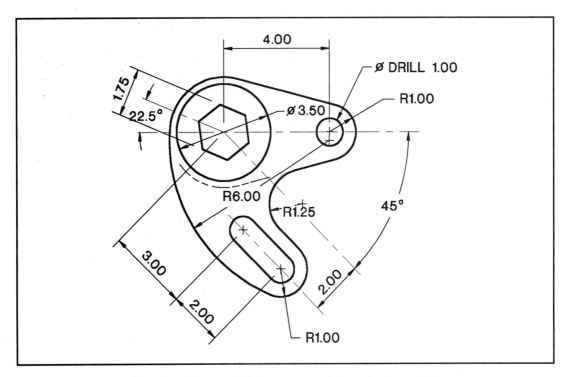

Figure 3-151 The Completed Drawing in AutoCAD

Fundamentals II

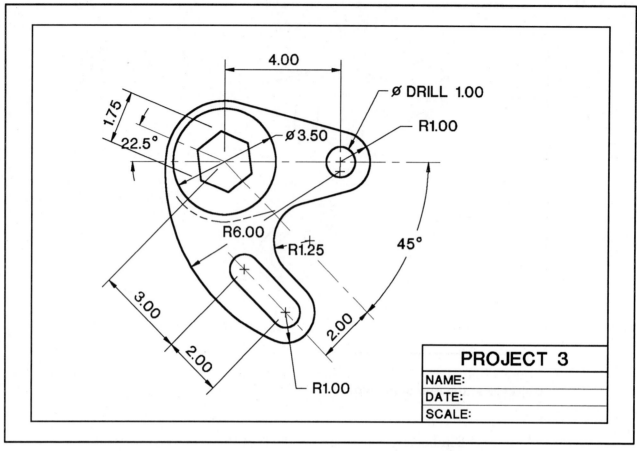

Figure 3–152 Drawing a Border to Create a Title Block for the Completed Drawing

STEP 21 Set the current layer to BORDER.

STEP 22 Draw a border and create a title block, as shown in Figure 3–152.

STEP 23 End the drawing.

CHAPTER 4

Fundamentals III

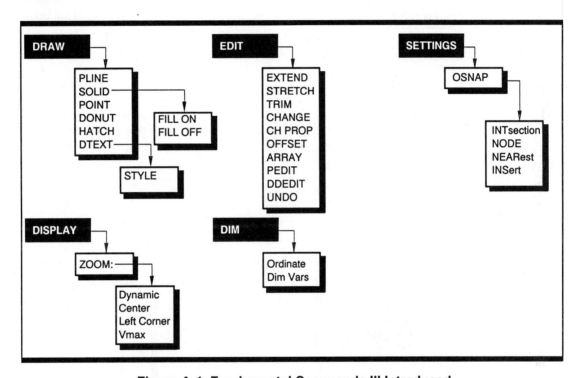

Figure 4-1 Fundamental Commands III Introduced

In this chapter additional DRAW and EDIT commands are covered, which include PLINE, POINT, SOLID, HATCH and STRETCH, EXTEND, TRIM, and CHANGE. In addition, advanced options of the DISPLAY-ZOOM command are explained. See Figure 4-1 for the commands and options that are covered in this chapter.

DRAW COMMANDS

In this chapter, additional DRAW commands are explained, including PLINE, POINT, SOLID, DOUGHNUT, HATCH, and DTEXT, in addition to the commands explained in Chapters 2 and 3.

PLINE (Polyline) Command

The "poly" in Polyline means multiple connected straight line and/or arc segments. They are drawn by invoking the PLINE command and then selecting a series of points. In this respect, PLINE functions much like the LINE command. However, when completed, the segments act like a single entity when operated by certain EDIT commands. You can specify the endpoints using only 2D (x,y) coordinates.

The versatile PLINE command can also be used to draw wide lines of different linetypes, arcs, tapered lines, and a filled circle.

The area and perimeter of a 2D Polyline can be calculated.

Where to Start Invoke the PLINE command from the Screen Root Menu Draw, (Figure 4–2), the pull-down menu Draw (Figure 4–3), or at the "Command:" prompt, you can type in **PLINE** and press ⏎ or spacebar.

    Command: **pline**
    From point:

You can specify the start point of the line by absolute coordinates or by using your pointing device. As soon as you select the start point of the Polyline, the current line-width is displayed:

    Current line-width is 0.0000.

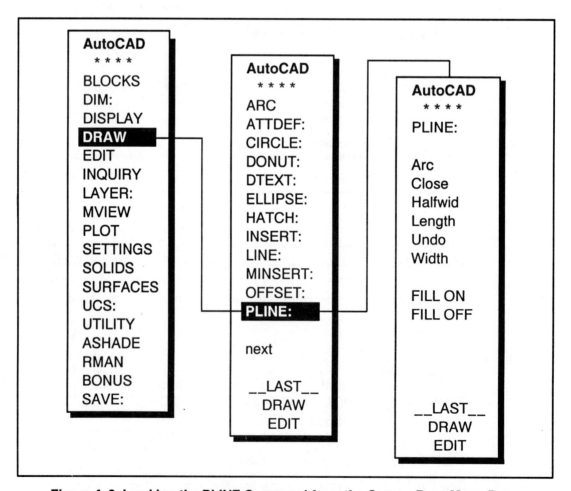

Figure 4–2 Invoking the PLINE Command from the Screen Root Menu Draw

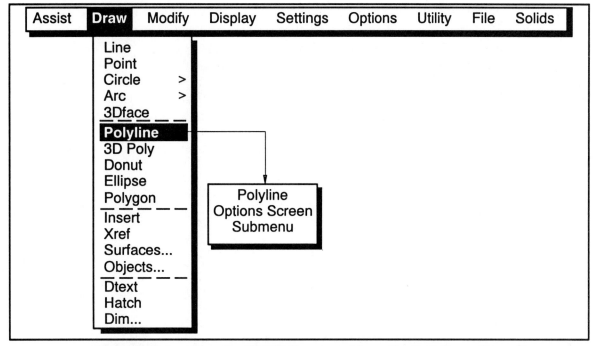

Figure 4–3 Invoking the PLINE Command from the Pull-Down Menu Draw

This width will remain the same for all the following Polyline segments until you select a different width. AutoCAD continues with the prompt:

Arc/Close/Halfwidth/Length/Undo/Width/<Endpoint of line>:

Where to from Here?   The default option "<Endpoint of line>" assumes you are going to enter straight-line segments. Therefore, it expects another point to be given to complete the line segment. You can specify the end of the line by absolute coordinates, relative coordinates, or by using your pointing device to pick the end of the line on the screen. Again, AutoCAD will repeat the prompt:

Arc/Close/Halfwidth/Length/Undo/Width<Endpoint of line>:

Having drawn a connected series of lines, you can give a null reply (press ⏎) to terminate the PLINE command. The resulting figure is recognized by AutoCAD editing commands as a single entity.

To access other features of the PLINE command select either the options from the screen menu or enter just a capitalized initial letter indicated in the prompt.

For example, the following command sequence shows placement of connected lines, as shown in Figure 4–4.

Fundamentals III

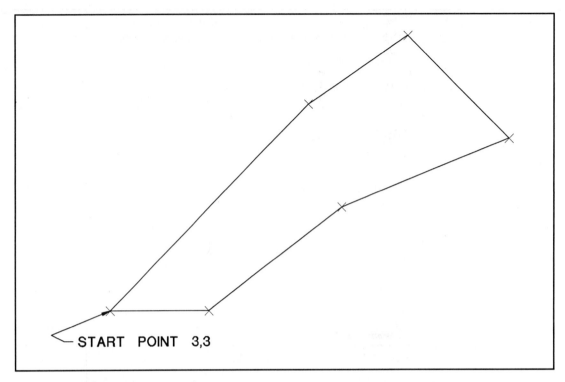

START POINT 3,3

Figure 4-4 Using the PLINE Command to Place Connected Lines

Command: **pline**
From point: **3,3**
Current line-width 0.0
Arc/Close/Halfwidth/Length/Undo/Width/<Endpoint of line>: **@3,0**
Arc/Close/Halfwidth/Length/Undo/Width/<Endpoint of line>: **@4,3**
Arc/Close/Halfwidth/Length/Undo/Width/<Endpoint of line>: **@3,2**
Arc/Close/Halfwidth/Length/Undo/Width/<Endpoint of line>: **@5,2**
Arc/Close/Halfwidth/Length/Undo/Width/<Endpoint of line>: **@-3,3**
Arc/Close/Halfwidth/Length/Undo/Width/<Endpoint of line>: **@-3,-2**
Arc/Close/Halfwidth/Length/Undo/Width/<Endpoint of line>: ⏎

Close and Undo Options Close and Undo options work similar to the LINE command.

Width Option After selecting a starting point you may enter a **W** or pick width from the menu to specify a starting and ending width for a wide segment. When you select this option, AutoCAD prompts:

Starting width <default>:
Ending width <default>:

You can specify a width by selecting a point on the screen. AutoCAD will use the distance from the starting point of the Polyline to the point selected as the starting width. You can accept the default value for the starting width by providing a null response, or type in a new value. The starting width you enter becomes the default for the ending width. If necessary, you can change the ending width to

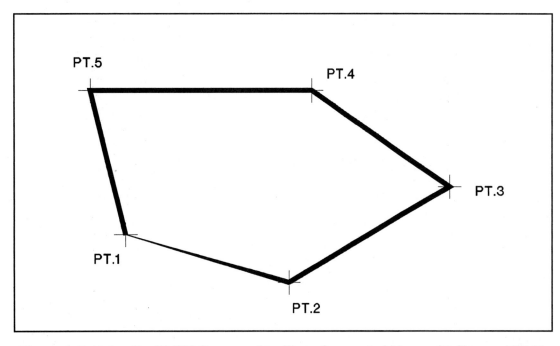

Figure 4-5 Using the PLINE Command to Place Connected Lines with Tapered Width

draw a tapered segment or an arrow. The ending width, in turn, becomes the uniform width for all subsequent segments until you change the width again.

For example, the following command sequence shows placement of connected lines with tapered width, as shown in Figure 4-5.

```
Command:  pline
From point:  pick point 1
Current line-width 0.0
Arc/Close/Halfwidth/Length/Undo/Width/<Endpoint of line>: w
Starting width <0.000>:  .1
Ending width <0.125>: .25
Arc/Close/Halfwidth/Length/Undo/Width/<Endpoint of line>: pick point 2
Arc/Close/Halfwidth/Length/Undo/Width/<Endpoint of line>: pick point 3
Arc/Close/Halfwidth/Length/Undo/Width/<Endpoint of line>: pick point 4
Arc/Close/Halfwidth/Length/Undo/Width/<Endpoint of line>: c
```

Halfwidth Option This option is similar to the width option including the prompts, except this lets you specify the width from the center of a wide Polyline to one of its edges. In other words, you specify half of the total width required to draw. For example, it is easier to input 1.021756 as the halfwidth rather than to figure out the total width by doubling. You can specify a halfwidth by selecting a point on the screen in the same manner used to specify a width.

ARC Option The Arc option allows you to draw a Polyline arc. When you select the Arc option AutoCAD displays another submenu:

```
Angle/CEnter/Close/Direction/Halfwidth/Line/Second pt/Undo/Width/<Endpoint
    of arc>: a
```

Fundamentals III

If you respond with a point, it is interpreted as the endpoint of the arc. The endpoint of the previous segment will be the starting point of the arc and the starting direction of the new arc will be the ending direction of the previous segment (whether the previous segment is a line or an arc). This resembles the ARC command's Start, End, Direction (S,E,D) option, but requires only the endpoint to be specified or selected on the screen.

The CLose, Width, Halfwidth, and Undo options are similar to the straight-line segments described above.

The Angle option lets you specify the included angle by prompting:

Included angle:

The arc will be drawn counterclockwise if the value is positive, clockwise if it is negative. After the angle is specified AutoCAD will prompt you for the endpoint of the arc.

The CEnter option lets you override the location of the center of the arc and AutoCAD prompts:

Center point:

When you provide the center point of the arc, AutoCAD prompts you for additional information:

Angle/Length/<Endpoint>:

If you respond with a point, it is interpreted as the endpoint of the arc. Selecting A (Angle) or L (Length) allows you to specify the arc's included angle or chord length.

The Direction option lets you override the direction of the last segment and AutoCAD prompts:

Direction from starting point:

If you respond with a point, it is interpreted as the starting point of the direction and AutoCAD will prompt you for the endpoint for the direction.

The Line option reverts to drawing straight line segments.

The Radius option allows you to specify the radius by prompting:

Radius:

After the radius is specified, you will be prompted for the endpoint of the arc.

The Second point option causes AutoCAD to use the three-point method of drawing an arc by prompting:

Second point:

If you respond with a point, it is interpreted as the second point and then you will be prompted for the endpoint of the arc. This resembles the ARC command's Three-Point option.

Length Option The Length option continues a Polyline in the same direction as the last segment for a specified distance.

POINT Command

The POINT command draws points on the drawing and these points are drawn on the plotted drawing sheet with a single "pen down." Drafter/designers usually enter such points to be used as reference points for Osnapping to when necessary. When the drawing is finished simply erase them from the drawing or freeze the layer they are on. Points can be entered by specifying coordinates or with your pointing device. You can Osnap to a point by using the Node option of the Object Snap (OSNAP) feature.

The POINT command is invoked from the Screen Root Menu Draw (Figure 4-6), pull-down menu Draw (Figure 4-7) or at the "Command:" prompt type in **POINT** and press ↵.

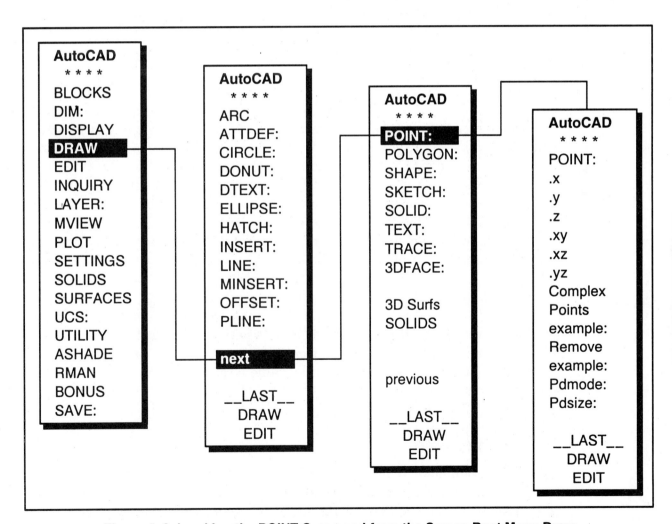

Figure 4-6 Invoking the POINT Command from the Screen Root Menu Draw

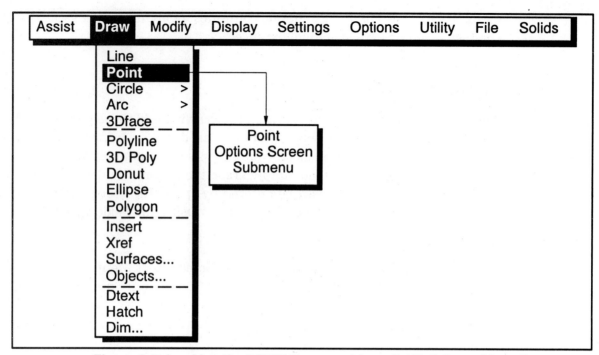

Figure 4-7 Invoking the POINT Command from the Pull-Down Menu Draw

Command: **point**
Point: *enter coordinates or specify a point with the pointing device*

Point modes When you draw the point it will appear on the display as a blip (+), if BLIPMODE is on. After a REDRAW command it will change to its default mode and appear as a dot (.). You can make the point appear as a +, x, 0, or | by changing the system variable PDMODE. This can be done by using the SETVAR command. You can also use the pull-down icon menu shown in Figure 4-8 to set PDMODE values. The default value of PDMODE is zero. If the PDMODE is changed, all previous points will remain the same until you regenerate the drawing. After a screen regeneration all points will appear as the last PDMODE value entered.

Point size The size that the point appears on the screen depends on the value to which the system variable PDSIZE is set. Again, you can set this size by the SETVAR command or select PDSIZE from the point submenu. Like PDMODE the default for PDSIZE is zero. Any positive value larger than this will increase the size of the point accordingly.

SOLID Command

The SOLID command creates a solid filled (straight sided) area whose outline is determined by points you specify on the screen. Two important factors should be kept in mind when using the SOLID command. One, the points must be selected in a specified order or else the four corners might cause a bowtie to be generated

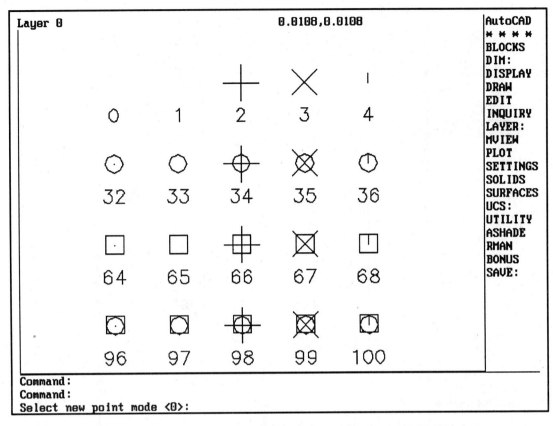

```
Layer 0                          0.0108,0.0108        AutoCAD
                                                      * * * *
                                                      BLOCKS
                                                      DIM:
                                                      DISPLAY
                                                      DRAW
                                                      EDIT
         0       1       2       3       4            INQUIRY
                                                      LAYER:
                                                      MVIEW
                                                      PLOT
                                                      SETTINGS
                                                      SOLIDS
         32      33      34      35      36           SURFACES
                                                      UCS:
                                                      UTILITY
                                                      ASHADE
                                                      RMAN
                                                      BONUS
         64      65      66      67      68           SAVE:



         96      97      98      99      100


Command:
Command:
Select new point mode <0>:
```

Figure 4-8 Using the Pull-Down Icon Menu to Set PDMODE Values

instead of a rectangle. Two, the polygon generated will have straight sides. But further study will reveal that even filled doughnuts and PLINE-generated curved areas are actually straight sided, just as arcs and circles generate as straight line segments of small enough length to appear smooth.

> ***NOTE:*** Be sure the Fill mode is ON. To check at the "Command:" prompt type in **FILL** and press ⏎. AutoCAD will respond that Fill is ON or OFF. If Fill is OFF the PLINE, TRACE, SOLID, and DOUGHNUT commands will display the outline of the shapes. With Fill ON, the shapes you create with these commands will all appear solid. If Fill is reset to ON after it has been OFF you must initiate a REGEN for the screen to display as filled any unfilled shapes created by these commands. Remember, Fill is only a toggle switch. Switching between ON-OFF affects only the appearance of shapes created with TRACE, PLINE, SOLID, and the DOUGHNUT commands. Solids can only be selected or identified by picking the outlines. The solid area is not recognized as an entity.

Fundamentals III

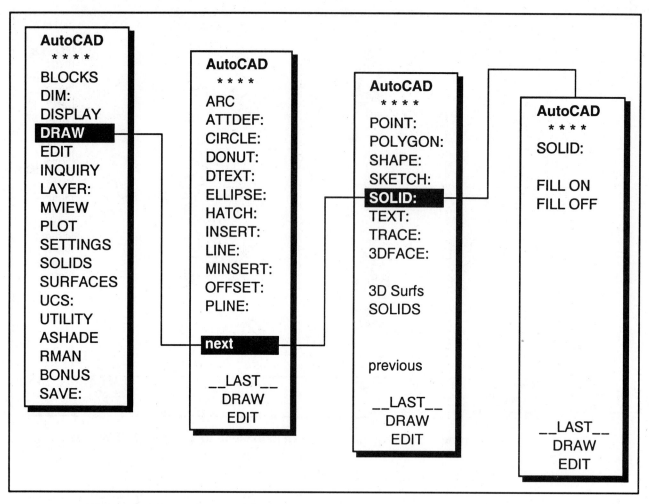

Figure 4-9 Invoking the SOLID Command from the Screen Root Menu Draw

The SOLID command is invoked from the Screen Root Menu Draw (Figure 4-9), or, at the "Command:" prompt type in **SOLID** and press ⏎.

Command: **solid**
First point: ⏎

Figure 4-10 shows an example of how to create a solid rectangular shape.

Command: **solid**
First point: *pick point 1*
Second point: *pick point 2*
Third point: *pick point 3*
Fourth point: *pick point 4*

To create the solid shape, notice that the odd picks must be on one side and the even picks on the other side. If not, you get one of the following effects, as shown in Figure 4-11.

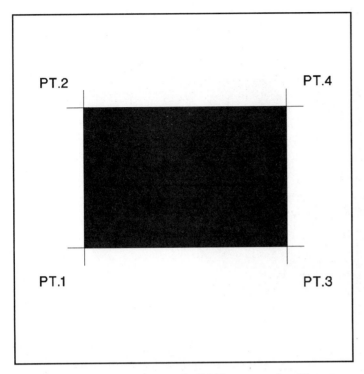

Figure 4-10 Creating a Solid Rectangular Shape

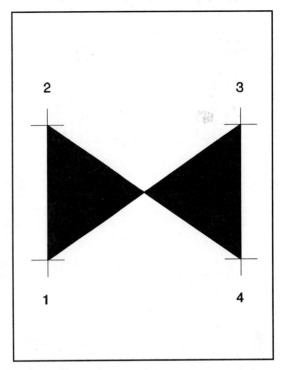

Figure 4-11 Results of Using the SOLID Command When Odd/Even Points Are Not Specified Correctly

You can use the SOLID command to create an arrowhead or triangle shape, as shown in Figure 4-12.

Polygon shapes can be created with the SOLID command by keeping the odd picks along one side and the even picks along the other side of the object, as shown in Figure 4-13.

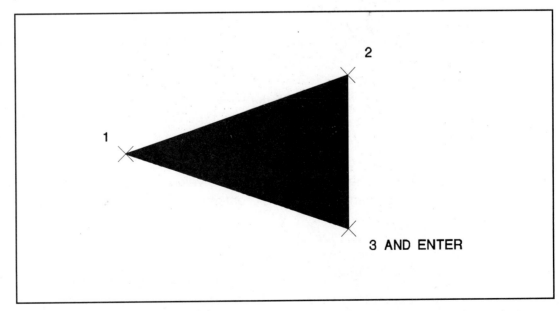

Figure 4-12 Using the SOLID Command to Create Arrowhead or Triangle Shapes

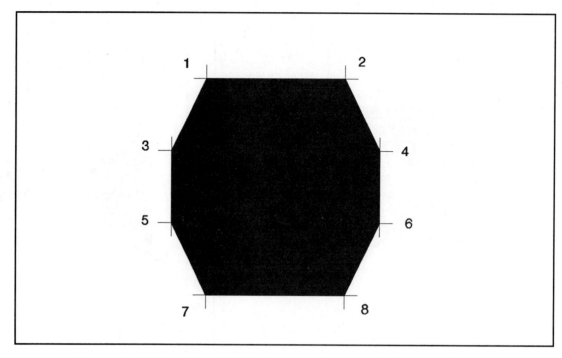

Figure 4-13 Using the SOLID Command to Create Polygon Shapes

Turn the Fill mode OFF and enter the REGEN command. Notice that only the outline of the shape appears. Now set Fill to ON and enter the REGEN command. Now the shapes are filled in again.

DOUGHNUT Command

The DOUGHNUT (or DONUT) command lets you draw a solid filled circle or ring by specifying outer and inner diameters of the filled area. A filled circle is generated by specifying zero as the value of the inner circle.

The DOUGHNUT command is invoked from the Screen Root Menu Draw (Figure 4-14), or at the "Command:" prompt type in **DOUGHNUT** or **DONUT** and press ⏎.

> Command: **doughnut**
> Inside diameter <current>: *enter a value 0 or greater*
> Outside diameter <current>: *enter a value greater than inside diameter*

The diameters of your last selection appear as the current default. To give a new diameter enter a numeric value or select two points on the display to show AutoCAD the diameter. After entering the diameters AutoCAD prompts you to enter:

> Center of doughnut:

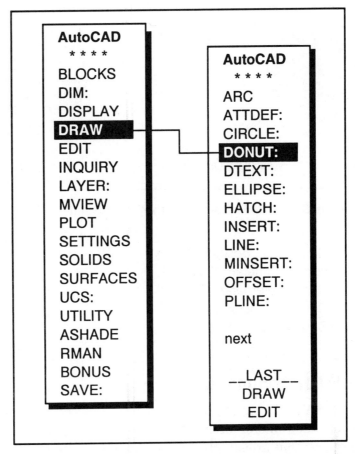

Figure 4-14 Invoking the DOUGHNUT Command from the Screen Root Menu Draw

You may select the center point specifying its coordinates or by picking it with your pointing device. After selecting the center point AutoCAD prompts for the center of the next doughnut and so on. To terminate the command enter a null response.

> *NOTE:* Be sure Fill is set to ON or the circles will not appear solid.

For example, the following command sequence shows placement of a solid filled circle, as shown in Figure 4-15, by using the DOUGHNUT command.

```
Command: doughnut
Inside diameter <.5>: 0
Outside diameter <1>: 1
Center of doughnut: 3,2
Center of doughnut: ⏎
```

The following command sequence show placement of a filled circular shape, as shown in Figure 4-15, by using the DOUGHNUT command.

Figure 4-15 Using the DOUGHNUT Command to Place a Solid Filled Circle and a Filled Circular Shape

Command: **doughnut**
Inside diameter <0.0>: **.5**
Outside diameter <0.0>: **1**
Center of doughnut: **6,4**
Center of doughnut: ⏎

HATCH Command

The HATCH command is used to fill closed areas with repeating patterns of continuous and/or broken parallel lines or groups of these lines. You can use patterns that are supplied in an AutoCAD support file called ACAD.PAT, patterns in files available from third-party custom developers, or you can create your own custom hatch patterns. See Appendix I for the list of patterns supplied with ACAD.PAT.

HATCH patterns are drawn as line segment groups. But, if properly defined, they can appear as repeated shapes made up of straight line segments.

Hatching as a Block AutoCAD normally combines the lines generated during one HATCH command into an anonymous Block. This means you can use the ERASE, COPY, MOVE, CHANGE, or other commands that will operate on a Block to edit a group created during one HATCH command as though it were a single entity. Commands like BREAK and OFFSET will not work on a HATCH pattern. A group can, however, be separated into its individual lines and segments by using the EXPLODE command and selecting one of the segments of the group. The segments, when exploded, are not parts of a defined hatch pattern, but separate from each other. Another method to have hatching drawn as separate entities, instead of as a Block, is to use the asterisk (*) to prefix the pattern name when responding to the prompt.

Hatching is put in the current construction plane, that is, in the current User Coordinate System, and at the current ELEVATION and THICKNESS. However, the extrusion will be in the direction of the WCS positive Z direction.

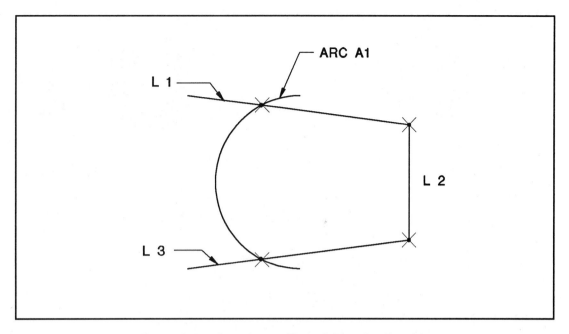

Figure 4-16 Creating a Closed Area for Hatching

Hatched Area Outlines The area selected for the outline used by the HATCH command must be recognized by AutoCAD as being closed. The segments that determine the area must also all meet at their endpoints. For example, the arc and three-segment polyline in Figure 4-16 create a closed area.

But the entities do not all connect at endpoints. In order for the closed area to be valid for hatching it would require the arc and lines to meet, as shown in Figure 4-17.

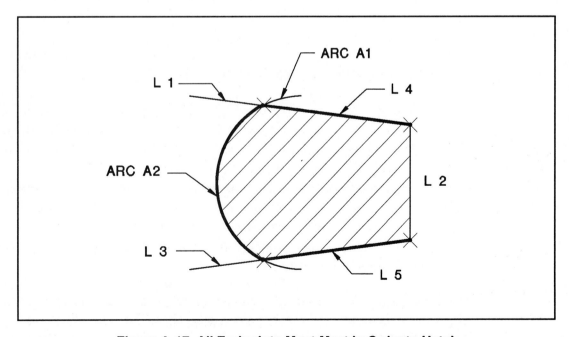

Figure 4-17 All Endpoints Must Meet in Order to Hatch

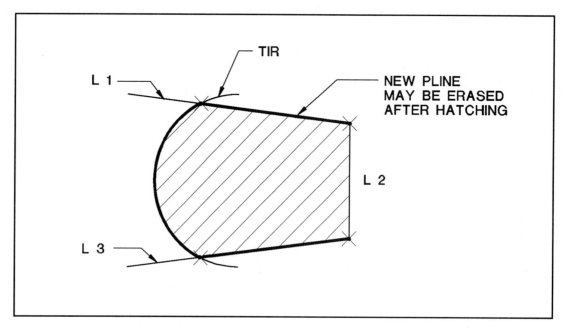

Figure 4-18 Creating All Boundary Segments with One PLINE in Order to Select the Resulting Polyline with One Pick

Therefore, it would be necessary to draw A2, L4, and L5 as separate entities and select them instead of A1, L1, and L3 for determining the area to be hatched. L2 would be acceptable as it is for one of the segments enclosing the area. When this type of area is needed to be hatched, it is often a good practice to draw all of the boundary segments with one PLINE command so you can select the resulting Polyline with one pick. Figure 4-18 shows how you may draw a Polyline, hatch the enclosed area, and then either erase the Polyline or put it on a layer that is turned off.

Don't forget that even the longer straight segments must be drawn over the existing lines in order to close the desired areas.

> **NOTE:** To determine an area for hatching, entities selected must be connected at their endpoints. They must NOT overlap. They must NOT leave a gap.

Hatching Styles An area selected for hatching may be between two closed polygons, such as in Figure 4-19.

When a group of entities is selected during the HATCH command, the style specified determines how AutoCAD will perform the hatching. The styles available are Normal, Outermost, and Ignore.

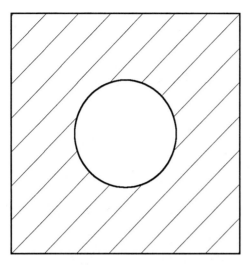

Figure 4-19 An Area Selected for Hatching between Two Polygons

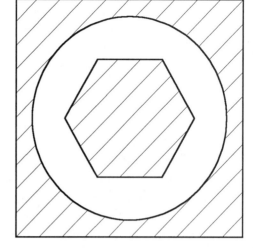

Figure 4-20 Hatching Using the Normal Style

The Normal style will cause AutoCAD to hatch between alternate areas starting with the outermost area, as shown in Figure 4-20.

The Outermost style will hatch only the outermost area, as shown in Figure 4-21.

> **NOTE:** For the above Normal and Outermost areas to perform as shown, all of the boundaries must be included in the selection. This can be done by selecting them individually or by including them all in a window or crossing.

The Ignore option causes AutoCAD to hatch the entire area enclosed by the outermost boundary, as shown in Figure 4-22. This is almost the same as if you retained the Normal style and selected only the outermost boundary.

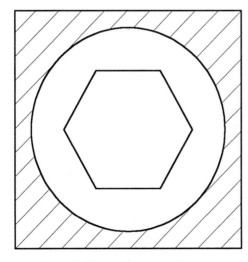

Figure 4-21 Hatching Using the Outermost Style

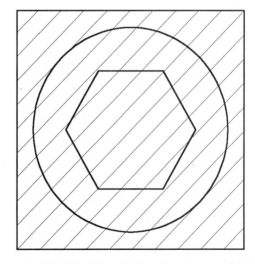

Figure 4-22 Hatching Using the Ignore Style

But, if the outermost boundary were part of a Block that had inner entities, then just using the Normal style would hatch alternate areas. For these cases, the Ignore style will cause the hatching to fill the entire area, regardless of how you select the Block, as long as its outermost entities comprise a closed polygon and are joined at their endpoints.

Caution must be observed when hatching over dimensioning.

The dimensions may be included in selecting the entities and will not affect the hatching as long as the dimension variable DIMASO was on when the hatching was created and it has not been exploded. The DIMASO toggles the associative dimensioning. If the dimensions had been drawn with DIMASO off or had been exploded into individual entities, then the lines (dimension and extension) would have an unpredictable (and undesirable) effect on a hatching pattern if they had been included in the group selected. Therefore, the selecting in this case should be done by picking the individual entities on the screen.

Hatching and Special Selected Entities   Certain entities have special effects on hatching under certain conditions. First of all, in order for any entity to have any possible effect, that entity must be included in the selected group.

Blocks are hatched as though they were separate entities. Note, however, that when you select a Block, all entities that make up the Block will be selected as part of the group to be considered for hatching.

Text, Shapes, and Attributes   If the selected items include Text, Shape, and/or Attribute entities, AutoCAD will not hatch through these items if identified in the selection process. AutoCAD leaves an unhatched area around the entity so it can be clearly viewed, as shown in Figure 4–23. Using the Ignore style will negate this feature and the hatching will not be interrupted when passing through the Text, Shape, and Attribute entities.

Figure 4–23 Hatching in an Area Where There Is Text

Hatching around Traces and Solids When a filled solid or trace with width is selected in a group to be hatched, AutoCAD will not hatch inside that solid or trace. However, the hatching will stop at the outline of the filled object, not leaving a clear space around the entity as it does around Text, Shape and Attributes. Again, these objects will be hatched over unless they are selected.

Viewport edges in Paper Space can be selected as boundaries for hatching.

Invoke the HATCH command from the Screen Root Menu Draw (Figure 4-24), pull-down menu Draw (Figure 4-25), or at the "Command:" prompt, you can type in **HATCH** and press ⏎.

> Command: **hatch**
> Pattern (? or name/U,style)<default>: *hatch pattern name*

You may use one of the patterns in the ACAD.PAT file by entering its name. See Appendix I for the list of pattern names. Patterns not in the ACAD.PAT file can be in a file with the pattern name followed by a .PAT extension. See Chapter 15 on customizing for how to create and store your own custom hatch patterns.

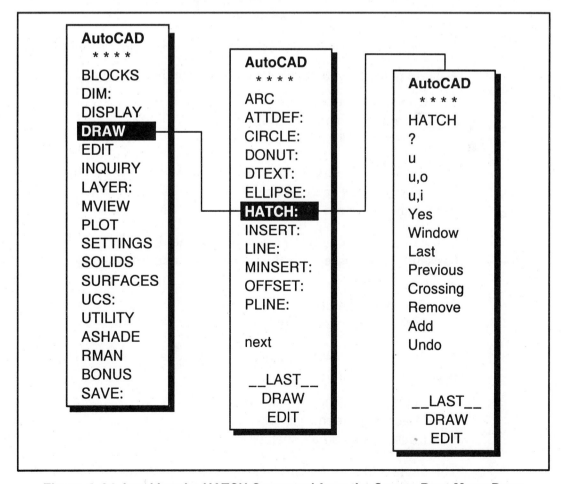

Figure 4-24 Invoking the HATCH Command from the Screen Root Menu Draw

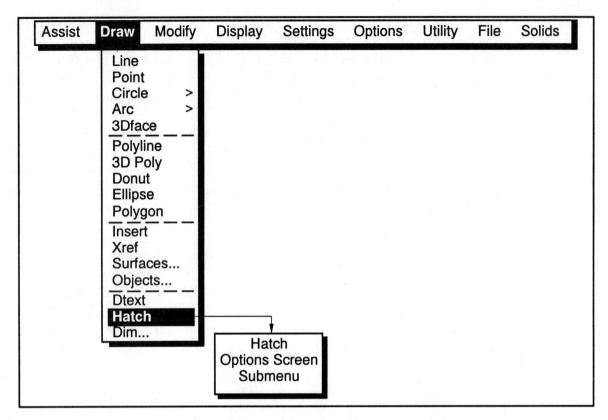

Figure 4-25 Invoking the HATCH Command from the Pull-Down Menu Draw

A list of patterns can be displayed by responding as follows:

Command: **hatch**
Pattern (? or name/U,style)<default>: **?**
Pattern(s) to list <*>:

Pressing ⏎ will cause all patterns in the ACAD.PAT file to be listed. Or, you can reply with a name or a combination of characters and wild cards (*, ?, or other wild card) to have certain patterns or groups of patterns listed.

You can specify a simple pattern of parallel lines or two groups of parallel lines (crossing at 90 degrees) at the spacing and angle desired by selecting the **U** option as shown below:

Command: **hatch**
Pattern (? or name/U,style)<default>: **u**

After responding with **U**, AutoCAD provides the means to customize the hatch pattern with the following prompts:

Angle for crosshatch lines <default>:
Spacing between lines <default>:
Double hatch area? <default>:

The angle and spacing can be specified by entering numeric values or by picking two points on the screen. A **Y** or **N** specifies whether double hatching (second family of parallel lines at 90 degrees) is drawn or not. Values of the previous hatch are the defaults.

By giving a line space value followed by XP while in Model Space, AutoCAD uses an equivalent Paper Space spacing.

When you specify the pattern name, you have the freedom to select one of the three styles explained earlier. To invoke the Normal style, just type the name of the style and press ⏎. To invoke the Outermost style, type the name of the pattern followed by a comma (,) and the letter **o**. To invoke the Ignore style, type the name of the pattern followed by a comma (,) and the letter **i**.

Once you specify the type of pattern, and the style, AutoCAD responds with two additional prompts:

    Scale for pattern <default>:
    Angle for pattern <default>:

Each pattern is defined with a real world spacing and definition, and with a rotation angle of zero degrees. If necessary, you can change the scale and rotation angle. The rotation angle is given in reference to positive X Axis.

After you choose the pattern scale and rotation angle, AutoCAD prompts:

    Select objects:

Select objects by any of the standard object selection methods.

> **NOTE:** The selection of objects for hatching must be done with awareness of how each entity will affect or be affected by the HATCH command. Complex hatching of large areas can be time consuming. Forgetting to select a vital entity can change the whole effect of hatching. You can terminate hatching before it is completed by pressing ⌃Ctrl + C.

Hatching Base Point and Angle Different areas hatched with the same (or similar) pattern at the same scale and angle will have corresponding lines lined up with each other in adjacent areas. This is because the families of lines were defined in the pattern(s) with the same base point and angle, no matter where the areas to be filled are in the drawing. This causes hatching lines to line up in adjacent hatched areas. But if you wish to offset the lines in adjacent areas, you can make the base point in one of the areas different from the base point in the adjacent area. You can change the Snap base point by using either the SNAP command and the Rotation option or the SETVAR command to change the system variable called SNAPBASE. This is also useful to improve the look of hatching in any one area.

Changing the SNAPANG system variable or base angle (from the SNAP/Rotate command/option) will affect the angles of lines in a hatching pattern. This capability is also possible when responding to the HATCH command's "Angle for pattern <default>:" prompt.

Multiple Hatching When you have finished hatching an area and press ⏎ to repeat the HATCH command, AutoCAD prompts only for the objects to be selected. The optional parameters of pattern, mode, scale, and angle remain unchanged. In order to change any item, you must use another means of reinvoking the HATCH command, such as selecting it from a Menu device, typing in **HATCH**, or using another command like REDRAW (Ctrl + C and ⏎ will not nullify automatic repeating).

OBJECT SELECTION

All editing commands include the Object Selection subcommand. Object Selection in most of the editing commands permits any number of objects to be selected for being edited. The BREAK, PEDIT, DIVIDE, and MEASURE commands are restricted to only one object, as is the Linear Dimensioning option that permits dimensioning an object by just selecting that object. The FILLET and CHAMFER commands require exactly two objects. The DIST and ID Inquiry commands actually require point selection, while the AREA command permits either point or object selection. The options covered in this section give you more flexibility and ease of use when you are prompted to select objects for use by the above commands.

This section will cover the Multiple, Box, Auto, Undo, Add, Remove, and Single options in addition to the options that are explained in Chapter 2.

Multiple Option

The Multiple option to the Object Selection subcommand helps you overcome the limitations of the Pointing, Window, and Crossing options. The Pointing option is time-consuming for use in selecting many objects. AutoCAD does a complete scan of the screen each time a point is picked. By using the Multiple modifier option, you can pick many points without delay and when you press ⏎, AutoCAD applies all of the points during one scan.

Selecting one or more objects from a crowded group of entities is sometimes difficult with the Pointing option. It is often impossible with the Window option. For example, if two objects are very close together and you wish to point to select them both, AutoCAD will normally select the last one drawn no matter how many times you select a point that touches them both. By using the Multiple option, AutoCAD excludes an object from being selected once it has been included in the selection set. An alternative to this is to use the Crossing option to cover both objects. If this is not feasible, then the Multiple modifier may be the best choice.

Box Option

The Box option is usually employed in a menu string to give the user a double option of Window and Crossing depending on how and where the picks are made on the screen. It must be spelled out (BOX) completely and not applied as an abbreviation like you may do with the others; i.e., W for Window. Because of this, you normally would not go to the trouble to use the Box option from the keyboard when a single key (W or C) will provide an already decided option.

When the Box modifier is invoked as a response to a prompt to select an object, the options are applied as follows:

> If the picks are left to right (the first point is to the left of the second), then the two points become diagonally opposite corners of a rectangle that is used as a Window option. That is, all visible objects totally within the rectangle are part of that selection.

> If the picks are right to left, then the subsequent rectangle becomes a Crossing option rectangle. That is, all visible objects that are within or partially within the rectangle are part of that selection.

> If the Window option is in effect, the dragged rectangle is displayed by a solid line. If the Crossing option is in effect, the lines are dotted.

Auto Option

The Auto option to the Object Selection subcommand offers a triple option. It includes the Pointing option with the two Box options. If the target box touches an object, then that object is selected as you would in using the Pointing option. If the target box does not touch an object, then the selection becomes either a Window or Crossing option depending upon where the second point is picked in relation to the first.

Undo Option

The Undo option to the Object Selection subcommand allows you to remove the last item(s) selected from the selection set without aborting the Object Selection subcommand and then continue adding to the selection set. It is a short way to use the combined Remove/Last/.../Add sequence of options. It should be noted that if the last option to the selection process included more than one object, the Undo option will remove all the objects from the selection set that were selected by that last option.

Add Option

The Add option to the Object Selection subcommand lets you switch back from the Remove mode in order to continue adding objects to the selection set by whatever and however many options you wish to use.

Remove Option

The Remove option to the Object Selection subcommand lets you remove objects from the selection set. The Object Selection subcommand always starts in the Add mode. The Remove mode is a switch from the Add mode, not a standard option. Once invoked, the objects selected by whatever and however many options you use will be removed from the selection set. It will be in effect until reversed by using the Add option.

Single Option

The Single option to the Object Selection subcommand causes the Object Selection to terminate and the command in progress to proceed after you use only one

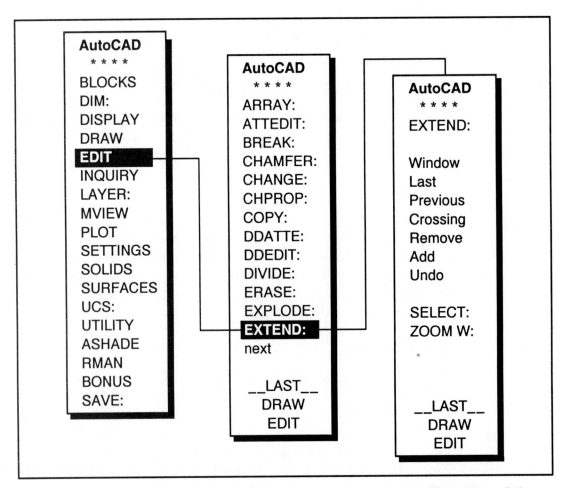

Figure 4-26 Invoking the EXTEND Command from the Screen Root Menu Edit

Object Selection option. It does not matter if one object is selected or a group is selected with that option. If no object is selected and the point selected cannot be the first point of a Window or Crossing rectangle, AutoCAD will not abort the command in progress; however, once there is a successful selection, the command will proceed.

EDIT COMMANDS

In this chapter eight additional EDIT commands are explained, including EXTEND, STRETCH, TRIM, CHANGE, CHPROP, OFFSET, ARRAY, and PEDIT, in addition to the commands explained in chapters 2 and 3.

EXTEND Command

The EXTEND command is used to change one or both endpoints of selected lines to extend to a selected line or arc. Arcs, if possible, can also be extended to reach a specified line or other arc.

The EXTEND command is invoked from the Screen Root Menu Edit (Figure 4-26), pull-down menu Modify (Figure 4-27), or at the "Command:" prompt, you can type in **EXTEND** and press ⏎ or spacebar.

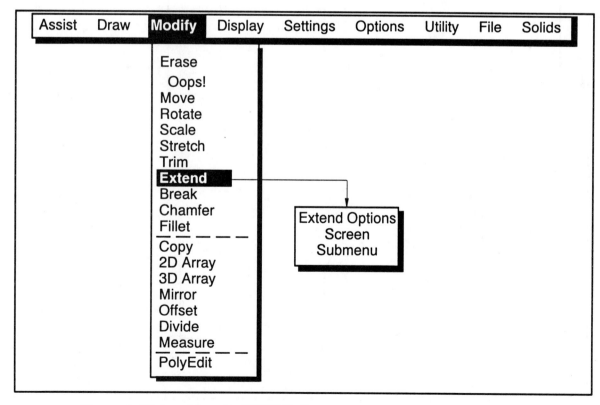

Figure 4-27 Invoking the EXTEND Command from the Pull-Down Menu Modify

Command: **extend**
Select boundary edge(s). . .
Select objects: *select an object to extend to*
Select objects: *press ⏎ if selection is completed*
Select object to extend: *select an object to extend*
Select object to extend: press ⏎ *if selection is completed*

The EXTEND command first prompts you to "Select boundary edge(s). . ." These are edges that you want to extend a line or arc to meet. After selecting the boundary edges, give a null response and then AutoCAD will prompt you to select the objects to extend. You can select one or more objects to extend and then give a null response to terminate the command.

Figure 4-28 shows examples of the use of the EXTEND command.

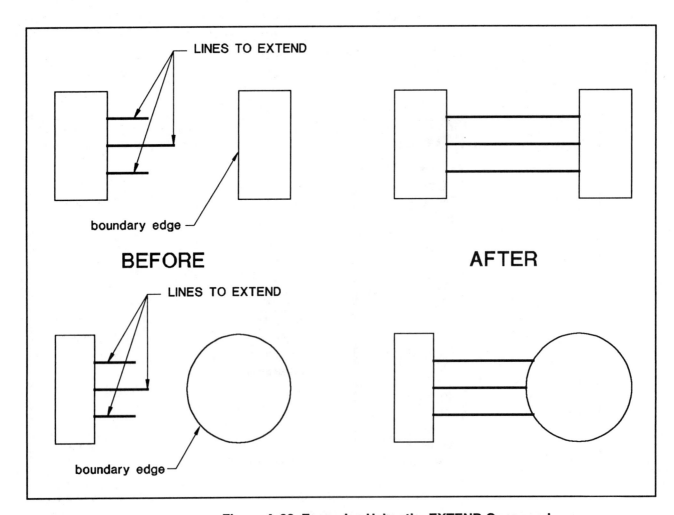

Figure 4-28 Examples Using the EXTEND Command

STRETCH Command

The STRETCH command allows you to stretch the shape of an object without affecting other crucial parts that remain unchanged. A common example is to stretch a square into a rectangle. The length is changed while the width remains the same.

The STRETCH command is invoked from the Screen Root Menu Edit (Figure 4-29), pull-down menu Modify (Figure 4-30), or at the "Command:" prompt type in **STRETCH** and press ↵ or spacebar.

NOTE: When STRETCH is selected from the menu it defaults to the Crossing option for "Selecting objects."

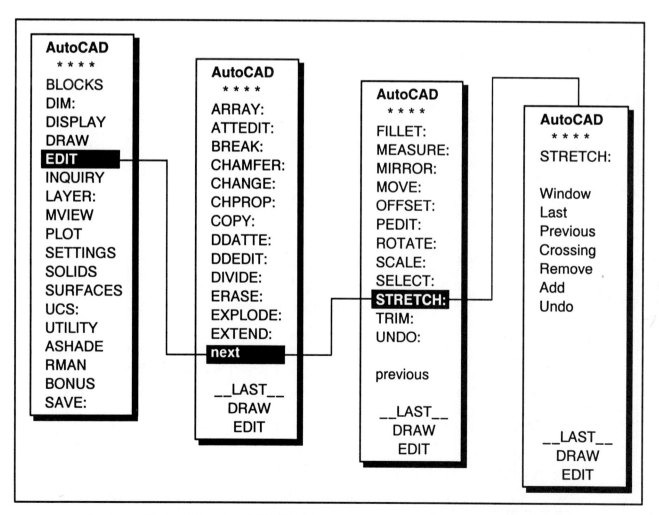

Figure 4-29 Invoking the STRETCH Command from the Screen Root Menu Edit

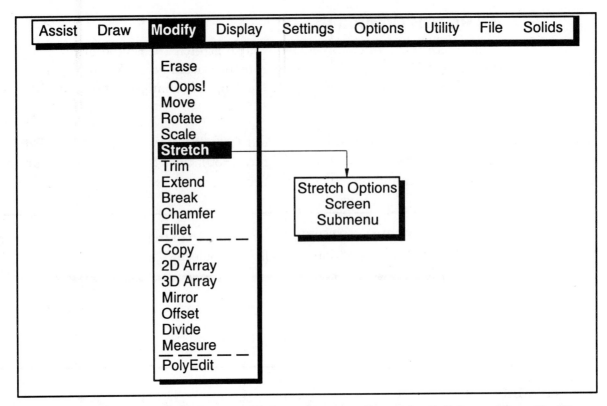

Figure 4-30 Invoking the STRETCH Command from the Pull-Down Menu Modify

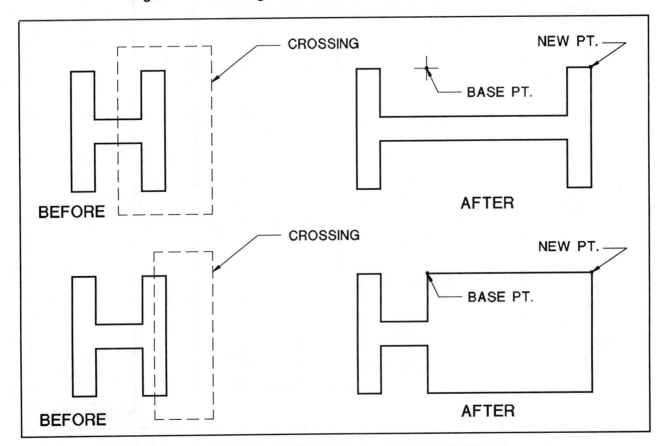

Figure 4-31 Examples Using the STRETCH Command

Command: **stretch**
Select objects to stretch by window . . .
Select objects: **c**
First corner: *select the first corner of the crossing box*
Other corner: *select the second corner*
Select objects: ⏎
Base point: *select the base point for the stretch to begin*
New point: *select the new point to stretch*

Figure 4–31 shows examples of using the STRETCH command.

TRIM Command

The TRIM command, like the EXTEND command, changes the endpoint(s) of lines, circles, and arcs. TRIM, however, is used for segments that extend past a selected cutting edge. The TRIM command will remove the portion of the object(s) that is drawn past the cutting edge.

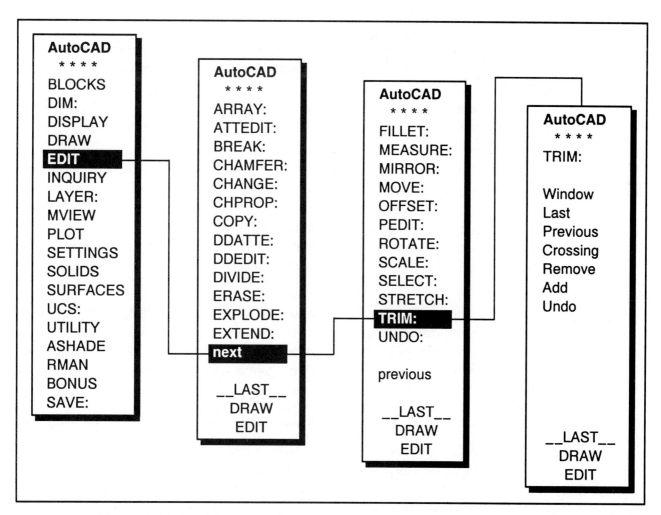

Figure 4–32 Invoking the TRIM Command from the Screen Root Menu Edit

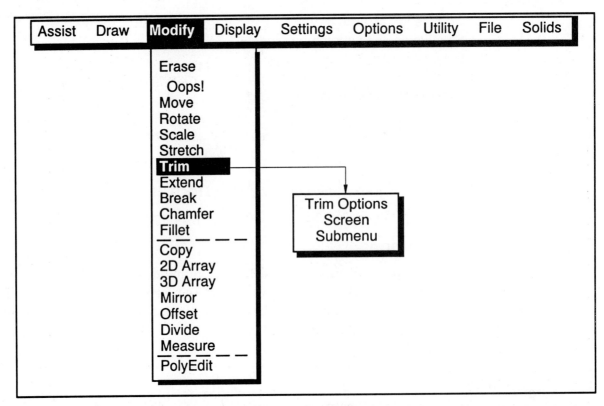

Figure 4-33 Invoking the TRIM Command from the Pull-Down Menu Modify

The TRIM command is invoked from the Screen Root Menu Edit (Figure 4-32), pull-down menu Modify (Figure 4-33), or at the "Command:" prompt you can type in **TRIM** and press ⏎.

```
Command: trim
Select cutting edge(s). . .
Select objects: select the cutting edge
Select objects: press ⏎ if selection is completed
Select object to trim: select the object to trim
Select object to trim: press ⏎ if selection is completed
```

The TRIM command initially prompts you to "Select cutting edge(s)..." After selecting one or more cutting edges to trim, then give a null response. After pressing ⏎ you are prompted to "Select object to trim:" in which case you select one or more objects to trim and then give a null response to terminate the command.

NOTE: Don't forget to press ⏎ after selecting the cutting edge(s). Otherwise, the program will not respond as expected. In fact, it continues expecting more cutting edges until you terminate the edge selecting mode.

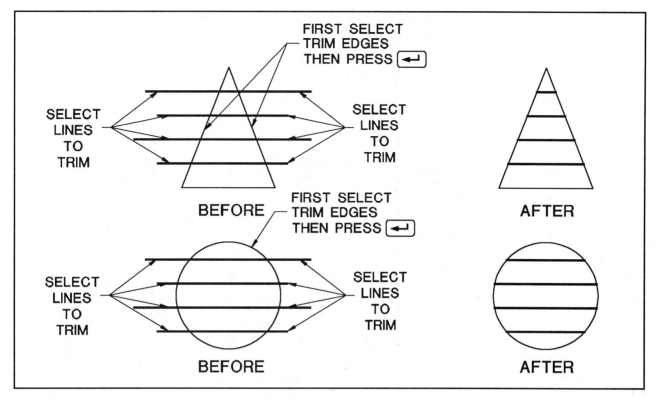

Figure 4-34 Examples Using the TRIM Command

TRIM and EXTEND are very similar in this method of selecting. With TRIM you are prompted to select a cutting edge with EXTEND you are prompted to select a boundary edge to extend to.

Figure 4-34 shows examples of using the TRIM command.

CHANGE Command

The CHANGE command lets you modify some of the characteristics of lines, circles, text, and Blocks. It also allows you to change certain properties of the objects you have selected, such as their color, linetype, and thickness and also allows you to move the objects to a different layer.

The CHANGE command is invoked from the Screen Root Menu Edit (Figure 4-35), or at the "Command:" prompt type in **CHANGE** and press ⏎.

Command: **change**
Select objects: *select the objects*
Properties/<Change point>:

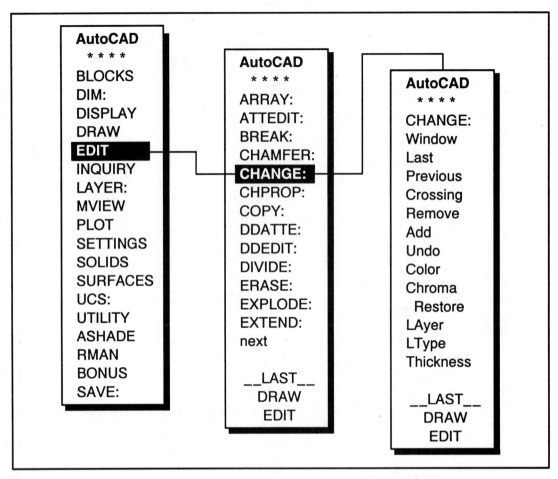

Figure 4-35 Invoking the CHANGE Command from the Screen Root Menu Edit

Change Point Option The default option is the Change point option which allows you to modify some of the characteristics of lines, circles, text, and Blocks.

Line – If you select one or more lines, the closest endpoint(s) of the entities selected will be moved to the new change point, as shown in Figure 4-36.

Circle – If you select a circle, the new circle will pass through the new change point, as shown in Figure 4-36. The distance from the center to the point selected determines the new radius.

Text – If you select a text, AutoCAD will allow you to change one or more parameters as shown in the following prompt sequence:

    Enter text insertion point: *select a new point or press* ⏎
    Name of the style or ⏎ for no change:
    New height <default>:
    New rotation angle <default>:
    New text <text>:

If you do not wish to change any of the above parameters, press ⏎ (null response) to accept the default.

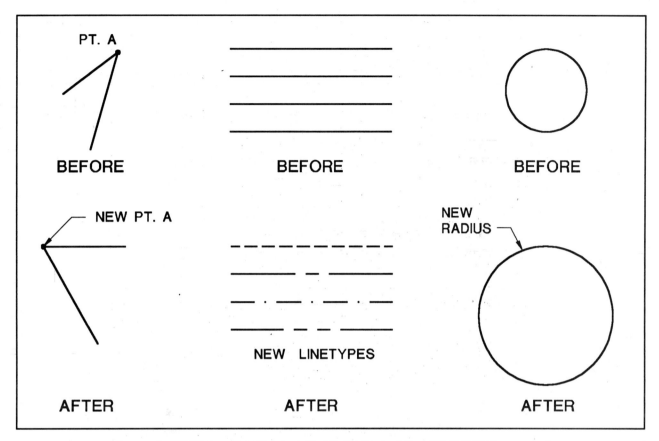

Figure 4-36 Using the Change Point Option of the CHANGE Command

Block – If you select a Block, the change point you select becomes the new origin of the Block. As with text, you may press ⏎ when prompted for a new change point. Doing this will leave the Block in the same location and you will then be prompted for a new scale factor and rotation angle. If you do not wish to change any of the above parameters, press ⏎ (null response) to accept the default.

Properties Option This option allows you to change one or more properties of the selected entities. The properties include Color, Layer, Linetype, and Thickness.

Color – This option under the Properties allows you to change an object's color. Enter a color number or name to change. To make the object inherit the color of the layer, enter BYLAYER or, to inherit the color of the Block upon insertion, enter BYBLOCK.

LAyer – This option under the Properties allows you to move an object from one layer to another. The layer you enter must already exist.

LType - This option under the Properties allows you to change an object's linetype. Enter the desired linetype name. To make the object inherit the linetype of the layer, enter BYLAYER or, to inherit the linetype of the Block upon insertion, enter BYBLOCK.

Fundamentals III

Thickness – This option under the Properties allows you to change an object's extrusion thickness. Enter a numeric value. This option does not have any effect on entities that are drawn with 3DFACE, 3DPLINE, MESH, dimensions, or viewport entities.

The following command sequence shows changing the color and layer of an object to BYLAYER and to layer text, respectively.

```
Command: change
Select objects: select the objects
Properties/<Change point>: p
Change what property (Color/LAyer/LType/Thickness)? c
New color <default>: bylayer
Change what property (Color/LAyer/LType/Thickness)? la
New layer <default>: text
Change what property (Color/LAyer/LType/Thickness)? ↵
```

CHPROP Command

The CHPROP command is quicker to use if you are going to change the properties of objects. The choices are exactly the same as the CHANGE command's Properties option.

The CHPROP command is invoked from the Screen Root Menu Edit, or at the "Command:" prompt type in **CHPROP** and press ↵ or spacebar.

```
Command: chprop
Select objects: select the objects
Change what property (Color/LAyer/LType/Thickness)?
```

Enter the desired option to change the properties of the selected object(s).

OFFSET Command

The OFFSET command is used to generate entities that are similar and parallel to existing entities. There are several rules that must be followed when using the OFFSET command. There are also some "rules of thumb" to prevent unpredictable results from occurring when using the OFFSET command on arbitrary curve/line combinations in Polylines.

The OFFSET command is invoked from the Screen Root Menu Edit (Figure 4-37), pull-down menu Modify (Figure 4-38), or at the "Command:" prompt type in **OFFSET** and press ↵.

```
Command: offset
Offset distance or Through<last>: specify distance
Select object to offset: select object
Side to offset?: pick a point to one side of the object
Select object to offset: ↵
```

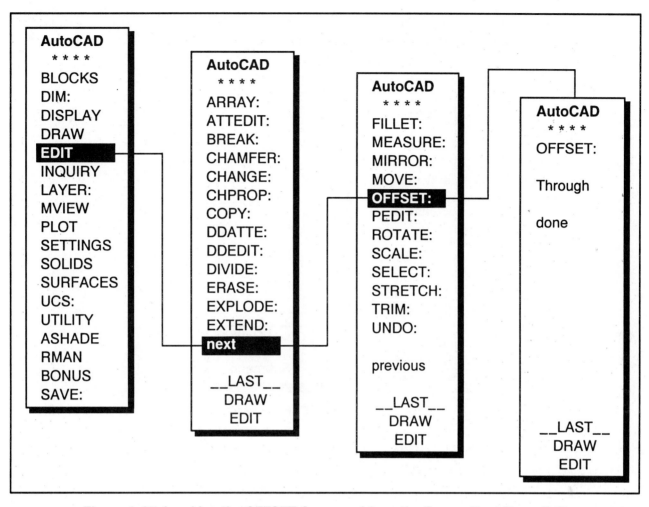

Figure 4-37 Invoking the OFFSET Command from the Screen Root Menu Edit

Valid Entities to Offset Valid entities include the Line, Arc, Circle, and 2D Polyline. If you select another type of entity, such as Text, you will get the following error message:

Cannot offset that entity.

The entity selected for offsetting must be in a plane parallel to the current coordinate system. Otherwise you will get the following error message:

Entity not parallel with UCS.

Repeating Command Once you specify the side, the object selected is offset. You are then prompted to select another object for offsetting. In order to return to the "Command:" prompt, you must press ↵ or CANCEL.

Figure 4-39 shows examples of using the OFFSET command.

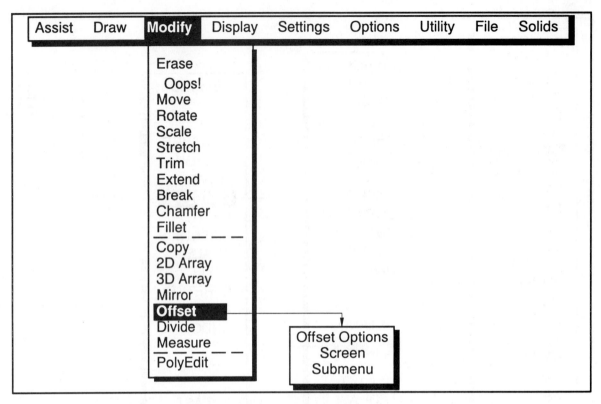

Figure 4-38 Invoking the OFFSET Command from the Pull-Down Menu Modify

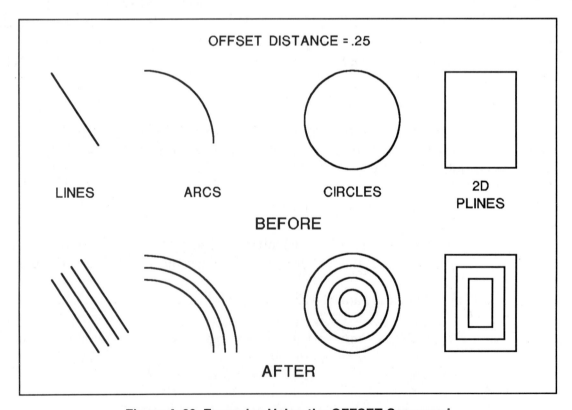

Figure 4-39 Examples Using the OFFSET Command

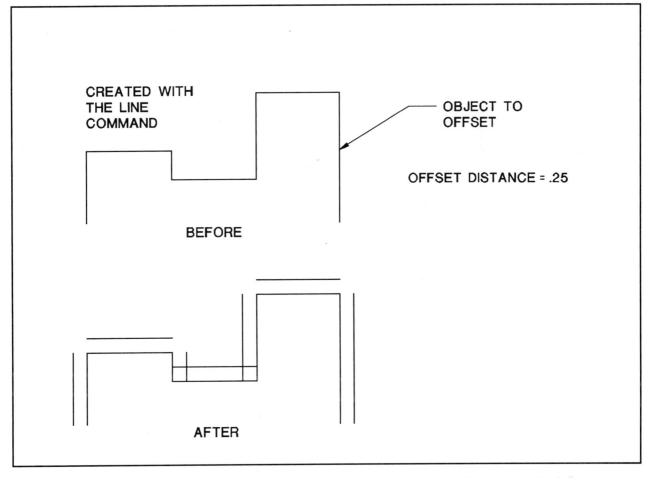

Figure 4-40 Using the OFFSET Command with Single Entities as Opposed to Polylines

Offsetting Miters and Tangencies The OFFSET command affects single entities in a manner different from a Polyline made up of the same entities. Also, Polylines whose arcs join lines and other arcs in a tangent manner are affected differently than Polylines with nontangent connecting points. For example, in Figure 4-40 the seven lines are separate entities. When OFFSET to the side shown, there are gaps and overlaps at the ends of the newly created lines.

In Figure 4-41, the lines have been joined together (see the next section on PEDIT) as a single Polyline. See how the OFFSET command affects the corners where the new Polyline segments join.

CAUTION! NONTANGENT POLYLINE CONNECTIONS

The results of offsetting Polylines with arc segments that connect other arc segments and/or line segments in dissimilar (nontangent) directions might be unpredictable. Examples of offsetting such Polylines are shown in Figure 4-42.

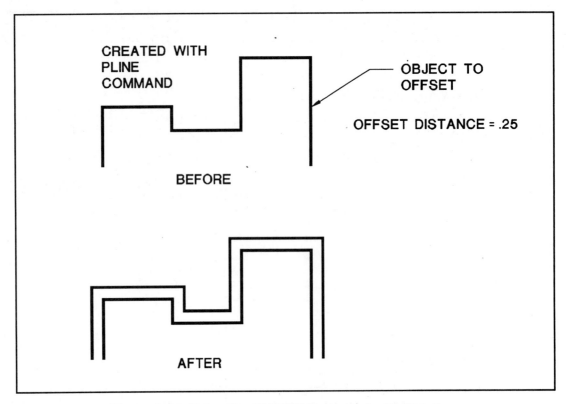

Figure 4-41 Using the OFFSET Command with Polylines

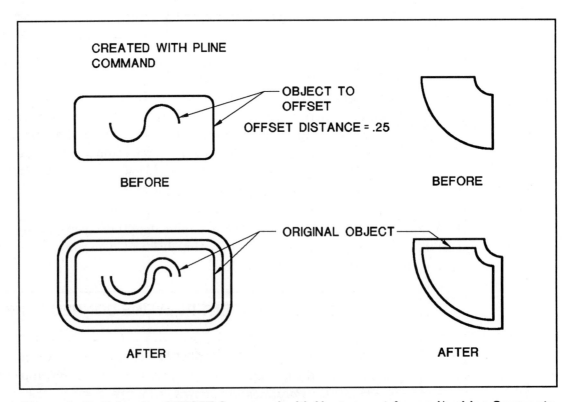

Figure 4-42 Using the OFFSET Command with Nontangent Arc and/or Line Segments

If you are not satisfied with the resulting new Polyline configuration, you can use the PEDIT command to edit it. Or, you can EXPLODE the Polyline and edit the individual segments.

ARRAY Command

The ARRAY command is used to make multiple copies of selected objects in either rectangular or polar arrays. In the rectangular array, you can specify the number of rows, the number of columns, and the spacing between rows and columns (row and column spacing may differ). The whole rectangular array can be rotated at a selected angle. In the polar array, you can determine the angular intervals, the number of copies, the angle that the group covers, and whether or not the objects are rotated about the center of the group.

The ARRAY command is invoked from the Screen Root Menu Edit (Figure 4-43), pull-down menu Modify (called as 2DARRAY) (Figure 4-44), or at the "Command:" prompt type in **ARRAY** and press ⏎.

Command: **array**
Select objects: *select objects*
Rectangular or Polar array (R/P):

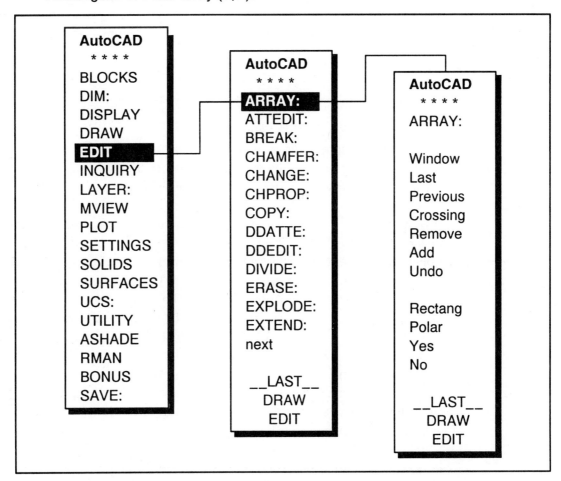

Figure 4-43 Invoking the ARRAY Command from the Screen Root Menu Edit

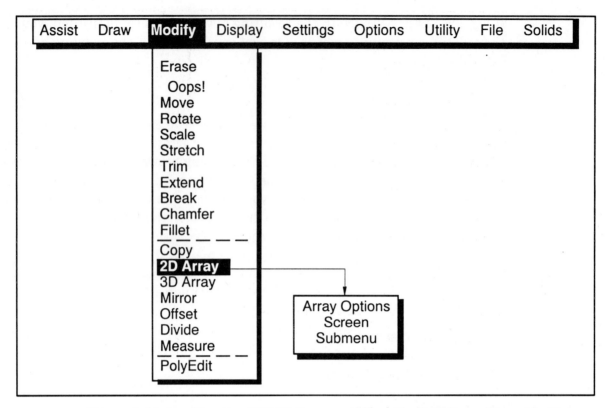

Figure 4-44 Invoking the ARRAY Command from the Pull-Down Menu Modify

Enter **R** for rectangular array and AutoCAD prompts:

Number of rows (---) <1>: *enter a number*
Number of columns (||||) <1>: *enter a number*
Unit cell or distance between rows <--->: *specify the distance*
Distance between columns <|||>: *specify the distance*

Any combination of whole numbers of rows and columns may be entered (except both 1 row and 1 column which would not create any copies). AutoCAD includes the original element in the number you enter. The next prompt(s) requests the distances of the spacing between elements to be arrayed. Row and column spaces can be different from each other. They can be entered separately when prompted, or you may select two points which specify the opposite corners of a rectangle called a unit cell. AutoCAD uses the width of the unit cell as the horizontal distance(s) between columns and the height as the vertical distance(s) between rows. A positive number for the column and row spacing will cause the elements to array toward the right and upward, respectively. Negative numbers for the column and row spacing will cause the elements to array toward the left and downward, respectively.

The following command sequence shows an example of placing a rectangular array with 6 rows and 4 columns, as shown in Figure 4-45.

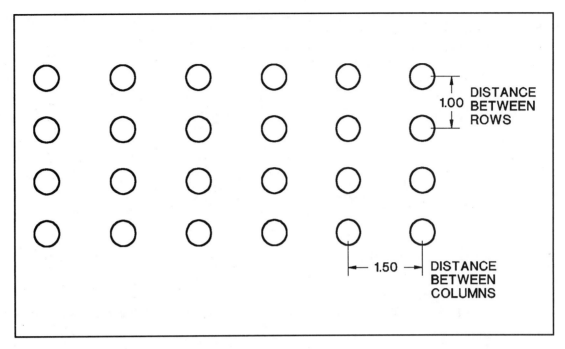

Figure 4-45 Using the ARRAY Command to Place a Rectangular Array

Command: **array**
Select objects: *select objects*
Rectangular or Polar array (R/P): **r**
Number of rows (---)<1>: **6**
Number of columns (||||)<1>: **4**
Unit cell or distance between rows <--->: **1**
Distance between columns <||||>: **1.5**

To create a polar array, enter **P** for polar to the array type prompt and AutoCAD prompts:

Center point of array:

Enter the point around which you want the array to form. To create the polar array AutoCAD needs information on two of the three parameters as described below:

1. Specify the number of items in the array (include the original item).

2. Specify the angle to fill and a positive value specifies counterclockwise rotation and a negative value for clockwise rotation.

3. Specify the angle between items.

If you specify two of the above mentioned parameters, then the array is completely specified. But, if you specify only one of the first two parameters, AutoCAD will prompt you for the third parameter.

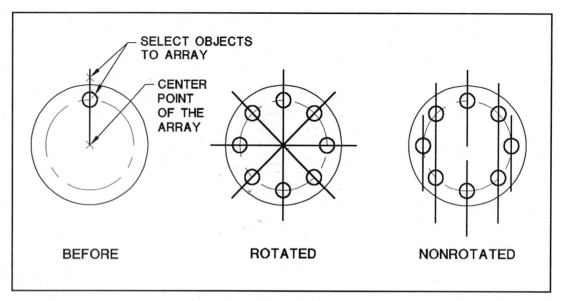

Figure 4-46 Using the ARRAY Command to Place Rotated and Nonrotated Polar Arrays

The last prompt in the case of a polar array is:

Rotate objects as they are copied? <Y>:

A **Y** response will rotate the objects as they are copied.

The following command sequence shows an example of placing a rotated polar array.

Command: **array**
Select objects: *select objects*
Rectangular or Polar array (R/P): **p**
Center point of array: *specify the center point*
Number of items: **8**
Angle to fill (+=CCW, -=CW) <360>: **270**
Rotate objects as they copied? <Y>: ⏎

In Figure 4-46 both nonrotated and rotated polar arrays are shown.

PEDIT Command

The PEDIT command is used to edit Polylines. Other editing commands such as MOVE, COPY, BREAK, TRIM, and EXTEND can also be used on Polylines. But, because Polylines are complex combinations of joined lines and/or arcs that may or may not have varying widths, AutoCAD has made available special editing features in one command for dealing with the unique properties of Polylines. This one command (PEDIT) has a multioption menu with several associated multioption submenus.

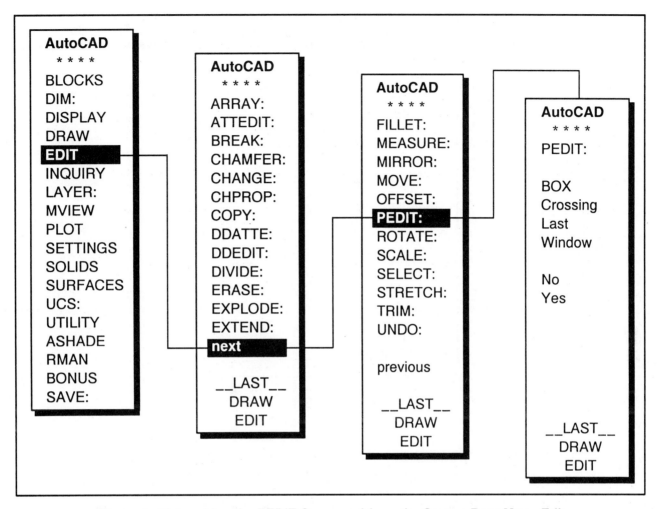

Figure 4-47 Invoking the PEDIT Command from the Screen Root Menu Edit

Invoke the PEDIT command from the Screen Root Menu Edit (Figure 4-47), pull-down menu Modify (Figure 4-48), or at the "Command:" prompt you can type in **PEDIT** and press ⏎.

    Command: **pedit**
    Select polyline: *select line or arc or polyline*

If you select a line or arc instead of a Polyline, you will be prompted as follows:

    Entity selected is not a polyline.
    Do you want it to turn into one? <Y>

Responding **Y** or pressing ⏎ will turn the selected line or arc into a single segment Polyline which can then be edited. Normally this is done in order to use the Join option to add other connected segments which, if not Polylines, will also be transformed. It should be emphasized at this time that in order to Join segments together into a Polyline, their endpoints must coincide. This occurs during line-line, line-arc, arc-line, and arc-arc continuation operations. You can

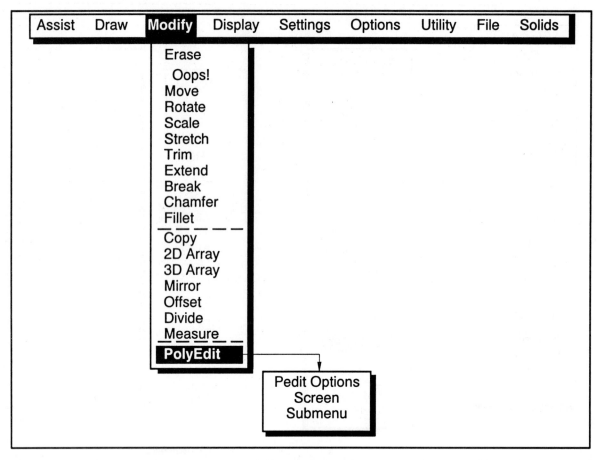

Figure 4-48 Invoking the PEDIT Command from the Pull-Down Menu Modify

also connect segments with the OSNAP mode called Endpoint, or you can key in exact coordinates for the endpoint of one segment that coincides with the coordinates for the endpoint of another. Joining segments to create one Polyline can be done by using the following sequence:

Command: **pedit**
Select polyline: *select line or arc*
Entity selected is not a polyline.
Do you want it to turn into one? <Y>
Close/Join/Width/Edit vertex/Fit curve/Spline curve/Decurve/Undo/eXit <X>: **j**
Select objects: *proceed with object selection*

The second prompt above will not appear if the first segment selected is already a Polyline. It may even be a multisegment Polyline. After the object selection process you will be returned to the multi-option prompt. Another reason for turning a line or an arc into a Polyline or Polyarc is to be able to give it width.

This section will cover those features of the PEDIT command that affect 2D Polylines.

Close Option This option performs in a manner similar to the Close option of the LINE command. If, however, the last segment was a Polyarc (or Polyline Arc),

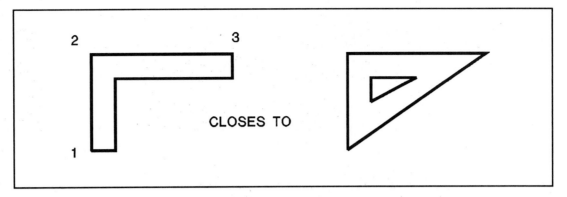

Figure 4-49 Using the PEDIT Close Option #1

then the next segment will be similar to the arc-arc continuation, using the direction of the last Polyarc as the starting direction and draws another Polyarc with the first point of the first segment as the ending point of the closing Polyarc.

Figure 4-49 and Figure 4-50 show examples of the application of the Close option.

Open Option   This option deletes the segment that was drawn with the Close option. If the Polyline had been closed by drawing the last segment to the first point of the first segment without using the Close option then the Open option will not have a visible effect.

Join Option   This option takes selected Lines, Arcs, and/or Polylines and combines them with a previously selected Polyline into a single Polyline if all segments are connected at sequential and coincidental endpoints.

Width Option   This option permits uniform or varying widths to be specified for Polyline segments.

Edit Vertex Option   A vertex is the point where two segments join. When you select this option, the visible vertices are marked with an X to indicate which one is to be modified. You can modify vertices of Polylines in several ways. When you select the Edit vertex option, AutoCAD prompts you with additional suboptions:

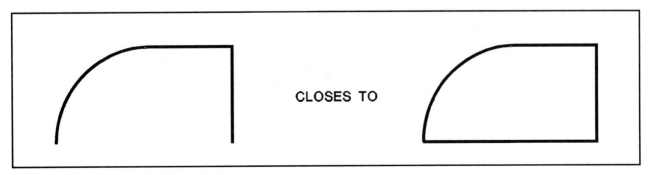

Figure 4-50 Using the PEDIT Close Option #2

Command: **pedit**
Select polyline: *select a polyline*
Close/Join/Width/Edit vertex/Fit curve/Spline curve/Decurve/Undo/eXit<X>: **e**
Next/Previous/Break/Insert/Move/Regen/Straighten/Tangent/Width/eXit <N>:

Next and Previous – Whether or not you have modified the marked vertex, when you wish to move the mark to the next or previous vertex, you can use the N (Next) or P (Previous) option.

Break – The Break option establishes the marked text as one vertex for the Break option and then prompts:

Next/Previous/Go/eXit <N>:

These choices of the Break option permit you to step to another vertex for the second break point, or to initialize the break, or to exit the option. If two vertices are selected, you may use the Go option to have the segment(s) between the vertices removed. If you select the endpoints of a Polyline, this option will not work. If you select the Go option immediately after the Break option, the Polyline will be divided into two separate Polylines. Or, if it is a closed Polyline, it will be opened at that point.

Insert – This option allows you to specify a point and have the segment between the marked vertex and the next vertex become two segments meeting at the specified point. The selected point does not have to be on the Polyline segment.

For example, the following command sequence shows the application of the Insert option, as shown in Figure 4–51.

Command: **pedit**
Select polyline: *select a polyline*
Close/Join/Width/Edit vertex/Fit curve/Spline curve/Decurve/Undo/eXit<X>: **e**
Next/Previous/Break/Insert/Move/Regen/Straighten/Tangent/Width/eXit <N>: **i**
Enter location of new vertex: *select a new vertex*

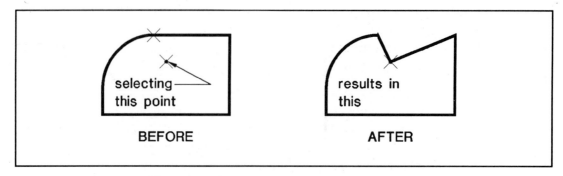

Figure 4–51 Using the PEDIT Insert Option

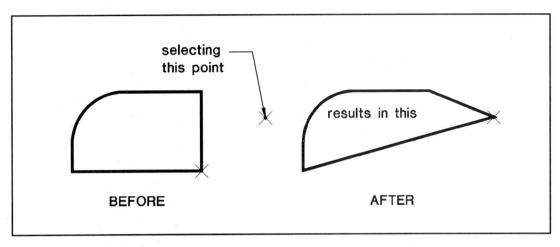

Figure 4-52 Using the PEDIT Move Option

Move – This option allows you to specify a point and have the marked vertex be relocated to the selected point.

For example, the following command sequence shows the application of the Move option, as shown in Figure 4-52.

Command: **pedit**
Select polyline: *select a polyline*
Close/Join/Width/Edit vertex/Fit curve/Spline curve/Decurve/Undo/eXit<X>: **e**
Next/Previous/Break/Insert/Move/Regen/Straighten/Tangent/Width/eXit<N>: **m**
Enter new location: *specify the new location*

Regen – The Regen option regenerates the Polyline.

Straighten – The Straighten option establishes the marked vertex as one vertex for the Straighten option and then prompts:

Next/Previous/Go/eXit <N>:

These choices of the Straighten option permit you to first step to another vertex for the second point, or to exit the option. When the two vertices are selected, you may use the Go option to have the segment(s) between the vertices replaced with a single straight line segment.

For example, the following command sequence shows the application of the Straighten option, as shown in Figure 4-53.

Command: **pedit**
Select polyline: *select a polyline*
Close/Join/Width/Edit vertex/Fit curve/Spline curve/Decurve/Undo/eXit <X>: **e**
Next/Previous/Break/Insert/Move/Regen/Straighten/Tangent/Width/eXit <N>: **s**
Next/Previous/Go/eXit <N>: **n**
Next/Previous/Go/eXit <N>: **n**

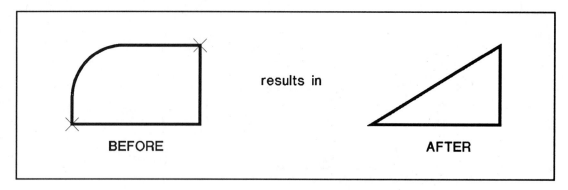

Figure 4-53 Using the PEDIT Straighten Option

Next/Previous/Go/eXit <N>: **x**
Tangent – This option permits you to assign to the marked vertex a tangent direction that can be used for the curve fitting option. The prompt is as follows:

Direction of tangent:

You can specify the direction with a point or key it in from the keyboard.

Width – This option permits you to specify the starting and ending width of the segment between the marked vertex and the next vertex. The prompt is as follows:

Enter new width for all segments <current>:

For example, the following command sequence shows the application of the Width option, as shown in Figure 4-54.

Command: **pedit**
Select polyline: *select a polyline*
Close/Join/Width/Edit vertex/Fit curve/Spline curve/Decurve/Undo/eXit <X>: **e**
Next/Previous/Break/Insert/Move/Regen/Straighten/Tangent/Width/eXit <N>: **w**
Enter new width for segments<default>: **.25**

eXit – This option exits from the Vertex editing option and returns to the multi-option PEDIT prompt.

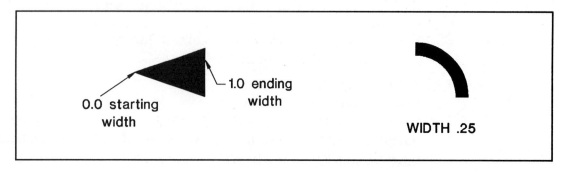

Figure 4-54 Using the PEDIT Width Option

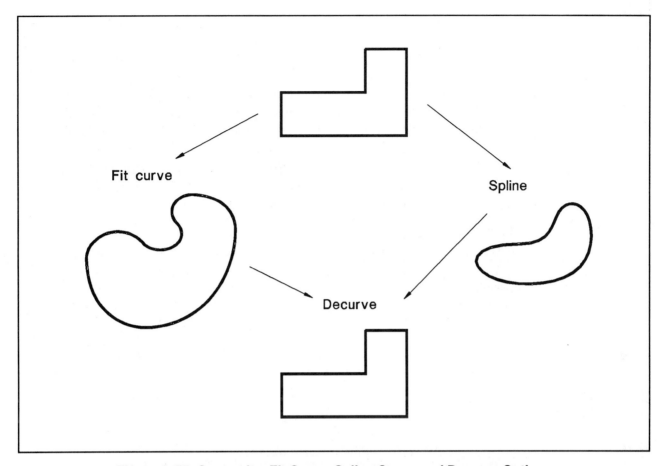

Figure 4-55 Comparing Fit Curve, Spline Curve, and Decurve Options

Fit curve option This option draws a smooth curve through the vertices, using any specified tangents.

Spline curve option This option provides several ways to draw a curve based on the Polyline being edited. These include Quadratic B-spline and Cubic B-spline curve drawing.

Decurve option This option returns the Polyline to the way it was originally drawn.

See Figure 4-55 for differences between fit curve, spline, and decurve.

Undo option This option reverses the latest PEDIT operation.

eXit option This option exits the PEDIT command.

DISPLAY COMMAND
ZOOM

In this section four additional options of the ZOOM command are explained, including ZOOM Dynamic, ZOOM Center, ZOOM Left, and ZOOM Vmax, in addition to the options explained in Chapter 2.

Fundamentals III

Dynamic Option AutoCAD's ZOOM Dynamic provides a quick and easy method of moving to another view of the drawing. With the ZOOM Dynamic you can see the entire drawing extents and then select the location and size of the next view by simple cursor manipulations. Using ZOOM Dynamic is the only means by which you can visually select a new display area that is not entirely within the current display. The only other method of visually selecting the entire new display is ZOOM Window, which is restricted to an area inside the current display. Other methods of visually selecting part of the new display within the current area are ZOOM Left Corner and ZOOM Center. But these methods (Window, Center, and Left Corner) do not permit visual selections that are entirely outside the current display. The command sequence is as follows:

Command: **zoom**
All/Center/Dynamic/Extents/Left/Previous/Vmax/Window/<Scale(X/XP): **d**

The current viewport is then transformed into a selecting view that displays the drawing extents, as shown in Figure 4–56.

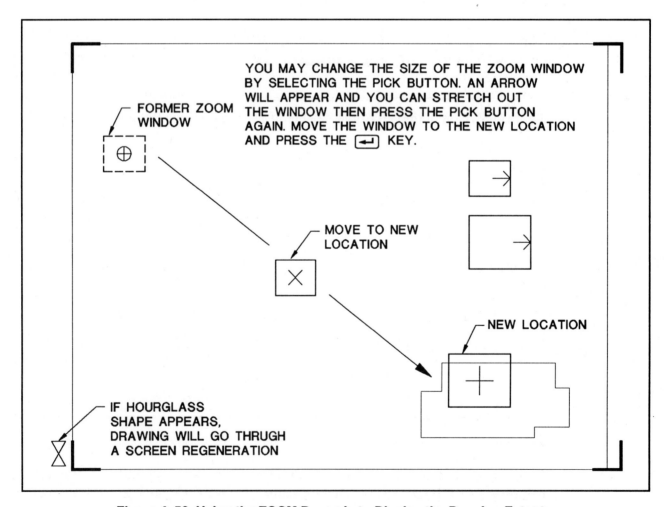

Figure 4-56 Using the ZOOM Dynamic to Display the Drawing Extents

When the selecting view has been displayed, you will see the drawing extents marked by a white or black box, the current display marked by a green or magenta dotted box, and the generated area marked at the corners in red. A new view box, the same size as the current display, will appear. Its location can be controlled by movement of the pointing device. Its size can be controlled by a combination of the pick button and cursor movement. When the new view box has an X in the center, the box will pan around in response to cursor movement. After pressing the pick button on the pointing device the X will disappear and an arrow will appear at the right edge of the box. The new view box is now in ZOOM mode. While the arrow is in the box, moving the cursor left will decrease the box size and moving the cursor right will increase the size.

When the desired size has been chosen, press the pick button again to pan or press ⏎ to accept the view defined by the location/size of the new view box. Pressing ⟨Ctrl⟩ + ⟨C⟩ will cancel the ZOOM Dynamic and return you to the current view.

> ***REGEN or REDRAW in ZOOM Dynamic*** The hourglass symbol will appear when the new view being selected is not entirely within the area defined by the four corners of the generated area. This means that a REGEN will be necessary, thus requiring more time than REDRAW. If used transparently, AutoCAD will not permit this and will display a message:
>
> Requires regen, cannot be transparent

Center Option The Center option of the ZOOM command lets you select a new view by specifying its center point and the height of the view in current units. The following command sequence shows an example of the Center option, as shown in Figure 4-57.

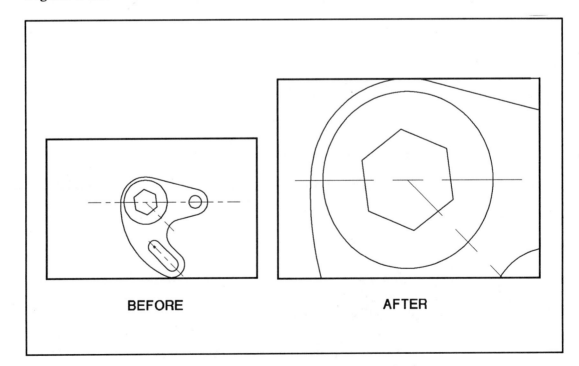

BEFORE   AFTER

Figure 4-57 Using the ZOOM Center Option

```
Command: zoom
All/Center/Dynamic/Extents/Left/Previous/Vmax/Window/<Scale(X/XP): c
Center point: 8,6
Magnification or Height <current height>: 4
```

The center point may be picked on the screen. The height may be specified in terms of the current view height by specifying the magnification value followed by an X. A response of 3X will make the new view height three times as large as the current height. The Model Space view height may be specified in terms of Paper Space by entering a value followed by XP.

Left Corner Option The Left Corner option of the ZOOM command operates exactly like ZOOM Center, except the point specified will become the lower left corner of the new view instead of the center. X and XP magnification are used in the same manner as in the Center option.

Vmax Option The Vmax option of the ZOOM command causes the new view to be the same as the current viewport's Virtual Screen. This provides the largest display without causing a regeneration.

TEXT COMMANDS

In this section additional TEXT commands and options are explained in addition to those options explained in Chapter 2.

DTEXT Command — Dynamic Text

The DTEXT command functions exactly as the TEXT command with one major difference; DTEXT lets you see the text on the screen as you type it in from the keyboard.

You will notice the same sequence of prompts that you used in the TEXT command. After you select your Start point <default> or select any of the justification options, you will then be prompted to enter a height and a rotation angle. At this time a cursor box will appear on the screen at the starting point you have selected.

When you have entered the line of text and pressed ⏎, you will notice the box cursor drop down to the next line anticipating that you wish to enter more text. If this is the case, simply type in the next line of text or when you are through, give a null response to terminate the command.

If you are in the DTEXT command when you notice a mistake or simply want to change a value or word you may backspace to the text you want to change. This will, however, delete all of the text you backspaced over to get back to the point you want to change. If this would involve erasing several lines of text it may be faster to use the CHANGE or DDEDIT command to adjust the text string.

One feature of DTEXT that will speed up your entry of text on your drawing is the ability to move the screen cross-hairs to a new point on the drawing while staying in the DTEXT command. As you move the screen cross-hairs to a new point on your drawing and pick point with your pointing device, you will notice the cursor box move to this new point allowing you to enter a new string of text and quickly move the cursor to the next point to enter more text. However, you must remember to give a null response to terminate the command.

The DTEXT command is invoked from the Screen Root Menu Draw (Figure 4–58), pull-down menu Draw (Figure 4–59), or at the "Command:" prompt type in **DTEXT** and press ⏎ or spacebar.

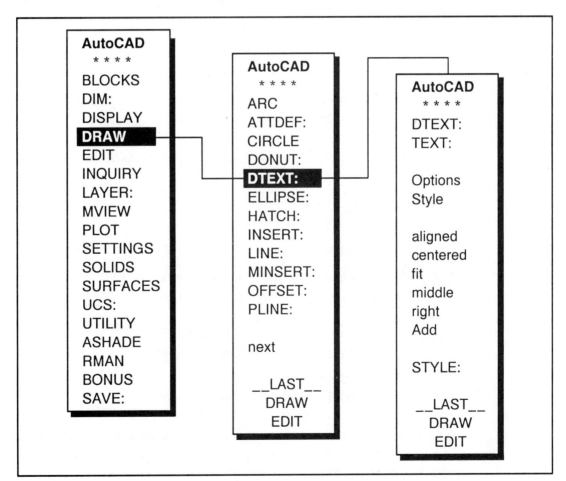

Figure 4–58 Invoking the DTEXT Command from the Screen Root Menu Draw

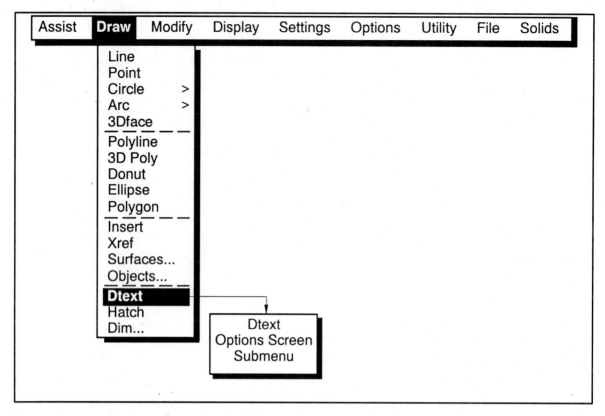

Figure 4-59 Invoking the DTEXT Command from the Pull-Down Menu Draw

Command: **dtext**
Justify/Style/<Start point>:

The options are similar to the TEXT command, explained in Chapter 2. All the options that are available to the TEXT command are available to the DTEXT command.

DDEDIT Command

The DDEDIT command allows you to edit text using the Advanced User Interface (AUI) if your display device supports the AUI.

The DDEDIT command is invoked from the Screen Root Menu Edit (Figure 4-60), or at the "Command:" prompt type in **DDEDIT** and press ↵ or spacebar.

Command: **ddedit**
<Select a TEXT or ATTDEF object>/Undo:

When you select a line of text, a dialogue box appears highlighting the text string to be changed. Place the arrow cursor on the line of text and pick it with your pointing device. You now can edit the text string as you desire using the backspace, insert, and delete keys on the keyboard to make the necessary changes.

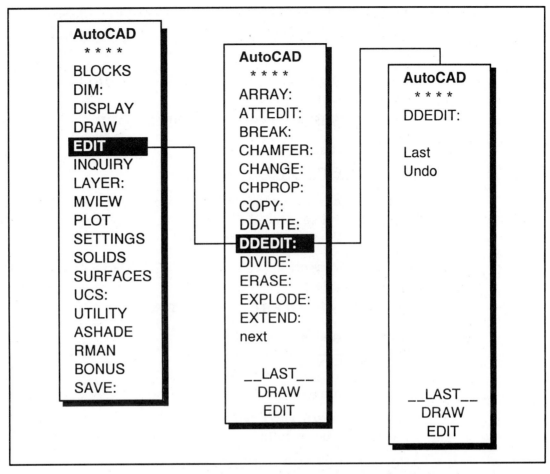

Figure 4-60 Invoking the DDEDIT Command from the Screen Root Menu Edit

When you are finished select OK. You are again prompted for a new text string to edit or you can enter a **U** to undo the last change made to the text. To terminate the command, give a null response.

Special Text Character and Symbol Options

In order to draw special symbols for text and dimensions, AutoCAD requires a sequence of control characters. For instance, to draw degree symbol (°), AutoCAD requires the control characters to precede the text string. The control characters for a symbol begin with a double percent sign (%%). The next character you enter represents the symbol. The following control sequences have been defined:

%%u	Toggle underscore mode on/off
%%o	Toggle overscore mode on/off
%%d	Draw degree symbol (°)
%%p	Draw plus/minus tolerance symbol (±)
%%c	Draw circle diameter dimensioning symbol (Ø)
%%%	Force a single percent sign (%)
%%*nnn*	Draw special character number *nnn* (ASCII)

Fundamentals III

%%u mode The %%u control string allows you to underscore (underline) a text string. The control sequence has to be in the beginning of the string from where the underlining of the text string will begin.

For example, to underscore the string of words "THIS IS A TEST FOR UNDER-SCORE," type the text as follows:

> **%%uTHIS IS A TEST FOR UNDERSCORE**

The resulting text string will appear:

> THIS IS A TEST FOR UNDERSCORE

%%o mode The %%o control string allows you to overscore (line above) a text string. The control sequence has to be in the beginning of the string from where the overscore of the text string will begin.

For example, to overscore the string of words "THIS IS A TEST FOR OVERSCORE," type the text as follows:

> **%%oTHIS IS A TEST FOR OVERSCORE**

The resulting text string will appear:

> THIS IS A TEST FOR OVERSCORE

You can underscore or overscore part of a line as follows:

> THIS IS %%uA TEST %%
> for underscore results in

> THIS IS A TEST FOR UNDERSCORE

%%d mode The %%d control string allows you to draw a degree symbol. For example, to draw the string "104.5°F," type the text as follows:

> **104.5%%dF**

%%p mode The %%p control string allows you to draw a plus/minus tolerance symbol. For example, to draw the string "34.5±3," type the note as follows:

> **34.5%%p3**

%%c mode The %%c control string allows you to draw a diameter symbol ($\emptyset$). For example, to draw the string "56.06$\emptyset$," type the text as follows:

> **56.06%%c**

%%% mode The %%% control string allows you to draw a single percent sign. This is necessary only when you must precede another control sequence. For example, to draw the string "34.67%±1.5," type the text as follows:

> **34.67%%%%%p1.5**

%%nnn mode The %%nnn control string allows you to draw special symbols by entering %% followed by a three-number code. For example, to draw the @ symbol, type the control string as follows:

> **%%064**

QTEXT Command

The QTEXT command is a support command for TEXT and DTEXT that is designed to reduce the redraw and regeneration time of a drawing. Regeneration times become a significant factor if the drawing contains a great deal of text and attribute information and/or if a fancy text font is used. Using QTEXT, the text is replaced with rectangular boxes of a height corresponding to the text height. These boxes are regenerated in a fraction of the time required for the actual text.

If a drawing contains many text and attribute items, it is advisable to switch QTEXT ON. However, before plotting the final drawing, or inspection of text details, the QTEXT command is turned OFF and is followed by the REGEN command.

The QTEXT command is invoked from the Screen Root Menu Settings (Figure 4–61), or at the "Command:" prompt type in **QTEXT** and press the ⏎ key.

    Command: **qtext**
    ON/OFF:

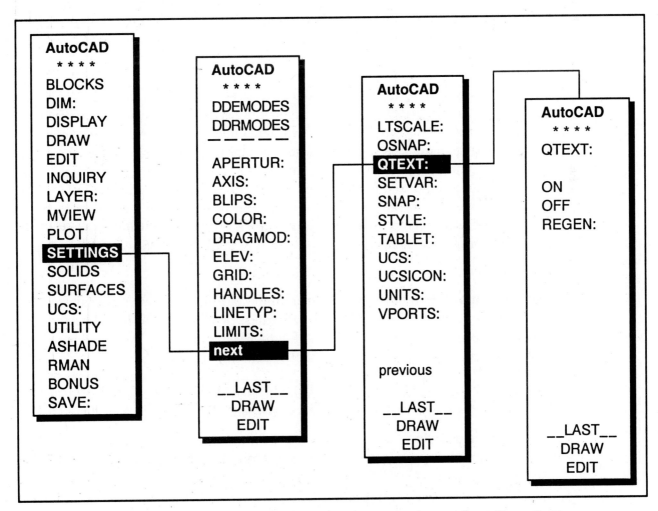

Figure 4–61 Invoking the QTEXT Command from the Screen Root Menu Settings

Fundamentals III

TEXT STYLES

The Style option to the TEXT command in conjunction with the STYLE command lets you determine how text characters and symbols appear other than adjusting the usual height, slant and angle of rotation. In order to be able to specify a text style from the Style option of the TEXT command, it must first be defined by using the STYLE command. In other words, the STYLE command will help you to create a new style or modify an existing style. The Style option under the TEXT command will allow you to choose a specific style from available styles.

STYLE Command

There are three areas of consideration when using the STYLE command.

First, you must make up a name for a style that you wish to define. Style names may contain up to 31 characters, numbers, and special characters ($, -, and _). Names like "titleblock," "notes," or "billofmaterials" can remind you of the purpose for which the particular style was designed. Abbreviated names like "tb," "n," or "bom" for the above would be easier to enter if used very often, but might be harder to determine their purpose. Arriving at a suitable name for text styles like layers, Blocks, and other named items often means deciding between ease of use and ease of recognition.

Second, you may apply a particular font to a STYLE. The font that AutoCAD uses as a default is called TXT. It has blocky looking characters, which are economical to store in memory. But the TXT.SHX font, made up entirely of straight line (noncurved) segments, is not considered as attractive or readable. Other fonts offer many variations in characters, including those for foreign languages. All fonts are stored for use in files of their font name with an extension of .SHX. The most effective way to get a distinctive appearance in text strings is to use a specially designed font. See Appendix J for a list of fonts that come with the AutoCAD program. If necessary, you can buy additional fonts from third-party vendors.

The third application of the STYLE command is in how AutoCAD treats general physical properties of the characters, regardless of the font that is selected. These properties are the Height, Width-to-Height ratio, Obliquing Angle, Backwards, Upside-down, and Orientation (horizontal/vertical) options.

The STYLE command is invoked from the Screen Root Menu Draw, or at the "Command:" prompt type in **STYLE** and press ⏎ or spacebar.

```
Command: style
Text Style name (or ?) <current>: specify the style name
Font file <default>: specify the filename
Height: specify the text height
Width factor <default>: specify the scale factor
```

Obliquing angle <default>: *specify the angle*
Backwards? <Y/N> *yes or no*
Upside-down? <Y/N> *yes or no*
Vertical? <Y/N> *yes or no*

The options and effects are discussed in the following sections.

Text Height If you respond with 0 (zero), then when you use this style in a TEXT command, you will be given an opportunity to change the text height with each occurrence of the command. If you give any other value, then that value will be used for all usages of this style and you will not be prompted for a text height during the TEXT command.

Width Factor Font characters will be drawn using the width/height factor of their definitions if the width factor is 1 (one). If you enter a value such as .5, then the characters will be drawn at half the defined width for the defined height. That is, they will be tall and thin. If the width factor is 3, the characters will be three times wider than normal for the given height.

Obliquing Angle This option is contrary to AutoCAD's normal angle measuring convention. To have the characters drawn slanted, enter the angle in degrees. Zero degrees is vertically upward (or AutoCAD's 90 degrees). A positive value will slant the top of the characters toward the right, or in a clockwise direction. A negative value will slant the characters in a counterclockwise direction. Remember, this positive/clockwise and negative/counterclockwise convention is opposite to AutoCAD's default convention for applying angles in drawing. See Figure 4–62 for the differences in oblique angles.

Backwards and Upside-down Options Responding **Y** to either of these options will cause the text to be drawn right-to-left (with the characters backwards) or upside-down (left-to-right), respectively. See Figure 4–63 for examples of backwards and upside-down text.

Vertical Option Responding **Y** to this orientation option will cause the text to be drawn vertically downward with each character centered below the previous one. See Figure 4–64 for examples of vertical orientation text.

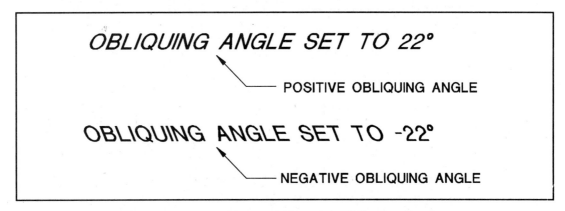

Figure 4–62 Positive and Negative Obliquing Angles

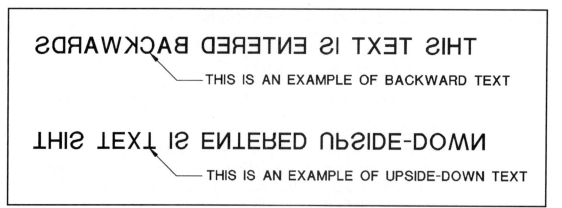

Figure 4-63 Examples of Backwards and Upside-Down Text

```
T              E              V              T
H              X              E              E
I              A              R              X
S              M              T              T
               P              I
I              L              C
S              E              A
                              L
I              O
S              F

A
N
```

Figure 4-64 Examples of Vertical Orientation Text

When you have responded to each of the above options by entering a new value or by providing a null response to keep the default value, the following will appear in the prompt area:

(Style name) is now the current text style.

The newly created style will become default style for the TEXT and DTEXT commands. If necessary, you can select a specific style from the available styles with the help of the Style option of the TEXT and DTEXT commands. The Style option is invoked as follows:

Command: **text**
Justify/Style/<Start point>: **s**
Style name(or ?)<STANDARD>: **style name**
Justify/Style/<Start point>:

After specifying a predefined style, you can continue with the TEXT command.

STANDARD is the default text style that is provided in the prototype drawing ACAD and is used for all text items including dimensioning and attributes unless specified otherwise.

UNDO, U, AND REDO COMMANDS

The UNDO command undoes the effects of the previous command or group of commands, depending upon the option employed. The U command is a one-time UNDO, and the REDO command is a one-time reversal of the effects of the previous UNDO.

U Command

The U command undoes the effects of the previous command, displaying the name of that command. Pressing ⏎ after using the U command will then undo the next previous command, and continue stepping back with each repetition until it reaches the state of the drawing at the beginning of the current editing session. The U command is invoked at the "Command:" prompt by typing in **U** and pressing ⏎.

> Command: **u**

For example, if the previous command sequences drew a circle and then copied it, two U commands in sequence will be as follows:

> Command: **u**
> COPY
> Command: ⏎
> CIRCLE

Using the U command after commands that involve transparent commands or subcommands will cause the entire sequence to be undone. For example, when you set a dimension variable and then perform a dimension command, a subsequent U command will nullify the dimension drawn and the change in the setting of the dimension variable.

UNDO Command

The UNDO command permits you to select a specified number or marked group of prior commands for undoing. The UNDO command is invoked from the Screen Root Menu Edit (Figure 4-65), or at the "Command:" prompt type in **UNDO** and press ⏎ or spacebar.

> Command: **undo**
> Auto/Back/Control/End/Group/Mark/<Number>:

The number options can be shortened by using the UNDO Control option as follows:

> Command: **undo**
> Auto/Back/Control/End/Group/Mark/<Number>: **c**
> All/None/One <All>:

All – This option enables all Undo options and is the default option of the UNDO command.

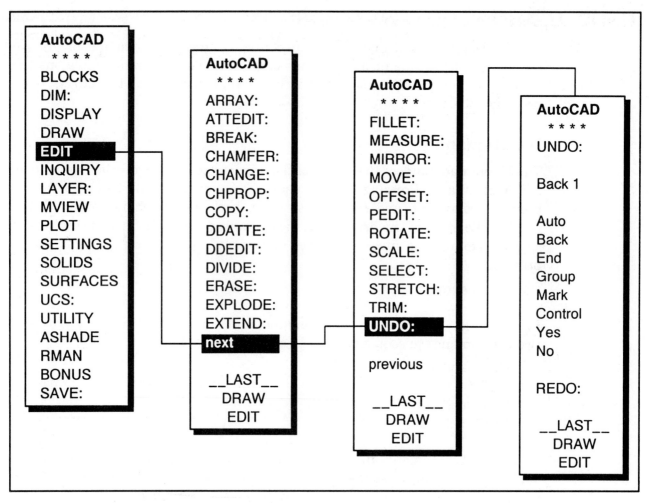

Figure 4-65 Invoking the UNDO Command from the Screen Root Menu Edit

None – This option disables the U and UNDO commands except the Control option of the UNDO command that can re-enable options.

One – This option prevents the U and UNDO commands from being used for multiple usage.

Limiting the U and UNDO commands frees the disk space that is otherwise being reserved to make multiple undoing possible. You are cautioned that changes to the drawing cannot be undone except for the most recent one with the One option. With the None option, no reversal is available.

Number Option The Number option allows you to enter a number; e.g., 3, at the full prompt (when Control is set to All) as follows:

Command: **undo**
Auto/Back/Control/End/Group/Mark/<Number>: **3**

The above sequence will cause the three previous operations to be undone. This is similar to using the U command three times in a row. The advantage of UNDO Number over multiple U's is that multiple screen regenerations will not occur, thus saving time.

Mark and Back Options If you are at a point in the editing session from which you would like to experiment, but would like the option of undoing the experiment, you can mark that point. An example of the Mark and Back option is demonstrated as follows:

> Command: **line** *draw a line*
> Command: **circle** *draw a circle*
> Command: **undo**
> Auto/Back/Control/End/Group/Mark/<Number>: **m**
> Command: **text** *enter text*
> Command: **arc** *draw an arc*
> Command: **undo**
> Auto/Back/Control/End/Group/Mark/<Number>: **b**

The Back option will return you to the state of the drawing that has the line and the circle. Following this UNDO Back with U will remove the circle. Another U will remove the line. Another U will display the prompt:

> Everything has been undone

Using the Back option when no Mark has been established will prompt:

> This will undo everything. OK? <Y>

Responding **Y** will undo everything since the current editing session was begun or since the last SAVE command.

CAUTION

Because the default is Y, think twice before giving a null response.

Group and End Options AutoCAD's U and UNDO commands treat the operations between an UNDO Group and an UNDO End as one command. A Group option entered after another Group option (before an UNDO End) will automatically invoke an UNDO End option, thereby grouping the operations since that prior Group option. If the UNDO Control has been set to None or One, the Group option will not work. Using the U command is permissible after Group and before an UNDO End, to undo operations, but only back to the UNDO Group.

The Group and End options are normally intended for use in strings of menu commands where a menu pick involves several operations.

Auto Option The Auto option causes multiple operations invoked by a single menu pick to be treated as one command by the U or UNDO command. UNDO Group should be placed at the beginning of a menu string with UNDO End at the end of the string. It has no effect if the UNDO Control has been set to None or One, however.

The effects of the following commands cannot be undone:

AREA, ATTEXT, DBLIST, DELAY, DIST, DXFOUT, END, FILES, FILMROLL, GRAPHSCR, HELP, HIDE, ID, IGESOUT, LIST, MSLIDE, PLOT, PRPLOT, QUIT, REDRAW, REDRAWALL, REGENALL, RESUME, SAVE, SHADE, SHELL, STATUS, and TEXTSCR.

Fundamentals III

REDO Command

The REDO command permits one reversal of a prior U or UNDO command. This will undo the undo. To undo the undo, the REDO command should be used immediately after using the U or UNDO command. The REDO command is invoked from the Screen Root Menu Edit, or at the "Command:" prompt type in **REDO** and press ⏎ or spacebar.

    Command: **redo**

The REDO command does not have any options.

OSNAP INTERSECTION, NODE, NEAREST, AND INSERT MODES

In this chapter four OSNAP modes are explained, including INTersection, NODE, NEArest, and INSert, in addition to OSNAP modes explained in Chapters 2 and 3.

INTERSECTION Mode

The INTERSECTION OSNAP mode lets you specify an intersection of two entities in response to a prompt requiring a point. Figure 4-66 shows valid intersections that can be selected by using the OSNAP INT mode.

NODE Mode

The NODE OSNAP mode lets you specify a Point entity in response to a prompt requiring a point.

> ***NOTE:*** A point drawn by using the POINT command is an entity. It should not be confused with a location in space that AutoCAD calls a point for purposes of identifying ends of lines and arcs, centers of circles and arcs, starting locations of text, and reference location/points for use in inserting Blocks and shapes. The point entity that can be OSNAPped to (using the NODE OSNAP mode) can be used as a location point, just like an intersection can be used as a location point. Neither location point is an entity. It just so happens that the first one is at the same location as the entity called Point. So, by using the NODE OSNAP mode, you can specify a location point that coincides with a Point entity.

NEAREST Mode

The NEAREST OSNAP mode lets you specify any entity (except text and shape items) in response to a prompt for a point and AutoCAD will use the point on that entity nearest the cursor. Some part of the entity must be in the aperture box for a point on that entity to be used.

INSERT Mode

The INSERT OSNAP mode lets you specify the insertion point of a Block, text item, or shape in response to a prompt for a point. The insertion point of a text

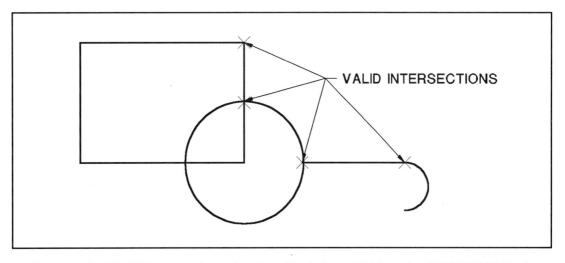

Figure 4–66 Valid Intersections that Can Be Selected Using the OSNAP INT Mode

item will be the one specified when it was drawn, such as Center, Right, Middle, etc.

ORDINATE DIMENSIONING

Ordinate dimensioning allows the user to display the X or Y coordinate of a feature (point) along with a simple leader line. Ordinate dimensioning is commonly used in mechanical application drawings. All the ordinate dimensions are displayed in reference to World Coordinate System (lower-left corner of the screen) or User Coordinate System (UCS), whichever is current. By default, you will be working on the World Coordinate System. UCS allows you to set your own coordinate system. For a detailed explanation of UCS, refer to Chapter 13.

The DIM: command can be invoked from the Screen Root Menu and then you can invoke Ordinate to get into Ordinate option, or at the "DIM:" prompt you can also type **ORD** and press ⏎ to get into ordinate dimensioning. AutoCAD prompts:

> DIM: **ord**
> Select feature:

Identify the feature to be dimensioned. If the feature is the corner of the object, identify the point with OSNAP endpoint or INTersect. After identifying the feature, AutoCAD prompts:

> Leader endpoint (Xdatum/Ydatum):

Designate the point for the leader endpoint. AutoCAD uses the difference between the feature location and the leader endpoint to determine whether it is an X or Y type of ordinate dimension. For example, if points selected for the first two prompts of the ORDINATE command indicate a horizontal direction relative to the current UCS, a Y datum dimension is drawn, as shown in Figure 4–67.

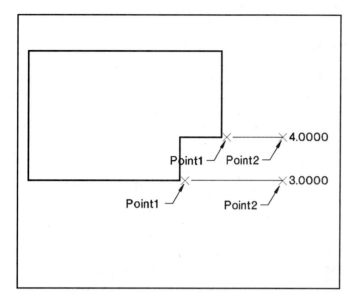

Figure 4-67 Y Datum Dimension

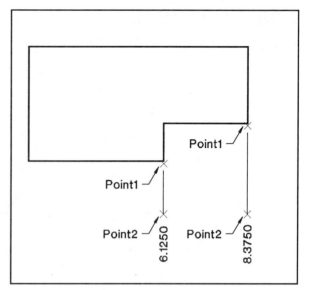

Figure 4-68 X Datum Dimension

If you pick two points in response to the first two prompts of the ORDINATE command that indicate a vertical direction relative to the current UCS, a X datum dimension is drawn, as shown in Figure 4-68.

Instead of providing the second point, you can explicitly indicate Xdatum or Ydatum dimensions for the leader endpoint prompt. This will be useful when the object being dimensioned contains crowded features and leaders must be routed to avoid collisions between adjacent dimension text. Subsequently, AutoCAD will prompt you for the leader endpoint.

Once you have given the location for the leader endpoint, AutoCAD measures the appropriate coordinate and prompts:

Dimension text <coordinate>:

A null response will cause AutoCAD to use the measured coordinate (X or Y) as the dimension text. If necessary, you can override the calculated dimensioning text. You can supply the text by typing it in from the keyboard.

The following command sequence shows an example of placing ordinate dimensioning by explicitly specifying X ordinate:

Command: **dim**
DIM: *pick ordinate from the screen menu*
Select Feature: *pick the feature*
Leader endpoint (Xdatum/Ydatum): **x**
Leader endpoint: *pick the endpoint of the leader*
Dimension text <default>: ⏎

LAB EXERCISES

Lab Exercise 4-1

For exercise 4-1, draw the front of the objects as a section view to practice using the HATCH command. Use a B-size sheet or PROTO-B drawing created in Chapter 2.

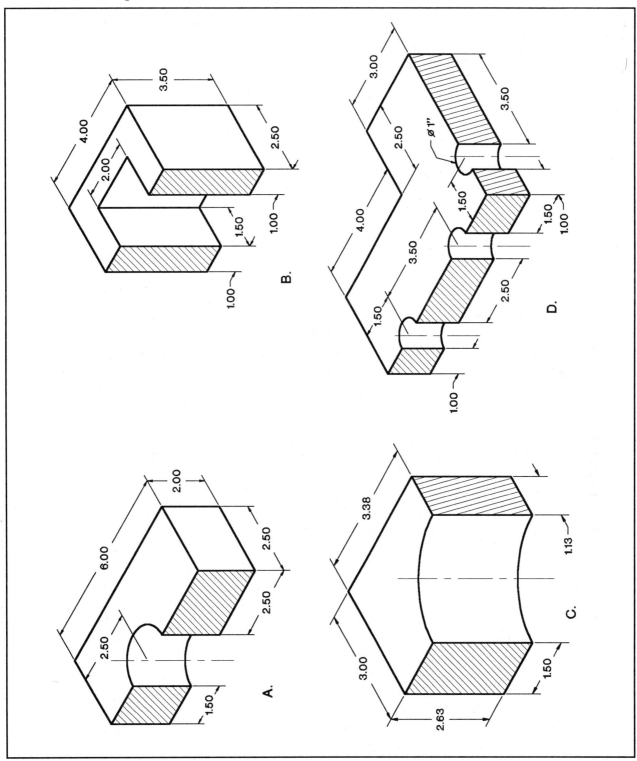

Lab Exercise 4-2

For exercise 4-2, draw the circle and divide it into three parts. Each segment must be separated from the others. Label each part. Use the HATCH command to hatch each part.

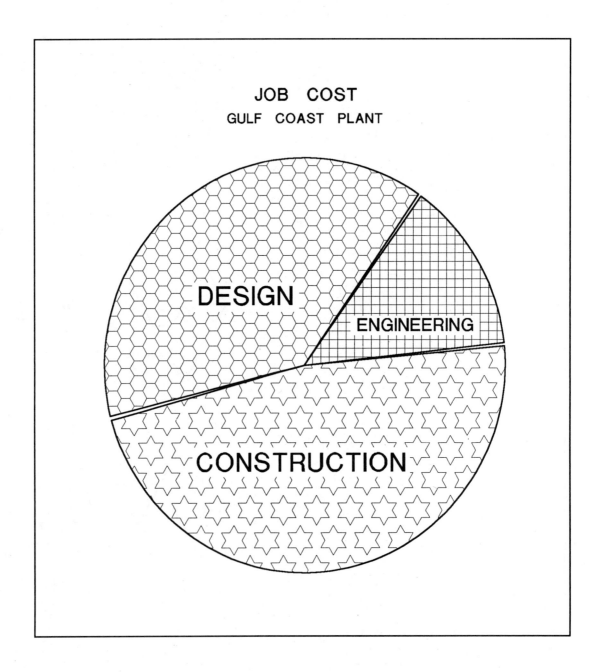

Lab Exercise 4-3

For exercise 4-3, lay out the top, front, and right side views. Draw the front view as a section. Show the cutting-plane line and all dimensions and callouts.

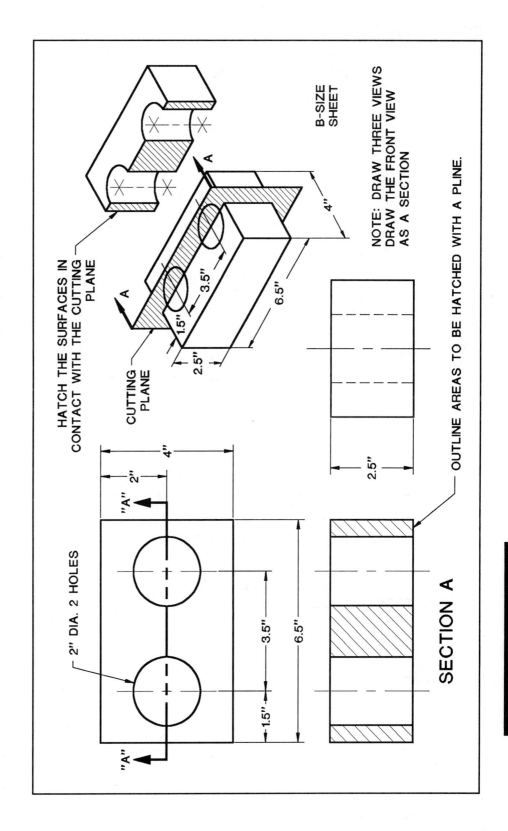

HATCH THE SURFACES IN CONTACT WITH THE CUTTING PLANE

CUTTING PLANE

B-SIZE SHEET

NOTE: DRAW THREE VIEWS DRAW THE FRONT VIEW AS A SECTION

OUTLINE AREAS TO BE HATCHED WITH A PLINE.

2" DIA. 2 HOLES

SECTION A

Lab Exercise 4-4

For exercise 4-4, lay out the top and front views. Draw the front view as a section view. Show the cutting-plane line and all dimensions and callouts.

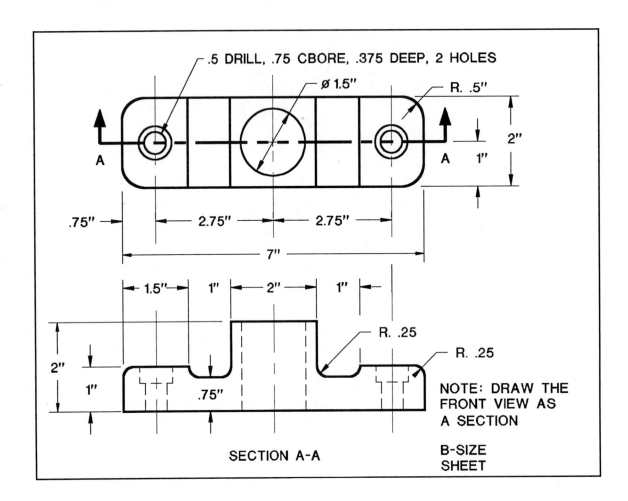

SECTION A-A

Lab Exercise 4-5

For exercise 4-5, lay out the top and front views. Draw the front view as a half section. Add all hatching, the cutting-plane line, and all dimensions and callouts. Use a B-size sheet or PROTO-B drawing.

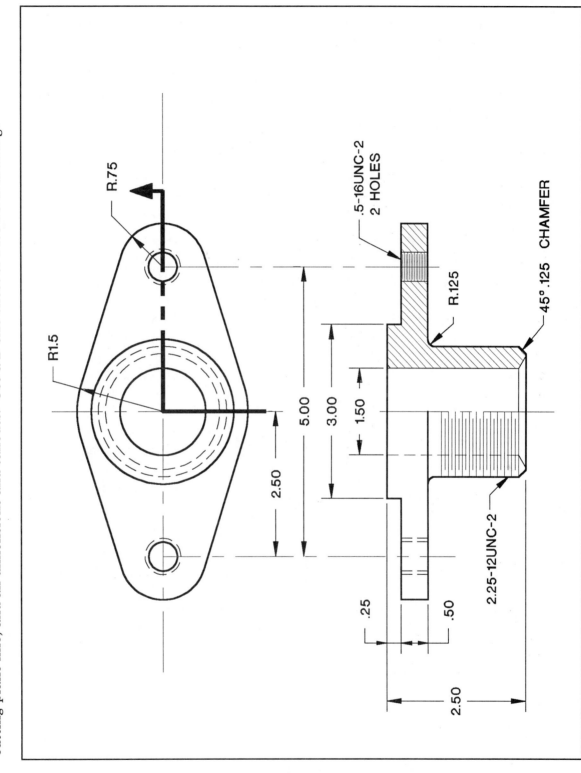

Lab Exercises 4-6 and 4-7

For exercises 4-6 and 4-7, lay out the front and left side views. Draw the left side view as a half section. Use a C-size drawing or use a PROTO-C drawing created in Chapter 2. Add all hatching, the cutting-plane line, dimensions, and callouts. Make the necessary changes to the dimensioning variables as noted on the drawing.

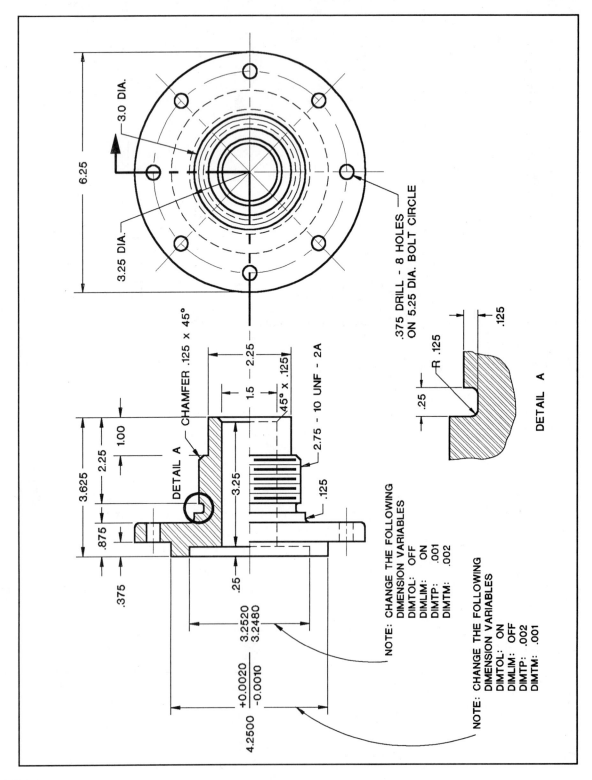

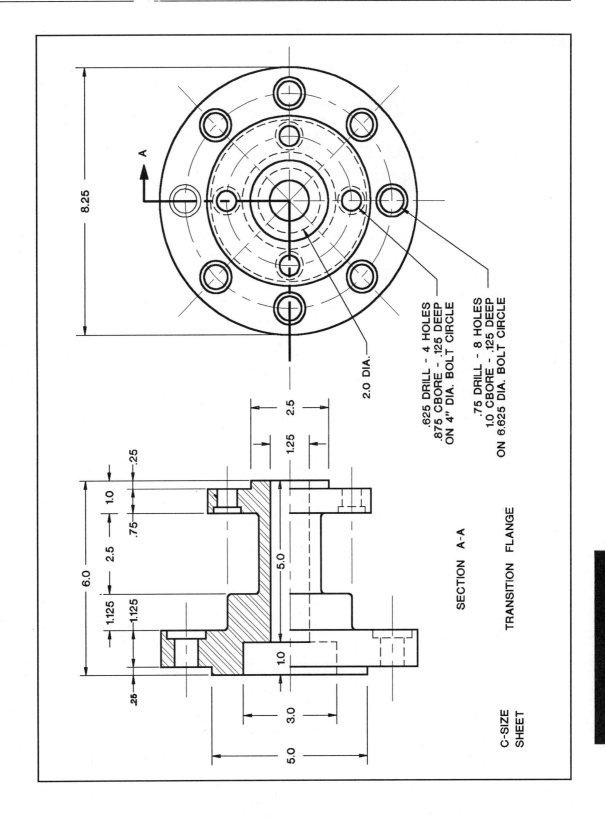

8.25

2.0 DIA.

.625 DRILL - 4 HOLES
.875 CBORE - .125 DEEP
ON 4" DIA. BOLT CIRCLE

.75 DRILL - 8 HOLES
1.0 CBORE - .125 DEEP
ON 6.625 DIA. BOLT CIRCLE

2.5
1.25

.25
1.0
.75
2.5
6.0
1.125
1.125
.25

5.0
1.0
3.0
5.0

SECTION A-A

TRANSITION FLANGE

C-SIZE
SHEET

Lab Exercise 4-8

For exercise 4-8, lay out the cabin floor plan to the dimensions shown on the drawing.

Set limits   lower left: 0,0

                         upper right: 60',50'

Set units to Architectural

Set DIMSCALE = 30

Set text height = 6"

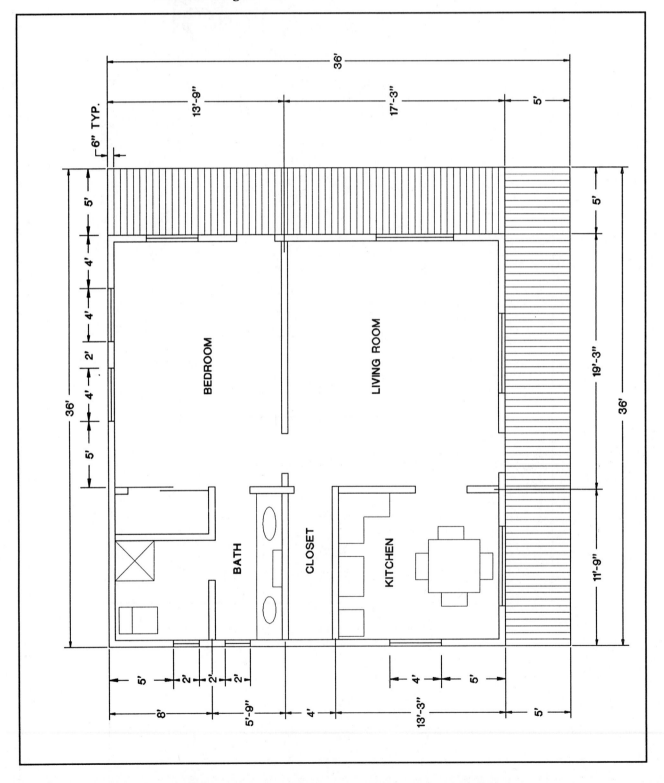

Lab Exercise 4-9

For exercise 4-9, lay out the front and right side view of the cabin. Logs are turned to a uniform 6" diameter.

Set limits   lower left: 0,0
                  upper right: 100', 50'

Set units to Architectural

Set DIMSCALE = 48

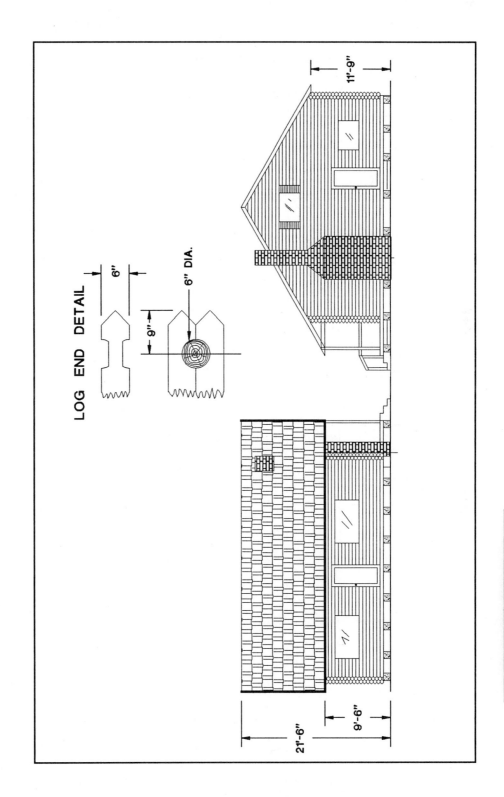

Lab Exercise 4-10

For exercise 4-10, lay out the foundation plan for the cabin using the dimensions given on the foundation. Use the ARRAY command.

      Set limits lower left: 0,0
      Set DIMSCALE = 30
      Set text height = 6"

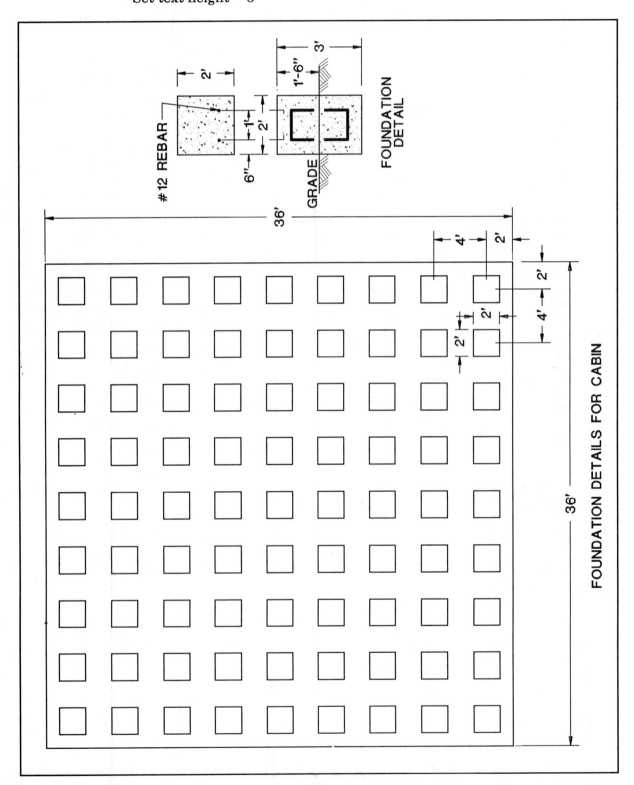

CHAPTER 5

Plotting and Printing

(Photos courtesy of CalComp Inc.)

One task has not changed much in the transition from board drafting to CAD, and that is obtaining a hard copy. The term "hard copy" describes a tangible reproduction of a screen image. The hard copy is usually a reproducible medium from which prints are made and it can take many forms, including slides, videotape, prints, or plots. This chapter describes the two most commonly used processes for getting a hard copy: plotting and printing.

In manual drafting, if you need your drawing to be done in two different scales, you have to physically draw the drawing for two different scales. Whereas in CAD, with minor modifications, you can plot or print the same drawing in different scale factors on different size paper. In AutoCAD Release 11, you can even compose your drawing in Paper Space limits that equal your sheet size and plot it at 1:1 scale.

PLANNING THE PLOTTED SHEET

Planning ahead is still required in laying out the objects to be drawn on the final sheet. The objects drawn on the plotted sheet must be arranged. At least in CAD, with its true-size capability, an object can be started without first laying out a plotted sheet. But eventually, some limits or at least a displayed area must be determined. If this is done arbitrarily, the chances of the drawing being plotted to any standard scale are very slight. For schematics, diagrams, and graphs, plotted scale is of little concern. But for architectural, civil, and mechanical drawings, plotting to a conventional scale is a professionally accepted practice that should not be abandoned just because it can be circumvented.

Setting up the drawing limits must take the plotted sheet into consideration in order to get the entire view of the object(s) on the sheet. So, even with all the power of the CAD system, some thought must still be given to the concept of scale, which is the ratio of true size to the size plotted. In other words, before you start drawing, you should have an idea at what scale the final drawing will be plotted or printed on a given size paper.

The limits should correspond to some factor of the plotted sheet. If the objects will fit on a 24" × 18" sheet at full size with room for a border, title block, bill of materials, dimensioning, and general notes, then set up your limits to (0,0) (lower left corner) and (24,18) (upper right corner). This can be plotted or printed at 1:1 scale, or one object unit equals one plotted unit.

Plot scales can be expressed in several different formats. Each of the following five plot scales is exactly the same. Only the display formats differ.

    1/4" = 1'-0"
    1" = 4'
    1 = 48
    1:48
    1/48

A plot scale of 1:48 means that a line 48 units long in AutoCAD will plot with a length of 1 unit. By default, plotting units in AutoCAD are inches.

Variables

There are four variables that control the relationship between the size of objects in an AutoCAD drawing and their sizes on a sheet of paper produced by an AutoCAD plot.

The four variables to consider are:

1. Size of the object in AutoCAD. For simplification it will be referred to as ACAD_size.

2. Size of the object on the plot. For simplification it will be referred to as ACAD_plot .

3. Maximum available plot area for a given sheet of paper. For simplification it will be referred to as ACAD_max_plot.

4. Plot scale. For simplification it will be referred as to ACAD_scale.

The relationship between the variables can be described in the following three algebraic formulas:

$$ACAD\_scale = ACAD\_plot / ACAD\_size$$
$$ACAD\_plot = ACAD\_size * ACAD\_scale$$
$$ACAD\_size = ACAD\_plot / ACAD\_scale$$

Example to Compute Plot Scale, Plot Size, and Limits

An architectural elevation of a building 48' wide and 24' high must be plotted on a 36" × 24" sheet. First, you have to determine the plotter's maximum available plot area for the given sheet size. This depends on the kind of plotter you are using to plot your drawings.

Some experimentation is required to ascertain the actual size of the plotter's maximum available plot area. An easy way to determine these limits is to plot a line drawn from (0,0) along the X axis, using the plot to FIT option. The resulting width of the plot will be the maximum width the plotter can address at the chosen size. To determine the maximum height for a chosen size, plot to FIT a line drawn from (0,0) along the Y axis.

In the case of a Houston Instruments plotter, the available area for 36" × 24" is 33.5" × 21.5". Next, you have to determine the area needed for the title block, general notes, and other items such as an area for revision notes and a list of reference drawings. For the given example, let's say that an area of 27" × 16" is available for the drawing.

The objective is to arrive at one of the standard architectural scales in the form of x in. = 1 ft. The usual range is from 1/16" = 1'-0" for plans of large structures to 3" = 1'-0" for small details. To determine the plot scale, substitute these values for the appropriate variables in the formula:

$$ACAD\_scale = ACAD\_plot / ACAD\_size$$
$$ACAD\_scale = 27"/48' \text{ for X axis}$$
$$= 0.5625"/1'-0" \text{ or } 0.5625"=1'-0"$$

The closest standard architectural scale that can be used in the given situation is 1/2" = 1'-0" (0.5" = 1'-0", 1/24 or 1:24).

To determine the size of the object on the plot, substitute these values for the appropriate variables in the formula:

$$\text{ACAD\_plot} = \text{ACAD\_size} * \text{ACAD\_scale}$$

$$\text{ACAD\_plot} = 48' * (0.5''/1') \text{ for X axis}$$

$$= 24'' \text{ (less than the 27'' maximum allowable space on the paper)}$$

$$\text{ACAD\_plot} = 24' * (0.5''/1') \text{ for Y axis}$$

$$= 12'' \text{ (less than the 16'' maximum allowable space on the paper)}$$

Instead of 1/2" = 1'-0" scale, if we go with a 3/4" = 1'-0" scale, then the size of the object on the plot will be 48' * (0.75"/1') = 36" for the X axis, which is more than the available space on the given paper. The drawing will not fit on the given size paper. You must select a larger paper size.

Once the plot scale is determined and verified that the drawing will fit on the given paper size, the drafter can now determine the drawing limits for the plotted sheet size of 33.5" × 21.5".

To determine the limits for the X and Y axis, substitute the appropriate values in the formula:

$$\text{ACAD\_limits (X axis)} = \text{ACAD\_max\_plot} / \text{ACAD\_plot}$$

$$= 33.5'' / (0.5''/1'-0'')$$

$$= 67'$$

$$\text{ACAD\_limits (Y axis)} = 21.5'' / (0.5''/1'-0'')$$

$$= 43'$$

Appropriate LIMITS settings in AutoCAD for a 36" × 24" sheet with a maximum available plot area of 33.5" × 21.5" at a plot scale of 0.5" = 1'-0" would be:

lower left corner: 0,0
upper right corner: 67',43'

Another consideration in setting up a drawing for user convenience is to be able to have the (0,0) coordinates at some point other than the lower left corner of the drawing sheet. Many objects have a reference point from which other parts of the object are dimensioned. Being able to set that reference point to (0,0) is very helpful. In many cases, the location of (0,0) is optional. In other cases, the coordinates should coincide with real coordinates, such as those on an industrial plant area block. In another cases, only one set of coordinates might be a governing factor.

In this example, the 48' wide × 24' high front elevation of the building is to be plotted on a 36" × 24" sheet at a scale of 1/2" = 1'-0". It has been determined that (0,0) should be at the lower left corner of the front elevation view as shown in Figure 5-1.

Centering the view on the sheet requires a few minutes of layout time. Several approaches will allow the drafter to arrive at the location of (0,0) relative to the lower left corner of the plotted sheet or limits. Having computed the limits to be 67' wide × 43' high, the half-width and half-height (dimensions from the center) of the sheet are 33.5' and 21.5' to scale, respectively. Subtracting the half-width of the building from the half-width of the limits will set the X coordinate of the lower

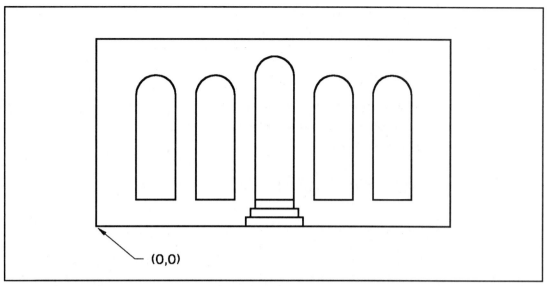

Figure 5-1 Setting the Reference Point to (0,0) Coordinates in a Location Other than the Lower Left Corner

left corner at -9.5' (from the equation 24'-33.5'). The same is done for the Y coordinate -9.5' (12'-21.5'). Therefore, the lower left corner of the limits will be at (-9.5',-9.5').

Appropriate LIMITS settings in AutoCAD for a 36" × 24" sheet with a maximum available plot area of 33.5" × 21.5" by centering the view at a plot scale of 0.5" = 1'-0" (see Figure 5-2) would be:

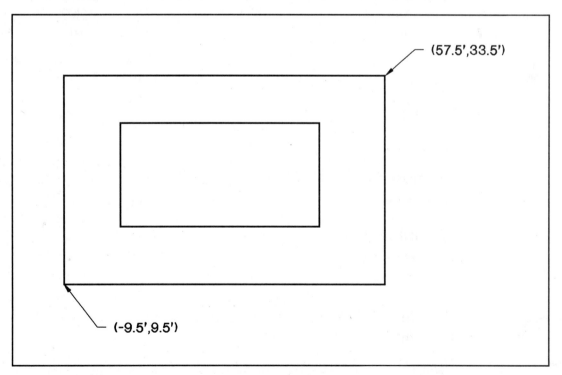

Figure 5-2 Setting the Limits to the Maximum Available Plot Area by Centering the View

lower left corner: -9.5',-9.5'
upper right corner: 57.5',33.5'

Setting for LTSCALE

As explained earlier in Chapter 2 LTSCALE provides a method of adjusting the linetypes to a meaningful scale for your actual drawing. This sets the length of dashes in linetypes. When LTSCALE is set to the reciprocal of the plot scale, provided default linetypes plot out on paper the sizes they are defined in ACAD.LIN.

LTSCALE = 1 / ACAD_scale

Setting for DIMSCALE

As explained earlier in Chapter 2, AutoCAD provides a set of dimensioning variables, that control the way it draws dimensions. The dimension variable DIMSCALE is applied globally to all dimension variables which govern sizes or distances, as an overall scaling factor. The default DIMSCALE is 1. When DIMSCALE is set to the reciprocal of the plot scale, it will apply globally to all dimension variables for the plot scale factor.

DIMSCALE = 1 / ACAD_scale

If necessary, you can set individual dimensioning variables to the size that you would actually want the dimension to appear on the paper by substituting the appropriate values in the formula:

size of the plotted dimvars_value = dimvars_value * ACAD_scale * DIMSCALE

As an example, to determine the arrow size DIMASZ for a plot scale of 1/2" = 1'-0", DIMSCALE of 1 and default DIMASZ is 0.18", then

size of the plotted arrow = 0.18" * (1/24) * 1
= 0.0075"

Scaling Annotations and Symbols

How can you determine what size your text and symbols (Blocks) will plot? As mentioned earlier, you almost always draw objects actual size, or real-world dimensions. Even in the case of text and placement of Blocks, you place them to the real-world dimensions. In the previous example, the architectural elevation of a building 48' × 24' is drawn to actual size and plotted to a scale of 1/2" = 1'-0'. Let's say you wanted your text size to plot at 1/4" high. If you were to create your text and annotations at 1/4", they would be so small relative to the elevation drawing itself that you could not read them.

Before you start placing the text, you need to know at what scale you will eventually plot the drawing. In the previous example of architectural elevation, the plot scale is 1/2" = 1'-0" and you want your text size to plot at 1/4" high. You

Table 5-1 Text Height Conversion Chart

DESIRED HEIGHT		1/16"	3/32"	1/8"	3/16"	1/4"	5/16"	3/8"	1/2"	5/8"
Scale	Factor									
1/16" = 1'-0"	192	12"	18"	24"	36"	48"	60"	66"	96"	120"
1/8" = 1'-0"	96	6"	9"	12"	18"	24"	30"	36"	48"	60"
3/16" = 1'-0"	64	4"	6"	8"	12"	16"	20"	24"	32"	40"
1/4" = 1'-0"	48	3"	4.5"	6"	9"	12"	15"	18"	24"	30"
3/8" = 1'-0"	32	2"	3"	4"	6"	8"	10"	12"	16"	20"
1/2" = 1'-0"	24	1.5"	2.25"	3"	4.5"	6"	7.5"	9"	12"	15"
3/4" = 1'-0"	16	1"	1.5"	2"	3"	4"	5"	6"	8"	10"
1" = 1'-0"	12	0.75"	1.13"	1.5"	2.25"	3"	3.75"	4.5"	6"	7.5"
1 1/2" = 1'-0"	8	0.5"	.75"	1"	1.5"	2"	2.5"	3"	4"	5"
3" = 1'-0"	4	0.25"	.375"	0.5"	0.75"	1"	1.25"	1.5"	2"	2.5"
1" = 10'	120	7.5"	11.25"	15"	22.5"	30"	37.5"	45"	60"	75"
1" = 20'	240	15"	22.5"	30"	45"	60"	75"	90"	120"	150"
1" = 30'	360	22.5"	33.75"	45"	67.5"	90"	112.5"	135"	180"	225"
1" = 40'	480	30"	45"	60"	90"	120"	150"	180"	240"	300"
1" = 50'	600	37.5"	56.25"	75"	112.5"	150"	187.5"	225"	300"	375"
1" = 60'	720	45"	67.5"	90"	135"	180"	225"	270"	360"	450"
1" = 70'	840	52.5"	78.75"	105"	157.5"	210"	262.5"	315"	420"	525"
1" = 80'	960	60"	90"	120"	180"	240"	300"	360"	480"	600"
1" = 90'	1080	67.5"	101.25"	135"	202.5"	270"	337.5"	405"	540"	675"
1" = 100'	1200	75"	112.5"	150"	225"	300"	375"	450"	600"	750"

need to find a relationship between 1/4" on the paper and the size of the text for real-world dimensions in the drawing (model). If 1/2" on the paper equals 12" in the model, then 1/4"-high text on the paper equals 6", so text and annotations should be placed at 6" high in the drawing (model) to plot at 1/4" high to a scale of 1/2" = 1'-0". Similarly, you can calculate the various text sizes for a given plot scale.

Table 5-1 shows the model text size needed to achieve a specific plotted text size at some common scales.

Composing Border and Title Block

As mentioned earlier, you always draw objects actual size, or in real-world dimensions. After drawing your model, you can add a border and title block, just like adding any other entities in your model. Instead of monotonously creating a border and title block for every new model you will be drawing in AutoCAD, you can create a stand-alone title block of appropriate paper size limits (electronic sheet) and insert it as a Block to a proper scale factor.

Plotting and Printing

Create the border and title block full size (12" × 9", 18" × 12", 24" × 18", 36" × 24" or 48" × 36"). When creating the border, make sure to set the limits to the plotter's maximum available plot area for the given sheet size. This depends on the kind of plotter you are using to plot your drawings.

Once the plotter's maximum available plot area is determined for a given paper size, a border and title can be drawn that match these proportions. All text, attribute tags, logos, lines, and so forth should be drawn at the size they will plot. If necessary, you can also define attributes in the title block.

You can insert the border and title to your model drawing as a Block, to a scale factor, which is inverse of the scale that you would use to plot the drawing. Let's look at an example.

We'll take the same example we used before—architectural elevation of a building 48' wide and 24' high plotted on a 36" × 24" sheet to a plot scale of 1/2" = 1'-0" (1/24 or 1:24). Insert the border and title drawing into the model and scale it 24 times (inverse of the plot scale factor 1/24) larger to fit around the elevation drawing. It will scale back to its original size when the drawing is plotted.

If 1/8" plotted on the paper is to represent 1" of the drawing geometry, the scale factor of the border and title block insertion will be 8. If 1/8" plotted on the paper is to represent 1' of the drawing geometry, the scale factor of the border and title block insertion will be 96. This method can be used even when the object is very small and needs to be enlarged on the final plot. For a plot scale factor of 2"= 1", then scale factor of the border and title block insertion will be 0.5.

The second approach would be to scale the model drawing down and insert it into the title block before you plot. This will allow you to plot at 1=1 scale, and "What You See is What You'll Plot (WYSWYP)."

You can create a 1=1 border and title drawing as explained earlier, and insert the model drawing file into it at the appropriate scale. If you make changes to the model drawing file, reinsert it with an equal sign to redefine it.

You can create the model drawing in real-size dimensions. Then, create a block of the entire drawing with the help of BLOCK command. Next, insert your title block at 1=1 scale on its own layer and zoom to the title block. Then, insert your entire drawing into the border and title drawing at the scale that you would have used to plot in the previously discussed method. If you need to make changes in the model, you can explode, then reblock to the same name.

Creating a Plot in Paper Space

One of the most useful new features of AutoCAD Release 11 is the option to work on your drawing in two different environments, Model or Paper Space. In Paper

Space you can compose the drawing at different scale factors and plot at a 1:1 scale. For a detailed explanation, refer to Chapter 8.

Plotting Options

The PLOT or PRPLOT (for printer plot) commands are invoked from the Screen Root Menu Plot, pull-down menu File, or at the "Command:" prompt type in **PLOT** or **PRPLOT**, depending on whether you want to plot on a plotter or printer plotter, and press ⏎.

The prompts are identical for both PLOT and PRPLOT commands except in the case of PLOT, where AutoCAD prompts for information concerning pen colors and linetypes.

> Command: **plot**
> What to plot--Display, Extents, Limits, View, or Window <default>:

These options allow you to specify what to plot.

Display Option This option will plot what is currently displayed on the screen. An important point to remember is that the lower left corner of the current display is the origin point of the plot. This option is useful if you want to plot only part of the drawing. Before you select this option, make sure the view you want is displayed on the screen by using ZOOM and PAN commands.

Extents Option This option will plot the entire drawing. This option forces the lower left corner of the entire drawing, rather than the display, to become the origin of the plot. This option is similar to ZOOM Extents and ensures that the entire drawing is plotted, regardless of the setting of the LIMITS command.

Limits Option This option plots the drawing to its limits. In general, this makes the origin of the drawing equal to the origin of the plot.

View Option This option plots a previously saved view. If you plot a previously created view, the plot is identical to the screen image after the VIEW Restore command is used to bring the view on-screen. View plotting makes it easy to plot predefined areas of a drawing. When you select this option, AutoCAD prompts:

> View name:

Window Option This option allows you to pick a window on the screen and plot the entities that are inside the window. The lower left corner of the window becomes the origin of the plot. This is similar to using the ZOOM Window

Plotting and Printing

command to zoom into a specific portion of the drawing, and then using the Display option of the PLOT command to plot. When you select this option, AutoCAD prompts:

First corner: *pick a point or enter coordinates*
Other corner: *pick a point or enter a coordinates*

Once you have chosen the portion of the drawing to be plotted and pressed ⏎, AutoCAD switches to the text screen and displays the basic plot specifications as shown below and prompts you if you want to change any of them.

Plot will NOT be written to a selected file
Sizes are in Inches
Plot origin is at (0.00,0.00)
Plotting area is 36.00 wide by 24.00 high (D size)
Plot is NOT rotated
Pen width is 0.010
Area fill will NOT be adjusted for pen width
Hidden lines will NOT be removed
Plot will be scaled to 1=1
Do you want to change anything? <N>

If you give a null response or press **N** and press ⏎, AutoCAD will prompt you to position the paper in the plotter and begin plotting to the default settings.

Instead, if you want to change one or more specifications, enter **Y** or **YES** and press ⏎. As a first step, AutoCAD will display a pen-assignment table.

Selecting Pen Assignments

Table 5-2 shows which pen colors, plotter linetypes, and pen speeds are used.

The entity color in the first column of this list is the color you have assigned to an object in your drawing. Usually an object is automatically assigned the color of

Table 5-2 Pen Color, Plotter Linetype, and Pen Speed Chart

Entity Color	Pen No.	Linetype	Pen Speed
1 (red)	1	0	36
2 (yellow)	1	0	36
3 (green)	1	0	36
4 (cyan)	1	0	36
5 (blue)	1	0	36
6 (magenta)	1	0	36
7 (white)	1	0	36
8	1	0	36

the layer on which it is drawn. Instead, you can also assign a color to an object independent of the layer on which it is drawn. It is highly recommended to draw the objects by following color assignments to the layers.

The second column shows the assignment of pen numbers for various colors. You can plot the object in either the same color you used in the drawing file or in a different color. Generally, it is easier to keep track of your colors and pens if you have the same color. If necessary, you can assign the same pen number to all the colors, and the plotting will be done in one color. If you have a single-pen plotter and you want to do a multiple-pen plot, AutoCAD stops the plotter and prompts you to change pens whenever a different pen is called for.

The third column shows the assignment of linetypes for various colors. Some plotters are capable of generating their own linetypes. This feature is very seldom used because it is simpler to assign linetypes to layers directly in the drawing.

The fourth column controls the pen speed setting. This is important because different pens have different speed requirements. Refillable technical pens generally require slower speeds, while roller pens are capable of very high speeds.

You can also alternate the pen assignment feature to serve a different purpose. For example, if you want a few of the entities to be plotted wider than others you can draw those specific entities in a specific color, say red, then assign the color red to a pen number that has a pen that can plot wide lines.

If you want to change pen assignments, enter **y** or **yes** and press ⏎ in response to the prompt:

> Do you want to change any of these parameters? <N>

The following prompt appears:

> Enter values. blank=Next value, Cn=Color n, S=Show current values, X=Exit

Entity Color	Pen No.	Line Type	Pen Speed	
1(red)	1	0	60	Pen number <1>:

This prompt duplicates the information on the first color listed in the previous prompt. If necessary, you can change the pen number, linetype, or pen speed for individual entity color. If you want to leave a setting as is, press ⏎, or type a new value. AutoCAD will not let you type invalid numbers, such as a negative pen number or a pen speed that is too high. At any time you can jump to prompts related to a specifc entity color by typing **C** followed by entity color number. To see the full list of pen assignments at any time, press **S**. Once you are satisfied with your pen assignments, enter **X** to exit pen assignments.

Creating a Plot File

In order to create a plot file, the following prompt appears:

Write the plot to a file? <N>

At this prompt you can tell AutoCAD to send the plot information to a plot file instead of to the plotter by typing **y** and pressing ⏎. Or, press ⏎ to accept the default No. The creation of a plot file is useful if you need to use a plotter connected to another computer. You can copy the file to a floppy disk and then transfer the disk to the other computer. AutoCAD creates the plot file with PLT as an extension to the given filename.

Setting the Units

The next prompt is regarding the selection of a base unit of measurement. The following prompt appears:

Size units (Inches or Millimeters) <Inches>:

AutoCAD lets you plot your drawing in inches or millimeters. Press ⏎ to accept the default Inches. If you did your drawing relative to millimeters, you would select millimeters. You cannot do a drawing relative to inches, then pick millimeters at this prompt and expect to get a scale drawing.

Setting the Origin for Plot

The next prompt is regarding the position of the origin on the paper. The following prompt appears:

Plot origin in inches <0.00, 0.00>:

This prompt allows you to move the origin of the plotted drawing. The origin is the position on the plotted sheet where you tell AutoCAD to place the lower left corner of the drawing. By default, the lower left corner of the paper is the location of the origin. To change the location of the origin, and thus change the location of the drawing on the sheet, you can give a coordinate in inches or millimeters to the prompt. Make sure to use the same measurement system you chose at the previous prompt. Moving the origin is helpful if you want to plot several drawings on a single paper. Press ⏎ to accept the default origin location.

Selecting the Paper Size

The next prompt is regarding the selection of the paper size. The following prompt appears:

```
Standard values for plotting size
Size        Width      Height
A           10.50       8.00
B           16.00      10.00
C           21.00      16.00
D           33.00      21.00
E           43.00      33.00
MAX         44.72      35.31
Enter the Size or Width, Height (in inches) <A>:
```

The list of sizes depends on your plotter. You can select a listed size by entering either its American National Standards Institute (ANSI) designation, A, B, C, etc. or you can specify a width, height by entering a numeric value at this prompt; e.g., 14.5,9.5. AutoCAD remembers the 14.5 × 9.5 dimension and presents it as the USER option the next time you plot. If you enter a size that is too large, you will get an error message

Warning plotter area exceeds plotter maximum
Plotting area truncated to maximum

before the last prompt in this sequence. If you still continue to plot, AutoCAD will truncate part of the drawing to fit on the given paper.

Rotating the Plot

The next prompt is regarding rotation of the drawing from its normal position. The following prompt appears:

Rotate plot 0/90/180/270 <0>:

AutoCAD lets you change the orientation of the drawing. Press ↵ for a normal plot, enter 90 to rotate the plot by 90 degrees, or rotation of 180 or 270 turns the plot upside down. You can also answer this prompt with **Y** or **N**. If you answer **Y** to this prompt, the plot is rotated 270 degrees on the paper and **N** will plot the drawing as a normal plot (0 degrees).

Selecting the Pen Width

The next prompt allows you to select the thickness of individual lines being plotted in solid-filled areas. The following prompt appears:

Pen width <0.010>:

AutoCAD allows you to control how wide the lines will be drawn in solid-filled areas (trace, pline, solid, and doughnut). If the value you give here is too high, the solid area will come out as a vertical/horizontal hatch pattern. If it is too low, the plotter will waste time drawing over areas it has already covered. The default pen width 0.010 is adequate in most conditions.

Adjusting Area Fill Boundaries

The Next prompt allows you to compensate for pen width around the edges of a solid-filled area. The following prompt appears:

Adjust area fill boundaries for pen width <N>:

When the plotter draws a solid-filled area, it finishes the area by drawing the boundary with the given pen width. If the plotter uses a wide-width pen, the solid area will be too large. You can tell AutoCAD to compensate by typing **Y** to the prompt and pressing ⏎. Generally, compensation for pen width is critical only when you are producing drawings, such as printed circuit artwork, photo etching, or similar artwork. Press ⏎ for the default.

Hidden Line Removal

The next prompt allows you to remove hidden lines from 3D drawings. The following prompt appears:

Remove hidden lines? <N>:

Respond **Y** and press ⏎ if you want to remove hidden lines. Hidden lines are those that normally would be obscured by objects placed in front of them. This option is not applicable to 2D drawings. Press ⏎ for the default.

Selecting the Scale

The next prompt allows you to select the scale to plot your drawing. The following prompt appears:

Specify scale by entering:
Plotted Inches=Drawing units or Fit or ? <F>:

Here you decide at what scale you want to plot your drawing. There are three options to respond to the prompt.

1. You can respond with a plot inches or millimeters=drawing units. As explained earlier, you can express the plot scale in several different formats. For example, if you want to plot your drawing to a scale of 1/4"=1'-0", you can enter 1:48 or .25=12.

2. You can respond with option fit and press ⏎. This allows you to plot the drawing to fit on the given sheet of paper.

3. If you enter ? to the prompt and press ⏎, AutoCAD displays a brief help screen describing the available options for scaling your plot.

Start Plotting

The next prompt allows you to position the paper in the plotter. The following prompt appears:

Effective plotting area: 13.5 wide by 9.5 high
Position paper in plotter.
Press RETURN to continue or S to Stop for hardware setup.

This prompt tells you the size of your plotting area and reminds you to put paper in your plotter. If you have to change any of the options on the plotter hardware, type **S** and set up your options. If you try setting up your plotter without using the S option, AutoCAD overrides your settings when it starts to send its information to the plotter. Once you are through with setting up the paper, press ⏎.

AutoCAD reports its progress as it converts the drawing into the plotter's graphics language by displaying the number of vectors processed.

If something goes wrong or if you want to stop abruptly, press ⟨Ctrl⟩ + ⟨C⟩ at any time. AutoCAD will cancel the plotting.

Once the plot is done, the last prompt appears:

Plot complete.
Press RETURN to continue.

Press ⏎ to take you back to the Drawing Editor.

Plotting and Print Plotting from the Main Menu

If you prefer, you can plot and print plot from the AutoCAD Main Menu. From the Main Menu, enter **3** to plot a drawing, enter **4** to print plot a drawing. AutoCAD will prompt you for the name of the drawing. The rest of the options are identical to the plotting from the Drawing Editor, except when you want to use the PLOT Window option. You cannot use your pointing device to pick the window; instead, you must provide a pair of coordinates for the window's corner.

Printing from the Main Menu is useful if you have several drawings to be plotted or print plotted, without having to open and close the files.

LAB EXERCISES

Lab Exercise 5-1

Load one of the drawings from Chapter 2 into the Drawing Editor. Use the PLOT command to plot it to fit on a B-size sheet.

Lab Exercise 5-2

Plot the same drawing used in exercise 5-1 using the Limits option on a B-size sheet.

Plotting and Printing

Lab Exercise 5-3

Plot the project drawing from Chapter 2 on an A-size sheet to a scale of 3/16" = 1'-0".

Lab Exercise 5-4

Load one of the drawings from Chapter 3 into the Drawing Editor. Display the drawing the way you want to plot, and use the PLOT command to plot using the Display option to fit on a C-size sheet.

Lab Exercise 5-5

Plot the same drawing used in exercise 5-4 using the Extents option on a C-size sheet.

Lab Exercise 5-6

Plot the project drawing from Chapter 3 on a B-size sheet to a scale of 1=1.

CHAPTER
6

Blocks and Attributes

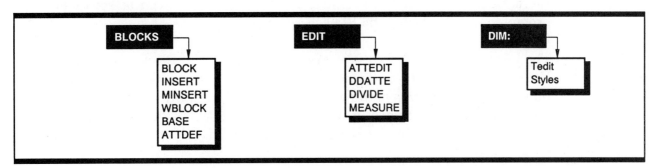

Figure 6-1 The Block and Attribute Commands and Options

AutoCAD has a very powerful BLOCK command. It permits you to group entities under a user-determined name and perform certain editing commands on the group as though they were a single entity. In this chapter the BLOCK command and other related commands are explained, including WBLOCK and Attributes. See Figure 6-1 for a list of the commands and options that are covered in this chapter.

AutoCAD's BLOCK command feature provides a powerful design/drafting tool. Even though it can be made up of more than one entity, a Block acts as a single unit when operated on by certain Editing commands like MOVE, COPY, ERASE, ROTATE, ARRAY, and MIRROR. The BLOCK command enables a designer to create an object from one or more entities, save it under a user-determined name, and later place it back into the drawing. When Blocks are inserted in the drawing they can be scaled up or down in both or either of the X or Y axes. They can also be rotated as they are inserted on the drawing. Blocks can best be compared with their manual drafting counterpart, the template. You can also export a Block to become a drawing file outside your current drawing and create a symbol library from which Blocks can be inserted into other drawings. Like the plastic template, Blocks greatly reduce repetitious work.

Using the BLOCK command can save time by not having to draw the same object(s) more than once. Blocks save computer storage by only having to store the entity descriptions once. When inserting Blocks, you can change the scale and/or proportions of the original object(s).

417

CREATION OF BLOCKS

When you use the BLOCK command to create a Block, AutoCAD refers to this as defining the Block. The resulting definition is stored in the drawing data base. The same Block can be inserted as many times as needed.

Blocks may comprise one or more entities. The first step in creating Blocks is the creation of a Block Definition. In order to do this, the entities that make up the Block must be visible on the screen. That is, the entities that will make up the Block Definition must have already been drawn so you can select them when prompted to do so during the BLOCK command.

The layer the individual entities are on comprising the Block is very important. Entities that are on layer 0 when the Block is created will assume the color and linetype of any future layer on which the Block is inserted. Entities on any layer other than 0 when included in the Block Definition will retain the characteristics of that layer, even when the Block is inserted on a different layer. See Figure 6-2 for an example.

Note the warning at the end of Chapter 1 concerning the use of the COLOR command. You should also be careful when using the CHPROP command to change the color or linetype of elements of a Block. It is best to keep the color and linetype of Blocks and the entities that comprise them in the BYLAYER state.

Examples of some common uses of Blocks in various disciplines are shown in Figure 6-3.

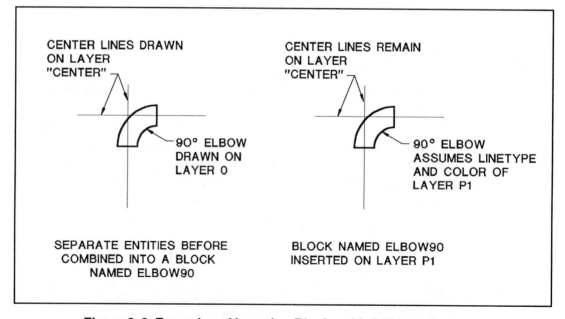

Figure 6-2 Examples of Inserting Blocks with Different Formats

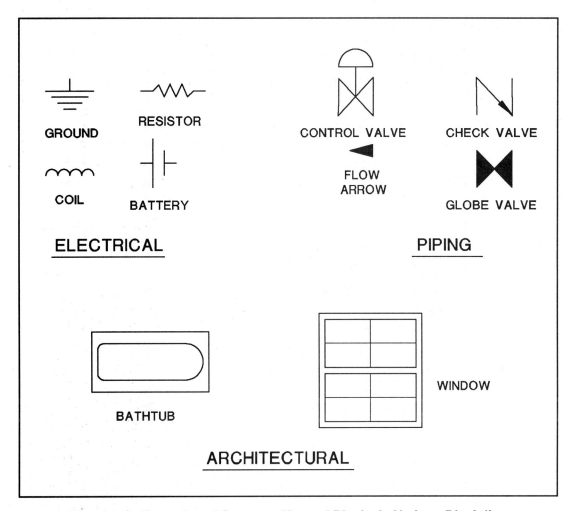

Figure 6-3 Examples of Common Uses of Blocks in Various Disciplines

BLOCK COMMAND

The BLOCK command is invoked from the Screen Root Menu Blocks (Figure 6-4), or at the "Command:" prompt type in **BLOCK** and press ⏎.

    Command: **block**
    Block name (or ?):

At this point you can enter a Block name up to 31 characters long. The Block name may contain letters, digits, and the special characters $ (dollar), - (hyphen), and _ (underscore). All letters are converted to uppercase. If this name has been previously used, AutoCAD prompts:

    Block <name> already exists.
    Redefine it? <N>

If you accept the default by pressing ⏎, the BLOCK command will end without changing anything. Should you respond by entering **Y** (for yes) the Block Definition with that same name will be redefined. Once the drawing is regenerated, any

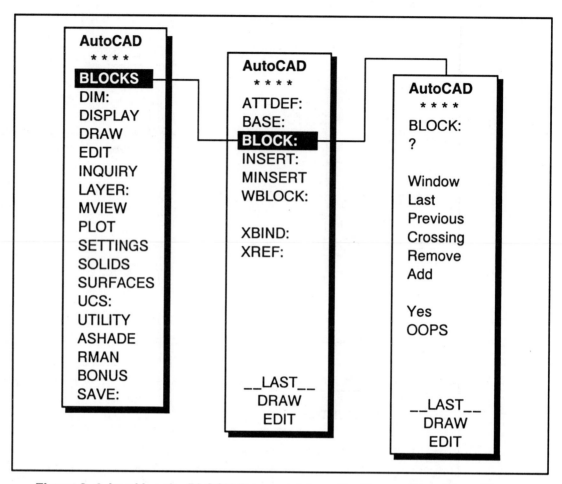

Figure 6-4 Invoking the BLOCK Command from the Screen Root Menu Blocks

existing Blocks on the drawing with this name will be redefined to the new symbol.

After the Block has been named, AutoCAD prompts:

Insertion base point:

The insertion point specified during the creation of the Block becomes the base point for future insertions of this Block. It is also the point that the Block can be rotated or scaled about during insertion. When determining where to locate the base insertion point it is important to consider what will be on the drawing BEFORE you insert the Block. So you must anticipate this preinsertion state of the drawing. It is sometimes more convenient for the insertion point to be somewhere off of the object than on it. Select the point or enter the X and Y coordinate from the keyboard.

After entering the Block name and selecting the insertion point the next step is to select the set of entities that will be included in the Block. AutoCAD now prompts:

Select objects:

CREATION OF A BLOCK

1. DRAW THE FIGURE.

2. INVOKE THE BLOCK COMMAND AND RESPOND WITH THE BLOCK NAME.

3. SPECIFY THE INSERTION POINT.

4. SELECT THE ENTITIES THAT WILL MAKE UP THE BLOCK.

WINDOW

5. TERMINATE THE SELECTION PROCESS BY PRESSING THE [↵] KEY.

Figure 6-5 Steps for Creating a Block

At this time you can use any of AutoCAD's entity selection methods. Upon selecting the entities that will comprise the new Block, AutoCAD confirms the process of creating the Block by erasing the entities that make up the definition (all of the entities selected) from the screen. Refer to Figure 6-5 to review the steps for the creation of a Block.

1. Draw the entities that will comprise the Block.
2. Invoke the BLOCK command and respond with a name of your choice.
3. Specify the insertion point. (You may select it with a pointing device or specify coordinates.)
4. Select the entities that will make up the Block.

> **NOTE:** It is possible to press ↵ out of sequence (before any entities have been selected) and inadvertently create a Block without any entities. Just start over again, noting that you will be redefining the "no-entity" Block you may have just created.

5. Terminate the selection process by pressing ↵ or null response.

INSERT COMMAND

You can insert previously defined blocks in the current drawing by invoking the INSERT command. If there is no Block Definition with the specified name in the current drawing, AutoCAD will search the drives and directories on the path (see the Appendix concerning DOS) for a drawing of that name and insert it instead.

> ***NOTE:*** If Blocks were created and stored in a prototype drawing, and you make your new drawing equal to the prototype, those Blocks will be in the new drawing ready to insert. Any drawing inserted into the current drawing will bring with it all of its Block definitions whether they have been inserted or are only stored as definitions.

The INSERT command is invoked from the Screen Root Menu Blocks (Figure 6-6); or at the "Command:" prompt type in **INSERT** and press ⏎.

Command: **insert**
Block name (or ?): *block name*

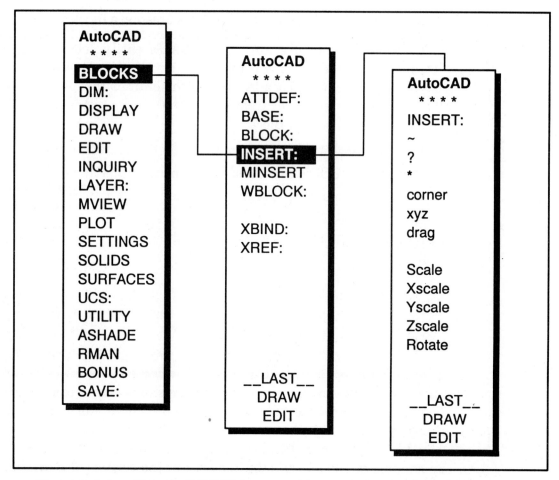

Figure 6-6 Invoking the INSERT Command from the Screen Root Menu Blocks

AutoCAD will prompt you for the name of the Block. Type in the name of the existing Block. If you are not sure, you can type **?**, and AutoCAD will provide you a list of the available Blocks in the current drawing.

Once you type in the appropriate name of the Block, AutoCAD will prompt:

Insertion point: *pick the point*
X scale factor <1> / Corner / XYZ: *type a number or pick a point*
Y scale factor (default=X): *type a number or null response*
Rotation angle <0>: *type a number or pick a point*

A copy of the specified Block is inserted at the designated point in the current drawing to the specified scale. The default scale factor is 1 (full scale). You can specify a scale factor between 0 and 1 to insert the Block smaller than the original size of the Block. If necessary, you can specify different X and Y scale factors for insertion of the Block. By default, Y scale factor is the same as X scale factor. It is possible to enter a negative value for the X and Y scale factors. A scale factor of a negative value causes a mirror image of the Block to be inserted about the insertion point. As a matter of fact, if -1 were used for both scale factors, it would "double mirror" the object, the equivalent of rotating it 180 degrees.

The rotation angle causes the Block to be inserted at any desired angle. To rotate the Block, give a positive or negative angle referencing the Block in its original position or drag the Block to the correct angle and pick the position.

NESTED BLOCKS

Blocks can contain other Blocks. That is, when using the BLOCK command to combine entities into a single object, one or more of the selected entities may themselves be Blocks. And, the Blocks selected can have Blocks nested within them. There is no limitation to the depth of nesting. You may not, however, use the name of any of the nested Blocks as the name of the Block being defined. This would mean that you were trying to redefine a Block, using its old definition in the new.

Any entities within Blocks (as nested Blocks) that were on layer 0 when made into a Block will assume the color and linetype of the layer on which the Block is inserted. If an entity (originally on layer 0 when included in a Block Definition) is in a Block that has been inserted on a layer other than layer 0, it will retain the color and linetype of the layer it was on when its Block was included in a higher level Block. For example, you draw a circle on layer 0 and include it in a Block named Z1. Then, you insert Z1 on layer R, whose color is red. The circle would then assume the color of layer R (in this case it will be red). Create another Block called Y3 by including the Block Z1. If you insert Block Y3 on a layer whose color is blue, the Block Y3 will retain the current color of layer R (in this case it will be red) instead of taking up the color of blue.

EXPLODE COMMAND

The EXPLODE command causes Blocks and associative dimensioning to be turned into the separate entities from which they were created. It also causes Polylines/ Polyarcs to separate into individual simple line and arc entities. It causes 3D Polygon meshes to become 3DFaces, and 3D Polyface meshes to become 3DFaces, and simple line and point entities. When an object is exploded, the new separate entities are created in the space (Model or Paper) of the exploded objects.

The EXPLODE command is invoked from the Screen Root Menu EDIT or at the "Command:" prompt type in explode and press ⏎.

    Command: **explode**
    Select block reference, polyline, dimension, or mesh: *select object*

Only one object may be exploded per command operation. The object selected must be eligible for exploding or an error message will appear. An eligible object may or may not change its appearance when exploded.

Possible Changes Caused by the EXPLODE Command

A Polyline/Polyarc segment having width will revert to a zero-width line and/or arc. Any tangent information associated with individual segments will be lost. If exploded Polyline/Polyarc segments have width or tangent information, the EX-PLODE command will be followed by the message:

    Exploding this polyline has lost (width/tangent) information.
    The UNDO command will restore it.

Individual elements within Blocks that were on layer 0 when created (and whose color was BYLAYER), but were inserted on a layer with a color different than that of layer 0, will revert to the color of layer zero.

Attributes are special text entities that, when included in a Block Definition, take on the values (names and numbers) specified at the time the Block is inserted. The power and usage of Attributes are discussed later in this chapter. To understand the effect of the EXPLODE command on Blocks that include Attributes, it is sufficient to know that the fundamental entity from which an Attribute is created is called an Attribute Definition. It is displayed in the form of an Attribute Tag before it is included in the Block.

An Attribute within a Block will revert to the Attribute Definition and will be represented on the screen by its Tag only. The value of the Attribute specified at the time of insertion will be lost. The group will revert to those elements created by the ATTDEF command prior to combining them into a Block with the BLOCK command.

In brief, an Attribute Definition is turned into an Attribute when the Block in which it is a part is inserted, and conversely, an Attribute is turned back into an Attribute Definition when the block is exploded.

Exploding Blocks with Nested Elements

Blocks containing other Blocks and/or Polylines/Polyarcs will be separated for one level only. That is, the highest level Block will be exploded, but any nested Blocks or Polylines/Polyarcs will remain Blocks and Polylines/Polyarcs. They in turn can be exploded when they come to the highest level.

Blocks inserted with the MINSERT command or with unequal X, Y, and Z scale factors cannot be exploded, nor can Xrefs and their dependent Blocks.

Viewport entities in a Block Definition cannot be turned on after being exploded unless they were inserted in Paper Space.

MINSERT COMMAND

The MINSERT (multiple insert) command is used to insert Blocks in a rectangular array. The total pattern takes the characteristics of a Block, except the group cannot be exploded. This command works similar to the rectangular ARRAY command.

The MINSERT command is invoked from the Screen Root Menu Blocks (Figure 6-7), or at the "Command:" prompt type in **MINSERT** and press ⏎.

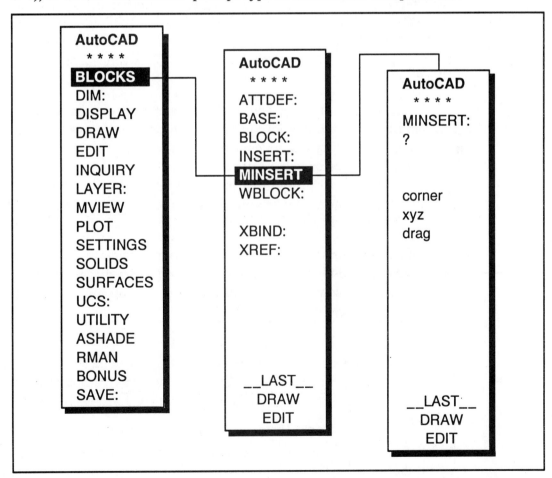

Figure 6-7 Invoking the MINSERT Command from the Screen Root Menu Blocks

Command: **minsert**
Block name (or ?): *name of the block*
Insertion point: *pick the point*
X scale factor <1> / Corner / XYZ: *type a number or pick a point*
Y scale factor (default=X): *type a number or null response*
Rotation angle <0>: *type a number or pick a point*
Number of rows (---) <default>: *specify the number of rows*
Number of columns (|||): *specify the number of columns*
Unit cell or distance between rows (---): *specify the distance between rows*
Distance between columns (|||): *specify the distance between columns*

The row/column spacing can be specified by the delta-x/delta-y distances between two points picked on the screen. For example, if, in response to the "Distance" prompt, you selected points 2,1 and 6,4 for the first and second points, respectively, the row spacing would be 3 (4-1) and the column spacing would be 4 (6-2).

INSERTING UNIT BLOCKS

Groups of entities often need to be duplicated within a drawing. The BLOCK command earlier showed how AutoCAD makes this task easier. The task of transferring Blocks or groups of entities to another drawing is demonstrated in the section on the WBLOCK command. This section will cover additional aspects of creating Blocks in anticipation of inserting them later with a change in scale factors (sometimes with x and y unequal). This concept is referred to as a Unit Block.

Doors and windows are a few of the objects that can be stored as Blocks in a symbol library. But, Blocks can be used in different ways to suit differing situations. The following examples are offered as procedures that are used without customizing menus or using AutoLISP routines to enhance the process. It should be noted that these procedures may be improved either with customization or possibly with some variations in using standard commands and features. Also, the symbology and names of items are subject to variation.

You can use a variety of symbols to represent windows in an architectural plan view. Horizontal sliding windows may need to be distinguished from single- or double-hung windows, as shown in Figure 6–8. You may also wish to have more

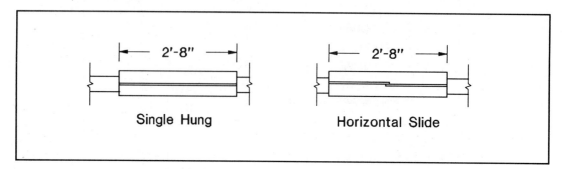

Figure 6–8 Two Different Windows Shown as Blocks

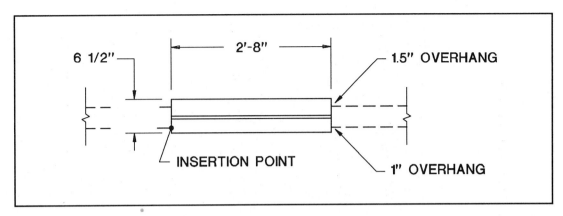

Figure 6-9 Changing the Width of a Window by Changing the X Scale Factor of a Block

than one option as to how you will insert a window. You may wish to use as its insertion point the center of the window sometimes or one of its edges at other times.

Because there are windows of varying widths, you might have to create a separate Block for each width. A group of windows might be 1'-0", 1'-6", 2'-0", 2'-8", 3'-0", 3'-4", 4'-0", 5'-4", 6'-0", and 8'-0" and some widths in between. You would have to make a Block for each width in addition to the different types. The above symbol for the 2'-8"-wide window could be drawn with the Snap set a 0.5 (1/2") to the dimensions shown in Figure 6-9.

The above entities could be saved as a Block named WDW32 (for a 32"-wide window). This window could be inserted from its corner as shown if you have established that intersection in the wall in which it is to be drawn.

The preceding method requires a separate Block for each window width. Another method is to make a drawing of a window in which the X and/or Y dimension is one unit in anticipation of using the final desired dimension as the X and/or Y scale factor during insertion. The following Unit Block symbol for the window can be used for any width window, as shown in Figure 6-10.

This group of entities might be made into a Block named WDW1. Then, in order to use it for a 2'-8" window, the INSERT command will be as follows:

```
Command: insert
Block name: wdw1
Insertion point: select IP the same as above
X scale factor <1>: 32
Y scale factor <default=X>: 1
Rotation angle:
```

Note that when you specify a value for the X scale factor, AutoCAD assumes you wish to apply the same value to the Y scale factor, making the resulting shape of

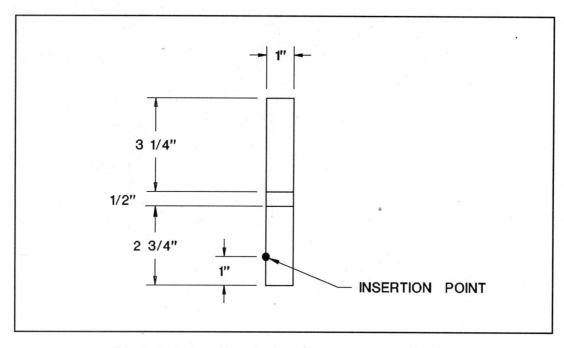

Figure 6-10 Creating a Unit Block Symbol for a Window

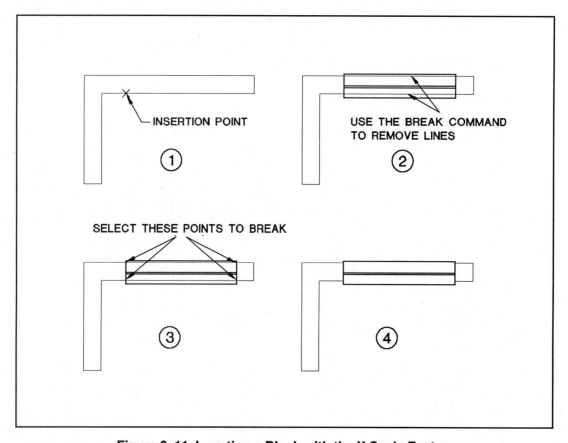

Figure 6-11 Inserting a Block with the X Scale Factor

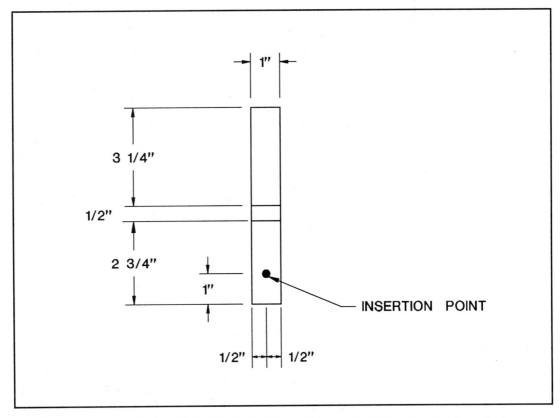

Figure 6-12 Using Unit Blocks by Specifying a Point for Center Insertion

the object(s) proportional to the Unit Block from which it was generated. That is why the Y scale factor defaults to the X scale factor (which defaults to 1). Therefore, if you wish to insert the Block with the X scale factor different from the Y scale factor you must input a Y scale factor even if it is to be a factor of 1. The Block WDW1 can be used for any width window by using the desired width (in inches) as the X scale factor and then using 1 as the Y scale factor. Figure 6-11 shows the window inserted in its location with the proper X scale factor. Also shown is the clean-up that can be done with the BREAK command.

Another variation on the Unit Block WDW1 would be to use the same shape for center insertion. It would be drawn the same but the insertion point would be chosen as shown in Figure 6-12. Figure 6-13 shows the window inserted.

Window symbols in plan lend themselves to the one-way scaling Unit Block application. As demonstrated, they vary only in the X scale and not the Y scale from one size to another. Doors, however, present a special problem when trying to apply the Unit Block method. A symbol for a 2'-8"-wide door might look like Figure 6-14.

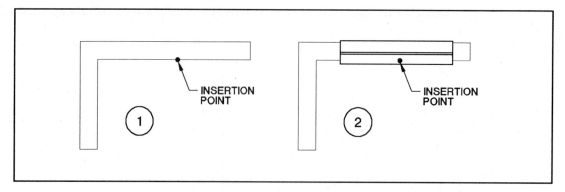

Figure 6-13 The Window Inserted Using Unit Blocks

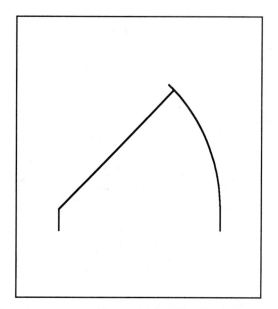

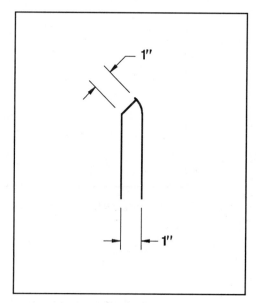

Figure 6-14 Creating a Unit Block Symbol for a Door

Figure 6-15 A Base Block 1 Unit Wide Simplified Door Symbol

In both cases the 2'-8"-wide door is drawn half open or swung at 45 degrees to the wall. Therefore, if you used an approach on the door that was used on the window Unit Block, some problems will be encountered. First, a base Block 1 unit wide simplified door symbol would not be practical. Note the Unit Block in Figure 6-15.

The Unit Block in Figure 6-16, if inserted with an X scale factor of 32 and a Y scale factor of 1, would appear as in Figure 6-16.

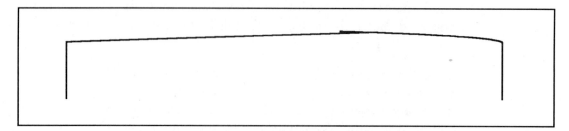

Figure 6-16 A Unit Block Inserted with X and Y Scale Factors

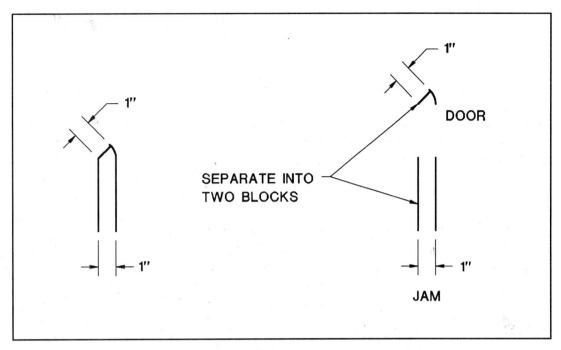

Figure 6-17 Separating Unit Blocks for One Symbol

Even though the 4"-lines that represent the jambs are acceptable, the "door" part of the symbol will not retain its 45-degree swing if not inserted with equal X and Y scale factors. Equal X and Y scale factors present another problem. Using a Y scale factor other than 1 would make the 4"-wide jamb incorrect. Therefore, combining the jambs with the door in the same symbol presents problems that might be impossible to overcome when trying to use a Unit Block approach to permit one Block to be used for all sizes of doors.

Separate Unit Blocks for One Symbol

The solution to the jambs being adaptable to one-way scaling Blocks (while the door is not) may be to make these two (jambs and door) into two Blocks as shown in Figure 6-17.

Now you can insert the Blocks separately as follows (see Figure 6-18):

```
Command: insert
Block name: jmb
Insertion point: pick a point
X scale factor <1>: 32
Y scale factor <default=X>: 1
Rotation angle <default>: ⏎
Command: insert
Block name: dr
Insertion point: pick a point
X scale factor <1>: 32
Y scale factor <default=X>: ⏎
Rotation angle <default>: ⏎
```

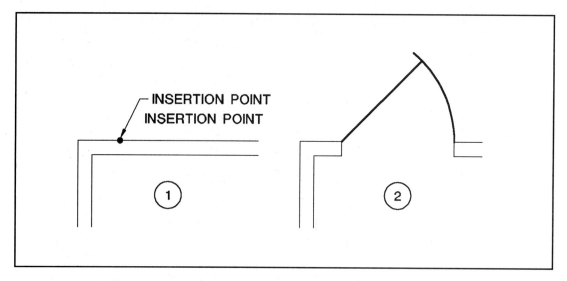

Figure 6-18 Two Unit Blocks Separated for One Symbol

> *NOTE:* When you intend to apply the concept of the Unit Block, whether it is to be scaled uniformly (X scale equal to Y scale) or not, be sure that shapes and sizes of all items in the symbol will be correct at their new scale.

Columns from Chapter 2 as Unit Blocks

Another Unit Block application is when both X and Y scale factors are changed, but not at the same factor. From Chapter 2 the columns, as shown in Figure 6-19, can be created from a Unit Block as follows:

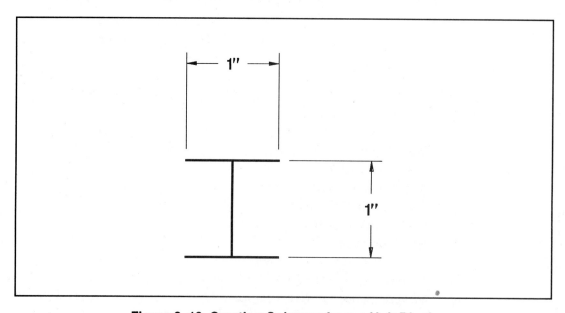

Figure 6-19 Creating Columns from a Unit Block

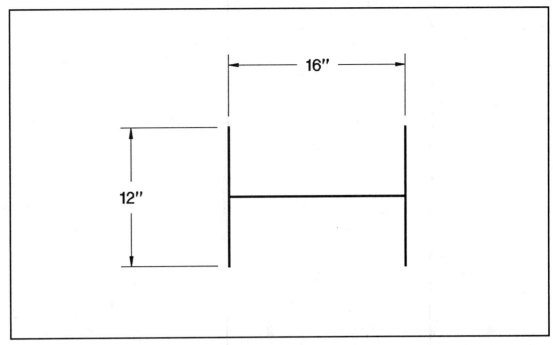

Figure 6-20 Converting a Rotated Column into a Block for Insertion

The column can be made into a Block named CoL1 and can be inserted for a 10 × 8-wide flange symbol as follows:

Command: **insert**
Block name: **coL1**
Insertion point: *pick a point*
X scale factor <1>: **8**
Y scale factor <default=X>: **10**
Rotation angle: ⏎

This can also be done for a 16 x 12 column rotated at 90 degrees as shown in Figure 6-20.

Command: **insert**
Block name: **coL1**
Insertion point: *pick a point*
X scale factor <1>: **12**
Y scale factor <default=X>: **16**
Rotation angle: **90**

Note the 90-degree rotation. But don't forget that the X and Y scale factors are applied to the Block in the respective X and Y directions that were in effect when it was created, not to the X and Y directions after a rotated insertion.

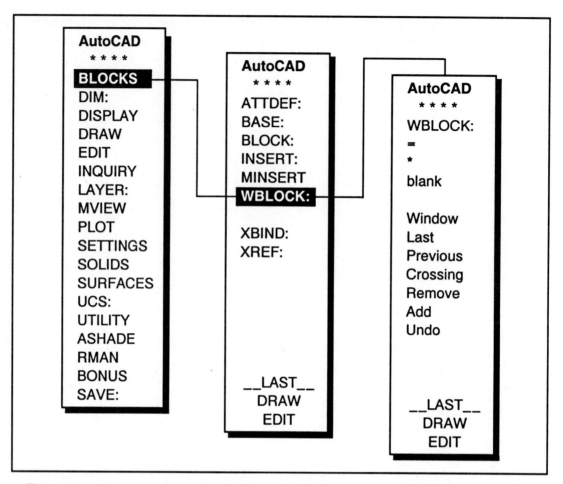

Figure 6-21 Invoking the WBLOCK Command from the Screen Root Menu Blocks

CREATING ONE DRAWING FROM ANOTHER — THE WBLOCK COMMAND

The WBLOCK command permits you to group entities in a manner similar to the BLOCK command. But, in addition, WBLOCK causes the group to be exported to a file, which, in fact, becomes a new and separate drawing. The new drawing (created by using the WBLOCK command) might consist of a selected Block in the current drawing. Or it might be made up of selected entities in the current drawing. You can even export the complete current drawing to the new drawing file. Whichever of the above you choose to WBLOCK, the new drawing will assume the Layers, Linetypes, Styles, and other environmental items like system variable settings of the current drawing.

The WBLOCK command is invoked from the Screen Root Menu Blocks (Figure 6-21), or at the "Command:" prompt type in **WBLOCK** and press ↵.

    Command: wblock
    Filename: ↵

Here is where you will provide a drawing name as you do when you begin a new drawing. You should type in only the keyname and not the extension. AutoCAD will append the .DWG automatically. The name given should comply with the requirements of valid characters (maximum of eight) and should be unique for drawings on the specified directory/path. Otherwise you will get the message:

"Warning! Drawing (name) already exists. Do you want to replace it with the new drawing? <N>."

If you wished to use existing objects in the current drawing to create a new foundation drawing named Slab1 your response would be as follows:

    Command: **wblock**
    Filename: **slab1**

After providing a valid filename (Slab1 in this case), you will be prompted:

    Block name:

Optional replies to the "Block name:" prompt include the following:

1. BLOCK (Block name)
2. = (equal sign)
3. * (asterisk)
4. ⏎ (RETURN)

Each of the four options is explained below:

1. Block name: **block**

If you had created a Block from entities in the current drawing and named it Frame1, you could reply to the "Block name:" prompt with the name of the Block as follows:

    Command: **wblock**
    Filename: **slab1**
    Block name: **frame1**

The above sequence would have created a new drawing named Slab1 that would include the entities in the Block named Frame1. It should be noted that when the new drawing is called up for editing, the entities would no longer be combined into one Block, but would be separate entities, just as they were in the current drawing before being made into the Block. In addition, the new drawing Slab1 would assume the environmental settings of the current drawing from which the Block named Frame1 is being WBLOCKed.

2. Block name: **=**

If you wanted to name the new drawing Frame1, the same as the Block you had just created, you would respond as follows:

```
Command: wblock
Filename: frame1
Block name: =
```

The difference between the = response and the previous Slab1 response is that the resulting name of the new drawing will be Frame1 instead of Slab1.

3. Block name: *

If you wished to have the entire current drawing duplicated into a new one (whether or not any entities have been made into a Block), you would respond as follows:

```
Command: wblock
File name: slab1
Block name: *
```

If existing objects had been made into a Block named Frame1 and it is the only entity in the drawing, then responding with the asterisk (*) is similar to the equal sign (=). The asterisk response will cause all entities to be written, whether visible or not, and whether in Blocks or not.

This method of creating one drawing from another is similar to responding to the Main Menu item no. 1 (Begin a new drawing) with new-drawing-name=other-drawing-name with one main difference. The Main Menu method copies all of the named objects from the other drawing, even those that are not being used. An example of objects not being used is when a Block has been defined but has not been inserted, or a layer (other that the current one) exists but nothing has been drawn on it.

One advantage of using the WBLOCK with the asterisk (*) response is that when the drawing is written to a file, all of the unused Blocks, Layers, Linetypes, and other unused named objects are not written. That is, the drawing is automatically purged. This means that unused items will not be written to the new drawing file. For example, unused items include Block Definitions that have not been inserted, noncurrent Layers that have no entities drawn on them and Styles that are not being used. This can be useful if you just wish to clean up a cluttered drawing, especially one that has had other drawing files inserted into it, each bringing with it various unused named objects.

4. Block name: ⏎

If you do not wish to make a Block in the current drawing, you can still make a separate drawing out of selected entities by pressing ⏎ in response to the "Block name:" prompt. You will then be prompted to select the objects to be written to the drawing file. Like the sequence of prompts in the BLOCK command you will also be prompted for an insertion point as shown below:

Command: **wblock**
Filename: **slab1**
Block name: ⏎
Insertion point: *pick a point*
Select objects: *select objects to be written to the new drawing*

New for Release 11

XREFS and Model/Paper Space in Release 11 must be considered when using the WBLOCK command. A complete description of Model/Paper Space is found in Chapter 7. A named Block (to be written to the new drawing) will be written to Model Space. An external reference or one of its Blocks cannot be WBLOCKed to a file. Using the optional equal (=) response or selecting objects after a ⏎ response to the "Block name:" prompt also writes to Model Space. When you use the asterisk (*) option, writing the entire drawing to a file, Model Space entities are written to Model Space in the new drawing and Paper Space entities are written to Paper Space.

BASE COMMAND

The BASE command allows you to establish a base insertion point for the whole drawing in the same manner that you specify a base insertion point when using the BLOCK command to combine elements into a Block. The purpose of establishing this base point is primarily so that the drawing can be inserted into another drawing using the INSERT command and having the specified base point coincide with the specified insertion point. The default base point is the origin (0,0,0). You can specify a 2D point and AutoCAD will use the current elevation as the base Z coordinate. Or you can specify the full 3D point. The command sequence is as follows:

Command: **base**
Base point <current>: *specify point*

ATTRIBUTES

Attributes can be used for automatic annotation during insertion of a Block. Attributes are special text entities that can be included in a Block Definition. Attributes must be defined themselves beforehand and then selected at the proper time during the BLOCK command. This will include the Attribute(s) selected in the Block Definition in a similar manner to other selected entities like lines, circles, arcs and regular text.

The two primary features of Attributes are as follows:

The first use of Attributes permits annotation during insertion of the Block to which the Attribute(s) will be attached. Depending upon how you define the Attribute, you can cause it to appear automatically either with a preset (constant) text string, or have it prompt you (or other user) for a string to be written as the Block is inserted. This feature permits you to insert each Block with a string of preset text or with its own unique string.

The second (perhaps the most important) purpose of attaching Attributes to a Block is to have extractable data about the Block stored in the drawing data base file. Then, when the drawing is complete (or even before) you can use the ATTEXT (attribute extract) command and have Attribute data extracted from the drawing and written to a file in a form that data base handling programs can use. You can have as many Attributes attached to a Block as you wish. As mentioned above, the text string that makes up an Attribute can be either constant or user specified at the time of insertion.

A Definition within a Definition

When creating a Block you select entities to be included. Entities such as Lines, Circles, and Arcs are drawn by using their respective commands. Normal text is drawn by using the TEXT or DTEXT command.

Similar to drawing entities, Attributes must also be drawn before they can be included in the Block. It is complicated and requires additional steps to place them in the drawing; AutoCAD calls this procedure defining the Attribute. Therefore, an Attribute Definition is simply the result of defining an Attribute by using the ATTDEF command. The Attribute Definition is the entity that is selected during the BLOCK command. Later, when the Block is inserted, the Attributes that are attached to it and the manner in which they become a part of the drawing are a result of how you created the Attribute.

Visibility

If an Attribute is to be used only to store information, then you can, as part of the definition of the Attribute, specify whether or not it will be visible. If you plan to use an Attribute with a Block as a note, label, or call out, you should be alert to the effect of scaling (whether equal or unequal X/Y factors) on the text that will be displayed. The scaling factor(s) on the Attribute will be the same as on the Block. Therefore, be sure that it will result in size and proportions desired. You should also be aware of the effect of rotation on visible Attribute text. Attribute text that is defined as horizontal in a Block will be displayed vertical when that Block is inserted with a 90-degree angle of rotation.

Visibility and Plotting

Note that, like any other entity or object in the drawing, it must be visible on the screen (or would be if the plotted view were the current display) for that entity or object to be eligible for plotting.

TAG, VALUE, PROMPT, AND DEFAULT

Four components associated with Attributes should be understood before attempting a definition. The purpose of each is described as follows.

Tag

An Attribute Definition has a tag just as a layer or a linetype has a name. The tag is the identifier of the Attribute Definition and is displayed where this Attribute Definition is located, depicting text size, style and angle of rotation. The tag cannot contain spaces. Two Attributes with the same tag should not be included in the same Block. Tags appear in the definition only, not after the Block is inserted. However, if you explode a Block, the Attribute value (described herein) changes back into the tag.

If multiple Attributes are used in one Block, each must have a unique tag in that Block. This restriction is similar to each layer, linetype, Block, and other named object having a unique name within one drawing. An Attribute's tag is its identifier at the time that Attribute is being defined, before it is combined with other entities and Attributes by the BLOCK command.

Value

The value of an Attribute is the actual string of text that appears (if the visibility mode is ON) when the Block (of which it is a part) is inserted. Whether visible or not the value is tied directly to the Attribute, which in turn associates it with the Block. It is this value that you will want written to a data base file. It might be a door or window size or, in a piping drawing, the flange rating, weight, or cost of a valve or fitting.

> **NOTE:** When an extraction of Attribute data is performed, it is the value of an Attribute that is written to a file, but it is the tag that directs the extraction operation to that value. This will be described in detail as part of the ATTEXT command.

Prompt

The prompt is what you see when inserting a Block with an Attribute whose value is not constant or preset. During the definition of an Attribute, you can specify a string of characters that will appear during the insertion of the Block to prompt you to enter the appropriate value. What the prompt says to you during insertion is what you told it to say when you defined the Attribute.

Default

You can specify a default value for the Attribute during the definition procedure. Then, during insertion of the Block, it will appear behind the prompt in brackets;

i.e., <default>. It will automatically become the value if ⏎ is pressed in response to the prompt for a value.

ATTRIBUTE COMMANDS

The four primary commands to manage Attributes are:

1. ATTDEF — Attribute definition
2. ATTDISP — Attribute display
3. ATTEDIT — Attribute edit
4. ATTEXT — Attribute extract

As explained earlier, the ATTDEF command creates an attribute definition, which is an entity that is selected during the BLOCK command.

The ATTDISP command controls the visibility of the attributes.

The ATTEDIT command provides a variety of ways to edit without exploding the Block.

The ATTEXT command allows you to extract the data from the drawing and have it written to a file in a form that data base handling programs can use as shown below.

DOORS

SIZE	THKNS	CORE	FINISH	LOCKSET	HINGES	INSET
3070	1.750	SOLID	PAINT	PASSAGE	4 X 4	—
3070	1.750	SOLID	VARNISH	KEYED	4 X 4	20 X 20
2868	1.375	HOLLOW	PAINT	PRIVACY	3 X 3	—

ROOM FINISHES

NAME	WALL	CEILING	FLOOR	BASE	REMARKS
LIVING	GYPSUM	GYPSUM	CARPET	NONE	PAINT
FAMILY	PANEL	ACOUSTICAL	TILE	STAIN	STAIN
BATH	PAPER	GYPSUM	TILE	COVE	4'_CERAMIC_TILE
GARAGE	GYPSUM	GYPSUM	CONCRETE	NONE	TAPE_FLOAT_ONLY

You can include an Attribute in the WDW Block to record the size of the window. A suggested procedure would be to zoom in near the insertion point and create an Attribute Definition with a tag that reads WDW-SIZE, as shown in Figure 6–22.

If, during the insertion of the WDW Block, you respond to the prompt for the SIZE Attribute with 2054 for a 2'-0" wide × 5'-4" high window, the resulting Block entity would be as shown in Figure 6–23, with the normally invisible Attribute value shown here for illustration purposes.

Even though the value displayed is distorted, that will not affect the string when extracted to a data base file for a bill of materials.

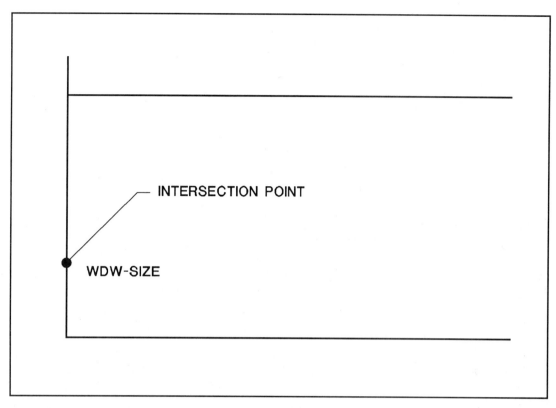

Figure 6–22 Including Attributes in Blocks by Creating an Attribute Definition

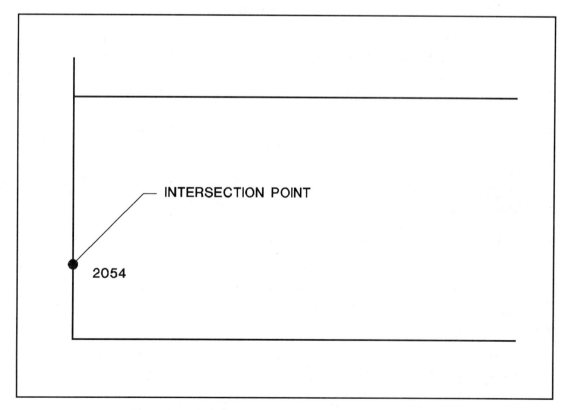

Figure 6–23 The Attribute Value Visible in a Block Entity

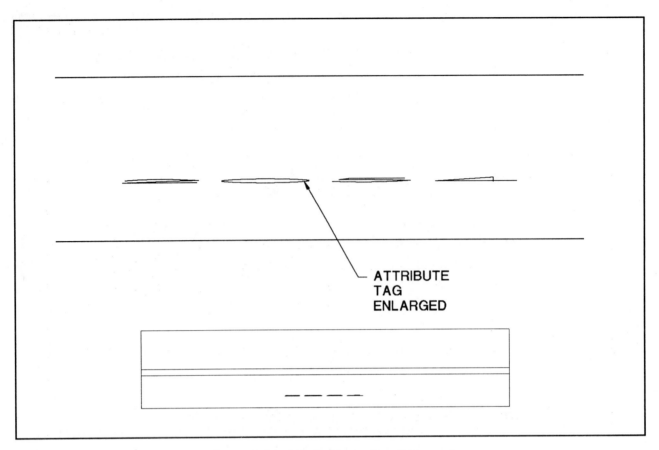

Figure 6-24 The Attribute Tag Enlarged

To solve the distortion and rotation problem, if you wish to have an Attribute displayed for rotational purposes, you can create a Block that contains Attributes only, or only one Attribute. Then it can be inserted at the desired location and rotated for readability to produce the results shown in Figure 6-25:

Attribute Definitions would be created as shown in Figure 6-25 and inserted as shown in Figure 6-26.

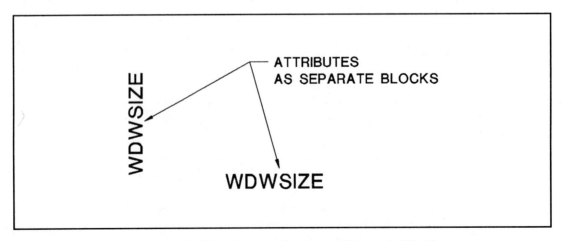

Figure 6-25 Showing Attributes as Separate Blocks

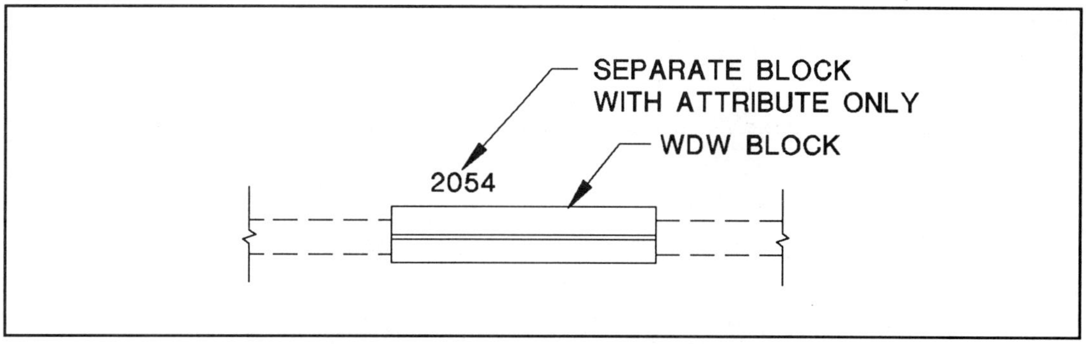

Figure 6-26 A Separate Block with Attribute Only

The insertion points selected would correspond to the midpoint of the outside line that would result from the insertion of the WDW Block. The SIZE Attributes could be defined into Blocks called WDWSIZE and inserted separately with each WDW Block, therefore providing both annotation and data extraction.

CAUTION!

The main caution in having an Attribute Block separate from the symbol (WDW) Block is in editing. Erasing, copying, and moving the symbol Block without the Attribute Block could mean that the data extraction would result in the wrong quantity.

There is another solution to the problem of a visible Attribute not being located or rotated properly in the inserted Block. If the Attribute is not constant, you can edit it independently after the Block has been inserted with the ATTEDIT command. It permits changing an Attribute's height, position, angle, value, and other properties. The ATTEDIT command will be covered in detail later in this chapter, but it should be noted here that the height editing option applies to the X and Y scales of the text. Therefore, for text in the definition of a Block that was inserted with unequal X and Y scale factors, you will not be able to edit its proportions back to equal X and Y scale factors.

ATTDEF Command

Creating an Attribute Definition is accomplished by using the ATTDEF command. As with the Block, defining an Attribute must take into consideration the conditions under which the Block (to which it is attached) will be inserted.

The ATTDEF command is invoked from the Screen Root Menu Blocks (Figure 6-27), or at the "Command:" prompt type in **ATTDEF** and press ⏎.

> Command: **attdef**
> Attribute modes -- Invisible:N Constant:N Verify:N Preset:N
> Enter (ICVP) to change, RETURN when done:

The setting of each mode is changed by entering its initial. For example, the Invisible mode can be changed from "N" to "Y" by entering I. Only one mode can be changed at a time.

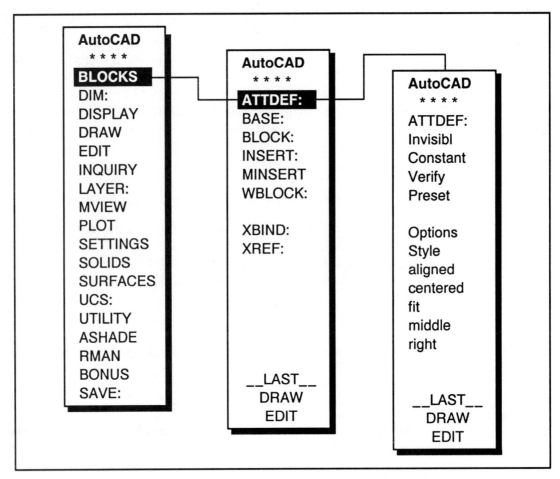

Figure 6-27 Invoking the ATTDEF Command from the Screen Root Menu Blocks

Once the modes are in the desired status press ⏎ and the next prompt will appear.

Attribute Modes

Invisible — Setting the Invisible mode to Y (yes) causes the Attribute value to NOT be displayed when the Block insertion is completed. Even if visible, the value will not appear until the insertion is completed. Attributes needed only for data extraction should be invisible to quicken regeneration and keep from cluttering your drawing. You can use the ATTDISP command to override the Invisible mode setting. The Invisible mode being Y does not affect the visibility of the tag in the Attribute Definition.

Constant — If the Constant mode is set to Y (yes), you must enter the value of the Attribute while defining it. That value will be used for that Attribute every time the Block to which it is attached is inserted. There will be no prompt for the value during insertion and you cannot change the value. You can duplicate an Attribute Definition, using the COPY command and use it for more than one Block. Or you can explode a Block and retain one or more of its Attribute Definitions for use in subsequent Blocks.

Verify — If the Verify mode is set to Y (yes), you will be able to verify its value when the Block is inserted. For example, if a Block with three (nonconstant value) Attributes is inserted, once you have completed all prompt/ value sequences that have displayed the original defaults, you will be prompted again with the latest values as new defaults, giving a second chance to be sure the values are correct before the INSERT command is completed. Even if you press ⏎ to accept an original default value, it appears as the second chance default also. If you, however, make a change during the verify sequence, you will not get a third chance, that is, a second verify sequence.

Preset — If the Preset mode is set to Y (yes), the Attribute automatically takes the value of the default that was specified at the time of defining the Attribute. During a normal insertion of the Block, you will not be prompted for the value. You must be careful to specify a default during the ATTDEF command or the Attribute value will be blank. A Block consisting of only Attributes whose defaults were blank and Preset modes were Y (yes) could be inserted, but would not display anything and cannot be purged from the drawing. The only adverse effect would be that of adding to the space taken in memory. One way to get rid of a nondisplayable Block like this is to use a visible entity to create a Block with the same name, thereby redefining it to something that can be edited; i.e., erased and subsequently purged.

Once the modes are in the desired status, press ⏎ and the following prompts will appear:

> Attribute tag: *enter the tag name*

If you press ⏎ you will get the message:

> "Tag cannot be null."

> Attribute prompt: *Enter prompt*

This option is available if the Constant mode is set to N (no). If you respond by pressing ⏎, the prompt will be the same as the tag.

> Default Attribute value: *enter value or null response*

The above prompt will appear unless the constant mode is set to Y (yes), in which case the prompt will be:

> Attribute value: *enter value*

In the case above (constant mode set to Y) you will not be prompted for a value during Block insertion.

For any value entry (from a default value entry) you can force one of more leading spaces by beginning the string with a backslash (\). A leading backslash (\) can be forced by beginning with two backslashes (\\).

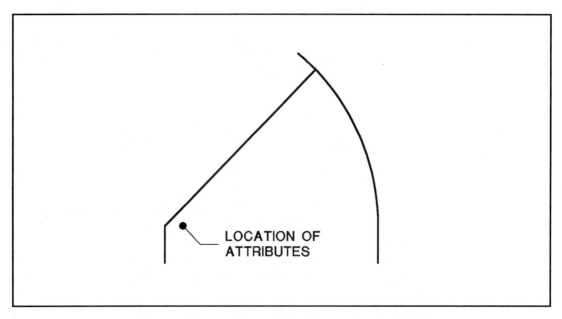

Figure 6-28 Predrawn Door Block with Attributes

After the above ATTDEF prompts have been answered you will be prompted to place the tag in the same manner as you would for placing text, except AutoCAD will use the tag in place of the text string. Subsequent Attributes can be placed in a manner similar to placing lines of text, using the insertion point and line spacing as left justified, centered, aligned, or right justified lines of text. Simply press ⏎ to invoke a repeating Attribute Definition.

A predrawn 2'-0"-wide door is made into a Block with Attributes, as shown in Figure 6-28.

> **NOTE:** In this example the Block is drawn to true size with jambs so it can be inserted with X and Y scale factors equal to 1 (one). But, the Attributes will all be invisible, because the door might be inserted at a rotation incompatible with acceptable text orientations. The Attributes can also be very small, located at a point that will be easy to find if they must be made visible in order to read (Figure 6-29).

The Attributes might be entered as follows (Figures 6-30 and 6-31):

```
Command: attdef
Attribute modes -- Invisible:N  Constant:N  Verify:N  Preset:N
Enter (ICVP) to change, RETURN when done: i
Attribute modes -- Invisible:Y  Constant:N  Verify:N  Preset:N
Enter (ICVP) to change, RETURN when done: c
Attribute modes -- Invisible:Y  Constant:Y  Verify:N  Preset:N
Enter (ICVP) to change, RETURN when done: ⏎
```

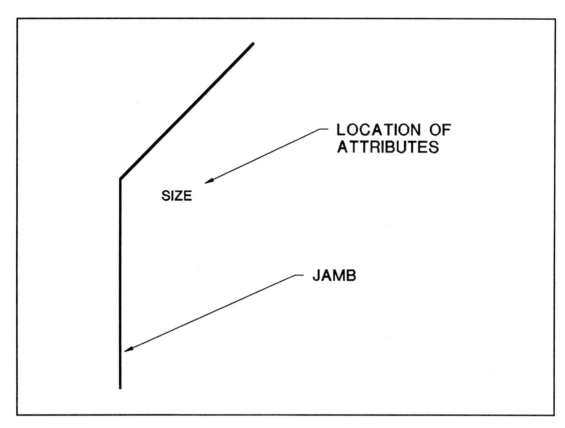

Figure 6–29 Predrawn Jamb Block with Attributes

Attribute tag: **size**
Attribute value: **26681.375** *for 2'-6" × 6'-8" × 1-3/8"*
Justify/Style/<start point>: *select point*
Height <default>: **1/16**
Rotation angle <default>: ⏎
Text:

NOTE: The values given for the various Attributes can be written just as any string of text is written. You should note that these strings, when written to a data base handling file, might eventually need to be interpreted as numbers rather than characters. The difference is primarily of concern to the person who will use the data in a data base handling program. So, if you are not familiar with data types such as numeric, character, date, etc., you might wish to consult with someone (or study a book on data bases) if you are entering the values. For example, an architectural distance such as 12'-6 1/2" may need to be written in decimal feet (12.54) without the apostrophe or in decimal inches (150.5) without the inch mark if it is going to be used mathematically once extracted.

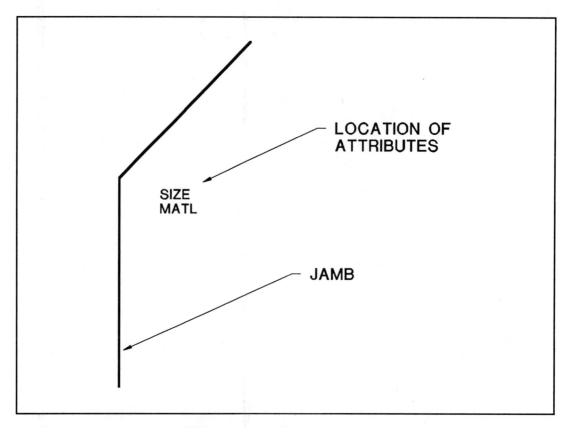

Figure 6-30 Predrawn Jamb Block with Character Attributes

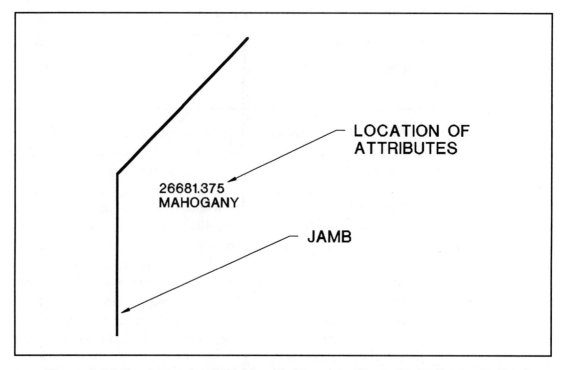

Figure 6-31 Predrawn Jamb Block with Character/Numeric Attributes Defined

Command: ⏎
Attribute modes -- Invisible:Y Constant:Y Verify:N Preset:N
Enter (ICVP) to change, RETURN when done: **c**
Attribute modes -- Invisible:Y Constant:N Verify:N Preset:N
Enter (ICVP) to change, RETURN when done: ⏎
Attribute tag: **matl**
Attribute prompt: **material**
Attribute default value: **mahogany**
Justify/Style/<start point>: *select point*
Text:
Command: ⏎

You can continue to define additional Attributes in the same manner for the L.H./ R.H. SWING, PAINT/VARNISH FINISH, Type of HINGE, Type of LOCKSET, etc. (Figure 6–32).

Inserting a Block with Attributes

Blocks with Attributes may be inserted in the standard manner. If there are any nonconstant Attributes you will be prompted to enter the value for each. You may set the system variable called ATTREQ to 0 (zero), thereby suppressing the prompts for Attribute values. In this case the values will either be blank or be set

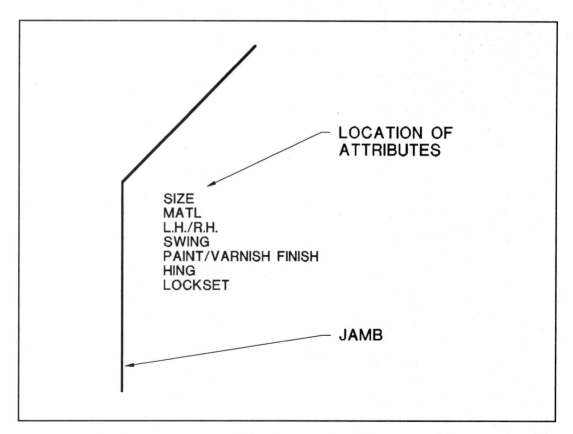

SIZE
MATL
L.H./R.H.
SWING
PAINT/VARNISH FINISH
HING
LOCKSET

LOCATION OF ATTRIBUTES

JAMB

Figure 6–32 Predrawn Jamb Block with Additional Character Attributes Defined

to the default values if they exist. You can later use either the DDATTE or ATTEDIT command (described herein) to establish or change values.

You can set the system variable called ATTDIA to a nonzero value and have a dialogue box be displayed for Attribute value input. The AUI must be available in order to use this feature.

ATTDISP Command

The ATTDISP command controls the visibility of Attributes. Attributes will normally be visible if the Invisible mode is set to N (no) when they are defined. The ATTDISP command is invoked from the Screen Root Menu Display (Figure 6-33) or at the "Command:" prompt type in **ATTDEF** and press ⏎.

    Command: **attdisp**
    Normal/ON/OFF <current value>:

Responding ON makes all Attributes visible, OFF makes all Attributes invisible. The option Normal will display the attributes as you created them. The system variable called ATTMODE is affected by the ATTDISP setting. If REGENAUTO is ON, changing the ATTDISP setting causes drawing regeneration.

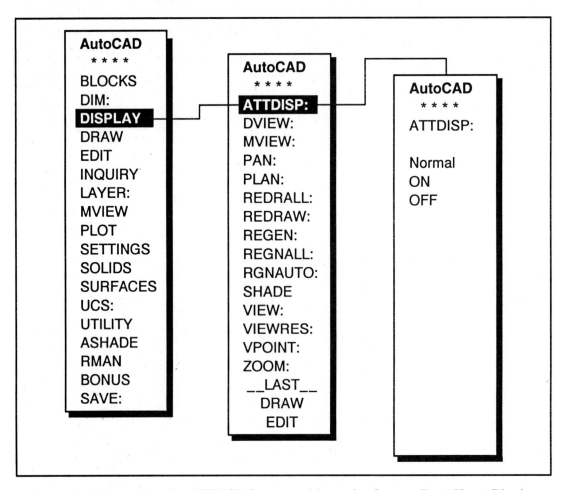

Figure 6-33 Invoking the ATTDISP Command from the Screen Root Menu Display

ATTEDIT Command

Unlike other entities in an inserted Block, Attributes can be edited independently of the Block and other Attributes. You can, however, edit groups of Attributes collectively. This permits you to insert a Block with generic Attributes, that is, the default values can be used in anticipation of changing them to the desired values later. Or, you can copy an existing Block that may need only one or two Attribute changes to make it correct for its new location. And, of course, there is always the chance that either an error was made in entering the value or design changes necessitate subsequent changes.

The ATTEDIT command provides a variety of ways to specify Attributes to be edited. It also allows various properties of the selected Attributes to be edited. It should be noted that Attributes with constant values cannot be edited in this manner.

The ATTEDIT command is invoked from the Screen Root Menu Edit (Figure 6-34) or at the "Command:" prompt type in **ATTDEF** and press ⏎.

Command: **attedit**
Edit Attributes one at a time? <Y>:

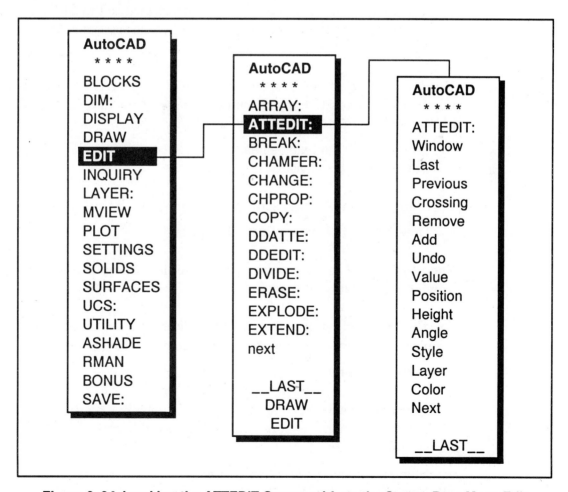

Figure 6-34 Invoking the ATTEDIT Command from the Screen Root Menu Edit

Responding **Y** permits you to edit visible Attributes individually. You can limit those Attributes eligible for selection by specifying Block name, tag, or value. In addition to an Attribute's value, other properties that can be changed during this one-at-a-time mode include its position, height, and angle of rotation.

Responding **N** permits global (or mass) editing of Attributes. Again, you can limit those eligible for editing to specified Block name, tag, and value. However, this mode permits editing of Attribute values only and no other properties.

After responding **Y** or **N** you will be prompted to specify eligible Attributes as follows:

> Block name specification <*>:
> Attribute tag specification <*>:
> Attribute value specification <*>:

For any Attribute to be eligible for editing, the Block name, Attribute tag, and Attribute value must all match the name, tag, and value specified. Use of "*" or "?" wild card characters will allow more than one string to match. Pressing ⏎ in response to the "Block name specification" prompt will default to the asterisk, which will make all Attributes eligible with regard to the Block name restriction. Attributes would still have to match tag and value responses in order to be eligible for editing.

Global Editing If you responded to the "Edit attributes one at a time? <Y>:" prompt with **N** (no), thereby choosing global editing, and set the Block name, tag, and value limitations, the following prompts appear:

> Global edit of Attribute values.
> Edit only Attributes visible on screen? <Y>

An N reply will cause a flip screen to text mode with the following message:

> Drawing must be regenerated afterwards.

When the editing for this command is completed (and if AUTOREGEN is ON) a drawing regeneration will occur.

If at the "Edit only Attributes visible on screen? <Y>" prompt, you respond **Y** (or default to **Y** by pressing ⏎) you will be prompted as follows:

> Select Attributes:

Attributes may now be selected either by picking on the screen or window, crossing, or last method. Eligible Attributes are then highlighted and the following prompt appears:

> String to change:
> New string:

> **NOTE:** The changes you specify will affect a group of Attributes all at one time. You should take care that unintended changes do not occur.

The responses to "String to change:" cause AutoCAD to search eligible selected Attribute strings for matching strings. Each matching string will be changed to your response to "New string:." For example, Blocks named WDW20, having tags named SIZE, and values of 2054 (for 2'-0" × 5'-4") can be changed to 2060 by the following sequence:

> String to change: **54**
> New string: **60**

If you did not limit the Attributes by Block name, tag, and value you might unintentionally change a window whose SIZE is 5440 (for 5'-4" × 4'-0") to 6040.

If you respond to "String to change:" by pressing ⏎, it will cause any response to "New string:" to be placed ahead of all eligible Attribute value strings. For instance, if you specified only Block name WDW20 with an Attribute value of 2054 to be eligible for editing, you can make an addition to the value by the following sequence:

> String to change: ⏎
> New string: **dbl hung**

The value 2054 will be changed to read DBL HUNG 2054. You should be sure to add a space behind the G if you do not want the result to be DBL HUNG2054.

Editing Attributes One at a Time If you responded to the "Edit attributes one at a time? <Y>" prompt by pressing ⏎ (defaulting to **Y**), and have specified the eligible Attributes through the Block name, tag, and value sequences, you will be prompted:

> Select Attributes:

You may select Attributes by picking them on the screen, or the window, crossing, or last method. The eligible selected Attributes with nonconstant values will be marked sequentially with an X. The next prompt is as follows:

> Value/Position/Height/Angle/Style/Layer/Color/Next <N>:

Angle is not an option for an Attribute defined as FIT text, nor are Angle and Height options for Aligned Attributes. Entering any option's initial letter permits a change relative to that option followed by the repeated prompt for the list of options until you default to **N** for the next Attribute.

The Value option, if chosen, will prompt you as follows:

> Change or Replace? <R>

Defaulting to **R** causes the following prompt:

New Attribute value:

Any string entered will become the new value. Even a null response will become a null (blank) value. Entering **C** at the "Change or Replace? <R>" prompt will cause the following prompt to appear:

String to change:
New string:

Responses to these prompts follow the same rules described in the previous section on global editing. In addition to the "Position/Height/Angle" options normally established during Attribute definition, you can change those preset properties such as "Style/Layer/Color" with the ATTEDIT command.

Dialogue Box Editing of Attributes When you invoke the DDATTE command from the Screen Root Menu Edit, or at the "Command:" prompt type in **DDATTE** and press ⏎, a dialogue appears when you select a Block having nonconstant Attributes. Selecting entities that are not Blocks or Blocks that contain no Attributes will cause an error message to appear.

Using the pointing device, you can select values to be changed in the dialogue box. Type in the new values and accept the value by picking **OK** or pressing ⏎. **Ctrl** + **C** or selecting Cancel will terminate the command, returning all values unchanged.

You can use the DDATTE command to just look at the values of a selected Attribute without making changes. Or, you can employ repeated editing or repeated inquiry looks at Attribute values by modifying the DDATTE command with the MULTIPLE command as follows:

Command: **multiple ddatte**

Using the dialogue box limits the length of the Attribute tag and Attribute value that can be displayed to 24 characters and 34 characters, respectively. If you wish to use the dialogue box method of changing values, it also limits the length of a new Attribute value that can be input to 34 characters. However, a longer value will not be shortened by just viewing its first 34 characters (the maximum viewable).

ATTEXT Command

Extracting data from a drawing is one of the foremost innovations in CAD. Paper copies of drawings have long been used to communicate more than just how objects look. In addition to dimensions, drawings tell builders or fabricators what materials to use, quantities of objects to make, manufacturers' names and models of parts in an assembly, coordinate locations of objects in a general area, and what types of finishes to apply to surfaces. But, until computers came into the picture (or pictures came into the computer), extracting data from manual drawings

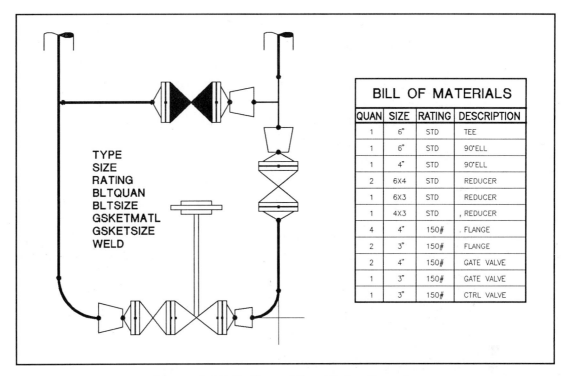

Figure 6-35 Refinery Plant Piping Complex

involved making lists (usually by hand) while studying the drawing, often checking off the data with a marker. AutoCAD's Attribute feature and the ATTEXT command combine to allow complete, fast, and accurate extraction of (1) data consciously put in for the purpose of extraction, (2) data used during the drawing process, and (3) data that AutoCAD maintains about all entities (Blocks in this case).

The CAD drawing in Figure 6-35 shows a small part of a refinery plant piping complex. The seventeen valves and fittings are a fraction of those that might be on a large drawing. Each symbol is a Block with Attributes attached to it. Values that have been assigned to each Attribute tag record the type (TEE, ELL, RE-DUCER, FLANGE, GATE VALVE, or CONTROL VALVE), size (3", 4", or 6"), rating (STD or 150#), weld (length of weld) and many other vital bits of specific data. Keeping track of hundreds of valves, fittings, and even cut lengths of pipe is a time-consuming task subject to omissions and errors if done manually, even if the drawing is plotted from CAD. Just as important as extracting data from the original drawing is the need to update a list of data when the drawing is changed. Few drawings, if any, remain unchanged. AutoCAD's Attribute feature makes the job fast, thorough, and accurate. An example of some of the Blocks with Attributes in their definition state and their corresponding inserted state is shown in Figure 6-36.

Figure 6-36 shows three examples of Blocks as defined and as inserted, each Attribute having been given a value during the INSERT command. Remember, it is the value that will be extracted in accordance with how the template specifies the tags. By using the ATTEXT command, a complete listing of all valves and fittings in the drawing can be written to a file as shown in Table 6-1.

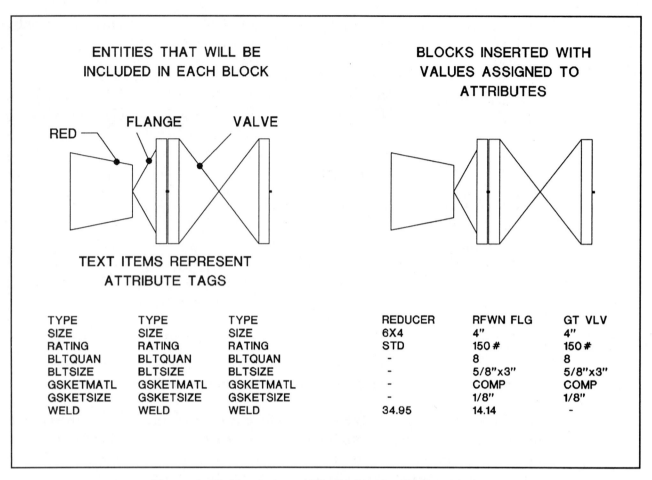

Figure 6-36 Examples of Blocks Having Defined Values

Table 6-1 A List of Inventory as Specified by the ATTEXT Command and Tags

TYPE	SIZE	RATING	BLTQUAN	BLTSIZE	GSKETMATL	GSKETSIZE	WELD
TEE	6"	STD	—	—	—	—	62.44
ELL	6"	STD	—	—	—	—	41.63
ELL	4"	STD	—	—	—	—	14.14
RED	6X4	STD	—	—	—	—	34.95
RED	6X4	STD	—	—	—	—	34.95
RED	6X3	STD	—	—	—	—	31.81
RED	4X3	STD	—	—	—	—	25.13
FLG	4"	150#	8	5/8"X3"	COMP	1/8"	14.14
FLG	4"	150#	8	5/8"X3"	COMP	1/8"	14.14
FLG	4"	150#	8	5/8"X3"	COMP	1/8"	14.14
FLG	4"	150#	8	5/8"X3"	COMP	1/8"	14.14
FLG	3"	150#	4	5/8"X3"	COMP	1/8"	11.00
FLG	3"	150#	4	5/8"X3"	COMP	1/8"	11.00
GVL	4"	150#	16	5/8"X3"	COMP	1/8"	—
GVL	4"	150#	16	5/8"X3"	COMP	1/8"	—
GVL	3"	150#	8	5/8"X3"	COMP	1/8"	—
CVL	3"	150#	8	5/8"X3"	COMP	1/8"	—

The headings above each column in Table 6-1 are for your information only. These will not be written to the extract file by the ATTEXT command. They signify the tags whose corresponding values will be extracted.

When operated on by a data base program, this file can be used to sort valves and fittings by type, size, or other value. The scope of this book is too limited to cover data base applications properly. But generating a file like Table 6-1 that a data base program can use is the important linkage between computer drafting and computer management of data for inventory control, material takeoff, flow analysis, cost, maintenance and many other applications. The CAD drafter can apply the ATTEXT feature to perform this task.

Files Using the ATTEXT command involves concepts of computer applications other than CAD (although not necessarily more advanced). Some fundamental understanding of the computer's operating system (DOS in the majority of cases) is needed. The operating system is used to manipulate and store files.

Many different types of files or groups of files are involved in using the ATTEXT command.

1. AutoCAD program files are being used in the Editor to perform the Attribute extraction.
2. The drawing file is a data file that contains the Blocks and their associated Attributes whose values are eligible for extraction.
3. A template file must be created to tell AutoCAD what type of data to extract.
4. A line editor or word processor is used to create the template file.
5. The extraction process creates a FILENAME.TXT file containing the data in accordance with the instructions received from the template file.
6. A set of database program files usually can operate on the extracted file.
7. The program files in the operating system files make it all possible.

Data Base Extracted data can be manipulated by a data base application program. The telephone directory, a data base, is an alphabetical listing of names, each followed by a first name (or initial), an address, and a phone number. A listing of pipe, valves, and fittings in a piping system can be a data base if each item has essential data associated with it such as its size, flange rating, weight, material of manufacture, product that it handles, cost, location within the system, and many others.

Records and Fields The two elementary terms used in a data base are the record and the field. A record is like one listing in the phone book made up of a name and its associated first name, address, and phone number. The name Jones with its data is one record. Another Jones with a different first name (or initials) is another record. Another Jones with the same first name or initials at a different address is still another record. Each listing is a record. The types of data that may be in a record come under the heading of a field. Name is a field. All the names in the list come under the name field. Address is a field. Phone number is a field. And even though some names may have first names and some may not, first name is a field. It is possible to take the telephone directory that is listed alphabetically by name, feed it into a computer data base program, and generate the same list in numerical order by phone number. You can generate a partial list of all the Joneses sorted alphabetically by the first name. Or you can generate a list of everyone who lives on Elm Street. The primary purpose of the ATTEXT command is to generate the main list that includes all of the desired objects to which the data base program manipulations can be applied.

Creating A Template

Template The template is a file saved in ASCII format and lists the fields that specify the tags and determine which Blocks will have their Attribute data extracted. The template must be a file on an accessible path with the extension of .TXT. When you use a text editor or word processor in the ASCII mode, you must add this extension when you name the file.

Field Name The field name must correspond exactly to the Attribute tag if you wish for that Attribute's value to be extracted. If the Attribute tag is called **type**, then there must be a field name in the template called **type**. A field name called **ratings** will not cause a tag name called **rating** to have its values written to the extract file.

Character-numeric The template tells the ATTEXT command to classify the data written to a particular field either as numeric or as character type. Characters (a, b, c, A, #, ", etc.) are always character type, but numbers do not always have to be numeric type. Characters occupy less memory space in the computer. Sometimes numbers, like an address and phone number, are better stored as characters unless they are to be operated on by mathematical functions (addition, subtraction, etc.). The only relative significance of numbers as characters is their order (1 2 3 ....) for sorting purposes by the data base program. Characters (a b c ...) have that same significance. The template contains two elements for each field. The first is the field name. The second is the character-numeric element.

Numbers in strategic spaces in the character-numeric element of the template file specify the number of spaces to allow for the values to be written in the extract file. Others also specify how many decimal places to carry numeric values.

The format is as follows:

fieldname	Nwwwddd	for numeric values with decimal allowance
fieldname	Nwww000	for numeric values without decimal allowance
fieldname	Cwww000	for character values

Each line in the template is one field. The w's and d's are to be filled in with the necessary digits when the template file is created. The order of fields listed in the template does not have to coincide with the order that Attribute tags appear in a Block. Any group of fields, in any order is acceptable. The only requirement for a Block to be eligible for extraction by the ATTEXT command is that there be at least one tag-field match.

A template for the example in Figure 6–35 would be written as follows:

TYPE	C008000
SIZE	C008000
RATING	C006000
BLTQUAN	N004000
BLTSIZE	C010000
GSKETMATL	C006000
GSKETSIZE	C006000
WELD	N006002

> **NOTE:** Word processors add coded characters (often hidden) to files unless specifically set up to write in the ASCII format. These coded characters are not acceptable in the template. Be sure that the text editor or word processor being used is in the proper mode. Also, do not use the ⬭TAB⬭ to line up the second column elements, but key in the necessary spaces, as the ⬭TAB⬭ involves coded characters.

From the extracted file in Table 6–1, a data base program can generate a sorted list whose items correspond to selected values. The procedure (again, to explain would take another book entirely) might list only 3"-flanges, or all 3"-fittings, or all reducers, or any combination of available records required corresponding to tag-field association.

BL:xxxxxx Nonattribute Fields Available If necessary, additional data is also automatically stored with each inserted block. The descriptions of each and the suggested format in a template file is shown below:

BL:LEVEL	Nwww000	*(Block nesting level)*
BL:NAME	Cwww000	*(Block name)*
BL:X	Nwwwddd	*(X coordinate of Block insertion point)*
BL:Y	Nwwwddd	*(Y coordinate)*
BL:Z	Nwwwddd	*(Z coordinate)*
BL:NUMBER	Nwww000	*(Block counter; same for all members of a MINSERT)*
BL:HANDLE	Cwww000	*(Block's handle; same for all members of a MINSERT)*
BL:LAYER	Cwww000	*(Block insertion layer name)*
BL:ORIENT	Nwwwddd	*(Block rotation angle)*
BL:XSCALE	Nwwwddd	*(X scale factor of Block)*
BL:YSCALE	Nwwwddd	*(Y scale factor)*
BL:ZSCALE	Nwwwddd	*(Z scale factor)*
BL:XEXTRUDE	Nwwwddd	*(X component of Block's extrusion direction)*
BL:YEXTRUDE	Nwwwddd	*(Y component)*
BL:ZEXTRUDE	Nwwwddd	*(Z component)*

The comments in the parentheses above are for your information and must not be included in the template file. The first column element is the name of the field, for example "BL:ORIENT." The second column element begins with a C or an N, denoting character or numeric data, respectively. The next three digits denote the width of the field, that is, how many spaces are to be allowed in the extract file for values to be written under this particular field. If the value to be written under this field for any record is too long for the width allowed, AutoCAD truncates the data written, proceeds with the extraction, and displays the following error message:

**Field overflow in record <record number>

The last three digits in the second column element of the field format denote the number of decimal places to which numeric values will be written. Character fields should have zeros in these three places. When fields are specified to be numeric, the Attribute values must be numbers, or AutoCAD will display an error message.

The ATTEXT command is invoked from the Screen Root Menu Blocks (Figure 6-37), or at the "Command:" prompt type in **ATTEXT** and press ⏎.

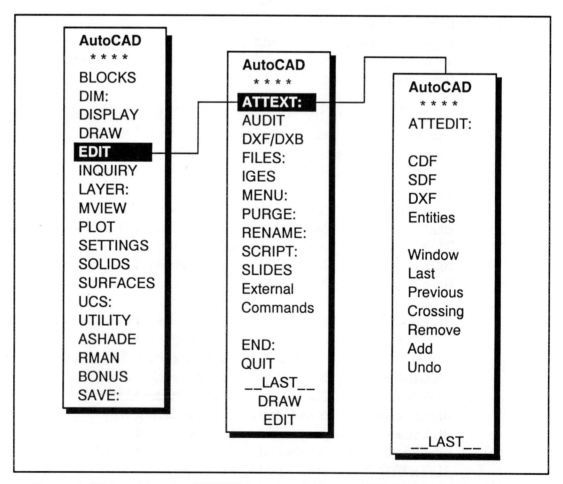

Figure 6-37 Invoking the ATTEXT Command from the Screen Root Menu Blocks

Command: **attext**
CDF,SDF or DXF Attribute extract (or Entities)? <C>

The default Comma Delimited Format (CDF) generates a file containing no more than one record for each Block Reference in the drawing. The values written under the fields in the extract files are separated by commas, with the character fields enclosed in single quotes.

The Standard Delimited Format (SDF) writes the values lined up in the widths allowed, and it is possible for adjacent mixed fields (characters and numeric) to not have spaces between them. It may be necessary to add dummy fields to provide spaces in these cases.

The AutoCAD Drawing Interchange File format is called DXF. Unlike the DXFOUT command, extraction files generated by the ATTEXT command contain only Block Reference, Attribute, and End-of-Sequence entities.

Entities is a option that allows you to select the entities for extraction of their Attributes. Once selection if complete, the prompt reverts to the CDF, SDF, or DXF prompt without the Entities option.

When the CDF and SDF formats are used, the next prompt is for the name of the TEMPLATE file:

Template file <default>:

At this prompt, enter the keyname of the template file without the .TXT extension. The next prompt is for the name of the file to which the values will be written:

Extract file name <drawing name>:

Pressing ⏎ will cause the keyname of the extract file to be the same as the keyname of the drawing, except AutoCAD will automatically append the .TXT extension. DOS permits a filename of con, for writing to the screen, or a filename of prn, for writing to a printer. In this case, a printer must be connected and ready to print.

Duplications The example extract file listed some records whose values in every field were the same. This would serve no purpose in a telephone directory, but in a list of objects in a drawing, it is possible that the only difference between two objects is their location in the drawing. In a bill of materials, the purchasing agent is not concerned with where, but how many duplicate objects there are. If it were essential to distinguish every object, the BL:X, BL:Y, and BL:Z fields could be included in the template to identify each object. Multiple insertions of the same Block in the same location could still be distinguished by their BL:HANDLE field if the handles system variable were ON, or by their BL:NUMBER if they were inserted with the MINSERT command.

Also, to the experienced pipe estimator (or astute novice) there are other duplications that are possible if not taken into account. Counting bolts and weld lengths for every fitting and valve could result in twice the quantities required. Mating flanges, each having 4 bolt holes, only require 4 bolts to assemble. An ell welded to a tee likewise requires the specified weld length only once. Therefore, Attribute value quantities associated with corresponding tags should take into account this and similar problems in mating assemblies.

Also, if the same fittings (in the form of Blocks with Attributes) are shown in more than one view in a drawing, some mechanism should be provided to prevent duplication of quantities in this case. As you can see, advanced features (Attributes) that provide solutions to complex problems (data extraction) often require carefully planned implementation.

Changing Entities in a Block Without Losing Attribute Values Sometimes it might be desirable to make changes to the entities within Blocks that have been inserted with Attributes and have had values assigned to the Attributes. Remember that the values of the Attributes can be edited with the DDATTE command. But, in order to change the geometry of a Block, it normally requires that you explode the Block, make the necessary changes, and then redefine the Block again. As long as the Attribute Definitions keep the same tags in the new definition, the redefined Blocks that have already been inserted in the drawing will retain those Attributes with the original definitions.

Another method of having a new Block definition applied to existing Blocks is to create a new drawing with the new Block definition. This can be done by using the WBLOCK command to create a drawing that conforms to the old definition and then edit that drawing. Or you can start a new drawing with the name of the Block that you wish to change.

In order to apply the new definition to the existing Block, you can call up the drawing from the Main Menu, and then use the INSERT command with the Block name: **option.** For example, if you wish to change the geometry of a Block named Part_1, and the changes have been made and stored in a separate drawing with the same name (Part_1), the sequence of prompts is as follows:

```
Command: insert
Block name <default>: part_1=
Block "Part_1" redefined
Regenerating drawing.
Insertion point: Ctrl + c
Command:
```

It is not necessary to specify an insertion point or respond to scale factor and rotation angles. Simply inserting the Block with the = (equals) behind the name will cause the definition of the drawing to become the new definition of the Block with the same name residing in the current drawing.

EDIT AND INQUIRY COMMANDS

In this section two more EDIT commands are explained — DIVIDE and MEASURE — in addition to the commands explained in Chapters 2, 3, and 4.

DIVIDE Command

The DIVIDE command causes AutoCAD to divide an entity into equal length segments, placing markers at the dividing points. Entities eligible for application of the DIVIDE command are the Line, Arc, Circle, and Polyline. Selecting an entity other that one of these will cause an error message to appear and you will be returned to the "Command:" prompt.

The sequence of prompts is as follows:

> Command: **divide**
> Select object to divide: *select a line, arc, circle, or polyline*
> <Number of segments>/Block:

You may respond with an integer from 2 to 32767, causing points to be placed along the selected entity at equal distances, but not actually separating the object. Logically, there will be one less point placed than the number entered, except in the case of a circle. The circle will have the first point placed at the angle from the center of the current Snap rotation angle. A closed Polyline will have the first point placed at the first point drawn in the Polyline. The total length of the Polyline will be divided in the number of segments entered without regard to the length of the individual segments that make up the Polyline. An example of a closed Polyline is shown in Figure 6–38.

> *NOTE:* It is advisable to set the system variables PDSIZE and PDMODE to values that will cause the points to be visible.

The Block option allows a named Block to be placed at the dividing points instead of a point. The sequence of prompts is as follows:

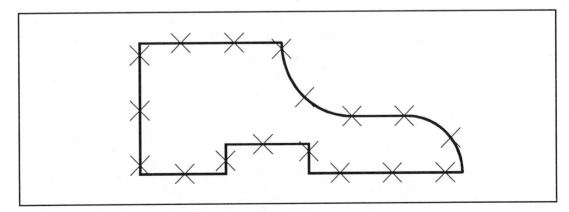

Figure 6–38 The DIVIDE Command as Used with a Closed Polyline

```
Command: divide
Select object to divide: select a line, arc, circle, or polyline
<Number of segments>/Block: block (or just b)
Block name to insert: enter the name of the Block
Align block with object? <Y>
Number of segments:
```

If you respond with **No** or **N** to the "Align block with object?" prompt, all of the blocks inserted will have a zero angle of rotation. If you default to **Yes**, the angle of rotation of each inserted block will correspond to the direction of the linear part of the object at its point of insertion or to that of a line tangent to a circular part of an object at the point of insertion.

MEASURE Command

The MEASURE command causes AutoCAD to divide an entity into specified length segments, placing markers at the measured points. Entities eligible for application of the MEASURE command are the Line, Arc, Circle, and Polyline. Selecting an entity other than one of these will cause an error message to appear and you will be returned to the "Command:" prompt.

The sequence of prompts is as follows:

```
Command: measure
Select object to measure: select a line, arc, circle, or polyline
<Number of segments>/Block:
```

You may respond with an integer from 2 to 32767, causing points to be placed along the selected entity at equal distances, but not actually separating the object. Logically, there will be one less point placed than the number entered, except in the case of a circle. The circle will have the first point placed at the angle from the center of the current Snap rotation angle. A closed Polyline will have the first point placed at the first point drawn in the Polyline. The total length of the Polyline will be measured in the number of segments entered without regard to the length of the individual segments that make up the Polyline.

> **NOTE:** It is advisable to set the system variables PDSIZE and PDMODE to values that will cause the points to be visible.

The Block option of the MEASURE command is similar to the Block option of the DIVIDE command.

DIMENSIONING UTILITY COMMANDS

The following dimensioning utility commands let you make various changes to associative dimension entities. Each of these commands prompts you to "Select objects:". You can use any of the Object Selection options such as Window and Crossing.

Tedit

The Tedit subcommand of the DIMENSION command allows you to move or rotate dimension text entities in associative dimensions. The sequence of prompts is as follows:

> Command: **dim**
> DIM: **tedit**
> Select dimension: *select an associative dimension*
> Enter text location (Left/Right/Home/Angle):

After selecting an associative dimension, the text string drags with cursor movement to show its placement if you pick a point on the screen. This occurs if the dimension variable DIMSHO is set to ON.

The Left and Right options cause the text to left- or right-justify along the dimension line on linear, radial, and diameter dimensions only. Final positions depend upon the settings of the DIMTAD and DIMTVP dimension variables. The Home option causes the position and rotation to be set to the defaults. The Angle option allows you to rotate the text. The prompt is as follows:

> Text angle:

You may respond with the value of the new angle or you can select two points to specify the angle.

Trotate

The Trotate subcommand of the DIMENSION command allows you to rotate dimension text entities in associative dimensions. This command is similar to that of the Angle option of the TEDIT command, except that this command can operate on more than one dimension at a time. The sequence of prompts is as follows:

> Command: **dim**
> DIM: **trotate**
> Enter new text angle: *specify the rotation angle*
> Select objects: *select the dimension objects and press* ⏎

Hometext

The Hometext subcommand of the DIMENSION command allows you to return the text to its default (home position) if you have moved the text from its default position by TEDIT or TROTATE commands. The sequence of prompts is as follows:

> Command: **dim**
> DIM: **hometext**
> Select objects: *select the dimension objects and press* ⏎

Newtext

The Newtext subcommand of the DIMENSION command allows you to change the dimension text for existing dimension entities. The sequence of prompts is as follows:

```
Command: dim
DIM: newtext
Enter new dimension text: specify the new text
Select objects: select the dimension objects and press ⏎
```

Update

The Update subcommand of the DIMENSION command allows you to update existing dimensions entities to use the current settings of the dimension variables, current text style, current Units settings and dimension style. The sequence of prompts is as follows:

```
Command: dim
DIM: update
Select objects: Select the dimension objects and press ⏎
```

Dimension Styles

Dimension variable settings are used to make the look of the dimensions conform to various drafting conventions or adjust the size of dimension components, such as the arrow size, text size, extension line offset, and general overall scale of the dimensions as a whole.

In one drawing a combination of dimension variable settings might be applied to one group of dimensions and another combination of settings might be applied to another group. Changing from one combination of settings to another often requires changing more than just one or two individual settings. It could be time-consuming to not only make the necessary changes, but just to verify that any questionable settings are correct. AutoCAD's Style subcommand to the DIMEN-SION command allows you to save the current combination of dimension variable settings and give it a name by which it can be recalled later.

Saving a dimension style can be accomplished by the following:

```
Command: dim
DIM: save
?/Name for new dimension style: unique name for style
```

The combination of settings is saved under the name given. It includes all dimension variables except DIMSHO and DIMASO. Any time a particular style is in effect and one of the dimension variable settings is changed, the current style becomes *UNNAMED.

A style that has been created previously can be recalled by using the Restore option as follows:

Command: **dim**
DIM: **restore**
Current dimension style: *enter style name*
?/Enter dimension style name or RETURN to select dimension:

Responding with **?** causes the following prompt to appear:

Dimension style(s) to list <*>: *enter name(s)*

You can respond with ⏎ to have all styles listed or use names or wild cards to list styles.

Responding with a dimension style name preceded by a tilde (~) causes AutoCAD to display a list showing the differences between the current settings and the settings of the named style.

The Override option allows you to change dimension variable settings for a particular dimension with or without affecting the settings of its style. The sequence of prompts is as follows:

Command: **dim**
DIM: **override**
Dimension variable to override: *enter variable name*
Current value <value> New value: *enter new value*
Dimension variable to override: ⏎
Select objects:

If one or more of the dimensions selected are associated with a particular style, the following prompt will appear:

Modify dimension style "style name"? <N>: *enter y or n*

If you respond with **Y**, AutoCAD will change the settings in the named style to the new values and all other dimensions associated with that style will also be updated.

If you respond with **N**, only the dimension selected is changed and is no longer associated with a style.

LAB EXERCISES

Lab Exercises 6-1 through 6-4

Create all of the Blocks shown in Figure 6-39 and Figure 6-40. Set your Grid to .125 and snap to .0625 while making the BLOCKS or WBLOCKS, whichever you prefer. If you create them as Blocks as part of the prototype drawing, then they will come with the prototype when you make your new drawing equal to the prototype. These exercises are all schematic drawings. They are not drawn to any scale.

Lay out exercise 6-1 and exercise 6-3 on a B-size sheet.

Lay out exercise 6-2 on a C-size sheet.

Lay out exercise 6-4 on an A-size sheet.

Set Grid .25 or .5 and Snap .125 or .25.

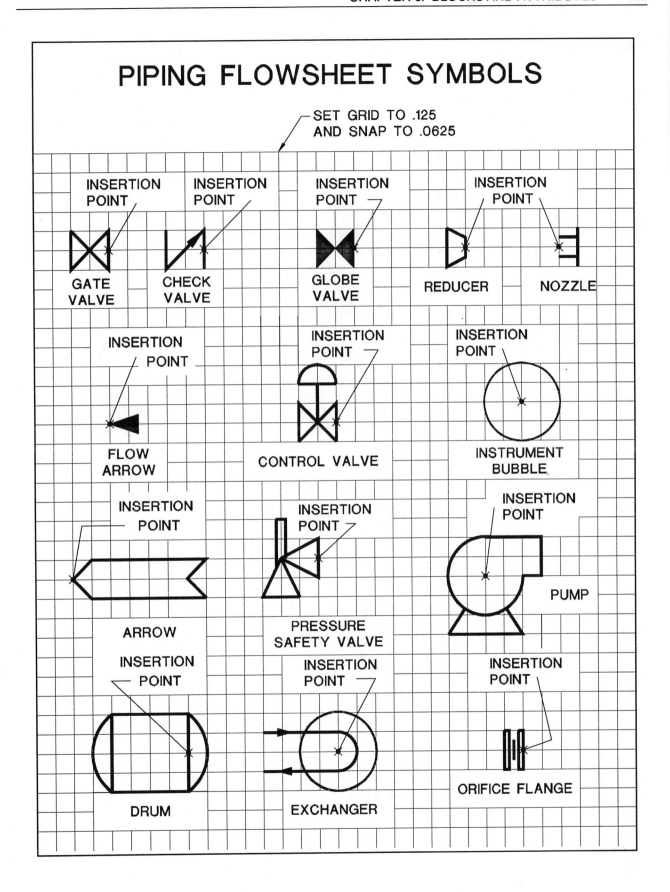

Figure 6-39 Piping Flowsheet Symbols

BLOCKS WITH ATTRIBUTES

SET GRID TO .125
AND SNAP TO .0625

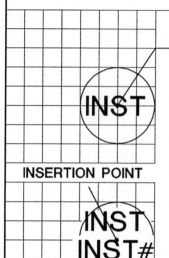

INSERTION POINT

INSERTION POINT

1. CREATE FIGURE
2. SELECT ATTDEF COMMAND
   ATTRIBUTE DEFINITION
3. SELECT ATTRIBUTE MODES
4. ATTRIBUTE TAG: INST (INSTRUMENT)
5. ATTRIBUTE PROMPT: ENTER INST. TAG
6. DEFAULT ATTRIBUTE VALVUE: RETURN
7. JUSTIFY/STYLE/ <START POINT> MIDDLE
8. SELECT MIDDLE POINT
9. HEIGHT <0.125>: ENTER HEIGHT
10. ROTATION ANGLE <0>: ENTER ANGLE
11. SELECT BLOCK OR WBLOCK COMMAND
12. ENTER BLOCK NAME
13. SELECT INSERTION POINT
14. SELECT FIGURE AND INCLUDE
    ATTRIBUTE TAG.

NOTE: IF THERE ARE TWO OR MORE ATTRIBUTES
      REPEAT #2 THRU #10 FOR EACH ATTRIBUTE
      BEFORE GOING ON TO #11.

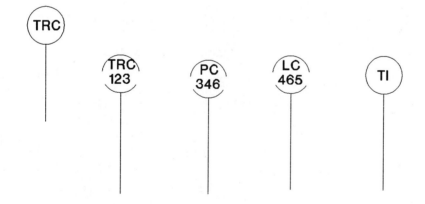

EXAMPLES

Figure 6-40 Examples of Blocks with Attributes

Blocks and Attributes

Lab Exercise 6-1

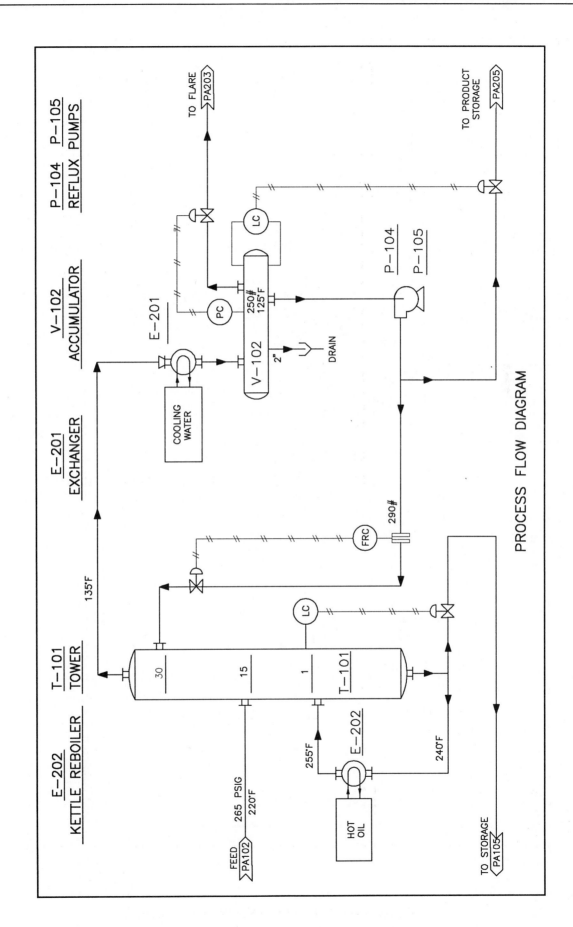

PROCESS FLOW DIAGRAM

Lab Exercise 6-2

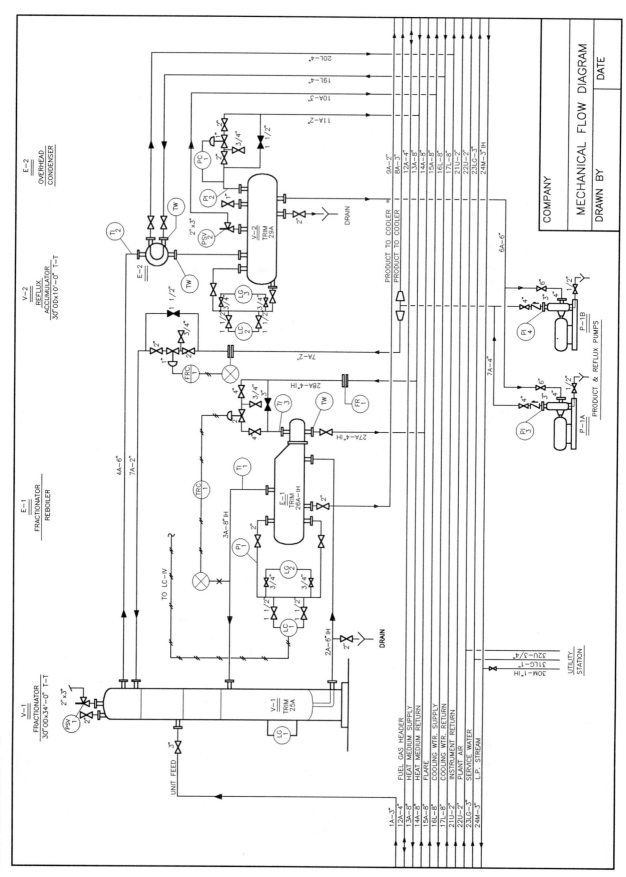

Lab Exercise 6-3

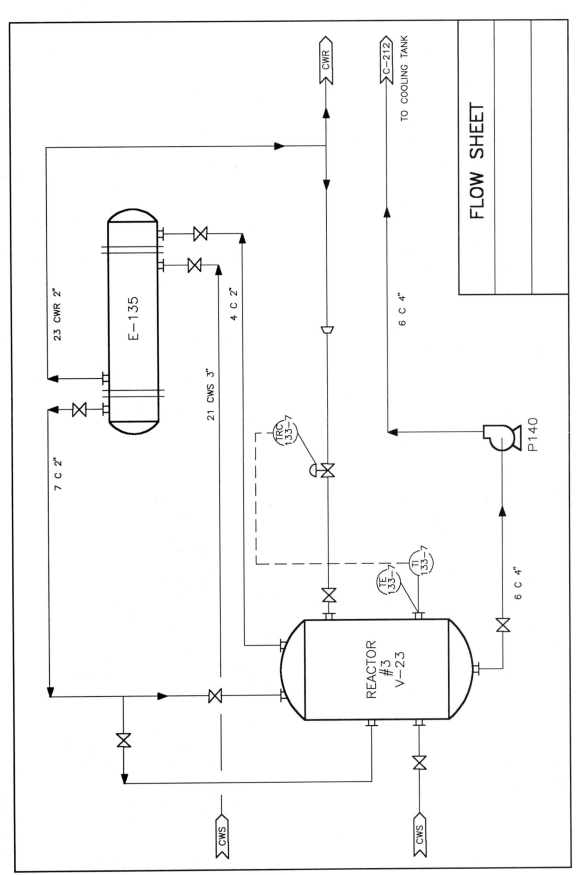

Lab Exercise 6-4

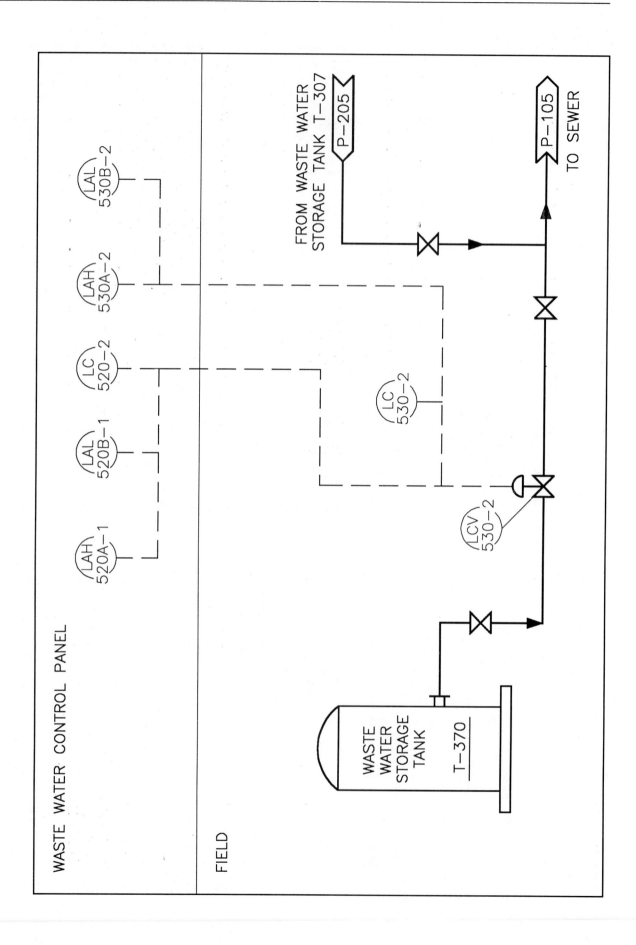

Lab Exercises 6-5 through 6-7

For exercises 6-5 through 6-7, set up a prototype drawing for the layout. Create all of the blocks shown in Figure 6-41. Set your Grid to .125 and Snap to .0625 while making the BLOCKS or WBLOCKS. If you create them as Blocks on your prototype drawing, then they will come with the prototype when you make your new drawing equal to the prototype. These exercises are all schematic drawings. They are not drawn to any scale.

Lay out exercises 6-5, 6-6, and 6-7 on a B-size sheet.

Set Grid .25 or .5 and Snap .125 or .25.

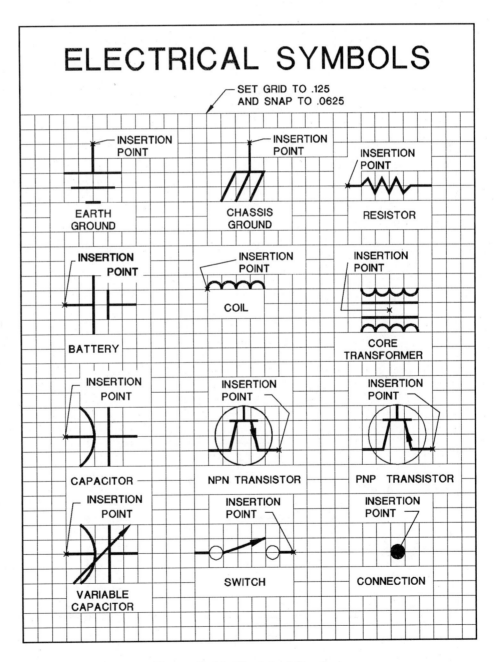

Figure 6-41 Electrical Symbols

Lab Exercise 6-5

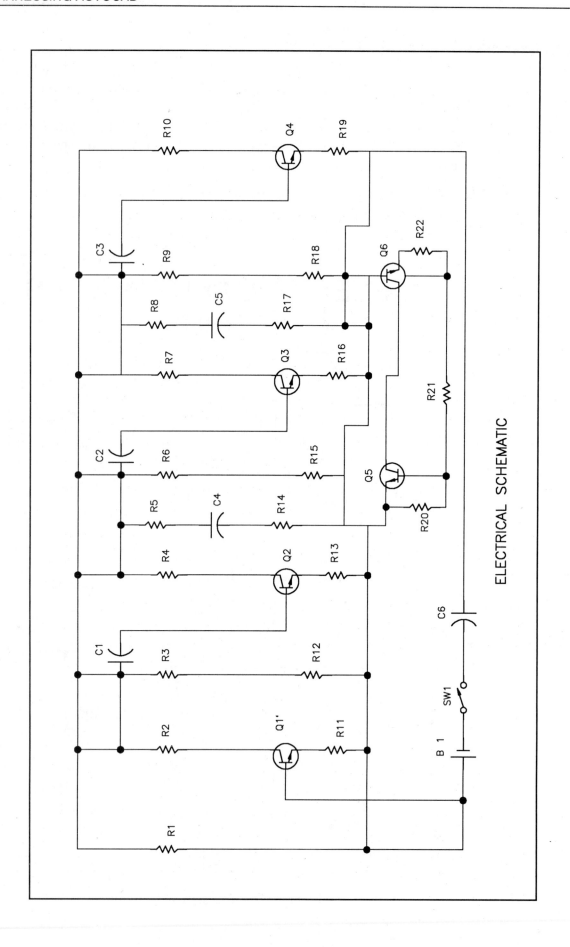

ELECTRICAL SCHEMATIC

Lab Exercise 6–6

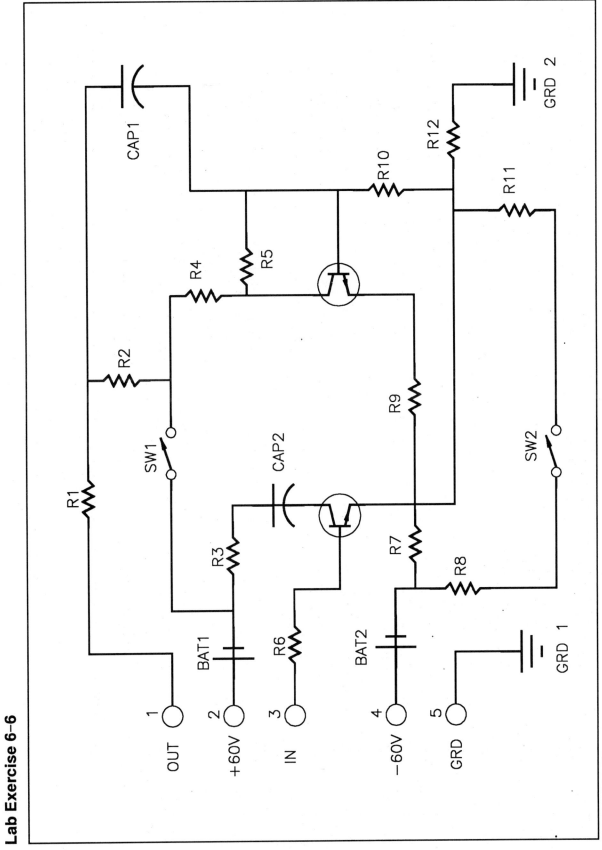

Lab Exercise 6-7

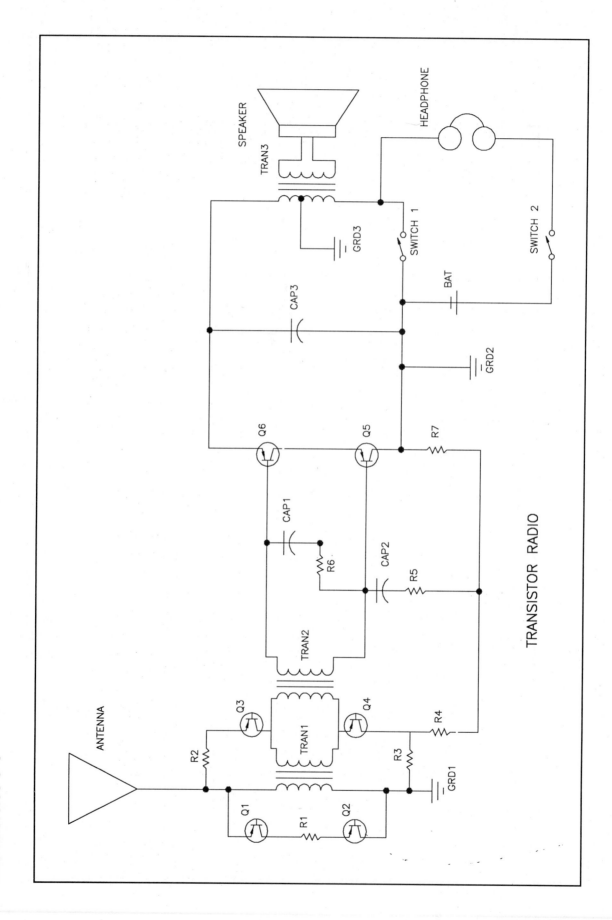

CHAPTER 7

External References

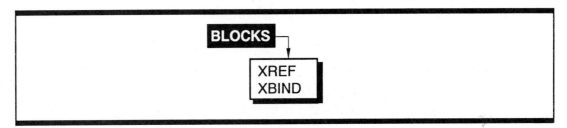

Figure 7-1 The Xref and Xbind Commands

In this chapter the commands and options that are related to external references are explained. This is a Release 11 feature. See Figure 7-1 for the list of commands that are covered in this chapter.

One of most powerful time-saving features of AutoCAD is the ability to combine one drawing with another. With Release 11, AutoCAD supports a feature that lets you display or view the contents of an unlimited number of drawing files while working in your current drawing file. This function is in the form of the external reference (Xref).

Prior to Release 11, existing AutoCAD drawings could be combined in only one way: by using the INSERT command to insert one drawing into another. When one drawing is inserted into another, the inserted drawing becomes a permanent part of the drawing it is inserted into. The data from the inserted drawing is merged with the data of the current drawing. Once the drawing is inserted, no link or association remains between the original drawing from which the inserted drawing came and the drawing it has been inserted into.

The INSERT command and the new Release 11 Xref command give users a choice of methods for combining existing drawing files. The new external reference feature does not make Block insertion of drawings obsolete; users can decide which method is more appropriate for the current application.

When a drawing is externally referenced (instead of inserted as a Block), the user can view and Osnap to the referenced drawing from the current drawing, but each drawing's data is still stored and maintained in a separate drawing file. The only information in the reference drawing that becomes a permanent part of the current drawing is the name of the reference drawing and its directory path. If

479

necessary, externally referenced files may be scaled, moved, copied, mirrored, or rotated by using the AutoCAD EDIT commands. You can control the visibility, color, and linetype of the layers belonging to an external drawing file. This lets you control which portions of the external drawing file are displayed, and how. No matter how complex an external reference drawing may be, it is treated as a single entity by AutoCAD. If you invoke the MOVE command and point to one line, for instance, the entire object moves, not just the line you pointed to. You cannot explode the externally referenced drawing. All the manipulations performed on a reference file will not affect the original drawing file because a reference file is only an image, however scaled or rotated.

Borders are an excellent example of drawing files that are useful as external reference files. The entities that make up a border will use considerable space in a file, and commonly amount to around 20,000 bytes. If a border is drawn in each drawing file, this would waste a large amount of bytes, especially if you multiply 20,000 bytes by 100 drawing files. If external reference files are used correctly, they can save a large amount of disk space.

Accuracy and efficient drawing time are other important design features that are enhanced through external reference files. When an addition or change is made to a drawing file that is being used as an external reference file, all the drawings that use the file will reflect the modifications. For example, if you alter the title block of a border, all the drawing files that use that border as an external reference file will automatically display the title block revisions. (Can you imagine accessing 100 drawing files to correct one small detail?) External reference files will save time, and ensure the drawing accuracy required to produce a professional product.

There is no limit to the number of external references you can add to a drawing. If necessary, you can even nest them so that loading one external reference automatically causes another external reference to be loaded. When you attach a drawing file as an external reference file, it is permanently attached until it is detached or bound to the current drawing. When you load your drawing into the Drawing Editor (or plot the drawing from the Main Menu), AutoCAD automatically reloads each external reference drawing file; thus, each external drawing file reflects the latest state of the referenced drawing file.

The Xref command, when combined with the networking capability of AutoCAD Release 11, gives the project manager powerful new features to cope with the realities of file management. The project manager can see the work of the various departments or designers working on a particular aspect of the contract instantaneously. If necessary, you can overlay a drawing where appropriate, track the progress, and maintain document integrity. At the same time, departments need not lose control over individual designs and details.

XREF'S DEPENDENT SYMBOLS

The symbols that are carried into a drawing by an Xref are called dependent symbols because they depend on the external file, not the current drawing, for their characteristics. The symbols have arbitrary names and include Blocks, layers, linetypes, text styles, and dimension styles.

When you attach an external reference drawing, AutoCAD automatically renames an Xref's dependent symbols. AutoCAD forms a temporary name for each symbol by combining its original name with the name of the Xref itself. The two names are separated by the vertical bar (|) character. Renaming the symbols prevents the Xref's entities from taking on the characteristics of existing symbols in the drawing.

For instance, you created a drawing called PLAN1 with layers 0, first-fL, dim, and text and in addition to Blocks arrow and monument. If you attach PLAN1 drawing as an external reference file, the layer first-fL will be renamed as PLAN1|first-fL, dim as PLAN1|dim, and text as PLAN1|text, as shown in Figure 7-2. Blocks arrow and monument will be renamed as PLAN1|arrow and PLAN1|monument. The only exceptions to renaming are unambiguous defaults like layer 0, and linetype continuous. The information on the layer 0 from the reference file will be placed on the layer 0 of the current drawing. It will take the characteristics of the current drawing.

This prefixing is carried to nested Xref's. For example, if the external file PLAN1 included an Xref named Title that has a layer legend, it would get the symbol name PLAN1|title|legend if PLAN1 was attached to another drawing.

This automatic renaming of Xref's dependent symbols has two benefits:

1. It allows you to see at a glance which named objects belong to which external reference file.
2. It allows dependent symbols to have the same name in both the current drawing and an external reference, and to coexist without any conflict.

```
   Layer name         State     Color       Linetype
-----------------    -------   ---------   -----------
8                      On      7 (white)   CONTINUOUS
PLAN1|DIM              On      3 (green)   CONTINUOUS    Xdep: PLAN1
PLAN1|FIRST-FL         On      1 (red)     CONTINUOUS    Xdep: PLAN1
PLAN1|TEXT             On      5 (blue)    CONTINUOUS    Xdep: PLAN1

Current layer: 0

?/Make/Set/New/ON/OFF/Color/Ltype/Freeze/Thaw:
```

Figure 7-2 Attaching an External Reference File

The AutoCAD commands and dialogue boxes for manipulating named objects do not let you select Xref's dependent symbols. Usually, dialogue boxes display these entries using grayed-out text.

For example, you cannot insert a Block that belongs to an external reference drawing in your current drawing nor can you make a dependent layer the current layer and begin creating new entities on it.

You can control the visibility of the layers (ON/OFF) of an external reference drawing and, if necessary, you can even change the color and linetype. Any changes you make to these settings, though, apply only to the current drawing session; they are discarded when you end the drawing.

There may be times when you want to make your Xref data a permanent part of your current drawing. To make an Xref drawing a permanent part of the current drawing, use the Bind option of the Xref command. When you use the Bind option, all layers and other symbols, including the data, become part of the current drawing. This is similar to inserting a drawing with the INSERT command.

If necessary, you can make dependent symbols such as layers, linetypes, text styles, and dim styles part of the current drawing by using the Xbind command instead of binding the whole drawing. This allows you to work with the symbol just as if you had defined it in the current drawing.

XREF COMMAND

The Xref command has many options. The Xref command is invoked from the Screen Root Menu Blocks (Figure 7-3), pull-down menu Draw (Figure 7-4), or at the "Command:" prompt type in **Xref** and press ⏎.

> Command: **xref**
> ?/Bind/Detach/Path/Reload/<Attach>:

Attach Option

This is the default option of the Xref command. Use it when you want to attach a new external reference file or to insert a copy of the Xref file already attached to the current drawing file. When you select this option, AutoCAD will prompt:

> Xref to Attach <default>:

You can enter a drawing name or a drawing name preceded by an explicit path specification. You also can enter the tilde (~) at the prompt to display the Select Drawing File dialogue box and select the drawing file you want to attach to the current drawing.

Once you enter a name, AutoCAD prompts you for an insertion point, scale, and rotation angle, as described for the INSERT command, earlier in Chapter 6.

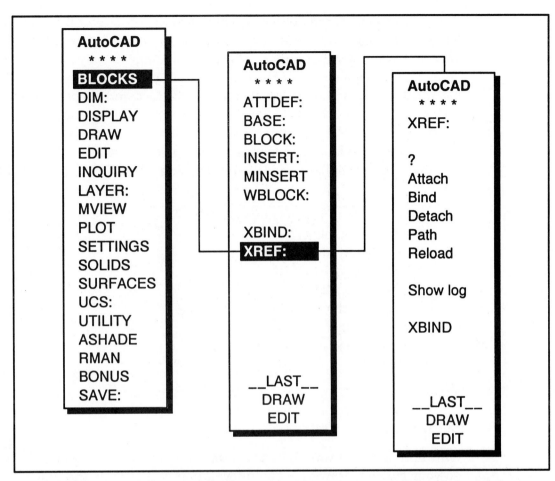

Figure 7–3 Invoking the Xref Command from the Screen Root Menu Blocks

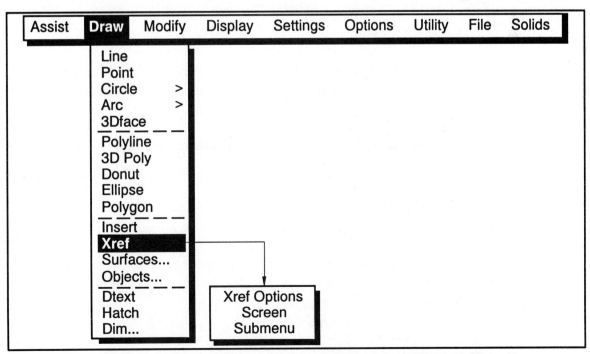

Figure 7–4 The Xref Command Invoked from the Pull-Down Menu Draw

Before AutoCAD prompts for the insertion point, it checks to see if a standard Block of the same name already exists in the drawing, or if it has already been attached as an Xref. If a Block of the same name already exists, AutoCAD issues an error message and ends the command. If you specify an Xref that has already been attached, AutoCAD alerts you to this fact and then prompts for insertion point.

For instance, the following command sequence will attach a drawing PLAN1 as an external reference file to the current drawing ELECT-1:

```
Command: xref
?/Bind/Detach/Path/Reload/<Attach>: ⏎
Xref to Attach: plan1
Attach Xref PLAN1: plan1
PLAN1 loaded.
Insertion point: 0,0
   X scale factor <1> / Corner / XYZ: ⏎
   Y scale factor <default=X>: ⏎
   Rotation angle <0>: ⏎
Command:
```

? Option

This option allows you to list the names of Xrefs that have already been attached to your current drawing. The information will include the name of the external reference file, the pathname used to load it, and the number of Xrefs currently attached to your drawing. When you select this option, AutoCAD will prompt:

```
Xref(s) to list <*>:
```

You can specify wild card characters to list multiple names, enter multiple names separated by commas, or press ⏎ in response to the prompt. AutoCAD will list all the Xrefs currently attached to the drawing.

For instance, the following command sequence lists the Xrefs attached to the current drawing:

```
Command: xref
?/Bind/Detach/Path/Reload/<Attach>: ?
Xref(s) to list <*>: ⏎
```

Xref Name	Path
PLAN1	/dwg/proj1/plan1
TITLE	/dwg/title

```
Total Xref(s): 2
```

Bind Option

This option will allow you to make your Xref data a permanent part of your current drawing. This has the same effect as inserting the drawing. When you select this option, AutoCAD will prompt:

Xref(s) to bind:

Enter a single Xref name, list of names separated by comma, or any valid wild card characters for an Xref(s) you want to bind.

When you bind an external reference, it becomes an ordinary Block in your current drawing. You can insert this Block just like any other Block. Bind also adds the dependent symbols to your drawing, letting you use them as you would any other named objects. In the process, AutoCAD renames the dependent symbols. The vertical bar (|) is replaced with three characters: $, a number, and another $. The number is assigned by AutoCAD to ensure that the named object will have a unique name.

For instance, if you bind an Xref named PLan1, which has a dependent layer pLan1|first-fL., AutoCAD will try to rename the layer to pLan1$0$first-fL. If there is already a layer by that name in your current drawing, then AutoCAD will try to rename the layer to plan1$1$first-fL and so on, until there is no duplicate.

If you do not want to bind the entire Xref, but only specific dependent symbols (a layer, linetype, Block, dim style, or text style), then you can use the Xbind command, explained later in the chapter.

Detach Option

This option removes an Xref from your drawing. If the Xref is currently being displayed as part of the current drawing, it will disappear when you detach it. When you select this option, AutoCAD will prompt:

Xref(s) to detach:

Enter a single Xref name, list of names separated by comma, or any valid wild card characters for an Xref(s) you want to detach.

Path Option

This option allows you to change the path to the Xref's source file. This can be useful if the external drawing file has moved from its original location or been renamed since you first attached it. When you select this option, AutoCAD will prompt:

Edit path for which Xref(s):

Enter a single Xref name, a list of names separated by comma, or any valid wild card characters for an Xref(s) filename whose path you want to change.

Once you enter a name, AutoCAD displays the current pathname of the Xref file and prompts you for a new pathname. When you enter a new pathname, AutoCAD tries to locate the file; if it cannot find the file you specified, it discards the new filename and lets you try again. When you have finished changing the specified pathname, AutoCAD automatically reloads (updates) the specified file.

For instance, the following command sequence shows steps in changing the path for an external reference file PLan1:

```
Command: xref
?/Bind/Detach/Path/Reload/<Attach>: path
Edit path for which Xref(s): plan1
old path: C:\dwg\proj1\plan1
new path: C:\dwg\proj2\plan1
Command:
```

Reload Option

This option allows you to update one or more Xrefs any time while the current drawing is in the Drawing Editor. When you select this option, AutoCAD will prompt:

```
Xref(s) to reload:
```

Enter a single Xref name, a list of names separated by comma, or any valid wild card characters for an Xref(s) you want to reload.

When you load a drawing into the Drawing Editor, it automatically reloads any external references attached. The Reload option has been provided to reread the external drawing from the external drawing file whenever it is desirable to do so from within the Drawing Editor. This option will be helpful, especially in a network environment to get the latest version of the reference drawing while you are in the Drawing Editor.

MANAGEMENT OF EXTERNAL REFERENCES

Several tools have been implemented to help in the management and tracking of external references.

One of the tracking mechanisms is an external ASCII log file that is maintained on each drawing which contains external references. This file, which AutoCAD generates and maintains automatically, has the same name as the current drawing and a file extension .XLG. You can examine the file with any text editor and/or print it. The log file registers each Attach, Bind, Detach, and Reload of each external reference for the current drawing. AutoCAD writes a title block to the log

```
Loading FIG8-2 into Drawing Editor.
Resolving Xref(s).

Xref:  PLAN1 -- (existing)

Resolve Xref PLAN1: plan1

    Update Block symbol table:
    Block update complete.

    Update Ltype symbol table:
    Ltype update complete.

    Update Layer symbol table:
       Overwrite symbol:  PLAN1|FIRST-FL
       Overwrite symbol:  PLAN1|DIM
       Overwrite symbol:  PLAN1|TEXT
    Layer update complete.

    Update Style Symbol table:
       Appending symbol:  PLAN1|STANDARD
```

Figure 7–5 Log File Entries Generated When an External Drawing File is Attached to an Existing Drawing

file that contains the name of the current drawing, the date and time, and the operation being performed. Once a log file has been created for a drawing, AutoCAD continues to append to it. The log file is always placed in the same directory as the current drawing.

See Figure 7–5 for a partial listing of the log file entries generated when an external drawing file PLAN1 is attached to the current drawing, ELEC-fl.

External references are also reported in response to the ? option of the Xref command and the BLOCK command.

Because of the external reference feature, the contents of a drawing may now be stored in multiple drawing files. This means that new backup procedures are required to handle drawings linked in external reference partnerships. Three possible solutions are:

1. Make the external reference drawing a permanent part of the current drawing prior to archiving with the Bind option of the Xref command.

2. Modify the current drawing's path to the external reference drawing so that they are both stored in the same directory, then archive them together.

3. Archive the directory location of the external reference drawing with the drawing which references it. Tape backup machines do this automatically.

XBIND COMMAND — ADDING DEPENDENT SYMBOLS TO THE CURRENT DRAWING

The Xbind command lets you add a selected subset of Xref's dependent symbols to your current drawing permanently. The dependent symbols include the Block, layer, linetype, dim style, and text style. Once the dependent symbol is added to the current drawing, it will behave as if it was created in the current drawing and saved with the drawing when you ended the drawing session. While adding the dependent symbol to the current drawing, AutoCAD removes the vertical bar symbol (|) from each dependent symbol's name, replacing it with three new characters: a $, a number, and another $ symbol.

For instance, you might want to use a Block that is defined in an external reference. Instead of binding the whole external reference with the Bind option of the Xref command, it is advisable to use the Xbind command. By using the Xbind command, the Block and the layers associated with the Block will be added to the current drawing. If the Block's Definition contains reference to an external reference, AutoCAD binds that Xref and all its dependent symbols as well. After binding the necessary dependent symbols, you can detach the external reference file.

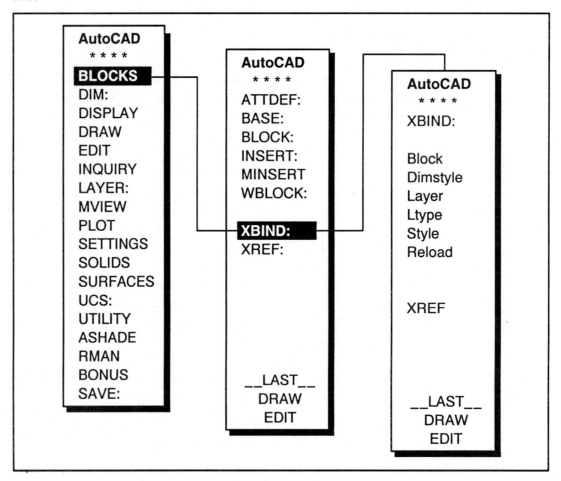

Figure 7-6 Invoking the Xbind Command from the Screen Root Menu Blocks

The Xbind command is invoked from the Screen Root Menu Blocks (Figure 7–6), or at the "Command:" prompt type in **Xbind** and ⏎.

> Command: **xbind**
> Block/Dimstyle/Layer/Ltype/Style:

Select the type of dependent symbol you want to bind. AutoCAD then prompts you for the name(s) of the dependent symbols. Enter a single symbol name, list of names separated by comma, or any valid wild card characters for symbols you want to bind to the current drawing.

The following command sequence shows steps in binding the Block arrow from an external reference file PLan1:

> Command: **xbind**
> Block/Dimstyle/Layer/Ltype/Style: **block**
> Dependent Block name(s): **plan1|arrow**
> Scanning...
> 1 Block(s) bound
> Command:

External References

LAB EXERCISES

Lab Exercise 7-1

For exercise 7-1, lay out the pipe-rack as shown. See detail "1" for steel dimensions. Starting point is 2',5'. Do not dimension the drawing. Put all callouts and coordinates as indicated.

> Drawing units set to Architectural
> Drawing Limits   lower left: 0',0'
>   upper right: 27',35'
>
> Starting Point 2',5'
> Set dimscale=32
> Set LTSCALE=32
> Set text height=4"

When you Xref this drawing into the final project, use insertion point 0',0'. The drawing will appear as shown in exercise 7-1a.

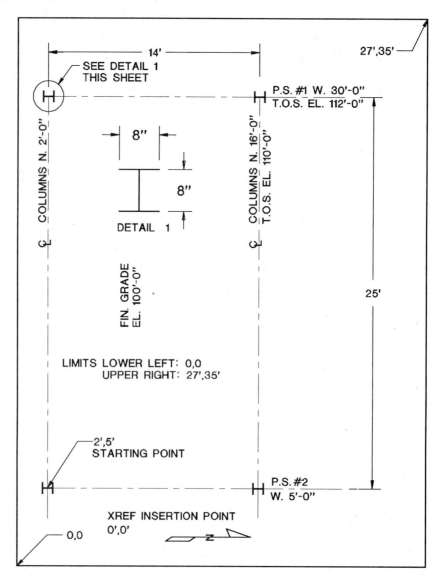

Lab Exercise 7–1a

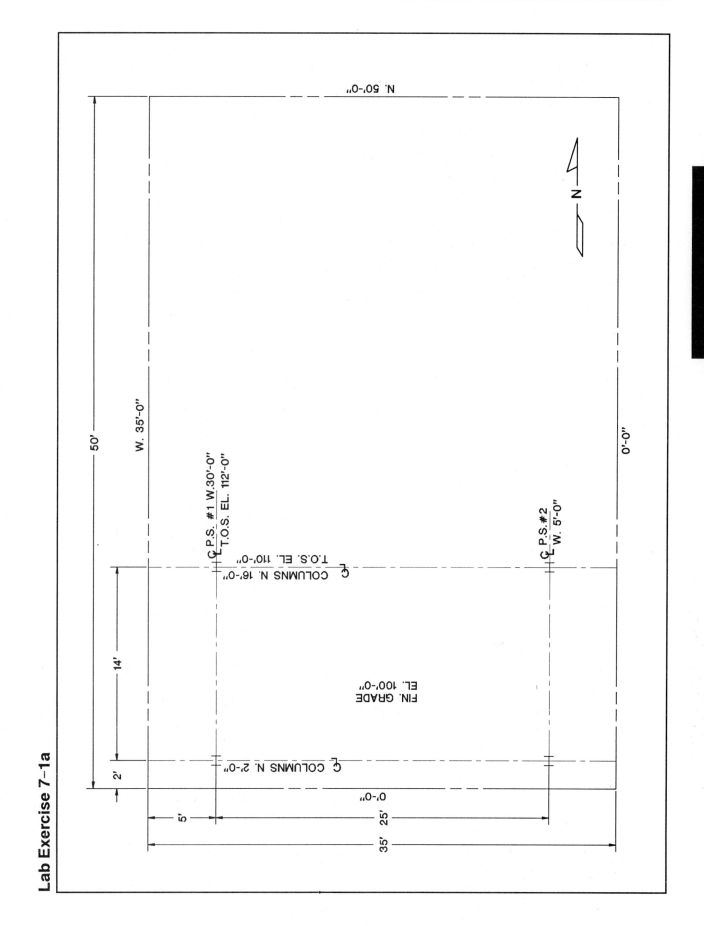

External References

Lab Exercise 7–2

For exercise 7–2, lay out the pumps as shown. Starting point is 17'-6", 7'. Do not dimension the drawing. Put all callouts and coordinates as indicated.

Drawing units set to Architectural
Drawing Limits   lower left: 0',0'
                               upper right: 28',21'
Starting Point 17'-6",7'
Set dimscale=32
Set LTSCALE=32
Set text height=4"

When you Xref this drawing into the final project, use insertion point 0',0'. The drawing will appear as shown in exercise 7–2a.

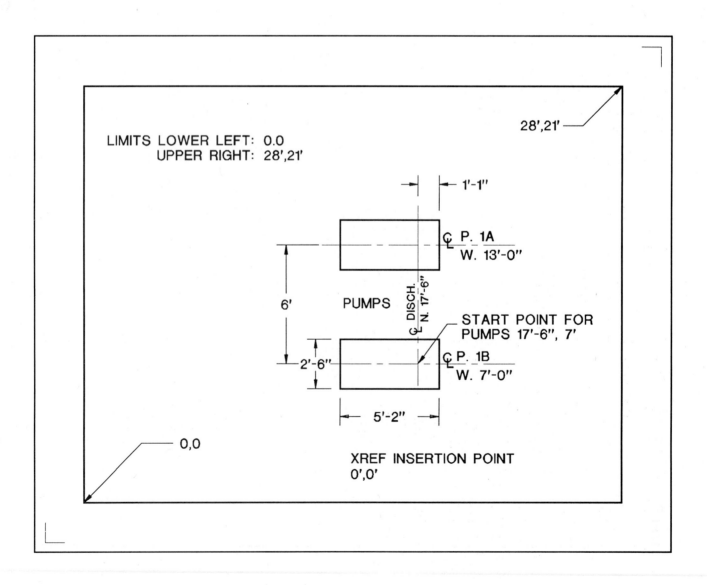

Lab Exercise 7-2a

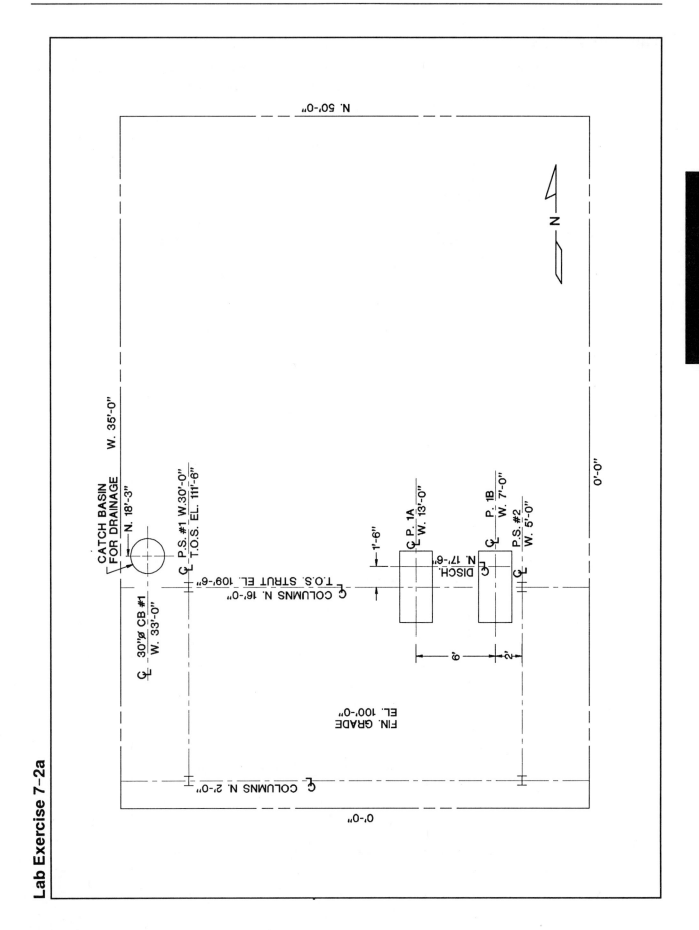

Lab Exercise 7-3

For exercise 7-3, lay out the pipe supports as shown. Starting point is 8'-6", 14'-6". Do not dimension the drawing. Put all callouts and coordinates as indicated.

Drawing units set to Architectural
Drawing Limits   lower left: 0',0'
                                 upper right: 23',35'
Starting Point 8'-6",14'-6"
Set dimscale=32
Set LTSCALE=32
Set text height=4"

When you Xref this drawing into the final project, use insertion point 30',0'. The drawing will appear as shown in exercise 7-3a.

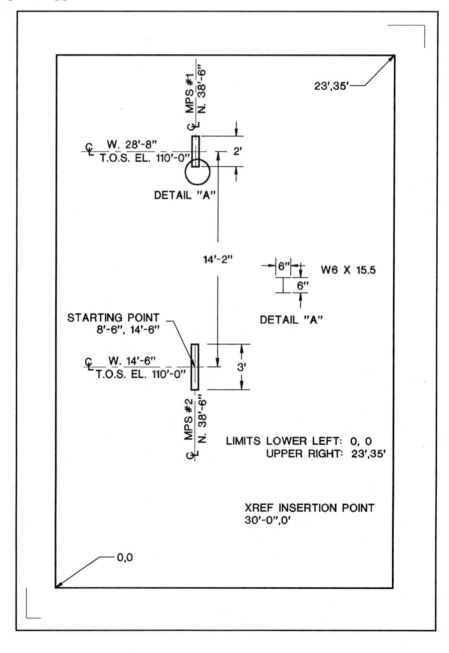

Lab Exercise 7-3a

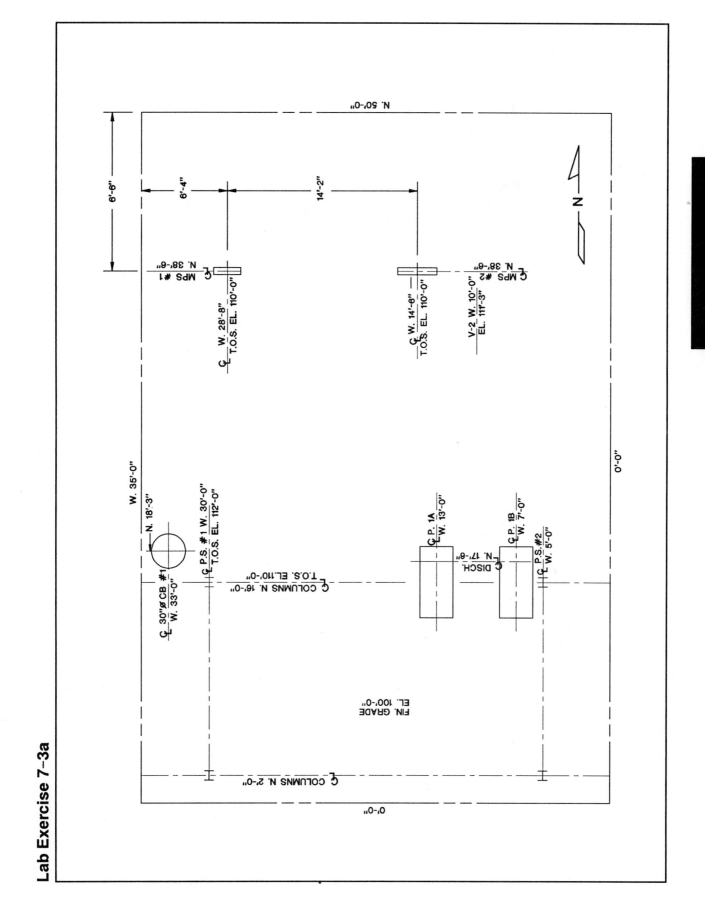

External References

Lab Exercise 7-4

For exercise 7-4, lay out the exchangers E-1 and E-2 as shown. See exercise 7-4a for detailed dimensions and exercise 7-4b for details on drawing vessel heads. Starting point is 7', 15'-7". Do not dimension the drawing. Put all callouts and coordinates as indicated.

Drawing units set to Architectural
Drawing Limits   lower left: 0',0'
                            upper right: 36',36'
Starting Point 7', 15'-7"
Set dimscale=32
Set LTSCALE=32
Set text height=4"

When you Xref this drawing into the final project, use insertion point 17'-6",0'. The drawing will appear as shown in exercise 7-4c.

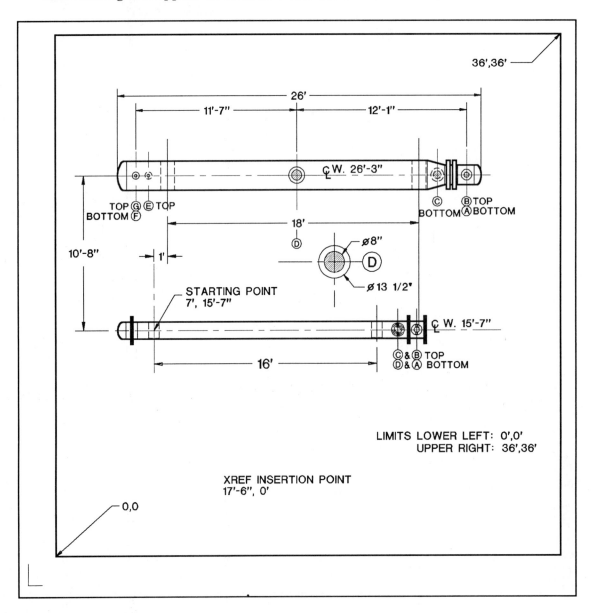

Lab Exercise 7-4a

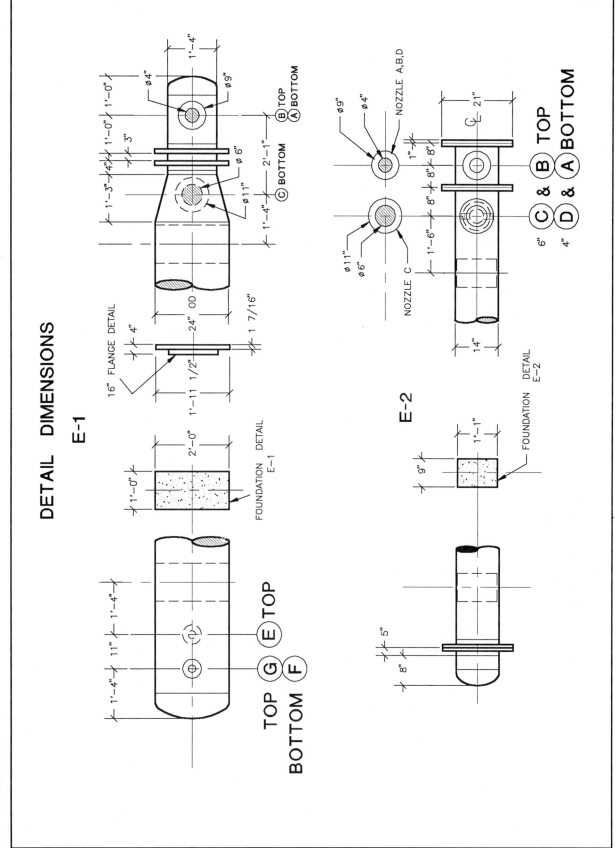

DETAIL DIMENSIONS

E-1

E-2

Lab Exercise 7-4b

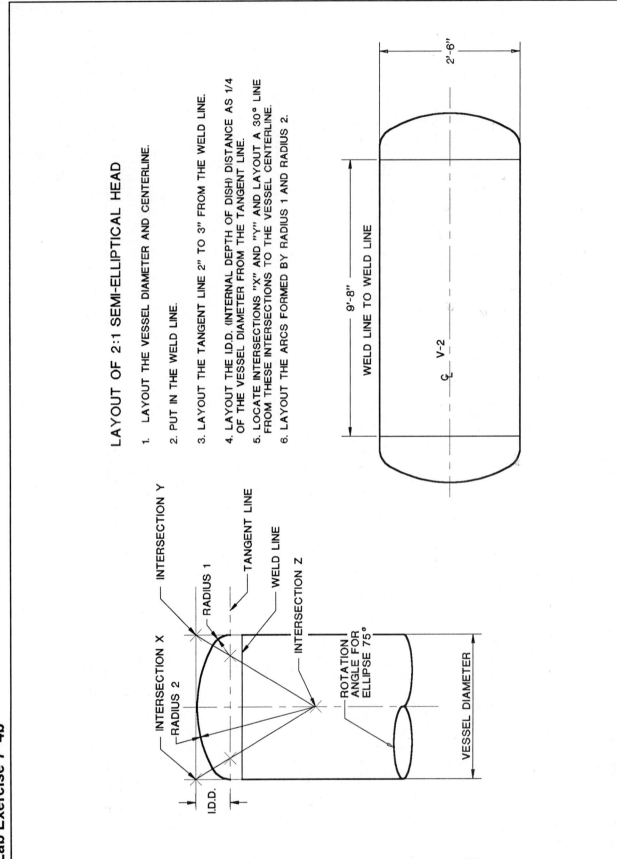

LAYOUT OF 2:1 SEMI-ELLIPTICAL HEAD

1. LAYOUT THE VESSEL DIAMETER AND CENTERLINE.

2. PUT IN THE WELD LINE.

3. LAYOUT THE TANGENT LINE 2" TO 3" FROM THE WELD LINE.

4. LAYOUT THE I.D.D. (INTERNAL DEPTH OF DISH) DISTANCE AS 1/4 OF THE VESSEL DIAMETER FROM THE TANGENT LINE.

5. LOCATE INTERSECTIONS "X" AND "Y" AND LAYOUT A 30° LINE FROM THESE INTERSECTIONS TO THE VESSEL CENTERLINE.

6. LAYOUT THE ARCS FORMED BY RADIUS 1 AND RADIUS 2.

Lab Exercise 7-4c

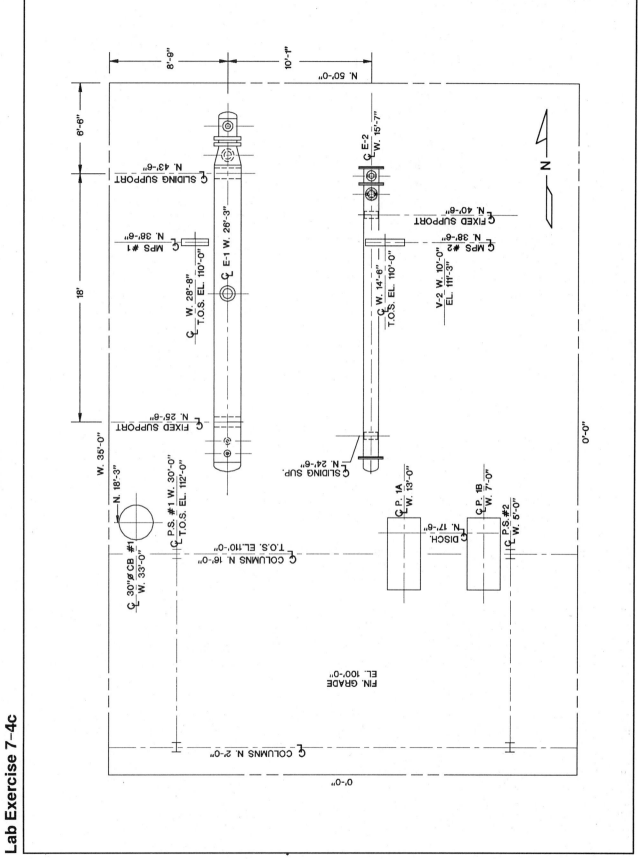

Lab Exercise 7-5

For exercise 7-5, lay out the horizontal vessel V-2 as shown. See exercises 7-5a and exercise 7-5b for detailed dimensions. Starting point is 7',10'. Do not dimension the drawing. Put all callouts and coordinates as indicated.

Drawing units set to Architectural
Drawing Limits   lower left: 0',0'
                        upper right: 24',18'
Starting Point 7', 10'
Set dimscale=32
Set LTSCALE=32
Set text height=4"

When you Xref this drawing into the final project, use insertion point 17'-6",0'. The drawing will appear as shown in exercise 7-5c.

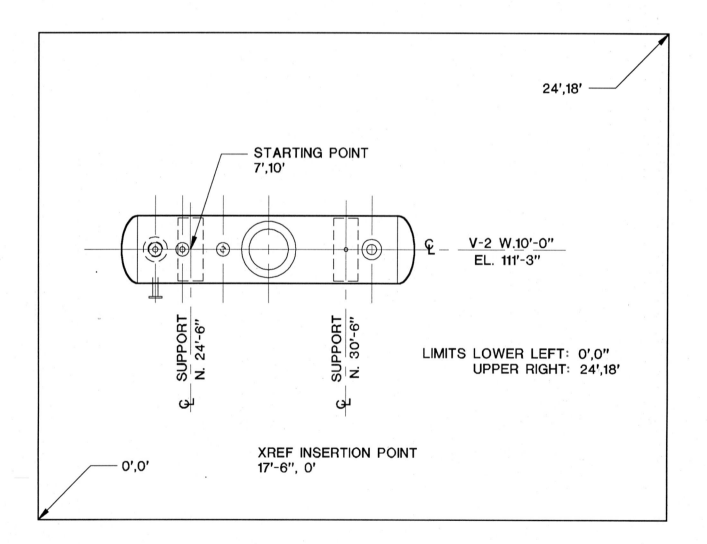

Lab Exercise 7-5a

HORIZONTAL VESSEL

Lab Exercise 7-5b

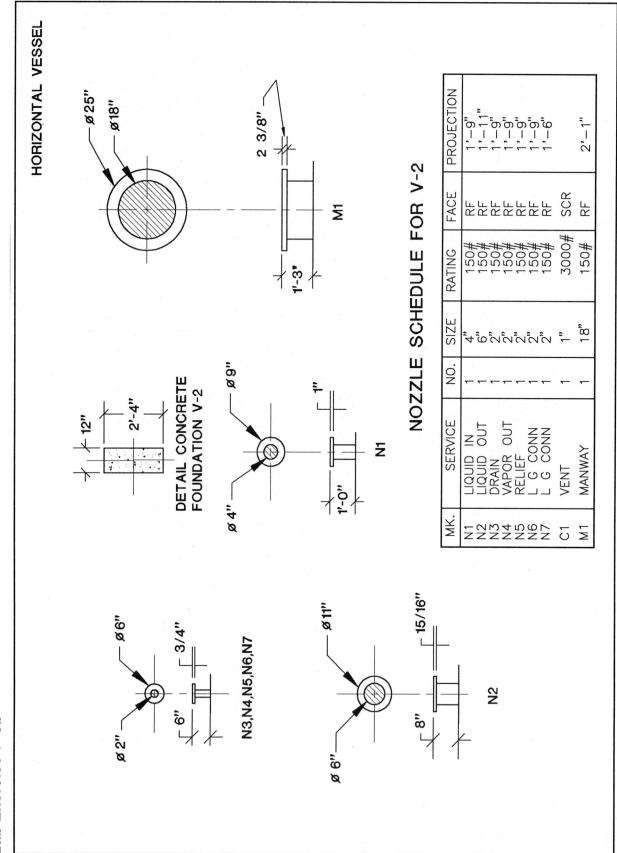

HORIZONTAL VESSEL

DETAIL CONCRETE FOUNDATION V-2

NOZZLE SCHEDULE FOR V-2

MK.	SERVICE	NO.	SIZE	RATING	FACE	PROJECTION
N1	LIQUID IN	1	4"	150#	RF	1'-9"
N2	LIQUID OUT	1	6"	150#	RF	1'-11"
N3	DRAIN	1	2"	150#	RF	1'-9"
N4	VAPOR OUT	1	2"	150#	RF	1'-9"
N5	RELIEF	1	2"	150#	RF	1'-9"
N6	L G CONN	1	2"	150#	RF	1'-9"
N7	L G CONN	1	2"	150#	RF	1'-6"
C1	VENT	1	1"	3000#	SCR	
M1	MANWAY	1	18"	150#	RF	2'-1"

Lab Exercise 7–5c

External References

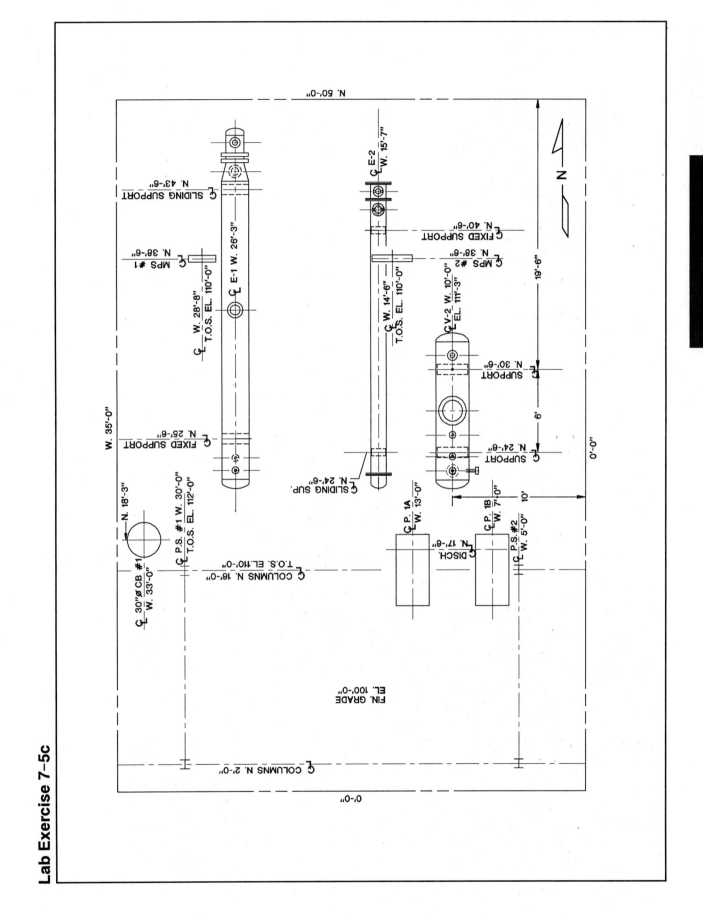

Lab Exercise 7-6

For exercise 7-6, lay out the vertical vessel V-1 as shown. See exercise 7-6a for detailed dimensions. Starting point is 8'-9",8'-6". Do not dimension the drawing. Put all callouts and coordinates as indicated.

Drawing units set to Architectural
Drawing Limits   lower left: 0',0'
                        upper right: 20',15'
Starting Point 8'-9", 8'-6"
Set dimscale=32
Set LTSCALE=32
Set text height=4"

When you Xref this drawing into the final project, use insertion point 17'-6",13'. The drawing will appear as shown in exercise 7-6b.

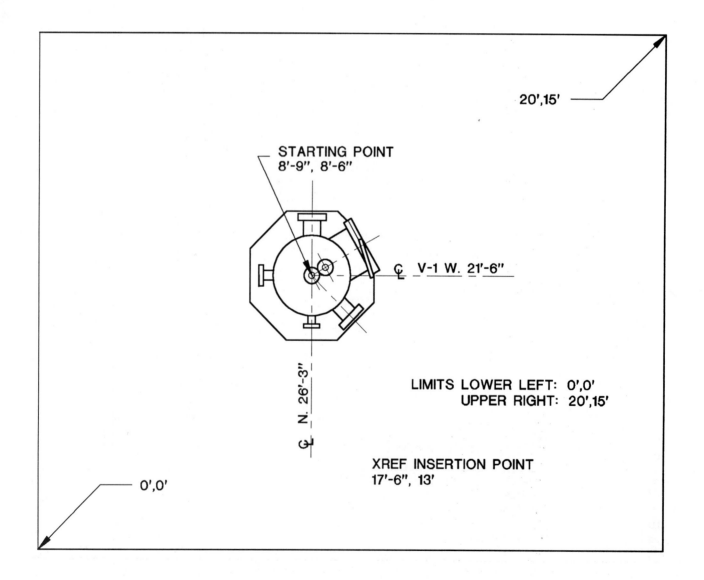

Lab Exercise 7-6a

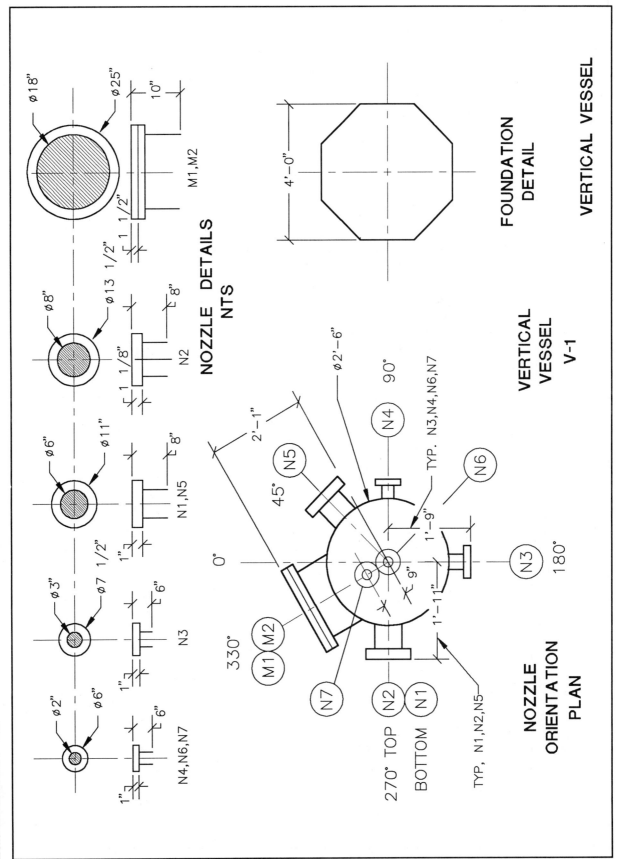

NOZZLE DETAILS
NTS

FOUNDATION
DETAIL

VERTICAL VESSEL

VERTICAL
VESSEL
V-1

NOZZLE
ORIENTATION
PLAN

Lab Exercise 7-6b

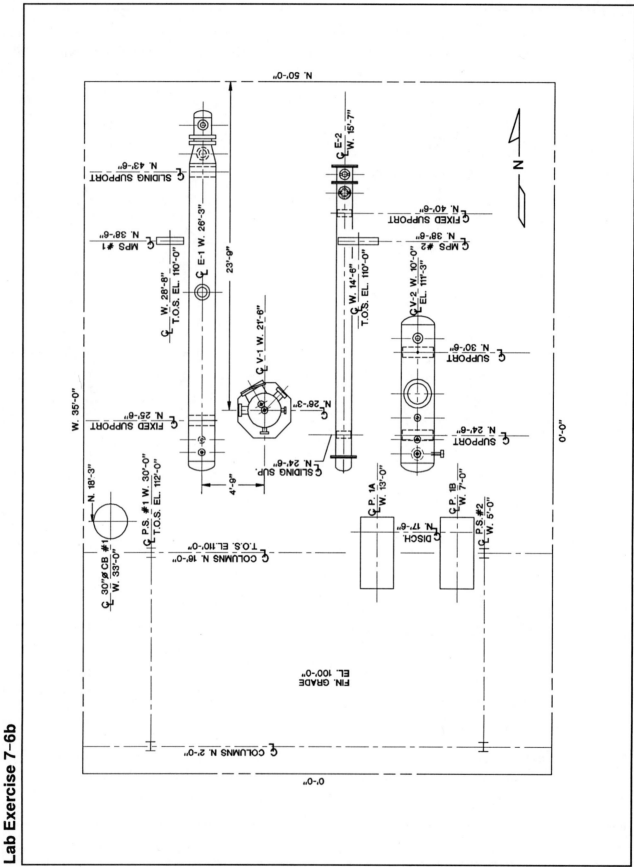

Lab Exercise 7-7

For exercise 7-7, set up a new drawing as shown. Lay out the title block and match line border to the dimensions given. Do not dimension the drawing. Name the drawing EQUIPLOC.DWG (Equipment Location Dwg.).

Drawing units set to Architectural

Drawing Limits	lower left:	-3',-5'
	upper right:	54',42'

Set dimscale=32
Set LTSCALE=32
Set text height=4"

When you Xref all of the exercises, 7-1 to 7-6, into the drawing, it will appear as shown in exercise 7-7a.

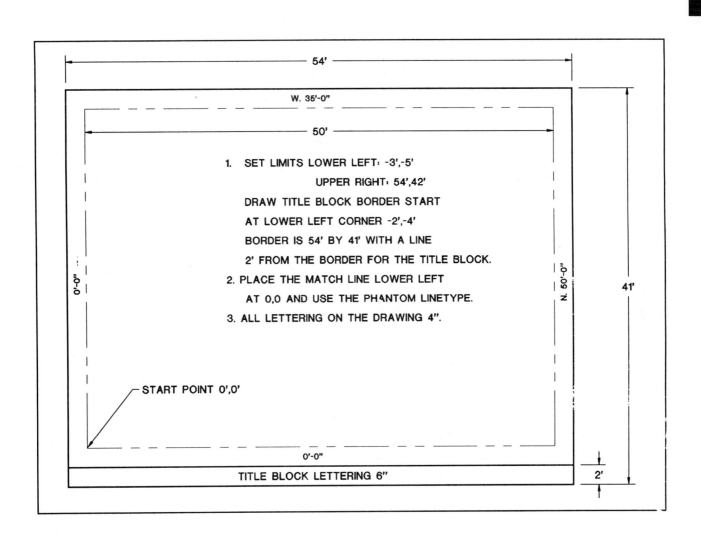

1. SET LIMITS LOWER LEFT: -3',-5'
   UPPER RIGHT: 54',42'
   DRAW TITLE BLOCK BORDER START
   AT LOWER LEFT CORNER -2',-4'
   BORDER IS 54' BY 41' WITH A LINE
   2' FROM THE BORDER FOR THE TITLE BLOCK.
2. PLACE THE MATCH LINE LOWER LEFT
   AT 0,0 AND USE THE PHANTOM LINETYPE.
3. ALL LETTERING ON THE DRAWING 4".

START POINT 0',0'

TITLE BLOCK LETTERING 6"

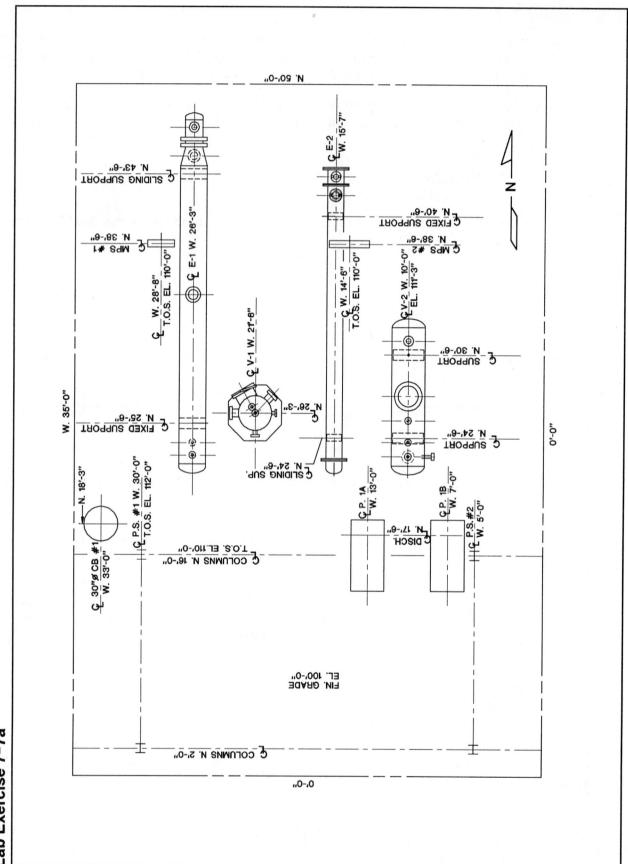

CHAPTER

8 Drawing Environments

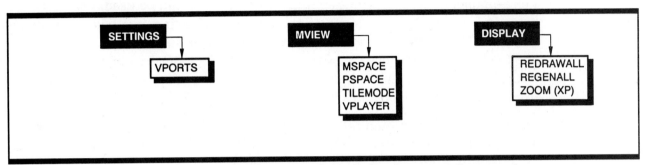

Figure 8-1 The Drawing Environment Commands

In this chapter a detailed explanation is provided for the two drawing environments, Model and Paper Space, new features of Release 11. See Figure 8-1 for the list of commands covered in this chapter.

One of the most useful new features of AutoCAD Release 11 is the option to work on your drawing in two different environments, Model Space or Paper Space. You will do most of your drafting and design work in Model Space. You will use Paper Space to arrange, annotate, and plot various views of your model. While Model Space is a 3D environment, Paper Space is a 2D environment for arranging views of your model. Prior to Release 11 the drawings were created entirely in the Model Space.

It does not matter whether you are working on a 2D or 3D model, you will do most of your drawing in Model Space. You will draw in Paper Space when you add standard items like title blocks, tables, and some types of dimensioning or annotation. If necessary, dimensioning and annotation in 3D drawing can be done in Paper Space. But there is no way to view Paper Space other than in plan view. You can draw 3D objects in Paper Space, but with no way to view them, it makes little sense to do so.

VIEWPORTS

One of the most useful features of AutoCAD is the ability to split the display into two or more separate viewports. Multiple viewports work by dividing your drawing screen into rectangles, making several different drawing areas instead of one. It is like having a multiple zoom lens camera, and each one is used to look at

509

different portions of the drawing. You can have up to 16 viewports (or cameras) visible at once. (In Release 10, you are limited to four viewports visible at once on DOS machines, 16 on UNIX and other systems). You retain your screen and pull-down menus and "Command" prompt area.

Each viewport maintains a display of the current drawing independent of the display shown by other viewports. You can simultaneously display a viewport showing the entire drawing, and another viewport showing a part of the drawing in greater detail. You can draw as well edit the entities between the viewports. For example, in a 2D drawing with three viewports could be used, two of them to zoom in on two separate parts of the drawing, showing two widely separated features in a great amount of detail on the screen simultaneously; and the third one to show the entire drawing (see Figure 8-2). In a 3D drawing, four viewports could be used to display simultaneously four views of a wire-frame model: top, front, right side, and isometric as shown in Figure 8-3.

You can create and manipulate viewports in two different ways: TILED viewports and UNTILED viewports. (Release 10 is limited to TILED viewports).

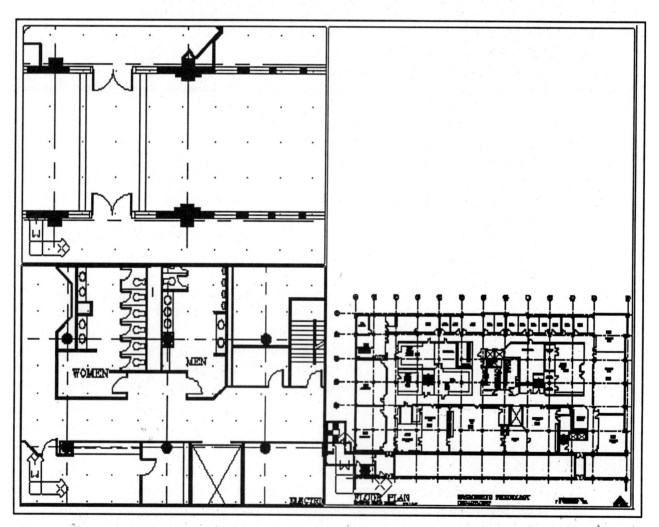

Figure 8-2 Using Viewports to Show an Entire 2D Drawing

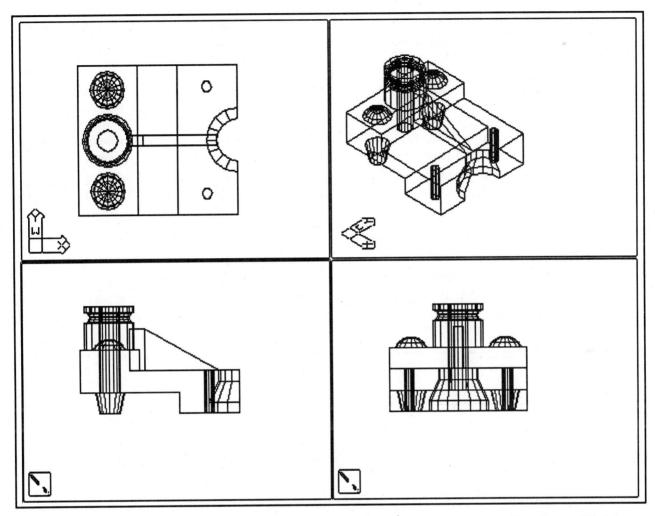

Figure 8-3 Using Viewports to Show Four Views Simultaneously for a 3D Wire-Frame Model

TILED Viewports

When the system variable TILEMODE is set to 1 (on), you can divide the graphics area of your display screen into multiple, nonoverlapping TILED viewports, as shown in Figures 8-2 and 8-3. You can create the TILED viewports using the VPORTS command.

You can work in only one viewport at a time. This is called the current viewport. You set the current viewport by picking in it with your pointing device. You can even switch viewports in midcommand. When a viewport is current, its border will be thicker than the others. The cross-hairs will appear only in the current viewport, if you move your pointing device outside the current viewport, the cursor appears as an arrow pointer.

Display commands like ZOOM and PAN, and drawing tools like GRID, SNAP, and ORTHO are controlled independently by each viewport. The most important thing to remember is that the images shown in multiple viewports are the multiple images of the same data. An object added to or edited in one viewport will affect its image in the other viewports. You are not making copies of your drawing, just putting its image in different viewports.

When you are working in TILED viewports visibility of the layers is controlled globally in all the viewports. If you turn off a layer, AutoCAD turns it off in all the viewports.

When the system variable TILEMODE is set to 1 (on), you can work in TILED viewports and in Model Space environment only. If you change the TILEMODE variable to 0 (off), then you can work in UNTILED viewports and in either Model or Paper Space environment. The default value for TILEMODE is 1 (on), unless the prototype drawing has been changed.

UNTILED Viewports

If the system variable TILEMODE is set to 0 (off), you can divide the graphics area of your display screen into multiple, overlapping, contiguous, or separated UNTILED viewports, as shown in Figure 8-4. You can create UNTILED viewports by using the MVIEW command.

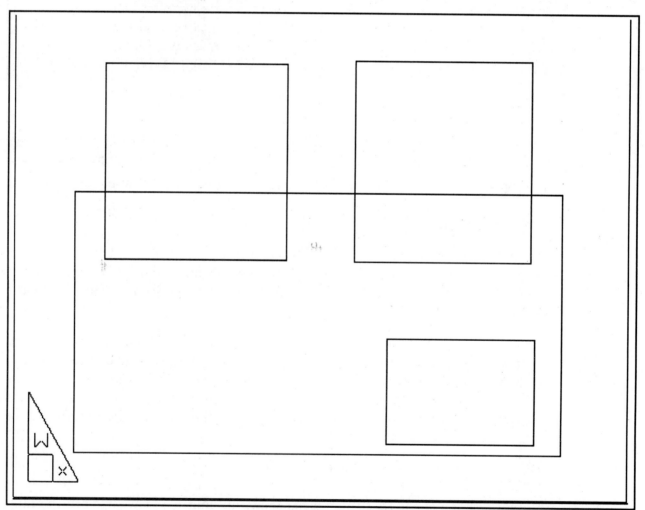

Figure 8-4 Setting TILEMODE to Display Multiple, Overlapping, Contiguous Untiled Viewports

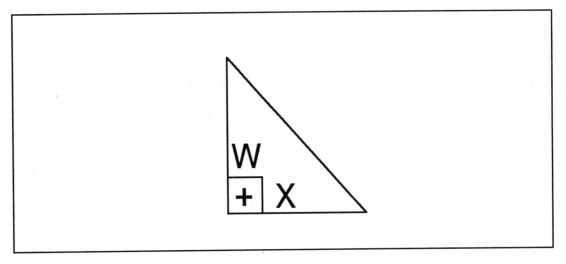

Figure 8-5 The Paper Space Icon

AutoCAD treats UNTILED viewports like any other entity such as lines, arcs, and text. You can use any of the standard AutoCAD editing commands, such as MOVE, COPY, STRETCH, SCALE, and ERASE, to manipulate the UNTILED viewports. For instance, you can use the MOVE command to grab a viewport and move it around on the screen without affecting other viewports. Viewports can be of any size and located anywhere in Paper Space.

When you are working in UNTILED viewports, you can switch back and forth between Model and Paper Space by using the MSPACE and PSPACE commands, respectively. When you are in Model Space, you can work in only one viewport at a time, similar to TILED viewports.

When you are working in Paper Space, the cursor cross-hairs span the entire graphics screen and do not change when you position the cursor over a viewport. When you are working in Paper Space, the letter P appears in the status to show that you are working in Paper Space. In addition, AutoCAD displays the Paper Space icon (unless you turned off the icon by using the UCSICON command), as shown in Figure 8-5.

What you draw in Paper Space appears only in UNTILED viewports. It will disappear if you change over to TILED viewports. What you draw in Model Space will be seen when you switch over to TILED viewports.

You can control the visibility of the layers by viewport, rather than globally, when you are working in UNTILED viewports Model Space by using the VPLAYER command. This lets you freeze a layer in one viewport while leaving it thawed in another. All the drawing features found in TILED viewports, like the ability to draw from one viewport to another, are possible in this mode. You cannot use MVIEW, VPLAYER, MSPACE and PSPACE commands unless the TILEMODE variable is set to off (0).

Drawing Environments

TILEMODE SYSTEM VARIABLE

The TILEMODE system variable allows you to work on either TILED or UNTILED viewports when the variable is set to on (1) or off (0), respectively. To change the value of the TILEMODE system variable you have to invoke the SETVAR command from the Screen Root Menu Settings, or at the "Command:" prompt type in **TILEMODE** and press ⏎.

For example, the following command sequence shows steps to change the TILEMODE system variable from 1 (on) to 0 (off):

```
Command: tilemode
New value for TILEMODE <1>: 0
Command:
```

When you change TILEMODE to 0 (off) in a drawing for the first time, AutoCAD switches to Paper Space, clears the graphics area, and prompts you to create one or more viewports. Since no viewport entities are currently in the drawing, you cannot see your model until you create at least one viewport. Use the MVIEW command to create one or more viewports. If you subsequently toggle TILEMODE to 1 (on) and then to 0 (off) again, AutoCAD displays the Paper Space view that was current before you last turned TILEMODE to 1 (on).

VPORTS COMMAND

The VPORTS command is used to create TILED viewports and can be invoked only when TILEMODE is on (1). The VPORTS command offers several options that you can use to build your screen display by adding, deleting, and joining viewports. The VPORTS command is invoked from the Screen Root Menu Settings (Figure 8-6), or at the "Command:" prompt type in **VPORTS** and press ⏎.

```
Command: vports
Save/Restore/Delete/Join/SIngle/?/2/<3>/4:
```

Options

Save Option This option allows you to save the current viewport configuration. The configuration includes the number and placement of active viewports and their associated settings. You can save any number of configurations with the drawing to be recalled at any time. When you select this option, AutoCAD prompts:

```
?/Name for new viewport configuration:
```

You can use the same naming conventions to name your configuration that you use for layer names. Instead of providing the name, you can respond with **?** to request a list of saved viewport configurations.

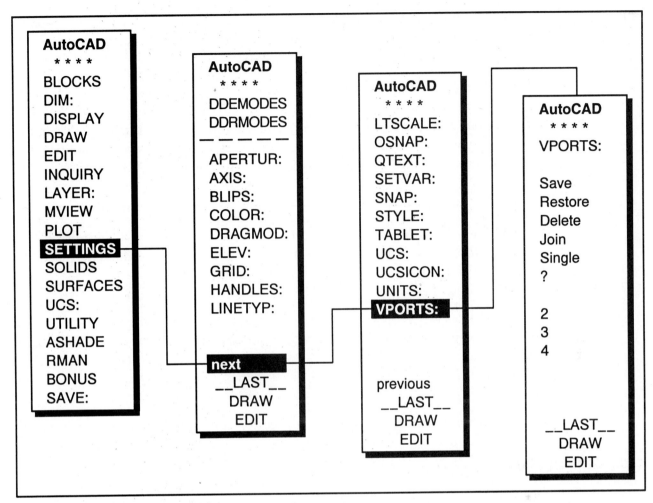

Figure 8-6 Invoking the VPORTS Command from the Screen Root Menu Settings

Restore Option This option allows you to redisplay a saved viewport configuration. When you select this option, AutoCAD prompts:

?/Name of viewport configuration to restore:

Provide the name of the viewport configuration you want to restore.

Delete Option This option deletes a named viewport configuration. When you select this option, AutoCAD prompts:

?/Name of viewport configuration to delete:

Provide the name of the viewport configuration you want to delete.

Join Option This option combines two adjoining viewports into a single viewport. The view for the resulting viewport is inherited from the dominant viewport. When you select this option, AutoCAD prompts:

Select dominant viewport <current>:

You can give a null response to show the current viewport as the dominant viewport or you can move the cursor to the desired viewport and press the pick button. Once you identify the dominant viewport, then AutoCAD prompts:

Select viewport to join:

Move the cursor to the desired viewport to join and press the pick button. If the two viewports selected are not adjacent or do not form a rectangle, AutoCAD displays an error message and reissues the prompts.

SIngle Option This option allows you to make the current viewport as the single viewport.

? Option This option displays the identification numbers and screen positions of the active viewports. When you select this option, AutoCAD prompts:

Viewport configuration(s) to list <*>:

To list all save configurations, give a null response. You also can use wild cards to list saved viewport names. All viewports are given an identification number by AutoCAD. This number is independent of any name you might give the viewport configuration. Each viewport is given a coordinate location, in respect to 0.0000,0.0000 as the lower left corner of the graphics area and 1.0000,1.0000 as the upper right corner.

2 Option This option splits the current viewport in half. When you select this option, AutoCAD prompts:

Horizontal/<vertical>:

You can select the Horizontal or Vertical split. Vertical is the default as shown in Figure 8-7.

3 Option This option divides the current viewport into three viewports. This is the default option. When you select this option, AutoCAD prompts:

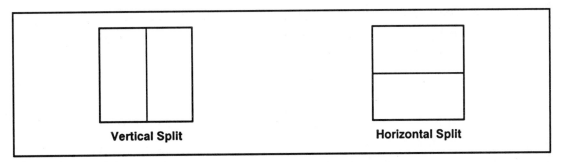

Figure 8-7 Using the 2 Option to Split a Current Viewport in Half by Horizontal or Vertical Division

Horizontal/Vertical/Above/Below/Left/<Right>:

You can select the Horizontal or Vertical option to split the current viewport into thirds by horizontal or vertical division as shown in Figure 8-8. The other options let you split into two small ones and one large one, specifying whether the large is to be placed above, below, left or right (see Figure 8-8).

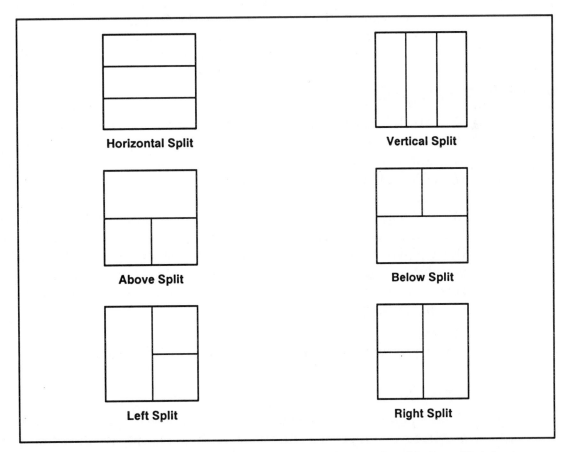

Figure 8-8 Using the 3 Option to Split a Current Viewport into Various Divisions

Drawing Environments

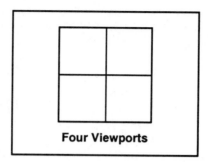

Figure 8-9 Using the 4 Option to Split a Current Viewport into Four Viewports of Equal Size

4 Option This option divides the current viewport into four viewports equal in size both horizontally and vertically, as shown in Figure 8-9.

REDRAWALL AND REGENALL COMMANDS

When you are working in multiple viewports, the REDRAW or REGEN commands will only affect the current viewport. To redraw or regen all the viewports simultaneously use the REDRAWALL or REGENALL commands.

MVIEW COMMAND

The MVIEW command is used to create new UNTILED viewports, turn their display on or off, and instruct AutoCAD to perform hidden line removal on a viewport's contents during a Paper Space plot. This command can be invoked only when TILEMODE is off (0).

MVIEW command is invoked from the Screen Root Menu Display (Figure 8-10) or from the pull-down menu Display. When you select the MVIEW command from the pull-down menu Display, AutoCAD first changes the TILEMODE system variable to 0 (off) and then executes the MVIEW command. It also changes the Display menu to the MVIEW pull-down menu. Or, at the "Command:" prompt type in **MVIEW** and press ↵.

    Command: **mview**
    ON/OFF/Hideplot/Fit/2/3/4/Restore/<First Point>: ↵

Options

First Point Option The default option lets you create a single new viewport by providing two diagonal data points. Pick two points to define a rectangular boundary, and the viewport is created to fill that area.

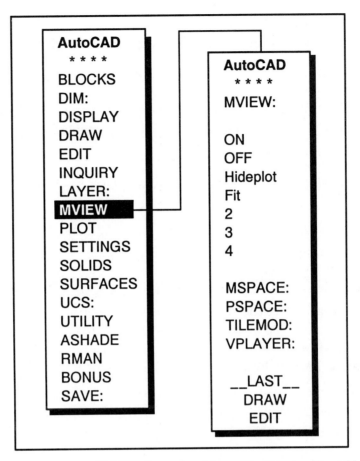

Figure 8-10 Invoking the MVIEW Command from the Screen Root Menu Display

ON Option This option turns on a model view inside the viewport. When you create a viewport, the model view is turned on by default. If it is on, AutoCAD automatically regenerates. When you select this option, AutoCAD prompts you to select the viewport to turn it on.

OFF Option This option turns off a model view inside the viewport. This clears the Model Space view and does not regenerate it again until the model view inside the viewport is turned on again. By turning the model view off, you can move, resize, and otherwise edit the viewport in Paper Space. When you select this option, AutoCAD prompts you to select the viewport to turn off.

Hideplot Option This option instructs AutoCAD to turn on or off the hidden line removal on the contents of the selected viewport when plotting in Paper Space. When you select this option, AutoCAD prompts for on or off. Subsequently, AutoCAD prompts you to select the viewport.

Fit Option This option creates a single viewport to fill the display. This can be convenient when you simply want the new viewport to fill the available display area.

2 Option This option lets you create two viewports within a rectangular area you specify. When you select this option, AutoCAD prompts:

Horizontal/<vertical>:

You can divide horizontally or vertically. Vertical is the default.

3 Option This option lets you create three viewports in a rectangular area. When you select this option, AutoCAD prompts:

Horizontal/Vertical/Above/Below/Left/<Right>:

You can select the Horizontal or Vertical option; AutoCAD creates three viewports stacked on top of each other or side by side. The other options let you create into two small ones and one large one, specifying whether the large is to be placed above, below, left, or right.

4 Option This option lets you create four viewports in a rectangular area, either by specifying the area, or fitting the four viewports to the display.

MSPACE COMMAND

This command lets you switch from Paper Space to Model Space. The TILEMODE system variable must be set to 0 (off) before this command can be used. In order for AutoCAD to switch from Paper Space to Model Space, there must be at least one viewport on and active.

The MSPACE command is invoked from the Screen Root Menu Mview, or at the "Command:" prompt type in **MSPACE** and press ⏎ or spacebar.

Command: **mspace**

PSPACE COMMAND

This command lets you switch from Model Space to Paper Space. The TILEMODE system variable must be set to 0 (off) before this command can be used. The PSPACE command is invoked from the Screen Root Menu Mview, or at the "Command:" prompt type in **PSPACE** and press ⏎ or the spacebar.

Command: **pspace**

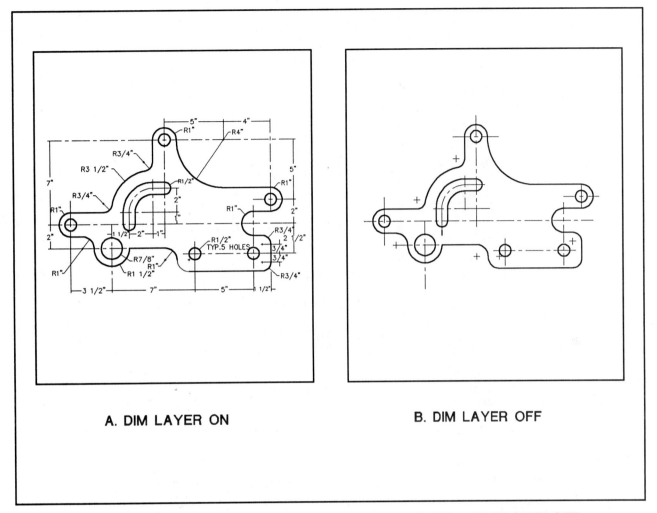

A. DIM LAYER ON   B. DIM LAYER OFF

Figure 8-11 A Viewport with DIMLAYER ON and DIMLAYER OFF

VPLAYER COMMAND

As described earlier, the VPLAYER (ViewPortLAYER) command controls the visibility of layers in a single viewport or in a set of viewports. This allows you to select a viewport and freeze a layer in it, while still allowing the contents of that layer to appear in another viewport. See Figure 8-11 in which two viewports contain the same view of the drawing, but in one viewport, the layer containing the dimensioning is on, and in another it is off by using the VPLAYER command. To use the VPLAYER command the system variable TILEMODE must be set to 0 (off).

The VPLAYER command can be executed from either Model Space or Paper Space. Several options in the VPLAYER command require you to select one or more viewports in which to make your changes. AutoCAD prompts:

    All/Select/<Current>:

To accept the default option, you have to be in Model Space; AutoCAD applies changes in the current viewport. If you opt for the select option and you are in

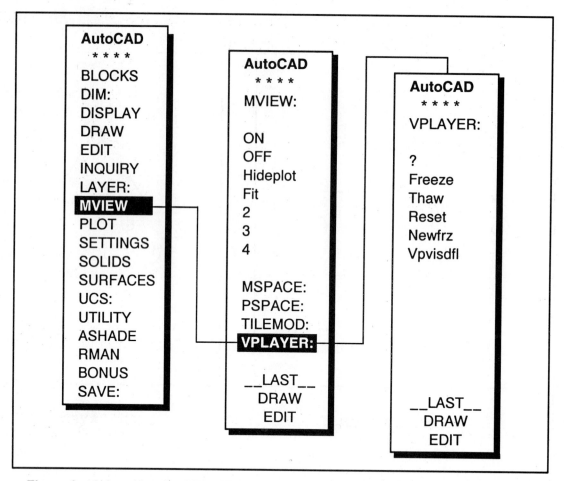

Figure 8-12 Invoking the VPLAYER Command from the Screen Root Menu Mview

Model Space, AutoCAD temporarily switches to Paper Space so you can select a viewport. The All option applies your changes to all Paper Space viewports.

If you set your TILEMODE to 1 (on), the global layer settings take precedence over any VPLAYER settings.

The VPLAYER command is invoked from the Screen Root Menu Mview (Figure 8-12) or at the "Command:" prompt type in **VPLAYER** and press ⏎ or the spacebar.

    Command: **vplayer**
    ?/Freeze/Thaw/Reset/Newfrz/Vpvisdflt:

Options

? Option This option displays the names of layers in a specific viewport that are frozen. When you select this option, AutoCAD prompts:

    Select a viewport:

Pick a single viewport. If you are in Model Space, AutoCAD will switch temporarily to Paper Space to let you select a viewport.

Freeze Option This option allows you to specify one or more layers to freeze in the selected viewport. When you select this option, AutoCAD prompts:

> Layer(s) to freeze:

You can respond to this prompt with a single layer name, a list of layer names separated by commas, or any valid wild card specification. Then AutoCAD prompts:

> All/Select/<current>:

Select the viewport(s) in which to freeze the selected layers.

Thaw Option This option allows you to specify one or more layers to thaw that were frozen by the VPLAYER command in specific viewports. When you select this option, AutoCAD prompts:

> Layer(s) to thaw:

You can respond to this prompt with a single layer name, a list of layer names separated by commas, or any valid wild card specification. Then AutoCAD prompts:

> All/Select/<current>:

Select the viewport(s) in which to thaw the selected layers.

Reset Option This option allows you to restore the default visibility setting for a layer in a given viewport. The default visibility is controlled by Vpvisdflt option, explained later in the chapter. When you select this option, AutoCAD prompts:

> Layer(s) to Reset:

You can respond to this prompt with a single layer name, a list of layer names separated by commas, or any valid wild card specification. Then AutoCAD prompts:

> All/Select/<current>:

Select the viewport(s) in which to reset the selected layers.

Newfrz (New Freeze) Option This option allows you to create new layers that are frozen in all viewports. If you create a new viewport, the layers that are created by the Newfrz option will be frozen by default. The layer can be thawed in the chosen viewport by using the Thaw option. When you select this option, AutoCAD prompts:

New viewport frozen layer name(s):

You can respond to this prompt with a single layer name or a list of layer names separated by commas.

Vpvisdflt (ViewPort Visibility Default) Option This option allows you to set a default visibility for one or more existing layers. This default determines the frozen/thawed state of an existing layer in newly created viewports. When you select this option, AutoCAD prompts:

Layer name(s) to change default viewport visibility:

You can respond to this prompt with a single layer name, a list of layer names separated by commas, or any wild card specification. Then AutoCAD prompts:

Change default viewport visibility to Frozen/<Thawed>:

You can respond to this prompt with a null response to set the default visibility to thaw or enter **F** to set the default visibility to freeze.

Freezing Layers in Viewports from Layer Control Dialogue Box

If the TILEMODE is off (0), you can freeze layers selectively by viewport from the Layer Control dialogue box selected from the pull-down menu Settings. This can be done with the two columns that are provided in the dialogue box, as shown in Figure 8-13 under the heading VP Frz (viewport freeze).

The columns under the subheading Cur (current) will allow you to selectively freeze layers under current Model Space viewport. The layer may be visible in other viewports and Paper Space. Freezing a layer in this way overrides the global setting. The columns under subheading New allow you to selectively freeze layers for all new viewport entities created. In Figure 8-14 the layers object, text, and dim are frozen in the current viewport and dim and hidden will be frozen in all the new viewport entities.

Dimensioning in Model Space and Paper Space

Dimensioning can be done in both Model Space and Paper Space. There are no restrictions on the dimensioning commands by the current mode or the Drawing Editor. It is advisable to draw associative dimensions in Model Space, since AutoCAD places the defining points of the dimension in the space where the dimension is drawn. If the model geometry is edited with commands such as STRETCH, EXTEND, or TRIM, the dimensions will be updated automatically.

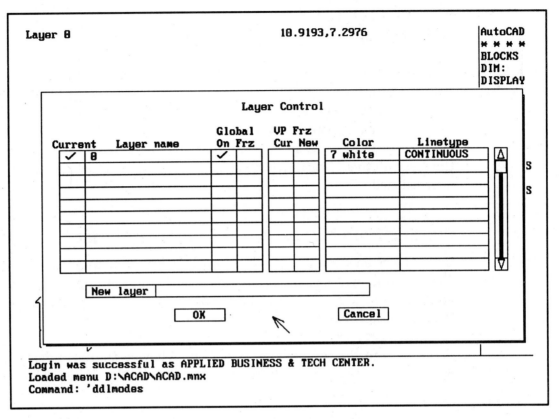

Figure 8-13 Freezing Layers by Viewport from the Layer Dialogue Box

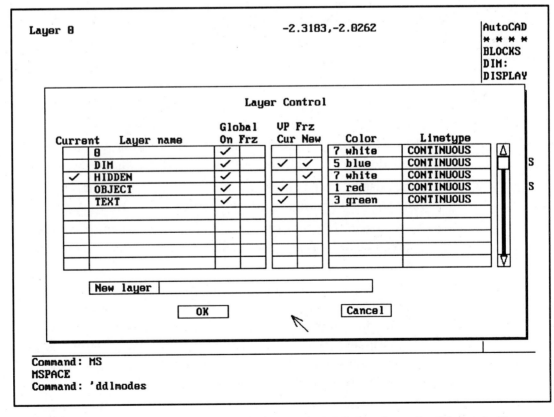

Figure 8-14 Freezing New Layers under Model Space from the Dialogue Box

Drawing Environments

Whereas, if the dimensions are drawn in Paper Space, the Paper Space dimension does not change if the model geometry is edited.

When you do dimensioning in Model Space, the DIMSCALE factor should be set to 0.0. This causes AutoCAD to compute a scale factor based on the scaling between Paper Space and current Model Space viewport. If dimensioning that describes model geometry should be created in Paper Space, then the dimension variable scale factor DIMLFAC should be based on Model Space viewport. It is important that the length scaling must be set to a value that is appropriate for the view being dimensioned.

Plotting from Model Space and Paper Space

In Model Space, the plot is based on how much of the drawing in the current viewport falls within the plot option chosen. In Paper Space, the plot is based on how much of the drawing, including any viewports and their contents, falls within the plot option chosen.

Following are the ten golden steps to be followed to plot a drawing from Paper Space at 1=1 scale after drawing the model in the Model Space to real-world dimensions:

1. Set the LIMITS in Paper Space equal to plotter's maximum available plot area for the given sheet size.
2. After setting the LIMITS, ZOOM All in Paper Space.
3. Set appropriate GRID and SNAP values (this may be different from the values in the Model Space).
4. Insert a border and title block, if you already have one, at 1=1 scale or attach it as an Xref. If not, draw the appropriate border and title on its own layer so you can freeze it as you work on your drawing.
5. Create as many viewports as you need using the MVIEW command on a separate layer for the various views and details you want to plot.
6. If necessary, resize, stretch, and move the viewports to be plotted to match your planned arrangement in the sheet.
7. Enter Model Space and create or modify, drawing your views and details. You can control the layers independently in each viewport by the VPLAYER command.
8. Establish the proper model-to-paper display units scale for each viewport. This can be done with a new option that is introduced in Release 11 for the ZOOM command called the XP option. The XP option is only valid while you are in Model Space and the TILEMODE is set to 0 (off). If you try to use this option when you are in Paper Space or TILEMODE is set to 1 (on), AutoCAD will generate an error message.

    Entering a scale factor followed by XP will cause the image to display relative to your Paper Space units. Typing 1/24XP or 0.04167XP (1/24=0.04167) will

Table 8-1 Typical Architectural Display Scaling for Paper Space Viewports

Plotting Scale	Display Factors
3" = 1'	ZOOM 1/4XP
3/4" = 1'	ZOOM 1/16XP
1/2" = 1'	ZOOM 1/24XP
3/8" = 1'	ZOOM 1/32XP
1/4" = 1'	ZOOM 1/48XP
1/8" = 1'	ZOOM 1/96XP

display an image to a scale of 1/2"= 1'-0", which is the same as 1:24 or 1/24. You determine the ZOOM XP scale factor as a reciprocal of the plot scale that you would use if you plot from Model Space when TILEMODE is set to 1 (on). For example, if you would like to display an image to plot scale 1/4" = 1'-0", then you would enter a scale factor of 1/48 followed by XP to cause the image to display relative to your Paper Space units. See Table 8-1 for factors for the XP option to various plotting scale factors.

After you use ZOOM XP, be careful not to do other ZOOMS in or out in Model Space. Panning is safe and good for fine-tuning the view. The most important thing to remember is that it is the viewport display that is scaled, not the plot.

9. Enter Paper Space. Add any annotations or dimensions that you wish to do in Paper Space. Fill in your title block information.

10. Plot or printer plot at a scale of 1:1.

> **NOTE:** Partially visible viewports are not plotted. Viewports that have been turned off are not plotted. The "remove hidden lines" option applies only to Model Space entities, and each viewport is processed for hidden lines according to its own Hideplot setting.

LAB EXERCISES

Lab Exercise 8-1

For exercise 8-1, plot the project drawing from Chapter 2 by displaying the drawing to 3/16" = 1'-0" on Paper Space and plotting to 1=1 (what you see is what you get) on an A-size sheet by following the steps below:

1. Change the TILEMODE system variable from 1 to 0 to get into Paper Space.
2. Set LIMITS in Paper Space for lower left corner to (0,0) and upper right corner to (12,9).

3. Set Grid and Snap to .5 and .25, respectively.
4. Insert a border and title block (SIZE A), if you already have one, at 1=1 scale or attach it as an Xref. If not, draw the appropriate border and title on its own layer so you can freeze it as you work on your drawing.
5. Create a viewport by MVIEW command to a size 7.5" × 4.5".
6. Enter Model Space using the MSPACE command.
7. Set the display of the model by using the ZOOM command to a scale factor of 1/64XP. (DO NOT ZOOM IN OR OUT IN MODEL SPACE AFTER SETTING THE DISPLAY TO THE APPROPRIATE DISPLAY FACTOR).
8. Enter Paper Space using the PSPACE command.
9. Plot the drawing to a scale of 1=1 on an A-size sheet.

Lab Exercise 8-2

For exercise 8-2, plot the project drawing from Chapter 3 by displaying the drawing to 1 = 1 on Paper Space and plotting to 1=1 (what you see is what you get) on a C-size sheet. Set LIMITS in Paper Space for lower left corner to (0,0) and upper right corner (22,17). Create a viewport by MVIEW command to a size of 18" × 12" and scale the display to a scale factor of 1XP. Make sure you have an appropriate border and title block, and plot is set to 1=1.

Lab Exercise 8-3

For exercise 8-3, load the drawing from Lab Exercise 7-7a (Equipment Location Drawing) into the Drawing Editor. Plot the drawing using PLOT command by displaying the complete drawing to 3/8" = 1'-0" on Paper Space in one viewport and in another viewport displaying just the vertical vessel (exercise7-6) and plotting to 1=1 (what you see is what you get) on a D-size sheet. Set LIMITS in Paper Space for lower left corner to (0,0) and upper right corner (34,22). Create a viewport by the MVIEW command to a size of 22" × 18" and scale the display to a scale factor of 1/32XP. Create another viewport to a size of 4" × 3" and display the vertical vessel in the viewport. Make sure you have the appropriate border and title block, and plot is set to 1=1.

CHAPTER
9
Utility Commands

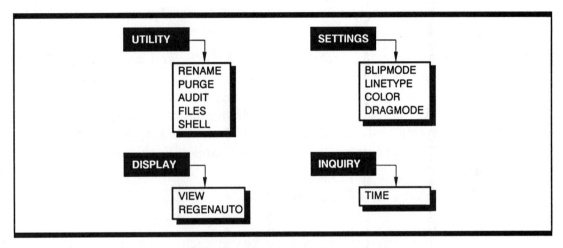

Figure 9-1 The Utility Commands

In this chapter a detailed explanation is provided for the various Utility commands. See Figure 9-1 for the list of commands that are covered in this chapter.

RENAME COMMAND — MANAGING NAMED OBJECTS

The RENAME command allows you to change the names of Blocks, dimension styles, layers, linetypes, text styles, views, User Coordinate Systems, or viewport configurations. The RENAME command is invoked from the Screen Root Menu Utility or at the "Command:" prompt type in **RENAME** and press ⏎ or the spacebar.

Command: **rename**
Block/Dimstyle/LAyer/LType/Style/Ucs/VIew/VPort:

Select the type of object option to be renamed, then AutoCAD will prompt:

Old (object option) name:
New (object option) name:

Respond with the old and new name for the object, respectively. Except for the layer named 0 and the linetype named CONTINUOUS, you can change the name of any of the named objects. You can rename external references, which causes AutoCAD to rename all its dependent named objects.

PURGE COMMAND — DELETING UNUSED NAMED OBJECTS

The PURGE command is used to selectively delete any unused named objects. The PURGE command can be used when the drawing is first called up from the Main Menu as long as no changes have been made to the drawing data base, such as adding or deleting entities. The PURGE command is invoked from the Screen Root Menu Utility or at the "Command:" prompt, type in **PURGE** and press ⏎ or the spacebar.

    Command: **purge**
    Purge unused Blocks/Dimstyles/LAyers/LTypes/SHapes/STyles/All:

Except layer 0, linetype CONTINUOUS, and text style STANDARD, you can purge any or all of the unused named objects by responding to the first prompt with the type, or the initial(s) corresponding to the type of the named object or A (for All), respectively. After specifying the type of objects, AutoCAD prompts with the name of all eligible (unused) objects of that type with a default of No as in the following example of unused layers named PLAN and SIDEVIEW:

    Purge layer PLAN? <N>
    Purge layer SIDEVIEW? <N>

You can respond with a **Y** or **Yes** at each object and it will be purged from the drawing or you can press ⏎ and the object will remain unpurged. If a Block has nested Blocks, the PURGE command will remove the outer Block Definition only. To remove second, third, or deeper level Blocks-within-Blocks, you must PURGE the outer one, END the drawing, call it back from the Main Menu, and repeat the process until all depths are purged. It may be that deeper nested Blocks are being used elsewhere in the drawing, and that makes them ineligible for PURGING. Individual shapes are part of a .SHX file. They cannot be renamed, but references to those that are not being used can be purged. Views, User Coordinate Systems, and viewport configurations cannot be purged, but the commands that manage them provide options to delete those that are not being used.

COMMAND MODIFIER — MULTIPLE

MULTIPLE is not a command, but when used with another AutoCAD commands, it causes automatic recalling of that command when it is completed. You must enter ⎈Ctrl + C to terminate this repeating process. Some of the commands from the pull-down menu are programmed to use the MULTIPLE modifier. An example of using this modifier to cause automatic repeating of the ARC command is as follows:

    Command: **multiple arc**

You can use the MULTIPLE command modifier with any of the Draw, Edit, and Inquiry commands. However, PLOT and PRPLOT will ignore the MULTIPLE command modifier.

UTILITY DISPLAY COMMANDS

The Utility display commands include VIEW, REGENAUTO, DRAGMODE, and BLIPMODE.

VIEW Command

The VIEW command allows you to give a name to the display in the current viewport and have it saved as a view. You can recall a view later by using the VIEW command and responding with the name of the view desired. This is useful for moving back quickly to needed areas in the drawing without having to resort to zooms and pans. It is also useful for plotting a named view in a drawing from the Main Menu without having to enter the AutoCAD editor and display that view. The VIEW command is invoked from the Screen Root Menu Display or at the "Command:" prompt type in **VIEW** and press ⏎ or the spacebar.

    Command: **view**
    ?/Delete/Restore/Save/Window:

The options and responses are as outlined in the following sections.

? Option This option causes AutoCAD to display a list of named views according to the response to the next prompt:

    View(s) to list <*>:

The default response is the global symbol, the asterisk, which will cause all the named views to be listed. Other typical restrictions of the names can be specified by using whole names or combinations of characters and wild card symbols such as the asterisk and/or the question mark. AutoCAD will include in the list the space (M for Model or P for Paper) in which each view was defined.

Delete Option This option permits deleting specified views according to names or character/wild card specifications given.

Restore Option This option causes the named view to replace the current display in a manner similar to the combined action of the VPOINT command and the ZOOM Dynamic.

Model Space views restored to Paper Space will be placed in the viewport of your choice by responding to the following prompt:

Restoring model space View.
Select viewport:

The desired viewport (which must be on and active) can be chosen by picking its border. AutoCAD will automatically change to Model Space. Restoring a Paper Space view while working in Model Space causes AutoCAD to change automatically to Paper Space. The system variable TILEMODE must be off to restore a Paper Space view.

Save Option This option prompts for a name and saves the display in the current viewport by that name, replacing any view with that name.

Window Option This option prompts for two points to specify the diagonally opposite corners of a rectangle, which will be the display used in the same manner as the Save option.

> *NOTE:* Restoring a view whose shape does not coincide with the current display might not cover all the current display, leaving parts showing around the restored view. This will not, however, affect the plotting of the view.

REGENAUTO Command

The REGENAUTO command has two settings, ON and OFF. The setting determines whether automatic regeneration occurs when certain commands are completed. Drawing a line or circle on the screen is immediately apparent (unless the current layer is turned off) and does not require regeneration. But, redefining a Block or font for a text style can cause regeneration. The REGENAUTO command is invoked from the Screen Root Menu Display, or at the "Command:" prompt type in **REGENAUTO** and press ⏎ or the spacebar.

Command: **regenauto**
ON/OFF<current>:

When you turn REGENAUTO off, what you see on the screen may not always represent the current state of the drawing. When changes are made by certain commands the display will be updated only after using the REGEN command. But, waiting time can be avoided as long as you are aware of the status of the display. Turning the REGENAUTO setting back to ON will cause a regeneration. While the REGENAUTO is off and commands requires a regeneration you will be prompted:

About to regen, proceed? <Y>

Responding with **No** will abort the command. Exceptions to this are the ZOOM Vmax command, which does not require a regeneration, and ZOOM All, ZOOM Extents, REGEN, and VIEW Restore, which do require regeneration.

DRAGMODE Command

The DRAGMODE command has three settings, ON, OFF, and Auto. Certain Draw and Edit commands display highlighted dynamic (cursor following) representations of the objects being drawn or edited. This can slow down the drawing process if it is not really required. Turning the DRAGMODE setting to OFF will turn off dragging. The DRAGMODE command is invoked from the Screen Root Menu Settings, or at the "Command:" prompt type in **DRAGMODE** and press ⏎ or the spacebar.

Command: **dragmode**
ON/OFF/Auto <current>:

When DRAGMODE is turned off, all calls for dragging will be ignored. Turning the DRAGMODE on allows dragging by use of the DRAG command modifier. Setting the DRAGMODE to Auto causes dragging wherever possible.

When DRAGMODE is turned on the DRAG command modifier can be used wherever dragging is permitted. For example, during the MOVE prompt you can use the following:

Command: **move**
Select objects: *select the objects*
Base point or displacement: *specify base point*
Second point of displacement: **drag**

At this point the selected objects will follow the cursor movement in highlighted display.

BLIPMODE Command

The BLIPMODE command has two settings, ON and OFF. When the BLIPMODE setting is on, a small cross mark is displayed when points on the screen are picked with the cursor or specified by entering their coordinates. Turning the BLIPMODE setting to OFF prevents the marks from being placed. After editing for a while, the drawing can become cluttered with these blips. They have no effect other than visual reference and can be removed at any time by using the REDRAW, REGEN, ZOOM, or PAN commands. Pressing the (F7) key or (Ctrl) + (G) twice (Grid ON/OFF) will also quickly remove the blips. Any other command requiring regeneration will cause the blips to be removed. The BLIPMODE command is invoked from the Screen Root Menu Settings, or at the "Command:" prompt type in **BLIPMODE** and press ⏎ or the spacebar.

534 • *HARNESSING AUTOCAD*

Command: **blipmode**
ON/OFF<current>:

ENTITY PROPERTIES

There are two important properties, color and linetype, that control the appearance of entities. You can specify the color and linetype for the entities to be drawn, with the help of the LAYER command as explained in Chapter 3. You can do the same using the COLOR and LINETYPE commands.

COLOR Command

The COLOR command allows you to specify a color for the entities to be drawn, separate from the layer color. The COLOR command is invoked from the Screen Root Menu Settings, or at the "Command:" prompt type in **COLOR** and press ⏎ or the spacebar.

Command: **color**
New entity color<current>:

The color may be entered as a standard name (red, green, cyan) or by the number code. Or, you can respond with BYLAYER or BYBLOCK. BYLAYER is the default. If you reply with a standard name or number code, this becomes the current color. All new entities you create will be drawn with this color, regardless of which layer is current, until you again set the color to BYLAYER or BYBLOCK. BYLAYER causes the entity drawn to assume the color of the layer on which it is drawn. BYBLOCK causes entities to be drawn in white until selected for inclusion in a Block Definition. Subsequent insertion of a Block that contains entities drawn under the BYBLOCK option will cause those entities to assume the color of the layer on which the BLOCK is inserted. You can use the CHANGE command to change the color of existing objects.

> **NOTE:** As noted in Chapter 2, the options to specify colors by both layer and by the COLOR command can cause confusion in a large drawing, especially one containing Blocks and nested Blocks. You are advised not to mix the two methods of specifying colors in the same drawing.

LINETYPE Command

The LINETYPE command allows you to draw lines with different dash/dot/space combinations. It is used to load linetype definitions from a library or lets you create custom linetypes.

The only entities that different linetypes can be applied to are Lines, Circles, Arcs, and 2D Polylines. A linetype must exist in a library file and be loaded before you can apply it to an entity or layer. Standard linetypes are in the library file called ACAD.LIN and are loaded automatically with the LAYER command Ltype option when the command is selected from the side menu, not from the pull-down menu.

Linetypes are combinations of dashes, dots, and spaces. AutoCAD does not permit "out of line" objects in a linetype such as circles, wavy lines, Blocks, and skew segments. All parts of the line must be "on the line." You can, however, use Trace and Polyline widths or wide plotter pens, giving width to all parts of a line.

Dash, dot, and space combinations eventually repeat themselves. For example, a six-unit long dash, followed by a dot between two one-unit long spaces will repeat itself according to the overall length of the line drawn and the LTSCALE setting.

Lines with dashes (not all dots) usually have dashes at both ends. AutoCAD automatically adjusts the lengths of end dashes to reach the endpoints of the adjoining line. Intermediate dashes will be the lengths specified in the definition. If the overall length of the line is not long enough to permit the breaks, the line will be drawn continuous.

There is no guarantee that any segments of the line will fall at some particular location. For example, when placing a centerline through circle centers, you cannot be sure that the short dashes will be centered on the circle centers as most conventions call for. To achieve this effect, the short and long dashes will have to be created by either drawing them individually or by BREAKing a continuous line to create the spaces between the dashes. This also creates multiple in-line lines instead of one line of a particular linetype. Or you can use the DIMENSION command Center option to place the desired mark.

Individual linetype names and definitions are stored in one or more files whose extension is .LIN. The same name may be defined differently in two different files. Selecting the desired one requires proper responses to the prompts in the Load option of the LINETYPE command. If you redefine a linetype, loading it with the LINETYPE command will cause objects drawn on layers assigned to that linetype to assume the new definition.

Mastering the use of linetypes involves using the LAYER command, the LINETYPE command, the LTSCALE command and knowing what files contain the linetype definition(s) desired. Also, with the LINETYPE command you can define custom linetypes.

The LINETYPE command is invoked from the Screen Root Menu Settings, or at the "Command:" prompt type in **LINETYPE** and press ⏎ or the spacebar.

```
Command: linetype
?/Create/Load/Set:
```

The options and responses are as described in the following sections.

? Option This option displays a list of the linetypes in a specified file with graphic descriptions.

```
Command: linetype
?/Create/Load/Set: ?
File to list <default>: ⏎ or specify filename
```

You can press ⏎ to designate the default file or enter the name of another file. Do not add the .LIN extension to the name of the file. AutoCAD assumes this. The display flips to the text screen and lists all the linetypes in a specified file.

Create Option This option allows you to create new linetypes and store them in a library file. For a detailed explanation about creating linetypes, see Chapter 14, Customizing AutoCAD.

Load Option This option allows you to load explicitly a linetype into your current drawing. Standard linetypes from the library file ACAD.LIN are loaded automatically with the LAYER command Ltype option when the command is selected from the side menu.

Set Option This option allows you to set the current linetype for subsequently drawn entities. If you reply with a standard name, this becomes the current linetype. All new entities you create will be drawn with this linetype, despite which layer is current, until you again set the linetype to BYLAYER or BYBLOCK. BYLAYER is the default. BYLAYER causes the entity drawn to assume the linetype of the layer on which it is drawn. BYBLOCK causes entities to be drawn in continuous until selected for inclusion in a Block Definition. Subsequent insertion of a Block that contains entities drawn under the BYBLOCK option will cause those entities to assume the linetype of the layer on which the Block is inserted. You can use the CHANGE command to change the linetype of existing objects.

> **NOTE:** As noted in Chapter 2, the options to specify linetypes by both layer and by the LINETYPE command can cause confusion in a large drawing, especially one containing Blocks and nested Blocks. You are advised not to mix the two methods of specifying linetypes in the same drawing.

DRAWING AID X, Y, AND Z FILTERS — AN ENHANCEMENT TO OSNAP

AutoCAD's filters feature allows you to establish a 2D point by specifying the individual (X and Y) coordinates one at a time in separate steps. In the case of a

3D point you can specify the individual (X, Y, and Z) coordinates in three steps. Or you can specify one of the three coordinate values in one step and a point in another step, from which AutoCAD will extract the other two coordinate values for use in the point being established.

The filters feature is used when being prompted to establish a point, as in the starting point of a line, the center of a circle, drawing a node with the POINT command, or specifying a base or second point in displacement for the MOVE or COPY command, to mention just a few.

During the application of the filters feature there are steps where you can input either single coordinate values or points, and there are steps where you can input only points. It is necessary to understand these restrictions and options and when one type of input is more desirable than the other.

When selecting points during the use of filters, you need to know which coordinates of the specified point are going to be used in the point being established. It is also essential to know how to combine OSNAP modes with those steps that use point input.

The filters feature is actually an enhancement to either the OSNAP or the @ (last point) feature. Using AutoCAD's ability to establish a point by snapping to a point on an existing object is one of the most powerful features in CAD, and being able to have AutoCAD Snap to such an existing point and then filter out selected coordinates for use in establishing a new point adds to that power. Therefore, in most cases, you will not use the filters feature if it is practical to type in all of the coordinates from the keyboard, because typing in all coordinates can be done in a single step. The filters feature is a multistep process, and each step might include substeps; one to specify the coordinate(s) to be filtered out and another to designate the OSNAP mode involved.

Filters with @

When AutoCAD is prompting for a point, the filters feature is initiated by entering a period followed by the letter designation for the coordinate(s) to be filtered out. For example, if you draw a point starting at (0,0) and use the relative polar coordinate response @3<45 to determine the endpoint, you can use filters to establish another point whose X coordinate is the same X coordinate as the end of the line just drawn. It works for Y and Z coordinates and combinations of XY, XZ, and YZ coordinates also. The following command sequence shows how to apply filter to a line that needs to be started at a point whose X coordinate is the same as the end of the previous line and the Y coordinate is 1.25. The line will be drawn horizontally 3 units long. The sequence will be as follows:

Utility Commands

```
Command: line
From point: 0,0
To point: @3<45
To point: ⏎
Command: line or ⏎
From point: .x
of @
(need YZ): 0,1.25
To point: @3<0
```

Entering .x initiates the filters feature. AutoCAD then prompts you to specify a point from which it can extract the X coordinate. The @ (last point) does this. The new line will have a starting point whose X coordinate is the same as that of the last point drawn. By using the filters feature to extract the X coordinate, that starting point will be on an imaginary vertical line through the point specified by @ in response to the "of" prompt.

When you initiate filters with a single coordinate (.x in the example above) and respond with a point (@), the prompt that follows asks for a point also. From it (the second point specified) AutoCAD will extract the other two coordinates for the new point.

Even though the prompt is for "YZ," the point may be specified in 2D format as 0,1.25 (the X and Y coordinates) from which AutoCAD takes the second value as the needed Y coordinate. The Z coordinate is assumed to be the elevation of the current coordinate system.

You can use the two-coordinate response to initiate filters, specify a point and then all that AutoCAD requires is a single value for the final coordinate. An example of this would be as follows:

```
Command: line
From point: 0,0
To point: @3<45
To point: ⏎
Command: line or ⏎
From point: .xz
of @
(need Y): 1.25
To point: @3<0
```

You can also specify a point in response to the prompt "(need Y)" as follows:

(need Y): **0,1.25** *or pick a point on the screen*

In this case, AutoCAD will use the Y coordinate of the point specified as the Y coordinate of the new point.

Remember, it is an individual coordinate in 2D (one or two coordinates in 3D) of an existing point that you wish AutoCAD to extract and use for the new point. In most cases you will be Osnapping to a point for the response. Otherwise, if you knew the value of the coordinate needed, you would probably type it in from the keyboard.

Filters with OSNAP

Without filters, an OSNAP mode establishes a new point to coincide with one on an existing object. With filters, an OSNAP mode establishes selected coordinates of a new point to coincide with corresponding coordinates of one on an existing object.

Extracting one or more coordinate values to be applied to corresponding coordinate values of a point that you are being prompted to establish is shown in the following example. In Figure 9-2 a 2.75" × 7.1875" rectangle has a 0.875"-diameter hole in its center. A board drafter would determine the center of a square or rectangle by drawing diagonals and centering the circle at their intersection. AutoCAD drafters (without filters) could do the same, or might draw orthogonal lines from the midpoint of a horizontal line and from the midpoint of one of the vertical lines to establish a centering intersection. The following command sequence shows steps in drawing a rectangle with a circle in the center using filters.

```
Command: line
From point: select point p1
To point: @2.75<90
To point: @7.1875<0
To point: @2.75<270
To point: c
Command: circle
3P/2P/TTR/<Center point>: .x
of mid
of select line 1
(need YZ): mid
of select line 2
Diameter/<Radius>: d
Diameter: .875
```

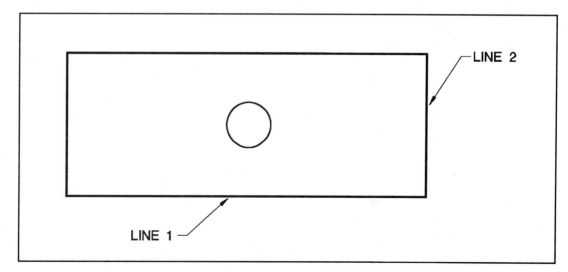

Figure 9-2 Extracting Coordinate Values to Be Applied to Corresponding Coordinate Values

SHELL COMMAND

The SHELL command allows you to execute utility programs while you are in the Drawing Editor. You can execute any of the utility programs as long as there is sufficient memory to execute. The SHELL command is invoked from the Screen Root Menu Utility or at the "Command:" prompt type in **SHELL** and press ⏎ or the spacebar.

    Command: **shell**
    OS Command:

You can reply with any command that would be a valid response to the operating system's command prompt. When the utility program is finished, AutoCAD takes you back to the "Command:" prompt. If you need to execute more than one DOS command, then give a null response to the "DOS command:" prompt. AutoCAD responds with the following message:

    Type EXIT to return to AutoCAD

and then displays the DOS prompt followed by two greater-than signs instead of one, as shown below:

    C>>

You can now enter as many DOS commands as you wish. When you are finished, you may return to the AutoCAD Drawing Editor by typing **EXIT**. It will take you back to the "Command:" prompt.

If there is not enough free memory for the SHELL command, the following message will appear:

    Shell error: insufficient memory for command.

Where there is insufficient memory, you can execute the SH command instead of the SHELL command. SH requires less memory than the SHELL command and can be used to access internal DOS commands such DIR, COPY, and TYPE. If the need arises, you can adjust the amount of memory required for the SH and SHELL commands by modifiying the ACAD.PGP file. For additional information, see Chapter 14 on Customizing AutoCAD.

> **NOTE:** Do not delete the AutoCAD lock files or temporary files created for the current drawing when you are at the operating system prompt. Do not use the CHKDSK command with /F option. Do not run programs that reset the serial I/O ports on the computer.

FILES COMMAND

The FILES command will allow you to execute some of the DOS commands while you are in the Drawing Editor. The DOS commands include listings of files from a specific drive or directory, and enable you to delete, rename, copy or unlock specific files. You can also perform the same operations with the help of the SHELL command.

The FILES command is invoked from the Screen Root Menu Utility or at the "Command:" prompt type in **FILES** and press ⏎ or the spacebar.

Command: **files**

AutoCAD will display the File Utility Menu as shown below.

File Utility Menu
0. Exit File Utility Menu
1. List Drawing files
2. List user specified files
3. Delete files
4. Rename files
5. Copy files
6. Unlock files

Enter selection (0 to 6) <0>:

This is the same menu that is displayed when you select option 6 from the Main Menu. For a detailed explanation of the Utility Menu, see Appendix E.

TIME COMMAND

The TIME command displays the current time and date related to your current drawing session. In addition, you also can find out how long you have been working in the Drawing Editor. This command uses the clock in your computer to keep track of the time functions and displays to the nearest millisecond using 24-hour military format. The TIME command is invoked from the Screen Root Menu Inquiry or at the "Command:" prompt type in **TIME** and press ⏎ or the spacebar.

Command: **time**

The following listing is displayed in the text screen followed by a prompt:

Current time: 11 July 1991 at 11:54:15.340
Drawing created: 11 July 1991 at 10:31:12.230
Drawing last updated: 11 July 1991 at 10:31:12.230
Time in drawing editor: 0 days 01:23:03:110
Elapsed timer: 0 days 01:23:03:110
Timer on.

Display/ON/OFF/Reset:

The first line gives information about today's date and time.

The second line gives information about the date and time the current drawing was initially created. The drawing time starts when you initially begin a new drawing from Main Menu option number 1. If the drawing was created by using the WBLOCK command, the date and time is taken into consideration at the time the command was executed.

The third line provides information about the date and time the drawing was last updated. This is initially set to the drawing creation time. This is updated each time when you use the END or SAVE command.

The fourth line provides the information about the time you are in the Drawing Editor. This timer is continuously updated by AutoCAD while you are in the Drawing Editor, excluding plotting and printer plot time. This timer cannot be stopped or reset.

The fifth line provides the information about the stopwatch timer. You can turn this timer ON or OFF and reset to zero. This timer is independent of other functions.

Display Option

This option redisplays the time functions with updated times.

ON Option

This option will turn the stopwatch timer to ON, if it is OFF. By default it is ON.

OFF Option

This option will turn the stopwatch timer to OFF and will display the accumulated time.

Reset Option

This option will reset the stopwatch timer to zero.

To exit the TIME command, give a null response or (Ctrl) + (C) to the prompt.

AUDIT COMMAND

The AUDIT command can be used as a diagnostic tool to correct any errors or defects in the data base of the current drawing. AutoCAD generates an extensive report of the problems and for every error detected, AutoCAD recommends action to correct it.

The AUDIT command is invoked from the Screen Root Menu Utility, or at the "Command:" prompt type in **AUDIT** and press (⏎).

    Command: **audit**
    Fix any errors detected? <N>:

If you respond with **Y** or **Yes**, AutoCAD will fix all the errors detected, and display an audit report with the detailed information about the errors detected and fixing them. If you answer with **N** or **No**, AutoCAD will just display a report and will not fix any errors.

Also in addition, AutoCAD creates an ASCII report file with the description of problems and the action taken. It will save the file in the current directory, using the current drawing's name with the file extension .ADT. You can use the regular DOS commands TYPE or PRINT to display the report file on the screen or print it on the printer.

CHAPTER
10

Special Features — Slides and Scripts

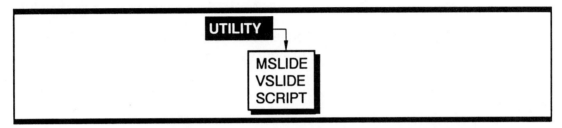

Figure 10-1 The Utility Commands MSLIDE, VSLIDE, and SCRIPT

In this chapter a detailed explanation is provided for the special features of AutoCAD, which include slides and script files. See Figure 10-1 for a list of commands that are covered in this chapter.

Slides are quickly viewable, noneditable views of a drawing or parts of a drawing. There are two primary uses for slides. One is to have a quick and ready picture to display symbols, objects, or written data for information purposes only. The other very useful application of slides is to be able to display a series of pictures, organized in a prearranged sequence for a timed slide show. This is a very useful tool for demonstrations to clients or in a showroom. This feature supplements time-consuming calling up of views required when using the AutoCAD editor ZOOM, PAN, and other Display commands. It can be implemented through use of the SCRIPT command (described later in this chapter).

It should be noted that a slide merely masks the current display. Any cursor movement or editor functions employed while a slide is being displayed will affect the current drawing under the slide and not the slide itself. However, if objects are erased under the slide, parts of objects on the slide that coincide with them will also disappear from view.

MSLIDE — MAKING A SLIDE

The current display can be made into a slide with the MSLIDE command. The current viewport becomes the slide while working in Model Space. The entire display, including all viewports, becomes the slide when using MSLIDE while working in Paper Space. The MSLIDE command takes a picture of the current display, and stores it in a file, so be sure it is the correct view. The MSLIDE command is invoked from the Screen Root Menu Utility, or at the "Command:" prompt type in **MSLIDE** and press ⏎ or the spacebar.

Command: **mslide**
Slide file <default>:

The default will be the drawing name, which can be used as the slide filename by pressing ⏎. Or, you can type any other name, as long as you are within the limitations of the DOS file naming convention. AutoCAD automatically appends the extension .SLD. Only objects that are visible on the screen drawing area (or in the current viewport when in Model Space) are made into the slide.

If you plan to show the slide on different systems you should use a full-screen view with a high resolution display for creating the slide.

SLIDE LIBRARIES

While in DOS (and your SLIDELIB.EXE file is in the ACAD directory), you can invoke the SLIDELIB command to create a slide library file. The command is as follows:

C:\ACAD>slidelib slidefile <slide-list>

The SLIDELIB command is used in conjunction with a list of slide filenames. Each slide filename must correspond to an actual slide whose extension is .SLD. The list of filenames is on a separate file, written in ASCII format with each slide filename on a separate line by itself. The filenames in the list may or may not include the .SLD extension, but must include the path (drive and/or directory) for the SLIDELIB command to access the proper file for inclusion in the library.

A file named SLDLIST could read as follows:

```
pic_1
A:pic_2.sld
c:\dwgs\pic_3.sld
b:\other\pic_6
```

Each line represents a slide name, some with extensions, some without. Each one has a different path. When the SLIDELIB command is used (from the DOS prompt) to address this file, all the slides listed will be included in the library that you specify. Their paths will not be included when used with the SLIDELIB command. If there were a PIC_2.SLD on another path it would not be included or conflict with the one specified for its particular library file. This allows for control of which slides will be used if the same slide filename exists in several drive/ directory locations. The SLIDELIB command appends .SLB to the library file it creates from the slide list.

The above listing file can be used to create a library file named ALLPICS.SLB by the following sequence:

C:\ACAD>slidelib allpics <sldlist>

> **NOTE:** The name of the library file does not include the extension .SLB. Also, the less than sign (<) is a DOS function that redirects the names in the file to be used as the list of slides in the library.

VSLIDE — VIEWING A SLIDE

The VSLIDE command displays a slide in the current viewport. The VSLIDE command is invoked from the Screen Root Menu Utility or at the "Command:" prompt type in **VSLIDE** and press ⏎ or the spacebar.

Command: **vslide**
Slide file <default>:

The default is the current drawing name. If you have made a slide with that name, you can have it displayed by pressing ⏎. If you had stored the slide in a library file and are calling it up for view you can use the library file keyname followed by the slide name in parentheses. For example, if the slide named PIC_1 (actually stored under the filename pic_1.sld) is in a library file called ALLPICS.SLB, you can use the following response format:

Command: **vslide**
Slide file <default>: **allpics(pic_1)**

> **NOTE:** The library file only lists the address of each slide. It can be on a path or directory other than that of the slide(s) listed in it. It is not necessary to specify the path in front of the slide name. For example, the ALLPICS.SLB might be on the working directory, while the slide PIC_1 is on drive F in the directory SL1, and the slide PIC_2 is on drive F in the directory SL2. The sequences to call them into view would be as follows:

Command: **vslide**
Slide file <default>: **allpics(pic_1)**
Command: **vslide**
Slide file <default>: **allpics(pic_2)**

If the ALLPICS.SLB is on drive F in the subdirectory called SLB the sequences would be as follows:

Command: **vslide**
Slide file <default>: **f:\slb\allpics(pic_1)**
Command: **vslide**
Slide file <default>: **f:\slb\allpics(pic_2)**

SCRIPT

Of the many means available to enhance AutoCAD through customization, scripts are perhaps the easiest to create. Scripts are similar to the macros that can be created to enhance word processing programs. They permit you to combine a sequence of commands and data into one or two entries. Creating a script, like most enhancements to AutoCAD, requires that you use a line editor or word processor to generate a file (with the extension of .SCR) which will contain the instructions and data for the SCRIPT command feature to follow.

Scripts are used in two basic ways. One is while in the Autocad editor and the other is as part of the start-up sequence that invokes the ACAD.EXE program which displays the Main Menu.

Because script files are written for use at a later time, you must anticipate the conditions under which they will be used. Therefore, familiarity with sequences of prompts that will occur and the types of responses required is necessary to have the script function properly. Writing a script is a form of programming.

The Script Text

A script text file must be written in ASCII format. That is, it must not have any embedded print codes or control characters that are automatically written in files when created with a word processor in the document mode. If you are not using the line editor called EDLIN or EDIT (DOS Ver. 5.0), be sure that you are in the nondocument, programmer, or ASCII mode of your word processor when creating or saving the file. One way to make sure there are no hidden characters in your file is to use the DOS command TYPE or PRINT to display the file. This will reveal such characters.

Each command can occupy a separate line or you can combine several command/data responses on one line. Each space between commands and data is read as a ⏎ just as it does when pressing the spacebar while in the AutoCAD editor. The end of a line of text is also the same as a ⏎.

Scripts with the ACAD.EXE Initiation

A special form of the ACAD program command permits you to include the name of a script file and have it automatically invoke the AutoCAD editor and go into action with whatever commands and data entries you have programmed it to do. For example, if you wish to have the script feature to create a new drawing called PLAN1 and draw a two-unit radius circle at coordinates 4,7 a script file called PC.SCR would be written as follows:

```
1
    (this line left blank)
circle 4,7 2
```

The blank line is permissible in this case for entering the drawing name when invoking the script feature. Invoke the AutoCAD program with the name of the drawing followed by the name of the script file as shown below:

C:\ACAD>**acad plan1 pc**

If a drawing of the same name already exists, you would get a message that would interrupt and terminate the sequence.

Spaces and End-of-Lines in Script Files

The following script file has several commands and data (the response ON, coordinates and distances). The first line of AutoCAD editor entries includes the GRID, LINE, and CIRCLE commands and their responses. Note that there are two spaces after the 5,5 response which are required to simulate the double ↵. One thing that is not obvious is that there is an extra space following the 5,0 response in the second LINE command. This extra space and the END-OF-LINE code that even EDLIN must include combine to simulate pressing the space bar twice. This is necessary, again, to exit the LINE command.

```
1

GRID ON LINE 0,0 5,5  CIRCLE 3,3 3
LINE 0,5 5,0
CIRCLE 5,2.5 1
```

Changing Block Definitions with a Script File

Using a script from DOS to perform a repetitive task is illustrated in the following example. This application also offers some insight on changing the entities in an inserted Block with Attributes without affecting the Attribute values.

Figure 10-2 shows a group of drawings which all utilize a common Block with Attribute values in one insertion that are different from the Attribute values of those in other drawings. In this case, the border/title block is a Block named BRDR. It was originally drawn with the short lines around and outside of the main border line. It was discovered that these lines interfered with the rollers on the plotter and needed to be removed. The BRDR Block Definition is shown in Figure 10-3. Remember, the insertion of this Block has different Attribute values in each drawing, such as drawing number, date, title, etc.

If you wish to change entities in the Block but maintain the Attribute values as they are, there are two approaches to redefinition. One is to find a clear place in the drawing and insert the Block with an asterisk (*). This is the same as inserting and exploding the Block. Then, make the necessary changes in the entities and make the revised group into a Block with the same Block name. This redefines all insertions of Blocks with that same name in the drawing. In this case there is only one insertion. You must be careful how any changes to Attributes might affect the already inserted Block of that name.

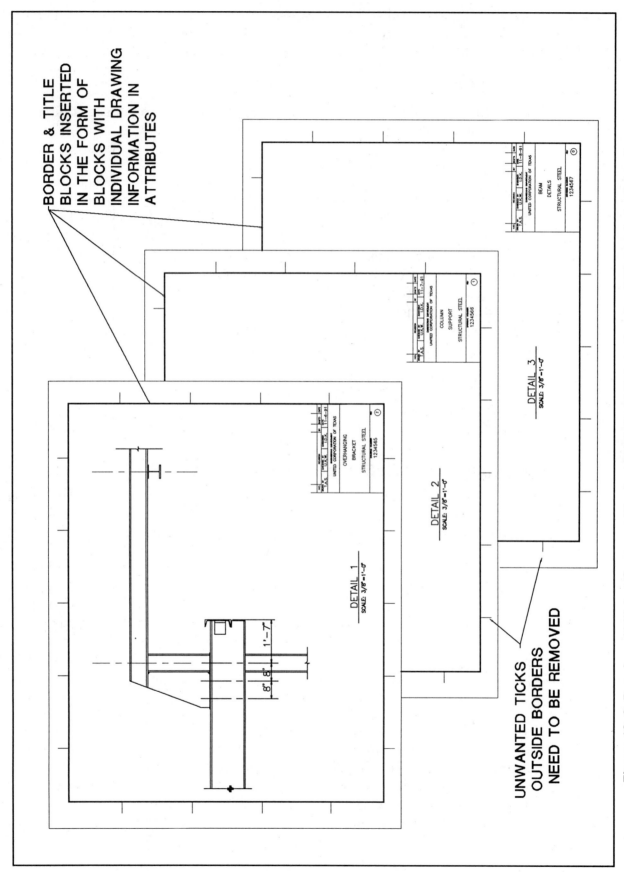

Figure 10-2 Drawings Utilizing Common Block and Attribute Values that Are Different from Other Drawings

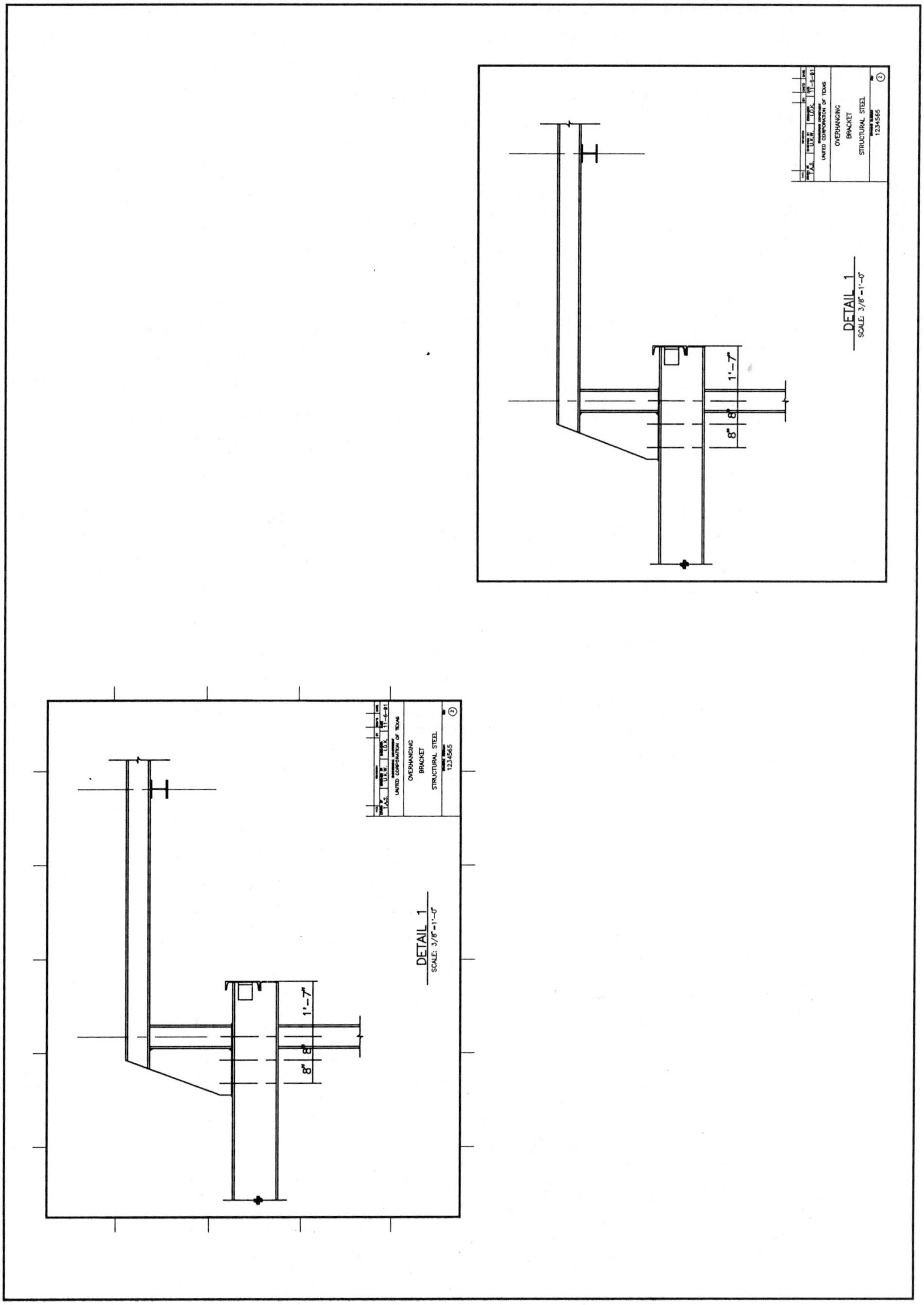

Figure 10-3 A Block Definition

The second method is to WBLOCK the Block to a file with the same name. This makes a new and separate drawing of the Block. Then exit the current drawing, call up the newly created drawing, and make the required changes in the entities and END the drawing that was created by the WBLOCK. Then you re-enter the drawing in which the Block entities need to be changed. You can now use the INSERT command and respond with "blockname=" and have the Block redefined without losing the Attribute values. For example, if the Block name is BRDR, the sequence would be as follows:

```
Command: insert
Block name: BRDR=
Block BRDR redefined
Regenerating drawing.
Insertion point: Ctrl + C displays *Cancel*
```

The key to the above sequence is the equal sign (=) following the Block name. This causes AutoCAD to change the definition of the Block named BRDR to be that of the drawing named BRDR, but maintains the Attribute values as long as Attribute Definitions remain unchanged.

If the above procedure must be repeated many times, this is where a script file can be employed to automate the process. In the following example, we will show how to apply the script to a drawing named PLAN_1. The sequence included a Cancel as it was described above to be used while in the Drawing Editor. This expedited the operation by not actually having the Block inserted, but only its Definition brought into the drawing. Because a Cancel or Ctrl + C during the running of a SCRIPT command will cause it to terminate, it cannot be in the middle of a script. Besides, invoking Ctrl + C in a SCRIPT command requires using the AutoLISP function "(command)." Therefore, using the script to make the change in the Block from the initiation of the ACAD command from DOS will require a different approach. It can be written in a file (called BRDRCHNG.SCR for this example) in ASCII format as follows:

```
2

INSERT
BRDR=
0,0     the 0,0 is followed by 6 spaces
ERASE L the L is followed by 1 space
REDRAW
END
0
```

Now, from DOS (and on the directory that ACAD.EXE is on), you can apply the script to drawing PLAN_1 by responding as follows:

```
C:\ACAD>acad plan_1 brdrchng
```

There are several important aspects of the above sequence to be noted.

Line 1—The "2" invokes the Main Menu item 2, "Edit an Existing Drawing."

Line 2—The following space causes the script to pause for the drawing name to be entered.

Lines 3–4—This is where you might enter ⟨Ctrl⟩ + ⟨C⟩ if you were not in a SCRIPT command and have the definition of the Block named BRDR take on that of the drawing BRDR without having to actually continue with the insertion in the drawing. In this case, 0,0 as the insertion point is arbitrary because the inserted Block is going to be erased anyway.

Line 5—Special attention is to given to the six spaces following the insertion point. These are the same as pressing the spacebar or ⏎ six times in response to the "X-scale," "Y-scale," and "Rotation angle" prompts, and the number of spaces (⏎s) that follow must correspond to the number of Attributes that require responses for values. In this example there were three Attributes. Again, the fact that the responses are null is immaterial because this insertion will not be kept.

Line 6—The ERASE L is self-explanatory, but do not forget that after the "L" you must have another space (⏎) to terminate the object selection process and complete the ERASE command.

Lines 7–9—The REDRAW command is not really required except to show the user for a second time that the changes have been made before the END command completes the script. The "0" exits the Main Menu.

Scripts from within the Editor

Invoking a SCRIPT command while in the AutoCAD editor is simple. The sequence is as follows:

> Command: **script**
> Script file <default>: *script filename*

The default will be the drawing name, which can be used as the script filename by pressing ⏎. AutoCAD automatically appends the extension .SCR. The example above will cause a script (by the name entered) to begin. The commands and responses in the named script file will be executed unless terminated by invalid entries or the user presses ⟨Ctrl⟩ + ⟨C⟩ or the ⟨Backspace⟩. The name entered becomes the default when the command is completed.

Utility Commands for Script

Following are the Utility commands that may be used within a script file.

DELAY Subcommand The DELAY subcommand causes the script to pause for the number of milliseconds that have been specified after the delay. A line to delay the script for five seconds would be written as follows:

> DELAY 5000

RESUME Subcommand The RESUME subcommand causes the script to resume running after the user has pressed either ⟨Ctrl⟩ + ⟨C⟩ or the ⟨Backspace⟩ key to interrupt the script. It may be entered as follows:

> Command: **resume**

GRAPHSCR and TEXTSCR Subcommands The GRAPHSCR and TEXTSCR subcommands are used to flip or toggle the screen to the Graphics or Text mode, respectively, during the running of the script. They are simply entered as a command in the script as follows:

Command: **graphscr**

or

Command: **textscr**

These two screen toggle commands can be used transparently by preceding them with an apostrophe. These commands have no effect on dual-screen installations.

RSCRIPT Subcommand The RSCRIPT subcommand, when placed at the end of a script, causes the script to repeat itself. With this feature you can have a slide show run continuously until terminated by Ctrl + C or a Backspace.

A repeating demonstration can be set up to show some sequences of commands and responses as follows:

GRID ON
LIMITS 0,0 24,24
ZOOM A
CIRCLE 12,12 4
DELAY 2000
COPY L M 12,12 18,12 12,18 6,12 12,6 *an extra space at the end*
DELAY 5000
ERASE W 0,0 24,24 *an extra space at the end*
DELAY 2000
LIMITS 0,0 12,9
ZOOM A
GRID OFF
TEXT 1,1 .5 0 THAT'S ALL FOLKS!
ERASE L *an extra space at the end*
RSCRIPT

The above script file utilizes the DELAY and the RSCRIPT subcommands. Note the extra spaces where continuation of some actions must be terminated. The RSCRIPT subcommand is not feasible when invoking the SCRIPT from the Main Menu because it requires a QUIT or END command, after which a RSCRIPT would not be read.

The SCRIPT command can be used to show a series of slides as shown in the following sequence:

VSLIDE SLD_A
VSLIDE *SLD_B
DELAY 5000
VSLIDE
VSLIDE *SLD_C
DELAY 5000
VSLIDE
DELAY 10000

The above script uses the asterisk (*) before the slide name prior to the delay. This causes AutoCAD to load the slide, ready for viewing. Otherwise, there would be a blank screen between slides while the next one is being loaded.

CHAPTER
11

Isometric Drawing

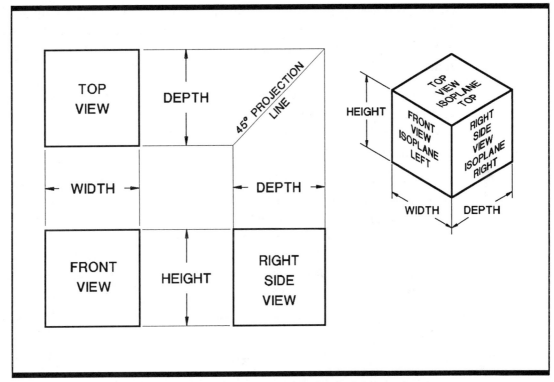

Figure 11-1 A 2D Isometric Pictorial Drawing

This chapter covers isometric drawings. While an isometric drawing shows a representation of all three dimensions—height, width, and depth—it is not a true 3D drawing. It is only 2D, composed of only 2D entities as shown in Figure 11-1. In a true 3D drawing, you can rotate the model on the display screen to show any view needed. The 3D drawing is covered in Chapter 12.

The isometric drawing is a representation of an object whose object lines have been projected onto a flat plane. Isometric means "one" (iso) "measurement" (metric). Functionally, it means that an object (usually demonstrated by a cube), when viewed in isometric projection, will have units of equal length in each Axis (X, Y, and Z) and project equal length lines on the drawing plane.

Isometric drawings are a quick way to give shop or field personnel 3D pictorial drawings to help understand the 2D plan and elevations. It is standard practice to draw an isometric drawing of each individual pipeline in a refinery. Also, in machine and tool design, an isometric drawing is often included to aid the shop in acquiring a quick understanding of the 2D layout.

Other pictorial drawings include perspective drawings. The perspective drawing is utilized mainly in architectural and interior design. It is used mainly to present (camera's eye) renderings of buildings or interior room design and will not be considered in this chapter. It must be noted that many engineering disciplines are in the process of converting from a 2D to a 3D world. Once the 3D model is completed, it can be viewed in plan, in elevation, or in any angle.

In an isometric drawing, horizontal lines are represented by lines drawn 30-degrees up from the horizontal plane or X Axis. All vertical lines are vertical on the isometric plane. All parallel lines that are parallel in any orthographic view remain parallel in isometric views, as shown in Figure 11-2.

However, angles do not appear as true angles in isometric. All dimensions can be laid out full scale along the vertical or horizontal isometric Axes. Any lines that are not parallel to the isometric Axis cannot be measured, but must be drawn in after entering the other isometric lines, as shown in Figure 11-3.

Remember, there are no true angles in isometric drawings; therefore, you must draw all of the lines that are parallel to the isometric axes first and then connect the incline or oblique lines last. Note that all vertical lines on the orthographic drawing are vertical on the isometric drawing. All horizontal lines on the orthographic drawing are 30-degrees from horizontal. All lines that are not parallel to an isometric axis cannot be measured at the same scale and are considered nonisometric lines, as shown in Figure 11-4.

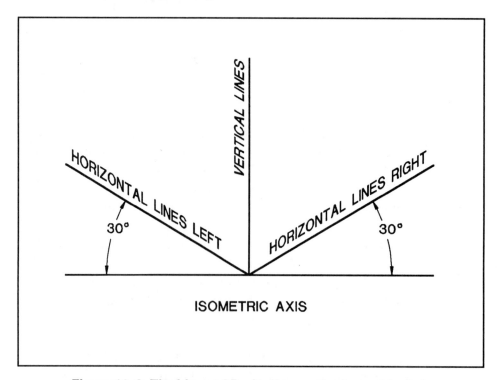

Figure 11-2 The Lines of Projection on the Isometric Axis

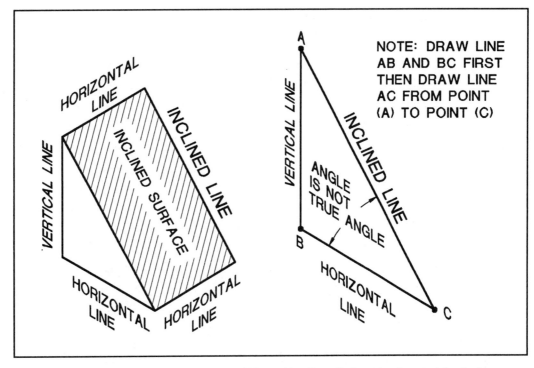

Figure 11-3 Drawing in Lines When Not Parallel to the Isometric Axis

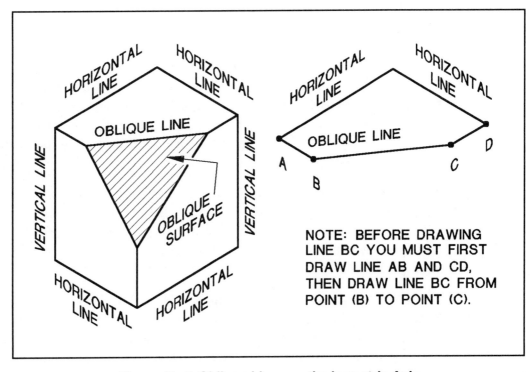

Figure 11-4 Oblique Lines on the Isometric Axis

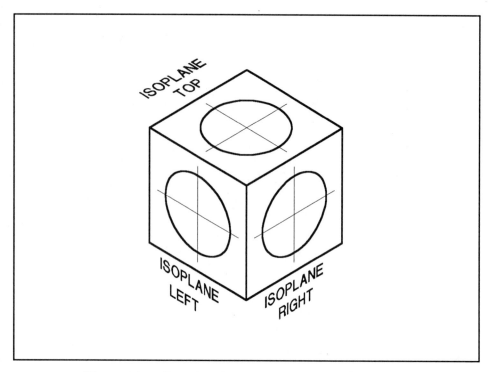

Figure 11-5 Drawing Circles on Isometric Drawings

Circles are represented by ellipses on isometric drawings and must be oriented on one of the three isometric planes in a proper way or they will appear distorted. The three surfaces will be noted as isoplane left, isoplane top, and isoplane right, as shown in Figure 11-5.

DRAWING TOOLS

The drawing tools available for 2D orthographic drawings are also available for isometric drawings. Set appropriate Grid spacing using the GRID command. Next, invoke the SNAP command and select the Style option. AutoCAD prompts you to select standard or isometric style. Enter an **I** for isometric. Then AutoCAD prompts for the vertical spacing of the Grid dots, and it will be displayed as shown in Figure 11-6.

After you change the style to isometric, the Grid dots on the display screen will change to an isometric Grid. You will also notice the cross-hairs appear at an isometric angle as an aid to you in your layout. The cross-hairs toggle between the three isometric planes: isoplane left, isoplane top, and isoplane right, as shown in Figure 11-7.

While you do not have to toggle them to draw in any other plane, it is helpful to have them aligned and oriented to the plane in which you are currently working. The cross-hairs can be oriented with the isoplane command or you may toggle them by pressing (Ctrl) & (E). The cross-hairs will always appear in one of the three isoplane positions unless you are using the window to select objects while

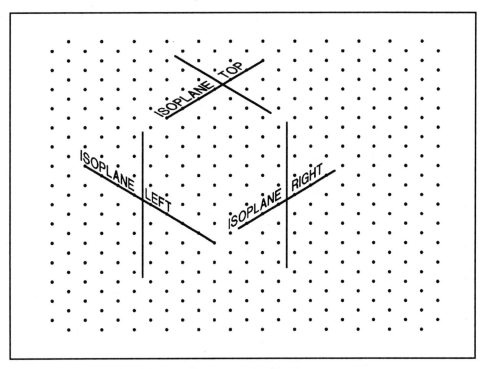

Figure 11-6 Setting the Grid for Isometric Drawing

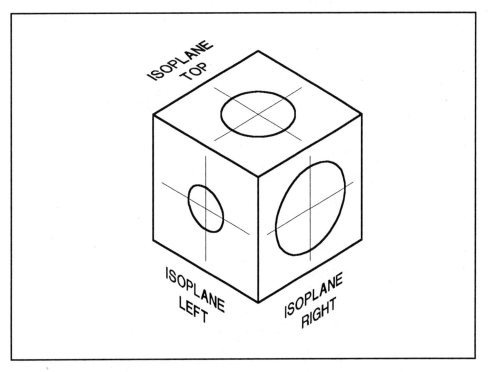

Figure 11-7 The Cross-hairs on the Isometric Plane

using an editing command. Then the cross-hairs revert back to vertical and horizontal while your window is being created.

You can use the ORTHO mode to draw lines parallel to one of the two axes of the current isoplane.

ISOMETRIC CIRCLES

To draw a circle on one of the three isoplanes you may use the ELLIPSE command. After invoking the ELLIPSE command, select the Iso option. Then AutoCAD prompts you for the center point of the circle and subsequently prompts for the radius of the circle.

NOTE: 1. The circle will be oriented according to the current isoplane. Toggle the cross-hairs to the correct isoplane in which you intend to place the isocircle.

2. You may drag the isocircle and pick a point on the circle or enter a radius or **D** for diameter and then enter the diameter.

3. When you press ↵ after entering an isocircle, AutoCAD defaults back to ellipse. You must select isocircle for every circle you are entering on the isometric drawing.

ISOMETRIC TEXT

Any text that is added to the isometric drawings should conform to isometric standards. For example, horizontal text in the right isoplane should be drawn using a text font with a slant angle of 30°.

To accomplish this it is necessary to create several text styles and set the obliquing angle to the correct setting depending on which isoplane the text is to be used, as shown in Figure 11-8.

ISOMETRIC DIMENSIONING

When dimensioning the isometric drawings use linear aligned dimensions. Later these dimensions can be adjusted to the proper obliquing angle using the command oblique under the dimensioning submenu, as shown in Figure 11-9.

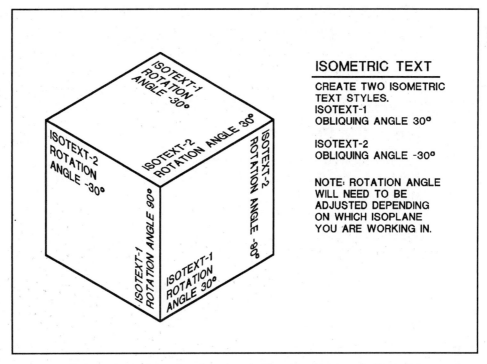

Figure 11-8 Creating Isometric Text for Isometric Drawing

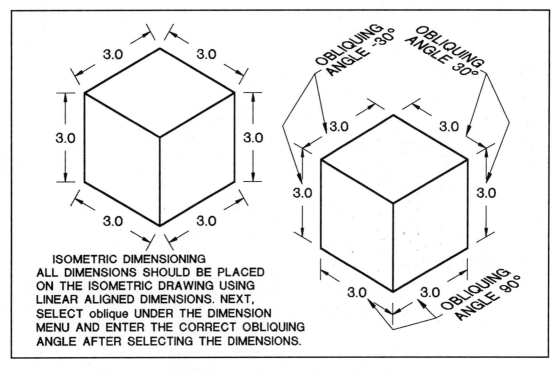

Figure 11-9 Isometric Dimensioning

Chapter 11 Project Exercise

CREATING THE PROJECT DRAWING

Isometric Project

Skills required to set up this project are explained in this chapter. These include setting up an isometric grid, controlling the isometric cursor and dimensioning the isometric drawing.

The object of this project is to set up a 12" × 9" sheet for drawing the part shown in Figure 11-10 at full scale.

Step 1   Begin a new drawing called iso.

Step 2   Set up.

The drawing will be plotted at full scale on an A-size sheet. The location of the start point at 1.52, 2.88 will allow room for dimensioning and callouts as shown in Figure 11-10.

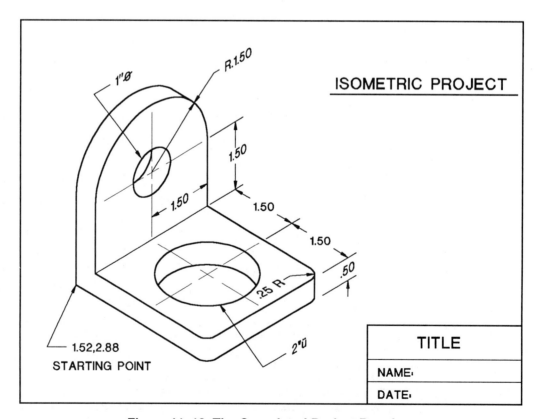

Figure 11-10 The Completed Project Drawing

Isometric Drawing

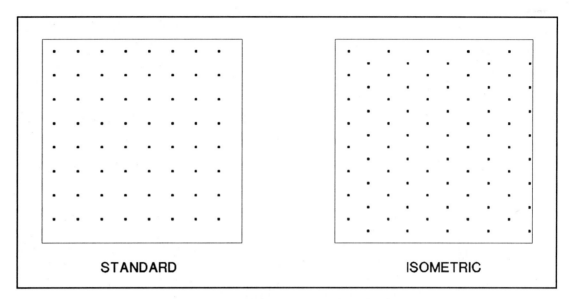

STANDARD   ISOMETRIC

Figure 11-11 Setting Up the Isometric Grid

Step 3   Set the units to decimal with two decimal places.

Create the following layers with appropriate colors and linetypes as shown below:

Object	white	continuous
Center	yellow	center
Layout	red	phantom
Dimension	magenta	continuous
Text	green	continuous

Set layer LAYOUT to be the current layer.

Step 4   Set GRID and SNAP to .25, and change SNAP to isometric style.

Command: **snap**
Snap spacing or ON/Off/Aspect/Rotate/Style <0.25>: **s**
Standard/ISOMETRIC<S>: **i**
Vertical spacing <0.25>: ⏎

See Figure 11-11.

Step 5   Begin the layout of the object by drawing the outline of it, as shown in Figure 11-12. Invoke the LINE command and start at point 1.52,2.88. Use the dimensions shown in Figure 11-12 and lay out the lines using your pointing device. Count the .25" Grid units or use the polar coordinate system to get the exact lengths.

NOTE: Ctrl + E will toggle the cursor to left, right, or top.

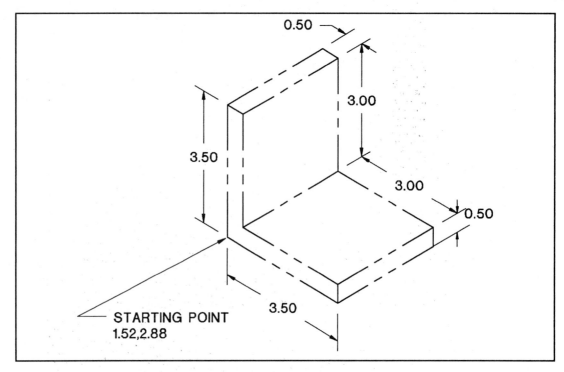

0.50

3.00

3.50

3.00

0.50

STARTING POINT
1.52,2.88

3.50

Figure 11-12 Layout of the Object

Command: **line**
From point: **1.52, 2.88**
To point: *count the Grid squares when selecting points*

Step 6   Set layer CENTER to be the current layer. Using the LINE command, draw in the center lines shown in Figure 11-13.

> ***NOTE:*** Use OSNAP midpoint to midpoint to draw the lines.

Step 7   Set layer OBJECT to be the current layer.

Using the ELLIPSE command (Isocircle) draw the circles shown in Figure 11-14. The center of the 2" circle is located at point 4.55,3.13 and the center of the 1" circle is located at 3.25,5.38. You may also pick the center of the circles using the OSNAP INTERSECTION mode.

Lay out the isometric circles as follows:

Command: **ellipse**
<Axis endpoint 1>/ Center/Isocircle: **i**
Center of circle: *select intersection of the center lines*
<Circle radius>/Diameter: *enter the radius or* **"D"** *for diameter*

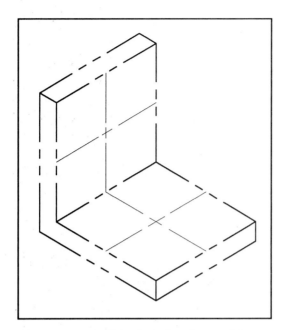

Figure 11-13 Drawing the Center Lines

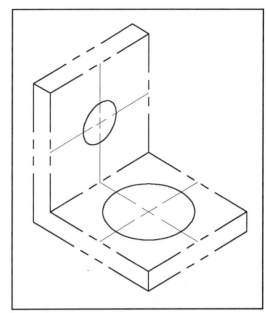

Figure 11-14 Drawing the Isocircles

> **NOTE:** For the circles on the right vertical plane, be sure to toggle using `Ctrl` + `E` to Isoplane Right. If you do not do this the circle will not appear correctly on this vertical plane.

Step 8 Lay out a construction line perpendicular to the two center lines, as shown in Figure 11-15.

Copy the isocircles from where they are located to the new position at the end of the construction line, as shown in Figure 11-16.

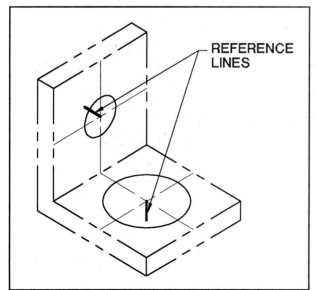

Figure 11-15 Laying Out a Construction Line Perpendicular to the Two Center Lines

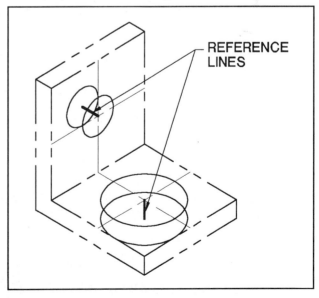

Figure 11-16 Copying the Isocircles to the End of the Construction Line

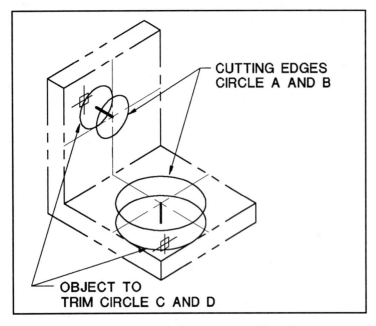

Figure 11-17 Trimming the Specified Circles

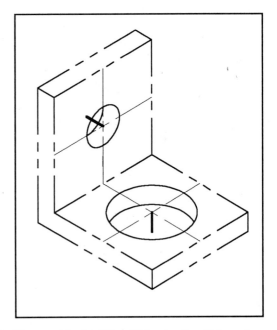

Figure 11-18 The Object after Trimming the Specified Circles

> **NOTE:** If you are familiar with isometric drawings, you can copy the circles and pick the center point as the base point and use a polar coordinate to copy them where they should go. The 1" circle @.5<150 and the 2" circle @.5<270.

Step 9 Trim the circles located in the background selecting circles A and B as the trim edge and circle C and D as the circles to trim, shown in Figure 11-17.

When complete, the object should appear as shown in Figure 11-18.

Step 10 Invoke the ELLIPSE command and select isocircle to add the arc whose edge represents the top of the object, as shown in Figure 11-19.

Step 11 Using the TRIM command, select the horizontal center line as a cutting edge and trim out the lower half of the isocircle, as shown in Figure 11-20.

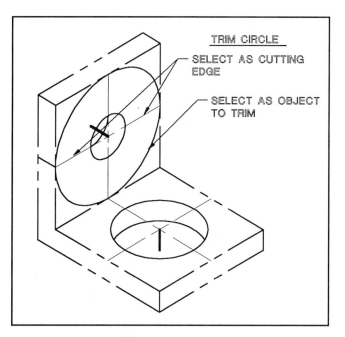

Figure 11-19 Adding an Arc at the Top of the Object Using the ELLIPSE Command

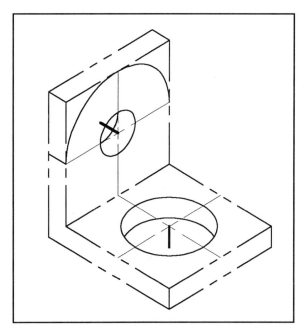

Figure 11-20 Trimming Out the Lower Half of the Isocircle

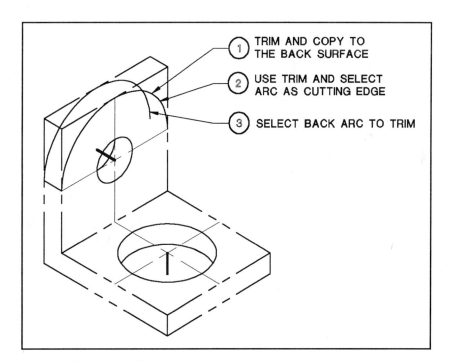

Figure 11-21 Copying the Arc to the Back Surface

Step 12   Copy the arc to the back surface using OSNAP and the cursor or the polar coordinate system as shown in Figure 11-21. When this step is complete, the drawing should look like Figure 11-22.

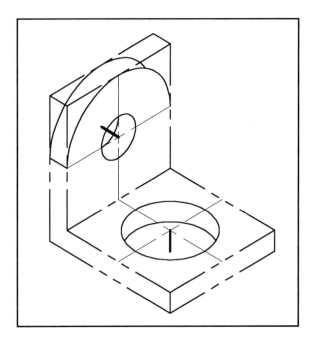

Figure 11-22 The Object after Copying the Arc to the Back Surface

Step 13   Draw the line, as shown in Figure 11-23, connecting the front surface to the back surface. Use the LINE command and draw a line (OSNAP) tangent to tangent, or construct the boxes as shown in this figure and draw the line (OSNAP) intersection to intersection.

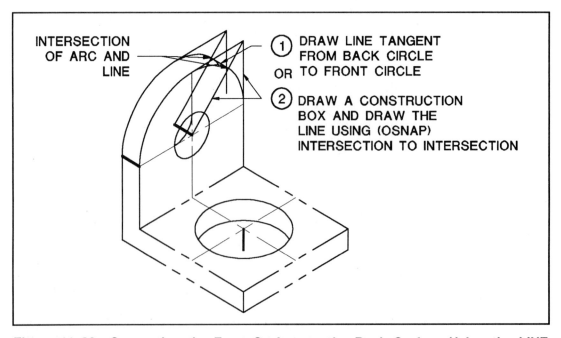

Figure 11-23   Connecting the Front Surface to the Back Surface Using the LINE Command

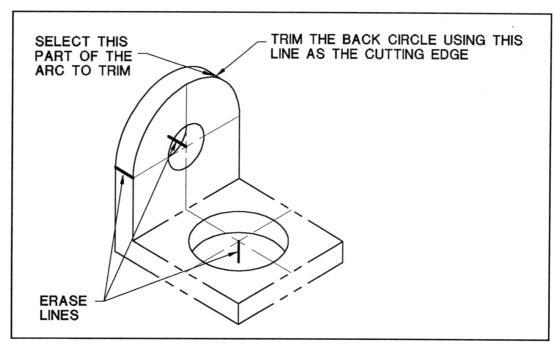

Figure 11-24 Trimming the Circle on the Back Surface

Step 14 Trim back the circle on the back surface, as shown in Figure 11-24, and erase the small construction lines as they are no longer needed. The object should now appear as shown in Figure 11-25 .

Step 15 Change to the OBJECT layer and draw over the lines laid out with the phantom lines in layer LAYOUT, as shown in Figure 11-26.

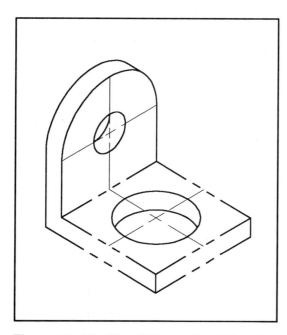

Figure 11-25 The Object after Trimming the Circle on the Back Surface

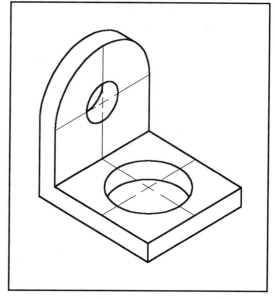

Figure 11-26 Drawing over the Construction Lines on the OBJECT Layer that Were Established in the LAYOUT Layer

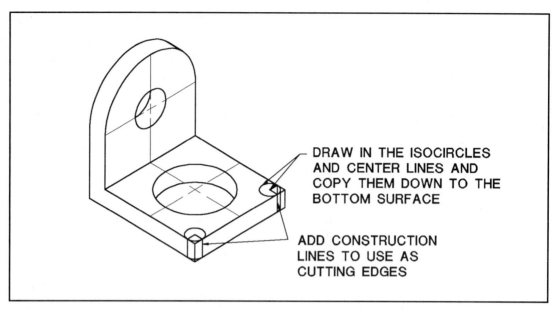

DRAW IN THE ISOCIRCLES
AND CENTER LINES AND
COPY THEM DOWN TO THE
BOTTOM SURFACE

ADD CONSTRUCTION
LINES TO USE AS
CUTTING EDGES

Figure 11-27 Adding Construction Lines Using the ELLIPSE Command and the LINE Command

Step 16 Using the ELLIPSE command in Isocircle mode, lay out the isocircles and use the LINE command to add the construction lines shown in Figure 11-27.

Step 17 Trim the isocircles using the construction lines as cutting edges, as shown in Figure 11-28.

Step 18 Trim out the corners of the object and erase the construction lines, as shown in Figure 11-29.

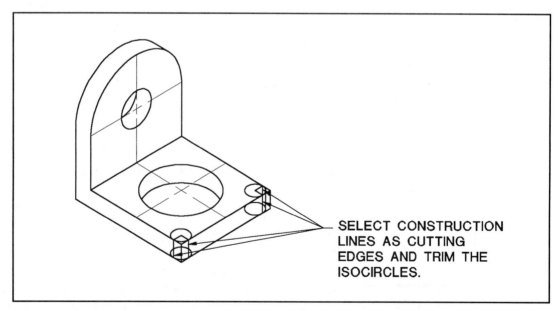

SELECT CONSTRUCTION
LINES AS CUTTING
EDGES AND TRIM THE
ISOCIRCLES.

Figure 11-28 Trimming the Isocircles Using the Construction Lines as Cutting Edges

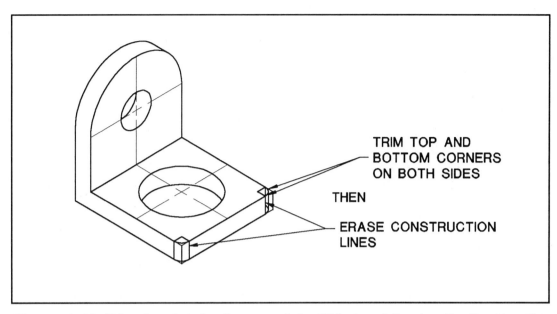

Figure 11-29 Trimming Out the Corners of the Object and Erasing the Construction Lines

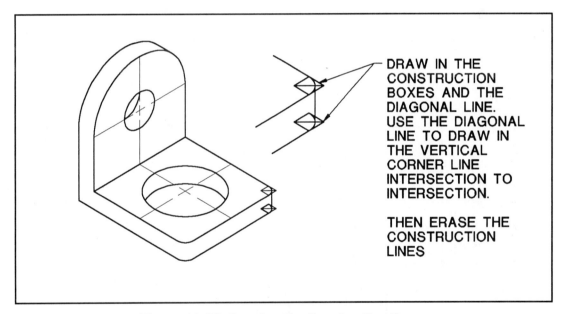

Figure 11-30 Drawing the Construction Boxes

Step 19 Draw the construction boxes shown in Figure 11-30 and add the vertical corner line. Use the LINE command with OSNAP to draw this line from intersection to intersection.

Step 20 Use the BREAK command to delete the back of the lower isocircle, as shown in Figure 11-31. When this is done, the object should appear as shown in Figure 11-32.

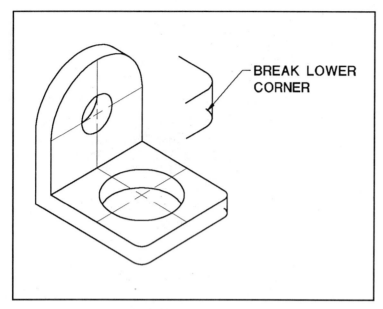

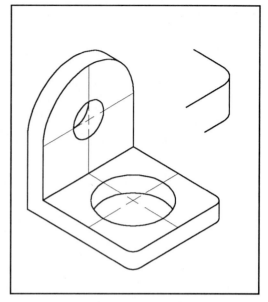

Figure 11-31 Using the BREAK Command to Delete the Back of the Lower Isocircle

Figure 11-32 The Object After Deleting the Back of the Lower Isocircle

Step 21 Finally, as shown in Figure 11-33, add the necessary dimensions and callouts.

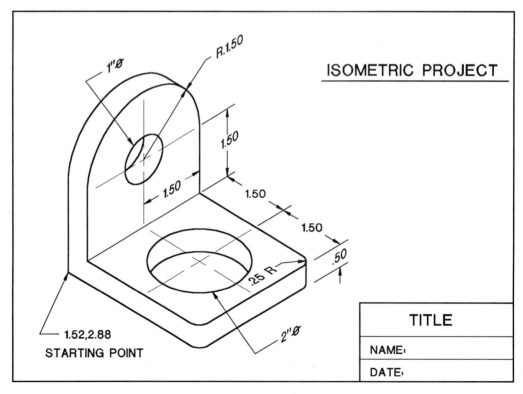

Figure 11-33 Adding the Dimensions and Callouts to Complete the Drawing

LAB EXERCISES

Lab Exercises 11-1 through 11-5

Using the information provided in Chapter 11 and the isometric project, complete exercises 11-1 through 11-5. Add dimensions and callouts where necessary.

Lab Exercise 11-1

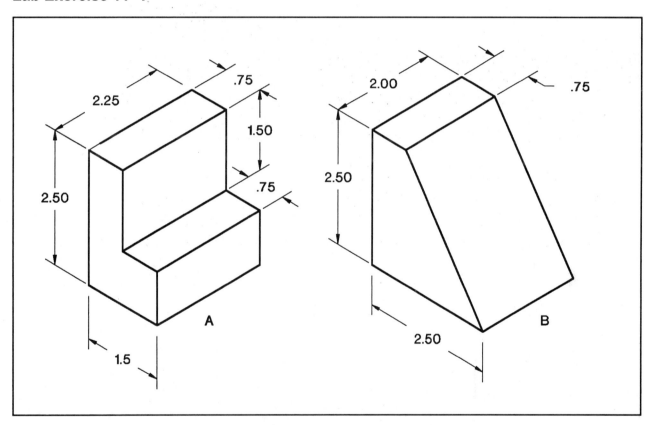

Lab Exercise 11-2

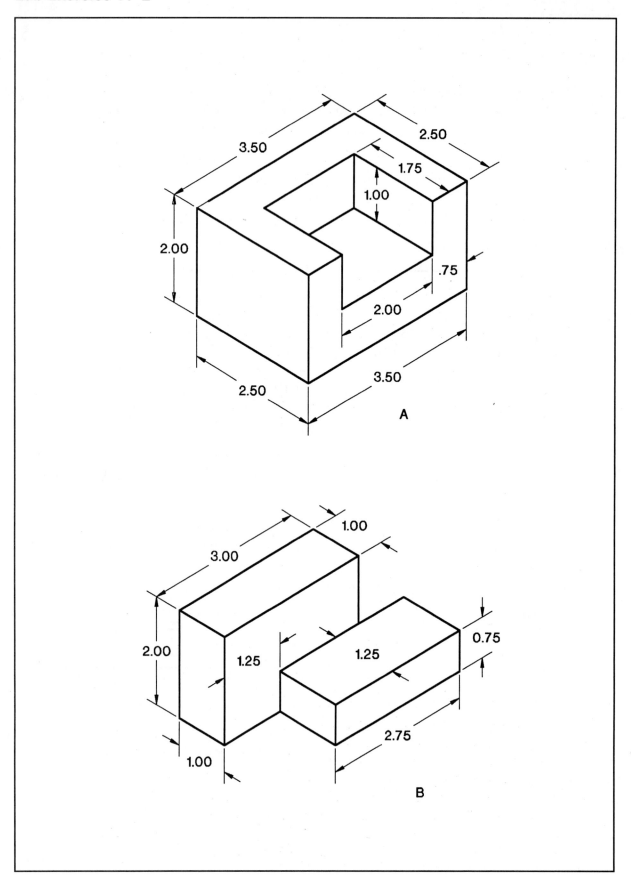

Lab Exercise 11-3

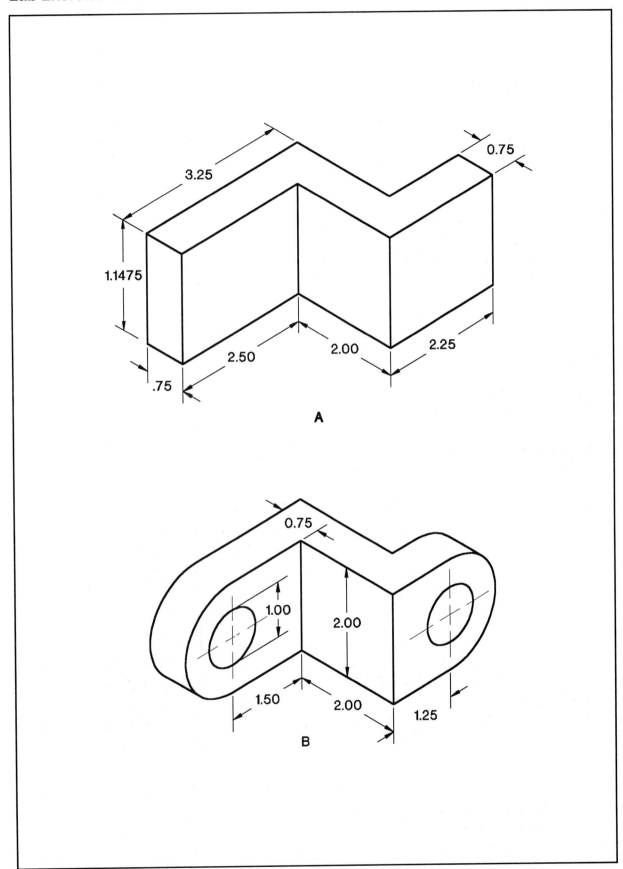

3.25

0.75

1.1475

2.50

2.00

2.25

.75

A

0.75

1.00

2.00

1.50

2.00

1.25

B

Lab Exercise 11-4

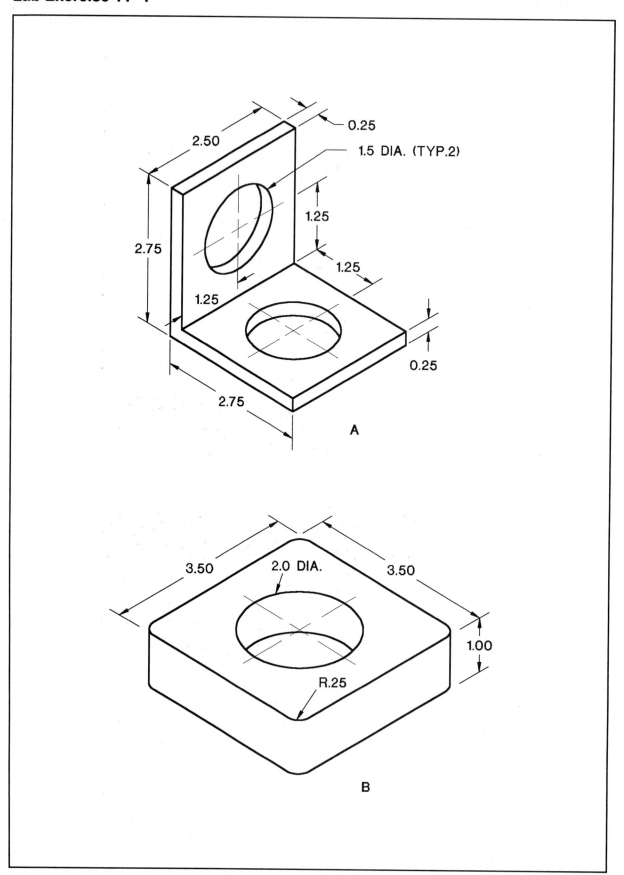

Lab Exercise 11-5

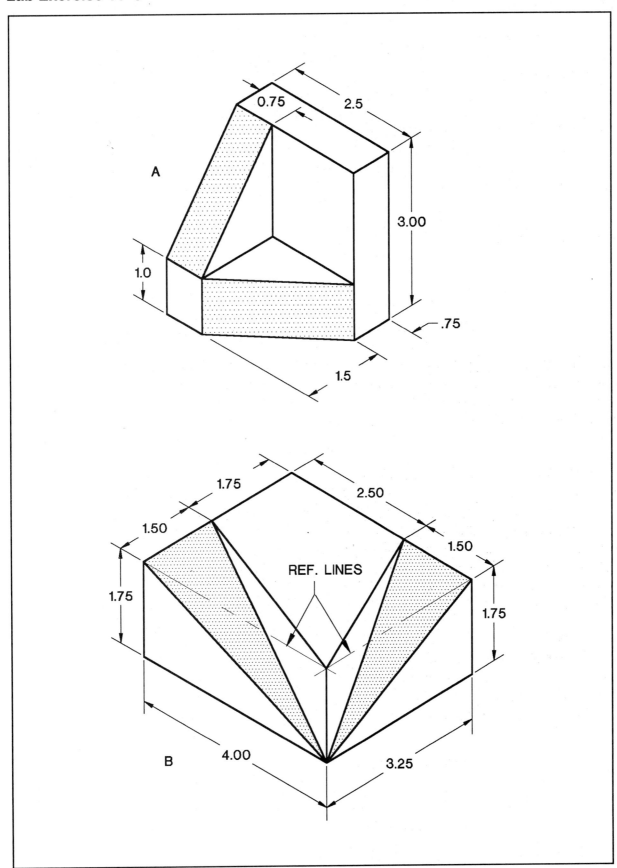

Lab Exercises 11-6 and 11-7

1. After drawing the piping fittings, flanges, and valves as shown in Figures 11-34 through 11-39, you must rotate them at -30 degrees about the insertion point before you WBLOCK or BLOCK them.

2. After making the WBLOCKS, start a new drawing for exercises 11-6 and 11-7. Insert the Blocks as shown in the exercise figure. After inserting the WBLOCKS into the drawing, DRAG them to the correct rotation angle. Be sure to keep Snap and ORTHO On while doing this.

Isometric Drawing

MAKING PIPING
ISOMETRIC BLOCKS

STEP 1
SET UP A .125 ISOMETRIC GRID, AND SET THE
SNAP VALUE TO .0625 WHILE DRAWING OBJECTS.

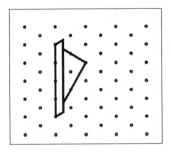

NOTE:
PIPING ISOMETRICS ARE NOT
DRAWN TO SCALE. FOR THE
CREATION OF WBLOCKS SET
GRID AND SNAP TO THE
SETTINGS INDICATED ABOVE
AND COUNT THE GRID DOTS
TO MAKE WBLOCKS THE
CORRECT SIZE.

STEP 2
ROTATE THE OBJECT TO A HORIZONTAL POSITION
BEFORE MAKING IT A WBLOCK.

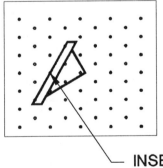

NOTE:
THIS IS A VERY IMPORTANT
STEP IF YOU WANT TO
INSERT THE WBLOCK AT THE
CORRECT ISOMETRIC ANGLE.

INSERTION POINT
ROTATE OBJECT -30° ABOUT
THIS POINT

Figure 11-34 Making Piping Isometric Blocks

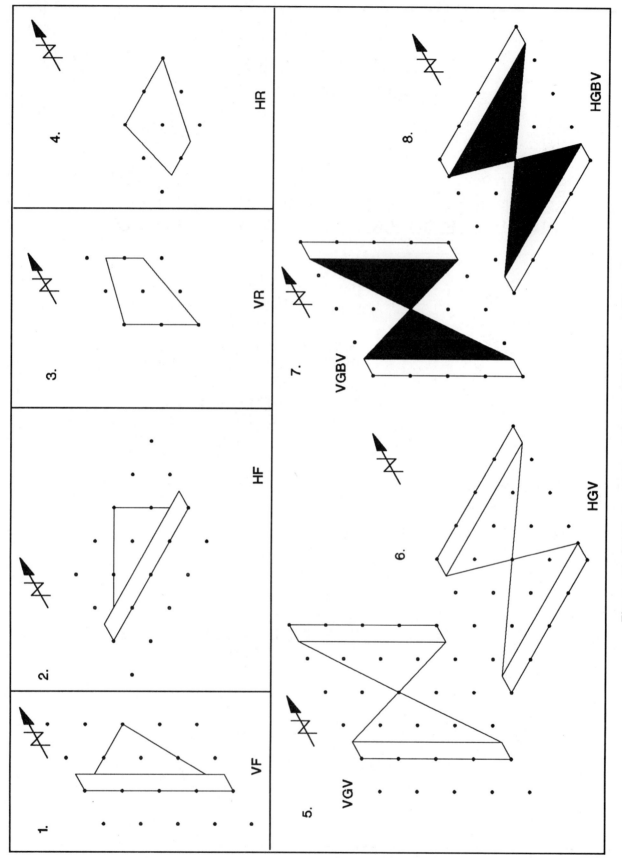

Figure 11-35 Horizontal and Vertical Valves and Fittings

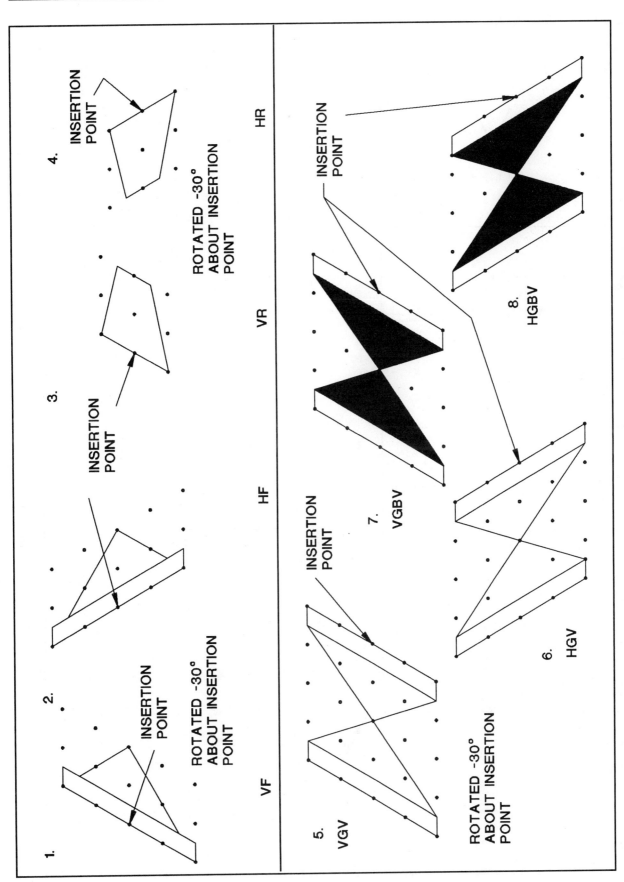

Figure 11–36 Horizontal and Vertical Valves and Fittings

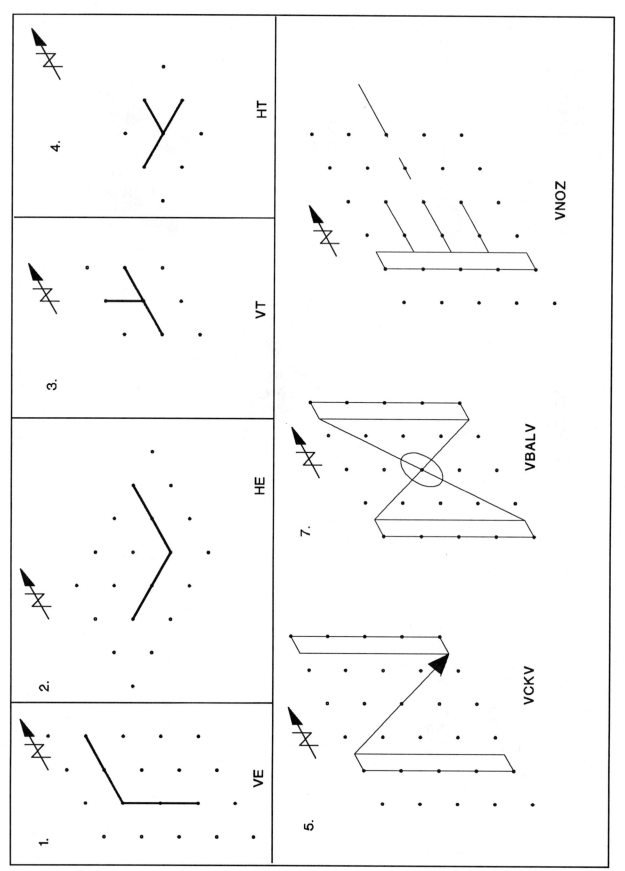

Figure 11-37 Horizontal and Vertical Valves and Fittings

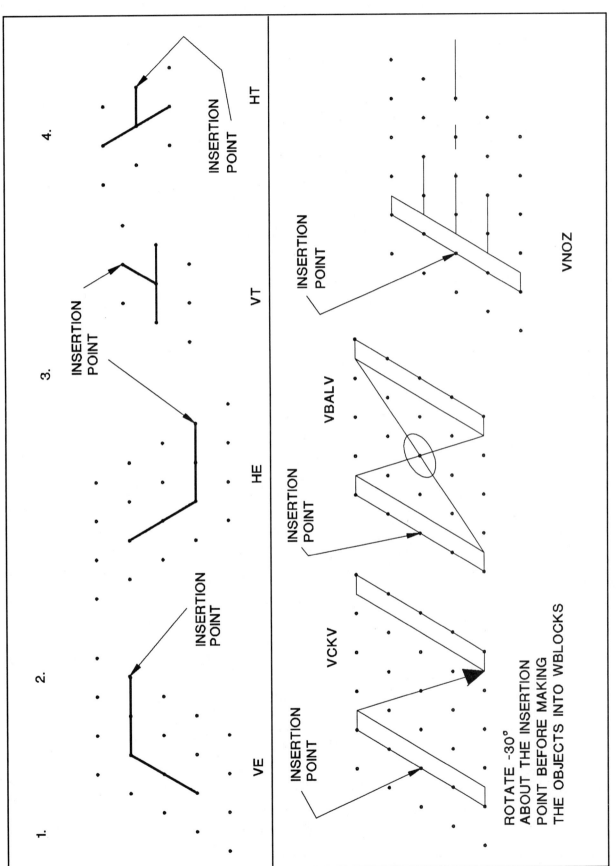

Figure 11-38 Horizontal and Vertical Valves and Fittings

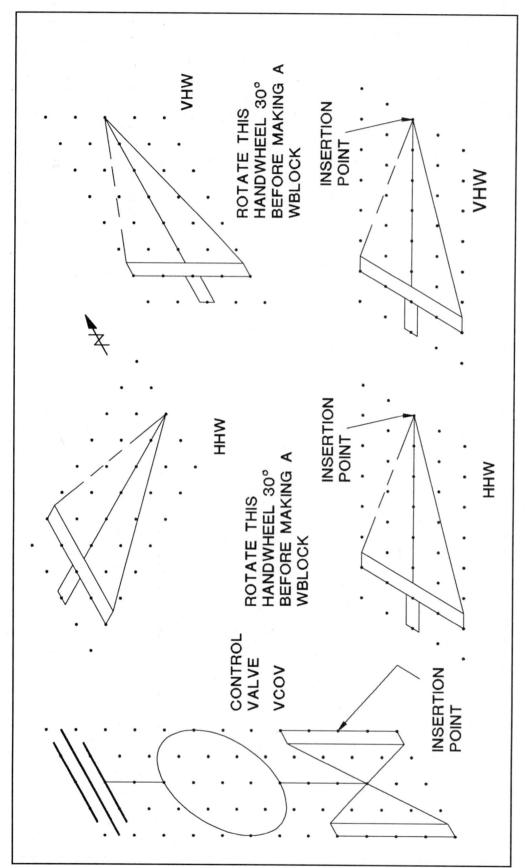

Figure 11-39 Horizontal and Vertical Valves and Stems

Isometric Drawing

Lab Exercise 11-6

CONTROL SET

NAME

DATE

4'-3 5/16"

2'-8 3/8"

1'-3 3/8"

1'-0 1/2"

6"X4" RED.

1'-2"

1'-8"

4"300#
RF.

TRC
121

1'-5 1/2"

1'-2 1/2"

1'-5 1/2"

6"X4" RED. TEE

6"

6"X4" RED.
(TYP. 2)

℄ EL. 102'-0"

Lab Exercise 11-7

PUMP SUCTION

NAME

DATE

FOR CONT. SEE
DWG.# 12-C-8"

3'-0"

4'-0"
(TYP. 2)

8"

1'-2 1/4"

F.O.F. EL. 104'-6"

CEL.103'-0"
P-102B

8"x6" RED.
(TYP. 2)

P-102A

CHAPTER
12   AutoCAD 3D

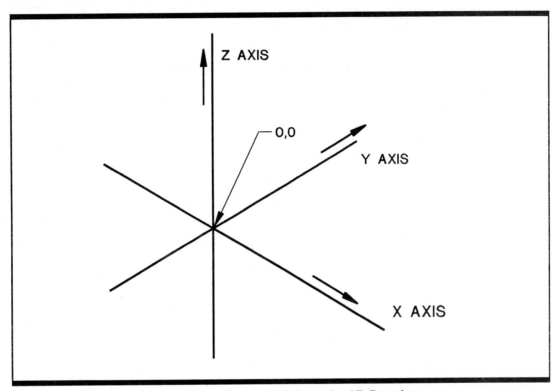

Figure 12-1 X, Y, and Z Axes for 3D Drawing

WHAT IS 3D?

In 2D drawing you have been working with two axes, X and Y. In 3D drawing, in addition to the X and Y axes, you will be working on the Z Axis, as shown in Figure 12-1. Plan views, sections, and elevations represent only two dimensions. Isometric, perspective, and axonometric drawings, on the other hand, represent all three dimensions. For example, to create three views of a cube, the cube is simply drawn as a square with thickness. This is referred to as extruded 2D. Only objects that are extrudable can be drawn by this method. Any other views are achieved by simply rotating the viewpoint or the object, just as if one were physically holding the cube. You can also can get an isometric or perspective view by simply changing the viewpoint.

585

Whether you realize it or not, all drawings you have done in previous chapters are created in true 3D. What this means is that with every line, circle, or arc that you have drawn, even if you think you have drawn them in 2D, are really stored with three coordinates. By default, AutoCAD stores the Z value as your current elevation. What you think of now as 2D is really only one of an infinite number of views of your drawing in 3D space.

Drawing objects in 3D provides three major advantages:

1. An object can be drawn once and then can be viewed and plotted from any angle (viewpoint).
2. A 3D object holds mathematical information, which can be used in engineering analysis such as finite element analysis and computer numerical control (CNC) machinery.
3. Shading for visualization.

There are two major limitations in working in 3D. Whenever you want to input 3D coordinates whose Z coordinate is different from the current construction plane's elevation, you have to use the keyboard instead of your pointing device. One exception is to OSNAP to an object not in the current construction plane. The input device (mouse or digitizer) can only supply AutoCAD with two of the three coordinates at a time. Three-dimensional input devices exist but there is no practical support for them at this time. So, you are limited to using the keyboard. The second limitation is determining where you are in relationship to an object in 3D space.

This chapter provides a detailed explanation of the tools and specific commands used for 3D drawing.

VIEWING

Until now, you have been working on the plan view or XY plane. You have been looking down at the plan view from a certain distance along the Z Axis. The direction from which you view your drawing or model is called the viewpoint. You can view a drawing from any point in Model Space. From your selected viewpoint, you can add entities, edit existing entities, or suppress the hidden lines from the drawing.

The VPOINT and DVIEW commands are used to control viewing of a model from any point in Model Space.

VPOINT Command

To view a model in 3D, you may have to change the viewpoint. The location of the viewpoint can be controlled by the VPOINT command. The default viewpoint is 0,0,1; i.e., you are looking at the model from 0,0,1 (on the positive Z Axis above the model) to 0,0,0 (origin).

Table 12-1 Exercise for Rotating 3D Objects

VPOINT Setting	Displayed View(s)
0,0,1	Top
0,0,-1	Bottom
0,-1,0	Front
0,1,0	Rear
1,0,0	Right side
-1,0,0	Left side
1,-1,1	Top, Front, Right side
-1,-1,1	Top, Front, Left side
1,1,1	Top, Rear, Right side
-1,1,1	Top, Rear, Right side
1,-1,-1	Bottom, Front, Right side
-1,-1,-1	Bottom, Front, Left side
1,1,-1	Bottom, Rear, Right side
-1,1,-1	Bottom, Rear, Left side

The VPOINT command is invoked from the Screen Menu Settings, or at the "Command:" prompt type in **VPOINT** and press ⏎.

Command: **vpoint**
Rotate/<Viewpoint> <current>:

The default method requires you to enter X,Y,Z coordinates from the keyboard. These coordinates establish the viewpoint. From this viewpoint, you will be looking at the model in the space toward the model's origin. For example, a 1,-1,1 setting gives you a -45-degree angle projected in the XY plane and 35.264-degree angle above the XY plane (top, right and front views), looking at the model origin (0,0,0). You can set the VPOINT to any X,Y, and Z location. Table 12-1 lets you experiment with the rotation of 3D objects.

Instead of entering coordinates, give a null response (press ⏎) and a compass and axes tripod will appear on the screen, as shown in Figure 12-2.

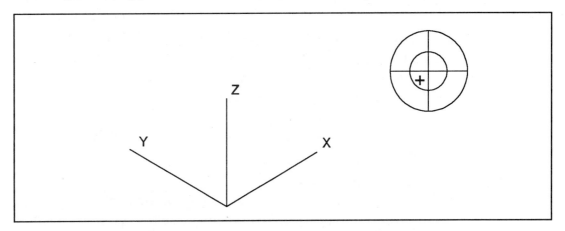

Figure 12-2 The Compass and Axes Tripod

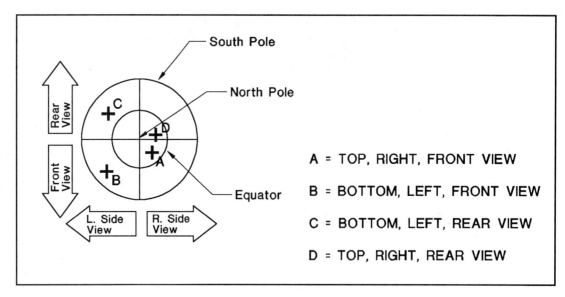

Figure 12-3 Components of the Compass and Its Poles

The compass, in the upper right of the screen, is a 2D representation of a globe. The center point of the circle being the north pole (0,0,1), the inner circle representing the equator, and the outer circle representing the south pole (0,0,-1), as shown in Figure 12-3.

A small cross is displayed on the compass. You can move the cross using your pointing device. If the cross is in the inner circle, you are above the equator, looking down on your model. If the cross is in the outer circle, you are looking from beneath your drawing, or from the southern hemisphere. By moving the cross, the axes tripod rotates to conform to the viewpoint indicated on the compass. When you achieve the desired viewpoint, press the pick button on your pointing device or press ⏎. Your drawing will regenerate to reflect your VPOINT position.

Rotate Option The Rotate option allows you to specify the location of the viewpoint in terms of two angles. The first angle determines the rotation in the XY plane from the X Axis (0 degrees) clockwise or counterclockwise. And the second angle determines the angle from XY plane up or down. When you select the Rotate option, AutoCAD prompts:

    Enter angle in X-Y plane from X axis <current>:
    Enter angle from X-Y plane <current>:

Specify the angles, and your drawing will regenerate to reflect your VPOINT position.

Using Icons AutoCAD provides a series of icons, shown in Figure 12-4, under Vpoint 3D... from the pull-down menu to select the predefined viewpoint directions. The Vpoint 3D... is invoked from the pull-down menu Display.

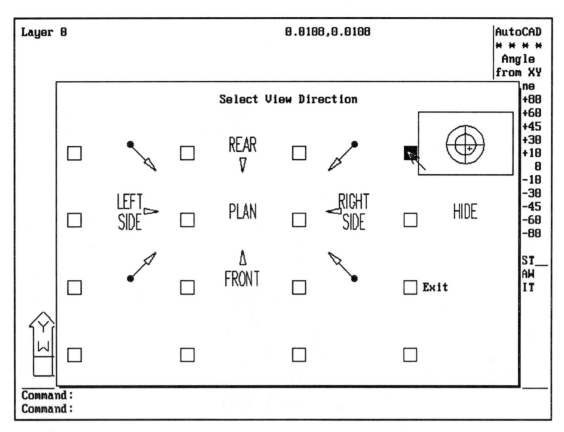

Figure 12-4 The Vpoint 3D Icons

Nine options are available, including the icon for PLAN. The other eight options position you away from your drawing at the sides indicated. Select the icon that you would like to view the model in the line-of-sight direction, then AutoCAD prompts:

Enter angle from X-Y plane <default>:

Specify the angle from which to view your drawing and AutoCAD will regenerate the drawing to reflect your VPOINT position.

> **NOTE:** By default, AutoCAD always places the model to your current VPOINT position in reference to WCS, not the current UCS. If necessary, you can change the system variable WORLDVIEW from 1 (default) to 0, then AutoCAD will place the model in reference to UCS for your current VPOINT position. It is recommended that you keep the WORLDVIEW set to 1 (default). Regardless of WORLDVIEW setting, you are always looking through your viewpoint to WCS origin.

DVIEW Command

The DVIEW command is an enhanced VPOINT command and here you can visually move around an object on the screen in dynamically viewing selected

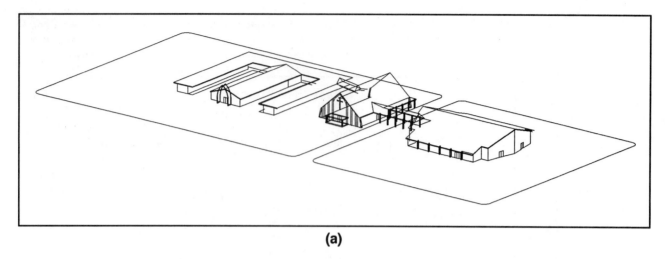

(a)

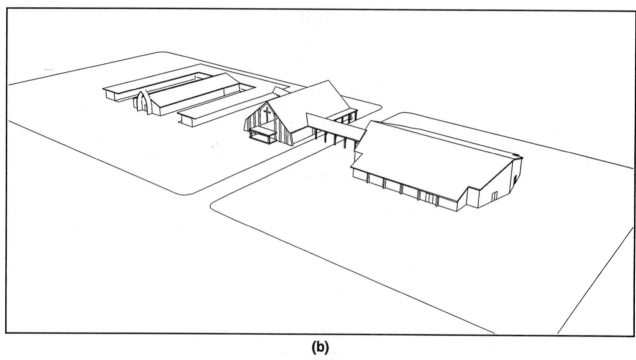

(b)

Figure 12-5 The DVIEW Command Parallel (a) and Perspective (b) Views

objects as the view changes. The DVIEW command provides either parallel or perspective views, whereas the VPOINT command provides only parallel views. In the case of a parallel view, parallel lines always remain parallel, whereas in perspective view, parallel lines converge from your view to a vanishing point. Figures 12-5a and 12-5b show parallel and perspective views, respectively, of a model. The viewing direction is the same in each case.

The DVIEW command is invoked from the Screen Menu Display or at the "Command:" prompt, type in **DVIEW** and press ⏎.

Command: **dview**
Select objects:

Select the objects by any of the selection sets used by AutoCAD. All or any part of the objects in the drawing can be selected for viewing during the DVIEW command process, but once you exit the DVIEW command, all objects in the drawing will be represented in the new view created. If your drawing is too large to display quickly in the DVIEW display, small portions can be selected and used to orient the entire drawing. The purpose of this is to save time on slower machines and still give dynamic rotation so that you can quickly and effortlessly adjust the view of your object before you begin working with it.

If you give a null response to the "Select objects:" prompt, AutoCAD provides you with a picture of a 3D house. Whatever you do to the 3D house under DVIEW will be done to your current drawing when you exit the DVIEW command.

Each time when you exit the DVIEW command, AutoCAD performs an unconditional regeneration. No matter what the current setting for REGENAUTO is, AutoCAD will automatically perform a REGEN.

After selecting the objects, give a null response. AutoCAD prompts you with the following options:

CAmera/TArget/Distance/POints/PAn/Zoom/TWist/CLip/Hide/Off/Undo/<eXit>:

CAmera Option The Camera option is one of the six options that adjust what is seen in the view. When using the Camera option, the drawing is stationary while the camera can move in two directions. It can move up and down (above or below) or it can move around the target to the left or right (clockwise or counterclockwise). When you are moving the camera, the target is fixed.

When you enter the Camera option, AutoCAD prompts:

Enter angle from X-Y plane <default>:

In addition to the prompt, you will also see a vertical bar on the right of the screen, as shown in Figure 12-6. Move your cursor to the right until it appears in this vertical bar and then move the cursor up and down slowly. The vertical bar is calibrated from 0 degrees in the middle to 90 degrees to the top and −90 degrees to the bottom, which represents the number of degrees the camera is above or below the target. When you move the cursor, you will see the object begin to dynamically rotate vertically. Move the cursor to the desired angle and then press the pick button. Or, you could also type the desired angle from the keyboard. Either way, you have selected an angle of view above or below the target.

Next, AutoCAD prompts for the desired rotation angle of the camera around the target:

Enter the angle in the X-Y plane from X axis <default>:

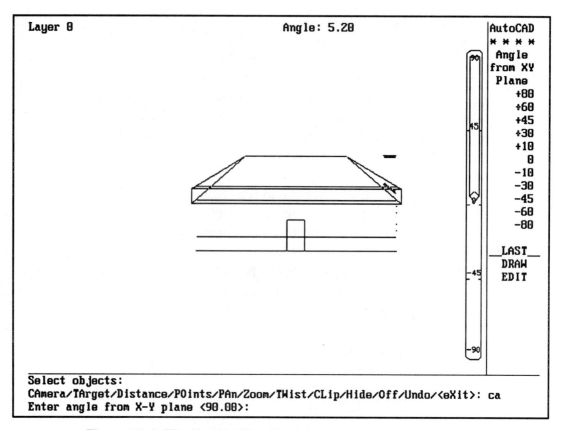

Figure 12-6 The Vertical Bar Displayed for the CAmera Option

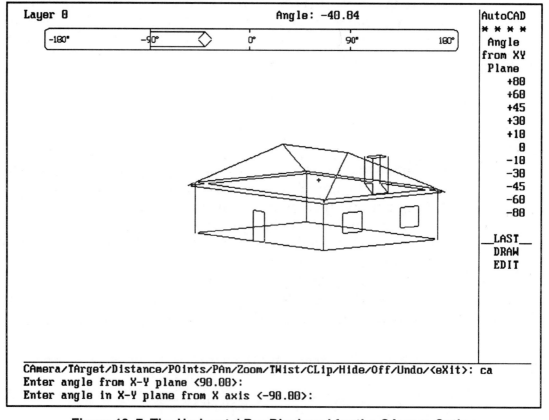

Figure 12-7 The Horizontal Bar Displayed for the CAmera Option

In addition to the prompt, you will also see a horizontal bar, shown in Figure 12-7, similar to the vertical bar appearing at the top of your screen. This bar is calibrated from −180 degrees to 180 degrees.

You can move the camera 180 degrees clockwise and 180 degrees counterclockwise around the target. Move your cursor on the bar to reach the desired angle and press the pick button. Or, you could also type in the desired angle from the keyboard. Either way, you have selected an angle of view around the target clockwise or counterclockwise.

AutoCAD will take you back to the 12-option prompt of the DVIEW command. When your angle of view is correct, you may exit by giving a null response, or selecting the Exit option. This will take you back to the "Command:" prompt.

When you exit DVIEW, your entire drawing will rotate to the same angle of view as the few objects that you selected.

The following command sequence shows an example of using the Camera option of the DVIEW command.

Command: **dview**
Select objects: *select the objects*
CAmera/TArget/Distance/POints/PAn/Zoom/TWist/CLip/Hide/Off/Undo/<eXit>:
    ca
Enter angle from X-Y plane <default>: **45**
Enter angle in X-Y plane from X axis <default>: **45**
CAmera/TArget/Distance/POints/PAn/Zoom/TWist/CLip/Hide/Off/Undo/<eXit>:

TArget Option The Target option is similar to the Camera option, but in this case, the target is rotated around the camera. The camera remains stationary except for maintaining its lens on the target point. The prompts are similar to the Camera option. It may seem that there is no difference between the Camera and Target options, but there is one minor difference in the actual angle of view. For instance, if you elevate the camera 75 degrees above the target, you are then looking at the target from the top down. On the other hand, if you raise the target 75 degrees above the camera, you are then looking at the target from the bottom up. The actual angles are reversed. The real difference comes if you are typing in the angles rather than visually picking them.

The following command sequence shows an example of using the Target option of the DVIEW command.

Command: **dview**
Select objects: *select the objects*
CAmera/TArget/Distance/POints/PAn/Zoom/TWist/CLip/Hide/Off/Undo/<eXit>:
    ta
Enter angle from X-Y plane <default>: **75**
Enter angle in X-Y plane from X axis <default>: **75**
CAmera/TArget/Distance/POints/PAn/Zoom/TWist/CLip/Hide/Off/Undo/<eXit>:

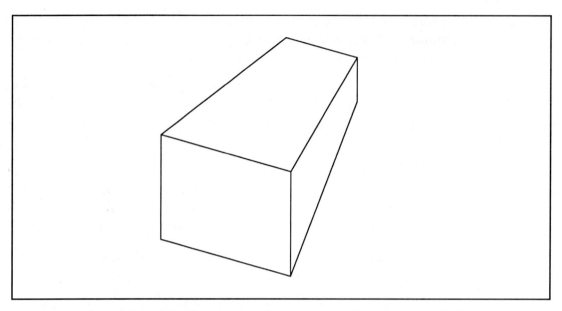

Figure 12-8 The Box Icon as It Appears for the Distance Option

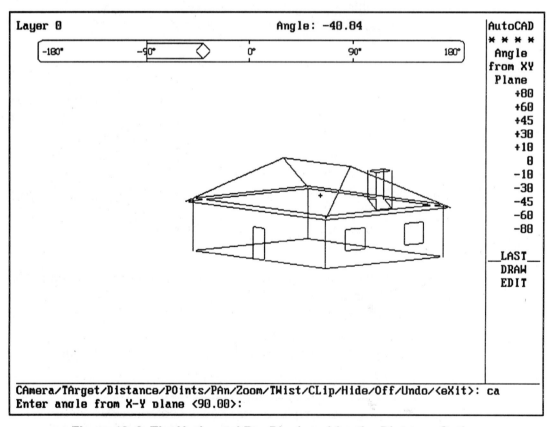

Figure 12-9 The Horizontal Bar Displayed for the Distance Option

Distance Option The Distance option is used to create a perspective projection from the current view. The only information required for this option is the distance from the camera to the target point. Once AutoCAD knows the distance, it will be able to apply the correct perspective. When perspective viewing is on, a box icon appears, as shown in Figure 12-8, in place of the UCS icon on the screen. Some commands (like ZOOM and PAN) will not work while perspective is on. You turn on the perspective just for visual purposes or for plotting.

When you select the Distance option, AutoCAD prompts:

New camera/target distance <default>:

In addition to the prompt, you will also see a horizontal bar, shown in Figure 12-9, at the top of the screen. The bar goes from 0x to 16x. These are factor distances times your current distance from the object. Moving the slider cursor toward the right increases the distance between the target and camera, and moving toward the left reduces the distance between the target and camera. The current distance is represented by 1x. For instance, moving the slider cursor to 3x represents the new distance to three times the previous distance. Or, you could also type the desired distance in the current linear units from the keyboard.

The following command sequence shows an example of using the Distance option of the DVIEW command.

Command: **dview**
Select objects: *select the objects*
CAmera/TArget/Distance/POints/PAn/Zoom/TWist/CLip/Hide/Off/Undo/<eXit>:
    d
New camera/target distance <default>: **75'**
CAmera/TArget/Distance/POints/PAn/Zoom/TWist/CLip/Hide/Off/Undo/<eXit>:
    ⏎

Off Option The Off option will allow you to turn off the perspective view. The following command sequence shows an example of using the Off option of the DVIEW command.

Command: **dview**
Select objects: *select the objects*
CAmera/TArget/Distance/POints/PAn/Zoom/TWist/CLip/Hide/Off/Undo/<eXit>:
    o
CAmera/TArget/Distance/POints/PAn/Zoom/TWist/CLip/Hide/Off/Undo/<eXit>:
    ⏎

> *NOTE:* To turn on the perspective again, select the Distance option and press ⏎ for all the defaults. There is no option called On to turn on the perspective view.

POints Option The Points option allows you to establish the location of the camera as well as target points. This gives AutoCAD the basic information needed to create the view. The location of the camera and target points must be specified in a parallel projection. If perspective is on, AutoCAD temporarily turns it off while you specify the new location for camera and target points, and then redisplays the image back in perspective.

When you select the Points option, AutoCAD prompts:

Enter Target point:
Enter Camera point:

Specify the target and camera locations. After the locations are defined, the screen shows the new view immediately.

The following command sequence shows an example of using the Points option of the DVIEW command.

Command: **dview**
Select objects: *select the objects*
CAmera/TArget/Distance/POints/PAn/Zoom/TWist/CLip/Hide/Off/Undo/<eXit>:
    po
Enter Target point: *specify a point*
Enter Camera point: *specify a point*
CAmera/TArget/Distance/POints/PAn/Zoom/TWist/CLip/Hide/Off/Undo/<eXit>:

PAn Option The Pan option will allow you to view a different location of the model by specifying the pan distance and direction. This option is similar to the regular PAN command. The following command sequence shows an example of using the Pan option of the DVIEW command.

Command: **dview**
Select objects: *select the objects*
CAmera/TArget/Distance/POints/PAn/Zoom/TWist/CLip/Hide/Off/Undo/<eXit>:
    pa
Displacement base point: *specify a point*
Second point: *specify a point*
CAmera/TArget/Distance/POints/PAn/Zoom/TWist/CLip/Hide/Off/Undo/<eXit>:

Zoom Option The Zoom option allows you to zoom in to a portion of the model. This option is similar to the regular AutoCAD ZOOM Center command, with the center point lying at the center of the current viewport. This option is controlled by a simple scale factor value.

When you select the Zoom option, AutoCAD prompts:

Adjust zoom scale factor <default>:

In addition to the prompt, you will also see a horizontal bar at the top of the screen. The slider bar lets you specify a zoom scale factor, with 1x being the current zoom level. Any value greater than 1 will increase the size of the objects in the view, while any decimal value less than 1 decreases the size.

> **NOTE:** When the perspective is on, the Zoom option prompts for a lens length rather than a zoom factor, but the effect is similar. The larger the lens size, the closer the object.

TWist Option The Twist option allows you to rotate or twist the view. It allows you to rotate the image around the line of sight at a given angle from zero with zero being to the right. The angle is measured counterclockwise.

The following command sequence shows an example of using the Twist option of the DVIEW command.

Command: **dview**
Select objects: *select the objects*
CAmera/TArget/Distance/POints/PAn/Zoom/TWist/CLip/Hide/Off/Undo/<eXit>:
    tw
New view twist <default>: *select a point*
CAmera/TArget/Distance/POints/PAn/Zoom/TWist/CLip/Hide/Off/Undo/<eXit>:

CLip Option The Clip option allows you to hide portions of the object in view so that the interior of the object can be seen, or parts of the complex object can be more clearly identified.

The Clip option has three suboptions, Back, Front, and Off. The Back suboption eliminates all parts of the object in view that are located beyond the designated point along the line of sight. The Front suboption eliminates all parts of the object in view that are located between the camera and the front clipping plane. The Off suboption turns off front and back clipping.

The following command sequence shows an example of using the Clip option of the DVIEW command.

Command: **dview**
Select objects: *select the objects*
CAmera/TArget/Distance/POints/PAn/Zoom/TWist/CLip/Hide/Off/Undo/<eXit>:
    cl
Back/Front/<Off>: **b**
On/Off/<Distance from Target> <default>: *specify the distance or turn on and*
    off the previously defined clipping plane
CAmera/TArget/Distance/POints/PAn/Zoom/TWist/CLip/Hide/Off/Undo/<eXit>:

AutoCAD 3D

Hide Option The Hide option is similar to the regular AutoCAD HIDE command.

Undo Option The Undo option will undo the last DVIEW operation. You can use it to step back multiple DVIEW operations.

eXit Option The Exit option will terminate the DVIEW command. It is the default option of the DVIEW command.

COORDINATE SYSTEMS

In AutoCAD there are two types of coordinate systems available. One is a single fixed coordinate system called the World Coordinate System and the other is a set of infinite user-defined coordinate systems available through the User Coordinate System.

The World Coordinate System (WCS) is fixed and cannot be changed. In this system, the X Axis starts at the point 0,0,0 and increases as the point moves to the operator's right; the Y Axis starts at 0,0,0 and increases as the point moves to the top of the screen; and finally, the Z Axis starts at the 0,0,0 point and gets larger as it comes toward the user. All drawings from previous chapters are created with reference to WCS. The WCS is still the basic system used in virtually all 2D AutoCAD drawings. However, because of the difficulty in calculating 3D points, the WCS is not suited for many 3D applications.

The User Coordinate System (UCS) allows the user to change the location and orientation of the X,Y, and Z axes to reduce the calculations needed to create 3D objects. The UCS command lets you redefine the origin in your drawing, and establish positive X and the positive Y axes. New users think of a coordinate system simply as the direction of positive X and positive Y. But once the directions X and Y are defined, the direction of Z will be defined as well. Thus, the user only has to be concerned with X and Y. As a result, when you are drawing in 2D, you are also somewhere in 3D space. For example, if a sloped roof of a house is drawn in detail using the WCS, each endpoint of each entity on the inclined roof plane must be calculated. On the other hand, if the UCS is set to the same plane as the roof, each object can be drawn as if were in the plan view. You can define any number of UCSs within the fixed WCS and save them, assigning each a user-determined name. But, at any given time only one coordinate system is current and all coordinate input and display is relative to it. If multiple viewports are active, they all share the same current UCS.

Right Hand Rule

The directions of the X,Y, and Z axes change when the UCS is altered, hence, the positive rotation direction of the Axes may become difficult to determine. The Right Hand Rule will help in determining the rotation direction when changing the UCS or using commands that require entity rotation.

To remember the orientation of the axes, perform the following:

1. Hold your right hand with the thumb, forefinger, and middle finger pointing at right angles to each other, as shown in Figure 12-10.
2. Consider the thumb to be pointing in the positive direction of the X Axis.

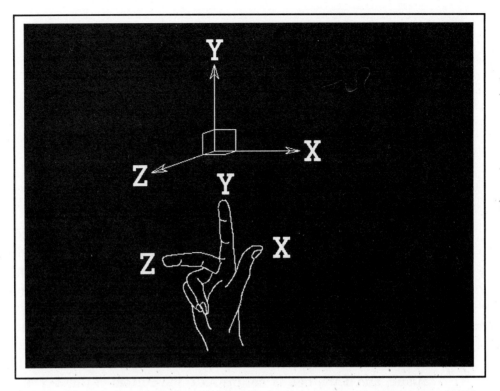

Figure 12-10 The Correct Hand Position when Using the Right Hand Rule

3. The forefinger points in the positive direction of the Y Axis.
4. The middle finger points in the positive direction of the Z Axis.

UCS Icon

The UCS icon provides a visual reminder of how the UCS axes are oriented, where the current UCS origin is, and the viewing direction relative to the UCS XY plane. AutoCAD displays different coordinate system icons in Paper Space and Model Space. When Model Space is current, AutoCAD displays the icon as shown in Figure 12-11a and when Paper Space is current, AutoCAD displays the icon as shown in Figure 12-11b.

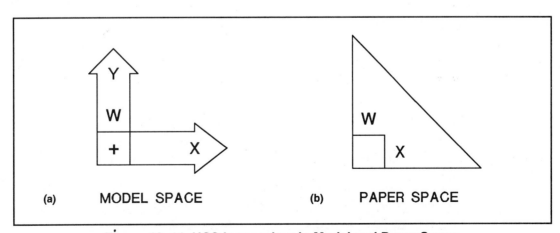

Figure 12-11 UCS Icons when in Model and Paper Space

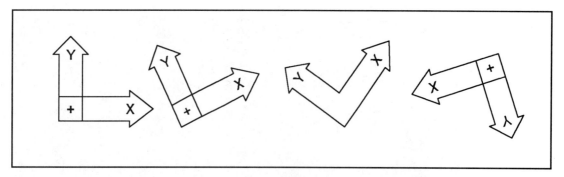

Figure 12-12 Various Orientations of the UCS Icon

The X and Y Axis directions are displayed using arrows labeled appropriately, and the Z Axis is displayed by the placement of the icon. The icon displays a W in the Y Axis arrow if the current UCS is the World Coordinate System, and a (+) appears at the base of the arrows if the icon is placed at the origin of the current coordinate system. When looking straight up or down on the Z plane, the icon seems flat. When viewed at any other angle, the icon looks skewed. The orientation of the Z Axis is defined further by the presence or absence of a box at the base of the arrows that create the icon. If the box is visible, you are looking down on the X-Y plane, and if the box is not present, the bottom of the X-Y plane is being viewed. See Figure 12-12 for all the different orientations of the UCS icon.

> ***NOTE:*** If the viewing angle comes within one degree of the Z Axis, the UCS icon will change to a "broken pencil," as shown in Figure 12-13. When this icon is showing in a view, it is recommended that you avoid trying to use the cursor to specify points in that view, because results may be unpredictable.

The display and placement on the origin of the UCS icon is handled by the UCSICON command. The UCSICON command is invoked from the Screen Menu Settings, or at the "Command:" prompt type in **UCSICON** and press ⏎.

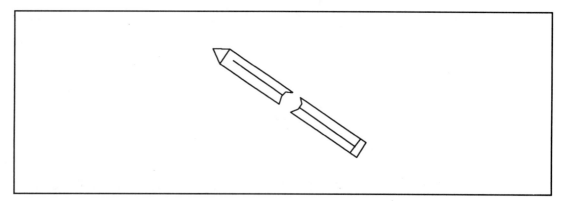

Figure 12-13 The UCS Icon as It Appears if the Viewing Angle Comes within One Degree of the Z Axis

```
Command: ucsicon
ON/OFF/All/Noorigin/ORigin <default>:
```

ON Option This option allows you to turn the icon ON if it is OFF in the current viewport.

OFF Option This option allows you to turn the icon OFF if it is ON in the current viewport.

Noorigin Option This option tells AutoCAD to display the icon at the lower left corner of the viewport, regardless of the location of the UCS origin. This is like parking the icon in the lower left corner. This is the default setting.

ORigin Option This option forces the icon to be displayed at the origin of the current coordinate system.

> *NOTE:* If the origin is off screen, the icon is displayed at the lower left corner of the viewport.

All Option This option determines whether the options that follow will affect all of the viewports or just the current active viewport. This option is issued before each and every option if you want to affect all viewports. For example, to turn ON the icon in all the viewports and display the icon on the origin, the following sequence of prompts is displayed:

```
Command: ucsicon
ON/OFF/All/Noorigin/ORigin <default>: all
ON/OFF/Noorigin/ORigin: on
Command: ⏎
ON/OFF/All/Noorigin/ORigin: all
ON/OFF/Noorigin/ORigin: origin
Command:
```

UCS Command

The UCS is the key to almost all 3D operations in AutoCAD, as mentioned earlier. Many commands in AutoCAD are traditionally thought to be 2D commands. They are used effectively in 3D because they are always relative to the current UCS. For example, Rotate will only rotate in the direction of X and Y. Therefore, if you wanted to rotate an object in the direction of Z, you would change your UCS so that X or Y is now in the direction what was previously Z. Then you could use the 2D ROTATE command.

The UCS command lets you redefine the origin in your drawing. Broadly, you can define origin by four methods:

1. Specifying a data point for an origin, a new XY plane by providing three data points, or providing a direction for the Z Axis.

2. Defining an origin relative to the orientation of an existing entity.

3. Defining an origin by aligning with the current viewing direction.

4. Defining an origin by rotating the current UCS around one of its axes.

The UCS command is invoked from the Screen Menu Settings or at the "Command:" prompt type in **UCS** and press ⏎.

Command: **ucs**
Origin/ZAxis/3point/Entity/View/X/Y/Z/Pre/Restore/Save/Del/?/<World>:

Origin Option This option defines a new UCS by shifting the origin of the current UCS, leaving the directions of X,Y, and Z axes unchanged. When you select this option, AutoCAD prompts:

Origin point (0,0,0):

Specify a new origin point relative to the origin of the current UCS, as shown in Figure 12-14.

ZAxis Option This option allows you to define an origin by giving a data point and the direction for the Z Axis. AutoCAD arbitrarily, but consistently, sets the direction of the X and Y axes in relation to the given Z Axis. When you select this option, AutoCAD prompts:

Origin point (0,0,0):
Point on positive portion of the Z axis <default>:

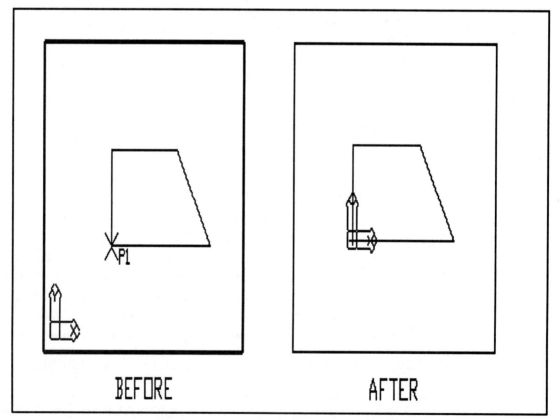

Figure 12-14 Specifying a New Origin Point Relative to the Origin of the Current UCS

Specify a data point and the direction for the positive Z Axis. If you give a null response to the second prompt, the Z Axis of the new coordinate system will be parallel to the previous one. This is similar to using the Origin option.

3point Option The 3point option is the easiest and most often used option for controlling the orientation of the UCS. This option allows the user to select three points to define the origin and the directions of the positive X and Y axes. The origin point acts as a base for the UCS rotation, and when a point is selected to define the direction of the positive X Axis, the direction of the Y Axis is limited because it is always perpendicular to the X Axis. When the X and Y axes are defined, the Z Axis is automatically placed perpendicular to the XY plane. When you select this option, AutoCAD prompts:

> Origin point (0,0,0):
> Point on positive portion of the X axis <default>:
> Point on positive-Y portion of the UCS X-Y plane <default>:

Specify a data point and the direction for positive X and Y axes, as shown in Figure 12-15. The points must not form a straight line. If you give a null response to the first prompt, the new UCS will have the same origin as the previous UCS. If you give a null response to the second or third prompt, then that Axis direction will be parallel to the corresponding Axis in the previous UCS.

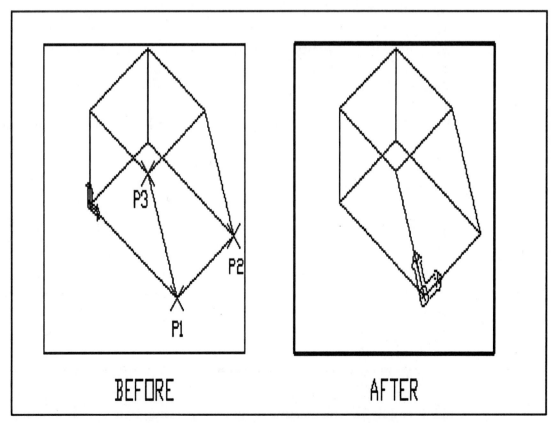

Figure 12–15 Specifying a Data Point and Direction for Positive X and Y Axes when Using the 3Point Option

Table 12-2 Locations of the Origin and Its X Axis for Different Types of Entities

Entity	Method of UCS Determination
Line	The nearest endpoint of the pick point becomes the new UCS origin. The new X Axis is chosen so that the line lies in the XZ plane of the new UCS.
Circle	The circle's center becomes the new UCS origin, and the X Axis passing through the pick point.
Arc	The arc's center becomes the new UCS origin, and the X Axis passes through the endpoint of the arc closest to the pick point.
2D Polyline	The Polyline's start point becomes the new UCS origin, with the X Axis extending from the start point to the next vertex.
Solid	The first point of the solid determines the new UCS origin, and the X Axis lies along the line between the first two points.
Dimension	The new UCS origin is the middle point of the dimension text and the direction of the X Axis is parallel to the X Axis of the UCS in effect when the dimension was drawn.

Entity Option This option lets you define a new coordinate system by pointing to an entity. The actual orientation of the UCS depends on how the entity was created. When the entity is selected, the UCS origin is placed at the first point used to create the entity (in the case of a line, it will be the closest endpoint; for a circle, it will be the center point of the circle); the X Axis is determined by the direction from the origin to the second point used to define the entity. And the Z-Axis direction is placed perpendicular to the XY plane in which the entity sits. Table 12-2 lists locations of the origin and its X Axis for different types of entities.

When you select this option, AutoCAD prompts:

    Select object:

Identify an entity to define a new coordinate system, as shown in Figure 12-16.

View Option This option places the XY plane parallel to the screen, and makes the Z Axis perpendicular. The UCS origin remains unchanged. This method is used mainly for labeling text, which you want to be aligned with the screen rather than with entities.

X/Y/Z Rotation Option The X/Y/Z rotation option lets you define a new coordinate system by rotating the X, Y, and Z axes independently of each other. You can show AutoCAD the desired angle by picking two points or you can enter the rotation angle from the keyboard. In either case, the new angle is specified relative to the X Axis of the current UCS. See Figures 12-17, 12-18, and 12-19 for examples in rotating the UCS around X, Y, and Z axes, respectively.

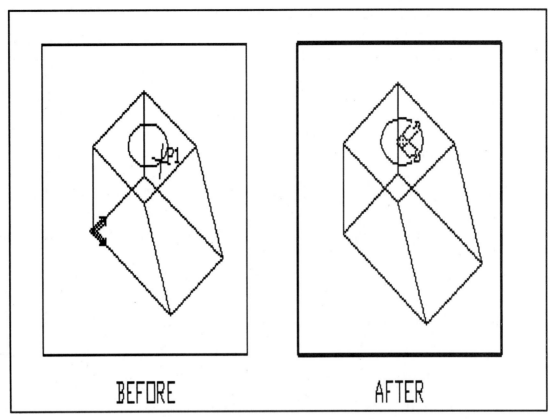

Figure 12-16 Defining a New Coordinate System

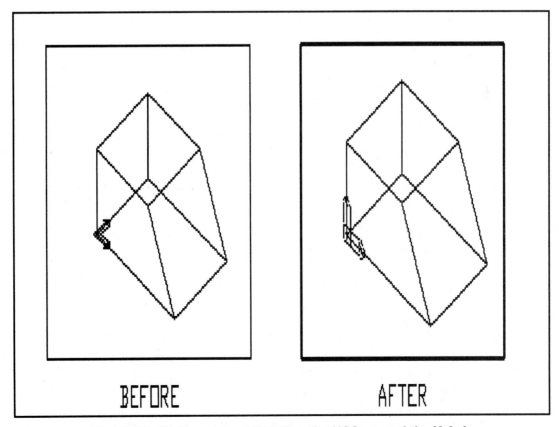

Figure 12-17 Example of Rotating the UCS around the X Axis

AutoCAD 3D

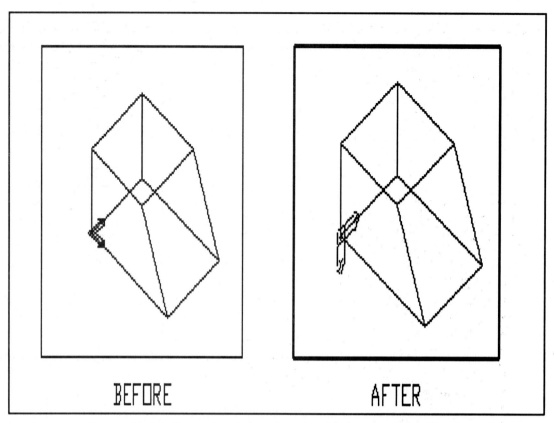

BEFORE   AFTER

Figure 12-18 Example of Rotating the UCS around the Y Axis

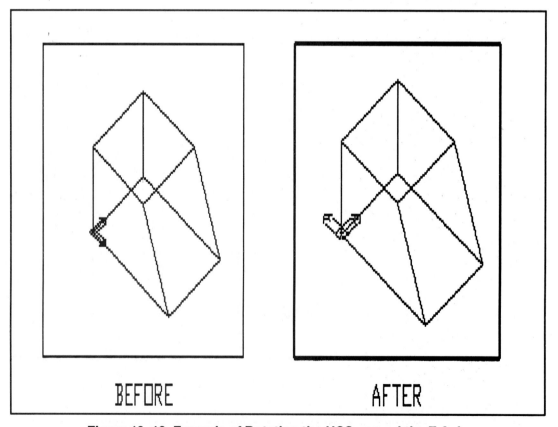

BEFORE   AFTER

Figure 12-19 Example of Rotating the UCS around the Z Axis

Previous Option This option is similar to the Previous option of the ZOOM command. AutoCAD saves the last ten coordinate systems in both Model and Paper Space. You can step back through them by using repeated Previous options.

Restore Option This option allows you to restore any previously saved UCS.

Save Option This option allows you to save the current UCS under a user-defined name.

Delete Option This option allows you to delete any saved UCS.

? Option This option lists the name of the UCS you specify, origin, and XYZ axes for each saved coordinate system, relative to the current UCS. To list all the UCS names, accept the default, or you can specify wild cards.

World Option This option returns you to the WCS.

UCS Dialogue Box

You can also define a UCS by selecting the UCS Control command from the Settings menu of the Pull-down menu. This will give you a dialogue box called UCS Control, as shown in Figure 12-20.

The dialogue box displays a list of the coordinate systems defined. The *WORLD* coordinate system is always the first entry in the list. A checkmark appears in the

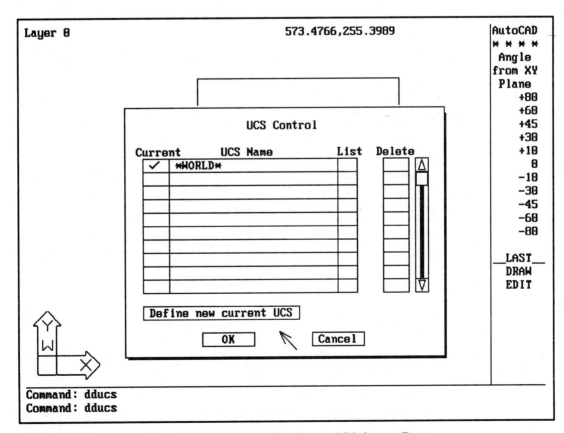

Figure 12-20 The UCS Control Dialogue Box

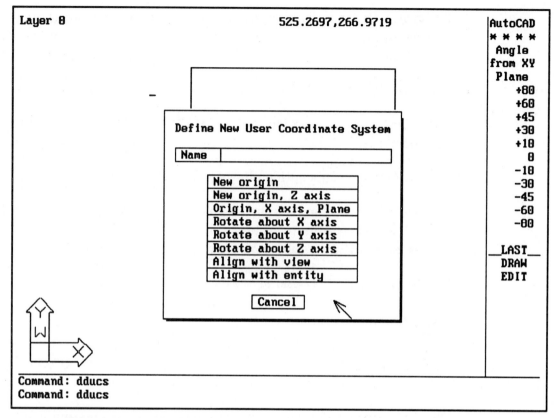

Figure 12-21 The Define New User Coordinate System Dialogue Box

Current column for the coordinate system currently in effect. You can make a different coordinate system current by placing a checkmark in its Current column. You can also name or rename a UCS by entering the new name in the coordinate system's UCS Name input command line. If necessary, you can delete a UCS by placing a checkmark in the Delete button next to its entry in the list.

Selecting the "Define new current UCS" button activates another dialogue box, as shown in Figure 12-21, that lets you define a new UCS. If you want to give a name to the new coordinate system, enter the name in the Name input button command line. Then select a method for defining a new UCS. It is easy to equate each of the options that are listed in the dialogue box for defining the new coordinate system with the options explained earlier, except one. The option Origin, X axis, Plane is the same as the 3point option.

PLAN Command

The PLAN command provides a convenient means of viewing the drawing from plan view. The definition of plan means that you are sitting at positive Z and looking down on X to the right and Y pointing up. You can select the plan view of the current UCS, a previously saved UCS, or the WCS. The PLAN command is invoked from the Screen Menu Settings, or at the "Command:" prompt type in **PLAN** and press ⏎.

Command: **plan**
<Current UCS>/Ucs/World:

Current UCS Option This option displays the plan view of the current UCS. This is the default option.

Ucs Option This option displays a plan view of a previously saved UCS. When you select this option, AutoCAD will prompt for a name of the UCS.

World Option This option displays the plan view of WCS.

2D DRAW Commands in 3D Space

You can use most of the DRAW commands discussed in previous chapters with a Z coordinate value. But 2D entities such as Polylines, circles, arcs, and solids are constrained to the X,Y plane of the current UCS. For these entities, the Z value is accepted only for the first coordinate to set the elevation of the 2D entity above or below the current plane. When you pick a point using an OSNAP mode, it assumes the Z value of the point to which you snapped.

Elevation and Thickness

You can create new entities by first setting up a default elevation or Z value. Subsequently, all the entities drawn will assume the current elevation as the Z value whenever a 3D point is expected but you supply only X and Y value. The current elevation is maintained separately in Model Space and Paper Space.

Similarly you can create new entities with extrusion thickness by presetting a value for the thickness. Subsequently, all the entities drawn such as lines, Polylines, arcs, circles, and solids will assume the current thickness and extrude in their Z direction. For example, you can draw a cylinder by drawing a circle with preset thickness, or to draw a cube, simply draw a square with preset thickness.

> **NOTE:** Thickness can be positive or negative. Thickness is in the direction of the Z Axis of 2D entities. For 3D entities that can accept thickness, it is always relative to the current UCS. They will appear oblique if they do not lie in or parallel to the current UCS. If thickness is added to a line drawn directly in the Z direction, it will appear that the line extends beyond its endpoint in the positive or negative thickness direction. Text and dimensions ignore the thickness setting.

The elevation and thickness can be set by ELEV command. The ELEV command is invoked from the Screen Menu Settings or at the "Command:" prompt type in **ELEV** and press ⏎.

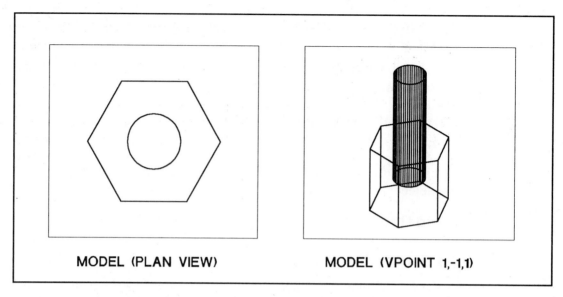

MODEL (PLAN VIEW)   MODEL (VPOINT 1,-1,1)

Figure 12-22 Specifying a New Current Elevation and Thickness

Command: **elev**
New current elevation <current>:
New current thickness <current>:

Specify the new current elevation and thickness. For example, the following are the command sequences to draw a six-sided polygon at zero elevation with a radius of 2.5 units and a height of 4.5 units and place a cylinder at the center of the polygon with a radius of 1.0 unit at an elevation of 2.0 units with a height of 7.5 units, as shown in Figure 12-22.

Command: **elev**
New current elevation <0.0000>: ⏎
New current thickness <0.0000>: **4.5**
Command: **polygon** *draw a polygon with a radius of 2.5 units*
Command: **elev**
New current elevation <0.0000>: **2.0**
New current thickness <0.0000>: **7.5**
Command: **circle** *draw a circle with a radius 1.0 unit*

You can change the thickness of the existing entities using the CHANGE or CHPROP commands.

You can change the elevation of the existing entities including text by the regular MOVE command. In AutoCAD Release 10, you can do the same by the CHANGE command Elevation option.

2D Edit Commands in 3D Space

The editing commands that you used from earlier chapters can also be used in 3D drawing. The MOVE and COPY commands accept 3D points or displacements.

The ROTATE command will rotate objects about a Z Axis in the current UCS. You can always change the UCS to rotate objects to any orientation in space. The STRETCH command can be used on 3D entities such as lines and cylinders and can be stretched from and to any point in 3D space regardless of current UCS. BREAK, TRIM, EXTEND, OFFSET, FILLET, and CHAMFER commands will work properly when the entities that have to be edited are parallel to the current UCS. The easiest way to use them is to use the UCS Entity option to set your UCS parallel to the entities you want to edit. In the case of the HATCH command, it is better to have UCS on the surface to be hatched and draw new boundary edges in which to hatch.

3D ELEMENTS

A limited number of 3D primitive commands are available specifically for 3D drawing. The commands include 3DPOLY, 3DFACE, and 3DMESH. In addition, AutoCAD provides a series of AutoLISP routines that automatically create geometric objects like spheres, cones, etc.

3DPOLY Command

The 3DPOLY command draws Polylines with independent X,Y, and Z Axis coordinates. The 3DPOLY command works similar to the PLINE command with a few exceptions. Unlike the PLINE command, 3DPOLY draws only straight line segments without variable width. Editing a 3D Polyline with the PEDIT command is similar to 2D Polyline, except for some options. 3D Polylines cannot be joined, curve fit with arc segments, or given a width or tangent.

3DFACE Command

When you create a 3D model, it is often necessary to have solid surfaces for hiding and shading. These surfaces are created with the 3DFACE command.

The 3DFACE command creates a solid surface and the command sequence is similar to the SOLID command. Unlike the SOLID command, you can give differing Z coordinates for the corner points of a face, forming a section of a plane in space. Unlike the SOLID command, a 3DFACE is drawn from corner to corner clockwise or counterclockwise around the object (and it does not draw a "bow tie"). A 3D face is a plane defined by either three or four points used to represent a surface. It provides a means of controlling which edges of a 3D face will be visible. You can describe complex, 3D polygons using multiple 3D faces and you can tell AutoCAD which edges you want to be drawn. If you have an object with curved surfaces, then the 3DFACE command is not suitable. One of the mesh commands will be more appropriate, as explained later in the chapter.

The 3DFACE command is invoked from the Screen Menu Settings or at the "Command:" prompt type in **3DFACE** and press ↵.

Command: **3dface**
First point:

Specify the first point, and AutoCAD will prompt you for the second, third, and fourth points in sequence. Then AutoCAD will close the face from the fourth point to the first point and prompt for the third point. If you give a null response to the third point, AutoCAD will close the 3Dface with three sides and then terminate the command and will take you to the "Command:" prompt.

If you want to draw additional faces in one command sequence, the last two points of the first face will become the first two points for the second face. And the last two points of the second face will become first two points of the third face and so on. You have to be very careful in drawing several faces in one command sequence since AutoCAD does not have an Undo option that works inside the 3DFACE command. A single mistake can cause the entire face to be redrawn. For this reason, it is a good idea to draw 3D faces one at a time.

For example, the following command sequence shows placement of 3D faces, as shown in Figure 12-23.

Command:**3dface**
First point: *select point A1*
Second point: *select point A2*
Third point: *select point A3*
Fourth point: *select point A4*
Third point: *select point A5*
Fourth point: *select point A6*
Third point: *select point A7*
Fourth point: *select point A8*
Third point: *select point A1*
Fourth point: *select point A2*
Third point: ⏎

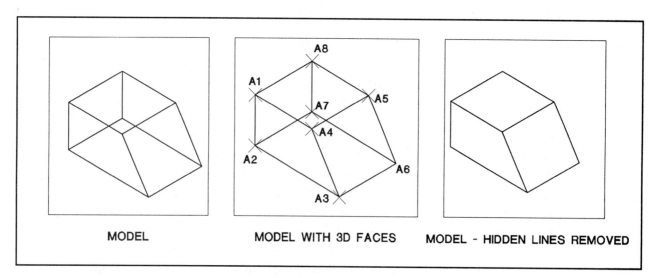

MODEL   MODEL WITH 3D FACES   MODEL - HIDDEN LINES REMOVED

Figure 12-23 Placing 3D Faces

The surface created, as shown in Figure 12-23, required four faces to cover it. Some of the faces are overlapping and this is not acceptable when viewing the object. The 3DFACE command allows face edges to be "invisible." To create an invisible edge, the letter **I** must be entered at the prompt for the first point of the edge to be invisible, and then the point can be entered.

The following command sequence shows placement of 3Dfaces for invisible edges, as shown in Figure 12-23.

> Command: **3dface**
> First point: *select point A1*
> Second point: *select point A8*
> Third point: *select point A5*
> Fourth point: *select point A4*
> Third point: *select point A3*
> Fourth point: *select point A6*
> Third point: *select point A7*
> Fourth point: i ⏎ *select point A8*
> Third point: *select point A1*
> Fourth point: *select point A2*
> Third point: *select point A3*
> Fourth point: *select point A4*
> Third point: ⏎

3DFACE commands ignore the thickness. The SPLFRAME system variable controls the display of invisible edges in 3D faces. If SPLFRAME is set to a nonzero value, all invisible edges of 3D faces are displayed.

3DFACE Editing The AutoCAD program does not supply a method of editing the endpoints of a 3D face directly. However, the CHFACE.LSP AutoLISP routine allows endpoints to be relocated. (The CHFACE.LSP file will be in your AutoCAD bonus diskette that comes with the program.)

3D POLYGON MESHES

A 3D mesh is a single entity. It defines a flat surface or approximates a curved one by placing multiple 3D faces on the surface of an object. It is a series of lines consisting of columns and rows. AutoCAD lets you determine the spacing between rows (M) and columns (N).

It is possible to create a mesh to a flat or curved surface by locating the boundaries or edges of the surface. Surfaces created in this fashion are called geometry-generated surfaces. Their size and shape depend on the boundaries used to define them, and the specific formula (or command) used to determine the location of the vertices between the boundaries. AutoCAD provides four different commands to create geometry-generated surfaces, which include RULESURF, REVSURF,

TABSURF, and EDGESURF. The differences between these types of meshes depend on the types of objects connecting the surfaces. In addition, AutoCAD provides two additional commands to create polygon mesh—3DMESH and PFACE commands. The key to using meshes effectively is to understand the purpose and requirement of each type of mesh and select the appropriate one for the given condition.

3DMESH Command

You can define a 3D polygon mesh by the 3DMESH command. Initially, it prompts you for the number of rows and columns in terms of Mesh M and Mesh N, respectively. Then it prompts you for the location of each vertex in the mesh. The product of M times N gives the number of vertices for the mesh.

The 3DMESH command is invoked from the Screen Menu Settings or at the "Command:" prompt type in **3DMESH** and press ⏎.

    Command: **3dmesh**
    Mesh M Size:
    Mesh N Size:

Specify an integer value between 2 and 256 for each dimension of the mesh. The points for each vertex must be entered separately, and the M value can be considered the number of lines that will be connected by faces, while the N value is the number of points each line consists of. Vertices may be specified as 2D or 3D points, and may be any distance from each other.

The following command sequence creates a simple 5 × 4 polygon mesh. The mesh is created between the first point of the first line, the first point of the second line, and so on, as shown in Figure 12-24.

    Command: **3dmesh**
    Mesh M Size: **5**
    Mesh N Size: **4**
    Vertex (0,0): *select point A1*
    Vertex (0,1): *select point A2*
    Vertex (0,2): *select point A3*
    Vertex (0,3): *select point A4*
    Vertex (1,0): *select point B1*
    Vertex (1,1): *select point B2*
    Vertex (1,2): *select point B3*
    Vertex (1,3): *select point B4*
    Vertex (2,0): *select point C1*
    Vertex (2,1): *select point C2*
    Vertex (2,2): *select point C3*
    Vertex (2,3): *select point C4*
    Vertex (3,0): *select point D1*
    Vertex (3,1): *select point D2*

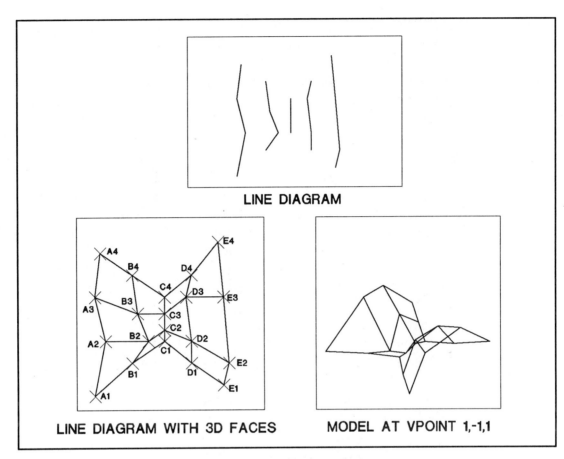

Figure 12-24 Creating a 3D Mesh

Vertex (3,2): *select point D3*
Vertex (3,3): *select point D4*
Vertex (4,0): *select point E1*
Vertex (4,1): *select point E2*
Vertex (4,2): *select point E3*
Vertex (4,3): *select point E4*

> **NOTE:** Specifying 3D mesh of any size can be time-consuming and tedious. It is preferable to use one of the geometry-generated surfaces such as the RULESURF, TABSURF, REVSURF, and EDGESURF commands. The 3DMESH command is primarily designed for AutoLISP and ADS applications.

PFACE Command

The PFACE command allows you to construct a mesh of any topology you desire. This command is similar to the 3DFACE command and creates surfaces with invisible interior divisions. You can specify any number of vertices and 3D faces, unlike other meshes. Producing this kind of mesh lets you conveniently avoid creating many unrelated 3D faces with the same vertices.

AutoCAD first prompts you to pick all the vertex points and then you create your faces by entering the vertex numbers that define their edges.

The PFACE command is invoked from the Screen Menu Settings or at the "Command:" prompt type in **PFACE** and press ⏎.

    Command: **pface**
    Vertex 1:

Specify all the vertices one after another used in the mesh, keeping track of the vertex numbers shown in the prompts. You can specify the vertices as 2D or 3D points and place them at any distance from one another. Enter a null response (press ⏎) after specifying all the vertices, then AutoCAD prompts for a vertex number that has to be assigned to each face. You can define any number of vertices for each face, and enter a null response (press ⏎). Then AutoCAD prompts for the next face. After all the vertex numbers for all the faces are defined, enter a null reponse (press ⏎), and AutoCAD draws the mesh.

The following command sequence creates a simple polyface to a given six-sided polygon with a circle of 1" radius drawn at the center of the polygon at a depth of −2, as shown in Figure 12–25.

    Command: **pface**
    Vertex 1: *select point A1*
    Vertex 2: *select point A2*
    Vertex 3: *select point A3*
    Vertex 4: *select point A4*
    Vertex 5: *select point A5*
    Vertex 6: *select point A6*
    Vertex 7: ⏎
    Face 1 Vertex 1: *type **1** and press* ⏎
    Face 1 Vertex 2: *type **2** and press* ⏎
    Face 1 Vertex 3: *type **1** and press* ⏎
    Face 1 Vertex 4: *type **2** and press* ⏎
    Face 1 Vertex 5: *type **1** and press* ⏎
    Face 1 Vertex 6: *type **2** and press* ⏎
    Face 1 Vertex 7: ⏎
    Face 2 Vertex 1: ⏎

If necessary, you can make an edge of the polyface mesh invisible by entering a negative number for the beginning vertex of the edge. By default, the faces will be drawn on the current layer and color. However, you can create the faces in layers and colors different from the original entity. You can assign a layer or color by responding to the prompt:

    Face n, Vertex n:

with L for layer or c for color. Then AutoCAD prompts for the name of the layer or color appropriately. It will continue with the prompts for vertex numbers. The

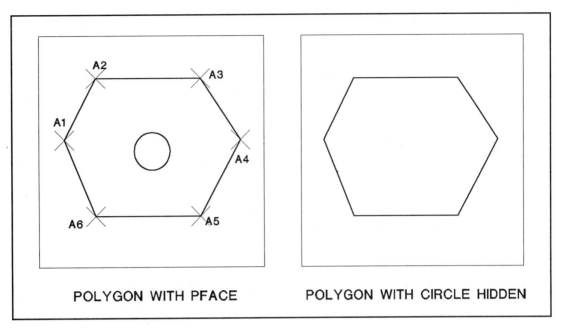

Figure 12-25 Creating a Polyface to a Given Six-Sided Polygon with a Circle at the Center

layer or color you enter will be used for the face you are currently defining and for any subsequent faces created.

> ***NOTE:*** Specifying the layer or color within the PFACE command does not change entity properties for subsequent commands. Specifying PFACE of any size can be time-consuming and tedious. It is preferable to use one of the geometry-generated surfaces such as the RULESURF, TABSURF, REVSURF, and EDGESURF commands. The PFACE command is primarily designed for AutoLISP and ADS applications.

RULESURF Command

The RULESURF command creates a polygon mesh between two entities. The two entities can be lines, points, arcs, circles, 2D Polylines, or 3D Polylines. If one entity is open, such as a line or arc, the other must also be open, too. If one is closed, such as circle, so must the other be. A point can be used as one entity, regardless of whether the other is open or closed. But, only one of the entities can be a point.

RULESURF creates an M by N mesh, the value of Mesh M is 2, which is constant. The value of Mesh N can be changed depending on the requirement of the number of faces. This can be done with the help of the system variable SURFTAB1. By default, the SURFTAB1 is set to 6.

The following command sequence shows how to change the value of the SURFTAB1 from 6 to 20:

Command: **surftab1**
New value for SURFTAB1 <6>: **20**

The RULESURF command is invoked from the Screen Menu Settings or at the "Command:" prompt type in **RULESURF** and press ⏎.

Command: **rulesurf**
Select first defining curve:
Select the second defining curve:

Identify the two entities to which a mesh has to be created. See Figure 12-26 in which an arc (A1-A2) and line (A3-A4) were identified and a mesh was created with SURFTAB1 set to 15. Two lines (B1-B2 and B3-B4) were identified and a mesh was created with SURFTAB1 set to 20. A cone was created by drawing a circle at an elevation of 0 and a point (C1) at an elevation of 5, followed by the application of RULESURF with a SURFTAB1 set to 20.

NOTE: When you identify the two entities, make sure to select on the same side of the entities, left or right. If you pick the left side of one of the sides and the right side of the other, you would get a bow-tie effect.

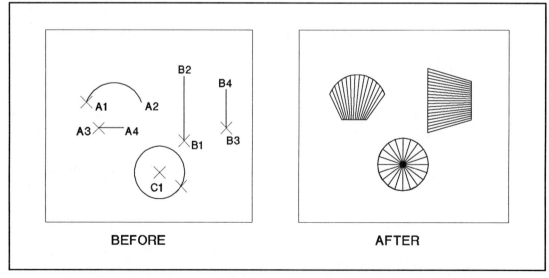

Figure 12-26 Creating a Mesh and a Cone by Identifying Two Entities

TABSURF Command

The TABSURF command creates a surface extrusion from an entity with a length and direction determined by the direction vector. The entity is called the defining curve and can be a line, arc, circle, 2D Polyline, or 3D Polyline. The direction vector can be a line or open Polyline. The endpoint of the direction vector nearest the point picked will be swept along the path curve, describing the surface. Once the mesh is created, the direction vector can be deleted. The number of intervals along the path curve is controlled by the system variable SURFTAB1, similar to the RULESURF command. By default, the SURFTAB1 is set to 6.

The TABSURF command is invoked from the Screen Menu Settings or at the "Command:" prompt type in **TABSURF** and press ⏎.

> Command: **tabsurf**
> Select path curve:
> Selection direction vector:

Identify the path curve and then the direction vector. The location at which the direction vector is selected determines the direction of the constructed mesh. The mesh will be created in the direction from the selection point to the nearest endpoint of the direction vector. In Figure 12-27, a mesh was created with SURFTAB1 set to 16 by identifying a Polyline as the path curve and the line as the direction vector.

> **NOTE:** The length of the 3D mesh will be the same as the direction vector.

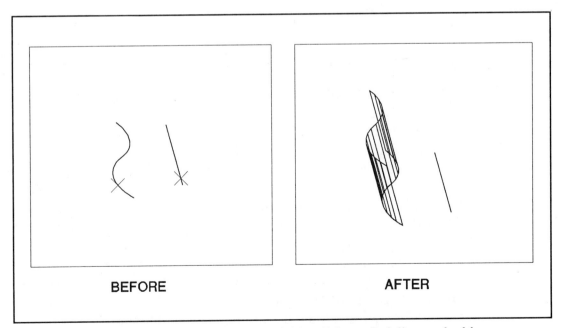

BEFORE   AFTER

Figure 12-27 Creating a Mesh by Identifying a Polyline and a Line

REVSURF Command

The REVSURF command is used to create a 3D mesh that follows the path defined by a path curve and is rotated around a center line. The entity used to define the path curve may be an arc, circle, line, 2D Polyline, or 3D Polyline. Complex shapes consisting of lines, arcs, or Polylines can be joined into one entity using the PEDIT command and then you can create a single rotated mesh instead of several individual meshes.

The center line can be a line or Polyline that defines the Axis around which the faces will be constructed. The center line can be of any length and at any orientation. If necessary, you can erase the center line after the construction of the mesh. So, it is recommended that you make the axis longer then the path curve so it is easy to erase after the rotation.

In the case of REVSURF, both the Mesh M size as well as Mesh N are controlled by system variables SURFTAB1 and SURFTAB2, respectively. The SURFTAB1 value determines how many faces will be placed around the rotation Axis and can be an integer value between 3 and 1024. The SURFTAB2 determines how many faces will be used to simulate the curves created by arcs or circles in the path curve. By default, SURFTAB1 and SURFTAB2 are set to 6.

The following command sequence shows how to change the value of the SURFTAB1 from 6 to 20 and SURFTAB2 from 6 to 15:

```
Command: surftab1
New value for SURFTAB1 <6>: 20

Command: surftab2
New value for SURFTAB1 <6>: 15
```

The REVSURF command is invoked from the Screen Menu Settings or at the "Command:" prompt type in **REVSURF** and press ⏎.

```
Command: revsurf
Select path curve:
Select axis of revolution:
Start angle <0>:
Included angle (+=ccw,-=cw) <Full circle>:
```

Identify the path curve and then the center line for the Axis of revolution. For the "Start Angle:" prompt, it does not matter if you are going to rotate the curve 360 degrees (full circle). If you want to rotate the curve only at a certain angle, then provide the start angle in reference to three o'clock (default) and then indicate the angle of rotation in clockwise (positive) and counterclockwise (negative). See Figure 12-28 in which a mesh was created with SURFTAB1 set to 16 and SURFTAB2 set to 12, by identifying a closed Polyline as the path curve and the vertical line as the axis of revolution, and then rotated 360 degrees.

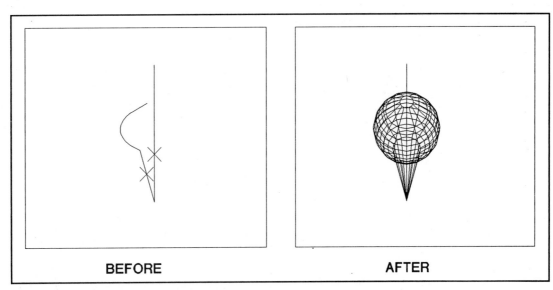

Figure 12-28 Creating a Mesh by Identifying a Closed Polyline and a Vertical Line as Axis of Revolution

EDGESURF Command

The EDGESURF command allows a mesh to be created with four adjoining sides defining its boundaries. The only requirement for EDGESURF is that it have exactly four sides. The sides can be lines, arcs, or any combination of Polylines and Polyarcs. Each side must join the adjacent one to create a closed boundary.

In EDGESURF, both the Mesh M size as well as Mesh N can be controlled by system variables SURFTAB1 and SURFTAB2, respectively, just as in REVSURF.

The EDGESURF command is invoked from the Screen Menu Settings or at the "Command:" prompt type in **EDGESURF** and press ⏎.

> Command: **edgesurf**
> Select edge 1:
> Select edge 2:
> Select edge 3:
> Select edge 4:

Identify all the four sides in a sequential order. When picking four sides, you must be consistent in picking the beginning of each polyline group. If you pick the beginning of one side and the end of another, the final mesh will cross and look strange. See Figure 12-29 in which a mesh was created with SURFTAB1 set to 25 and SURFTAB2 set to 20 by identifying four sides.

Editing Polymesh Surfaces

Like blocks, plines, hatch, and dimensioning, you can also explode a mesh. When you explode a mesh it separates into individual 3D faces. Meshes can also be altered by the PEDIT command similar to editing Polylines using the PEDIT

AutoCAD 3D

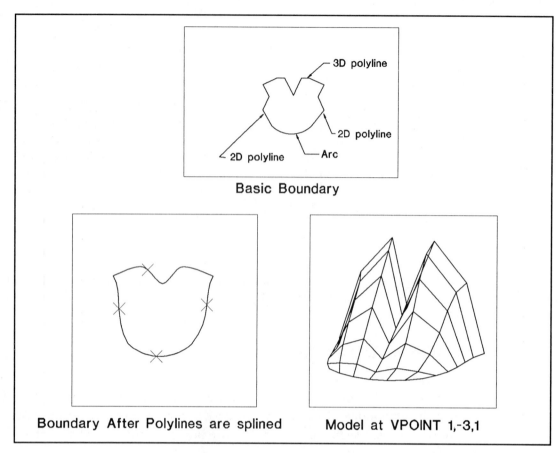

Basic Boundary

Boundary After Polylines are splined   **Model at VPOINT 1,-3,1**

Figure 12-29 Creating a Mesh by Identifying Four Sides

command. Most of the options under the PEDIT command can be applied to meshes, except giving width to the edges of the polymesh. For a detailed explanation of the PEDIT command, refer to Chapter 6.

HIDE Command

The HIDE command hides entities or displays in different colors that are behind other entities in the current viewport. Complex models are difficult to read in wire-frame form, and benefit in clarity when the model is displayed with hidden lines removed. HIDE considers circles, solids, traces, wide Polyline segments, 3D faces, polygon meshes, and the extruded edges of entities with a thickness to be opaque surfaces hiding objects that lie behind them. The HIDE command remains active only until the next time the display is regenerated. Depending on the complexity of the model, hiding may take from a few seconds to even several hours. Remember, the model must have solid surfaces before HIDE will work.

The HIDE command is invoked from the Screen Root Menu Display or at the "Command:" prompt type in **HIDE** and press ⏎.

Command: **hide**

There are no prompts to be answered. The current viewport goes blank for a period of time, depending on the complexity of the model, and is then redrawn with hidden lines removed temporarily. If necessary, you can instruct the HIDE command to display hidden lines on a separate layer with a different color rather than make them invisible. To do this, create layers with names identical to those of the existing layers in your current drawing, but with the prefix HIDDEN added. For example, if your drawing has layers OBJECT and PLAN, create new layers named HIDDENOBJECT and HIDDENPLAN. The HIDE command places all lines normally hidden on this new layer. You can control the visibility of the hidden layers by turning them ON and OFF.

Hidden line removal is lost during plotting unless you specify that AutoCAD remove hidden lines in the plotting configuration.

PLACEMENT OF MULTIVIEWS ON PAPER SPACE

When you create a 3D model, you can use the powerful capabilities of viewports to display the model from different viewpoints in each viewport and see the model take shape as you draw. Constructing a model is easier when displaying the model in various viewports and you can switch from one port to another while drawing and editing the objects.

The viewports are created by the VPORTS command when TILEMODE is 1 and with the MVIEW command when TILEMODE is 0. For a detailed explanation of creating viewports, refer to Chapter 7. It is recommended that you create four viewports and display the model in accordance with the third-angle projection and isometric view of the model. Third-angle projection requires that the view of the top of the object be placed above the view of the front of the object, and the view of the right side of the object be placed to the right of the front view. First-angle projection is more common in Europe, in which the top view is placed below the front view and the right side is placed on the left.

It is recommended that you create the necessary viewports and display the model from a different viewpoint in each viewport before you start drawing the model. The following are the steps in creating the viewports with appropriate limits for Model Space and Paper Space and setting up the viewpoints when TILEMODE is set to 0.

1. Set LIMITS in Paper Space equal to the plotter's maximum available plot area for the given sheet size.

2. Create a title block, or if you already have one, attach it as an XREF.

3. Create four viewports using the MVIEW command.

4. Enter Model Space and set the appropriate limits for the model to be drawn.

5. Make the top right viewport active and set the viewpoint to 1,-1,1 using the VPOINT command.

6. Make the top left viewport active and make sure it is set to 0,0,0 display.

7. Make the bottom left viewport active and set the viewpoint to 0,-1,0 using the VPOINT command, so that it will display the front view of the model.

8. Make the bottom right viewport active and set the viewpoint to 1,0,0 using the VPOINT command, so that it will display the right side view of the model.

9. Create the model by making the appropriate viewport active.

10. Enter Paper Space. Add any annotations or dimensions while in Paper Space. Fill in your title block information.

11. Plot or printer plot at a scale of 1:1.

LINING UP ORTHOGRAPHIC VIEWS

Standard drafting practice calls for main orthographic views and auxiliary views to be lined up. It does not matter which projection system is used, the main orthographic views and auxiliary views must be lined up precisely. All the views must be displayed with the same scale (or magnification), and corresponding features between views must line up along the same horizontal or vertical line for orthographic views, or along the same angular line for auxiliary views. This can be done using the ZOOM Center command and the XP option in Model Space. It works on the principle that if two viewports are the same size and are lined up, then the centers of these viewports are lined up. In Model Space, if the two different views in those viewports are centered around the same point and are the same scale in relation to Paper Space, then those views are lined up.

CHAPTER
13 Solid Modeling

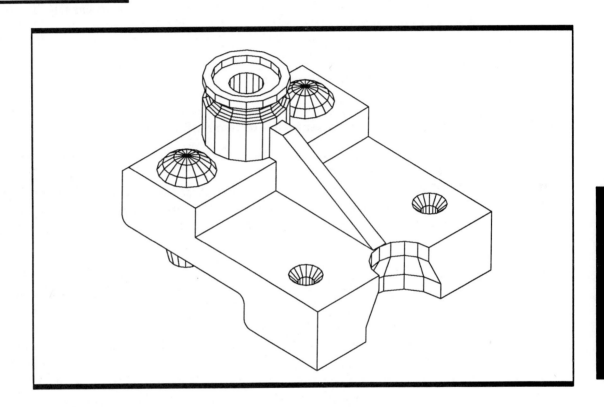

With the integration of Advanced Modeling Extension (AME) and AutoCAD, you can now combine solid and nonsolid geometries within the same file and use familiar AutoCAD commands to manipulate both.

WHAT IS SOLID MODELING?

A solid model is the unambiguous and informationally complete representation of the shape of a physical object. Fundamentally, solid modeling differs from wire-frame or surface modeling in two ways:

1. The information is more complete in the solid model.
2. The method of construction of the model itself is inherently straightforward.

In wire-frame or surface modeling (explained in Chapter 12) objects are created by positioning lines or surfaces in 3D space. In solid modeling you build the model as you would with building blocks. In solid modeling from beginning to the end, you think, draw, and communicate in 3D. One of the main benefits of solid modeling is its ability to be analyzed. You can calculate the mass properties of a solid object, such as its mass, center of gravity, surface area, moments of inertia, etc.

When 2D drawings are needed, you can always generate them from a solid model. Several commands let you extract 2D geometric shapes from the 3D solid model. For example, you can copy a face or generate a cross section of the model. The commands that are provided with AME make it easy to create 2D engineering drawings from a 3D solid model.

Structure of Solid Models

There are several different popular representations used in solid modeling. We can categorize the representation in two main categories:

1. Boundary Representation: Boundary Representation (B-Rep) model repre-sents the solid model in terms of its boundaries, including information regarding the nature of space on both inside and outside boundaries. A B-Rep model stores the mathematical data of the surface geometry on which the faces lie, the curve geometry on which edges lie, and the point coordinates of the vertices.

2. Constructive Solid Geometry (CSG): The Constructive Solid Geometry refers to the process of constructing complex solid objects from simpler ones. In CSG modeling the object is built from simple primitives such as Blocks, cylinders, cones, etc. into a complex model by Boolean operations. Thus, the solids have a CSG tree associated with them that keeps a record of the primitives and Boolean operations that were used to build them. You never see the CSG tree on the screen, but it is essential to understand the concept, because the sequence in which you apply the Boolean commands affects the structure of the tree.

AME is considered a hybrid modeler in the sense that it uses CSG techniques of modeling and stores boundary information as well.

AME and AMELite

The solid modeling commands can be divided into two groups:

1. The commands that come with Advanced Modeling Extension (AME) Version 1.0, available as an optional extension to AutoCAD Release 11. Formerly known as AutoSolid, AME is now fully integrated with AutoCAD.

2. The commands that come with AMELite, which are a subset of solids capa-bilities, that are provided free of charge to all registered AutoCAD Release 11 users. AMELite provides tools to create and render primitives only. Boolean operations are not supported by AMELite. Solids created by the full-blown

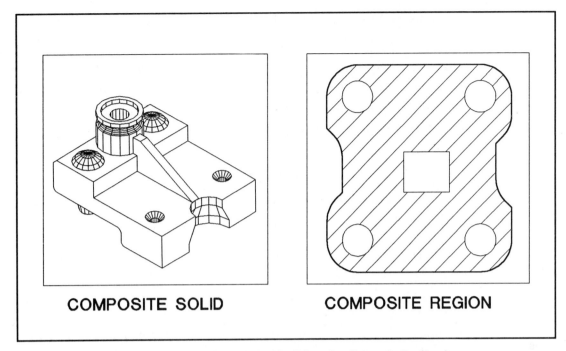

COMPOSITE SOLID   COMPOSITE REGION

Figure 13-1 A Composite Solid and a Composite Region

AME can be viewed, rendered, or plotted with AMELite. Users without AME can build most of a model's solid primitives, then hand the file over to an AME user to perform the Boolean operations and any required analysis.

AME Version 2.0

The AME Version 2.0 is available as an extension to Version 1.0. It is both a solid modeling and a region modeling package. Similar to Version 1.0, it lets you create a solid model—a 3D object. In addition, it lets you create a region—a closed, 2D area that can contain "holes." See Figure 13-1 for an example of a composite solid and a composite region.

You can create and edit regions as you do solids, except that they are two-dimensional. Both modelers use a building-block approach to constructing a solid or a region. You can join regions together to form a new composite region as you do in the case of solids. Similarly, you can also subtract and find the intersection in the case of regions. You can define a region's physical and material properties similar to solids. This allows you to analyze the object(s).

> **NOTE:** In some of the AME commands you can select both solids and regions, but solids are acted upon separately from regions, for instance, solids join with solids (union), and regions to regions, but never solids to regions, or vice versa.

Loading AME and AMELite

AME (Versions 1.0 and 2.0) and AMELite can be loaded manually or automatically. To load manually, invoke the Screen Root Menu Solids and select AME, from the pull-down menu Solids select AME, or at the "Command:" prompt type **(xload "ame")** and press ⏎.

Command: **("xload ame")**

NOTE: Use of the parentheses.

The same procedure can be followed for AMELite.

To automatically load AME or AMELite, include the following line in your ACAD.LSP or ACAD.ADS file:

(xload "ame") or **(xload "amelite")**

Whenever you start a new drawing, AME or AMELite is loaded automatically.

AME Menus

The AME commands can be entered at the keyboard, selecting from the AutoCAD screen menu, pull-down menus, and AutoCAD tablet menu. In this chapter, the pull-down menu is emphasized because of its ease of use.

AME contains six pull-down submenus under the title of AME. The default submenu under AME is strictly for loading the AME software. This submenu will not appear if AME is loaded automatically as explained in the previous section.

Once AME is loaded, then you have the option of using one of the five submenus, which contain the AME commands. Only one AME pull-down submenu appears on the menu bar at a time. At the bottom of each of the six submenus are the names of the five submenus not currently displayed. Selecting one of these menus displays the corresponding menu and hides the current one.

Following is a brief explanation of the submenus under the pull-down menu AME.

1. Setup: The Setup submenu allows you to set working units, display type, and wire density. You can select one of the four available units and in turn set the appropriate values for the corresponding system variables.

2. Primitives: The solid primitives are the basic building blocks that make up more complex solid models. Solid primitive commands can create solids of predefined shapes or user-defined shapes. They are the simplest elements in the CSG tree. The commands are provided under the submenu Primitives of the AME.

3. Composite Solids: A new composite from two or more existing solids or regions can be created by performing Boolean operations. There are three

different operations that can be performed in creating a composite solid or region. The commands are provided under the Modify submenu of the AME. Additional commands are provided under the Modify submenu for editing the structure of solid objects. These commands can change the physical characteristics of a solid and alter the CSG tree structure.

4. Inquiry: The commands that are provided under the Inquiry submenu of the AME let you obtain information about an existing solid or region. Additional commands are provided to set values to certain system variables.

5. Display: The commands that are provided under the Display submenu of the AME control the image of solids and regions in your drawing. Additional commands are provided under the Display submenu as drafting tools in displaying 2D objects from a 3D model.

6. Utility: The commands that are provided under the Utility submenu of the AME allow you to create and edit the materials used by AME, including the ability to change the material of an existing solid or region. Additional commands are provided for importing and exporting solids.

See Figures 13-2 and 13-3 for the list of commands available in various submenus via screen and pull-down, respectively.

> **NOTE**: The menu layout shown here is for Version 2.0. An asterisk (*) is shown next to the command name in the menu layout figures to indicate that they are available only in Version 2.0.

Using the standard ACAD.MNX file provided with AutoCAD, you can select the AME or AMELite solid modeling commands from the screen, pull-down, or tablet menus. AutoCAD provides aliases for many of the commands in the standard ACAD.PGP file. An alias is merely a nickname for the command. For a detailed explanation for creating your own alias names, refer to Chapter 15.

See Table 13-1 for a list of alias names for the solid modeling commands provided with Version 2.0 in the ACAD.PGP file. At any time, whenever you want to use AME or AMELite commands, you can just type the alias name instead of typing the whole command.

Construction Plane (CP) Option The CP option (available to all the AME commands) prompts you for the location of a point. This option lets you temporarily set a contruction plane and in turn changes the location and orientation of the UCS XY plane. In addition, the UCS icon is reoriented and displayed at the origin of the temporary construction plane. Once a point is located, the construction plane automatically returns to the location and orientation of the current UCS XY plane. The construction plane is, in effect, only for the location of one point.

Solid Modeling

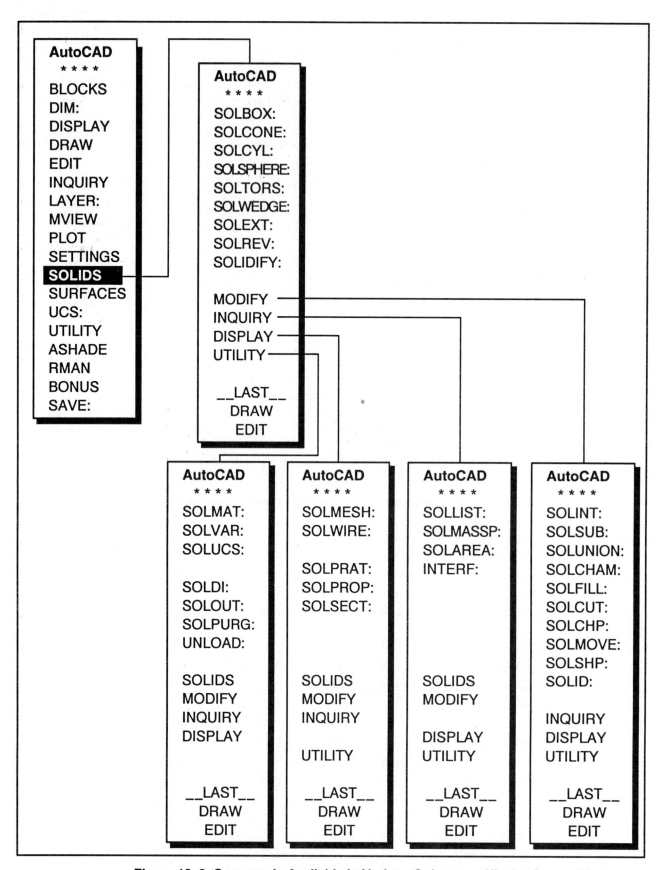

Figure 13-2 Commands Available in Various Submenus Via the Screen Menus

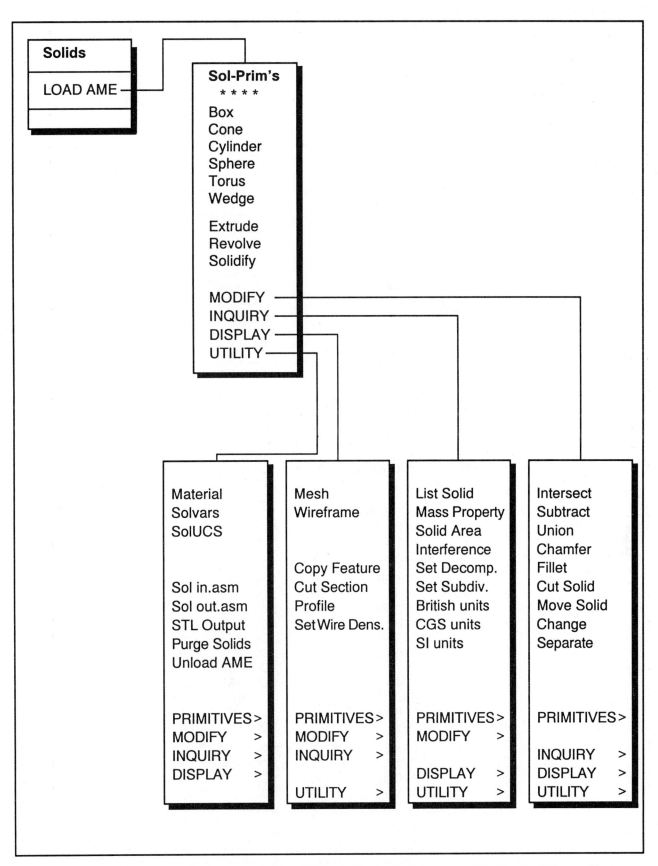

Figure 13-3 Commands Available in Various Submenus Via the Pull-Down Menus

Table 13-1 Alias Names for Solid Modeling Commands

ALIAS NAME	COMMAND NAME
BOX,	SOLBOX
WED,	SOLWEDGE
WEDGE,	SOLWEDGE
CON,	SOLCONE
CONE,	SOLCONE
CYL,	SOLCYL
CYLINDER,	SOLCYL
SPH,	SOLSPHERE
SPHERE,	SOLSPHERE
TOR,	SOLTORUS
TORUS,	SOLTORUS
FIL,	SOLFILL
SOLF,	SOLFILL
CHAM,	SOLCHAM
SOLC,	SOLCHAM
EXT,	SOLEXT
EXTRUDE,	SOLEXT
REV,	SOLREV
REVOLVE,	SOLREV
SOL,	SOLIDIFY
UNI,	SOLUNION
UNION,	SOLUNION
INT,	SOLINT
INTERSECT,	SOLINT
SUB,	SOLSUB
SUBTRACT,	SOLSUB
DIF,	SOLSUB
DIFF,	SOLSUB
DIFFERENCE,	SOLSUB
SEP,	SOLSEP
SEPARATE,	SOLSEP
SCHP,	SOLCHP
CHPRIM,	SOLCHP
MAT,	SOLMAT
MATERIAL,	SOLMAT
MOV,	SOLMOVE
SL,	SOLLIST
SLIST,	SOLLIST
MP,	SOLMASSP
MASSP,	SOLMASSP
SA,	SOLAREA
SAREA,	SOLAREA
SSV,	SOLVAR
FEAT,	SOLFEAT
PROF,	SOLPROF
PROFILE,	SOLPROF
SU,	SOLUCS
SUCS,	SOLUCS
SW,	SOLWIRE
WIRE,	SOLWIRE
SM,	SOLMESH
MESH,	SOLMESH

The CP option lets you locate points on different planes within a single AME command and is not listed with the regular options of the AME commands. This option can be used just like the X/Y/Z point filters are used.

When you enter CP at any prompt accepting point input, the following prompt will appear in order to select the appropriate options:

CP by Entity/Last/Zaxis/View/XY/YZ/ZX/<3point>:

Entity Option This option aligns the construction plane with a Polyline, circle, or arc.

Last Option This option aligns the construction plane to the plane last used by any of the CP options. If this is the first time the CP option has been used in this AutoCAD session, then you will see the following message and the main CP prompt is repeated:

No plane has been used before.

Zaxis Option This option defines the construction plane by locating its origin point and a point on the Z axis (normal) to the plane. This option is similar to the Zaxis option of the AutoCAD UCS command.

View Option This option aligns the construction plane with the viewing plane of the current viewport.

XY Option This option aligns the construction plane with the XY plane of the current UCS. The origin of the construction plane is located by a point. This option is similar to the Origin option of the AutoCAD UCS command.

YZ Option This option aligns the construction plane with the YZ plane of the current UCS. The X, Y, and Z axes of the construction plane are parallel to the Y, Z, and X axes of the current UCS, respectively. The origin of the construction plane is located by a point.

ZX Option This option aligns the construction plane with the ZX plane of the current UCS. The X, Y, and Z axes of the construction plane are parallel to the Z, X, and Y axes of the current UCS, respectively. The origin of the construction plane is located by a point.

3point Option This is the default option. This option defines the construction plane by locating three points. The first point is for the origin of the construction plane, the second one determines the positive direction of the X Axis, and the third determines the positive Y Axis portion of the plane. This option is similar to the 3point option of the AutoCAD UCS command.

> **NOTE:** The CP option is not available in AME Version 1.0.

Solid Modeling

SOLID PRIMITIVES

As mentioned earlier, solid primitives are the basic building blocks that make up more complex solid models. Solid primitive commands can create solids of pre-defined shapes or user-defined shapes.

The predefined solids include the BOX, CONE, CYLINDER, SPHERE, TORUS, and WEDGE.

With the Baseplane option available for all primitive commands (Version 2.0 feature), you can define a different plane in which to place the base of the primitives.

> **NOTE:** There are no region primitives, as they are created from regular 2D AutoCAD entities or from sections of solids.

The user-defined solids can be created by extruding or revolving 2D objects and regions to define a 3D solid. You can also solidify certain 2D AutoCAD objects that have a thickness value to form a user-defined solid. In addition, you can also solidify a 2D AutoCAD entity without a thickness into a region (AME Version 2.0 feature).

Creating a Box (SOLBOX Command)

The SOLBOX (alias BOX) command is used to create a solid box or cube. The base of the box by default is defined parallel to the current UCS. If necessary, you can use the Baseplane option to define a different plane. The SOLBOX command is invoked from the Screen Root Menu AME, the pull-down menu AME-PRIM'S, or at the "Command:" prompt type in **SOLBOX** or **BOX** and press ⏎.

    Command: **solbox**
    Baseplane/Center/<Corner of box>:

First, by default you are prompted for the starting corner of the box. Once you provide the starting corner, the box's dimensions can be entered in one of three ways.

The default option lets you create a box by locating the opposite corner of its base rectangle and then its height. The following command sequence defines a box, as shown in Figure 13-4, using the default option:

    Command: **solbox**
    Baseplane/Center/<Corner of box>: **3,3**
    Cube/Length/<Other corner>: **7,7**
    Height: **4**

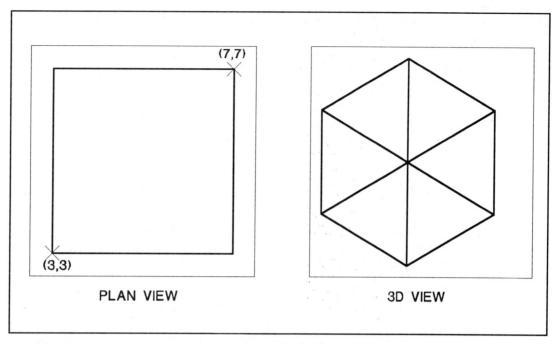

Figure 13-4 Creating a Box Using the Default Option of the SOLBOX Command

Cube Option The Cube option allows you to create a box in which all edges are of equal length. The following command sequence defines a box using the Cube option:

Command: **solbox**
Baseplane/Center/<Corner of box>: **3,3**
Cube/Length/<Other corner>: **c**
Length: **3**

Length Option The Length option lets you create a box by defining its length, width, and height. The following command sequence defines a box using the Length option:

Command: **solbox**
Baseplane/Center/<Corner of box>: **3,3**
Cube/Length/<Other corner>: **l**
Length: **3**
Width: **4**
Height: **3**

Center Option The Center option allows you to create a box by first locating its center point. Once you locate the center point, a line rubberbands from this point to help you visualize the size of the rectangle. Then AME prompts you to define the size of the box by entering one of the following options:

Cube/Length/<Other corner>:

Baseplane Option The Baseplane option lets you define the origin and orientation of the baseplane of the box. When you select the Baseplane option, AME prompts:

Baseplane by Entity/Last/Zaxis/View/XY/YZ/ZX/<3points>:

These options are the same as those of the Construction Plane (CP) option explained earlier in this chapter. After setting the baseplane, AME returns to the first SOLBOX prompt.

The Baseplane option remains in effect for the duration of the command, whereas with the CP option, once a point is located, the construction plane automatically returns to the location and orientation of the baseplane or current UCS XY plane.

> **NOTE:** The Baseplane option affects the extrusion direction of the box, while the CP option does not. The Baseplane and CP options are not available in AME Version 1.0.

Creating a Cone (SOLCONE Command)

The SOLCONE (alias CONE) command is used to create a cone both round and elliptical. By default, the base of the cone is parallel to the current UCS. If necessary, you can change the base of the cone by using the Baseplane option. Solid cones are symmetrical and come to a point along the Z Axis. The SOLCONE command is invoked from the Screen Root Menu AME, the pull-down menu AME-PRIM'S, or at the "Command:" prompt type in **SOLCONE** or **CONE** and press ⏎.

Command: **solcone**
Baseplane/Elliptical/<Center point>:

By default, AME prompts you for the center point of the base of the cone and assumes the base to be a circle. Subsequently, you are prompted for radius (or enter **D** for diameter). Enter the appropriate value and then it will prompt you for the height of the cone. For example, the following command sequence shows steps in drawing a cone, as shown in Figure 13–5, using the default option:

Command: **solcone**
Baseplane/Elliptical/<Center point>: **5,5**
Diameter/<Radius>: **3**
Height of cone: **4**

Elliptical Option Selecting this option indicates that the base of the cone is an ellipse. The prompts are identical to the regular AutoCAD ELLIPSE command. For example, the following command shows steps in drawing a cone using the Elliptical option:

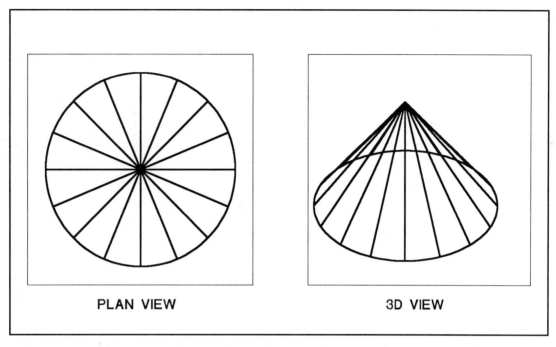

PLAN VIEW   3D VIEW

Figure 13-5 Creating a Cone Using the Default Option of the SOLCONE Command

Command: **solcone**
Baseplane/Elliptical/<Center point>: **e**
Axis endpoint 1>/Center: **3,3**
Axis endpoint 2: **6,6**
Other axis distance: **5,7**
Height of cone: **4**

Baseplane Option The Baseplane option lets you define the origin and orientation of the baseplane of the cone. When you select the Baseplane option, AME prompts:

Baseplane by Entity/Last/Zaxis/View/XY/YZ/ZX/<3points>:

These options are the same as those of the Construction Plane (CP) option explained earlier in this chapter. After setting the baseplane, AME returns to the first SOLCONE prompt.

> **NOTE:** The Baseplane option affects the central Axis direction of the cone, while the CP option does not. The Baseplane and CP options are not available in AME Version 1.0.

Creating a Cylinder (SOLCYL Command)

The SOLCYL (alias CYL) command is used to create a cylinder of equal diameter on each end and similar to an extruded circle or an ellipse. The SOLCYL command is invoked from the Screen Root Menu AME, the pull-down menu

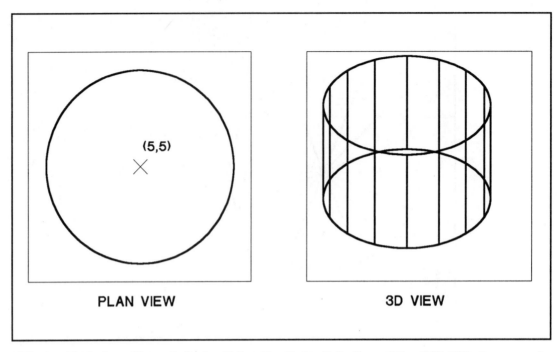

Figure 13-6 Creating a Cylinder Using the Default Option of the SOLCYL Command

AME-PRIM'S, or at the "Command:" prompt type in **SOLCYL** or **CYL** and press ⏎.

Command: **solcyl**
Baseplane/Elliptical/<Center point>:

The prompts are identical to those used for a cone. For example, the following command sequence shows steps in drawing a cylinder, as shown in Figure 13-6, using the default option:

Command: **solcyl**
Baseplane/Elliptical/<Center point>: **5,5**
Diameter/<Radius>: **3**
Center of other end/<Height of cylinder>: **4**

Creating a Sphere (SOLSPHERE Command)

The SOLSPHERE (alias SPHERE) command is used to create a 3D body in which all surface points are equidistant from the center. The sphere is drawn in such a way that its central Axis is coincident with the Z Axis of the current UCS. The SOLSPHERE command is invoked from the Screen Root Menu AME, the pull-down menu AME-PRIM'S, or at the "Command:" prompt type in **SOLSPHERE** or **SPHERE** and press ⏎.

Command: **solsphere**
Baseplane/<Center of sphere>:

First, AutoCAD prompts you for the center point of the sphere, then you can provide radius or diameter to define a sphere.

Baseplane Option The Baseplane option lets you define the origin and orientation of the baseplane of the sphere. When you select the Baseplane option, AME prompts:

Baseplane by Entity/Last/Zaxis/View/XY/YZ/ZX/<3points>:

These options are the same as those of the Construction Plane (CP) option explained earlier in this chapter. After setting the baseplane, AME returns to the first SOLSPHERE prompt.

> **NOTE:** The Baseplane option affects the central Axis direction of the sphere, while the CP option does not. The Baseplane and CP options are not available in AME Version 1.0.

For example, the following command sequence shows steps in drawing a sphere, as shown in Figure 13-7:

Command: **solsphere**
Baseplane/<Center point>: **5,5**
Diameter/<Radius>: **3**

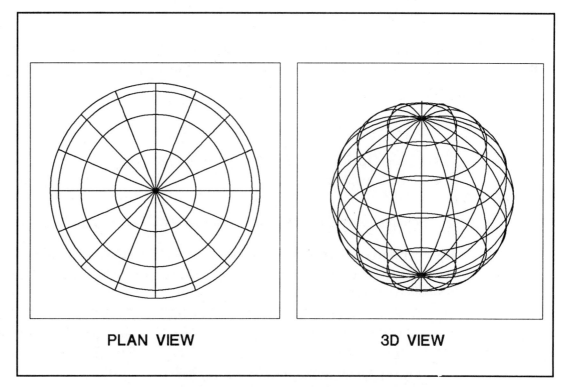

PLAN VIEW   3D VIEW

Figure 13-7 Creating a Sphere Using the SOLSPHERE Command

Solid Modeling

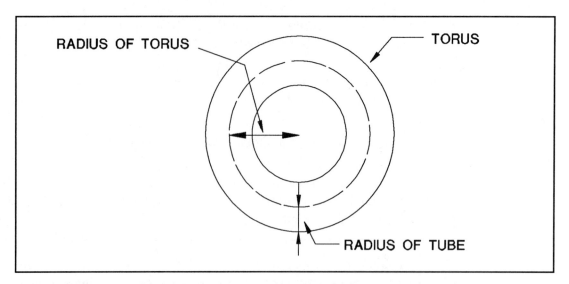

Figure 13-8 Creating a Torus with a Center Hole Using the SOLTORUS Command

Creating a Torus (SOLTORUS Command)

The SOLTORUS (alias TORUS) command is used to create a solid with a donut-like shape. If a torus were a wheel, the center point would be the hub. The torus is created lying parallel to and bisected by the XY plane of the current UCS. The SOLTORUS command is invoked from the Screen Root Menu AME, the pull-down menu AME-PRIM'S, or at the "Command:" prompt type in **SOLTORUS** or **TORUS** and press ⏎.

    Command: **soltorus**
    Baseplane/<Center of torus>:

AutoCAD prompts you for the center point of the torus, and then subsequently the diameter or radius of the torus and the diameter or radius of the tube, as shown in Figure 13-8. You can also draw a torus without a center hole as a result of the radius of the tube being greater than the radius of the torus. A negative torus radius would create a football-shaped solid.

Baseplane Option The Baseplane option lets you define the origin and orientation of the baseplane of the torus. When you select the Baseplane option, AME prompts:

    Baseplane by Entity/Last/Zaxis/View/XY/YZ/ZX/<3points>:

These options are the same as those of the Construction Plane (CP) option explained earlier in this chapter. After setting the baseplane, AME returns to the first SOLTORUS prompt.

> **NOTE:** The Baseplane option affects the central Axis direction of the torus, while the CP option does not. The Baseplane and CP options are not available in AME Version 1.0.

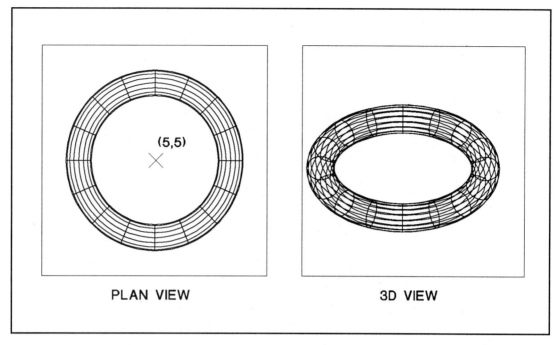

Figure 13-9 Creating a Torus by Specifying the Baseplane and Central Axis Direction Using the SOLTORUS Command

For example, the following command sequence shows steps in drawing a torus, as shown in Figure 13-9:

Command: **soltorus**
Baseplane/<Center of torus>: **5,5**
Diameter/<Radius> of torus: **3**
Diameter/<Radius> of tube: **.5**

Creating a Wedge (SOLWEDGE Command)

The SOLWEDGE (alias WEDGE) command is used to create a solid like a box that has been cut in half diagonally along one face. The face of the wedge is always drawn parallel to the current UCS and the sloped face tapering along the X Axis. The SOLWEDGE command is invoked from the Screen Root Menu AME, the pulldown menu AME-PRIM'S, or at the "Command:" prompt type in **SOLWEDGE** or **WEDGE** and press ⏎.

Command: **solwedge**
Baseplane/<Corner of wedge>:

First, you are prompted for the starting corner of the wedge. Once you provide that starting corner, the wedge dimensions can be entered in one of two ways.

The default option lets you create a wedge by locating the opposite corner of its base rectangle and then its height.

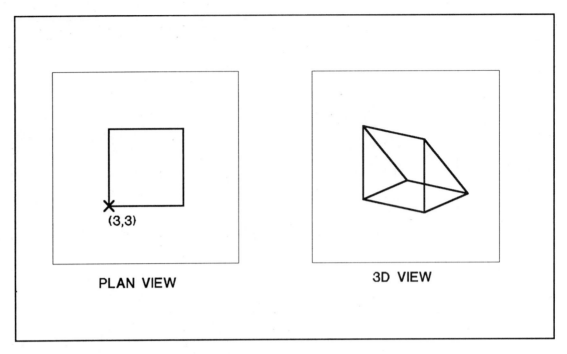

Figure 13-10 Creating a Wedge Using the Default Option of the SOLWEDGE Command

Length Option The Length option lets you create a wedge by defining its length, width, and height.

The prompts are similar to the SOLBOX command, except here there is no Cube option.

For example, the following command sequence shows steps in drawing a wedge by the default option, as shown in Figure 13-10:

```
Command: solwedge
Baseplane/<Corner of wedge> 3,3
Length/<Opposite corner>: 7,7
Height of the wedge: 4
```

Creating Solids from Existing 2D Objects (SOLEXT Command)

The SOLEXT (alias EXT) command is used to create unique solid primitives by extruding a circle, Polyline, polygon or 3Dpoly entity. Because a Polyline can have virtually any shape, the SOLEXT command allows you to create very irregular solids. With AME you can even taper the sides of the extrusion.

> **NOTE:** The Polyline must contain at least two line segments and none of the segments can cross each other. See Figure 13-11 for examples that cannot be extruded. If the selected Polyline is not closed, the SOLEXT command creates the extruded solid as if the Polyline were closed by a line.

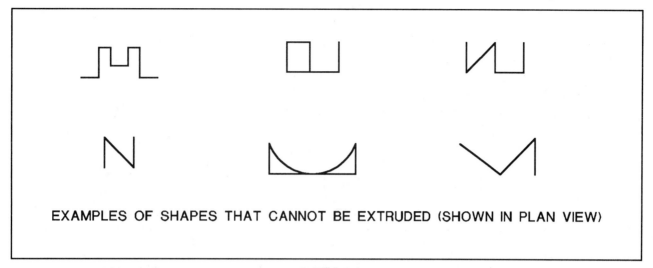

EXAMPLES OF SHAPES THAT CANNOT BE EXTRUDED (SHOWN IN PLAN VIEW)

Figure 13-11 Shapes that Cannot Be Extruded Using the SOLEXT Command

The extrusion is always perpendicular to the entity's plane. The SOLEXT command is invoked from the Screen Root Menu AME, the pull-down menu AME-PRIM'S, or at the "Command:" prompt type in **SOLEXT** or **EXT** and press ⏎.

> Command: **solext**
> Select regions, polylines and circles for extrusion...
> Select objects: *select the objects and press* ⏎

After selecting the objects (you can select multiple objects in a single use of the command), AutoCAD prompts:

> Extrusion Height:

Entering a positive value extrudes the objects along the positive Z Axis of the current UCS, and a negative value extrudes along the negative Z Axis. Finally, you are prompted:

> Extrusion taper angle from Zaxis <0>:

This angle is measured from the extrusion direction and must be zero or greater, but less than 90 degrees. If you enter zero as the taper angle, which is the default, the resulting solid's top will be the same size and shape as the base, and its edges will be perpendicular to the plane of the entity, as shown in Figure 13-12. Any other angle tapers from the base and produces a top that is smaller than the base, as shown in Figure 13-12.

If you include regions in the selection set, AME highlights them and asks you if you would like to extrude the individual region (or loops) to a different extrusion height. If you answer **YES**, then AME prompts you to select the loops that you want to have a common height, and then subsequently prompts for the height of the extrusion. After you provide the extrusion height of the loop(s), AME prompts

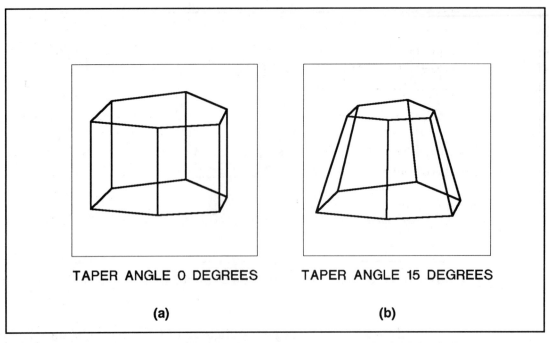

TAPER ANGLE 0 DEGREES   TAPER ANGLE 15 DEGREES

(a)   (b)

Figure 13-12   Creating a Solid Using Zero (a) and Fifteen Degrees (b) as the Taper Angle when Using the SOLEXT Command

you again to select loops. If you have no more loops to select, press ⏎ and the solid of extrusion is generated.

For example, the following command sequence shows steps in drawing an extrusion from a Polyline to a taper of zero degrees:

Command: **solext**
Select polylines and circles for extrusion...
Select objects: *select the polyline*
Select objects: ⏎
Height of extrusion: **5**
Extrusion taper angle from Z <0>: ⏎

> *NOTE:* The system variable SOLDELENT controls whether the selected objects are deleted or retained in your drawing after they are extruded. The following table explains the various settings for the SOLDELENT system variable.

SOLDELENT VALUE	RESULT
1	The Polyline will be retained after the solid is created.
2	AutoCAD prompts to ask you if you want the Polyline to be deleted.
3	The Polyline will be deleted.

Creating Solids from Revolution (SOLREV Command)

The SOLREV (alias REV) command is used to create unique solids by revolving or sweeping a circle, Polyline, polygon, or 3Dpoly entity around an Axis. The same closed Polyline rule applies as in the SOLEXT command. Only one entity can be revolved at any time. The SOLREV command is similar to the REVSURF command (explained in Chapter 12). The REVSURF command creates a surface of revolution, whereas SOLREV creates a solid of revolution. SOLREV provides several options for defining the Axis of revolution.

The SOLREV command is invoked from the Screen Root Menu AME, the pull-down menu AME-PRIM'S, or at the "Command:" prompt type in **SOLREV** or **REV** and press ⏎.

> Command: **solrev**
> Select polyline or circle for revolution...
> Select objects:

After selecting the object (you cannot select more than one object), AutoCAD prompts for:

> Axis of revolution - Entity/X/Y/<Start point of axis>:

Start Point of Axis Option This is the default option. AutoCAD prompts for two points for start and endpoints of the Axis, and the positive direction of rotation is based on the Right Hand Rule.

Entity Option The axis of revolution can be indicated by selecting an entity. The entity can be a line or single-segment Polyline.

X Axis Option This option uses the positive X Axis of the current UCS as the Axis of the revolution.

Y Axis Option This option uses the positive Y Axis of the current UCS as the Axis of the revolution.

After specifying the Axis of revolution, finally, AutoCAD prompts:

> Included angle <full circle>:

Specify the angle for revolution. The default is for full circle. You can specify any angle between 0 and 360 degrees.

> **NOTE:** The system variable SOLDELENT can be used to control the selected objects from being deleted from or retained in your drawing after they have been revolved.

Creating Solids from AutoCAD Entities (SOLIDIFY Command)

The SOLIDIFY (alias SOL) command converts AutoCAD entities into solids and regions. If the selected entity has thickness, then it is converted it into a solid; otherwise, AME converts it into a region. You can solidify only 2D Polyline, polygon, circle, ellipse, trace, donut, and AutoCAD 2D solid entities with a nonzero thickness. Solidify places the same requirements on Polylines that the SOLEXT command does.

> **NOTE:** If a selected polyline has width, the command ignores the width and solidifies the Polyline from the center of the Polyline width.

The SOLIDIFY command is invoked from the Screen Root Menu AME, the pull-down menu AME-PRIM'S, or at the "Command:" prompt type in **SOLIDIFY** or **SOL** and press ⏎.

    Command: **solidify**
    Select objects:

Select the objects that you want to be solidified. If you have selected the objects that cannot be solidified, AutoCAD highlights the objects and the following message appears:

    The highlighted objects cannot be solidified.
    Press space bar to continue...

> **NOTE:** The system variable SOLDELENT can be used to control the selected objects from being deleted or retained in your drawing after they have been solidified.

CREATING COMPOSITE SOLIDS

As mentioned earlier in this chapter, you can create a new composite solid or region by combining two or more solids or regions by Boolean operations. While the term Boolean implies that only two objects can be operated upon at once, AME lets you select many solid objects in a single Boolean command. There are three basic Boolean operations that can be performed in AME. They are as follows:

1. Union (SOLUNION)
2. Difference (SOLSUB)
3. Intersection (SOLINT)

The SOLUNION, SOLSUB, and SOLINT commands let you select both the solids and regions in a single use of the commands, but solids are combined with solids, and regions combined only with regions. Also, in the case of regions you can make composite regions only with those that lie in the same plane. This means that a single command can create a maximum of one composite solid, but might create many composite regions.

If necessary, you can even separate a composite model by using the SOLSEP command. This command undoes, in reverse order, the operations performed to create the composite model.

Union Operation

The union is the process of creating a new composite object from one or more original objects. The union operation joins the original solids or regions in such a way that there is no duplication of volume. Therefore, the total resulting volume can be equal or less than the sum of the volumes in the original solids or regions.

The SOLUNION command performs the union operation and is invoked from the Screen Root Menu AME, the pull-down menu AME-MODIFY, or at the "Command:" prompt type in **SOLUNION** or **UNION** and press ⏎.

> Command: **solunion**
> Select objects:

Select the objects you want to be unioned. You can select more than two objects at once. The objects (solids or regions) can be overlapping, adjacent, or nonadjacent. If you select an object that is not a solid or region, it is solidified according to the current setting of the system variable SOLSOLIDIFY.

For example, the following command sequence shows steps in creating a composite solid by joining two cylinders, as shown in Figure 13–13:

> Command: **solunion**
> Select objects: *select cylinders a and b and press* ⏎

Difference Operation

The difference is the process of forming a new composite object by starting with one object and removing from it any volume that it has in common with a second object. In the case of solids, they are created by subtracting the volume of one set of solids from another set. If the entire volume of the second solid is contained in the first solid, then what is left is the first solid minus the volume of the second solid. However, if only part of the volume of the second solid is contained within the first solid, then only that part that is duplicated in the two solids is subtracted. Similarly, in the case of regions, they are created by subtracting the common area of one set of existing regions from another set.

Solid Modeling

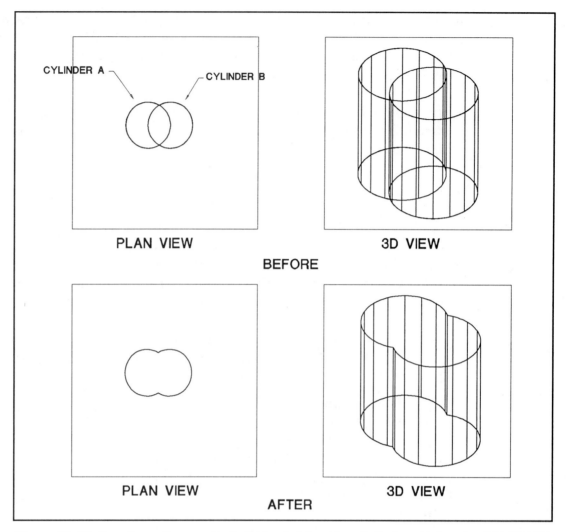

Figure 13-13 Creating a Composite Solid by Joining Two Cylinders Using the SOLUNION Command

The SOLSUB command performs the subtraction operation and is invoked from the Screen Root Menu AME, the pull-down menu AME-MODIFY, or at the "Command:" prompt type in **SOLSUB** or **SUB** and press ⏎.

    Command: **solsub**
    Source objects...
    Select objects:

Select the objects from which you will subtract other objects. You can select one or more as source objects. If you select more than one, they are automatically unioned. After selecting the source objects, press ⏎, and AME prompts you to select the objects to subtract from the source object.

    Objects to subtract from them...
    Select objects:

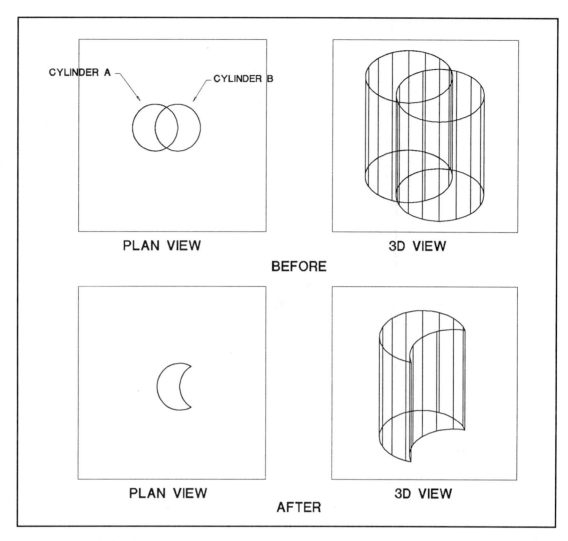

Figure 13-14 Creating a Composite Solid by Subtracting Cylinder B from Cylinder A Using the SOLSUB Command

If necessary, you can select one or more objects to subtract from the source object. If you select several, they are automatically unioned before they are subtracted from the source object.

> **NOTE:** Objects that are neither solids nor regions are ignored.

For example, the following command sequence shows steps in creating a composite solid by subtracting cylinder b from a, as shown in Figure 13-14.

Command: **solsub**
Select objects: *select cylinder a and press* ⏎
Objects to subtract from them...
Select objects: *select cylinder b and press* ⏎

Intersection Operation

The intersection is the process of forming a composite object from only the volume that is common to two or more original objects. In the case of solids, you can create a new composite solid by calculating the common volume of two or more existing solids. Whereas, in the case of regions, it is done by calculating the overlapping area of two or more existing regions.

The SOLINT command performs the intersection operation and is invoked from the Screen Root Menu AME, the pull-down menu AME-MODIFY, or at the "Command:" prompt type in **SOLINT** or **INT** and press ⏎.

> Command: **solint**
> Select objects:

Select the objects you want intersected. Only two objects can be selected at a time.

For example, the following command sequence shows steps in creating a composite solid by intersecting cylinder a with b, as shown in Figure 13-15:

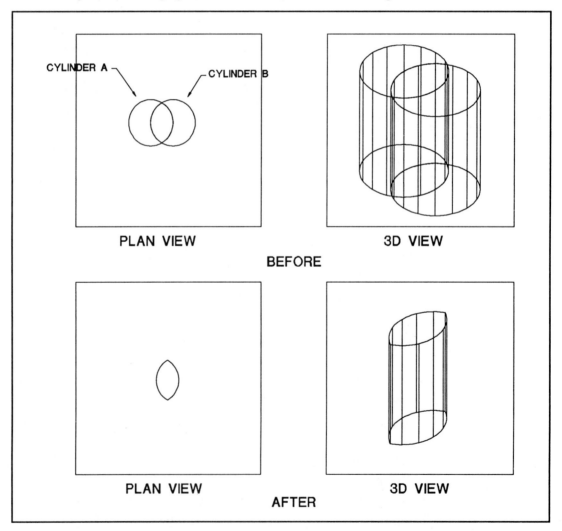

Figure 13-15 Creating a Composite Solid by Intersecting Cylinder A with Cylinder B Using the SOLINT Command

Command: **solint**
Select objects: *select cylinders a and b and press* ⏎

SEPARATION OF SOLIDS

The composite solids and regions created by the SOLUNION, SOLSUB, and SOLINT commands can be separated back to primitives. This can be done using the SOLSEP command. Each use of this command has the effect of undoing the last Boolean operation.

The SOLSEP command can be invoked from the Screen Root Menu AME, the pull-down menu AME-MODIFY, or at the "Command:" prompt type in **SOLSEP** or **SEP** and press ⏎.

Command: **solsep**
Select objects:

Select the objects that are to be disassembled. You can select several solids or regions to be separated at once. After the separation is completed, the component solids and regions are placed on the layers they were on prior to being used to create the composite solid.

EDITING SOLID MODELS

AME makes your job a little easier by providing editing tools that include chamfering or filleting the edges, moving the solid, and modifying the characteristics of the primitives. You can also use the regular AutoCAD editing commands such as MOVE, COPY, ROTATE, SCALE, and ARRAY to edit solids.

Solid Chamfer (SOLCHAM Command)

The SOLCHAM (alias CHAM) command allows the user to bevel the edges of an existing solid object. The chamfer primitive created by this command is automatically added to or subtracted from the selected existing solid. Similar to the AutoCAD CHAMFER command, SOLCHAM prompts you to supply different dimensions along each direction of the chamfer.

The SOLCHAM command can be invoked from the Screen Root Menu Solids, the pull-down menu Modify, or at the "Command:" prompt type in **SOLCHAM** or **CHAM** and press ⏎.

Command: **solcham**
Select base surface:

The SOLCHAM begins by prompting you to select the base surface containing the edges you want chamfered. If you pick an edge that is common to two surfaces, AME will highlight one of the surfaces and you will see this prompt:

<OK>/Next:

If this is the surface you want, press ⏎ to accept it. If it is not, enter **N** for next to highlight the adjoining surface and then press ⏎. Subsequently, AME prompts:

Select edges to be chamfered (press ⏎ when done):

Select the edges of the highlighted surface you want chamfered and then press ⏎. If you select an edge not adjacent to the highlighted surface, it will not be chamfered. Finally, you are prompted for the distances:

Enter distance along first surface <default>:
Enter distance along second surface <default>:

Enter a positive nonzero value or specify two points.

> **NOTE:** SOLCHAM will not work on regions. However, you can use the regular AutoCAD CHAMFER command on AutoCAD entities before they are converted into a region.

Solid Fillet (SOLFILL Command)

The SOLFILL (alias FIL) command gives the user the possibility of rounding the edges of an existing solid object. The fillet primitive created is automatically added to or subtracted from the selected existing solid. The fillets that are being created can be concave or convex.

The SOLFILL command can be invoked from the Screen Root Menu AME, the pull-down menu AME-MODIFY; or at the "Command:" prompt type in **SOLFILL** or **FIL** and press ⏎.

Command: **solfill**
Select edges to be filleted (press ⏎ when done):

Select the edges of the solids to be filleted. You can select one or more edges, and the edges can be on one or several solids. After selecting the edges, press ⏎. Then you are prompted for radius/diameter of the fillet as follows:

Diameter/<Radius> of fillet <default>:

By default, AME prompts you for a radius. If necessary, enter **D** for diameter and enter an appropriate diameter value. Then, AME creates the required fillet solid(s).

> **NOTE:** SOLFILL will not work on regions. However, you can use the regular AutoCAD FILLET command on AutoCAD entities before they are converted into a region.

Moving and Rotating Solids (SOLMOVE Command)

The SOLMOVE (alias MOV) command allows you to move and rotate the solids and regions based on the temporary Motion Coordinate System (MCS). The MCS icon appears while the SOLMOVE command is in effect. You can move and rotate the solids and regions in reference to MCS without defining an appropriate UCS. The MCS icon shows the orientation of the MCS's X, Y, and Z axes. The icon has a single arrow, double arrow, and a triple arrow pointing to the X, Y, and Z axes respectively.

The SOLMOVE command can be invoked from the Screen Root Menu AME, the pull-down menu AME-MODIFY, or at the "Command:" prompt type in **SOLMOVE** or **MOV** and press ⏎.

Command: **solmove**
Select objects:

Select the solid objects and/or regions to move or rotate. After selecting the objects, press ⏎. Then you are prompted for motion description as follows:

<Motion description>/?:

The motion description is a one- and/or two-letter code that lets you move and/or rotate the objects, or redefine the MCS origin. You can display a summary of the letters used in motion description codes on screen by entering **?** in response to the "Motion description" prompt and you can enter the motion description code as lowercase or uppercase.

The motion description codes can be divided into two categories. One category controls the moving and rotating of the objects and the second category is for redefining the MCS origin. Table 13-2 lists the motion description codes and gives a brief explanation of each code.

Table 13-2 Motion Description Codes

MOVING AND ROTATING OBJECTS

Code	Motion Description
TX	Translate along the X Axis
TY	Translate along the Y Axis
TZ	Translate along the Z Axis
RX	Rotate about the X Axis
RY	Rotate about the Y Axis
RZ	Rotate about the Z Axis

REDEFINING THE MCS ORIGIN

Code	Motion Description
AE	Align object and MCS with the edge
AF	Align object and MCS with the face
AU	Align object and MCS with the current UCS
AW	Align object and MCS with the WCS
E	Set axes to an edge
F	Set axes to face
U	Set axes to current UCS
W	Set axes to WCS
O	Restore MCS and SOLID to original location

Solid Modeling

> **NOTE:** You can enter several motion description codes at a single prompt by separating them with commas.

Changing a Primitive within a Composite (SOLCHP Command)

The SOLCHP (alias SCHP) command enables the user to edit complex solids or regions and make modifications to the individual primitives that make up the model or region. The modification to a selected primitive includes moving, copying, replacing, deleting, etc. After making appropriate modifications to the solid or region, AME automatically reevaluates the model reflecting the changes when you exit the command.

The SOLCHP command can be invoked from the Screen Root Menu AME, the pull-down menu AME-MODIFY, or at the "Command:" prompt type in **SOLCHP** or **SCHP** and press ⏎.

    Command: **solchp**
    Select solid or region:

Select a solid or region that you want to modify. Then you are prompted to select a primitive as follows:

    Select primitive:

Select the primitive that is part of the composite model you selected in the previous prompt. The primitive is highlighted and then you are prompted to select the appropriate option for modification as follows:

    Color/Delete/Evaluate/Instance/Move/Next/Pick/Replace/Size/eXit <N>:

Color Option This option allows you to change the color of the selected primitive.

Delete Option This option allows you to delete the selected primitive. If necessary, you can keep the detatched primitive as part of your drawing but not part of the composite solid.

Evaluate Option This option evaluates the model while you are still in the command to see the effects of modifications. This option is helpful when you have made many changes that affect the structure of a composite model and you want to see the changes before exiting the command. AME automatically evaluates when you exit the SOLCHP command.

Instance Option This option makes a copy of the selected primitive as a separate object. The copied primitive is placed at the same location in the drawing as the original primitive and on the current layer. Upon exiting the command, you can use the regular AutoCAD MOVE command to move the primitive.

Move Option This option allows you to relocate the selected primitive within the composite solid. The displacement is given with respect to the current UCS.

Next Option This is the default option and selects another primitive in the selected composite model. You can repeat this option until the primitive you want to operate upon is highlighted.

Pick Option This option allows you to identify a primitive in the selected composite model with your pointing device.

Replace Option This option replaces the selected primitive with another solid or region. A solid primitive can only be replaced with a solid and a region primitive can only be replaced with a region. If the original primitive is part of a composite model, it is replaced by the selected solid or region. If necessary, you can retain the detached primitive in the drawing.

Size Option This option allows you to change the size of the selected primitive. The subsequent prompts depend on the type of the selected primitive. For example, if the selected primitive is a box, then it will prompt you for X, Y, and Z dimensions; for a cylinder it will prompt you for radius and height.

eXit Option This option exits the SOLCHP command.

For example, the following command sequence shows steps in deleting selected primitives from a composite solid using the SOLCHP command, as shown in Figure 13-16:

```
Command: solchp
Select a solid: select the model
Select primitive: select one of the two cylinders
Color/Delete/Evaluate/Instance/Move/Next/Pick/Replace/Size/eXit <N>: d
Retain detached primitive? <N>: press ↵
Color/Delete/Evaluate/Instance/Move/Next/Pick/Replace/Size/eXit <N>: p
Select primitive: select the second cylinder
Color/Delete/Evaluate/Instance/Move/Next/Pick/Replace/Size/eXit <N>: d
Retain detached primitive? <N>: press ↵
Color/Delete/Evaluate/Instance/Move/Next/Pick/Replace/Size/eXit <N>: x
```

Cutting Solids with a Plane (SOLCUT Command)

The SOLCUT (alias CUT) command cuts one or more solids with reference to a construction plane. If necessary, you can retain both halves of the cut solids or just the half you specify. The cut solids retain the layer and color of the original solids. The cut solid will behave as if it were created as a separate composite solid.

The SOLCUT command can be invoked from the Screen Root Menu AME, the pull-down menu AME-MODIFY, or at the "Command:" prompt type in **SOLCUT** or **CUT** and press ↵.

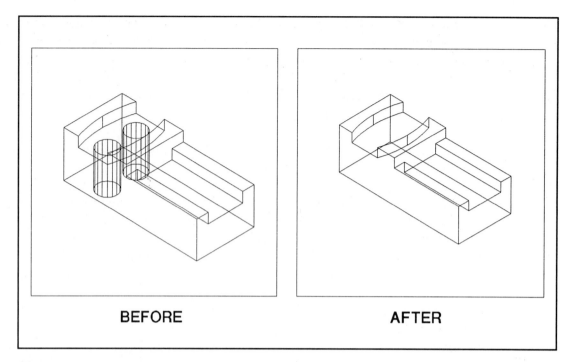

BEFORE   AFTER

Figure 13-16 Deleting Selected Primitives from a Composite Solid Using the SOLCHP Command

Command: **solcut**
Select objects:

Select one or more solids and press ⏎. AME next prompts you to define a cutting plane as follows:

Cutting plane by Entity/Last/Zaxis/View/XY/YZ/ZX/<3points>:

The options are the same as those of the Construction Plane (CP) option explained earlier in this chapter.

After defining the construction plane, AME prompts you to indicate which part of the cut solid is to be retained as follows:

Both sides/<Point on desired side of the plane>:

Point on Desired Side of the Plane Option This is the default option. With your pointing device indicate the side of the cut solid that has to be retained in your drawing.

Both Sides Option This option allows you retain both sides of the cut solids.

NOTE: The SOLCUT command is not available in AME Version 1.0 and it will not work on regions.

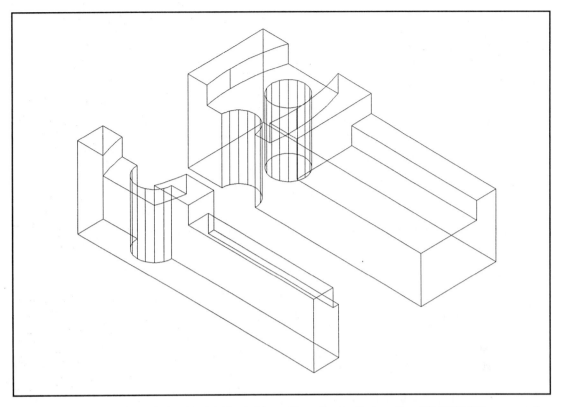

Figure 13-17 Cutting the Solid Model into Two Parts Using the SOLCUT Command

Solid Modeling

Figure 13-17 shows two parts of a solid model that have been cut using the SOLCUT command, and moved apart using the MOVE command.

INQUIRY COMMANDS

The group of commands that are available under Inquiry allows you to obtain information about solids or regions, including mass and area.

Information about a Solid/Region (SOLLIST Command)

The SOLLIST (alias SLIST) command is a specialized listing of information about a solid or region. The information includes the object's name, dimensions, handle, surface area, material, representation (wire-frame or mesh), and rigid-motion information. You can also use the regular AutoCAD LIST command to provide information about a solid or region. The AutoCAD LIST command information includes solids space (Model or Paper Space), handle, insertion point (location), scale factor, and rotation angle. Depending on what kind of information is needed, you can use either the SOLLIST or LIST commands.

The SOLLIST command can be invoked from the Screen Root Menu AME, the pull-down menu AME-INQUIRY, or at the "Command:" prompt type in **SOLLIST** or **SLIST** and press ⏎.

Command: **sollist**
Edge/Face/Tree/<Object>:

By default, you can select one or more objects. It can be a solid and/or region. If the solid is a primitive, then the name of the primitive will be displayed followed by dimensions in parentheses. However, if the solid or region is a composite, the type will be the Boolean operation and the handles of the top-level objects from which it was constructed will be listed. In addition, the information will include the surface area, representation (wire-frame or mesh), and a set of 16 numbers indicating the object's rigid motion.

Edge Option This option displays information about a selected edge of a solid or region.

Face Option This option displays information about a selected face of a solid or region.

Tree Option This option displays a composite solid's CSG tree. By studying the handles of each of the components, you can determine which ones are nested inside other components.

Mass Properties of a Solid/Region (SOLMASSP Command)

The SOLMASSP (alias MASSP) command calculates and displays the mass properties of selected solids and regions. The mass properties displayed for solids are mass, volume, bounding box, centroid, moments of inertia, products of inertia, radii of gyration, and principal moments with corresponding principal directions. The mass properties are calculated based on the current UCS.

The mass properties displayed for regions are area, centroid, bounding box, and perimeter. In addition, it will display information about moments of inertia, product of inertia, radii of gyration, principal moments, and principal direction if the regions are coplanar with the XY plane of the current UCS.

The SOLMASSP command can be invoked from the Screen Root Menu AME, the pull-down menu AME-INQUIRY, or at the "Command:" prompt type in **SOLMASSP** or **MASSP** and press ⏎.

Command: **solmassp**
Select objects:

Select the objects whose mass properties you want displayed. Several system variables control the units in which mass properties are calculated. The variables include SOLMASS, SOLVOLUME, SOLAREAU, and SOLLENGTH.

Area of a Solid/Region (SOLAREA Command)

The SOLAREA (alias SAREA) command calculates and displays the surface area of selected solids and the enclosed area of selected regions. If the solid is not already meshed, it is meshed temporarily for the purpose of calculating the surface area. The surface area of the solid is based on the sum of the areas of all the elements in the mesh and is only an approximation, especially in the case of curved surfaces. You can increase the wire density of the solids by changing the system variable SOLWDENS. The higher the value, the more accurate the mesh and the more accurate the calculation.

In the case of regions, the area is calculated by totaling the area enclosed by the boundaries of the selected regions minus area of any holes that are nested in the regions. The wire density does not affect the calculation of area for the region. The calculation of area for the region is exact, not an approximation as with solids.

The SOLAREA command can be invoked from the Screen Root Menu AME, the pull-down menu AME-INQUIRY, or at the "Command:" prompt type in **SOLAREA** or **SAREA** and press ⏎.

> Command: **solarea**
> Select objects:

Select the solids and/or regions. AME will display the area in the units selected by the SOLAREAU variable.

> **NOTE:** The British units, CGS units, and SI units commands available under the AME-SOLIDS pull-down menu allow you to set appropriate units for the mass property and solid area calculations. British units set the SOLLENGTH variable to feet, SOLAREAU to square feet, SOLVOLUME to cubic feet, and SOLMASS to pounds. CGS units set the SOLLENGTH variable to centimeters, SOLAREAU to square centimeters, SOLVOLUME to cubic centimeters, and SOLMASS to grams. SI units set the SOLLENGTH variable to meters, SOLAREAU to square meters, SOLVOLUME to cubic meters, and SOLMASS to kilograms.

Solid Interference (SOLINTERF Command)

The SOLINTERF (alias SINT) command checks the interference between two or more solids. In other words, it will determine if solids are touching one another. If necessary, AME will create a new solid on the current layer that is the intersection of the interfering solids.

There are two ways to determine the interference between solids.

1. Select two sets of solids, and AME will determine the interference between the first and second sets of solids.

2. Select one set of solids, instead of selecting two sets of solids, then AME will determine the interference between all of the solids in the set. They are checked against each other.

The SOLINTERF command can be invoked from the Screen Root Menu AME, the pull-down menu AME-INQUIRY, or at the "Command:" prompt type in **SOLINTERF** or **SINT** and press ⏎.

    Command: **solinterf**
    Select one set of solids...
    Select objects:

Select the first set of solids and press ⏎, then AME prompts:

    Select another set of solids...
    Select objects:

The second selection set is optional. Press ⏎ if you do not want to define the second selection set. If the same solid is included in both the selection sets, it is considered part of the first selection set and ignored in the second selection set. After selection of the solids, AME prompts:

    Calculate common volumes? <N>:

Enter **Y** to create a new solid on the current layer that is the intersection of the interfering solids. Entering **N**, which is the default, causes AME to prompt:

    Highlight interfering solids pairwise? <N>:

Enter **Y** to highlight two interfering solids at a time and AME displays the following prompt:

    eXit/<Next pair>:

By pressing ⏎ AME cycles through the interfering pairs in the selection set and displays one at a time. To exit the command, enter **X** and press ⏎.

> **NOTE:** The SOLINTERF command is not available in AME Version 1.0 and will not work on regions.

DISPLAY COMMANDS

The SOLMESH and SOLWIRE commands control the display representation of the solids and regions. The SOLMESH command displays an object in mesh representation and hides its wire-frame representation. The SOLWIRE command displays the wire-frame representation. You cannot display both mesh and wire-frame representations at the same time. The initial representation of a solid or region is controlled by the SOLDISPLAY variable. The default is wire-frame.

Polyface Entities (SOLMESH Command)

The SOLMESH (alias MESH) command displays solids and regions as polyface (Pface) entities (meshes). The mesh that is created approximates the surface of solids by creating multiedged faces. The mesh density of solids is controlled by the variable SOLWDENS. When a solid is meshed, all edge lines are straight line segments. So, you cannot use some of the object snaps like center, quadrant, etc. to snap to meshed arcs and circles. The solid has to be displayed in wire-frame representation.

The SOLMESH command can be invoked from the Screen Root Menu AME, the pull-down menu AME-DISPLAY, or at the "Command:" prompt type in **SOLMESH** or **MESH** and press ⏎.

> Command: **solmesh**
> Select solids to be meshed...
> Select objects:

Select the objects to be meshed and press ⏎. A mesh representation of the object will be displayed. After using the SOLMESH command, hidden lines are removed with the HIDE command. After the next regeneration, the hidden lines reappear but can be hidden again at any time with the HIDE command.

> **NOTE:** Solids and regions must be in a mesh representation before you can perform hidden line removal or shading using the AutoCAD HIDE and SHADE commands, respectively.

Wire-Frame Representation (SOLWIRE Command)

The SOLWIRE (alias WIRE) command displays solids and regions as wire-frame representations. A wire-frame approximates solids by displaying the edges of faces and the tessellation lines of curved surfaces.

The SOLWIRE command can be invoked from the Screen Root Menu AME, the pull-down menu AME-DISPLAY, or at the "Command:" prompt type in **SOLWIRE** or **WIRE** and press ⏎.

> Command: **solwire**
> Select objects:

Select the objects and press ⏎. A wire-frame display of the objects will be displayed.

Wire Density (SOLWDENS variable) The SOLWDENS variable sets the wire density of solids and regions at the time they are created. This variable applies to both primitives and composite solids and regions. The quality of shaded and hidden-line renderings can be improved by setting the SOLWDENS variable to a higher value. At the same time, rendering, union, intersection, and subtraction operations take longer and use more RAM. Increasing the wire density increases the accuracy of surface area calculations of solids but not for regions as they are derived from the boundary representation of the region, not its mesh.

To change the SOLWDENS variable value, select the Set Wire Dens. command from the AME-DISPLAY pull-down menu under AME, or at the "Command:" prompt type in **SOLWDENS** and press ⏎.

> Command: **solwdens**
> Wireframe mesh density (1 to 8) <current>:

Specify a number 1 through 8.

> **NOTE:** The SOLWDENS variable does not change the wire density of existing solids or regions; it affects only solids and regions created after its value is changed.

DISPLAYING THE 2D VIEW FEATURES

There are three AME commands that are available to extract views from solids and regions. The SOLFEAT command for extracting a feature (edges or faces) from a solid or region, the SOLSECT command for creating the cross section of multiple solids, and the SOLPROF command to create a profile image of solids with hidden lines.

Creating a 2D Object from a 3D Solid (SOLFEAT Command)

The SOLFEAT (alias FEAT) command allows you to create a 2D object from a 3D solid model. The SOLFEAT command creates a new entity in your current drawing from the face or edge of a selected solid or region. The newly created entity is an anonymous Block, created on the current layer and inserted at the same location of the feature it is replicating. The block can contain lines, arcs, circles, 2D Polylines, and 3D Polylines. The new entity can be manipulated by any of the AutoCAD commands by using the Last option.

The SOLFEAT command can be invoked from the Screen Root Menu AME, the pull-down menu AME-DISPLAY, or at the "Command:" prompt type in **SOLFEAT** or **FEAT** and press ⏎.

> Command: **solfeat**
> Edge/<Face>:

Face Option This option allows you to create new entities from the selected faces of solids or regions. This is the default option, and you can select this option by pressing ⏎ or entering **F** for face and pressing ⏎. Subsequently, AME prompts:

> All/<Select>:

The default option creates new entities from the selected faces of solids and regions.

The All option creates new entities for all faces of the solids and regions you select.

Edge Option This option allows you to create new entities from the selected edges of solids or regions. To select the Edge option, enter **E** and press ⏎. Subsequently, AME prompts:

    All/<Select>:

The default option creates new entities from the selected edges of solids and regions.

The All option creates new entities for all edges of the solids and regions you select.

If necessary, you can explode the anonymous Block and modify.

For example, the following command sequence shows steps in determining the creation of a feature with the help of the SOLFEAT command, as shown in Figure 13-18.

    Command: **solfeat**
    Edge/<Face>: ⏎
    All/<Select>: ⏎
    Select a face: *select point p1*
    <OK>/Next: ⏎
    Select a face: ⏎

> **NOTE:** In Figure 13-18 the face has been moved to a new position by using the MOVE command for clarification.

Creating a Cross Section of a Solid (SOLSECT Command)

The SOLSECT (alias SECT) command creates a cross section of one or more solids. The cross section is created as one or more unnamed Blocks or regions, depending on the setting of the system variable SOLSECTYPE. If the value is set to 1, the Block is created that contains lines, arcs, and circles; if set to 2, it creates a Block that contains Polylines, and if set to 3, it creates a region.

The Block or region is created on the current layer and is inserted at the location of the cross section. If you want the section to be crosshatched automatically, then set the variables SOLHPAT, SOLHSIZE, and SOLHANGLE to the name of the desired hatch pattern, size of the hatch pattern, and desired pattern angle, respectively.

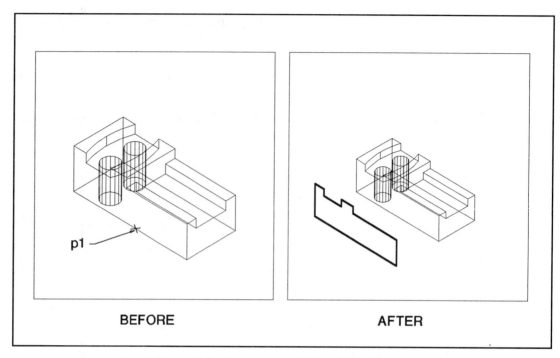

Figure 13-18 Creation of a Feature Using the SOLFEAT Command

The SOLSECT command can be invoked from the Screen Root Menu AME, the pull-down menu AME-DISPLAY, or at the "Command:" prompt type in **SOLSECT** or **SECT** and press ⏎.

        Command:**solsect**
        Select objects:

Select the objects from which you want cross sections. After selecting the objects, press ⏎ and AME prompts you to define the sectioning plane:

        Cutting plane by Entity/Last/Zaxis/View/XY/YZ/ZX/<3points>:

The options are the same as those of the Construction Plane (CP) option explained earlier in this chapter.

The new entity can be manipulated by any of the AutoCAD commands by using the Last option.

See Figure 13-19 for a hatched section produced with the SOLSECT command.

Creating a Profile Image of a Solid (SOLPROF Command)

The SOLPROF (alias PROF) command creates a profile image of a solid, including all of its edges according to the view in the current viewport. The profile image is

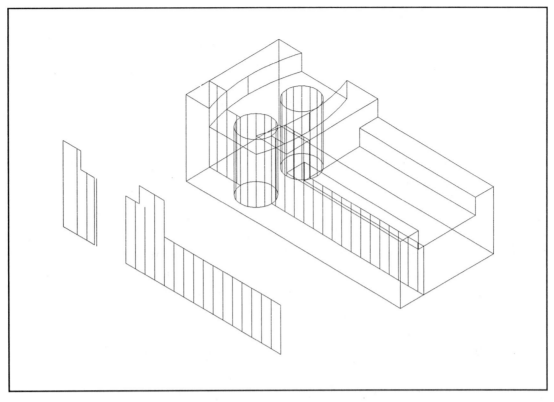

Figure 13-19 Creating a Hatched Section Using the SOLSECT Command

created from lines, circles, arcs, and/or Polylines. SOLPROF will not give correct results in perspective view; it is designed for parallel projections only.

The SOLPROF command will work only when TILEMODE is set to 0 (off) and you are in Model Space. The SOLPROF command can be invoked from the Screen Root Menu AME, the pull-down menu AME-DISPLAY, or at the "Command:" prompt type in **SOLPROF** or **PROF** and press ⏎.

> Command: **solprof**
> Select objects:

Select one or more solids and press ⏎. The next prompt lets you decide the placement of hidden lines of the profile on a separate layer.

> Display hidden profile lines on separate layer? <Y>:

Enter **Yes** or **No**. If you answer **Yes** (default option), two Block inserts are created—one for the visible lines in the same linetype as the original and the other for hidden lines in the hidden linetype. The visible lines are placed on a layer whose name is PV-(viewport handle of the current viewport). The hidden lines are placed on a layer whose name is PH-(viewport handle of the current viewport). If these layers do not exist, AME will create them. For example, if you create a profile in a viewport whose handle is 6, then visible lines will be placed on a layer PV-6 and hidden lines on layer PH-6. To control the visibility of the layers, you can turn the appropriate layers on and off.

The next prompt determines whether 2D or 3D entities are used to represent the visible and hidden lines of the profile.

Project profile lines onto a plane? <Y>:

Enter **Yes** or **No.** If you answer **Yes** (default option), AME creates the visible and hidden lines of the profile with 2D AutoCAD entities and **No** creates the visible and hidden lines of the profile with 3D AutoCAD entities.

Finally, AME asks you if you want tangential edges deleted. A tangential edge is an imaginary edge at which two faces meet and are tangent. In most of the drafting applications, the tangential edges are not shown. The prompt sequence is as follows for deleting the tangential edges:

Delete tangential edges? <Y>:

Enter **Yes** to delete the tangential edges and **No** to retain them.

For example, the following command sequence shows steps in creating a profile with the help of the SOLPROF command, as shown in Figure 13-20.

Command: **solprof**
Select objects: *select the solid*
Select objects: ⏎

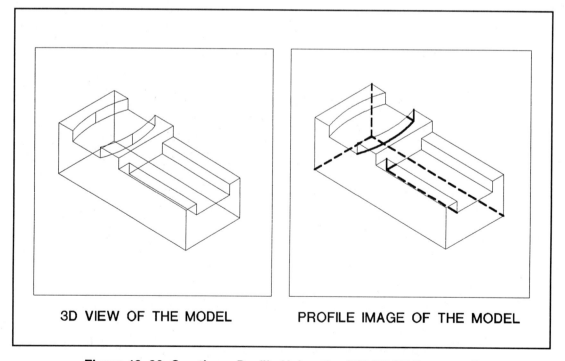

3D VIEW OF THE MODEL   PROFILE IMAGE OF THE MODEL

Figure 13-20 Creating a Profile Using the SOLPROF Command

Display hidden profile lines on separate layer?<Y> ⏎
Display profile lines onto a plane <Y>: ⏎
Delete tangential edges? <Y>:

UTILITY COMMANDS

The utility commands provide a variety of functions including creating, editing, and assigning materials to solids and regions, setting system variables related to AME, reorienting the UCS, and freeing memory used by your current drawing. In this section a brief explanation is given for the utility commands that are provided by AME.

Creating a Solid/Region of a Particular Material (SOLMAT Command)

The SOLMAT (alias MAT) command is used to assign a particular material to a given solid or region. In addition, you can also add a new material to a list and modify the definition of existing materials.

AME keeps a separate list of materials and their properties in an ASCII file called ACAD.MAT. If necessary, you can create another file with a different name with the extension .MAT.

The SOLMAT command can be invoked from the Screen Root Menu AME, the pull-down menu AME-UTILITY, or at the "Command:" prompt type in **SOLMAT** or **MAT** and press ⏎.

Command: **solmat**
Change/Edit/<eXit>/LIst/LOad/New/Remove/SAve/SEt/?:

Change Option This option lets you change a material that is assigned to a set of one or more existing solids or regions in your current drawing.

Edit Option This option lets you change the definition of a specific material in your current drawing.

LIst Option This option displays the definition of a material.

LOad Option This option loads a material definition into your current drawing from an external file.

New Option This option allows you to define a new material.

Remove Option This option deletes a material definition from your current drawing.

SAve Option This option allows you to save a material definition from your current drawing to an external ASCII file.

SEt Option This option sets the default material that is automatically assigned to a newly created solid or region.

? Option This option displays a list of the materials currently defined in the drawing and from an external file.

Setting the System Variables (SOLVAR Command)

The SOLVAR (alias SSV) command sets the system variables that control the AME environment. These variables control the operation of many solids and regions commands.

The SOLVAR command can be invoked from the Screen Root Menu AME, the pull-down menu AME-UTILITY, or at the "Command:" prompt type in **SOLVAR** or **SSV** and press ⮐.

```
Command: solvar
Variable name or ?:
```

This command works similar to the regular AutoCAD SETVAR command.

Aligning the UCS with a Solid/Region Face or Edge (SOLUCS Command)

The SOLUCS (alias SUCS) command aligns the UCS with the face or edge of an existing solid or an edge of an existing region.

The SOLUCS command can be invoked from the Screen Root Menu AME, the pull-down menu AME-UTILITY, or at the "Command:" prompt type in **SOLUCS** or **SUCS** and press ⮐.

```
Command: solucs
Edge/<Face>:
```

Face Option This option aligns the UCS to the face of a solid.

Edge Option This option aligns the UCS with the edge of a solid or region.

Removing Solids from Memory (SOLPURGE Command)

The SOLPURGE command removes solid objects from the memory that you may not be currently using. This in no way affects the objects that are already drawn in your current drawing. Removing the objects from the memory will speed up the processing and will help reduce the amount of memory and disk space required.

The SOLPURGE command is invoked from the Screen Root Menu AME, the pull-down menu AME-PRIM'S, or at the "Command:" prompt type in **SOLPURGE** and press ⏎.

    Command: **solpurge**
    Memory/Bfile/Pmesh/<Erased>:

Erased Option This is the default option, and allows you to recover memory occupied by secondary entities associated with an erased solid.

Memory Option This option allows you to free up the memory within the AME application that is associated with AME solids. This in no way deletes AutoCAD entities from your drawing. When you finish working with a group of related solids, you can use this option to remove from memory the related solids, and in turn increase the speed of processing.

Bfile Option This option allows you to purge Bfile information of solids from your drawing.

Pmesh Option This option allows you to purge Pmesh entities from your drawing. If you select a solid that is currently in mesh representation, it is returned to wire representation before the mesh is removed. By using the Pmesh option in conjunction with the Bfile option, you will reduce the size of your drawing as much as 50 percent.

UNLOADING AME

When you have finished using AME commands in your current drawing session, you can unload AME from the memory to increase processing speed. This can be done by invoking the UNLOAD command from the Screen Root Menu, the pull-down menu under AME-UTILITY, or at the "Command:" prompt type in (**xunload "ame"**) and press ⏎.

Solid Modeling

Project Exercises

CREATING THE PROJECT DRAWING

This project creates the bracket, as shown in Figure 13-21. The bracket is drawn entirely by using AutoCAD Solid Modeling features available in the AME package. By following the steps, you will be able to build the model by using various commands available in AME.

Step 1   Begin a NEW drawing called AME-PROJ.

Step 2   Set TILEMODE to 0. This automatically places you in Paper Space.

Step 3   Set UNITS to 2 decimal places.
Set LIMITS to 0,0 and 22,17.
ZOOM All.

Step 4   Create the following layers with appropriate colors and linetypes as shown below:

OBJECT	RED	CONTINUOUS
BORDER	GREEN	CONTINUOUS
DIM	BLUE	CONTINUOUS
VIEWPORTS	CYAN	CONTINUOUS

Set layer BORDER as the current layer.

Step 5   Draw the border and the title block.

Step 6   Set layer VIEWPORTS as the current layer.
Make four viewports.

```
Command: mview
On/OFF/Hideplot/Fit/2/3/4/Restore/<First Point>: 3.5,10
Other corner: 9.5,16
Command: ⏎
On/OFF/Hideplot/Fit/2/3/4/Restore/<First Point>: 11,10
Other corner: 17,16
Command: ⏎
On/OFF/Hideplot/Fit/2/3/4/Restore/<First Point>: 3.5,2.5
Other corner: 9.5,8.5
Command: ⏎
On/OFF/Hideplot/Fit/2/3/4/Restore/<First Point>: 11,2.5
Other corner: 17,8.5
```

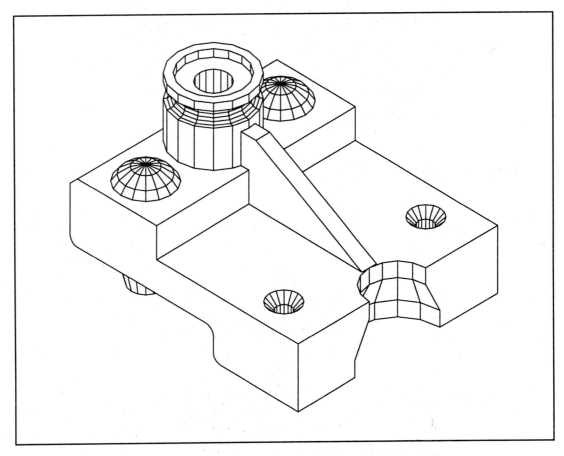

Figure 13-21 Creating a Bracket Using Solid Modeling

Step 7   Change to Model Space.

Command: **mspace**

Make the upper right viewport current.
Set Grid to .5 and Snap to .25.
Set Vpoint to 1,-1,1.

Step 8   Make the upper left viewport current.
Set Grid to .5 and Snap to .25.
Set Vpoint to 0,0,1.

Step 9   Make the lower left viewport current.
Set Grid to .5 and Snap to .25.
Set Vpoint to 0,-1,0.

Step 10   Make the lower right viewport current.
Set Grid to .5 and Snap to .25.
Set Vpoint to 1,0,0.

Step 11 If you have not already loaded AME, select the AME menu from the pull-down menu and select Load AME.

Set LAYER OBJECT as the current layer.

Begin the layout of the drawing by drawing four boxes using the SOLBOX command as shown below:

Command: **solbox**
Baseplane/Center/<Corner of box> <0,0,0>: **0,0,-2**
Cube/Length/<Other corner>: **l**
Length: **8**
Width: **7**
Height: **1**

Command: **solbox**
Baseplane/Center/<Corner of box> <0,0,0>: **0,0,–1**
Cube/Length/<Other corner>: **l**
Length: **3**
Width: **7**
Height: **1**

Command: **solbox**
Baseplane/Center/<Corner of box><0,0,0>: **5,0,–3**
Cube/Length/<Other corner>: **l**

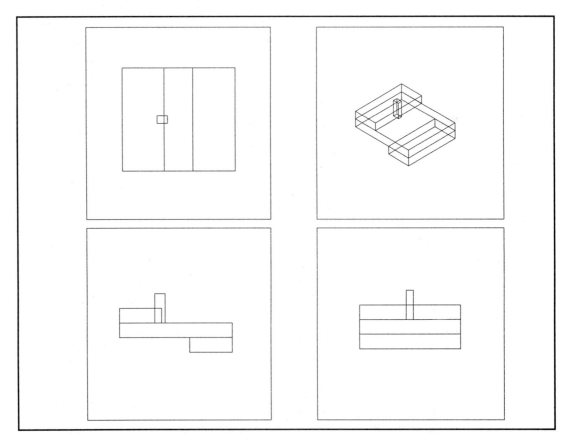

Figure 13–22 Creating the Basic Shape of the Bracket

Length: **3**
Width: **7**
Height: **1**

Command: **solbox**
Baseplane/Center/<Corner of box><0,0,0>: **2.5,3.25,–1**
Cube/Length/<Other corner>: **l**
Length: **.75**
Width: **.5**
Height: **2**

The above box constructions form the basic shape of the bracket, as shown in Figure 13–22.

Step 12 Use the SOLCYL command to create a cylinder as shown below:

Command: **solcyl**
Baseplane/Elliptical/<Center point> <0,0,0>: **1.5,3.5**
Diameter/<Radius>: **1.25**
Center of other end/<Height>: **2**

Step 13 Use the SOLWEDGE command to create a wedge as shown in Figure 13–23:

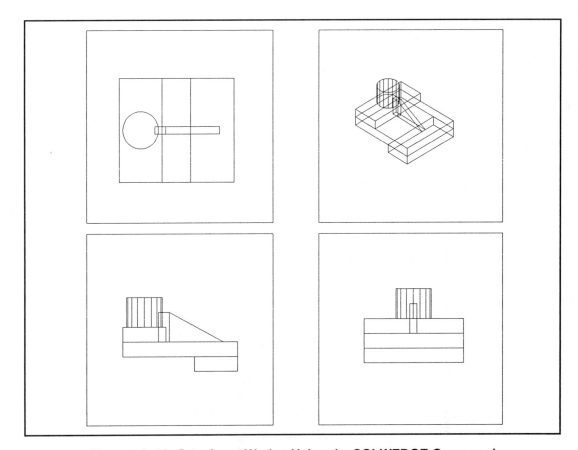

Figure 13–23 Creating a Wedge Using the SOLWEDGE Command

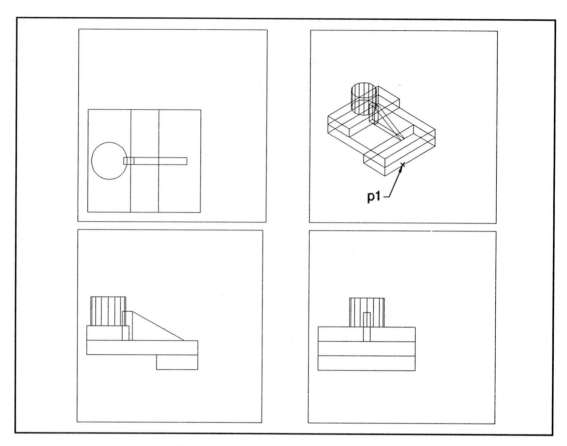

Figure 13-24 Creating a Solid UCS

Command: **solwedge**
Baseplane/<Corner of wedge> <0,0,0>: **3.25,3.25,-1**
Length/<Other corner>: **l**
Length: **3.75**
Width: **.5**
Height: **2**

Step 14   Set up a solid UCS, as shown in Figure 13-24, for solid modeling as follows:

Command: **solucs**
Edge/<Face>: ⏎
Select a face: *select the bottom edge of the end*
<OK>/Next: **n** *if not the end view*
<OK>/Next: ⏎

Next, relocate the icon as follows:

Command: **ucsicon**
ON/OFF/All/Noorigin/ORigin/<ON>: **or**

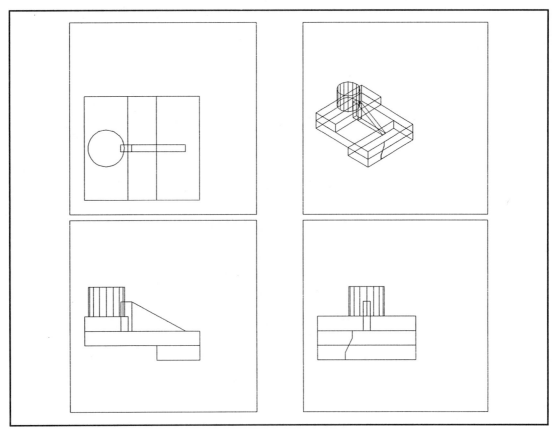

Figure 13–25 Drawing a Polyline to Specified Coordinates

Step 15   Draw a Polyline to the given coordinates, as shown in Figure 13–25:

Command: **pline**
From point: **3.5,–1**
Current line-width is 0.000
Arc/Close/Halfwidth/Length/Undo/Width/<Endpoint of line>:
    @1.0<0
Arc/Close/Halfwidth/Length/Undo/Width/<Endpoint of line>:
    @0.5<90
Arc/Close/Halfwidth/Length/Undo/Width/<Endpoint of line>:
    @0.5,1
Arc/Close/Halfwidth/Length/Undo/Width/<Endpoint of line>:
    @0.5<90
Arc/Close/Halfwidth/Length/Undo/Width/<Endpoint of line>:
    @1.5<180

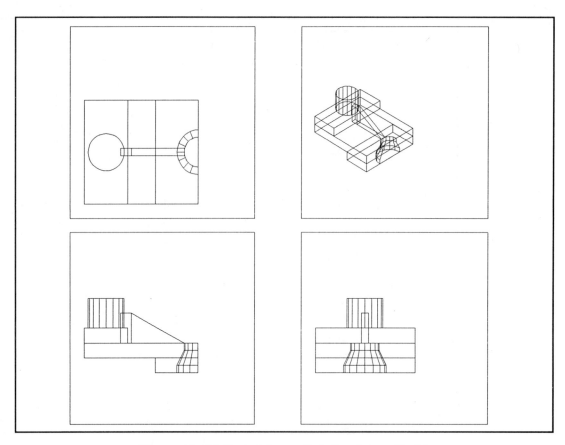

Figure 13-26 Revolving a Polyline into a Solid

Step 16   Revolve the Polyline just created into a solid, as shown in Figure 13-26:

> Command: **solrev**
> Select polyline or circle for revolution...
> Select objects: **l**
> Select object: ⏎
> Axis of revolution - Entity/X/Y/<Start point of axis>: **3.5,-1**
> Endpoint of axis: **3.5,1**
> Included angle <full circle>: **180**

Step 17   Create two spheres in reference to the WCS.

> Command: **ucs**
> Origin/ZAxis/3point/Entity/View/X/Y/Z/Prev/Restore/Save/Del/?/
>   <world>: ⏎
>
> Command: **solsphere**
> Baseplane/<Center of sphere> <0,0,0>: **1.5,1.125,-0.5**
> Diameter/<Radius of sphere>: **1**

Copy the sphere to a displacement of 0,4.75, as shown in Figure 13-27.

> Command: **copy**
> Select objects: **l**
> Select objects: ⏎

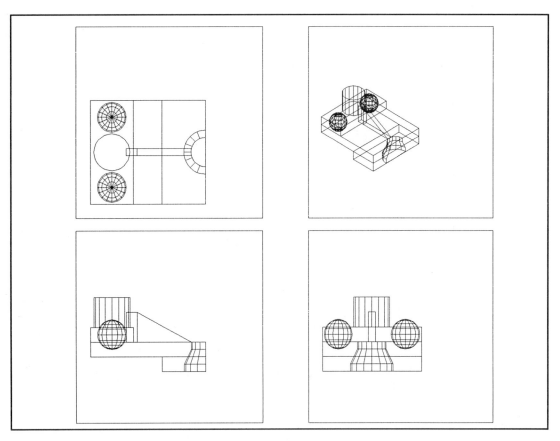

Figure 13-27 Copying a Sphere to a Specified Displacement

> \<Base point or displacement\>/Multiple: **0,0**
> Second point of displacement: **0,4.75**

Step 18   Place two cones by using the SOLCONE command, as shown in Figure 13-28.

> Command: **solcone**
> Baseplane/Elliptical/\<Center point\> \<0,0,0\>: **1.5,1.125,-2**
> Diameter/\<Radius\>: **0.75**
> Apex/\<Height\>: **-3**

Copy the cone to a displacement of 0,4.75.

Step 19   Starting at 0,0,-5, create a box that is 3 × 7 × 2, as shown in Figure 13-29.

Step 20   Create a .5-radius cylinder, centered at 1.5,3.5,-2, to a height of 4, as shown in Figure 13-30.

Step 21   Create a cylinder with radius 1, centered at 1.5,3.5,1.75 to a height of .25, as shown in Figure 13-31.

Step 22   Create a cylinder with radius .25, centered at 6.5,1.0,-3 to a height of 2, as shown in Figure 13-32.

Copy the cylinder to a displacement of 0,5.

Solid Modeling

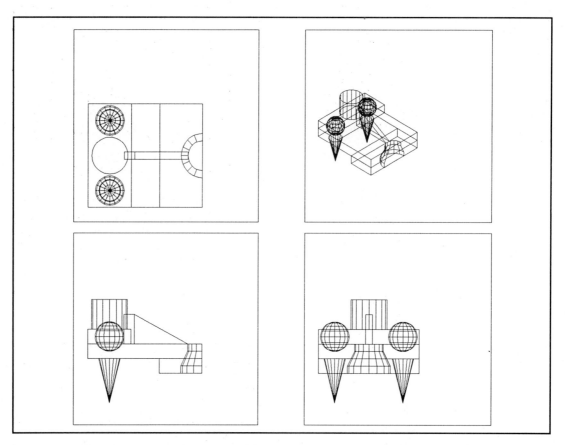

Figure 13-28 Placing Two Cones Using the SOLCONE Command

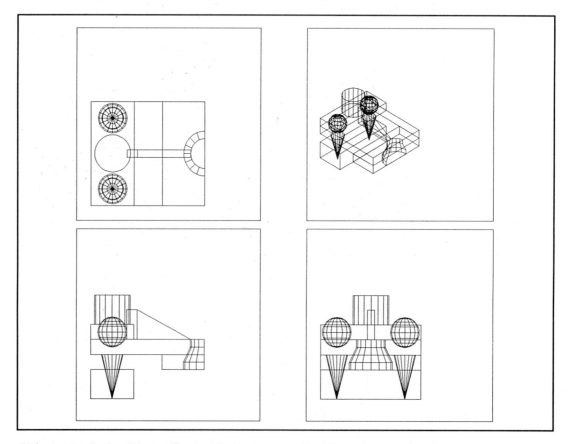

Figure 13-29 Creating a Box with the Starting Point 0,0,-5 and Dimensions of 3 × 7 × 2

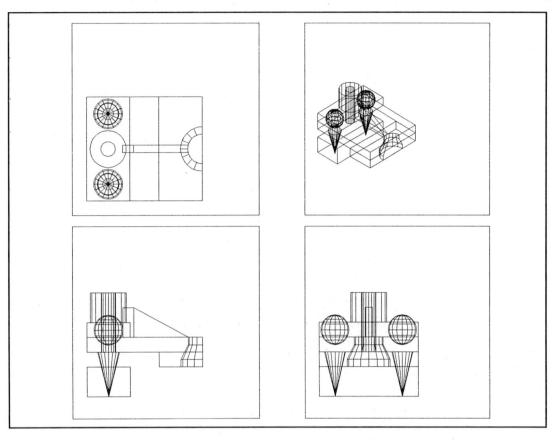

Figure 13-30 Creating a .5 Cylinder Centered at 1.5,3.5,-2 and a Height of 4

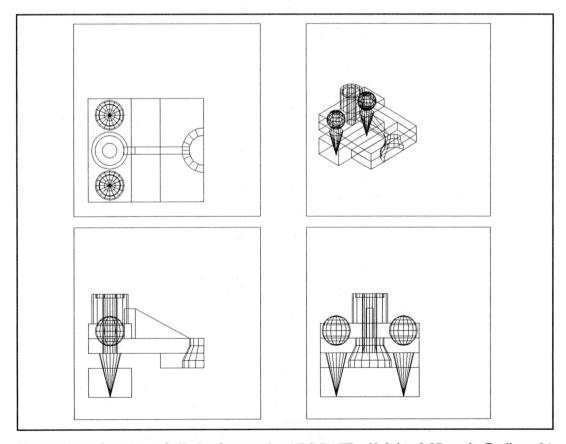

Figure 13-31 Creating a Cylinder Centered at 1.5,3.5,1.75, a Height of .25, and a Radius of 1

Solid Modeling

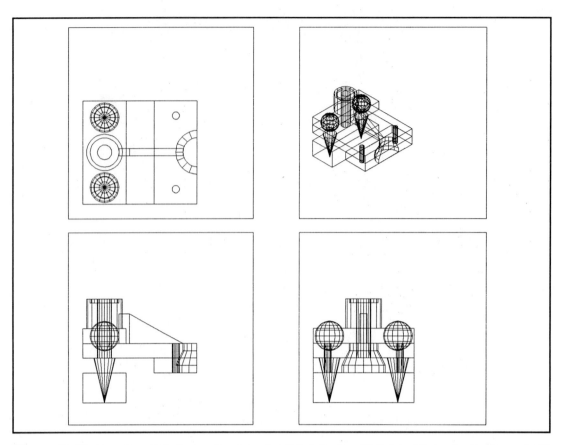

Figure 13-32 Creating a Cylinder Centered at 6.5,1.0,-3, a Height of 2, and a Radius of .25

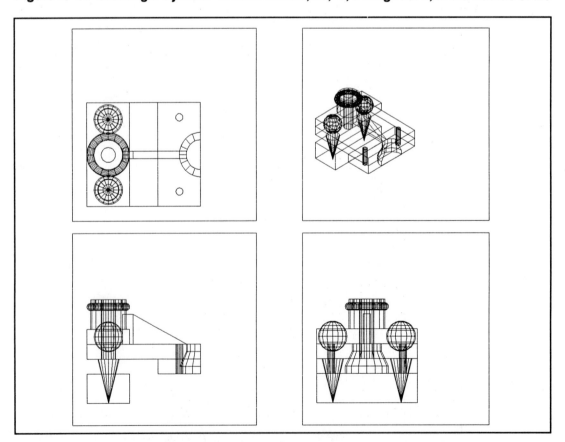

Figure 13-33 Creating a Torus Using the SOLTORUS Command

Step 23 Use the SOLTORUS command to create a torus, as shown in Figure 13-33:

> Command: **soltorus**
> Baseplane/<Center of torus> <0,0,0>: **1.5,3.5,1.5**
> Diameter/<Radius of torus>: **1.25**
> Diameter/<Radius of tube>: **.25**

Step 24 Select the connected boxes (except the box that was drawn in Step 19), the wedge, the large cylinder, the spheres, and the cones for use with the SOLUNION command. This is shown in Figure 13-34.

> Command: **solunion**
> Select objects: *select the boxes, wedge, large cylinder, spheres, cones and press* ⏎

Step 25 Select the resulting solid in response to the first SOLSUB prompt and then the remaining primitives to be subtracted from it. This is shown in Figure 13-35.

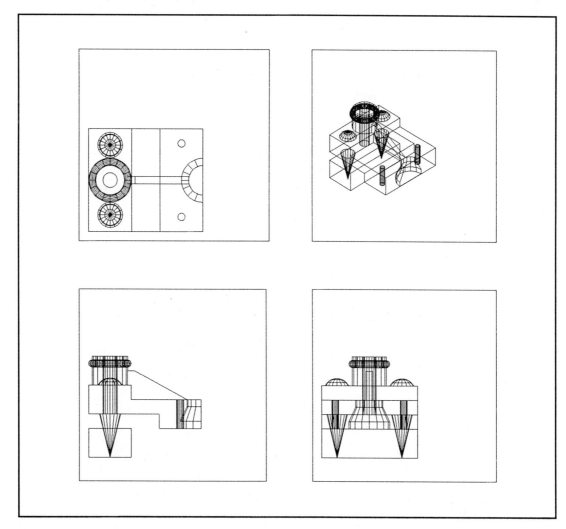

Figure 13-34 Using the SOLUNION Command to Unite the Wedge, Large Cylinder, Spheres, and Cones

Solid Modeling

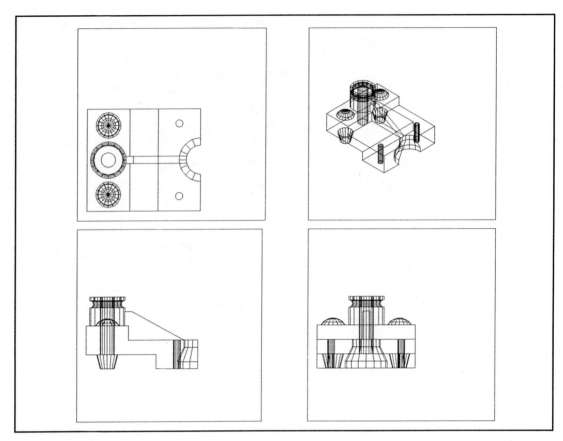

Figure 13-35 **Subtracting the Primitives from the Newly Created Solid Using the SOLSUB Command**

Command: **solsub**
Source objects...
Select objects: *select the resulting solid from Step 24*
Select objects: ⏎
Objects to subtract from them...
Select objects: *select the remaining primitives*
Select objects: ⏎

Step 26 Select the faces, as shown in Figure 13-36, for chamfer and fillet. Use the SOLCHAM and SOLFILL commands with .25 as the chamfer values and the radii on the respective selected objects. The end result should look as shown in Figure 13-37.

Step 27 After using the SOLMESH and HIDE commands, the result is as shown in Figure 13-38.

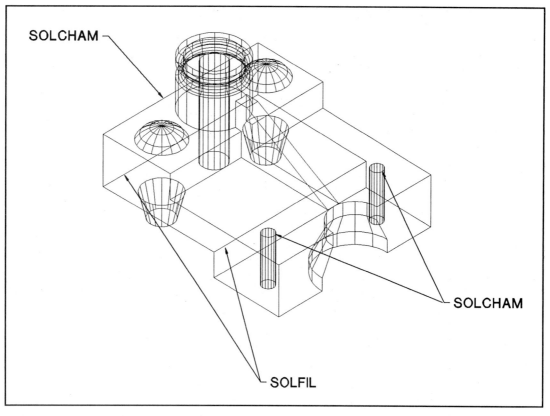

Figure 13-36 Using the SOLCHAM and SOLFILL Commands to Chamfer and Fillet the Faces

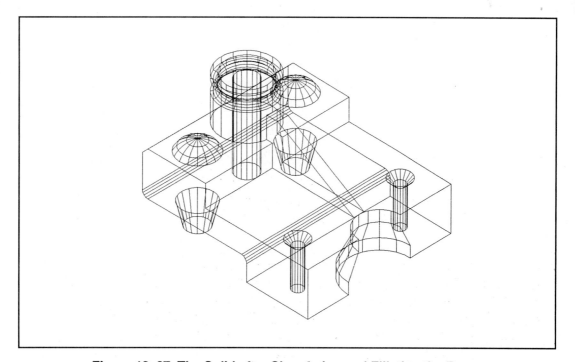

Figure 13-37 The Solid after Chamfering and Filleting the Faces

Solid Modeling

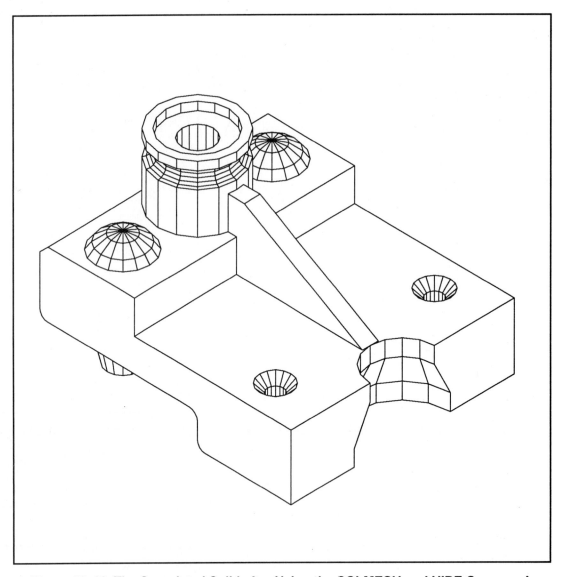

Figure 13-38 The Completed Solid after Using the SOLMESH and HIDE Commands

CHAPTER
14 The Tablet and Digitizing

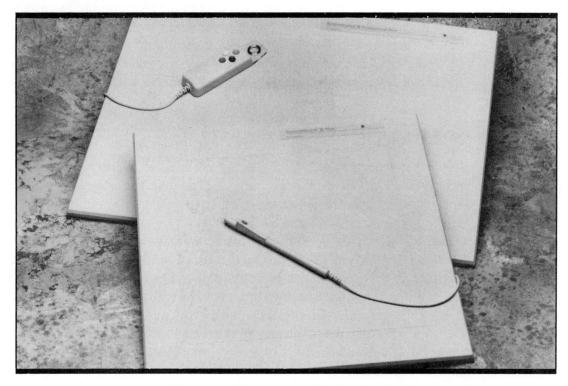

(Courtesy of Summagraphics Corporation)

The AutoCAD program consists of several major components in the form of program files along with many other supporting files. One major part of the program, the menu (in the form of a filename.MNX file), determines how various devices work with the program. The devices controlled by the menu include the buttons on the pointing device (mouse or tablet puck), the side screen menus, pull-down menus, function box keys (not commonly used) and tablet. This chapter covers configuring and using the tablet menu.

First, using the tablet part of any menu requires that the AutoCAD program be installed and configured for the particular make and model of digitizing tablet that is properly connected to the computer.

685

> ***NOTE:*** The installation configuration permits using only one digitizing device at a time. Because a mouse and a tablet are both digitizing devices, you must choose between one or the other at any one time. This pre-startup configuration is not to be confused with configuring the installed tablet with the TABLET command while in the AutoCAD Editor.

Second, a preprinted template with up to four rectangular menu areas should be used that has properly arranged columns and rows of pick areas within each menu area. Each pick area corresponds to a command or line of programming in the filename.MNX menu file in effect. It is also necessary to set aside a screen area on the tablet if you wish to control the screen cursor with the tablet's puck.

TABLET OPERATION

When a filename.MNX file, digitizing tablet, and overlay have been installed and properly set up to work together, you can use the attached puck on the tablet surface to achieve the following results.

Normal operation — The most common usage of a tablet is to allow the user to move the puck and press the pick button while pointing to one of the various commands or symbols on a preprinted overlay and be able to invoke that particular command or initiate a program (perhaps written by users themselves) that will draw that symbol. In addition, when the puck is moved within the overlay's designated screen area, the screen cursor will mimic the puck movement, thereby permitting you to specify points or select objects on the screen, including screen menu commands.

Mouse movement — Some tablets have an option that causes the puck to emulate mouse type rather than absolute movement. Mouse emulation means that if you pick the puck up off of the tablet surface and move it to another place in the screen area, the screen cursor does not move. The cursor moves only with puck movement while it is on the tablet and in the screen area. Absolute (normal) tablet-puck operation means that, once configured, each point in the tablet's screen area corresponds to only one point on the screen. So, while in the normal mode, if you pick the puck up and put it down at another point in the screen area, the cursor will immediately move to the screen's corresponding point.

Paper copying — By switching the TABLET mode to ON, you can cause points on the tablet to correspond to drawing coordinates rather than screen pixel locations as it does in the Normal or Mouse operations described above. This allows you to fix a drawing (like a map) on the tablet surface, select two points on the map, specify their coordinate locations on the map, after which the puck movement around the map will cause screen cursor movement to correspond to the same coordinates in the computer-generated drawing. Options and precautions for using this feature (referred to as digitizing) are discussed in this chapter.

The ACAD.MNX Tablet Configuration

The intended procedure is to have a preprinted template (the overlay) arranged on a sheet that can be fixed to the tablet. Tablet menu area(s) can then be configured to coincide with the template. Although you could try to configure a bare tablet, it would be difficult to select the required points for rectangular menu areas and also impractical to try and place a template on the tablet after it was configured in such a manner. However, if a tablet has been configured for one template, you can use another template in the same location without reconfiguring as long as the areas are the same. One benefit of this is being able to change from one set of icons/symbols or commands to another set without having to configure again. However, a change in the menu must be made in order to accommodate changes in the template, even if the configuration is the same.

The ACAD.MNX (compiled from ACAD.MNU) menu file supports a multibutton pointing device and the tablet overlay that is provided with the AutoCAD program package. That overlay is approximately 11" × 11" and has four areas for selecting icon/commands and a screen area, as shown in Figure 14-1. The pointing device (the puck furnished with every tablet) usually has three or more buttons (the menu supports up to a ten-button puck or mouse) and the cursor movement on the screen mimics the puck's movement in the tablet's configured screen area.

CUSTOM MENUS

Chapter 15 describes how to customize a menu file. Most of the explanations and examples refer to the screen menu primarily because of its complexity. The same principles of customizing the tablet portion of a menu can be applied.

The ACAD.MNX menu is programmed so that when you select a command from the tablet overlay, the screen's side menu is changed to an appropriate submenu of options for maximum productivity and ease of use. For example, if you select the LINE command from the tablet menu, the same accompanying screen side bar submenu will appear that appears when the LINE command is selected from a Draw menu on the screen (side bar or pull-down).

TABLET Command

The TABLET command is used to switch between digitizing paper drawings and normal command/icon/screen area selecting on a configured overlay. The TABLET command is also used to calibrate a paper drawing for digitizing or to configure the overlay to suit the current menu. The TABLET command is invoked

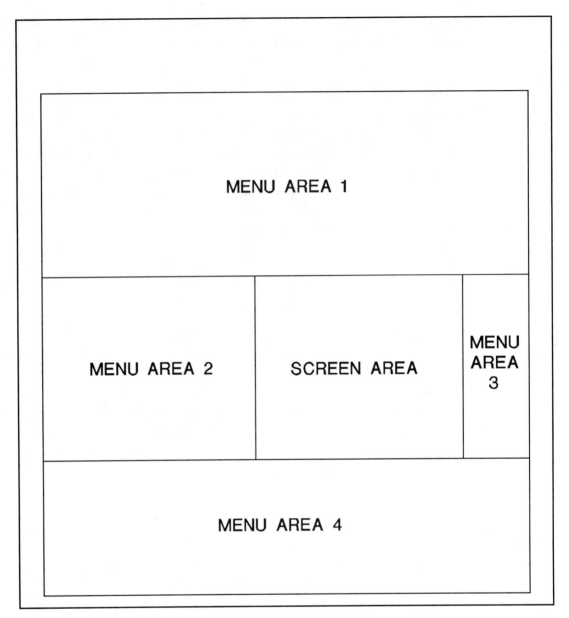

Figure 14-1 The Four Screen Areas of the Overlay

from the Screen Root Menu Settings or at the "Command:" prompt type in **TABLET** and press ⏎.

Command: **tablet**
Option (ON/OFF/CAL/CFG): ⏎

CFG (Configuration) Option The CFG option is used to set up the individual tablet menu areas and the screen pointing area. At this time a preprinted overlay should have been fixed to the tablet. Its menu areas should suit the menu you wish to use. The sequence of prompts is as follows:

Command: **tablet**
Option (ON/OFF/CAL/CFG): **cfg**
Enter number of tablet menus desired (0-4) <default>:

Select the number of individual menu areas desired (with a limit of 4). The next prompt asks:

Do you want to realign tablet menu areas? <N>:

If you respond **No** (**N** or press ⏎), the prompts will skip to selecting rows and columns. If you respond **Yes** (or **Y**), then for each of the menu areas specified you will be prompted to "point and pick" three corners as follows:

Digitize upper left corner of menu area n:
Digitize lower left corner of menu area n:
Digitize lower right corner of menu area n:

The "n" refers to tablet menu areas of the corresponding tablet number in the menu. If the three corners you digitize do not form a right angle (90 degrees), you will be prompted to try again. Individual areas may be skewed on the tablet and with each other, but such an arrangement usually does not provide the most efficient use of total tablet space. Tablet areas should not overlap.

The next prompts are as follows:

Enter the number of columns for menu area n:
Enter the number of rows for menu area n:

Enter the numbers from the keyboard. The area will be subdivided into equal rectangles determined by the row and column values you have entered. If the values you enter do not correspond to the overlay row/column values, the results will be unpredictable when trying to use the tablet. Remember also that the overlay must suit the menu being used.

The standard AutoCAD overlay is installed as follows:

Command: **tablet**
Option (ON/OFF/CAL/CFG): **cfg**
Enter number of tablet menus desired (0-4) <default>: **4**
Do you want to realign tablet menu areas? <N>: **y** *if required*

At this time, digitize areas 1 through 4, as shown in Figure 14-2. The values for columns and rows must be entered as follows:

MENU AREA	COLUMN	ROW
1	25	9
2	11	9
3	9	7
4	25	7

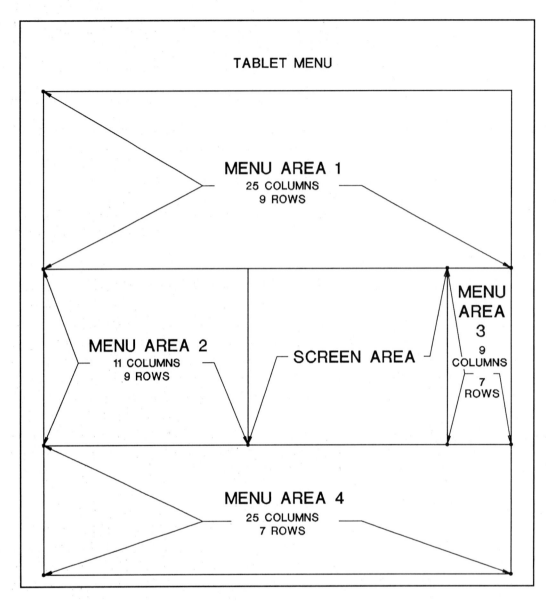

Figure 14-2 Digitizing the Screen Areas of the Tablet Menu

The above values are for the ACAD.MNX menu. Other menus may vary. To simplify installing the standard ACAD.MNX tablet, a screen menu option called RE-CFG automatically responds with the correct values for columns and rows as long as the areas 1 through 4 are selected in the proper sequence.

Once the tablet menu areas have been configured, you will be prompted to digitize the corners of the screen pointing area. With the overlay that accompanies the standard ACAD.MNX, there is an area set aside for screen pointing. Because there is no command/icon programming associated with the screen pointing area, it is not necessary to specify this particular area. It is, however, positioned for maximum productivity in tablet usage. You may specify a rectangular area anywhere on the tablet, as long as it does not overlap any of the tablet menu areas. On a large (table-sized) tablet, a large screen area may be specified. Too large an area, however, can become tiresome to use. An area about the size of the pad supplied with a mouse (8" × 6") is recommended. The drafting-table-sized tablets are used primarily for digitizing large maps and paper drawings without having to move and recalibrate. The prompts for specifying the screen area are as follows:

Do you want to respecify the screen pointing area? <N>

If you reply **Yes** (or **Y**), you will be prompted as follows:

Digitize lower left corner of screen pointing area:
Digitize upper right corner of screen pointing area:

ON/OFF Option The default setting of the TABLET mode is OFF. The OFF setting does not incapacitate the tablet as you might think, but means that you are not going to use the tablet for digitizing (making copies of paper drawings). With the TABLET mode set to OFF you may use the tablet to select command/ icons in the areas programmed accordingly. You may also use the puck in the screen area of the tablet to control the screen cursor.

In order to digitize paper drawings, you must respond to the prompt as follows:

Command: **tablet**
Option (ON/OFF/CAL/CFG): **on**

Most systems have a toggle key to switch the TABLET mode ON and OFF. With many PCs, the toggle is the function key F10 .

CAL Option If the tablet has been calibrated already, the last calibration coordinates will still be in effect. If not, or if you wish to change the calibration (necessary when you move the paper drawing on the tablet), you may respond as follows:

Option (ON/OFF/CAL/CFG): **cal**
Calibrate tablet for use...
Digitize first known point: *digitize the first known point*

The point on the paper drawing you select must be one whose coordinates you know. The next prompt asks you to enter the actual paper drawing coordinates of the point you just digitized as follows:

Enter coordinates for first point: *enter those known coordinates*

You are then prompted to digitize and specify coordinates for the second known point as follows:

Digitize second known point: *digitize the second known point*
Enter coordinates for second point: *enter those known coordinates*

An example of a drawing that might be digitized is a map as shown in Figure 14-3.

If for example, the map in Figure 14-3 has been printed on an 11" × 17" sheet and you wish to digitize it on a 12" × 12" digitizer, you can overlay and digitize on half of the map at a time. You may use the coordinates 10560,2640 and 7920,5280 for two calibrating points. But, because the X-coordinates increase toward the left, you must consider them as negative values in order to make them increase to the right. Therefore, in calibrating the map, you may use coordinates -10560,2640 and -7920,5280 to calibrate the first half and coordinates -7920,2640 and -5280,5280 for the second half.

The points on the paper should be selected so that the X values increase toward the right and the Y values increase upward.

SKETCHING — THE SKETCH COMMAND

The SKETCH command causes AutoCAD to draw connected lines of predetermined lengths immediately on the screen in response to mouse or puck movement. This feature makes a drawing that duplicates your tracing over a paper drawing fixed to a tablet or makes a sketch pad out of your computer screen with the cursor as your drawing implement, controlled by a mouse or puck.

Sketching may be used to generate irregular shapes not easily created through the more conventional means of placing entities. Maps and signatures are two examples of applications for sketching.

The connecting line segments that AutoCAD draws to create the sketch will be the length that you specify. The shorter the length you specify, the smoother the shapes will appear. But a large sketch with many long sketch lines of short segment lengths can result in a memory-hungry drawing. Therefore, it is recommended that you specify increment lengths no shorter than necessary to achieve a reasonably smooth plot appearance.

Although AutoCAD places no limit on the kilo- (or mega-) bytes that a drawing requires, disk storage limits might be a factor. For example, you may simulate a circle with a polygon of six straight-line segments or with 1024 segments. If smoothness is your goal, you must be prepared to deal with a larger drawing. This means longer REGENS and more memory required for storage. Also, the smoothness of the visible object on the screen may not reflect the smoothness of the plotted object. Therefore, it may be necessary to make a test plot to determine the optimum length of increments that you should specify.

SKETCH Command

Before using the SKETCH command you should turn ORTHO and SNAP modes OFF. The SKETCH command is invoked from the Screen Root Menu Draw or at the "Command:" prompt type in **SKETCH** and press ↵.

Command: **sketch**
Record increment <default>: ↵

You may respond with a value in drawing units or you may accept the default value by pressing ↵. The prototype drawing default setting is 0.10 units. The

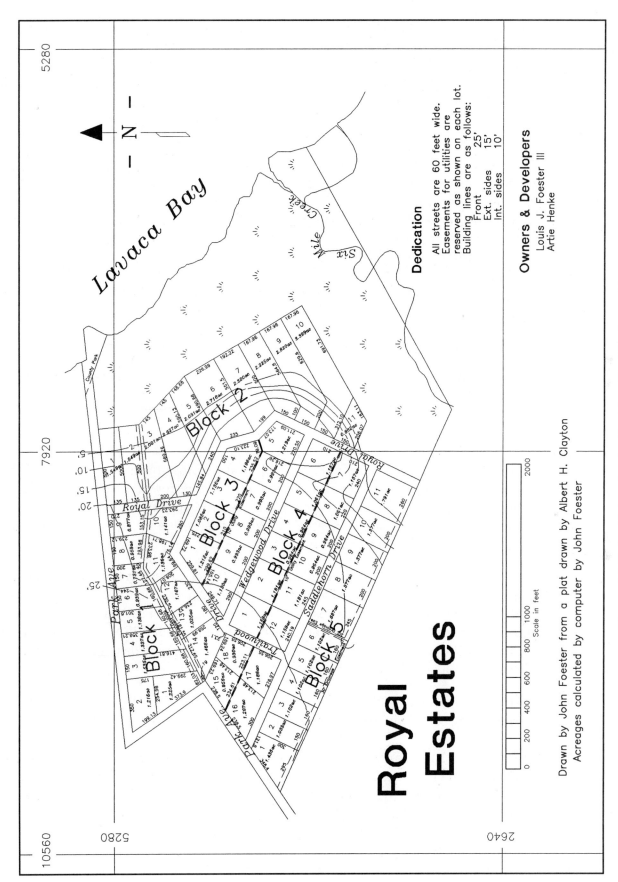

Drawn by John Foester from a plat drawn by Albert H. Clayton
Acreages calculated by computer by John Foester

Figure 14-3 An Example of a Drawing Digitized as a Map

The Tablet and Digitizing

current value is saved in the system variable called SKETCHING. You may also respond to the "Record increment <current>:" prompt by specifying two points, either keyed in or picked on the screen, causing AutoCAD to use the distance between the points as the "record (rec' ord) increment" (Note the accent). Once a record increment is specified, AutoCAD displays the following list of options:

Sketch   Pen   eXit   Quit   Record   Erase   Connect

Once you are in SKETCH mode, several optional subcommands can be used, created especially for the SKETCH mode. These are accessible as either single key entries, or as mouse/puck button, provided your mouse/puck has the number of buttons corresponding to the option. The table below shows the optional subcommands, their key, button number, and function. Normal button functions are not usable while in the SKETCH mode.

Command Character	Pointer Button	Function
P	Pick	Raise/lower pen
.(period)	1	Line to point
R	2	Record lines
X, Space or ↵	3	Record lines and exit
Q, or Ctrl + C	4	Discard lines and exit
E	5	Erase
C	6	Connect

Pen — Up/Down An imaginary pen follows the cross-hairs as you control the cursor with the mouse or tablet puck. When the pen is down, AutoCAD sketches a connected segment whenever the cursor moves the specified increment distance from the previously sketched segment. When the pen is up, the pen follows the cursor movement without drawing.

The pen is raised (up) and lowered (down) by either pressing the pick button on the mouse/puck or by pressing **P** on the keyboard. An exercise to demonstrate this is to press the pick button or press **P** on the keyboard several times while slowly moving the cursor across the screen. When you invoke a "PEN UP" the current location of the pen will be the endpoint of the last segment drawn, which will be shorter than a standard increment length.

A "PEN UP" does not take you out of the SKETCH mode. Nor does a "PEN UP" permanently record the lines drawn during the current SKETCH mode.

. (Period) — Line to Point While the pen is up, you can cause AutoCAD to draw a straight line from the last segment to the current cursor location and return to the "PEN UP" status by typing . (period) from the keyboard. This is convenient for long straight lines that might occur in the middle of irregular shapes.

R — Record Lines being displayed while the cursor is moved (with pen down) are only temporary. They will appear green (or red if the current color for that layer or entity is green) on color monitors until they are permanently recorded. These temporary segments are subject to being edited with special Sketch options until you press **R** to record the latest lines. These may include several groups of connected lines drawn during "PEN DOWN" sequences separated by "PEN UPs." When the Record option is invoked by pressing **R**, ⏎, or the third mouse/puck button, the total number of recorded segments is reported as follows:

> nnn lines recorded

E — Erase Prior to any group(s) of connected lines being recorded with the Record option above, you may use the E (Erase) option to remove any or all of the lines from the last segment back to the first. The sequence of prompts is as follows:

> Erase:
> Select end of delete

The pen is automatically set to up and you may then use the cross-hairs to remove segments, starting from the last segment. When you are satisfied with the lines remaining, press **P** or the pick button to accept the erasure. To abort the erasure and return to the SKETCH mode, press **E** again (or any other command) and the following will be displayed:

> Erase aborted

C — Connect Whenever a disconnect occurs (pen up or erase), you can reconnect and continue sketching from the point of the last disconnect as long as you have not exited the SKETCH command. The sequence is as follows:

> Connect:
> Move to endpoint of line.

At this prompt you can move the cross-hairs near the end of the last segment. When you are within a specified increment length, sketching begins, connected to that last endpoint. This option is meaningless if invoked during "PEN DOWN." A message will say so if you try. A message will also tell you:

> No last point known

if no last point exists. The Connect option can be canceled by pressing **C** a second time.

X — Record and Exit The X option exits the SKETCH mode after recording all temporary lines. This can also be accomplished by pressing either ⏎ or spacebar.

Q — Quit The Q option exits the SKETCH mode without recording any temporary lines. It is the same as ⒸⓉⓡⓛ + Ⓒ.

TABLET MODE AND SKETCHING

Sketching while in the TABLET mode operates similar to sketching with a mouse or on a tablet with the TABLET mode off. The difference is that the entire tablet surface is used for digitizing while the TABLET mode is on, making the maximum area available for tracing but making the screen menus inaccessible.

Editing Sketches

Once sketched lines have been recorded and the SKETCH command has been terminated, you can use regular AutoCAD Editor editing commands (like COPY, MOVE, ERASE) to edit the individual line segments or sketched Polylines (discussed next) just as though they had been drawn by the LINE or PLINE command. In the case of sketched Polylines, the PEDIT command can be used for editing.

Sketching in Polylines

You can cause AutoCAD to make the created sketch segments into Polylines instead of lines by setting the system variable SKPOLY to a nonzero value.

Linetypes in Sketching

You should use the CONTINUOUS linetype while sketching, whether using regular lines or Polylines.

COMPUTER RESPONSE AND SKETCH ACCURACY

A certain amount of computation is required each time AutoCAD must determine when and where an individual line segment is drawn. On slower systems, you must be careful not to run off and leave the computer behind when moving the cursor across the screen. It is possible that you could cause AutoCAD (primarily due to a slower computer reaction) to not react in time to draw a segment in the desired direction. This can occur if you "curve" the object line and move the cursor several increment lengths before AutoCAD computes an earlier segment's endpoint.

Some systems limit the numer of temporary segments that can be drawn before they are recorded. If you are about to overload the system, you will hear a continuous beep and be prompted:

Please raise the pen!

Invoke a "PEN UP" until you see the message:

Thank you. Lower the pen and continue.

Limited systems may display the following warning:

Warning—low memory—accuracy may be low.

This warning is the result of AutoCAD's memory requirements. It is not related to drawing size or sketch complexity. If you see a warning about low memory, you should stop tracing and save the current sketch before proceeding.

CHAPTER
15 Customizing AutoCAD

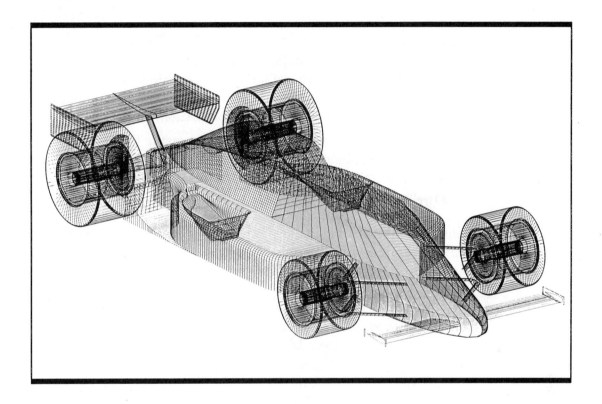

Off-the-shelf AutoCAD is extremely powerful. But, like many popular engineering and business software programs, it does not automatically do all things for all users. It does (probably better than any software available) permit users to make changes and additions to the core program to suit individual needs and applications. Word processors offer a feature by which you can save a combination of many keystrokes and invoke them at any time with just a few keystrokes. This is known as a macro. Data base management programs (as well as other types of programs) have their own library of users' functions that can also be combined and saved as a user-named, custom designed command. These programs also allow you to create and save standard blank forms for use later to be filled out as needed. Using these features to make your copy of a generic program unique and more powerful for your particular application is known as customizing.

Customizing AutoCAD can include several facets. Drafters can create custom linetypes while in the AutoCAD Editor. Custom hatch patterns, shapes, and text fonts can be created by the use of text editors in generating files conforming to special bit codes. Customizing menus, however, is less cryptic and, therefore, easier.

CUSTOM MENUS

The customizing that is the easiest to create for the AutoCAD operator is that of custom menus. Two reasons for menus being easy to customize are:

1. Custom menus can consist of AutoCAD commands that the AutoCAD operator should already be familiar with. Learning new names of functions is not necessary. Only a few special symbols for handling and identifying the menu devices are involved in menu customization.

2. Custom menus are written in text form, using the character strings, numeric input, and sequences normally used when performing drawing tasks from the keyboard and AutoCAD screen menus. It is not necessary to learn a new system of codes for inputting direction and distance.

Menu files are written as text files using keyboard characters. Each line of characters represents a line that may be invoked by picking the appropriate area on the screen menu, a tablet, or button on a mouse or function box.

Only one menu can be active at any one time. That one menu may include provisions for several different devices to be activated. Devices are the screen menu area, the digitizer buttons, tablet areas, and function boxes; and with AutoCAD's Release 9.0, came pull-down, pop-up, and icon menus, and dialogue boxes. In order to make any *filename*.MNX the current menu, invoke the MENU command and respond to the prompt for a menu name with the filename (without the .MNX extension). If you have created or placed a *filename*.MNU file on a path on a valid drive, and respond with the *filename*, AutoCAD will automatically compile the file into a filename.MNX file and load it for use in the Drawing Editor.

The Pick Button

The only nonprogrammable location on any menu device is the pick button on the buttons device. The first digitizer button is ALWAYS the pick, therefore when programming the buttons, the first programmable line is actually for the second button.

MENU LINES

One menu line represents a location on a device from where the user may invoke the commands on that line. For example, moving the cursor (with mouse or keyboard (**Ins**) and up or down arrows) to highlight a line in the screen menu area and then pressing either the digitizer pick button or the keyboard (⏎) key will cause that program line to be activated. Pressing the second button on the mouse or digitizer will activate the first program line in the BUTTONS section of the current menu. Placing the cross-hairs of the tablet mouse/puck over a particular rectangle on the digitizing tablet overlay and then pressing the pick button will cause the corresponding tablet menu program line to be activated, provided the digitizing tablet has been properly configured.

CAUTION!

Menu lines read and take meaning from every character and space. If you indent three spaces before typing a character, those three spaces are equivalent to pressing the spacebar (the same as striking (⏎)) three times when that line is picked. If you were not careful to "carriage return," and unintentionally left some spaces at the end of a line, some text editors will add unwanted spaces to ends of those lines. This interpretation of spaces on a line in a program file might vary from one type of file to another. AutoCAD's various customizable features each have their own syntax requirements. The embedded programmable language, AutoLISP, treats and uses characters and spaces differently from Menu, Hatch, and Linetype custom files. AutoLISP routines are not sensitive to added spaces and indentations outside of parentheses like Menu routines are.

More than One Text Line on a Program Line

One line represents one location. But it is possible to have one program line take up several text lines in a menu file. This is facilitated by using the (+) symbol as the last character of a text line when an extremely long string of commands and programming exceeds the width of the screen the programmer wishes to view. The seven text lines in the example below are considered to be one program line. The "[FIX]" will be displayed on the screen menu if the lines are placed accordingly. When you pick the "FIX" from the menu, all seven lines will be called because the first six lines end with a (+) symbol. This particular program line (remember, it is considered one line) takes a line that has been broken and puts it back together. It also mixes in AutoLISP.

```
[FIX](SETQ A (GETPOINT "NEAR FAR END OF ONE LINE:  ")) NEA;\+
(SETQ B (GETPOINT "NEAR FAR END OF OTHER LINE:  ")) NEA;\+
(SETQ P (OSNAP A "END"));+
(SETQ Q (OSNAP B "END"));+
ERASE !A !B;;+
LINE !P !Q;;
SCREEN MENU WITH BUTTONS
```

A copy of a menu file called ERASE.MNU is shown below.

Context:	Ref. Line Number
***BUTTONS	1
;	2
W	3
L	4
***SCREEN	5
ERASE	6 / 1
[ERASE]erase	7 / 2
[WIPE-OUT]erase	8 / 3
[ERASE-ABCDE]erase	9 / 4
erase	10 / 5
^Cerase	11 / 6
^C^Cerase	12 / 7
line	13 / 8
circle	14 / 9
arc	15 / 10
[CANCEL]^C	16 / 11
UNDO	17 / 12
[ERASE W]erase w	18 / 13
[ERASE L]erase l	19 / 14
[ERASE C]erase c	20 / 15
[ERL-ONLY]erase l;;	21 / 16
[]erase	22 / 17

The ERASE.MNU Line-by-Line Analysis

NOTE: Some of the lines in the ERASE.MNU are shown as examples of what NOT TO DO and WHY NOT.

Line 1   ***BUTTONS — The three asterisks (*) designate the device activated by the lines that follow. The buttons are those on the mouse or digitizer puck.

Line 2   The order of buttons starts with the first program line after ***BUTTONS corresponding to the second button on the mouse/puck. Remember, the first mouse or puck button is always the pick button and is not programmable. The semicolon (;) is the equivalent of the RETURN key.

Lines 3 & 4   These are the second and third program lines corresponding to the third and fourth mouse/puck buttons. "W" and "L" are handy for Window, Last, or Ltype (for LAYER).

> **NOTE:** On a stylus with no second button, all program lines following the ***BUTTONS (and before the next ***DEVICE) will be ignored. Similarly, on a three-button mouse/puck, the third program line (for the fourth button) will be ignored. In AutoCAD's ACAD.MNU there are nine program lines following the "***BUTTONS" line. In this case it will support a ten-button device including the pick button.

Line 5   ***SCREEN — All program lines following this line (and before the next ***DEVICE) will be displayed on lines in the menu area on the right side of the screen.

> **NOTE:** Screen submenus, when created, must take into consideration the number of lines available on the side screen menu areas. Many standard screen menu areas will display only 20 program lines.

Line 6/1   ERASE —This is the sixth line in the menu file and the 1st line in the screen menu. THIS IS NOT A VERY GOOD PROGRAM LINE. The problem with this line is that there are eight spaces before the command. This does two undesirable things:

1. The line will appear blank on the screen, when in fact, picking that line WILL invoke a command. It will be a blind command.
2. The eight spaces before the command will cause ⏎ to be pressed eight times before the command is entered. Remember that pressing ⏎ at the "Command:" prompt recalls the last used command. Pressing it several times inadvertently might be undesirable if the last command were UNDO.

Line 7 / 2   [ERASE]erase — The brackets are used to display a message on the screen. When used, the text in the program part of the line will not be visible on the screen.

Line 8 / 3   [WIPE-OUT]erase — The text message can say whatever you wish, but should explain what that program line does.

Line 9 / 4   [ERASE-ABCDE]erase — The message's visibility is limited to eight characters.

Line 10 / 5   erase — The command is now visible, but has the undesirable ⏎ space in front of it.

Line 11 / 6   ^Cerase — The ^C cancels any previous command and returns you to the "Command:" prompt before invoking the program line. This sets up the program line for immediate use.

Line 12 / 7   ^C^Cerase — Part of the command disappears from the display. The double cancel provides assurance of returning to the "Command:" before invoking the program line. For example, in the Dimension LEADER command it takes two [Cancel]s to return to the command status.

Line 13 / 8   line — "line" is both message and command.
Line 14 / 9   circle — "circle" is both message and command.
Line 15 / 10   arc — "arc" is both message and command.
Line 16 / 11   [CANCEL]^C — ^C is the same as (Ctrl) + (C).
Line 17 / 12   UNDO — UNDO is both message and command.
Line 18 / 13   [ERASE W]erase w — is a quick "ERASE WINDOW."
Line 19 / 14   [ERASE L]erase l — is a quick "ERASE LAST."
Line 20 / 15   [ERASE C]erase c — is a quick "ERASE CROSSING."
Line 21 / 16   [ERL-ONLY]erase l;; — is a quick "ERASE LAST" ONLY.
Line 22 / 17   []erase — This is only HALF AS BAD AS line 6 / 1. It is a BLIND command (displays nothing but does something), but at least it has no leading spaces.

> *NOTE:* With the "W" and "L" available on the buttons, lines 18 / 13, 19 / 14, and 21 / 16 may not be needed.

Review

The above menu demonstrates some DOs and DON'Ts of menu programming. Other devices are subject to the same conditions. Leading spaces on a program line in a tablet menu will also cause a corresponding number of ENTER strokes. The brackets are primarily used for devices that are visible on the screen. They can also be used within a tablet menu text for reference, as in the ACAD.MNU file for numbering all of the many locations of ***TABLET1.

Menu-to-Menu

The current menu may also call another menu to take its place and then be called back by that second menu in return. While a particular menu is active it may provide for devices to change back and forth between submenus, thereby causing different sets of commands to be invoked by their various pick areas. The best examples of this are the many nested screen menu configurations in the ACAD.MNU. All but the Root Menu are technically submenus but we will forego the "sub-" and refer to them as just menus.

Special Menu Symbology

There are some characters that have special meaning in a menu program line. These are listed below with a brief description. More detailed explanations will be given about these special symbols later in this chapter along with examples of their use.

[ ]	Items within leading brackets are nonfunctional. They may be used to display a message.
***	Three leading asterisks designate the beginning of a menu device such as SCREEN, TABLET, etc.
**	Two leading asterisks designate the beginning of a submenu within a particular device.
$S=	Activates and displays the previous submenu.
$S=SCREEN	Activates and displays the Screen Root Menu.
$S=S	Will display the Root Menu if the first item after the "***SCREEN" heading is the "**S" heading.
$S=<name>	Activates and displays the <name> submenu.
;	Presses ⏎.
space	Presses ⏎ in the same manner as striking the spacebar does from the keyboard.
\	Pauses for user input.
+	When placed at the end of a text line, it joins the next text line into that line as part of the same program line.
x^H*	Allows input of an asterisk for use as a global symbol in response to certain prompts. A leading asterisk, even if it by itself, will terminate the remainder of that particular submenu. The ^H is the control symbol for the backspace.
^C	(Ctrl) + (C) for [Cancel].
^B	ON/OFF TOGGLE for the SNAP mode.
^D	THREE WAY TOGGLE for the COORDINATE mode.
^E	LEFT/TOP/RIGHT TOGGLE for the ISOPLANE mode.
^G	ON/OFF TOGGLE for the GRID mode.
^O	ON/OFF TOGGLE for the ORTHO mode.
^T	ON/OFF TOGGLE for the TABLET mode.

AutoCAD's list of devices that can be configured as shown include the following:

> ***BUTTONS
> ***SCREEN
> ***TABLET1
> ***TABLET2
> ***TABLET3
> ***TABLET4
> ***AUX1
> ***POP1
>   thru
> ***POP10
>   and
> ***icon

Each three-star (***) heading designates the beginning of a particular device. Earlier in this chapter the BUTTONS and SCREEN menus were described. Remember, the second button on the mouse or digitizer puck activates the first program line after the ***BUTTONS heading. A single button stylus is not programmable. Any device will use only the number of lines that it has buttons or selection points for, regardless how many program lines are written into its menu. Excess lines are simply ignored.

Changing the Screen Menu

The screen menu area will accommodate 20 program lines. The lines in the menu normally coincide with the ones on the screen starting from the top. Studying a printout of the ACAD.MNU is an excellent way to see how the screen menu can be manipulated for the convenience of the drafter. But without some prior understanding of the different means of handling menus and commands simultaneously, you can neither appreciate the reasons for certain arrangements of menus nor the use of menu symbols.

It would be useful to make a diagram of menu hierarchies for a menu that is designed for a particular purpose. Later in this chapter you will be asked to diagram menu paths and then plan how to manipulate them on and off the screen to achieve the desired result.

Advanced Menu Programming

The previous examples illustrate basic menu display procedures. Some of the more intricate maneuvers covered in this chapter will show how the custom menu programmer can add to the user friendliness of overall function and command usage.

"Invalid Point," The Prompt that Won't Let Go

Many AutoCAD functions will not allow you to return to the "Command:" prompt without either entering the correct type of response(s) until the "Command:" prompt reappears, or pressing **Ctrl** + **C** to cancel. The persistent "Invalid point" or similar message lets you know that AutoCAD does not permit indiscriminate changing of one's mind. This could be a problem when you try to invoke a command from a menu device before another is completed. This is especially true with prior multiple prompt commands like LAYER, DIM, or PEDIT.

Note in the **SET submenu (shown later in this chapter), the ^C^C (double **Ctrl** + **C** or **Cancel**) entry for returning to a "Command:" status. The line is as follows:

    [APERTUR:]$S=X $S=APERTURE ^C^CAPERTURE

Note also that a space or (;) is not required behind the ^C's. The ^C's are "self ENTERing." Other **Ctrl** characters (those preceded by ^) like the TOGGLES ^D for COORDINATES, and the ^O for ORTHO are also "self ENTERing."

A Manageable List of Choices

Because many of AutoCAD's commands have a variety of possible responses that are nonnumerical (and do not make up a long list), the ACAD.MNU provides ready-made responses on screen submenus that appear automatically when the particular command is picked from a previous screen submenu. This convenience is also provided when a command is picked from an OVERLAY configured properly on a digitizing tablet. Picking LINE from the Draw submenu or from the Draw pull-down menu will cause the **LINE submenu to appear on the screen with its useful "close," "continue," "undo," and other ready-to-use responses. Picking DIMVARS while in the DIMENSIONING mode will cause the first of several long lists of possible dimensioning variables to appear on the screen. Also included are the "on" and "off" secondary responses required if certain dimensioning variables are selected.

Some commands either do not require responses or there is not a small (2 to 40) number of tailor-made responses that would fit reasonably on one or two screen lists. The LTSCALE command, when picked from the Settings submenu, for instance, does not cause another submenu to replace the Settings submenu because there are no acceptable responses except a real number, the range of which is infinite. Also, once the LTSCALE is set, the command is rarely used again.

Studying a printout of the Settings text portion of the ACAD.MNU shows that the LTSCALE and UNITS program lines are the only ones that do not perform multiple duties. Other selections like the QTEXT, for example, display another submenu (**QTEXT in this case) and at the same time invoke the prescribed command (QTEXT in this case). That menu line is written as follows:

[QTEXT:]$S=X $S=QTEXT ^C^CQTEXT

> **NOTE:** Not all submenus have the same name as their prompt and their command like QTEXT does.

Two Submenus at a Time

In the above example (QTEXT), the submenu is displayed by use of the "$S=QTEXT" mechanism. The purpose of "$S=X" will be explained later. For now, however, it is worthwhile to note that it is called up at the same time as the **QTEXT submenu. The mystery of how it is possible to display two submenus at the same time will unfold into a pleasing solution to the problem of saving space on the disk when writing menus.

Theory of Menu Choices

Many commands have a range of possible responses that is infinite. For example, how many possible points are there where you may begin a line? The classification of the response may be limited though. In the case of the line, the point must be in the form of a list comprising the X, Y, (and Z if 3D) coordinates in the proper order. But, the number of possible points available is infinite. Even responses that require a string, such as a layer name, are countless when you compute the combinations of characters available.

In spite of the above, there are many cases where the range of choices (of responses to commands) in normal usage is just a dozen or so. For example, many drawings require fewer than 20 layers, whose names have already been predetermined by the type used in a particular discipline. But this is not the best case for a custom program, that is, one that allows creation of layers by a list of predetermined names. This can be taken care of by using a prototype drawing having the layers already created. However, it would be convenient to have a screen menu of layer names that would facilitate setting those predetermined layers. A better case for a customized choice menu is for selecting from a list of standard door sizes. Most buildings require fewer than 20 different door sizes, even though there may be hundreds of doors in the building. Whatever the objective, a planning diagram, as shown in Figure 15–1, is helpful.

Example — Sizing a Drawing

A common task to all drafting is to determine what sheet size to use in plotting the hard copy. This task is ideally suited to custom programming, therefore AutoCAD added a special feature (the SETUP item) on the main screen menu to accomplish this. A special file called MVSETUP.LSP is included with AutoCAD's Release 11.0. The routine is designed to allow the user to set the drawing units, the scale, and the width and height of the sheet size in units.

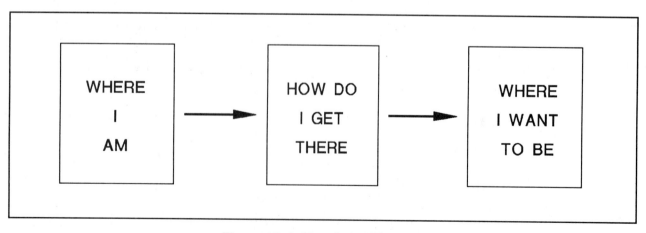

Figure 15–1 Planning a Diagram

The MVSETUP.LSP program contains some advanced AutoLISP commands, along with some menu manipulation. The primary purpose of this section is to demonstrate menu manipulation, therefore, a simpler routine will be introduced here that will only set the drawing sheet size.

Setting Limits The aspiring custom programmer should be far enough in AutoCAD to know that a drawing can be made to extend beyond the limits (and sometimes construction layout lines do so). Also, the entities may take up only a minute portion of the limits. Either case ignores the primary purpose of the limits feature, which was intended to establish the eventual hard copy sheet size on which the drawing is to be plotted.

Limited Range of Choices The main purpose in this example of menu planning, therefore, is to make it convenient for the user to establish the limits of the drawing. Like being able to choose between steak or lobster in the restaurant, the range of choices will include those sheet sizes commonly used to plot most of the CAD department's drawings. The text printout of a typical selection list (as typed out by using the text editor) might be as follows:

$$[8.5 \times 11]$$
$$[11 \times 8.5]$$
$$[17 \times 11]$$
$$[22 \times 17]$$
$$[34 \times 22]$$

> **NOTE:** The only programming in the above list is the use of the brackets "[ ]". But, this is a proper beginning.

Naming Submenus The screen submenu must have a unique name as its heading in the main device menu file. In this example, the purpose is to set standard limits, therefore an abbreviated name of SLIMITS will be given to our main course menu item.

```
**SLIMITS 3
[8.5 × 11]
[11 × 8.5]
[17 × 11]
[22 × 17]
[34 × 22]
8 blank lines
```

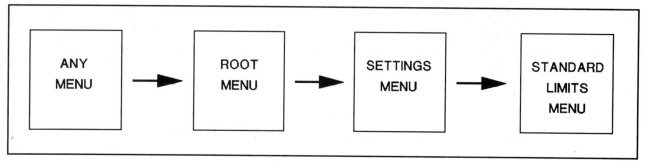

Figure 15-2 Planning a Customized Program

The reason for the "3" after the name and the blank lines will become evident soon. The diagram now taking shape in Figure 15-2 requires additional planning by the operator who will use the custom programming.

Accessing a Submenu A custom programmer must determine the best place from which to access this custom submenu called SLIMITS. AutoCAD separates functions into DRAW, EDIT, DISPLAY, etc. classifications. Therefore, the classification of the functions on the submenu must be considered. The functions on the SLIMITS submenu will probably fall into the Settings classification. They can be considered a refinement of the LIMITS command. With this in mind, the SLIMITS submenu will be accessed from the Settings subsubmenu, which has the heading **SET2 3.

Menus should also be analyzed using the frequency of use index. The purpose of a function on the SLIMITS submenu is to establish drawing sheet size. Once established, the sheet size for one drawing does not need to be changed, therefore, the frequency of use index will be low. A planning diagram is shown in Figure 15-3.

> *NOTE:* The headings are the submenu addresses.

> *NOTE:* The Settings submenu is accessible only from the main screen menu (AutoCAD or Root Menu) whose address in the text file is "**S" and is unique and special. It is the one that is displayed when the ACAD.MNU is first called up.

Customizing a Final Return Path Planning a custom menu should also include what will occur (menuwise) after a menu item is picked. In the case above, because of the low frequency index, it would be convenient to return to the main menu. Multiple use of the SLIMIT items is not anticipated. One alternative

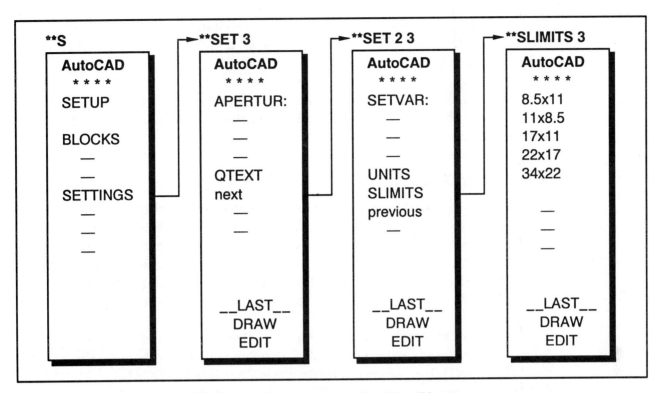

Figure 15-3 Example of a Planning Diagram

would be to return to the Settings submenu, as the SLIMITS program is often used in conjunction with other Settings submenu items. The following (more advanced) planning diagram in Figure 15-4 shows the final return path as determined by the custom programmer.

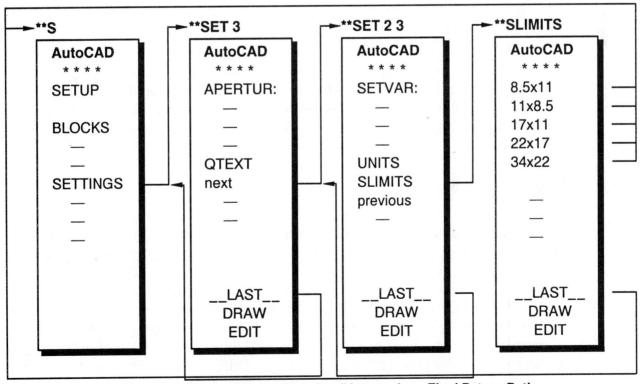

Figure 15-4 Customizing a Planning Diagram for a Final Return Path

This menu planning diagram is now complete and indicates that picking any of the [size]'s will return the "**S" menu back to the display. Also note the paths that picking [__LAST__] on either submenu will take.

So, before the MENU programmer starts programming the SLIMITS functions, the lead-in to the primary function menu and the return are all planned out on a diagram like the one above.

Multimenu Display

A refinement to MENU swapping is demonstrated by use of the "3" following the heading. (Note that in the heading the "3" is separated from the name of the submenu by a space.) As explained in the AutoCAD Reference Manual, a number in the heading causes the first line of programmed text to be displayed on the screen area line that corresponds to that number. The "3" will cause the first text line, [8.5 × 11] in this case, to begin on the third line of the screen menu area.

The purpose of this feature is to prevent the first two lines of the existing menu from being displaced (which would make them no longer readily accessible). When the ACAD.MNU first comes up, its first two lines are "AutoCAD" and " * * * * ." Studying the text of the ACAD.MNU will show that these two lines are not on the text of any of the other submenus, even though they are always displayed. The "3" at the heading of all the other submenus keeps these submenus from displacing the "AutoCAD" and " * * * * " on the screen. (A negative number in the heading following the name will provide the same result starting from the bottom of the screen menu area.)

__LAST__, DRAW, and EDIT

A heading suffix of "3" will keep "AutoCAD" and " * * * * * " displayed on any submenu without having to type it into the program text. A heading suffix of "- n" (n being some integer) will start a replacement menu so as to assure that (n - 1) lines at the bottom will not be displaced. There is another MENU programming feature that must be understood in order to be able to have the desired items displayed.

Blank Lines

Up to this point we have shown how the ACAD.MNU puts two lines at the top of the screen menu and uses the "3" mechanism in all the headings to keep it there. Note that when first called up, the ACAD.MNU screen display does not show the "__LAST__," "DRAW," and "EDIT" items at the bottom. These are displayed when an item is selected that has the "$S=X" in its string of menu functions. Note that the "$S=X" is the first program text item in almost all of the selections on the main menu. Therefore, a first pick of one of these selections will install the "**X" submenu on the screen, starting at the third line from the top and putting in 15 blank lines before the last three (__LAST__,DRAW, and EDIT).

Blank Lines Serve a Purpose

The blank lines before and after items in a menu text do serve a special purpose. A menu program line, whether blank or not, will displace any line currently being displayed on the corresponding line of the submenu its submenu replaces. By understanding (or not understanding) this, the custom programmer might create a submenu that affects whether or not parts of the current menu disappear.

The following example is a submenu of four lines (starting at line 3 by using the "3" in the heading). This submenu will displace the first six lines of a currently displayed submenu, leaving the remaining lines from 7 through 20 still being displayed. The text would be as follows:

```
**JUST4 3
[line 3]some function
[line 4]some other function
[line 5]still another function
[line 6]still another function
**THENEXTSUBMENU 3
```

> **NOTE:** There are no blank lines between "[line 6]...." and "**THE NEXT..." menu lines.

Let's say that **JUST4 is accessible from the **SET menu as shown below:

```
**SET 3
[APERTUR:]$S=X $S=APERTURE ^C^CAPERTURE
[AXIS:]$S=X $S=AXIS ^C^CAXIS
[BLIPS:]$S=X $S=BLIPMODE ^C^CBLIPMODE
[COLOR:]$S=X $S=COLOR ^C^CCOLOR
[DRAGMOD:]$S=X $S=DRAGMODE ^C^CDRAGMODE
[ELEV:]$S=X $S=ELEV ^C^CELEV
[GRID:]$S=X $S=GRID ^C^CGRID
[LINETYP:]$S=X $S=LINETYPE ^C^CLINETYPE
[LIMITS:]$S=X $S=LIMITS ^C^CLIMITS
[LTSCALE:]$S=X $S=LTSCALE
[OSNAP:]$S=X $S=OSNAPC ^C^COSNAP
[QTEXT:]$S=X $S=QTEXT ^C^CQTEXT
[JUST4:]$S=X $S=JUST4
[next]$S=SET2
```

```
**SET2 3
```

The display of the above submenu would look like this:

```
                    AutoCAD
                    * * * *
                    APERTUR
                    AXIS:
                    BLIPS:
                    COLOR:
                    DRAGMOD:
                    ELEV:
                    GRID:
                    LINETYP:
                    LIMITS:
                    LTSCALE:
                    OSNAP:
                    QTEXT:
                    JUST4:
                    next

                    _ _LAST_ _
                     DRAW
                     EDIT
```

The resulting display after picking "JUST4" from the above menu would be as follows:

```
                    AutoCAD
                    * * * *
                    line 3
                    line 4
                    line 5
                    line 6
                    DRAGMOD:
                    ELEV:
                    GRID:
                    LINETYP:
                    LIMITS:
                    LTSCALE:
                    OSNAP:
                    QTEXT:
                    JUST4:
                    next

                    _ _LAST_ _
                     DRAW
                     EDIT
```

The above results may or may not be desirable, depending on whether or not the programmer had wanted to have the 3rd through the 6th lines replaced and the next 14 remain unchanged.

A Poor Example of a Submenu

If the **JUST4 submenu were revised to **JUST4PLUS14 to have 14 blank lines after the fourth item ([line 6]), the text would appear as follows:

> **JUST4PLUS14 3
> [line 3]some function
> [line 4]some other function
> [line 5]still another function
> [line 6]still another function

**THENEXTSUBMENU 3

Too Many Lines

This submenu would not displace the "AutoCAD" or " * * * * " lines but it would displace the last three (_ _LAST_ _, DRAW, and EDIT) lines with the 14 blank lines.

One useful arrangement to use with the ACAD.MNU is to have each submenu start at line 3 and then include a total of 15 lines in the text file whether blank or not. If there were only four items in the menu, then it may be desirable to locate them lower in the screen menu area. Or, it may be desirable to have blank lines between items. A good working example would be as follows: (Note that submenu titles are limited to 31 characters with no spaces between.)

COUNT THE LINES

**SOME_PLUS_4_SPACED_PLUS_SOME 3	**Ref. Nos.**
	3
	4
	5
[line 6]some function	6
	7
[line 8]some other function	8
	9
[line 10]still another function	10
	11
[line 12]still another function	12
	13
	14
	15

**THENEXTSUBMENU 3

A review will show that the above is a common format of the screen submenus in the ACAD.MNU text file.

Getting to the Standard Limits Menu

The prior outline of menu arrangements should be kept in mind in the following example of customizing the ACAD.MNU for setting up standard limits. The first order of business is to arrange the menu so as to be able to get to the **SLIMITS submenu as outlined in the planning diagram. Access will be from the **SET2 submenu. Therefore, the revised text portion of the **SET2 submenu will be as follows:

```
**SET2 3
[SETVAR:]$S=X $S=SETVAR ^C^CSETVAR
[SNAP:]$S=X $S=SNAP ^C^CSNAP
[STYLE:]$S=X $S=STYLE ^C^CSTYLE
[TABLET:]$S=X $S=TABLET ^C^CTABLET
[UNITS:]^CUNITS
[SLIMITS:]$S=X $S=SLIMITS
```

**THENEXTSUBMENU 3

Before leaving the **SET2 submenu, some of its features are worthy of note. The first four items each have two menu-swapping expressions and an AutoCAD command (preceded by "^C^C"). These multiuse lines set up the **X submenu (with __LAST__, DRAW, and EDIT on the bottom three lines), set up the required submenu (**SETVAR in the case of SETVAR), and then invoke the necessary command (SETVAR in the same case).

Note that the UNITS command does not require a submenu. AutoCAD users know that the display switches to the text screen mode following the UNITS command. Note especially that our newly added (SLIMITS) program line only swaps menus and does not invoke a command. In this case, as will be brought out, the command will be invoked when a choice is made from the next submenu.

Multiple Purpose Menu Program Line

Most menu program lines perform multiple duties. As demonstrated in these examples, two separate types of tasks must be accomplished.

1. Menu Handling is getting from one "tool tray" to another. The "$S=" and "$S=name" expressions in a menu line cause the display to be changed as desired along with setting up or swapping the pick areas on other devices. A program line on the screen menu can manipulate pick areas on a tablet or pull-down menu, and they in turn can manipulate the screen menu and each other.

2. AutoCAD's standard commands may be invoked when properly arranged on a program line of any menu device. The user may also have AutoLISP routines in the program line. The programmer should know the sequence of responses required by each AutoCAD command along with the fact that some functions, like those which include the `Ctrl` (" ^ ") device require no response. In addition, these functions do not require a following semicolon (;), which is equivalent to ⏎. These are considered to be self-entering.

Double Returns

The "$S=" by itself returns the last displayed menu. In almost every case the last menu is the **X submenu. (Check the text to see how you got to the current display. It probably had a "$S=X" in it.) Therefore, using "$S=" one time will usually display blank lines between the " * * * * " and the "__LAST__" items because that is exactly what is on the **X submenu. So, in order to display the working submenu that you were using last, it requires a double last mechanism of "$S= $S=." This actually displays the **X submenu for a split second. It then displays the submenu that was the one you were on before getting to this one. It had, on the program line that you selected, a menu swapping device to get you where you are now. It almost takes double talk to describe this double return feature.

TABLET MENUS

The explanations and examples of the screen menu customization above can be applied to customizing the tablet menu area. One problem not encountered in a tablet menu is that of the display. The brackets that enclose nonactive items will not be visible except to someone who is reading the filename.MNU file from which the filename.MNX was compiled.

The main concern in customizing the tablet part of the menu is in placing the programming lines in the right order and in the right area so they will correspond to the preprinted overlay that will be configured on the tablet for use with the menu.

A menu may have up to four tablet areas. They will have the headings of ***TABLET1, ***TABLET2, ***TABLET3, and ***TABLET4. The first program line following a heading will correspond to the configured overlay's upper left column/row rectangle. Subsequent program lines will correspond the rectangle to the right in the same row as its predecessor until the end of the row is reached. Then the next program line will be on the extreme left rectangle of the next row. For example, a tablet menu area with 12 program lines might be in any one of the six following arrangements:

```
 1   2   3   4   5   6   7   8   9  10  11  12
```

```
 1   2   3   4   5   6
 7   8   9  10  11  12
```

```
 1   2   3   4
 5   6   7   8
 9  10  11  12
```

```
 1   2   3
 4   5   6
 7   8   9
10  11  12
```

```
 1   2
 3   4
 5   6
 7   8
 9  10
11  12
```

```
1
2
3
4
5
6
7
8
9
10
11
12
```

If there are more rectangles specified in the tablet configuration than there are program lines, the extras will be nonactive when picked. If there is an excess of program lines in the menu, they will, of course, not be accessible.

EXERCISES

1. What extension must a file have when writing a custom menu?

2. How many menus may be active simultaneously?

3. What AutoCAD command sequence will activate a menu written as a file named XYZ.MNU?

4. Under the ***BUTTONS menu, which program line corresponds to the second button on the mouse/puck?

5. Which menu manipulation symbology will return the screen back to the primary (formally Root Menu) display?

6. What symbology will connect multiple text lines into one program line on a menu?

7. Placing three blank spaces in a menu program line is equivalent to what action from the keyboard?

8. What symbology will return the screen display to the last menu displayed?

9. What is the purpose of the caret " ^ " in a menu program line?

10. What is the purpose of the "^C" at the beginning of a menu program line?

11. Explain how parts of two screen menus can be displayed at the same time.

12. Explain the reason for the space and the "3" following the screen submenu heading.

13. Create a menu file to include a program line that will draw a rectangle whose opposite corners are points whose coordinates are 1,1 and 5,2.

14. Create a menu file to include a program line that will draw a circle whose diameter is 2 units and center is a point whose coordinates are 3,3.

15. Create a menu file to include a program line that will array the previous circle in a polar array every 30 degrees with the center of the array at a point whose coordinates are 4,3.

16. Create a menu file to include a program line that will permit a line-arc-line continuation starting at point 1,1 with user picks for second, third, and fourth points.

17. Create a menu file to include a program line that will permit an arc-line-arc continuation starting at point 1,1 with user picks for second, third, and fourth points.

18. Write a menu file containing the following:
    a. Buttons for ⏎, Cancel , and ERASE LAST ONLY.
    b. Root Screen Menu having five DRAW commands.
    c. Screen submenu having five EDIT commands.
    d. Menu handling lines on each screen menu to activate the other.

19. To the above, include program lines that perform the following:
    a. Invoke the CIRCLE command.
    b. Call up a screen menu with five picks for five different points for the center of the above circle.
    c. Call up a screen menu with five picks for five different radii and returns to the Root Menu when picked.

20. Write lines that set UNITS as follows:
    a. Decimal to four-place display.
    b. Architectural to 1/8"-display.
    c. Each of the above to include a mechanism to return to the graph screen.

EXTERNAL COMMANDS AND ALIASES

AutoCAD allows you to run certain programs without having to exit the Drawing Editor. These include the internal and external DOS commands, word processors, data base and spreadsheet programs, and many others. In order to make these external programs possible to use from within the Editor, you must first list them with certain specifications in an ASCII file called ACAD.PGP.

The ACAD.PGP file might be considered a list of custom commands that you have determined should be accessible during an editing session. Each line in the ACAD.PGP file begins with the name by which the command may be invoked and the actual name of the program file itself. Also included on the line for a particular command is the amount of memory to be set aside for that command, the prompt by which you are notified to begin using that command, and in what state you will be returned to the Drawing Editor.

The format for a command line is as follows:

<Command name>,[<DOS request>],<Memory reserve>,[*]<Prompt>,<Return code>

An example of lines in an ACAD.PGP file for specifying external commands is as follows:

```
SH,,                  35000, *OS Command: ,0
SHELL,,               130000, *OS Command: ,0
TYPE,TYPE,            35000, File to type: ,0
CATALOG,DIR           /W,35000, File specification: ,0
DEL,DEL,              35000, File to erase: ,0
DIR,DIR,              35000, File specification: ,0
EDIT,,                45000, File to edit: ,0
```

The command name should not be the same as an AutoCAD editor command and should be in uppercase characters.

The memory amount specified should be at least 4K larger that the amount the program usually requires. The number must be present even if some operating systems or configurations will not require them.

The prompt is used to inform the operator if additional input is necessary. If the prompt is preceded by an asterisk (*), then the user's response may contain spaces. The response must be terminated by pressing ⏎. Otherwise, pressing the spacebar or ⏎ will terminate the response.

The return code is a bit-coded specification. The number you specify will represent one or more of the bit-codes. For example, if you specify 3, then bit-codes 1 and 2 will be in effect. If you specify 5, then bit-codes 1 and 4 will be in effect. The values are as follows:

1: Load DXB file — This causes a file named $cmd.cxb to be loaded into the drawing at the end of the command.

2: Construct block from DXB file — This causes the response to the prompt to become the name of a Block to be added to the drawing, consisting of entities in the $cmd.dxb file written by the file command. This code must be used in conjunction with bit-code 1. This may not be used to redefine a previously defined Block.

4: Restore text/graphics mode — If this bit-code is included, the mode that you were in (text or graphics) will be returned to when the command is completed; otherwise, you will be in the text mode.

In addition to specifying external programs in the ACAD.PGP file, you can also include aliases for regular AutoCAD commands. An alias is nothing but a nickname.

The format for a line to define an alias is as follows:

<Alias>,*<Full command name>

An example of lines in an ACAD.PGP file for specifying aliases (abbreviations) to AutoCAD commands is as follows:

Customizing AutoCAD

A,	*ARC
BL,	*BLOCK
BR,	*BREAK
C,	*CIRCLE
E,	*ERASE
EXT,	*EXTEND
H,	*HATCH
L,	*LINE
LA,	*LAYER
M,	*MOVE
P,	*PAN
PE,	*PEDIT
PL,	*PLINE
R,	*REDRAW
T,	*TRIM
Z,	*ZOOM

The abbreviation preceding the comma is the character or characters to be entered at the "Command:" prompt. The asterisk (*) must precede the command you wish invoked. It may be a standard AutoCAD command name, a custom command name that has been defined in and loaded with AutoLISP or ADS, or a display or machine driver command name.

HATCH PATTERNS

Certain concepts about hatch patterns should be understood before learning to create one.

1. Hatch patterns are made up of lines or line segment\space combinations. There are no circles or arcs available in hatch patterns like there are in shapes and fonts (which will be covered next).

2. A hatch pattern may be one or more series of repeated parallel lines or repeating dot or line segment/space combinations. That is, each line in one so-called family is like every other line in that same family. And each line has the same offset and stagger (if a segment/space combination) relative to its adjacent sibling as every other line.

3. One hatch pattern can contain multiple families of lines. One family of lines may or may not be parallel to other families. With properly specified base points, offsets, staggers, segment/space combinations, lengths, and relative angles, you can create a hatch pattern from multiple families of segment/space combinations that will display repeated closed polygons.

4. Each family of lines is drawn with offsets and staggers based on its own specified base point and angle.

5. All families of lines in a particular hatch pattern will be located (base point), rotated, and scaled as a group. These factors (location, angle of rotation, and scale factor) are determined when the hatch pattern is loaded by the HATCH command and used to fill a closed polygon in a drawing.

6. The pattern usually can be achieved by different ways of specifying parameters.

Hatch patterns are created by including their definition in a file whose extension is .PAT. This can be done by using a line editor such as EDLIN (EDIT in DOS 5.0) or a word processor in the nondocument (or programmer) mode which will save the text in ASCII format. Your hatch pattern definition can be also be added to the ACAD.PAT file. You can also create a new file specifically for a pattern.

Each pattern definition has one header line giving the pattern name/description and a separate specification line describing each family of lines in the pattern.

The header line has the following format:

*pattern-name[,description]

The pattern name will be the name for which you will be prompted when using the HATCH command. The description is optional and is for use only by someone reading the .PAT file to be able to identify the pattern. The description has no effect nor will it be displayed while using the HATCH command. The leading asterisk denotes the beginning of a hatch pattern.

The format for a line family is as follows:

angle, x-origin, y-origin, delta-x, delta-y [,dash-1, dash-2...]

The brackets "[]" denote optional segment/space specifications used for noncontinuous line families. Note also that any text following a semicolon (;) is for comment only and will be ignored. The angle, origins, and deltas are mandatory (even if their values are zero) in all definitions.

An example of continuous lines that are rotated at 30 degrees and separated by 0.25 units is as follows (see Figure 15–5):

```
*P30, 30 degree continuous
30, 0,0, 0,.25
```

The 30 specifies the angle.

The first and second zero specify the coordinates of the origin.

The third zero, though required, is meaningless for continuous lines.

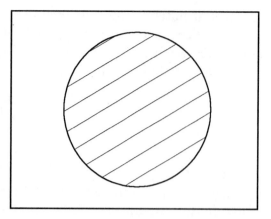

Figure 15-5 A Hatch Pattern with Continuous Lines Rotated at 30 Degrees and Separated by 0.25 Units

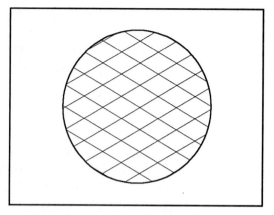

Figure 15-6 A Hatch Pattern with Continuous Lines Crossing at 60 Degrees to Each Other

The 0.25 specifies the distance between lines.

A pattern of continuous lines crossing at 60 degrees to each other could be written as follows (see Figure 15-6):

PX60,x-ing @ 60
30, 0,0, 0,.25
330, 0,0, 0,.25

A pattern of lines crossing at 90 degrees, but having different offsets is as follows (see Figure 15-7):

PX90, x-ing @ 90 w/ 2:1 rectangles
0, 0,0, 0,.25
90, 0,0, 0,.5

Note the effect of the delta-y. It is the amount of offset between lines in one family. Hatch patterns with continuous lines do not require a value (other than zero) for delta-x. Orthogonal continuous lines also do not require values for the x-origin unless used in a pattern that includes broken lines.

To illustrate the use of a value for the y-origin, two parallel families of lines can be written to define a hatch pattern for steel as follows (see Figure 15-8):

*steel
45, 0,0, 0,1
45, 0,.25, 0,1

Three concepts are worthy of note in the above example.

1. If the families were not parallel, then specifying origins other that zero would not serve a purpose.

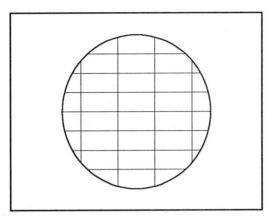

Figure 15-7 A Hatch Pattern with Lines Crossing at 90 Degrees Having Different Offsets

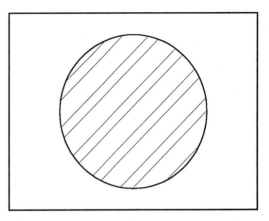

Figure 15-8 Defining a Hatch Pattern for Steel

2. Parallel families of lines should have the same delta-y offsets. Different offsets would serve little purpose.

3. Most importantly, the delta-y is at a right angle to the angle of rotation, but the y-origin is in the y direction of the coordinate system. The steel pattern as written above would fill a polygon, as shown in Figure 15-9. Note the dimensions when used with no changes to the scale factor of 1.0 or rotation angle of zero.

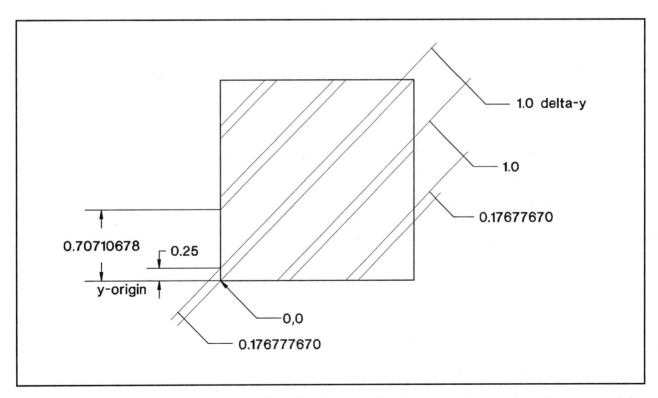

Figure 15-9 The Steel Hatch Pattern with the Delta-Y at a Right Angle to the Angle of Rotation and the Y-Origin in the Y Direction of the Coordinate System

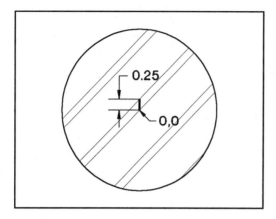

Figure 15-10 Hatch Pattern Dimensions Resulting from a 0.25 Value for the Delta-Y of the Second Line Family Definition

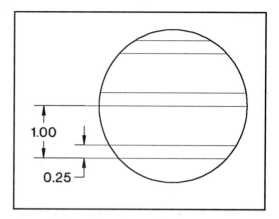

Figure 15-11 The Steel Hatch Pattern Defined with a 0.25 Separation between the Two Line Families

Custom Hatch Patterns and Trigonometry

The dimensions in the hatch pattern resulting from a 0.25 value for the delta-y of the second line family definition may not be what you expected, as shown in Figure 15-10. If you wished to have a 0.25 separation between the two line families (see Figure 15-11), then you must either know enough trigonometry/ geometry to predict accurate results or else put an additional burden on the user to reply to prompts with the correct responses to achieve those results. For example, you could write the definition as follows:

> *steel
> 0, 0,0, 0,1
> 0, 0,.25, 0,1

In order to use this pattern as shown the user will have to specify a 45-degree rotation when using it. This will maintain the ratio of 1 to .25 between the offset (delta-y) and the spacing between families (y-origin). However, if you wish to avoid this inconvenience to the user, but still wish to have the families separated by .25, you can write the definition as follows:

> *steel
> 45, 0,0, 0,1
> 45, 0,.353553391, 0,1

The value for the y-origin of .353553391 was obtained by dividing .25 by the sine (or cosine) of 45 degrees, which is .70710678. The x-origin and y-origin specify the coordinates of a point. Therefore, setting the origins of any family of continuous lines merely tells AutoCAD that the line must pass through that point. See Figure 15-12 for the trigonometry used.

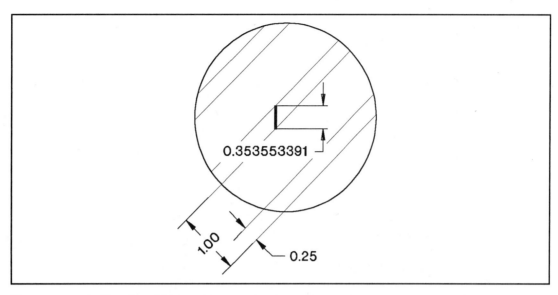

Figure 15-12 The Steel Hatch Pattern Defined with a 45-Degree Rotation to Maintain a 1:25 Offset Ratio

For families of lines that have segment/space distances, the point determined by the origins can tell AutoCAD not only that the line passes through that point, but that one of the segments will begin at that point. A dashed pattern can be written as follows (see Figure 15-13):

*dashed
0, 0,0, 0,.25, .25,-.25

Note that the value of the x-origin is zero, thus causing the dashes of one line to line up with the dashes of other lines. Staggers can be produced by giving a value to the x-origin as follows (see Figure 15-14):

*dashstagger
0, 0,0, .25,.25, .25,-.25

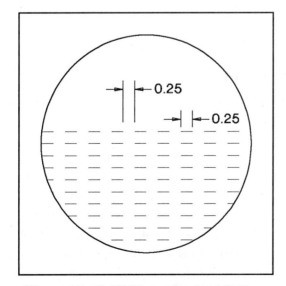

Figure 15-13 Writing a Dashed Pattern

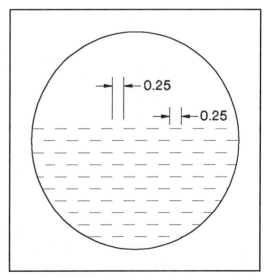

Figure 15-14 Writing a Staggered Dash Pattern

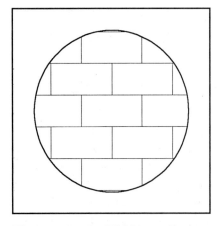 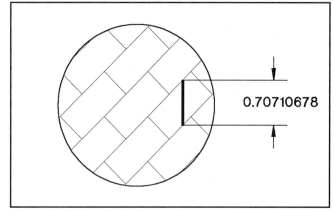

Figure 15-15 Writing a Pattern with Several Lengths of Segments and Spaces

Figure 15-16 Writing a Pattern with More Complex Hatch Patterns

In a manner similar to defining linetypes, you can cause lines in a family to have several lengths of segments and spaces (see Figure 15-15).

```
*simple
0, 0,0, 0,.5
90, 0,0, 0,1, .5,-.5
```

A similar, but more complex hatch pattern, could be written as follows (see Figure 15-16):

```
* complex
0, 0,0, 0,.5
45, 0,0, 0,1.414213562, 0,1.41421356
```

Repeating Closed Polygons

Creating hatch patterns with closed polygons requires planning. For example, a pattern of 45/90/45-degree triangles, as shown in Figure 15-17, should be started by first extending the lines, as shown in Figure 15-17a. Extend the construction lines through points of the object parallel to other lines of the object. Note the Grid that emerges when you use the lines and distances obtained to determine the pattern.

It is also helpful to sketch construction lines that are perpendicular to the object lines. This will assist you in specifying segment/space values.

In the example, two of the lines are perpendicular to each other, thus making this easier. Figures 15-18 through 15-21 illustrate potential patterns of triangles.

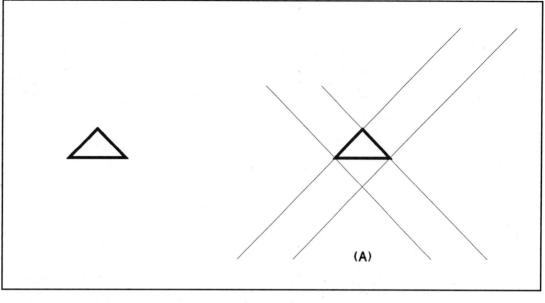

Figure 15-17 Closed Polygons

Once the pattern is selected, the Grid, and some knowledge of trigonometry, will assist you in specifying all of the values in the definition for each line family.

For pattern PA the horizontal line families can be written as follows (see Figure 15-22):

0, 0,0, 0,1, 1,-1

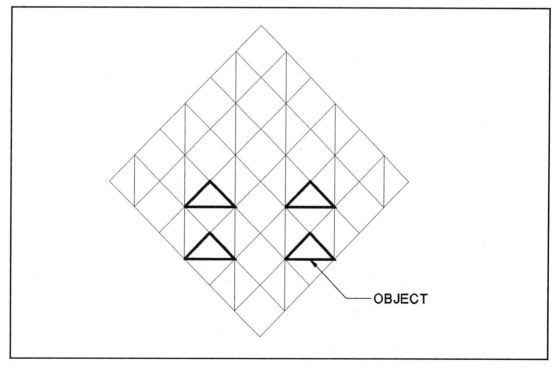

Figure 15-18 Creating Triangular Hatch Patterns – Method #1

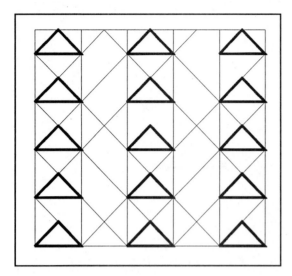

Figure 15-19 Creating Triangular Hatch Patterns – Method #2

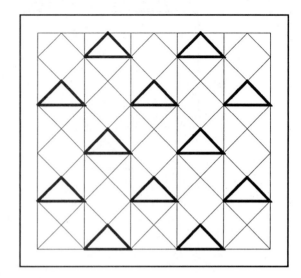

Figure 15-20 Creating Triangular Hatch Patterns – Method #3

The specifications for the 45-degree family of lines can be determined by using the following trigonometry:

$$\sin 45 \text{ degrees} = 0.70710678$$
$$s = 1$$
$$l = s \text{ times } \sin 45 \text{ degrees}$$
$$l = 1 \text{ times } \sin 45 \text{ degrees} = 0.70710678$$

Note that the trigonometry function is applied to the hypotenuse of the right triangle. In the example the hypotenuse is 1 unit. A different value would simply produce a proportional result, i.e., a hypotenuse of .5 would produce an L = S times

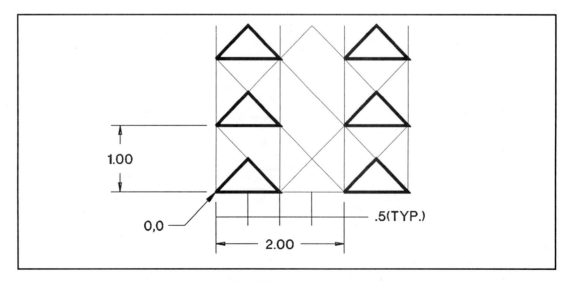

Figure 15-21 Creating Triangular Hatch Patterns – Method #4

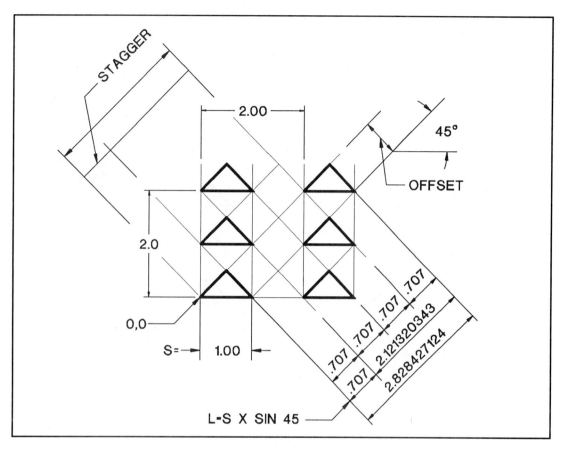

Figure 15-22 Triangular Patterns

0.70710678 = 0.353553391. The specifications for the 45-degree family of lines could be written as follows:

> 45, 0,0 0.70710678,0.70710678, 0.70710678,-2.121320343
> angle,origin,offset, stagger,   segment,   space

For the 135-degree family of lines, the offset, stagger, segment, and space have the same values (absolute) as the 45-degree family. Only the angle, the **x-origin** and the sign (+ or -) of the offset or stagger may need to be changed.

The 135-degree family of lines could be written as follows:

> 135, 1,0, -0.70710678,-0.70710678, 0.70710678,-2.121320343

Putting the three families of lines together under a header could be written as follows, and as shown in Figure 15-23.

> *PA,45/90/45 triangles stacked
> 0, 0,0, 0,1, 1,-1
> 45, 0,0 0.70710678,0.70710678, 0.70710678,-2.121320343
> 135, 1,0, -0.70710678,-0.70710678, 0.70710678,-2.121320343

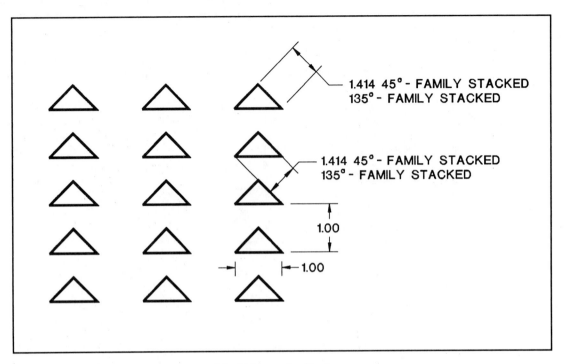

Figure 15-23 Triangular Patterns

Noting the "could be written" in the above statement tells you that there may be other ways to write the definitions. As an exercise, write the descriptions using 225 degrees instead of 45 degrees and 315 instead of 135 for the second and third families, respectively. As a hint, you determine the origin values of each family of lines from the standard coordinate system. But, to visualize the offset and stagger, orient the layout Grid so that the rotation angle coincides with the zero angle of the coordinate system. Then the signs and the values of delta-x and delta-y will be easier to establish along the standard plus for right/up and negatives for left/down directions.

Examples of two hatch patterns, PB and HONEYCOMB, follow.

The PB pattern can be written as follows, and as shown in Figure 15-24.

```
*PB, 45/90/45 triangle staggered
0, 0,0, 1,1, 1,-1
45, 0,0, 0,1.414213562, 0.70710678,0.70710678
135, 0,0, 0,1.414213562, 0.70710678,0.70710678
```

Note that this alignment simplifies the definitions of the second and third families of lines over the PA pattern.

The Honeycomb pattern can be written as follows, and as shown in Figure 15-25.

```
*HONEYCOMB
90, 0,0, 0,1, 0.577350264,-1.154700538
330, 0,0, 0,1, 0.577350264,-1.154700538
30, 0.5,-0.288675135, 0,1, 0.577350264,-1.154700538
```

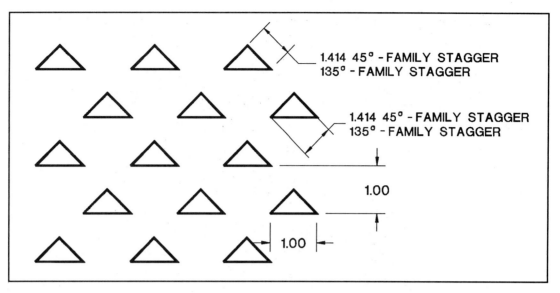

Figure 15-24 Example of the PB Hatch Pattern

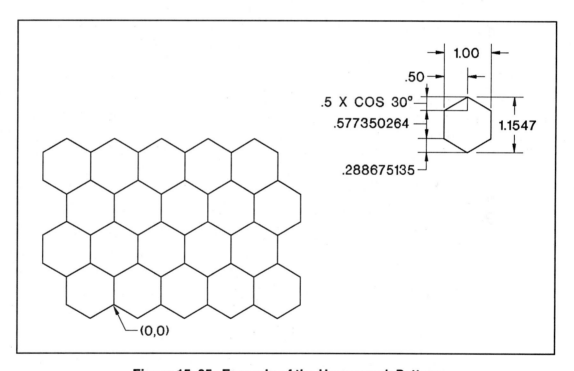

Figure 15-25 Example of the Honeycomb Pattern

SHAPES AND TEXT FONTS

Shapes and fonts are written in the same manner and are both stored in files with .SHP file extensions. The .SHP files must be compiled into .SHX files. This section covers how to create and save .SHP files and how to compile .SHP files into .SHX files. The main difference between shapes and fonts is in the commands used to place them in a drawing. Shapes are drawn by using the SHAPE command and fonts are drawn using commands that insert text, such as TEXT or DIM. Whether or not an object in a .SHP/.SHX file can be used with the SHAPE command or as a font character is partly determined by whether its shapename is written in uppercase or lowercase (explained herein).

Each shape or character in a font in a .SHP or .SHX file is made up of simplified entities. These entities are simplified lines, arcs, and circles. The reason they are referred to as simplified is because in specifying their directions and distances, you cannot use decimals or Architectural units. You must use only integers or integer fractions. For example, if the line distance needs to be equal to 1 divided by the square root of 2 (or .7071068), the fraction 70 divided by 99 (which equals .707070707) is as close as you can get. Rather than call the simplified lines and arcs "entities," we will refer to them as "primitives."

Individual shapes (and font characters) are written and stored in ASCII format. .SHP/.SHX files may contain up to 255 SHAPE-CHARACTERS. Each SHAPE-CHARACTER definition has a header line as follows:

*shape number, defbytes, shapename

The codes that describe the SHAPE-CHARACTER may take up one or more lines following the header. Most of the simple shapes can be written on one or two lines. The meaning of the items in the header is as follows:

The shape number may be from 1 to 255 with no duplications within one file.

Defbytes is the number of bytes used to define the individual SHAPE-CHARACTER, including the required zero that signals the end of a definition. The maximum allowable bytes in a SHAPE-CHARACTER definition is 2000. Defbytes (the bit-codes) in the definition are separated by commas. You may enclose pairs of bit-codes within parentheses for clarity of intent, but this does not affect the definition.

The shapename should be in uppercase if it is to be used by the SHAPE command. Like a Block name is used in the BLOCK command, you enter the shapename when prompted to do so during the SHAPE command. If the shape is a character in a font file, you may make any or all of the shapename characters lowercase, thereby causing the name to be ignored when compiled and stored in memory. It will serve for reference only in the .SHP file for someone reading that file.

Pen Movement Distances and Directions

The specifications for pen movement distances and directions (whether the pen is up or down) for drawing the primitives that will make up a SHAPE-CHARACTER are written in bit-codes. Each bit-code is considered one defbyte. Codes 0 through 16 are not DISTANCE-DIRECTION codes, but special instructions-to-AutoCAD codes that will be explained after DISTANCE-DIRECTION codes.

DISTANCE-DIRECTION codes have three characters beginning with a zero. The second character specifies distance. More specifically, it specifies vector length, which may be affected by a scale factor. Vector length and scale factor combine to

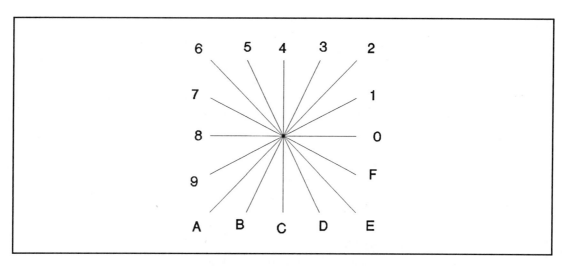

Figure 15-26 DISTANCE-DIRECTION Bit-Codes

determine actual distances. The third character specifies direction. There are 16 standard directions available through use of the DISTANCE-DIRECTION bit-code (or defbyte). Vectors of 1 unit in length are shown in the 16 standard directions in Figure 15-26.

Directions 0, 4, 8, and C are equivalent to the default 0, 90, 180, and 270 degrees, respectively. Directions 2, 6, A, and E are 45, 135, 225, and 315 degrees, respectively. But, the odd-numbered direction codes are NOT increments of 22.5 degrees, as you might think. They are directions that coincide with a line whose delta-x and delta-y ratio are 1 unit to 2 units. For example, the direction specified by code 1 is equivalent to drawing a line from 0,0 to 1,.5. This equates to approximately 26.56505118 degrees (or the arctangent of 0.5). The direction specified by code 3 equates to 63.434494882 degrees (or the arctangent of 2) and is the same as drawing a line from 0,0 to .5,1.

Distances specified will be measured on the nearest horizontal or vertical Axis. For example, 1 unit in the 1 direction specifies a vector that will project 1 unit on the horizontal Axis. Three units in the D direction will project 3 units on the vertical Axis (downward). So the vector specified 1 unit in the 1 direction will actually be 1.118033989 units long at an angle of 26.65606118 degrees and the vector specified 3 units in the D direction will be 3.354101967 units long at an angle of 296.5650512 degrees. See Figure 15-27 for examples of specifying direction.

To illustrate the DISTANCE-DIRECTION vector specifying codes, the following example is a definition for a shape called "oddity" that will draw the shape shown in Figure 15-28.

```
*200,7,ODDITY
014,012,020,029,02C,016,0
```

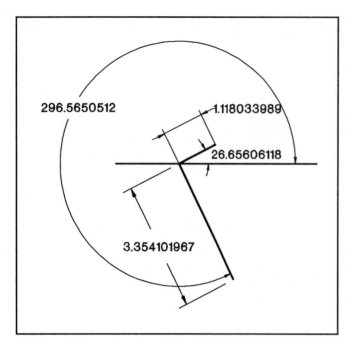

Figure 15-27 Specified Distances

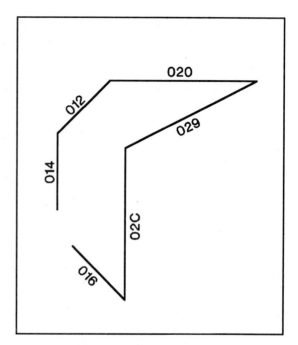

Figure 15-28   DISTANCE-DIRECTION Vector Specifying Codes

To draw the shape named oddity, you would first load the shape file that contains the definition and then use the SHAPE command as follows:

Command: **shape**
Name (or ?): **oddity**
Starting point: *specify a point*
Height <default>: *specify a scale factor*
Rotation angle <default>: *specify a rotation angle*

> **NOTE:** An alternative to standard DISTANCE-DIRECTION codes is to use Codes 8 and 9 to move the pen by paired (delta-x,delta-y) ordinate displacements. This is explained in the Special Codes section below.

Special Codes

Special codes may be written in decimal or hexadecimal. You may specify a special code as 0 through 16 or as 000 through 00E. A three-character defbyte with two leading zeros will be interpreted as a hexadecimal special code. A Code 10 is a special code in decimal. However, 010 is equivalent to decimal 16. But more importantly, it will be interpreted by AutoCAD as a DISTANCE-DIRECTION code with a vector length of 1 and a direction of 0. The hexadecimal equivalent to 10 is 00A. The code functions are as follows.

Code 0: End of Shape   The end of each separate shape definition must be marked with the Code 0.

Codes 1 and 2: Pen Up and Down   The "PEN DOWN" (or DRAW) mode is on at the beginning of each shape.   Code 2 turns the DRAW mode off or lifts the pen. This permits moving the pen without drawing.   Code 1 turns the DRAW mode on.

Note the relationship between the insertion point specified during the SHAPE command and where you wish the object and its primitives to be located.   If you wish for AutoCAD to begin drawing a primitive in the shape at a point remote from the insertion point, then you must lift the pen with a Code 2 and move the pen (with the proper codes) and then lower the pen with a Code 1.   Movement of the pen (directed by other codes) after a "PEN DOWN" Code 1 is what causes AutoCAD to draw primitives in a shape.

Codes 3 and 4: Scale Factors   Individual (and groups of) primitives within a shape can be increased or decreased in size by integer factors as follows: Code 3 tells AutoCAD to divide the subsequent vectors by the number that immediately follows the Code 3.   Code 4 tells AutoCAD to multiply the subsequent vectors by the number that immediately follows the Code 4.

CAUTION!

Scale factors are cumulative.   The advantage of this is that you can specify a scale factor that is the quotient of two integers.   A two-thirds scale factor can be achieved by a Code 4 followed by a factor of 2 followed by a Code 3 followed by a factor of 3.   But, the effects of scale factor codes must be reversed when they are no longer needed. They do not go away by themselves.   Therefore, at the end of the definition (or when you wish to return to normal or other scaling within the definition) the scale factor must be countered.   For example, when you wish to return to the normal scale from the two-thirds scale, you must use Code 3 followed by a factor of 3 followed by a Code 4 followed by a factor of 2.   There is no law that states you must always return to normal from a scaled mode.   You can, with Codes 3 and 4 and the correct factors, change from a two-thirds scale to a one-third scale for drawing additional primitives within the shape.   You should ALWAYS, however, return to the normal scale at the end of the definition.   A scale factor in effect at the end of one shape will carry over to the next shape.

Customizing AutoCAD

Codes 5 and 6: Saving and Recalling Locations Each location in a SHAPE definition is specified relative to a previous location. However, once the pen is at a particular location, you can store that location for later use within that SHAPE definition before moving on. This is handy when an object has several primitives starting or ending at the same location. For example, a wheel with spokes would be easier to define by using Code 5 to store the center location, draw a spoke, and then use Code 6 to return to the center.

Storing and recalling locations are known as pushing and popping them, respectively, in a stack. The stack storage is limited to four locations at any one time. The order in which they are popped is the reverse of the order in which they were pushed. Every location pushed must be popped.

More pushes than pops will result in the error message:

Position stack overflow in shape nnn

More pops than pushes will result in the error message:

Position stack underflow in shape nnn

Code 7: Subshape One shape in a .SHP/.SHX file can be included in the definition of another shape in the same file by using the Code 7 followed by the inserted shape's number.

Codes 8 and 9: X-Y Displacements Normal vector lengths range from 1 to 15 and can be drawn in one of the 16 standard directions unless you use a Code 8 or Code 9 to specify X-Y displacements. A Code 8 tells AutoCAD to use the next two bytes as the X and Y displacements, respectively. For example, 8, (7,-8) tells AutoCAD to move the pen a distance that is 7 in the X direction and 8 in the Y direction. The parentheses are optional for viewing effects only. After the displacement bytes, specifications revert to normal.

A Code 9 tells AutoCAD to use all following pairs of bytes as X-Y displacements until terminated by a pair of zeros. For example: 9,(7,-8),(14,9),(-17,3),(0,0) tells AutoCAD to use the three pairs of values for displacements for the current mode and then revert to normal after the (0,0) pair.

Code 00A: Octant Arc Code 00A (or 10) tells AutoCAD to use the next two bytes to define an arc. It is referred to as an octant (an increment of 45 degrees) arc. Octant arcs start and end on octant boundaries. Figure 15–29 shows the code numbers for the octants. The specification is written in the following format:

10, radius. (-)OSC

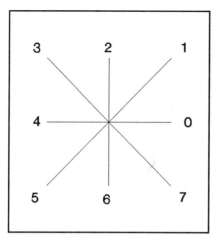

Figure 15-29   Code Numbers for Octants

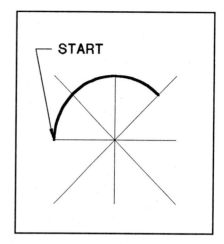

Figure 15-30 An Arc Drawn with Code 10, (2, -043)

The radius may range from 1 to 255. The second byte begins with zero and specifies the direction by its sign (clockwise if negative, counterclockwise otherwise), the starting octant (S) and the number of octants it spans (C) which may be written as 0 to 7 with 0 being 8 (a full circle). Figure 15-30 shows an arc drawn with the following codes:

$$10,(2,-043)$$

The arc has a radius of 2, begins at octant arc 4, and turns 135 degrees or 3 octants clockwise.

Code 00B: Fractional Arc   Code 00B (11) can be used to specify an arc that begins and ends at points other that the octants. The definition is written as follows:

$$11, \text{start-offset, end-offset, high-radius, low-radius, (-)0SC}$$

Start and end offsets specify how far from an octant the arc starts and ends. The high-radius, if not zero, specifies a radius greater than 255. The low-radius is specified in the same manner as the radius in a Code 10 arc, as are the starting octant and octants covering specifications in the last byte. The presence of the negative also signifies a clockwise direction.

The units of offset from an octant are a fraction of 1 degree times 45 divided by 256, or approximately .17578125 degrees. For example, if you wish to specify the starting value near 60 degrees the equation would be:

$$\text{offset} = (60-45)*(256/45) = 85.333333$$

So the specification value would be 85.

To end the arc at 102 degrees the equation would be:

$$offset = (102-90)*(256/45) = 68.2666667$$

So the specification value would be 68.

To draw an arc with a radius of 2 that starts near 60 degrees and ends near 102 degrees, the specifications would be as follows:

$$11,(85,68,0,2,012)$$

The last byte (012) specifies the starting octant to be 1 (45 degrees) and the ending octant to be 2 (90 degrees).

Codes 00C and 00D: Bulge-Specified Arc Codes 00C and 00D (12 and 13) are used to specify arcs in a different manner from octant codes. Codes 00C and 00D call out bulge factors to be applied to a vector displacement. The effect of using Code 00C or 00D involves specifying the endpoints of a flexible line by the X-Y displacement method and then specifying the bulge. The bulge determines the distance from the straight line between the endpoints and the extreme point on the arc. The bulge can range from −127 to 127. The maximum/minimum values (127 or −127) define a 180-degree arc, or half circle. Smaller values define proportionally smaller-degree arcs. That is, an arc specified some value, say x, will be x times 180 divided by 127 degrees. A bulge value of zero will define a straight line.

Code 00C precedes a single bulge defined arcs while 00D precedes multiple arcs. This is similar to the way Codes 008 and 009 work on X-Y displacement lines. Code 00D, like 009, must be terminated by a 0,0 byte pair. You can specify a series of bulge arcs and lines without exiting the Code 00D by using the zero bulge value for the lines.

Code 00E: Flag Vertical Text Command Code 00E (14) is only for dual-orientation text font descriptions, where a font might be used in either horizontal or vertical orientations. When Code 00E is encountered in the SHAPE definition, the next code will be ignored if the text is horizontal.

Text Fonts

Text fonts are special SHAPE files written for use with AutoCAD TEXT drawing commands. The shape numbers should correspond to ASCII codes for characters. Table 15-1 shows the ASCII codes.

Table 15-1 ASCII Codes for Text Fonts

32		space	64	@		96		left apostrophe
33	!		65	A		97	a	
34	"	double quote	66	B		98	b	
35	#		67	C		99	c	
36	$		68	D		100	d	
37	%		69	E		101	e	
38	&		70	F		102	f	
39	'	apostrophe	71	G		103	g	
40	(		72	H		104	h	
41	)		73	I		105	i	
42	*		74	J		106	j	
43	+		75	K		107	k	
44	,	comma	76	L		108	l	
45	-	hyphen	77	M		109	m	
46	.	period	78	N		110	n	
47	/		79	O		111	o	
48	0		80	P		112	p	
49	1		81	Q		113	q	
50	2		82	R		114	r	
51	3		83	S		115	s	
52	4		84	T		116	t	
53	5		85	U		117	u	
54	6		86	V		118	v	
55	7		87	W		119	w	
56	8		88	X		120	x	
57	9		89	Y		121	y	
58	:	colon	90	Z		122	z	
59	;	semicolon	91	[		123	{	
60	<		92	\	backslash	124			vertical bar
61	=		93	]		125	}	
62	>		94	^	caret	126	~	tilde
63	?		95	_	underscore			

Codes 1 to 31 are for control characters, only one of which is used in AutoCAD text fonts.

Codes 1 through 31 are reserved for special control characters. Only Code 10 (line feed) is used in AutoCAD. In order to be used as a font, the file must include a special shape number, 0, to describe the font. Its format is as follows:

> *0,4,fontname
> above, below, modes, 0

"Above" specifies the number of vector lengths that uppercase letters extend above the baseline, and "below" specifies the number of vector lengths that lowercase letters extend below the baseline. A modes byte value of zero (0) defines a horizontal (normal) mode and a value of two (2) defines dual-orientation (horizontal or vertical). A value of 2 must be present in order for the special Code 00E (14) to operate.

Standard AutoCAD fonts include special shape numbers 127, 128, and 129 for the degrees symbol, plus/minus symbol, and diameter dimensioning symbol, respectively.

The definition of a character from the TXT.SHP file is shown below. Note that the number 65 corresponds to the ASCII character that is an uppercase "A." The name "uca" (for uppercase a) is in lowercase to avoid taking up memory. As an exercise, you can follow the defbytes to see how the character is drawn.

```
*65,21,uca
2,14,8,(-2,-6),1,024,043,04D,02C,2,047,1,040,2,02E,14,8,(-4,
-3),0
```

The above character definition starts by lifting the pen. A font containing the alphanumeric characters must take into consideration the spaces between characters. This is done by having similar starting and stopping points based on each character's particular width.

CHAPTER

16 AutoLISP

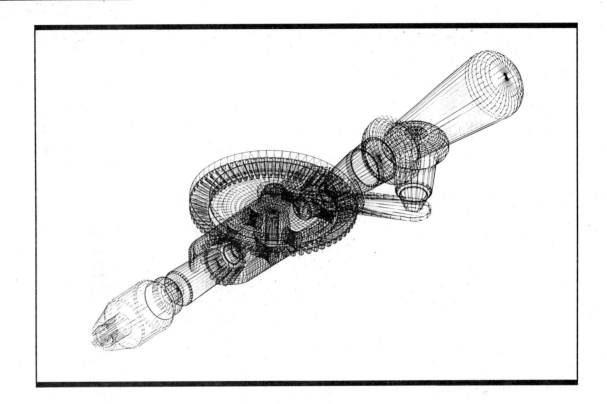

This chapter will cover the fundamental concepts of the AutoLISP programming language. Included are writing, storing, and loading .LSP files, the concepts of variables and expressions, the LIST, custom functions, and file handling.

VARIABLES AND EXPRESSIONS

In Version 2.1 (Release 6) in May, 1985, Autodesk first introduced its embedded programming language. It provided on board computational power for the operator while in the AutoCAD Editor. It also permitted true programming routines to be used by way of menu devices, including interactive functions to receive input from the operator in the form of keyboard entries and screen picks for use in the routine. In January, 1986, Version 2.18 included a full implementation of user-defined functions and custom commands, which added a whole new world of open architecture (meaning you can customize the program to suit your needs) to AutoCAD.

741

LOADING AUTOLISP INTO YOUR DRAWING

You do not have to learn how to write AutoLISP programs in order to be able to use them. AutoLISP programs are available from several sources. They are in the form of filename.LSP files. AutoCAD comes with program files that are ready to load and use in your drawing.

An AutoLISP file named RECTANG.LSP (which facilitates drawing a square or rectangle) can be loaded for use during the current editing session by using the AutoLISP function called load as follows:

Command: *(load "rectang")*

Note the following:

1. The use of the parentheses distinguishes AutoLISP functions and routines. This is especially important when using a function such as "load" for which there is an AutoCAD Editor command of the same name.

2. You should not include the .LSP extension. AutoCAD appends it automatically.

3. You may also specify a path if necessary. For example, if the RECTANG.LSP file is on the A: drive in a directory called Lisp the following response can be used:

Command: *(load "a:/lisp/rectang")*

Note the use of the nonstandard forward slashes to specify the directory path.

EXPRESSIONS AND VARIABLES

Expressions in AutoLISP should be understood before getting into variables. The simplest application of AutoLISP is to evaluate an equation by just typing it in and pressing ⏎. Of course, you must enter the equation in the proper format, which is somewhat different from ordinary algebraic notation. It involves a format that is unique among those used in other more popular computer programming languages. For example, if you wish to add 5 and 3, simply enter the following expression:

Command: **(+ 5 3)**

The integer 8 will be displayed in the prompt area. That is, AutoLISP evaluates the expression and returns the integer 8. Throughout this lesson, the word "return" will be used to describe the result of an evaluation. Another expression:

Command: **(+ 5 3 1 99)**

returns the integer 108.

Four things are worthy of note regarding these expressions and returns.

1. When AutoCAD sees an open parenthesis (unless responding to a prompt to enter text), it knows that it is entering an AutoLISP expression to be evaluated. The AutoLISP evaluator remains in effect until it encounters the closing parenthesis that is the mate of the first open parenthesis.

2. AutoLISP uses prefix notation, which means that expressions begin with the operator (after the opening parenthesis, of course). In the above examples, the plus sign (+) is the arithmetic operator. The operator tells AutoLISP what operation to perform on the items that follow. The items that follow the operator are known as the arguments.

3. As you can see by the second example, the plus operator can have more than the usual two arguments to which an algebraic plus sign is restricted.

4. Elements in an AutoLISP expression are separated by one or more spaces. Multiple adjoining spaces (unlike spaces in a menu line) are considered as one space in an AutoLISP routine.

Variables as Symbols and Symbols that Should Not Vary

Just as algebra uses letter names for the unknown-at-the-time values in an equation, AutoLISP utilizes symbols as variables, whose name you may select during the writing of the program. In algebra, for example, as sequence might be written as follows:

ALGEBRA	AutoLISP
a = 3	(setq a 3)
b = 7	(setq b 7)

therefore

| a + b = 10 | (+ a b) returns 10 |

and

| ab = 21 | (* a b) returns 21 |

naming and SETQing the value of an expression.

Assigning Names

Three reasons for assigning names are as follows:

1. Expressions

   Pi is the name for 3.14159 and so forth.

2. Variables

   A variable is an expression whose value is not known when originally written into the program. Variables will take on some value after the program has been called into use. The value of the variable is usually determined by some operation on some other value which the user has been prompted to enter while the program is in progress.

3. Custom-Defined Functions

   AutoCAD permits users to create and name a customized function and then use it in AutoCAD in a manner similar to a standard AutoCAD command.

TERMINOLOGY AND FUNDAMENTAL CONCEPTS

LISTS, OPERATORS, ARGUMENTS, TYPES, PARENTHESES, the EXCLAMA-TION POINT, and the concept of the FUNCTION-LIST comprise the basis of AutoLISP.

LISTs

Practically everything in AutoLISP is a list of some sort or another. Functions are usually represented as a list of expressions enclosed in parentheses. For example, (+ 1 2.0) is an AutoLISP function with three elements in it, the (+), the "1," and the "2.0." Other lists may be established by applying a function called LIST or by applying the single quote, such as '(1 2 3.0 a "b").

Operators and ARGUMENTS

Arguments are those items in a function-list on which the operator operates. For example, in the function-list (+ 1 2), the operator is (+) and the ARGUMENTs are "1" and "2."

TYPES

Arguments are classified by their TYPE. The ARGUMENTS in the example (+ 1 2) are of the type called INTEGER. In the function-list (+ 1.0 2.0), the ARGUMENTs are of the TYPE called REAL, signifying a real number.

The Parentheses

The primary mechanisms for entering and leaving AutoLISP from the Drawing Editor and entering expressions within AutoLISP are the open and closed parentheses.

CAUTION!

For every open parenthesis "(" there must be a closed parenthesis ")." If AutoCAD encounters a condition where the closed parentheses are one fewer than the open ones, the prompt will display the following:

1>

The above is caused most often by the need for one closed parenthesis. A display of 3> could indicate the need of three closed parentheses. The problem is usually remedied by just entering the specified number of closed parentheses. This type of error message can also be caused by having an odd number of double quotation marks inside of an AutoLISP expression, in which case one double quotation mark must be entered, followed by the required number of closed parentheses, in order to eliminate the error message in the prompt area. Further examination will usually reveal that the program line needs to be corrected to prevent the message from recurring.

The Exclamation Point

A leading exclamation point in response to a prompt is another mechanism of entering AutoLISP. This tells AutoCAD that the symbol that follows the exclamation point is an AutoLISP variable that has been set equal to some value and that AutoCAD should use the value of the variable as a response to the prompt.

The above terms and concepts are explained in detail with examples in the sections that follow.

Functions

The first function-list to be introduced involves three expressions: the operator SETQ, the variable that we have arbitrarily named "x," and the REAL number 2.5. Within this function SETQ will perform a special operation on the variable "x" and the REAL number 2.5. SETQ is probably AutoLISP's most common function. It means "set equal." By using SETQ as the first of three expressions, you will set the second expression equal to the third. We are accustomed to performing this operation by the conventional expression "x = 2.5." But as you will see in the example below, in order to write "x equals 2.5" in AutoLISP you must write in a special format "SET x EQUAL 2.5." It is done by writing three expressions in parentheses with the first being the operator SETQ, the second being "x," and the third being the value to which the variable named "x" is to be equal, for example:

Command: **(setq x 2.5)**

Having x = 2.5, or more properly, to have SET x EQUAL 2.5 is necessary only if you wish to use the value of the REAL number 2.5 later by just entering its name "x." If you have entered "(setq x 2.5)" at the "Command:" prompt earlier, then any time during that current editing session you may re-enter AutoLISP right from the keyboard by using ! before the name of the value in response to a prompt for some REAL number. If the prompt is asking for a name of something (like a layer name, which requires responding with something called a string variable), then trying to use a variable that has been set equal to a REAL number will cause an error message. The use of ! is another method of entering AutoLISP directly from the keyboard or in a string of custom menu commands and responses.

For example, you have created a unit Block named UB and wish to INSERT it with a scale factor of 2.5. The sequence of prompts and responses would be as follows:

Command: **insert**
Block name (or ?): **ub**
Insertion point: *pick an insertion point*
X scale factor <1> / Corner / XYZ: **!x**

Note at this point that the use of the name "x" and the fact that it is being applied to the "X scale" is purely coincidental.

By using the ! in front of the "x," you will have the value of x (or 2.5 in this case) used as a response to the prompt asking for the X scale.

This example is not very efficient. Entering !x appears to take only two key strokes, where entering 2.5 takes three. If that were true, you would save a key stroke. But, because entering the exclamation point ! requires the shift key, it is a double stroke requiring both hands. Along with the x it is actually less convenient than entering 2.5, which has three one-hand strokes. Additionally, the characters "2," "." and "5" are all accessible on AutoCAD's tablet overlay while the ! is not. Entering 2.5 will, however, give the same accuracy as entering 2.50000000000000.

> **NOTE:** If x has not previously been set equal to a value, then entering !x will return "nil." Believe it or not, advanced programming does make use of the "nil." Normally, variables and expressions retain their names and values only during the current editing session. They are lost when a drawing is ended. At the beginning of each session they must be re-established. But even this problem of saving variable values from one session to another can be addressed by a custom program.

NAMING AND SETQING THE VALUE OF AN EXPRESSION

Suppose the value you wish to enter is 1 divided by the square root of 2. This could be written as 0.7071068 depending on the accuracy desired. Now compare three key strokes using AutoLISP versus nine or 10 from the keyboard or tablet. Not only will a variable having a short name (and having been set equal to that value) save time in entering, but it will decrease the probability of errors in both reading and keying-in a long string of characters, for example:

   Command: **(setq x 0.7071068)**

If the value 0.7071068 is needed in response to a prompt, simply enter !x. Programming begins to appear both expedient and practical.

CAUTION!

You may respond with .7071068 outside AutoLISP, but while in AutoLISP, you must use some value (even if zero) on both sides of the decimal point. Expressions beginning or ending with a dot (.) have another special meaning. Before leaving this example, additional power of AutoLISP can be seen in a demonstration of using an expression within an expression within an expression. Two other AutoLISP operators will be introduced at this time. They are the SQRT and the "/" functions. The SQRT returns the square root of the argument following (it must be only one ARGUMENT and must be a nonnegative REAL number). The "/" function requires two ARGUMENTS and returns the quotient of the first divided by the second, for example:

   Command:**(sqrt 2)**

The above returns 1.414213562373...... You may now use this value as follows:

   Command: **(setq y (sqrt 2))**

This does two things. It sets y equal to the expression that follows, which is the square root of 2, and returns 1.414213562.

Having entered the above routine you may operate on y as follows:

   Command: **(/ 1.0 y)**

This expression will return the quotient of 1 divided by the value of y, which was previously set equal the square root of 2. Therefore, the expression evaluates to 0.7071068.

Using an AutoLISP function in this fashion neither sets values nor gives them names. It is of little use later but does return (display in the prompt area) the result of the prescribed computation for immediate viewing. Sometimes this is handier than picking up a hand-held calculator.

A two step use of AutoLISP could be written as follows:

Command: **(setq y (sqrt 2))**
Command: **(setq x (/ 1 y))**

The first step sets y equal to the square root of 2. The second step sets x equal to the inner expression, which uses the "/" operator (for division) and returns the value of 1 divided by the value of y. This two step sequence involves four operators (SQRT, /, and SETQ twice). It names y and sets it equal to the square root of 2. It names x and sets it equal to the reciprocal of y.

Instead of the above two-step routine, a simpler one-step routine is as follows:

Command: **(setq x (/ 1 (sqrt 2)))**

So in one step you can name an expression "x" and set it equal to the reciprocal of the square root of 2. It allows you to now respond to any prompt for a REAL number and apply this value by simply entering !x. This saves time and insures 14 decimal place accuracy, which is what CAD is all about in the first place—SPEED and ACCURACY.

Hands On

At the "Command:" prompt enter the following expression:

Command: **(setq a 1 b 2 c 99 d pi e 2.5)**

This expression is a function-list using the operator SETQ. Note the opening and closing parentheses that distinguish it as an individual expression. Unlike the (+...) function that performs a single operation of as many ARGUMENTs as you wish to furnish, the (setq...) must have pairs of ARGUMENTs. SETQ operates on each pair of ARGUMENTs individually. After entering the above, you may have AutoLISP evaluate equations by entering them as follows:

Command: **(setq x (+ a b))**   *returns 3*
Command: **(setq y (- a c))**   *returns -98*
Command: **(setq z (* b d))**   *returns 6.283185308*
Command: **(setq q (/ c e))**   *returns 39.6*

Perform the following exercises.

1. Name and give values to variables corresponding to the following algebraic equations.
   a = 4
   b = 7
   c = a × b
   d = b *with 2 as exponent*
   e = a   b   *square root of a squared plus b squared*

AutoLISP

Exercises from the Keyboard
Line

You should establish variables for the points p1 and p2 as follows (see Figure 16-1). Type in (**setq p1 (getpoint**)). Use the OSNAP mode Endpoint to pick one end of the line. Type in (**setq p2 (getpoint**)) and use the OSNAP mode Endpoint to pick the other endpoint of the line. Do not be alarmed that the prompt area is blank. When the points have been returned, record the X and Y coordinates on paper for use in the following exercises. For example, if (1.2345 6.7890 0.0000) is returned for p1, enter the following:

> Command: (**setq X1 1.2345**) *returns 1.2345*
> Command: (**setq Y1 6.7890**) *returns 6.7890*

Write in from keyboard routines to perform the following:

1. Set "dx" equal to the horizontal distance between p1 and p2.
2. Set "dy" equal to the vertical distance between p1 and p2.
3. Set "d" equal to the distance between p1 and p2.
4. Set "a" equal to the angle between p1 and p2 in radians.

Circle

Set variables to the center "c" of the circle and to one point "p" on the circle (see Figure 16-2). Write routines to perform the following:

1. Set "r" equal to the radius of the circle.
2. Set "d" equal to the diameter of the circle.
3. Set "p" equal to the perimeter of the circle.
4. Set "a" equal to the area of the circle.

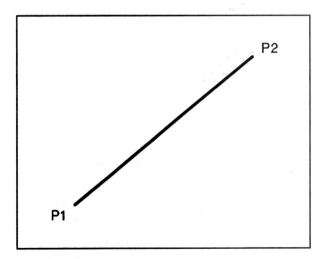

Figure 16-1 The Line for Writing a Routine

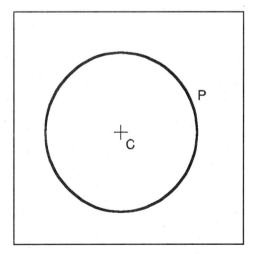

Figure 16-2 The Circle for Writing a Routine

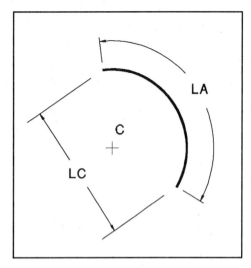

Figure 16-3 The Arc for Writing a Routine

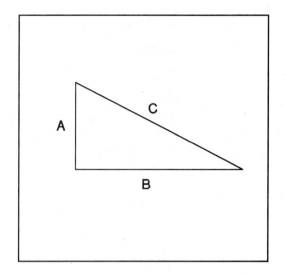

Figure 16-4 Right Triangle for Writing a Routine

Arc

Establish endpoints p1 and p2 and the center "c" of the arc (see Figure 16-3) as in the exercises on the Line above. Write routines to perform the following:

1. Set "r" equal to the radius of the arc.
2. Set "lc" equal to the chord length of the arc.
3. (A DOOZIE) Set "la" equal to the arc length of the arc.

Computation

Write routines to perform the following (see Figure 16-4):

1. If a = 1 and b = 2, then find c.
2. If b = 2 and c = 3, then find a.
3. Find the area of the triangle for question 1.
4. Find the area of the triangle for question 2.

According to Ben Shneiderman in his preface to Dan Friedman's "The Little LISPer," "The fundamental structure of the LISP programming language was derived from the abstract notions of lambda calculus and recursive function theory by John McCarthy. His goal was to produce a programming language with a powerful notation for defining and transforming functions. Instead of operating on numeric quantities, LISP was designed to manipulate abstract symbols, called atoms, and combinations of symbols, called lists. The expressive power was recognized by a small number of researchers who were primarily concerned with difficult symbolic manipulation problems in artificial intelligence."

Translating an algebraic word problem into a true algebraic expression demands a certain symbol classification and list processing also. Many algebra students can learn the process of solution to an algebraic expression (or at least memorize the procedures) once it is in the proper structure, but suffer a complete impasse when asked to "interpret" the word problem into that proper structure.

Words in a sentence or paragraph have characteristics similar to AutoLISP functions or expressions. Verbs act on subjects like subroutines act on variables and expressions. The conjunction "and" joins phrases like the "+" joins real numbers. A phrase like "out of here" has the subphrase "of here" in it.

SEPARATE THE LISTS
TYPEs of ARGUMENTs

While an ARGUMENT is defined in part by *The American Heritage Dictionary* as "A quarrel; contention," it also is defined under the heading of math as "The independent variable of a function." AutoCAD's Programmer's Reference consistently describes the variables upon whose value the function value depends as ARGUMENTs.

The LIST in AutoLISP is an ARGUMENT

When is a LIST NOT a LIST? As mentioned earlier, almost every function in AutoLISP is some form of a LIST. The AutoLISP interpreter operates on LISTs as they occur in a routine or program. The AutoLISP expression (setq x (/ 1 (sqrt 2))) is a LIST. To the AutoCAD lisp interpreter it is a LIST to be evaluated according to the operator "SETQ." Likewise, (/ 1 (sqrt 2)) and (sqrt 2) are a sublist and subsublist, respectively, to be evaluated. But none of these would be considered as the type of defined LIST (known as LIST to the TYPE function) that some of the AutoLISP function-lists, like (CAR <list>), normally require as their ARGUMENT. The LISTs that are acceptable ARGUMENTs to these certain functions might be looked upon as special LISTs within LISTs. They must take on a special format in order to satisfy the main function-list as the required ARGUMENT(s).

AutoLISP function-lists that require LISTs as one of their ARGUMENTs include the CAR, CADR, LAST, LENGTH, NTH, and REVERSE functions.

Whenever an AutoLISP function-list requires a LIST as one of its ARGUMENTs, then you must use one of the following procedures:

1. You may use the function-list that has as its operator the function called LIST. This function-list is written in the format (list <expr>...) as described in AutoCAD's Programmer's Reference. Typing in (list 1.0 2.0) will return (1.000000 2.000000). But more importantly, it will satisfy the requirements of this special LIST when needed for data input. Other function-lists (such as the one with the operator SQRT) most likely will NOT satisfy the special requirement of an ARGUMENT that must be of the TYPE called LIST.

2. If you must respond within AutoLISP with the special form of LIST required, writing (list 1.0 2.0) every time becomes laborious (like writing 3.14159 and so forth when the use of pi will do). Therefore, it is convenient to use the SETQ function and write:

(setq p (list 1.0 2.0))

The name "p" is strictly arbitrary in this case. Any unique variable name you would like to use will suffice. Then whenever your routine requires you to respond with a point whose X and Y coordinates are 1.0 and 2.0, respectively, you may respond with "p" within AutoLISP or "!p" directly from the keyboard while in the Drawing Editor. Try this exercise for an illustration of the above. The default limits of 0,0 and 12,9 as in the ACAD.DWG will be helpful. Type in at the "Command:" prompt the following:

```
Command:(setq p (list 1.0 2.0))
(1.000000 2.000000) will be displayed
Command: line
From point: (list 6.0 7.0)
To point: !p
```

CREATING A LIST

As explained earlier in this chapter, the (list <expr>..) function-list is often used under restrictive conditions. For example, using it as a response to some commands requiring a 2D point, the "<expr>..." part of the overall expression must be "<expr> <expr>" where both <expr>'s are REAL numbers.

Remember that an INTEGER can be entered in AutoLISP and AutoCAD will translate it into a REAL number under certain conditions. For a 3D point, the form of the response must be "<expr> <expr> <expr>." Using "<real> <real>," "<real> <int>," or "<int> <int>" may be considered as proper responses to a prompt for the starting point of a 2D line. This coincides with the type of entry required for a point even while NOT in AutoLISP.

For example, the following are considered appropriate while in the AutoCAD editor:

```
Command: line
From point: 1.5, .7081068
     or
From point: 3.1415, 5
     or
From point: 1, 1
```

A similar mixture of REALs and INTEGERs is evident in the following example from within AutoLISP:

Command: **line**
From point: **(list 1.5 0.7071068)**
    or
From point: **(list pi 5)**
    or
From point: **(list 1 1)**

Note two subtle differences! (Not the parentheses, because they are not subtle.) First, from within AutoLISP, any REAL number must begin with an INTEGER, NOT a decimal point.

Second, the two expressions comprising the list within each function are separated by a space, as in the last examples (within AutoLISP) instead of a comma, as in the first examples (not in AutoLISP).

A LIST THAT DOESN'T LOOK LIKE A LIST

Once a symbol (name of your choice) has been SETQed (set equal) to a LIST by the (setq <sym> (list <expr> <expr>...)) function, then that symbol becomes a defined LIST. It will evaluate to that (<expr> <expr>...) for use as a response within AutoLISP or out of AutoLISP by using the ! prefix. For example, entering (setq p1 (list 2.0 3.0)) returns (2.0000 3.0000). Using the TYPE command, as in entering (TYPE p1), will return "LIST." It will work for the following response to the LINE command:

From point: **!p1**

But if (setq p1 (list 2.0 "z")) has been entered as the prior routine instead of (setq p1 (list 2.0 3.0)), the above sequence will NOT accept !p1 as a valid response, even though (TYPE p1) still returns "LIST." Its ARGUMENT, (<expr> <expr>..), as a LIST is not (<real> <real>..) as points require.

Before you even considered programming in AutoLISP, you were using LISTs. If, in response to the "From point:" prompt, you entered "2,3.75" from the keyboard (or any form of "real,real," "real,integer," or "integer, integer") then you used a LIST. Even if you had entered "x1,2.5" or "3,y" you would have been using a LIST. But you would have found out that even though it was in a similar format, the elements of the entry were not of the proper classification. Once you understood that AutoCAD rejected anything except certain classifications of elements, you learned to work using that knowledge (or went back to the drawing board, literally!).

A disguised use of the LIST input is when you pick a point on the screen. AutoCAD defines that pick as a LIST in the proper format, (x-coordinate,y-coordinate), and enters it for you. It is a LIST in the acceptable format.

Association List

The following:

((a 097) (b 098) (c 099) (d 100)....(x 120) (y 121) (z 122))

is a LIST, but it is a very special LIST.

Each expression in the LIST similarly has two expressions enclosed in parentheses (making them each a LIST themselves) with the first being a lowercase letter, and the second being an INTEGER.

What makes the last LIST special is that it satisfies the requirements of an ASSOCIATION LIST. It may be used (like other qualified association lists) as an ARGUMENT in the AutoLISP function ASSOC. It takes the form of (assoc <item> <alist>).

Exercises

Determine if the evaluation results below satisfy the requirements of the expression of the TYPE LIST. If not, explain why.

a. 1 , 2
b. 1 2
c. (12)
d. (1 2)
e. (1.0 2)
f. (1.0 2.0)
g. ((1 2))
h. ((1 2)
i. (1 .2)
j. (1.0 0.2)
k. (1.0 2.0 3.0 x)
l. (1.0 2.0x3.0)
m. (* 2 4)
n. (-2 -4)

Pausing for User Input

There are very few AutoCAD commands that begin and end by just entering the command name. Except for END, REGEN, REDRAW, OOPS, UNDO, and the like, most commands pause for user input before they are completed. You can include this interactive capability in your AutoLISP routines through several input functions. The exercises in this section will introduce two such functions, (getpoint...) and (getreal...). The (getpoint) function pauses for input of a point (either from the keyboard or a pick on the screen) and returns that point in the form of a LIST of two REALs. The (getreal) function pauses for user input of a REAL number and returns that REAL number.

AutoLISP Functions — The Command Function

The function-list (command <args>...) provides a method of invoking an AutoCAD command from within AutoLISP. It is usually the culmination of the routine. The <args> are written in the same sequence as if entered from the keyboard from the AutoCAD. The AutoCAD command name that follows the (command ...) function must be enclosed in quotation marks as in the following example:

(setq p1 (list 1.0 1.0))
(setq p2 (list 2.0 2.75))
(command "line" p1 p2 "")

The above sequence, when included in an AutoLISP routine, will draw a line from 1,1 to 2,2.75.

Note that the double-double quotation mark is the equivalent of pressing ⏎ while in AutoLISP. It is referred to as the null STRING (""). It simulates pressing the spacebar.

In the (command ...) function-list, the arguments that are AutoCAD Editor entries are enclosed within quotation marks while AutoLISP symbols and expressions are NOT. One of the notable differences is illustrated in responding to a prompt for an angle. Remember, AutoLISP requires radians while the AutoCAD Editor normally uses degrees (unless the UNITS are set for angle input to be in radians). For this illustration certain symbols were named and SETQed to values as shown below:

(setq ublkname "UB1")
(setq inspt (list 2.0 2.0))
(setq xscal 2.5)
(setq yscal 2.5)
(setq ang 90)

Then a routine could be written in two different ways with the same results, as follows:

(command "insert" ublkname inspt xscal yscal ang)
or
(command "insert" "UB1" "2,2" "2.5" "" "90")

Although angular responses to normal AutoLISP functions must be in radians, this is an angular response while temporarily back in the AutoCAD Editor and therefore must be 90 for degrees.

The first program line uses AutoLISP symbols as responses to the INSERT command that the (command ...) function invoked. The second line uses AutoCAD Editor equivalents of the same responses. In the latter, the responses must be enclosed within quotation marks. This use of the quotation marks is different from their use to mark characters as a STRING type of ARGUMENT in function-lists other than the (command ...) function.

Two subtle lessons can be gotten from the above.

1. The use of quotation marks returns you to the AutoCAD Editor types of responses.
2. The double-double quotation marks (null STRING) is used to cause the Y scale factor to default to the X scale factor. This would not be appropriate if the Y scale needed to be different, of course. Using the null STRING in this manner is equivalent to returning to the AutoCAD Editor, striking the spacebar, and then returning back to AutoLISP.

The Pause Symbol

During a (command...) function you can cause a pause if you wish to allow the user to have input during that particular AutoCAD Editor command that you have called up. This is done by using the pause symbol in lieu of a variable or a fixed value where a particular response is required. For example, in the above program line you could have allowed the user to input a name and an angle:

(command "insert" pause inspt xscal yscal pause)

or

(command "insert" pause "2,2" "2.5" "" pause)

ANGLE BRACKETS AND OPTIONAL SQUARE BRACKETS

The function descriptions in this section include the operator (+ or − , for example), and the elements (ARGUMENTs) that must (or may) follow the operator. If the ARGUMENT(s) following the operator in the description are enclosed with angle <> brackets only, then those ARGUMENTs must follow the operator and must be of the TYPE specified. An ARGUMENT in square [ ] brackets following the operator (not necessarily immediately) is optional. When an ARGUMENT is followed by an ellipsis "...," then the operator will accept multiple ARGUMENTs of the type specified.

ELEMENTARY FUNCTIONS

(+ <number> <number>...)

This function returns the sum of the <number>s. There may be any quantity of <number>s.

(- <number> <number>...)

This function returns the difference of the <number>s. There may be any quantity of <number>s.

(* <number> <number>...)

This function returns the product of any quantity of <number>s.

(\ <number> <number>...)

This function returns the quotient of the first <number> divided by the second <number>, and if there are more than two ARGUMENTs, the quotient of the first and second will be divided by the third and so on.

RULES OF PROMOTION OF AN INTEGER TO A REAL

As noted in the Reference Manual, INTEGERs may range from −32768 to 32767. Adding or multiplying INTEGERs whose sum or product exceeds 32767 (or is less than −32768) will not provide an acceptable result.

1. If any ARGUMENT in one of the functions is entered as an INTEGER and that INTEGER is outside the integer limits, then the result is not usable.
2. If all of the number ARGUMENTs entered are INTEGERs, then the result will be an INTEGER, and if that result is outside the INTEGER limits, the result will be subject to error.
3. If any of the ARGUMENTs is entered as a REAL (and none is an INTEGER exceeding the INTEGER limits), then the result will be a REAL without limits.

MORE ELEMENTARY FUNCTIONS

(1+ <number>) and (1- <number>)

These functions are just different methods of writing (+ <number> 1) and (- <number> 1), respectively. For example:

> (1+ 7) returns 8
> (1- 7) returns 6

(abs <number>)

This function returns the absolute value of the <number>. For example:

> (abs (- 4 7)) returns 3

(ascii <string>)

This function returns the ASCII value of the first character of the <string>. For example:

> (ascii "All") returns 65
> (ascii "a") returns 97
> (ascii "B") returns 66

(chr <number>)

This function returns the character (as a one-character STRING) whose ASCII code is <number>. For example:

> (chr 65) returns "A"
> (chr 97) returns "a"
> (chr 100) returns "d"

(eval <expr>)

This function returns the result of evaluating <expr>, where <expr> is any LISP expression. For example:

> (setq z 6)
> (setq q 'z)
> (eval z) returns 6
> (eval q) returns 6

(exp <number>)

This function returns e raised to the <number> power (natural antilog). It returns a REAL. For example:

> (exp 1.0) returns 2.718282
> (exp -0.2) returns 0.818730753

(expt <base> <power>)

This function returns <base> raised to the specified <power>. If both ARGUMENTs are INTEGERs, the result is an INTEGER; otherwise, the result is a REAL. For example:

> (expt 3 4) returns 81

(log <number>)

This function returns the natural log of <number> as a REAL. For example:

> (log 3.74) returns 1.32175584
> (log 1.025) returns 0.024692613

(sqrt <number>)

This function returns the square root of <number> as a REAL. For example:

> (sqrt 16) returns 4.000000
> (sqrt 2.0) returns 1.414213562

(type <item>)

This function returns the TYPE of <item>, where TYPE is one of the following (as an atom):

REAL	floating point numbers
FILE	file descriptors
STR	strings
INT	integer
SYM	symbol
LIST	lists (and user functions)
SUBR	internal AutoLISP functions
PICKSET	AutoCAD selection sets
ENAME	AutoCAD entity names
PAGETB	Function paging table

TRIGONOMETRY

(sin <angle>)

This function returns the sine of <angle>, where <angle> is expressed in radians.

(cos <angle>)

This function returns the cosine of <angle>, where <angle> is expressed in radians. For example:

> (cos 1) returns .540302306
> (sin (/ pi 2)) returns 1.00000

(atan <num1> [<num2>])

If only <num1> is present, then (atan ...) returns the angle (in **radians**) whose tangent is <num1>. If <num1> and <num2> are present, then (atan ...) returns the angle whose tangent is the dividend of <num1> divided by <num2>. For example:

> (atan 0.75) returns 0.643501109
> (atan 1.0 2.0) returns 0.463647609

LIST HANDLING FUNCTIONS

(list <expr>...)

This function has expression(s) as its ARGUMENTs. It is included in this section because it is the function that creates the LISTs that the other functions in this section require as ARGUMENTs.

(list ...)

This function takes any number of expressions and makes them into a LIST. For example:

> (list 1 1) returns (1 1)

Remember! A created LIST in enclosed in parentheses.

A specific application of the (list ...) function is to combine two or three REALs in the format required by a function whose ARGUMENT is <pt> which is a 2D or 3D point. The point is a special form of a LIST.

For example:

> (setq p1 (list 1.0 1.0))
> (setq p2 (list 2.0 2.0))

allows the following:

> (setq a (angle p1 p2)) returns 0.785398163

but

> (setq p1 (list "you" 1.0))
> (setq p2 (list 2.0 2.0))

followed by

> (setq a (angle p1 p2)) returns

> error: bad point value

(angle <pt1> <pt2>)

This function returns the angle (in radians) between the base line of zero angle and the line from pt1 to pt2.

(distance <pt1> <pt2>)

This function returns the distance in decimal units from pt1 to pt2. If the UNITS are set to Architectural and the distance between two points is 6'-3", the (distance ...) function will return 75.000000.

(polar <pt> <angle> <distance>)

This function returns a point. It can be one of the most useful tools in the AutoLISP tool kit. The ARGUMENTs must be of the proper TYPE. The <pt> must evaluate to a LIST of two REALs. The <angle> and <distance> are each a REAL. The value of the <angle> is in radians.

(osnap <pt> <mode-string>)

This function returns a point. It allows OSNAPping to a point while in AutoLISP. Like the (polar ...) function, it returns a point in the form of a LIST of two or three REALs. For example, if a circle has been drawn using p1 and p2 in the 2P method as follows:

> (setq p1 (list 1.0 3.0))
> (setq p2 (list 4.0 3.0))
> (command "circle" "2P" p1 p2)

then

> (command "line" "0,0" (setq c (osnap p1 "center")) "")

returns (2.5 3.0) or the LIST or two REALs representing the center of the circle as the endpoint of the line.

(inters <pt1> <pt2> <pt3> <pt4> [<onseg>])

This function returns a point. It can be used for the following:

1. To determine if two nonparallel lines intersect.
2. If they intersect, the location of that point.
3. If they do not intersect, where they would intersect if one or both were extended until they intersected.

If the optional <onseg> ARGUMENT is present and is nil, the lines will be considered infinite in length and the function will return a LIST of three REALs designating that intersection point.

If the optional <onseg> ARGUMENT is not present or is not nil, then their intersection must be on both segments in order for a point to be returned; otherwise, the function will return nil.

CAR, CDR, AND COMBINATIONS

CAR and CDR are the primary functions that select and return element(s) of a LIST. Unlike the (angle ...) function and (distance ...) function, these functions will operate on a LIST comprised of elements of any TYPE. The elements can be atoms or LISTs within the LIST. The atoms can be REALs, INTEGERs, STRINGs, or symbols. The ARGUMENT to the CAR and CDR functions can even be a LIST of mixed types of elements. These were the foundation functions designed to analyze a LIST of symbols (which is what language is). In AutoLISP, these functions break down points into coordinates. For example:

> (setq p1 '(1.0 2.0)) returns (1.0 2.0)

then

> (car p1) returns 1.0, a real

but

> (cdr p1) returns (2.0), a list

Note the parentheses enclosing 2.0.

If

(setq L1 (list 1.0 2.0))

and

(setq L2 (list L1 3.0))

then

(car L2) returns (1.0 2.0), a list

Here is a LIST within a LIST. Or in the function-list (setq L2 (list L1 3.0)), L1 is a LIST within a LIST within a function-list.

The above expression is not used very often in AutoLISP, but its capability is worthy of note.

(car <list>) returns the first element of <list>.

(cdr <list>) returns <list> without the first element.

The TYPE of the return of the (car <list>) function depends upon the TYPE of the first element.

If

(setq L (list 1.0 2.0))

then

(car L) returns 1.0, a real

If

(setq L (list 1 2.0))

then

(car L) returns 1, an integer

If

(setq L (list "1" 2))

then

(car L) returns "1," a string

If the symbol "a" evaluates to nil and

(setq L (list a 2))

then

(car L) returns the symbol "a"

but, if

(setq a 1.0)

and

(setq L (list a 2.0))

then

(car L) returns 1.0, a real

While (car <list>) can return any type of expression, (cdr <list>) always returns a
LIST. The return may not look like a LIST, but its TYPE will be a LIST (even if
nil). For example:

(setq L1 (1.0 2.0))

(cdr L1) returns (2.0), a LIST

Remember, the parentheses designate the LIST and (car L1) returns 1.0, a
REAL; so, how can the LIST (2.0) be used as a REAL? By using the combination
of:

(car (cdr L1))

which is the same as

(car (2.0)) which returns 2.0, a REAL

Note how (car <list>) breaks the first expression out of the <list> and returns it
evaluated to its type.

So while (car <list>) and (cdr <list>) operate on the same LIST, (cdr <list>)
always returns a LIST. Consider:

(setq L1 (list 1.0)) returns (1.0), a LIST

(car L1) returns 1.0, a REAL

and

(cdr L1) returns nil;

it is the null LIST

or the same as (list ( ))

If

(setq L1 (list 1.0 2.0))

then

(car L1) returns 1.0

(cdr L1) returns (2.0)

and

(car (cdr L1)) returns 2.0

A short cut for the above is:

(cadr <list>)

or

(cadr L1) which returns 2.0, a REAL

CADR is one of several short forms of combinations of CAR and CDR.

REMEMBER!

(car <list>) may return any type

(cdr <list>) is a LIST

The short forms of CAR and CDR begin with "C" and end with "R." The characters between will be either an "A" or a "D" and will determine the sequence of combined CAR(s) and CDR(s). Some short forms are shown below:

CAAR	(car (car <list>))
CDDR	(cdr (cdr <list>))
CADR	(car (cdr <list>))
CDAR	(cdr (car <list>))

Any form that begins with "CA" will return an expression.
Any form that begins with "CD" will return a LIST.

All CARs and CDRs represented by "A's" and "D's" in such forms as CADAR and CDDAR, however deep, must have LISTs as their individual ARGUMENTs.

For example:

If

(setq L1 (list (1.0 2.0) 3.0)) returns ((1.0 2.0) 3.0)

(car L1) returns (1.0 2.0), a LIST

(cdr L1) returns (3.0), also a LIST

(list (1.0 2.0) 3.0) makes a LIST out of the LIST (1.0 2.0) and the atom 3.0. That is why the (car L1) returned a LIST, even though 3.0 is a REAL in the LIST "L1," (cdr <list>) always returns a LIST. The first element of L1 is (1.0 2.0) and when removed from ((1.0 2.0) 3.0), then (3.0) remains. And that is the function of (cdr L1), to return a LIST with its first element removed.

So

(caar L1)

is the same as

(car (car L1)) and returns 1.0, a REAL

but

(cdar L1)

which is the same as

(cdr (car L1)) returns (2.0), a LIST

Because 2.0 and 3.0 are not first elements, in order to return their values as REALs, they must first be returned as the first elements of a LIST as follows:

(cadar L1)

means

(car (cdr (car L1))) and returns 2.0

and is the same as

(car (cdr (1.0 2.0)))

and the same as

(car (2.0))

and

(cadr L1)

means

(car (cdr L1)) and returns 3.0

or

(car (3.0))

CAR and CADR Mainly for Graphics

(car ...) and (cadr ...) are the primary functions for accessing the X and Y coordinates of a point in AutoCAD. Remember if:

(setq L1 (list 1.0 2.0))

is entered, (cdr L1) returns the not-so-useful LIST (2.0)

but by using (cadr L1)

which means

(car (cdr L1))

in the following manner

(cadr L1) returns 2.0

which is no longer a LIST but a REAL.

Review

All forms of the CAR-CDR combination that begin with "CA" will return the first expression. All forms that begin with "CD" will return a LIST.

For graphics applications, LISTs represent the X and Y coordinates of a 2D point and the X, Y, and Z coordinates of a 3D point. Therefore, the more useful CAR-CDR combination forms are as follows:

in a 2D point

> (setq p2d (list 1.0 2.0))
> (car p2d) returns 1.0 the X coordinate
> (cadr p2d) returns 2.0 the Y coordinate
> (caddr p2d) returns nil

in a 3D point

> (setq p3d (list 1.0 2.0 3.0))
> (car p3d) returns 1.0 the X coordinate
> (cadr p3d) returns 2.0 the Y coordinate
> (caddr p3d) returns 3.0 the Z coordinate
> (cdr p2d) returns (2.0) a LIST

and

> (cdr p3d) returns (2.0 3.0), a LIST

neither of which is very useful unless the programmer wishes to project all of the 3D points on the Y-Z plane.

(last <list>) returns the last expression in the <list>. While (last <list>) can be used to return the Y coordinate of a 2D point and the Z coordinate of a 3D point, it is not recommended for that purpose. Because there might be an erroneous return, it is recommended that (cadr <list>) be used for the Y coordinate and (caddr <list>) for the Z coordinate.

(cons <new first element> <list>) returns the <first new element> and <list> combined into a new LIST, as in the following:

> (setq a 2.0)
> (setq b 3.0)
> (setq L1 (list a b))
> (cons 1.0 L1) returns (1.0 2.0 3.0)

(cons ...) will also return what is known as a "dotted pair" when there is an atom in place of the <list> ARGUMENT, as in the following:

> (cons 1.0 2.0) returns (1.000000 . 2.000000)

This special form of LIST requires less memory than ordinary LISTs.

(length <list>) returns the number of elements in <list> as in the following:

> (setq L1 (list "you" (1.0 2.0) 3.0))
> returns ("you" (1.0 2.0) 3.0)
> (length L1) returns 3
> (length (car L1)) returns nil because (car L1) is an atom
> (length (cddr)) returns 2
> (length (cadr)) returns 2
> (length (caddr)) returns nil

If

> (setq L1 (list "you" (1.0) 2.0))
> (length L1) returns 3
> (length (cadr L1)) returns 1

(nth <n> <list>) returns the "nth" element of <list>.
(Zero is the first element.) For example:

> (setq L1 (list "you" (1.0 2.0) 3))
> (nth 0 L1) returns "you," a STRING
> (nth 1 L1) returns (1.0 2.0), a LIST
> (nth 2 L1) returns 3, an INTEGER
> (nth 0 (cadr L1)) returns 1.0, a REAL
> (nth 1 (cadr L1)) returns 2.0, a REAL
> (nth 3 L1) returns nil

(reverse <list>) returns the <list> with the elements in reverse order, as in the following example:

> (setq L1 (list (1.0 2.0) 3.0))
> (reverse L1) returns (3 (1.0 2.0))
> (reverse (car L1)) returns (2.0 1.0)

TYPE CHANGING FUNCTIONS

In order for the AutoCAD operator, AutoCAD, and AutoLISP to properly communicate between each other (and within each internally), data is constantly exchanged. Of the different data TYPEs (as classified by AutoLISP) there are three TYPEs of data that may be stored as one TYPE, but need to be communicated as another TYPE. These are the INTEGER, the REAL, and the STRING.

Some AutoLISP functions are designed to take data of one TYPE as their ARGUMENT and return that data as another TYPE. The basic outline below, Figure 16-5, shows the functions and the TYPEs that they are designed to translate from and to.

		FROM		
		INTEGER	REAL	STRING
TO	INTEGER	(FIX)	FIX	ATOI
	REAL	FLOAT	(FLOAT)	ATOF
	STRING	ITOA	ANGTOS	
			RTOS	

Figure 16-5 The Basic Translation for Communication between AutoCAD and AutoLISP

(angtos <angle> [<mode> [<precision>]]) takes <angle> input as a REAL in radians and returns a STRING in the form determined by <mode>. The value of <mode> and its corresponding format is as follows:

ANGTOS MODE	FORMAT
0	Degrees
1	Degrees/Minutes/Seconds
2	Grads
3	Radians
4	Surveyor's Units

For example:

If

```
(setq p1 (1.0 1.0))
(setq p2 (2.0 2.0))
(setq a (angle p1 p2)) returns 0.78539816
```

then

```
(angtos a 0) returns "45"
(angtos a 1) returns "45.000000"
(angtos a 2) returns "45d0'0.0000""
(angtos a 3) returns "0.78539816r"
(angtos a 4) returns "N 45d0'0.0000 W""
```

The optional <precision> determines the decimal places to be displayed.

(atof <string>) takes a <string> and returns a REAL. For example:

```
(atof "3.75") returns 3.750000
(atof "4") returns 4.000000
```

(atoi <string>) takes a <string> and returns an INTEGER. For example:

```
(atoi "3.75") returns 3
(atoi "4") returns 4
```

(itoa <int>) takes an <integer> and returns a STRING. For example:

(itoa 33) returns "33"
(itoa -4) returns "-4"

The (rtos <number> [<mode> [<precision>]]) function takes a REAL input and returns a STRING in the form determined by <mode>. The value of <mode> and its corresponding format is as follows:

RTOS MODE	FORMAT
1	Scientific
2	Decimal
3	Engineering
4	Architectural
5	Arbitrary Fractional Units

The optional <precision> determines the decimal places to be displayed.

(fix <number>) takes a REAL or INTEGER and returns an INTEGER. For example:

(fix 4) returns 4
(fix 4.25) returns 4

(float <number>) takes a REAL or INTEGER and returns a REAL. For example:

(float 4) returns 4.000000
(float 4.25) returns 4.250000

INPUT FUNCTIONS

The INPUT functions cause a program to pause for user input of a particular TYPE and return data in the format of a specified TYPE.

The optional [<prompt>] in all (get ...) functions allows the programmer to display the <prompt> message in the prompt area on the screen. It will be demonstrated in the first (get ...) function description.

NOTE: The (getvar ...) function is NOT a function for user input.

CAUTION!

For all (get ...) functions, the user input CANNOT be in the form of an AutoLISP function.

(getangle [<pt>] [<prompt>]) will return an angle in radians between two points, the first of which may be the optional [<pt>] in the function. Note the option of either selecting two points or inputting the first point into the AutoLISP function and selecting the second point. This method is used in the (getdist ...) and the (getorient ...) functions and will be referred to in their descriptions. For example:

(setq a (getangle "PICK TWO POINTS: "))

will pause for the user to input 2 points, either of which may be typed in on the keyboard (as in 1'2,3'6-1/2 if in the Architectural UNITS mode), or picked on the screen. If the response to the above (getangle ...) function were 1,1 and 2,2 then the function would return 0.785398. Or if

(setq p1 (list 14.0 42.5))

then

(setq a (getangle p1 "PICK SECOND PT: "))

will use p1 for the first point and pause for the user to input the second point from the keyboard or on the screen.

If

(setq p1 (list 1 1))

and

(setq a (getangle p1 "PICK SECOND PT: "))

and 2,2 were entered, it would return 0.785398.

CAUTION!

Unlike the (angle ...) function, the angle returned by the (getangle ...) function is affected by a change in the ANGBASE system variable. If the ANGBASE were changed from 0 degrees to 45 degrees, the above (getangle p1 ...) function with a response of 2,2 would return 0.000000. (See the (getorient ...) function description.)

(getcorner <pt> [<prompt>]) returns a point selected during the pause. As the user places the cursor for selection, a rectangle is displayed with the <pt> as the lower left corner of the rectangle and the cursor location as the upper right corner.

(getdist [<pt>] [<prompt>]) returns the distance between two points in the same manner and with the same options as the (getangle ...) function returns an angle. The return will be a REAL. If the UNITS are set to Architectural a length of 3'-6 1/2" would be returned as 42.500000.

(getint [<prompt>]) pauses for an INTEGER input and returns that INTEGER.

(getkword [<prompt>]) pauses for user input of a keyword that must correspond to a word on a LIST set up by the (initget ...) function prior to using the (getkword ...) function. If the response is not appropriate then AutoCAD will retry. This function prevents a program from terminating prematurely due to the wrong type of data being input by mistake, and gives the user another chance. It also permits returning a STRING by just inputting initial letters. For example:

> (initget 1 "SET Make New")
> (setq g (getkword "LAYER CHOICES? (SET, M, or N): "))

AutoCAD will reject any response that does not comprise the initial uppercase characters of the options in the LIST set by (initget ...). The response may also include any and all of the lowercase characters in the STRING, but nothing in addition to the characters of any of the options. The responses that are valid to the above example are: SET, M, Ma, Mak, Make, N, Ne, and New, with any of the preceding in uppercase.

> (initget 1 "SET MaKe New")
> (getkword)

will accept "m" because the "K" was preceded by a lowercase "a."

> (initget 1 "SET MAke New")
> (getkword)

will not accept "m," but will accept "ma," "mak," or "make," but not "makeup."

(getorient [<pt>] [<prompt>]) will pause for the user to input two points, and will return an angle in radians between two points.

The point selection options are the same as the (getangle ...) function. Unlike the (getangle ...) function, the (getorient ...) function is not affected by an ANGBASE system variable change. It will return an angle determined by the line connecting the two input points. The angle will be measured between that line and the zero East baseline regardless of the ANGBASE setting.

(getpoint [<pt>] [<prompt>]) pauses for input of a point (either from the keyboard or a pick on the screen), and returns that point in the form of a LIST of two REALs.

The optional <pt>, if used, will cause a rubberband line from <pt> to the placement of the cursor until a pick is made.

(getreal [<prompt>]) pauses for user input of a REAL number and returns that REAL number.

(getstring [<cr>] [<prompt>]) pauses for keyboard characters to be entered and returns them as a STRING. It is not necessary to enclose the input in quotation marks. AutoLISP will do that automatically. The optional <cr>, if present and not nil, will permit the STRING to have blank spaces. The STRING must be terminated by striking ⏎. Otherwise, if <cr> is present and nil, striking the spacebar will terminate the entry.

(initget [<bits>] [<string>]) offers the programmer a one-time control of the user's response to the next (get ...) function, and that (get ...) function only.

This only means that any time control is needed for a (get ...) function, a new (initget ...) function must precede it.

The type of control that is offered by the (initget ...) function is as follows:

1. The program can be set up to reject responses of a certain unwanted type or value (without terminating the program) and offer the user a second chance to enter an acceptable response.
2. The program can be made to accept points outside of the limits even when LIMCHECK is on.
3. The program can be made to return 3D points rather than 2D points.
4. Dashed lines can be used when drawing a rubberband or a box.
5. The program can be made to accept a STRING when the (get ...) function normally requires a specific TYPE such as POINT or REAL.

The controls offered by using the <bits> option are shown in Figure 16-6. The <bits> may be a sum of whichever values in Figure 16-6 correspond to the controls desired for the next (get ...) function. For example:

> (setq p1 (list 0 0))
> (initget 9)
> (setq d (getdist p1 "SECOND POINT: "))

BITS VALUE	MEANING
1	REJECTS NULL INPUT
2	REJECTS ZERO VALUES
4	REJECTS NEGATIVE VALUES
8	ALLOWS INPUT OUTSIDE LIMITS
16	RETURNS 3D POINTS RATHER THAN 2D
32	USES DASHED LINES FOR RUBBERBAND/BOX

Figure 16-6 The Controls Offered by the Bits Option

The bits in the above line are a sum of 1 (rejects null input) and 8 (allows input outside limits). This will allow the second point to be outside the limits even if the LIMITS mode is ON. It also will not accept a null return.

CONDITIONAL AND LOGIC FUNCTIONS

AutoLISP's conditional and logic functions allow the user to have a program test certain conditions and proceed according to the result of those tests. Or, by using the WHILE function, a programmer's LOOP situation will allow iteration of a changing variable between the extents of a specified range.

The symbol "T" is used when an expression is needed that will never evaluate to nil.

(if <testexpr> <thenexpr> [<elseexpre>]) evaluates the <testexpr>. If the <textexpr> does not return nil, then the function returns the evaluation of the <thenexpr>. If the optional <elseexpr> is present and the <testexpr> evaluates to nil, then the function returns the evaluation of the <elseexpr>. Otherwise, the function returns nil. For example:

```
(setq q (getint "ENTER QUANTITY FROM 1-99: " ))
(if (< q 10)
    (setq c q)
    (setq c (fix (/ q 10))))
)
```

This program will take a number (from user input) and test to see if it is less than 10. If so, it will SETQ the symbol "c" to that number. If it is 10 or greater, it will divide the number by 10 and SETQ "c" to the whole number of the result, such as 37 becomes 3.7 becomes 3.

(cond (<test1> <result1> ...) ...) accepts any number of ARGUMENTs. The first item in each list is evaluated, and when one returns not nil, the following expressions in that list are evaluated and the function returns the value of the last expression. For example, a routine could be written to return the angle of a line to be only in the first or fourth quadrants, regardless of how it was originally selected. Note the four possibilities shown in Figure 16-7.

We will not consider the four ortho directions N, E, S, or W, in this example. If an angle is returned that was determined by the function (setq a (angle p1 p2)), then it could be in one of four quadrants. Then to assure that no matter which angle was set by p1-p2, the function would return an angle in the first or fourth quadrant. For example:

```
(setq a (angle p1 p2))
(cond
    ((and (> a pi) (< a (* 3 (/ pi 2)))) (setq a (- a pi))
    ((and (> a (/ pi 2)) (< a pi)) (setq a (+ a pi))
)
```

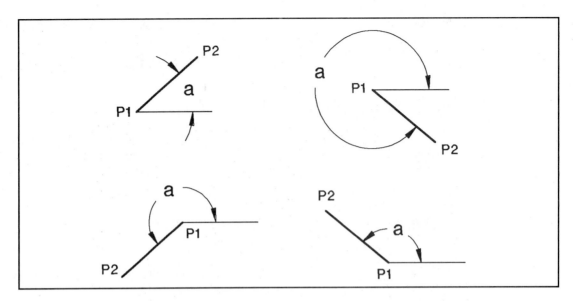

Figure 16-7 Conditional and Logic Function Return Possibilities

The (while <testexpr> <expr>...) function evaluates the <textexpr>, and if not nil, evaluates the following expressions and then repeats the procedure again with the <testexpr>.

This repetition continues until the <textexpr> evaluates to nil and then the function returns the evaluation of the <lastexpr>.

TEST EXPRESSIONS

The (if ...), (cond ...), and (while ...) functions normally use one of the logic functions as the <textexpr>. For example, the following program line was previously entered:

(setq a 10.0)

(if (null a) (setq a 6.0))

This sequence will not change the value of the symbol "a" because the evaluation of the expression (null a) is "nil." Therefore, the following expression will not be evaluated. Had "a" not been previously SETQed, the expression (null a) would evaluate to "T" (for TRUE), and the expression following would be evaluated and would have SETQed the symbol "a" to 6.0.

(= <atom> <atom> ...) returns T if all of the <atom>s evaluate to the same thing.

(/= <atom1> <atom2>) returns T if <atom1> is "not equal to" <atom2>. It is nil otherwise.

(< <atom> <atom> ...) returns T if each <atom> is "less than" the <atom> to its right. It is nil otherwise.

(<= <atom> <atom> ...) returns T if each <atom> is "less than or equal to" the <atom> to its right. It is nil otherwise.

(> \<atom\> \<atom\> ...) returns T if each \<atom\> is "greater than" the \<atom\> to its right. It is nil otherwise.

(>= \<atom\> \<atom\> ...) returns T if each \<atom\> is "greater than or equal to" the \<atom\> to its right. It is nil otherwise.

(and \<expr\>...) returns T if all \<expr\>s return T. It is nil otherwise.

(boundp \<atom\>) returns T if \<atom\> has a value bound to it. It is nil otherwise.

(eq \<expr1\> \<expr2\>) returns T if \<expr1\> and \<expr2\> are identical and are bound to the same object. It is nil otherwise.

(equal \<expr1\> \<expr2\>) returns T if \<expr1\> and \<expr2\> evaluate to the same thing. It is nil otherwise.

(not \<expr\>) returns T if \<expr\> is nil. Otherwise the function returns nil.

(null \<item\>) returns T if \<item\> is bound to nil. The function returns nil otherwise.

(or \<expr\>...) returns T if any of the \<expr\>s evaluate to something that is not nil. Otherwise the function returns nil.

EXERCISES

1. Identify the atoms in the following expressions:

   (if (not (null dfr)) (setq dfr (rtos rad)) (setq dfr "0"))

   Write the AutoLISP expression equivalent to the following:
2. a = 1
3. b = 2.0
4. c = a
5. d = 1 + 2
6. e = 2
7. f = 1 b
8. g = 7 + 9 + 3 + 7
9. h = (3 + 5 + 6) 7
10. i = (7 3) + (4 - (6 3))
11. j = 3 (7 + 6)
12. k = 3 + (7 6)
13. l = 5 – (7 + 2)
14. m = sin 0.75
15. n = cos 1.75
16. o = sin (pi 2)
17. p = absolute value of a
18. q = x
19. r = tan (3 pi 4)

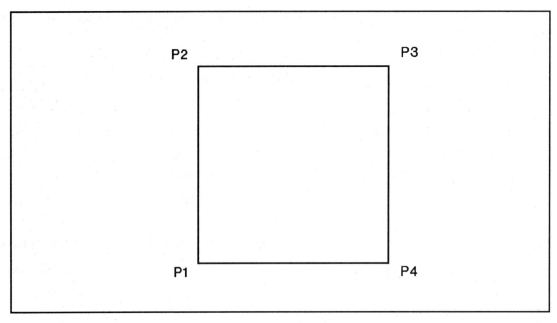

Figure 16-8 The Rectangle for Writing Expressions

In the rectangle shown in Figure 16-8, write the expressions that evaluate to the following:

20. the vertical distance between p1 and p3
21. the distance between p1 and p3
22. the horizontal distance between p2 and p4
23. the distance between p1 and p4
24. p2 in terms of p1 and p3
25. p3 in terms of p2 and p4
26. the sum of the four sides (perimeter)
27. the area enclosed by the four sides
28. the area of a triangle whose vertices are p1, p2, and p3
29. the angle between lines from p1 to p3 and from p1 to p4

Answer the following:

30. In (setq L1 (list 1.0 2.0)) what is (car L1)?
31. In (setq L2 (list 3.0 4.0)) what is (cdr L2)?
32. In (setq L3 (list 5.0 6.0)) what is (cadr L3)?

Example: (setq L5 (list 1.0 '(2.0 (3.0 4.0)) 5.0))

In the above example, write the combination of car and cdr that will return the following from the LIST L5:

33. 1.0
34. 2.0
35. 3.0
36. 4.0
37. 5.0

Give the evaluations of the following expressions:

38. (+ 1.0 2.0)		65. (/ 1.0 2)
39. (+ 3 4)		66. (/ 40000 2)
40. (+ 5 6.0)		67. (/ 2 40000)
41. (– 7 6)		68. (abs (+ 4 2))
42. (– 8 9)		69. (abs (– 4 2))
43. (+ 1 20 300)		70. (ascii "ABC")
44. (– 1 20 300)		71. (ascii "aBC")
45. (– 300 20 1)		72. (chr 66)
46. (– 30000 1.0)		73. (chr 98)
47. (+ 30000 30000)		74. (expt 3 2)
48. (* 1 2)		75. (expt 2 3)
49. (* 1.0 2.0)		76. (sqrt 9)
50. (* 3 4)		77. (sqrt (* 2 8))
51. (* 5.0 6)		78. (type 1)
52. (* 1 2 3)		79. (type pi)
53. (* 4 4 6.0)		80. (type 3.0)
54. (* 7 8000)		81. (type T)
55. (* 8.0 9000)		82. (sin 0)
56. (* 3 pi)		83. (cos (/ pi 2))
57. (* pi pi)		84. (atan 1)
58. (/ 2.0 1.0)		85. (angle (list 1.0 1.0) (list 2.0 2.0))
59. (/ 2.0 1)		86. (angle (list 2.0 1.0) (list 0.0 1.0))
60. (/ 2 1)		87. (distance (list 1.0 1.0) (list 3.5 1.0))
61. (/ 1 2)		88. (distance (list 6.0 5.0) (list 2.0 2.0))
62. (/ 3 2)		89. (polar (list 1.0 1.0) 0 2.0)
63. (/ 3.0 2)		90. (polar (list 2.0 3.0) pi 1)
64. (/ 3 2.0)		91. (inters (list 0.0 0.0) (list 3.0 3.0) (list 3.0 0.0) (list 0.0 3.0))

CUSTOM COMMANDS AND FUNCTIONS

(defun ...) and (defun C: ...)

This is an AutoLISP function that will create a custom-designed function called DEFUN. Its format is:

(defun <sym> <argument list> <expr>...).

The DEFUN function operates in a manner similar to the SETQ function. SETQ names a variable and sets it equal to a value. DEFUN names a new function so that when its name is entered in a routine, it will evaluate to the subsequent expression(s). In addition, it allows variables to be operated on by the function by entering the name of that defined function followed by a variable or group of variables.

The customizing power of this feature cannot be emphasized enough. What this means to the programmer is that when a routine has been worked out in AutoLISP, the entire routine can be given a name. Then when the routine needs to be used again, the programmer simply enters the name of the routine. This makes it a user-defined or custom-defined function.

The name of a custom-defined function can also be entered while in the AutoCAD Editor or it can be included in a MENU STRING by entering its name enclosed in parentheses.

In addition to having a one-word entry perform the task of many lines of programming, there is an optional feature that makes the custom-defined function even more effective. The user can define the custom function to perform the prescribed task on a dummy variable in the definition and then enter the defined function followed by some real variable later and have the task performed on the REAL variable. The dummy variables are listed in the <argument list>.

ARGUMENTS AND LOCAL SYMBOLS

Every custom-defined function and command must include the parentheses used to enclose the ARGUMENTs. Even if there are no ARGUMENTs or local symbols (which means the opening and closing parentheses would be empty), those opening and closing parentheses must follow the user-designated function name. Remember, however, that ARGUMENTs (the dummy variables) are not permitted in custom commands using the "C:FNAME" format. The following forms are examples of how function and command definitions may be written:

(defun fname ( )...def exprs...)	no ARGUMENTs or local symbols
(defun C:FNAME ( )...def exprs...)	no ARGUMENTs or local symbols
(defun fname (/ x y z)...def exprs...)	three local symbols only
(defun C:FNAME (/ x y z)...def exprs...)	three local symbols only
(defun fname (a b)...def exprs...)	two ARGUMENTs only
(defun fname (a b / x y z)...def exprs...)	two ARGUMENT and three local symbols

CAUTION!

If the ARGUMENTs enclosing parentheses are inadvertently omitted, AutoLISP will take whatever is in the first parentheses of the definition expressions and try to use them as ARGUMENTs and/or local symbols. This will naturally not oeprate as expected and result in an error message. Therefore, include parentheses as shown, even if empty.

Also, within the <argument list> optional local symbols may be listed (after the slash) to name symbols to be used within the function definition only, without having any effect on the same symbol name outside the defined function. This form of creating a defined function is for use within AutoLISP and cannot be entered without the enclosing parentheses. An added feature, to be discussed later, will allow the same user-defined function to be invoked in the same manner as AutoCAD commands. That is, with the added feature, they can be entered from the keyboard or in the menu without parentheses and then recalled immediately afterward by simply striking ⏎.

DEFINED FUNCTIONS AND COMMANDS

When one starts to delve into custom programs in many graphic applications, one of the first geometric-trigonometric stumbling blocks to overcome is the use of radians to measure angles. AutoCAD is no exception. Even if the use of radians is second nature to someone, using degrees seems to be first nature with almost all designer-drafters. The main problem is in converting from one to the other. This is often necessary because AutoCAD uses degrees in the Editor and radians in AutoLISP. Therefore, one of the first AutoLISP routines introduced in articles and books on AutoLISP is one that converts the value of an angle in degrees to its value in radians. The second routine is usually one that converts from radians back to degrees. The usual name for the degrees-to-radians function is an abbreviation called dtr. The dtr function is written as follows:

```
(defun dtr (a
  (* pi (/ a 180.0))
)
```

From the format:

```
(defun <sym> <argument list> <expr>...)
```

dtr is the symbol (<sym>), "a" is the only ARGUMENT in the ARGUMENT list, and the expression (<expr>) is:

```
(* pi (/ a 180.0)).
```

While (/ a 180.0) is an expression, it resides within the expression "(* pi (/ a 180.0))," and is not considered one of the separate "<expr>" expressions in the form:

```
(defun <sym> <argument list> <expr>...)
```

The "<expr>... " indicates there is no limit to the number of expressions possible in a defined function. While this is a very minor point, it may help in understanding what an expression is and how AutoLISP looks at them.

WRITING A DEFINED FUNCTION

The dtr function may be typed in from the keyboard while in the AutoCAD Drawing Editor as follows:

Command: **(defun dtr (a) (* pi (/ a 180.0)))**

This function may be used and applied to any real number in the following manner:

Command: **(dtr 90.0)**
returns 1.570796327
or
Command: **(dtr 180.0)**
returns 3.141592654
or
Command: **(dtr 7.5)**
returns 0.130899694

While entering the above from the keyboard will define the dtr function for use at any time during the current editing session, the definition will be lost when the drawing is ENDed. Although writing this routine is fairly simple, it is still not very economical. There is a better way.

WRITING AND STORING A DEFINED FUNCTION

Usually, any function that needs to be defined in one drawing will be useful enough to warrant saving the definition for instant re-use later in any drawing without having to type it in repeatedly.

Therefore, defined functions may be saved for loading into a drawing. By using a text editor or word processor in the programmer mode, the custom programmer can create a file having the file extension of .LSP, and then type in the routine. The example below is similar to the first example, only with a slight variation in format. It is as follows:

Filename: **ANGLE.LSP**

```
(defun dtr (a)           ;degrees to radians
    (* pi (/ a 180.0))   ;pi times "a" divided by 180
)                        ;leave function definition
```

The indentation is permissible in writing a defined function in a FILENAME.LSP file (unlike the program lines in a FILENAME.MNU file). It is even desirable in order to be able to easily identify the distinct elements and subelements of the function definition. The value of this procedure will become more evident with more elaborate definitions. The closing parenthesis, on a line by itself, is lined up with the opening parenthesis. This is an example of how indentation coincides with the depth of nesting of expressions.

In the last example, remarks have been written to the right, following semicolons. AutoLISP ignores anything on a line following a semicolon.

FUNCTION NAMES

The name of the file may or may not be the same as any of the function names it includes. It may even be the same as a function in another file, although that would not be logical. Uniqueness of names is critical within a group of named items, such as files, functions, variables, drawings on one directory, etc. But in most cases it is not a problem to duplicate names across groups, such as having a FILENM1.LSP and a FILENM1.DWG and a FILENM1.SHP at the same time along with defining a custom function as follows:

(defun filenm1 (.....

Duplication in this case is not only acceptable, but sometimes desirable in coordinating a group of specially named custom files and functions that are all in a single enhancement program being used for a singular purpose.

LOADING A DEFINED FUNCTION

As mentioned earlier in this chapter, custom-defined functions must be written into a FILENAME.LSP file in order to be saved and usable later. Once a custom-defined function is stored in that file, the user must load the file in order to use it. For example, the file named ANGLE.LSP has been created to store the custom-defined function named dtr as follows:

Filename: **ANGLE.LSP**

```
(defun dtr (a)            ;degrees to radians
   (* pi (/ a 180.0))     ;pi times a divided by 180
)                         ;leave function definition
```

In order to make dtr usable, the user must invoke the AutoLISP function named LOAD. It has the format of:

(load <filename>)

with <filename> being a STRING without the extension of .LSP. Therefore, the filename must be enclosed within quotations as follows:

(load "angle")

CAUTION!

The user is advised to be aware of the distinction between the AutoLISP function "load" and the AutoCAD command "load". The AutoCAD command named "LOAD" is used to load FILENAME.SHP (shape) files and is entered without the parentheses in the following manner:

Command: **LOAD**

The AutoLISP function named "load" is used to load FILENAME.LSP (AutoLISP) files and is entered with the parentheses in the following manner:

Command: **(load "angle")**

The above sequence will make the custom-defined function named dtr usable in the current editing session. The user must be careful when trying to load .LSP files from some other drive or directory. If the file named ANGLE.LSP is stored on the directory named "LISPFILE" then the format would be as follows:

Command: **(load "/lispfile/angle")**

Special note should be made of the forward slash versus the backslash. The filename is a STRING and a leading backslash in a STRING is itself a special control character used in conjunction with other code characters for specific operations on the STRING. Note from Chapter 1 that in order to have a backslash read as a backslash in a STRING, there must be a double backslash. Therefore, the forward slash is recommended in designating a directory path in PC-DOS/MS-DOS.

Drive specifications can also be included in the AutoLISP LOAD function format as follows:

Command: **(load "a:angle")**

or

Command: **(load "a:/lispfile/angle")**

The last entry may be used if the ANGLE.LSP file is in the lispfile directory on the A: drive.

If the custom programmer has created custom-defined functions in a file called "ACAD.LSP" and that file is accessible when a drawing is edited, AutoCAD will "load" that file automatically. Only functions that might be used in all drawings should be included in that file if it is created.

SIN AND COS, BUT NOT TAN!

Sometimes designer-drafters wish to determine some distances in the all-powerful RIGHT TRIANGLE (from which trigonometry is derived) by using the opposite and adjacent sides instead of the hypotenuse. So why doesn't AutoLISP have the TAN (tangent) function in addition to the SIN and COS? First of all, an angle is defined in *Webster's New Collegiate Dictionary* as "...a measure of the amount of turning necessary to bring one line or plane into coincidence with or parallel to another." Two special cases exist in computing the tangent of an angle, one of which causes a problem that the sine and cosine do not cause. When two lines exist, it is assumed that they must have length and therefore have a nonzero value. When considering the sine or cosine of an angle, the hypotenuse is always one of the existing nonzero lines. And in the sine and cosine of any angle the hypotenuse is always the divisor. So, even if the opposite side (in the case of the sine) or the adjacent side (in the case of the cosine) turn out to be zero, the worst that can happen is that the function will result in zero. In the case of the tangent where the divisor is the adjacent side, if it is zero, the result approaches infinity and is therefore not valid for use within the program. This occurs, of course, at 90 degrees.

The other special case is where the angle is zero and the tangent is zero. Zero may be a valid entry, where infinity cannot be. This problem does not occur in the sine and cosine functions because the results of either range from 1 to 0 to -1 and back to 1. All results within this range are valid for use within programs.

An approach to arriving at the tangent is possible by using existing AutoLISP functions named SIN and COS. The tangent can be expressed as the quotient of the sine divided by the cosine. But here again is the possibility of the divisor being zero because the cosine of 90 degrees is just that. If used for specific purposes where it is known that the value of the adjacent side involved is nonzero, then a custom-defined function that will return the tangent of an angle (along with a radians-to-degrees function) might be included in the ANGLE.LSP file as follows:

Filename: **ANGLE.LSP**

```
(vmon)
(defun dtr (a)                ;degrees to radians
   (* pi (/ a 180.0))         ;pi times a divided by 180
)                             ;leave function definition

(defun rtd (b)                ;radians to degrees
   (* 180.0 (/ b pi))         ;180 times b divided by pi
)                             ;leave function definition

(defun tan (c)                ;tangent
   (/ (sin c) (cos c))        ;sine divided by cosine
)                             ;leave function definition
```

DEFINED AUTOLISP COMMANDS

AutoCAD's programming features allow the creation of custom-defined AutoLISP commands with two characteristics similar to regular AutoCAD commands.

1. AutoLISP commands can be entered from the keyboard or within a menu string by just entering the name of the custom command without having to enclose it in parentheses.

2. If a particular AutoLISP command was the last command used, then striking ⏎ will recall that same command for immediate use.

CAUTION!

There are two characteristics of regular AutoCAD commands that are not attributable to AutoLISP commands. Therefore, care must be observed when planning a routine so as not to create an AutoLISP command in anticipation of these abilities. They are as follows:

1. While AutoCAD commands can be invoked from within AutoLISP routines and functions by using the COMMAND function, AutoLISP commands cannot be invoked from within AutoLISP functions or other AutoLISP commands. They can only be invoked from the keyboard or from menu STRINGs.

2. AutoLISP commands cannot operate on external variables (ARGUMENTs) of an <argument list>. However, local symbols are allowed.

WRITING AN AUTOLISP FUNCTION

The format used in creating an AutoLISP command is as follows:

(defun C:CMDNAME </ local symbols> <expr>...)

where "CMDNAME" may be a name of your choice as long as it does not duplicate the name of an existing AutoCAD command or function. Note two important things:

1. The command name "CMDNAME" must be preceded by "C:." While the Reference Manual states that the "C" must be in uppercase, some articles on AutoLISP have stated that it is not a requirement. If it is contingent on some future plans for AutoLISP, then perhaps following the instructions will prevent future problems. It should not be a major inconvenience to capitalize the prefix.

2. It does matter that the name of the command is in uppercase. This rule should be followed.

Other than the above dissimilarities, AutoLISP commands follow the same rules as custom-defined functions.

WHAT IS THE DATA BASE?

The file that stores information about the drawing includes TABLES and BLOCK sections that include data associated with linetype, layer, style (for text), view, UCS, viewport, and Blocks. These are accessible through the (tablenext...) and (tablesearch...) functions.

The ENTITIES section contains data associated individually with each entity in the drawing. There are functions that point to the entity data and that can use or manipulate that data.

ENTITY NAMES, ENTITY DATA, AND SELECTION SETS

Information is continually being updated during an editing session. An ongoing record is being kept for each new, modified, or deleted entity. The information or data concerning each entity is stored at some particular location in the drawing file. (This location is not to be confused with its X, Y, and Z coordinates.)

AutoLISP gains access to an entity's data through its entity name, which points to the location of the entity's data within the drawing file. The entity name is the address of that entity's data. You must grasp the concepts of entity name and entity data and be able to distinguish between the two.

ENTITY NAME FUNCTIONS

Entity name functions evaluate to an item whose DATA TYPE is called an AutoCAD entity name. An entity name can be used as a response when an AutoCAD command prompts you to "Select object:."

The (entnext [<ename>]) function, if performed with no ARGUMENTs, returns the entity name of the first nondeleted entity in the data base. If (entnext...) is performed with an entity name (which we will arbitrarily call en1 for illustration purposes) as the ARGUMENT, it returns the entity name of the first nondeleted entity that follows en1 in the data base.

WALKING THROUGH THE DATA BASE

Certain functions can search through the data base. The (entlast) function returns the entity name of the last nondeleted main entity in the data base. It may be used to return the entity name of a new entity that has just been added by a previous (command...) function.

The (entsel [<prompt>]) function returns a LIST which has the entity name as the first element and the point by which the entity was selected as the second element. Note that the second element (a point) is a LIST itself. For example:

Command: **line**
From point: **1,1**
to point: **4,4**
to point: ⏎
Command: **(setq es (entsel "Select an Entity: "))**
Select an Entity: **2.5,2.5**
returns (<Entity name: 60000018> (2.5 2.5 0.0))

While the evaluation of (entsel...) is a LIST and not an AutoCAD entity name, its first element is an entity name, obtainable by using the following:

Command: **(car es)**
returns <Entity name: 60000018>,
an entity name

Note that the address of the above entity is displayed in hexadecimal form "60000018" and is different for each different entity name. It will also differ from one editing session to the next for the same entity.

Point data is also obtainable by:

Command: **(cadr es)**
returns (2.5 2.5 0.0),
a LIST

and the X-coordinate is obtainable by:

Command: **(caadr es)**
returns 2.5,
a REAL

Note that:

Command: **(cdr es)**
returns ((2.5 2.5 0.0)),

which is a LIST whose only element is also the LIST (2.5 2.5 0.0).

The (handent <handle>) function returns the entity name associated with the specified handle. This more advanced concept will not be covered within the scope of this section. It is noteworthy, however, that the (handent...) function does assist in the problem of entities changing their names from one editing session to the next.

ENTITY DATA FUNCTIONS

These functions have entity names as their ARGUMENTs.

ENTGET Function

The primary entity data function is (entget <ename>). This function returns a LIST of entity data describing <ename> in that special format called an ASSO-CIATION LIST.

DATA TYPES FOR DATA BASE FUNCTIONS

Before continuing with detailed descriptions of the entity data functions and even before introducing selection sets, it would be convenient to discuss certain DATA TYPES which AutoLISP has set aside especially for use when accessing the data base. Some of the concepts used in this discussion of DATA TYPES will not be described in detail until later in this section. Therefore, the student will probably wish to refer back later for review after studying those concepts.

In a manner similar to INTEGERs, REALs, STRINGs, and LISTs, the special DATA TYPES called AutoCAD selection sets and AutoCAD entity names can be used as ARGUMENTs required by certain AutoLISP functions. It should be noted that the special functions designed to operate on these DATA TYPES can operate on them only. For example:

Having performed the following:

        (setq en1 (entnext))
        (setq ss1 (ssget "w" '(0 0) '(12 9))
        (setq od1 (list 1.0 2.0))
        (setq od2 "HELLO")

then

        (setq ed1 (entget en1))

and

        (setq en2 (ssname ss1 0))

are valid entries.

But

        (setq ed2 (entget od1))

and

        (setq ed3 (entget od2))

are not valid. The reason for the above valid and nonvalid entries are because en1 is an AutoCAD entity name which is the required DATA TYPE for an ARGUMENT to the (entget...) function, while od1 and od2 are other DATA TYPES and not valid as ARGUMENTs. Od1 is a LIST and od2 is a STRING.

Similarly, ss1 is a special DATA TYPE called AutoCAD selection set and is valid as an ARGUMENT to the (ssname...) function.

Further study will show that the (ssname...) function returns a value in the form of that special DATA TYPE called AutoCAD entity name. Therefore, if the above entries had been performed, then the following:

(setq ed4 (entget (ssname ss1 0)))

is a valid entry, returning the data (as an ASSOCIATION LIST) about the first entity in the drawing file that is included in a window whose corners are 0,0 and 12,9. Even if no entities had been found, and the above operation returned nil, the operation would still have been proper, having had the required DATA TYPE as an ARGUMENT to the (entget...) function.

BACK TO ENTGET

For an example let's say a newly created drawing had as the first entries, the following:

```
Command: line
From point: 1,1
To point: 4,4
To point: 

Command: line
From point: 1,4
To point: 4,1
To point: 
```

then:

(setq L1 (entget (entnext))

returns ((-1 . <Entity name: 60000018>) (0 . "LINE") (8 . "0") (10 1.0 1.0 0.0) (11 4.0 4.0 0.0) (210 0.0 0.0 1.0))

and

(setq L2 (entget (entlast))

or

(setq L2 (entget (entnext L1))

returns ((-1 . <Entity name: 60000030>) (0 . "LINE") (8 . "0") (10 1.0 4.0 0.0) (11 4.0 1.0 0.0) (210 0.0 0.0 1.0))

Also note the syntax in the following example:

Having entered:

> (setq en1 (entnext))

and

> (setq en2 (entlast))

then

> (setq L1 (entget en1))

returns the same as

> (setq L1 (entget (entnext)))

and

> (setq L2 (entget en2))

returns the same as

> (setq L2 (entget (entlast)))

or

> (setq L2 (entget (entnext L1)))

This is to emphasize that the entity names en1 and en2 are only addresses (or pointers) to where the data associated with the entities are located within the drawing file. The data list itself is gotten through the (entget...) function, which must have that address or entity name as its ARGUMENT.

THE ASSOCIATION LIST

Once the concepts of <ename>s and <elist>s are understood and the throes of creating those first routines to extract them are survived, the custom programmer must now deal with how to make use of the results.

The (assoc <item> <alist>) function is the primary mechanism used to extract specific data associated with a selected entity. In order to store data in an organized, efficient, and economical fashion, each common group of data is assigned what is called a GROUP CODE. That GROUP CODE is simply an INTEGER. For example, for a line, its starting point is a GROUP CODE 10 and its layer a GROUP CODE 8.

Using the first entity in the previous example, then you may enter the following sequence:

Command: **(setq ed1 (entget (entnext)))**

returns the ASSOCIATION LIST we saw earlier, which we will display as follows:

```
((-1 . <Entity name:60000018>)
   (0 . "LINE")
   (8 . "0")
   (10 1.0 1.0 0.0)
   (11 4.0 4.0 0.0)
   (210 0.0 0.0 1.0)
)
```

DOTTED PAIRS

The first and last parentheses enclose the ASSOCIATION LIST. The other matched pairs of parentheses each enclose LISTs, each comprising a specific GROUP CODE INTEGER as the first element followed by its associated value. In the case of the GROUP CODE 8, its value is the STRING "0," which is the name of the layer that this entity is on. Likewise, the value of the GROUP CODE 0 is the entity type which is the STRING "LINE." Note that these two sublists have a period between the GROUP CODE and its associated value (separated by spaces). This is a special list called a dotted pair, which requires less memory in storage. For economy, AutoCAD uses these dotted pairs where feasible. Some GROUP CODES, like the starting point, may be in the more common form of the LIST, such as (10 1.0 1.0 0.0) with the GROUP CODE as the first element followed by the X, Y, and Z coordinates, respectively.

GROUP CODES are broken down in accordance with the following tables:

GROUP CODE RANGE	FOLLOWING VALUE
0 - 9	STRING
10 - 59	FLOATING-POINT
60 - 79	INTEGER
210 - 239	FLOATING-POINT
999	COMMENT (STRING)

GROUP CODE	VALUE TYPE
0	Identifies the start of an entity, table entry, or file separator. The text value that follows indicates which.
1	The primary text value for an entity.
2	A name, Attribute tag, Block name, etc.
3-4	Other textual or name values.
5	Entity handle expressed as a hexadecimal string.
6	Linetype name (fixed).
7	Text style name (fixed).
8	Layer name (fixed).
9	Variable name identifier (used only in HEADER section of the DXF file).
10	Primary X coordinate (start point of a Line or Text entity, center of a circle, etc.).
11-18	Other X coordinates.
20	Primary Y coordinate. 2n values always correspond to 1n values and immediately follow them in the file.
21-28	Other Y coordinates.
30	Primary Z coordinate. 3n values correspond to 1n and 2n values and immediately follow them.
31-37	Other Z coordinates.
38	This entity's elevation if nonzero (fixed). Output only if system variable FLATLAND if set to 1.
39	This entity's thickness if nonzero (fixed).
40-48	Floating-point values (text height, scale, etc.).
49	Repeated value — multiple 49 groups may appear in one entity for variable length tables (such as the dash lengths in the LTYPE table).
50-58	Angles.
62	Color number (fixed).
66	"Entities follow" flag (fixed).
70-78	Integer values, such as repeat counts, modes.
210,220,230	X, Y, and Z components of extrusion direction.
999	Comments

Under the ENTITIES section of the .DXF format of the drawing file, the GROUP CODES and data associated with a few selected entities are as follows:

LINE   10, 20, 30 (start point), 11, 21, 31 (endpoints).

POINT   10, 20, 30 (point), 50 (angle of X Axis for the UCS in effect when the point was drawn-optional 0, for use when PDMODE is nonzero).

CIRCLE   10, 20, 30 (center), 40 (radius).

ARC   10, 20, 30 (center), 40 (radius), 50 (start angle) 51 (end angle).

TEXT   10, 20, 30 (insertion point), 40 (height), 1 (text value), 50 (rotation angle-optional 0), 41 (relative X scale factor-optional 1), 51 (obliquing angle-optional 0), 7 (text style name-optional "STANDARD"), 71 (text generation flags-optional 0), 72 (justification type-optional 0), 11, 21, 31 (alignment point-optional, appears only if 72 group is present and nonzero).

The above entities are shown for reference. The student is referred to the AutoCAD Reference Manual for the complete list of all related GROUP CODE information.

EXTRACTING DATA FROM A LIST

```
((-1 . <Entity name:60000018>)
    (0 . "LINE")
    (8 . "0")
    (10 1.0 1.0 0.0)
    (11 4.0 4.0 0.0)
    (210 0.0 0.0 1.0)
```

If the above list had been SETQed to the variable named ed1 then examples of the (assoc...) function would be as follows:

Command: **(assoc 0 ed1)**
returns (0 . "LINE")

Command: **(assoc 8 ed1)**
returns (8 . "0")

Command: **(assoc 10 ed1)**
returns (10 . (10 1.0 1.0 0.0))

The above results are LISTs. The first two are dotted pairs. In order to extract data from these, the following may be entered:

Command: **(cdr (assoc 0 ed1))**
returns "LINE,"
a STRING

Command: **(cdr (assoc 8 ed1))**
returns "0,"
also a STRING

but

> Command: **(cdr (assoc 10 ed1))**
> *returns (1.0 1.0 0.0),*
> *a LIST*

Therefore, in order to extract the X coordinate, enter:

> Command: **cadr (assoc 10 ed1))**
> *returns 1.0,*
> *a REAL*

Note how CDR returns the second element of a dotted pair as an atom while it requires CADR to return the second element of an ordinary LIST as an atom. CDR applied to an ordinary LIST returns a LIST (unless it is applied to a single element LIST).

OTHER ENTITY DATA FUNCTIONS

The (entdel <ename>) function deletes the entity specified by <ename> from the drawing or restores the entity previously deleted during the current editing session.

The (entmod <elist>) updates the data base information for the entity specified. Using this function in conjunction with the AutoLISP (subst...) function is a convenient method of making specific changes to selected entities.

The (entupd <ename>) function is used for more advanced handling of Block and Polyline subentities. The student is referred to the AutoLISP Programmer's Reference for use of this function.

SELECTION SETS

A selection set is a collection of entity names. It is the programmer's equivalent to a group of entities selected by one or more of the optional methods of selecting objects from the screen. Except that, by using the selection set functions, certain entities not visible on the screen may even be included in the group. It should be emphasized that a selection set comprises the entity names of the entities in the group. The selection set can be used in response to any AutoCAD command where selection by "Last" is valid. It also is a valid ARGUMENT to selection set functions that supply entity names to the (entget) function, which then returns entity data in the form of an ASSOCIATION LIST.

The (ssget [<mode>] [<pt1> [<pt2>]]) function returns the selection set and prompts something like <Selection set: 1>. This indicates that the selection set contains one or more entities. If no objects met the selection method, then nil would be returned.

The <mode>, if included, determines by what method the selection process is made. The "W," "L," "C," or "P" correspond to the window, last, crossing, or previous selection modes. Examples are as follows:

(ssget)	Asks the user for entity selection with one or more standard options.
(ssget "W" '(2 2) '(8 9))	Selects the entities inside the window from 2,2 to 8,9.
(ssget "L")	Selects last entity added to the data base.
(ssget "C" '(0 0) '(5 3))	Selects the entities crossing the box from 0,0 to 5,3.
(ssget "P")	Selects the most recently selected objects.
(ssget '(1.0 1.0))	Selects the entity passing through the point 1,1.
(ssget "X" <filter-list>)	Selects the entities matching the "filter-list."

SSGET Filters

The (ssget "X" <filter-list>) function provides a method of scanning the entire drawing file and selecting the entities having certain values associated with specified GROUP CODES. This function is used in conjunction with the (cons...) function. Note that while the (ssget...) function returns a group of entity names, it scans a group of ASSOCIATION LISTS (the drawing file, that is). So, the filter will be constructed in a manner that can be tested against entity data. Examples are as follows:

> (ssget "X" (list (cons 0 "CIRCLE")))

returns a selection set consisting of all the circles in the drawing.

> (ssget "X" (list (cons 8 "0")))

returns all entities on layer "0."

> (ssget "X" (list (cons 0 "CIRCLE") (cons 8 "0")))

returns all circles on layer "0."

The student should note at this time that the (ssget "X"...) function only selects from main entities. Special methods must be used to gain data about subentities such as attributes and Polyline vertices.

The (ssname <ss>) function returns an integer containing the number entities in selection set <ss>. For example:

> (setq sset (ssget "L"))
> (sslength sset)

returns 1.

The (ssname <ss> <index>) returns the entity name of the <index>'th element of selection set <ss>. The first element begins with number 0. For example, let's say that (setq sset (ssget)) results in five items:

> (setq en1 (ssname sset 0))
> returns the first entity.
> (setq en3 (ssname sset 2))
> returns the third entity.

The (ssadd [<ename> [<ss>]]) function without ARGUMENTs constructs a selection set with no members. If performed with a single entity name ARGUMENT, it constructs a new selection set containing that single entity name. If performed with an entity name and a selection set, it adds the named entity to the selection set.

The (ssdel <ename> <ss>) function deletes entity name <ename> from selection set <ss>.

The (ssmemb <ename> <ss>) function tests whether entity name <ename> is a member of selection-set <ss>.

ADVANCED ASSOCIATION LIST AND (SCANNING) FUNCTIONS

Examples of the (assoc <item> <alist>) have been demonstrated previously in this section. It will now be used in our custom-designed command.

The (subst <newitem> <olditem> <list>) function searches <list> for <olditem>, and returns a copy of <list> with <newitem> substituted in every place where <olditem> occurred.

Two sample routines are listed below. The TSAVE routine redefines the REDRAW command and then uses a time-checking part to cause the newly defined REDRAW command to invoke a SAVE command after a predetermined time has passed. The PARAB routine draws a parabola.

Saved in the file named TSAVE.LSP:

```
;————————————Autosave————————————
(defun S::STARTUP ( )
      (command "undefine" "redraw")
      (setq savetime 0.25)
)

(defun C:TSAVE ( )
      (setq temptime (getreal "ENTER INTERVAL OF TIME IN MINUTES
FOR SAVING: "))
   (setq savetime (/ temptime 60.0))
)

(defun C:REDRAW ( )
      (if (null cdate1)
            (setq cdate1 (decihr (getvar "cdate"))))
      (setq cdate2 (decihr (getvar "cdate")))
      (if (or (> (- cdate2 cdate1) savetime)
        (> cdate1 cdate2)
        )
        (progn
                  (setq tempex (getvar "expert"))
                  (setvar "expert" 2)
```

```
                    (command "save" "c:backup")
               (setq cdate1 cdate2)
               (setvar "expert" tempex)
          )
     )
          (command ".redraw")
)


(defun decihr (dt / hms dh dm ds hd)
     (setq hms (* (- dt (fix dt)) 10000.0))
     (setq dh (/ (fix hms) 100.0))
     (setq dm (/ (- dh (fix dh)) 0.6))
     (setq ds (/ (- hms (fix hms)) 36.0))
     (setq hd (+ (fix dh) dm ds))
)
```

Saved in the file named PARAB.LSP:

----------------------------- PARABOLA --

```
(defun c:parab ( )
   (setq point1 (getpoint "ENTER POINT: " ))
   (setq number (getint "ENTER ITERATIONS: "))
   (setq i (getreal "ENTER INCREMENTS: "))
   (setq p1 point1 p (car point1) counter 0)
   (while (< counter number)
     (setq p2
       (list
          (+ (car point1) i)
          (+ (cadr point1) (* 2.0 (sqrt (* p i))))
       )
   )
   (command "line" p1 p2 "")
   (setq p1 p2 counter (1+ counter) i (+ i i))
   )
)
```

AUTOCAD DEVELOPMENT SYSTEM (ADS)

The AutoCAD Development System (ADS) is a programming interface that, like AutoLISP, permits you to write or use applications for AutoCAD in high-level languages such as C. The applications are loaded in a similar manner to AutoLISP. AutoLISP is more appropriate for smaller applications, while ADS makes use of an extensive, powerful, and more complex library of programming functions. ADS, because of the large library, demands more of your system. ADS is not stand-alone, but tied to AutoLISP, and therefore, is not a good substitute for simpler tasks that can be so easily implemented with AutoLISP.

CHAPTER
17 AutoCAD for Windows

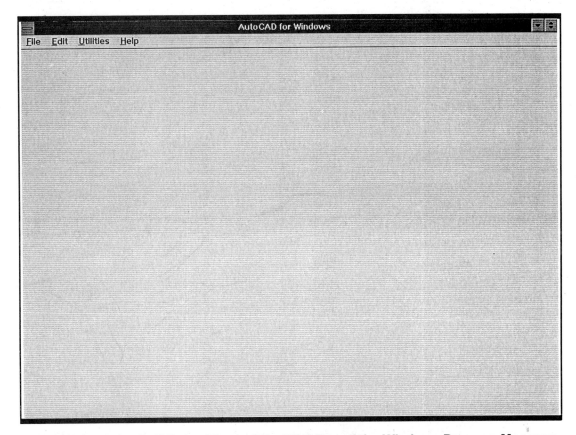

Figure 17–1 The Pull-Down Menu of the FILE Box of the Windows Program Manager

AutoCAD for Windows is a Windows-specific extension of AutoCAD Release 11 (386).   It provides a Graphical User Interface (GUI) which makes AutoCAD easy to learn and use while offering unique and useful features that are standard to the Windows environment. This chapter explains all the features that are unique to AutoCAD for Windows extension.

Reference manuals for Windows refer to GUI (pronounced "gooey") as an "easy-to-use graphical interface." The GUI is designed primarily to replace the typing of DOS command strings with a point and click interface that AutoCAD users are familiar with while in the Drawing Editor. Windows leads you visually through tasks in a way that alleviates having to memorize command names and syntax. For example, clicking the pointing device while the cursor is at the FILE box of the

Windows Program Manager causes a pull-down menu to be displayed, as shown in Figure 17-1.

Selecting an option like Open causes Windows to continue displaying sequential graphical option boxes in accordance with each step, ergo, a GUI.

In addition to implementing GUI standards, the open architecture of AutoCAD for Windows allows third-party developers to construct powerful applications that can dynamically link with other Windows applications like data bases and spreadsheets. Using Windows clipboard support, you can transfer information from AutoCAD to word processing and desktop publishing programs or vice versa.

WHAT IS WINDOWS?

Windows 3.0 is not a stand-alone operating system, but an interface between the text-based standard DOS and the user. The graphical nature of Windows relies on the human ability to visualize processes. The interface uses graphical objects to represent what, in the text-based world, may be a number of complex commands and procedures. The user is then allowed to pick that object and invoke a command, process, or even a complete program. One of the most powerful characteristics of the Windows interface is that the user has the option to create and change the graphical objects and the processes they invoke. Windows is also a nonpreemptive multitasking environment. This means that an AutoCAD operator is allowed to run many programs while AutoCAD is still running. System resources are virtually the only limit to the number of programs running simultaneously. This is the multitasking feature of Windows. The nonpreemptive feature means that Windows, not the running program, decides when each process will use the system resources. The next generation of GUIs will be Windows NT (NT stands for "New Technology"). This will be a complete stand-alone preemptive multitasking 32-bit operating system. It will greatly enhance the speed and graphics capabilities of AutoCAD for Windows. Windows NT is proposed to be fully compatible with existing Windows 3.0 applications.

Following are the key features for AutoCAD for Windows extension:

1. Full implementation of AutoCAD Release 11 features. Advanced Modeling Extension (AME) will not work because of the Windows memory architecture. Server authorization is not provided for the network license feature.

2. Implementation of Windows-standard GUI. This works like other Windows applications.

3. Customizable Tool Bar, which is an enhancement of the status line of the AutoCAD Drawing Editor. The tool bar consists of several push buttons, which can be programmed to execute various AutoCAD commands including macros.

4. AutoCAD commands in the menus can be represented with a series of icons that you can design and add to the menu.

5. While you are in the AutoCAD editor, you can resize, move, or do both to the AutoCAD drawing and text windows. If necessary, you can scroll the text window and send output to a specified file.

6. Using the Windows clipboard support, information can be exported to or imported from other applications into AutoCAD. AutoCAD for Windows has a PASTE command, which takes text from the Windows clipboard and sends it to the AutoCAD command line.

7. Context-sensitive hyper-text help is provided instantly on a command or AutoCAD prompt. The complete reference manual is available on-line; all sixteen megabytes of it.

8. Reconfiguration of the screen can be done from the AutoCAD editor. You can customize the AutoCAD screen environment and different aspects of the AutoCAD Windows interface.

9. Dynamic Data Exchange (DDE) is provided as a link between an external data source and the AutoCAD drawing data base. For instance, DDE linkage can be used to automatically update a Bill of Materials in a Windows spreadsheet when the AutoCAD drawing is edited. A great set of demos that show off the power of DDE is shipped with AutoCAD for Windows.

10. There are also a number of new development environments. One of these is Visual Basic from Microsoft. This programming environment takes full advantage of the Windows GUI while allowing extensive program development without the technical skill or knowledge of a professional programmer. One of the most useful implementations of Visual Basic is the creation of AutoCAD for Windows "floating icon menus."

11. AutoCAD for Windows reads and writes AutoCAD Release 11 drawing files so you can freely exchange files between platforms.

HARDWARE REQUIREMENTS

The hardware requirement is the same as that of AutoCAD Release 11 (386) except that you need at least four megabytes of RAM instead of two megabytes. One megabyte contains the 640K of conventional memory. The rest must be available as extended memory solely for AutoCAD for Windows. If you plan to work on large drawings, then it is advisable to increase the memory.

INSTALLATION AND CONFIGURATION

Follow the instructions provided in the Installation and Performance Guide that comes with the AutoCAD for Windows program for the installation and configuration of AutoCAD.

AutoCAD for Windows

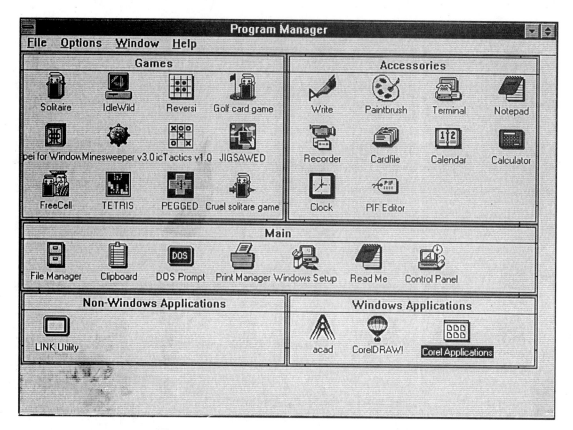

Figure 17-2 The Windows Program Icons

USING AUTOCAD FOR WINDOWS

Each time you start Windows, a special program called "the shell" runs. The shell shipped with Windows is the Program Manager. There are others developed by third-party software developers. One of the newest is Norton's Desktop from the same people who brought us the great utilities packages. The Program Manager is active all the time until you exit Windows from the Program Manager. Double-click the program group icon for the AutoCAD program and in turn Windows will display a set of icons corresponding to the programs they contain, as shown in Figure 17-2. To start AutoCAD, double-click the AutoCAD icon and the opening menu will appear.

OPENING MENU

The opening menu contains four pull-down menu items: File, Edit, Utilities, and Help, as shown in Figure 17-3, and replaces the traditional AutoCAD 386 Main Menu. However, by pressing the (F2) function key or by selecting the Show Text option under the Edit pull-down menu, you can display the traditional Main Menu text screen, as shown in Figure 17-4. File, Edit, and Help menus are also available when you are in the Drawing Editor. Utilities is the one pull-down menu that is available only from the opening menu.

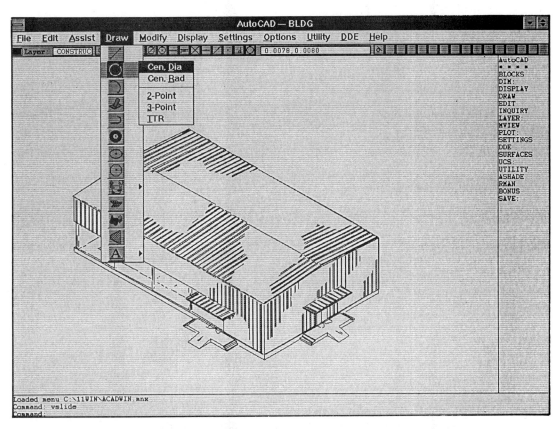

Figure 17-3 The Pull-Down Menu Items of the Opening Menu

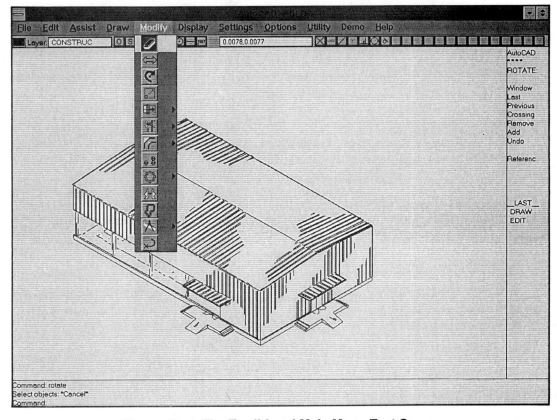

Figure 17-4 The Traditional Main Menu Text Screen

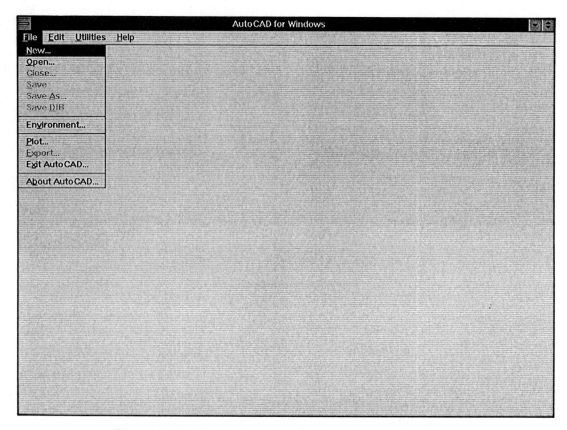

Figure 17-5 The Options Available under the File Menu

File Menu

Figure 17-5 shows various options that are available under the File Menu. Close, Save, Save As, Save DIB, and Export options are available only when you are in the Drawing Editor; otherwise, they will be grayed-out.

New... Option The New option allows you to create a new AutoCAD drawing. This option is similar to selecting item 1 under the Main Menu. When you select the New option, a dialogue box appears, as shown in Figure 17-6. Select the drive and directory in the appropriate box and then type the name of the drawing file you wish to create. Press ⏎ or select **OK** to create the file and open the Drawing Editor. If you select the Type It option, AutoCAD displays the old familiar DOS text Main Menu on the text screen and prompts for the name of the drawing.

Open... Option The Open option allows you to edit an existing drawing. This option is similar to selecting item 2 under the Main Menu. Select the drive and directory by selecting in the appropriate box and then select a drawing name. Press ⏎ or select **OK** to load the drawing.

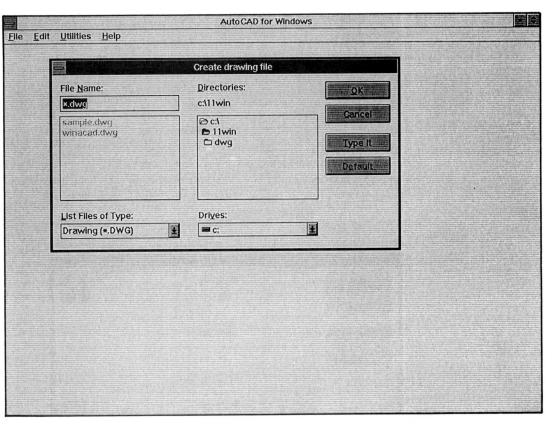

Figure 17-6 The New Option Dialogue Box

> *NOTE:* Whenever you wish to create a new drawing or edit an existing drawing from the Drawing Editor without exiting AutoCAD, select the New option or Open option, respectively, and provide the necessary information.

Close... Option The Close option allows you to exit the Drawing Editor and return to the opening menu after prompting you if you want to save changes to the drawing. This option is similar to the traditional AutoCAD QUIT command.

Save Option The Save option saves the current drawing and continues the editing session.

Save As... Option The Save As option prompts you for a name of a drawing or to accept the default name by displaying a file dialogue box. The Save As option is similar to the traditional AutoCAD SAVE command.

Save DIB Option The Save DIB option saves the entire graphic screen image as a Device Independent Bitmap (DIB). The image is saved as a new file with an extension .BMP in the same directory as the current drawing file.

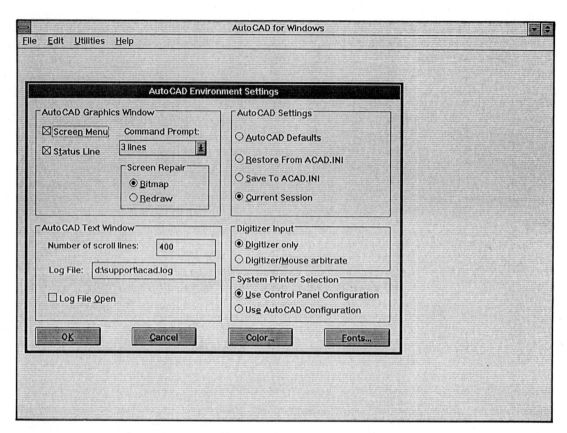

Figure 17-7 The Environment Settings Dialogue Box

Environment... Option   The Environment option displays the Environment Settings dialogue box, as shown in Figure 17-7. It allows you to customize the different aspects of the AutoCAD window interface.

The dialogue box has four different groups of options, which are explained below.

1. **AutoCAD Graphics Window** — The three check boxes under this window let you toggle the display of status line, Screen Menu, and File Dialogs on or off. The combo box under the "Command:" prompt lets you control the number of lines displayed between 0 and 3 lines. The Screen Repair option determines the mode in which the screen is repaired by the REDRAW command. The Bitmap option (default) is suitable for VGA and Super VGA screens. Use the Redraw option for a higher resolution screen.

2. **AutoCAD Text Window** — The option under this window allows you to configure the number of buffered scroll lines (includes the command prompts and responses) in the text window from 200 to 1500 lines. The default is 400 lines. If necessary, you can specify the name of a log file for recording the text. A check button is provided to turn on and off for recording.

3. **Digitizer Input Window** — There are two options provided under this window. Select the Digitizer Only option to accept the input from the configured digitizing device. By default, it will accept mouse input if no digitizer is configured. Select the Digitizer/Mouse arbitrate radio button and AutoCAD accepts input from whichever pointing device last moved.

4. **AutoCAD Settings Window** — There are four options provided under this window for saving to or restoring from the ACAD.INI file, the AutoCAD Environment Settings.

The AutoCAD default option restores the AutoCAD default settings from the ACAD.INI file for all of the items in the Environment dialogue box. If you have already modified the ACAD.INI file, then with a text editor, delete the entries under AutoCAD General, AutoCAD Graphics Screen, and AutoCAD Text Screen, and then restart AutoCAD to set the values back to the default. The Restore From ACAD.INI option restores all settings that were last saved to the ACAD.INI file. The Save to ACAD.INI option saves all current settings to the ACAD.INI file. The Current Session option allows you to use the settings only for the current session; they are not saved in the ACAD.INI file.

There are two additional options that are provided in the dialogue box — one is for Fonts... and the other one is for Color.... When you select the Fonts... button, a dialogue box appears and this allows you to select an appropriate Font, Font Style, and Size from the list boxes to control the Graphic or Text Screen appropriately. The Color... option also displays a dialogue box, which allows you to customize colors (separate from the Windows color facility) for the Drawing Editor.

After making all the necessary changes, click on **OK** to accept the changes or click on Cancel to disregard the changes and close the AutoCAD Environment Settings Dialogue box.

Plot Option The Plot option invokes the PLOT command. This option is similar to selecting item 3 under the Main Menu.

Export... Option The Export option first prompts you for a filename, and in turn prompts you for a selection set. The selected entities are copied to a Windows Metafile and saved under the given file name with an extension .WMF in the same directory as the drawing file.

Exit AutoCAD... Option The Exit AutoCAD option takes you back to the Windows Program Manager. If you select this option when you are in the Drawing Editor, first it will prompt you to save your changes, then exits AutoCAD, returning you to the Program Manager. If you select this option from the opening menu, then you exit AutoCAD and you are returned to the Program Manager.

About AutoCAD... Option The About AutoCAD option displays a pop-up window with the AutoCAD serial number, personalization data, and version number.

Edit Menu

Figure 17-8 shows various options that are available under the Edit Menu. Undo, Redo, Copy Image, and Copy Vectors options are available only when you are in the Drawing Editor; otherwise, they will be grayed-out.

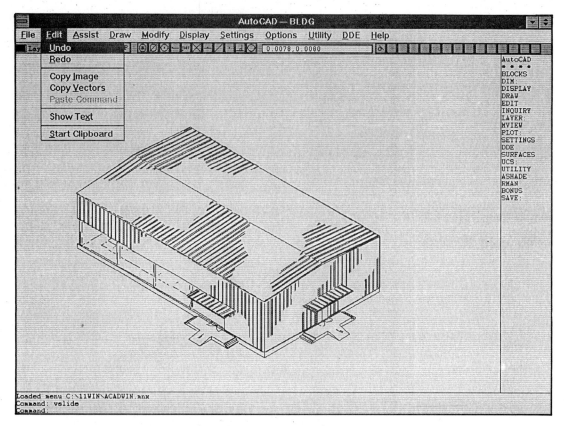

Figure 17-8 The Options Available under the Edit Menu

Undo Option The Undo option invokes the traditional AutoCAD UNDO command.

Redo Option The Redo option invokes the traditional AutoCAD REDO command.

Copy Image Option The Copy Image option lets you copy a screen image of selected objects to the clipboard in Windows Bitmap format. You can export the bitmap to another program.

Copy Vectors Option The Copy Vectors option lets you copy screen vectors of selected objects to the clipboard in a Windows Metafile format. You can export the vector image to another program.

Paste Command Option The Paste Command option sends text from the Windows clipboard to the AutoCAD command line. For instance, you can use the PASTE command to place the text when AutoCAD prompts for text during the DTEXT command.

Show Text Option The Show Text option brings the text window to the top and switches the option in this menu to Hide Text. By selecting the Hide Text option, the text window will be hidden. Toggling can also be performed by pressing the **F2** function key.

Start Clipboard Option The Start Clipboard option starts the Windows clipboard.

> ***NOTE:*** For a detailed explanation of the UNDO, REDO, and DTEXT commands, see chapter 4.

Utilities Menu

Figure 17–9 shows various options that are available under the Utilities Menu. The options that are provided allow you to change the AutoCAD default configuration values and perform various file-handling tasks.

Configure AutoCAD... Option The Configure AutoCAD option allows you to configure various devices to run the AutoCAD program. This option is similar to selecting item 5 under the Main Menu.

File Utilities Option The File Utilities option invokes the File Utility Menu. This option is similar to selecting item 6 under the Main Menu.

Compile Shape/Font File Option The Compile Shape/Font file option compiles shape or font description files. This option is similar to selecting item 7 under the Main Menu.

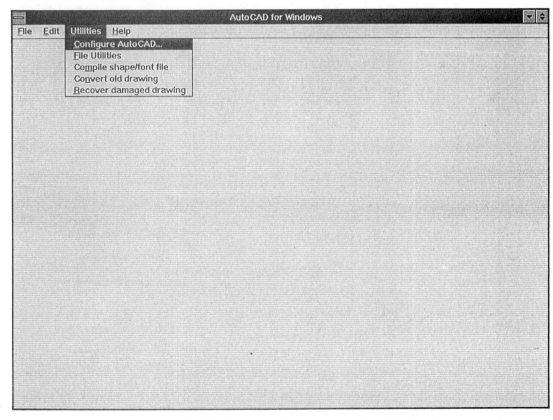

Figure 17–9 The Options Available under the Utilities Menu

Convert Old Drawing Option The Convert Old Drawing option converts old drawing files. This option is similar to selecting item 8 under the Main Menu.

Recover Damaged Drawing Option The Recover Damaged Drawing option invokes the AutoCAD drawing recovery facility. This option is similar to selecting item 9 under the Main Menu.

Help Menu

Figure 17–10 shows various options that are available under the Help Menu. Selecting the Help pull-down menu lets you access Enhanced Help.

Index Option The Index option displays a list of AutoCAD commands.

Keyboard Option The Keyboard option displays help for AutoCAD function keys.

Using Help Option The Using Help option describes how to use the Windows Help Manager.

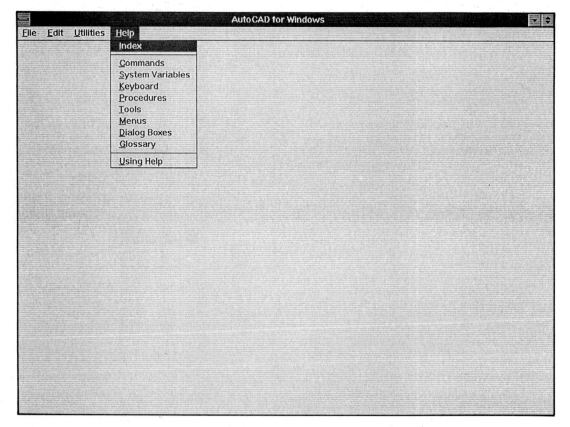

Figure 17–10 The Options Available under the Help Menu

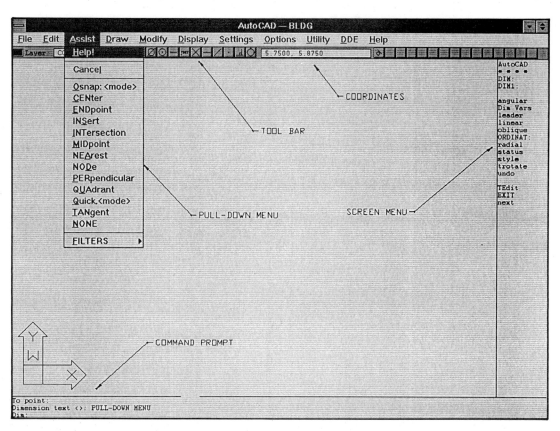

Figure 17-11 The Autocad Drawing Editor

DRAWING EDITOR

Once you respond with the name of the drawing from the AutoCAD opening menu, the opening menu is replaced by the Drawing Editor, as shown in Figure 17-11.

The Drawing Editor appears as a window. Below the title bar of the AutoCAD graphics window a Tool Bar appears. It is an enhancement to the traditional status line of the AutoCAD Drawing Editor. On the top as well as right-hand side of the Drawing Editor are the traditional Pull-down and Screen Menus, respectively. The pull-down menu contains the same options as AutoCAD Release 11 (386), except that the UNDO and REDO commands are in the Edit menu, and the Solids menu has been replaced by the DDE menu. In the screen menu, the DDE menu replaces the Solids menu. The traditional "Command:" prompt is located at the bottom of the Drawing Editor. You can toggle between text and graphics screens by pressing function key ⒡②. (In AutoCAD Release 11 you do the same by pressing function key ⒡①.)

Some titles of the pull-down menu and options have a letter underlined, indicating that the menu can be selected by pressing the ⒜ⓛⓣ key and the underlined letter at the same time. For instance, you can use ⒜ⓛⓣ + ⒟ to open the Draw menu.

Some of the pull-down menus use cascading menus. If you select a menu option with an arrow symbol pointing to the right, a submenu (child menu) appears to the side of the first menu, as shown in Figure 17-12.

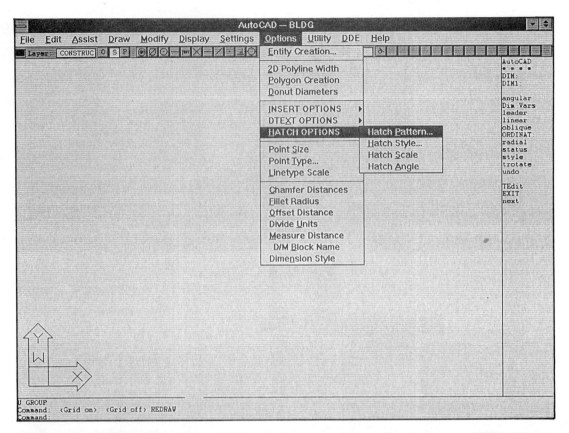

Figure 17-12 Selecting a Menu Option to Access a Cascading Submenu (Child Menu)

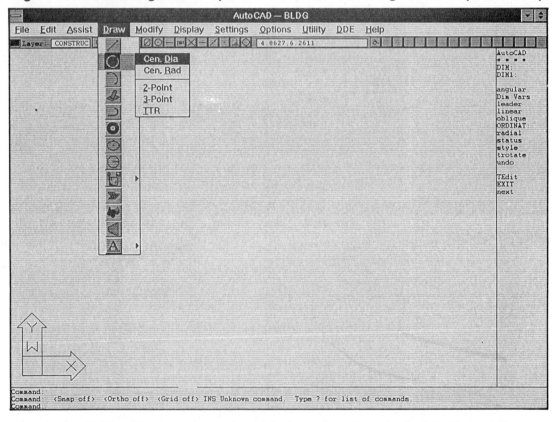

Figure 17-13 The Checkmark Displayed to Indicate a Toggle Switch Turned On or a Value Assigned to a Variable

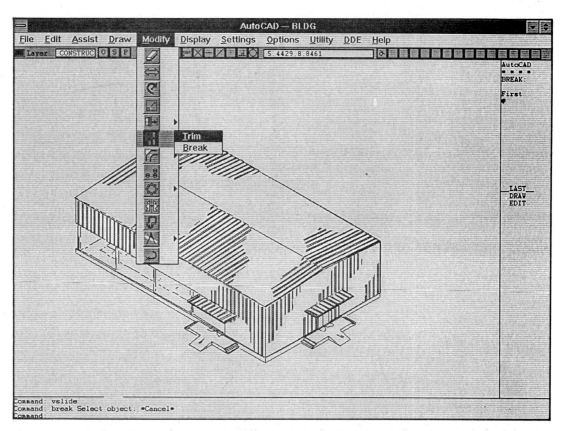

Figure 17-14 The Bitmap Icons for Draw, Modify, and the Tool Bar

When you select some of the options under the pull-down menu, a checkmark might appear to the left of the menu, as shown in Figure 17-13. The checkmark indicates a toggle switch that has been turned on, or that value is assigned to a variable.

The Draw and Modify pull-down menus and the Tool Bar contain bitmap icons that graphically represent AutoCAD commands as icons instead of words, as shown in Figure 17-14. To use any of the icons, just click on it and the icon appears to be pressed in after you select it.

The following table lists the keys assigned to various function keys.

Table 17-1 The Keys Assigned to Various Function Keys

Function Key	Other Keys	Function
F1		Help: calls the AutoCAD for Windows Help
F2		Toggle text screen
F4	Ctrl + T	Tablet Off
F5	Ctrl + E	Circular toggle of ISO plane
F6	Ctrl + D	Coordinate display control
F7	Ctrl + G	Grid mode On/Off
F8	Ctrl + O	Ortho mode On/Off
F9	Ctrl + B	Snap mode On/Off
F10 ⏎		Open File menu
	Ctrl + C	Cancel

> **NOTE:** Function keys (F1) and (F2) have been assigned differently as compared to the AutoCAD Release 11 (386) version.

WORKING WITH WINDOWS

One of the great things about Windows is that every program has essentially the same interface. Each window has the same elements and requires the same interface skills. The chapter on "Basic Skills" in the *Microsoft Windows User's Guide* gives a thorough treatment of the features.

The skills needed are as follows:

1. Clicking—This is the same as picking in AutoCA⌐ and requires a quick push of the mouse button.

2. Double-Clicking—This is two quick presses of the mouse button without moving the mouse. Many menus and elements may be double-clicked to invoke the default choice.

3. Click and Drag—This is done by picking and holding down the mouse button. The mouse is then moved to another position, which moves the object selected on the screen.

The elements of a window are as follows:

1. Mouse Pointer—This is normally an arrow pointing up and to the left. It changes, though, in context to what kind of area it is over (see Borders below).

2. Selection Cursor—When the mouse pointer is positioned over editable text, it changes into an I-beam appearance.

3. Insert Cursor—This is a flashing vertical bar found in editable text windows. It shows the place where typing will be placed. It can be move by using the cursor control keys or picking with the selection cursor on the desired position.

4. Hourglass Cursor—The mouse pointer changes into an hourglass while an application is doing internal processing such as saving a file. This tells the user to wait until the process is completed before further interaction is allowed.

5. Control-Menu Box—This contains a drop-down menu which can be used to close the window or switch to another window or application.

6. Title Bar—This contains the title of the document or application. The window may be dragged to a new position on the screen (or even almost completely off the screen leaving only a small part of the window showing). This is done by picking on the title bar and, while holding the mouse button down, moving the mouse. An outline of the window will appear to show the new position of the window. Releasing the button drops the window in the new position.

7. Menu Bar—This contains the drop-down menus. Documents do not have menu bars.

8. Minimize and Maximize Buttons—These are used to change the size of the window. When maximized, the window fills the screen. When minimized, the window changes to an icon. This means that the document or application may still be active, but user interaction is disabled. Icons may be picked and dragged to a new position on the screen. Double-clicking on the title bar will also toggle the window between maximize and normal sizes.

9. Window Borders and Corners—When the mouse pointer is moved over the borders or corners, it changes into a double arrow. The border may then be dragged to change the size of the window. This is accomplished by pressing the mouse button and holding it down while moving the mouse. An outline of the window will show the new size the window will be when the button is released.

10. Vertical and Horizontal Scroll Bars—These allow any text or image inside the window that is larger than the window to be scrolled or panned. Each bar has an arrow button on each end and a position button within a sliding track. Picking on the arrow button causes the window contents to pan in that direction. Picking and dragging the position button moves the image as far as the button is moved. The ends of the scroll bar represent the extremes of the window contents. Picking on the area on either side of the position button causes the window contents to move one full screen in that direction.

There are some specialized windows that do not use all the elements. One of these is a dialogue box. These are similiar to the AutoCAD dialogue boxes. They may contain any or all of the following.

1. Informative Messages—Give the user important information.

2. Edit Boxes—Allow the user to input appropriate data.

3. Option Buttons—Sometimes called radio buttons, these allow the selection of one of a list of choices.

4. Check Boxes—Allow a choice to toggled on or off.

5. List Boxes—These come in two types, scrollable and drop-down. The scrollable have a scroll bar on the side and allow a pick of a choice. The drop-down shows only one choice until the drop-down button is pressed. It then appears as a scrollable list box.

Tool Bar

The Tool Bar is an enhancement to the traditional status line of the AutoCAD Drawing Editor. The Tool Bar displays the current layer name, a box filled with current color, and the X, Y coordinate display, as shown in Figure 17-15.

Selecting in the coordinate area of the Tool Bar toggles between absolute, polar, and static coordinate display. In addition, the Tool Bar consists of several buttons. Three of the buttons are preprogrammed toggles for Ortho mode, Snap mode, and Paper Space, respectively. In addition to three preprogrammed buttons, 14

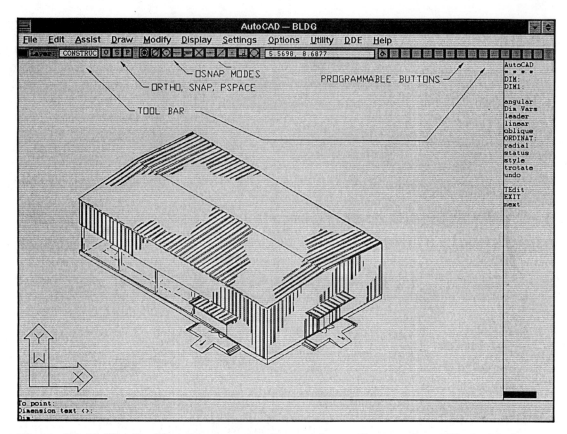

Figure 17–15 The Tool Bar Displays the Current Layer Name, a Box Filled with Current Color, and the X, Y Coordinate Display

additional buttons can appear in the Tool Bar and can be customized to execute any one or more AutoCAD commands. The number of push buttons visible depends on the size of the AutoCAD graphics window and the resolution of your display.

To program any one of the 14 buttons, refer to the section on Customizing AutoCAD for Windows.

Dialogue Boxes

The dialogue boxes let you input data to AutoCAD through the GUI provided by Windows. The dialogue boxes can be moved around the screen in the same way as graphics and text windows, as explained earlier in this chapter. Following is the brief description of the various dialogue boxes available in AutoCAD for Windows:

Drawing Tools Dialogue Box The Drawing Tools dialogue box will appear as shown in Figure 17–16 when you select the Drawing Tools option under the Settings pull-down menu. You can set the values and toggle on/off for various drawing tools available in AutoCAD.

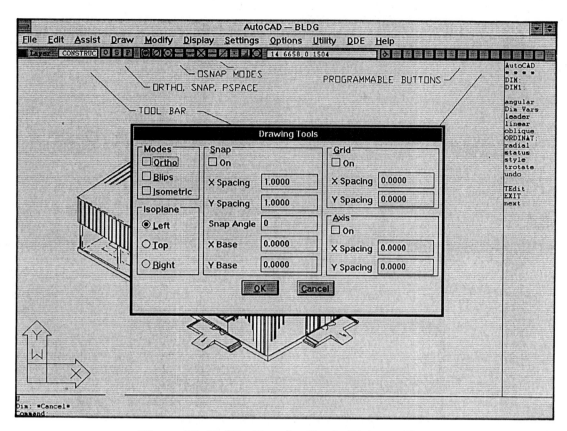

Figure 17-16 The Drawing Tools Dialogue Box

Layer Control Dialogue Box Layer control is provided through functions in the Modify Layer dialogue box and various subboxes. These include the Layer Name edit box, Select Color box, Set Ltype box, and Filters box. Layer controls include the following:

    Creating
    Setting (making current)
    Renaming
    Visibility (turning ON and OFF)
    Locking and unlocking
    Color
    Linetype
    Viewport visibility
    Filtering the lists of layers that appear in boxes

The Modify Layer dialogue box is accessible, as shown in Figure 17-17, through the Settings pull-down menu or by entering the DDLMODES command. The Modify Layer dialogue box includes a Layer Name list box. Layer names shown are eligible for editing. The layer names that appear can be restricted to only those desired by using the Filters feature described herein. On the line with each layer name is its State (ON/OFF/FROZEN), Color, and Linetype.

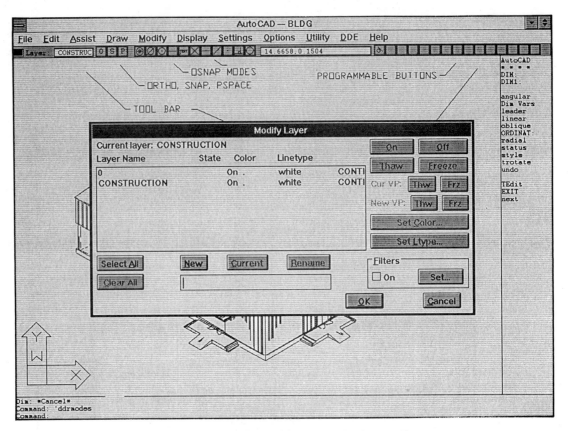

Figure 17-17 The Modify Layer Dialogue Box

The Layer Name edit box appears under the New, Current, and Rename buttons. The edit box is cleared if no layer names are selected. Optional layer editing features include the following:

1. New—To create new layers, enable the Layer Name edit box and then type in the name(s) (up to 31 characters per name with no wild cards). Multiple names are allowed (separated by commas) totalling up to 255 characters.

2. Current—One layer may be made current (similar to using the SET command) by clicking on its name in the list box (thereby highlighting it) and then selecting the Current button. The name will then appear behind "Current layer:" in the upper left corner of the Modify Layer box.

3. Rename—When a selected layer's name appears in the edit box, change its name by moving the cursor to the edit box, typing in the new name, and then selecting the Rename button.

The state of the selected layer(s) may be changed by selecting ON, OFF, FREEZE, or THAW in the upper right corner of the Modify Layer box. Layers that are ON will be noted as "ON"; OFF is noted as "."; and frozen is noted as "F."

To freeze or thaw layers only in selected viewports while in Model Space (or in all of Paper Space when in Paper Space), the TILEMODE system variable must be off (set to 0). This is accomplished with the Thw (Thaw) and Frz (Freeze) buttons associated with Cur (Current) VP: and New VP (viewport): in the right side of the Modify Layer box.

Selecting Frz or Thw, in the Cur VP, freezes or thaws selected layers in a Model Space current viewport. If the current viewport is in Paper Space, only Paper Space will be affected, not viewports.

Selecting Frz or Thw in the New VP, respectively, freezes or thaws for all new viewport entities.

The Select Color dialogue box appears when the Set Color.. button is selected and the selected layer name(s) appears in the Layer Name edit box. The Select Color dialogue box contains its own Color Code: edit box. You may select the color from the list or you may type in the name of the color. Select **OK** when the desired color is in the edit box or [Cancel] to terminate the Select Color process.

The Select Linetype dialogue box appears when the Set Ltype.. button is selected and the selected layer name(s) appears in the Layer Name edit box. The list of available linetypes displayed includes only those that have been loaded (CON-TINUOUS is always loaded). Additional linetypes cannot be loaded unless you exit the Modify Layer dialogue box. Select **OK** when the desired linetype has been selected or [Cancel] to terminate the Select Linetype process.

The Filters option lets you determine individual or groups of layer names to be included in or excluded from the list of layers eligible for editing in the Modify Layer dialogue box. The Filters option can be turned ON to limit the layers displayed or turned OFF to permit all layers to be displayed in the list.

The Set Layer Filters dialogue box appears when the Set.. button is selected. Whether or not a layer will be displayed in the list when Filters is toggled ON can be limited to those that are as follows:

    ON, OFF, or BOTH
    FROZEN, THAWED or BOTH
    FROZEN, THAWED or BOTH on the current viewport
    FROZEN, THAWED or BOTH on the new viewports
    Included in a list of eligible names (wild cards may control)
    Included in a list of eligible colors
    Included in a list of eligible linetypes (wild cards may control)

> **NOTE:** For a detailed explanation of the LAYER command, see Chapter 2.

Entity Creation Modes Dialogue Box The Entity Creation dialogue box will appear as shown in Figure 17-18 when you select the Entity Creation option under the Options pull-down menu.

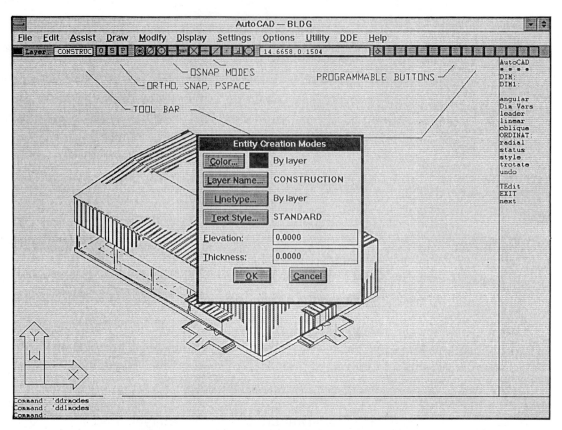

Figure 17-18 The Entity Creation Dialogue Box

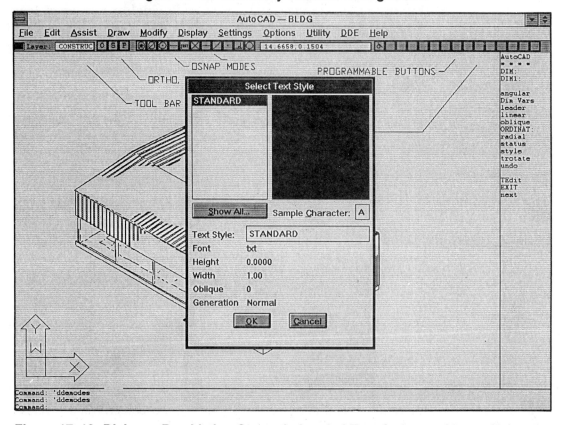

Figure 17-19 Dialogue Box Listing Currently Loaded Text Styles as Shown Using the Text Style Option

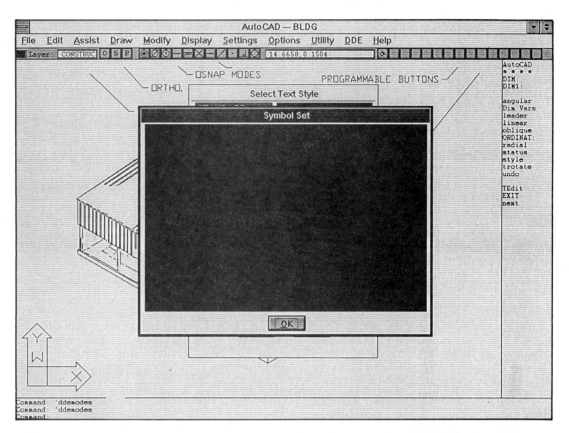

Figure 17-20 Dialogue Box Listing the Symbols Stored in the .SHX File that Make Up the Current Style

By selecting the Color option from the dialogue box, the Select Color dialogue box will pop up. Select the appropriate color. The default color is ByLayer. The Layer Name option will display a Select Layer dialogue box that lets you set the current layer. The Linetype option will display the Select Linetype dialogue box. Select the appropriate linetype. The default linetype is ByLayer. The Text Style option will display a dialogue box with a listing of all the text styles currently loaded in the Drawing Editor, as shown in Figure 17-19. If you click on Show All in the Select Text Style dialogue box, a window will pop up by displaying all the symbols stored in the .SHX file that make up the current style, as shown in Figure 17-20.

In addition to selecting the appropriate color, layer, linetype, and text style, you can also enter the appropriate values for Elevation and Thickness in the Entity Creation dialogue box.

Text Font Dialogue Box The Text Font dialogue box will appear as shown in Figure 17-21 when you select Dtext options under the Options pull-down menu. Select the appropriate font from the dialogue box by clicking on a font tile, and then click on **OK**. You can scan through the listing of fonts by clicking on **Previous** or **Next**.

> **NOTE:** The selected text font can be used only if you select the DTEXT command from the Draw pull-down menu.

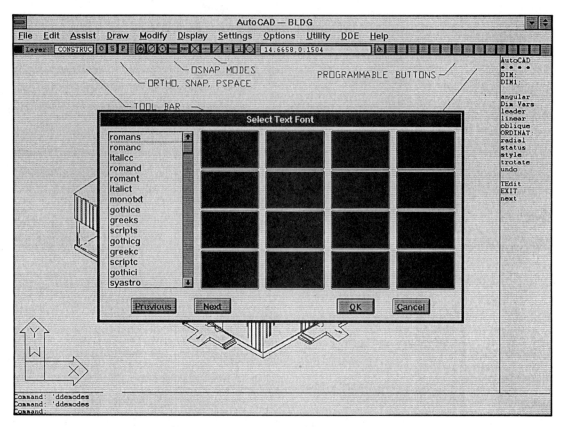

Figure 17-21 The Text Font Dialogue Box

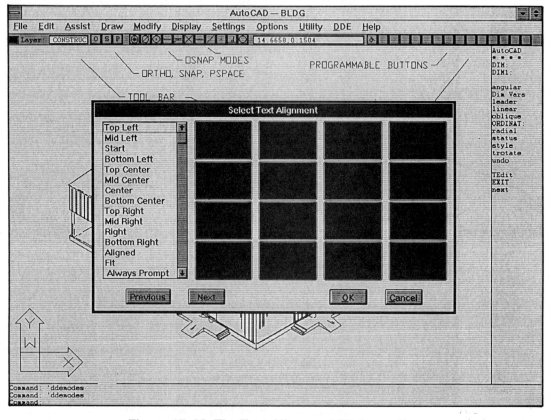

Figure 17-22 The Text Alignment Dialogue Box

Text Alignment Dialogue Box The Text Alignment dialogue box will appear as shown in Figure 17-22 when you select Dtext options under the Options pull-down menu. Select the appropriate alignment from the dialogue box by clicking on a tile, and then clicking on **OK**.

> **NOTE:** The selected text alignment can be used only if you select the DTEXT command from the Draw pull-down menu.

Hatch Pattern Dialogue Box The Hatch Pattern dialogue box will appear as shown in Figure 17-23 when you select Hatch options under the Options pull-down menu. Select the appropriate pattern from the dialogue box by clicking on a pattern tile, and then clicking on **OK**. You can scan through the listing of patterns by clicking on **Previous** or **Next**.

> **NOTE:** The selected hatch pattern can be used only if you select the HATCH command from the Draw pull-down menu.

Hatch Style Dialogue Box The Hatch Style dialogue box will appear as shown in Figure 17-24 when you select Hatch options under the Options pull-down menu. Select the appropriate hatch style from the dialogue box by clicking on a tile, and then clicking on **OK**.

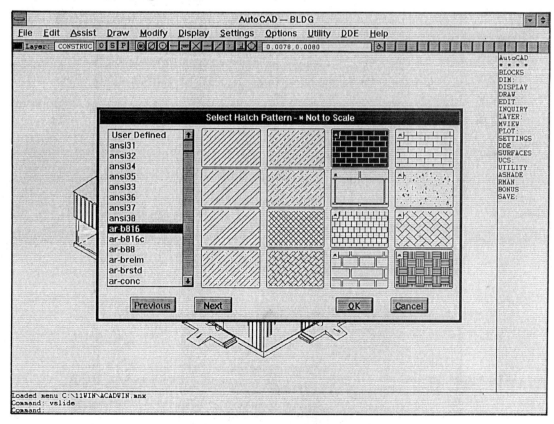

Figure 17-23 The Hatch Pattern Dialogue Box

AutoCAD for Windows

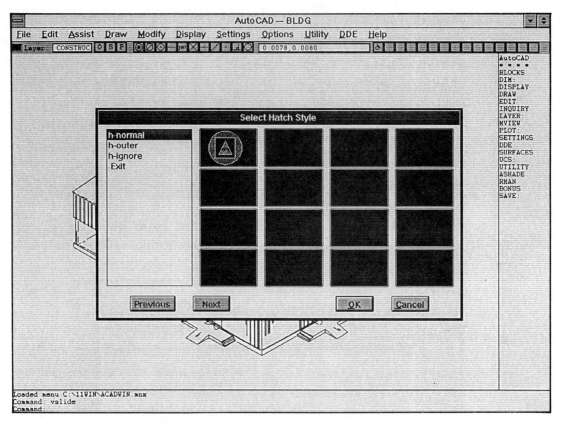

Figure 17-24 The Hatch Style Dialogue Box

NOTE: The selected hatch style can be used only if you select the HATCH command from the Draw pull-down menu.

Attribute Dialogue Box The Attribute dialogue box will be displayed as shown in Figure 17-25 for entering Attribute values during the insertion of a Block which contains Attributes. The same dialogue box will also appear for editing Attributes with the DDATTE command.

UCS Control Dialogue Box The UCS Control dialogue box will appear as shown in Figure 17-26 when you select the UCS Control... option under the Settings pull-down menu. This box is used for the creation of new user-defined coordinate systems and selecting a defined UCS as current.

AUTOCAD ENHANCED HELP

Selecting Help from the AutoCAD for Windows Editor Window causes the Help pull-down menu to be displayed, as shown in Figure 17-27.

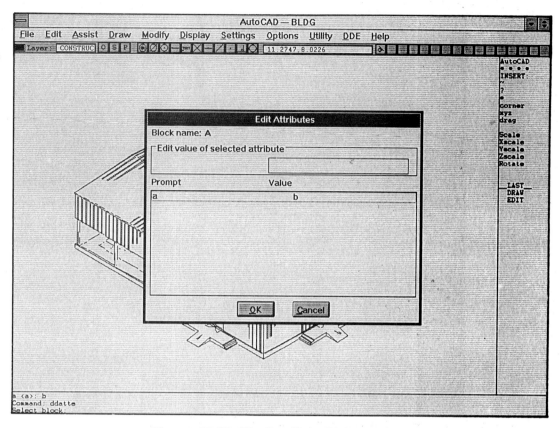

Figure 17-25 The Attribute Dialogue Box

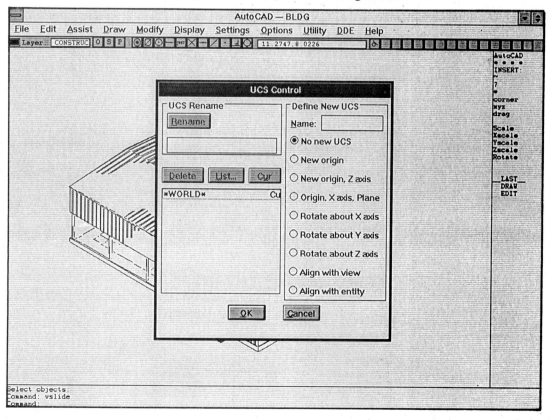

Figure 17-26 The UCS Control Dialogue Box

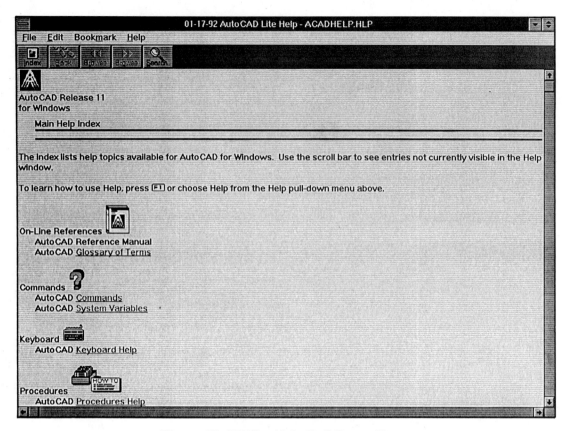

Figure 17-27 The Help Pull-Down Menu

From the pull-down menu you can select the Main Help Index or one of the other categories on the menu. Other methods of accessing the Enhanced Help include the following:

Press (F1) to open the Main Help Index.

Select one of the items from the pull-down Help menu.

Press (F1) while the cursor is highlighting a command on a screen or pull-down menu.

Press (F1) after typing a command name at the "Command:" prompt.

The Enhanced Help is available in two optional files. One is approximately 0.8 megabytes and the other is the same except that it contains the complete AutoCAD Reference Manual. The latter requires 16 megabytes. The smaller file is automatically installed with the AutoCAD program. You can install the larger file by responding to the appropriate prompts during the AutoCAD for Windows install program.

Once the Help Index menu is displayed you can access information on a particular topic by selecting the highlighted item, selecting one of the buttons at the top of the menu, or through one of the pull-down windows inside the Help window. These pull-down menus are under the headings of File, Edit, Bookmark, and Help.

The File pull-down menu lets you open another Windows Help file, print out a Help topic, or change the printer configuration.

The Edit pull-down menu lets you send text from a Help page to the clipboard or add your own notes to one of the pages.

The Bookmark pull-down menu lets you place a bookmark at the current location in the Help file and then list it with a user-defined name in the pull-down menu.

The Help pull-down menu has information on how to use the Help menus.

CUSTOMIZING AUTOCAD FOR WINDOWS

In addition to being able to customize AutoCAD menus, linetypes, hatch patterns, and being able to use AutoLISP and ADS to create special commands and program enhancements, AutoCAD for Windows has its own set of customizing features. They include provisions to customize the Windows-specific interface aspects, such as bitmaps (icons in menus), (Alt) + key macros, placing checkmarks at commands, graying-out inactive commands, locating and/or cascading menus, and programming certain buttons in the Tool Bar. These are all called metacharacters.

Menu names can be user-defined except the names File and Edit, which have been allocated permanently to the menus of those names.

Bitmaps and Underscores

An icon can be created with a paint program or icon editor. It can then be saved in a file with a .BMP extension and used in a menu area by enclosing its filename (without the .BMP extension) between carets (^). For example, a gate valve might be represented by a bitmap file called GV.BMP. It can then be displayed in the POP6 menu item as follows:

```
***POP6
[&Valves]
[^GV^GATE_VLV]^C^CInsert gate_vlv \;;\
```

The ampersand (&) preceding the valves causes the "V" in the heading to be underscored. By this mechanism (an underscored letter) the user can press that letter while holding the (Alt) key down and cause that menu to be "popped" onto the display.

Checkmarks and Graying

A leading exclamation point (!) will cause a checkmark to be placed by the item in a menu. This can be used to signify that a toggle is ON or that the option has a value assigned to it as shown below:

```
***POP6
[&Valves]
[!STD]^C^C(setq pipespec "STANDARD")
```

Preceding a menu item with an open parenthesis "(" causes that item to be grayed (or displayed with a reduced contrast) to signify that that item is currently inactive.

Cascading

A child menu can be displayed next to its parent by placing a hyphen/right arrow "->" by the item's name in the parent menu as follows:

```
***POP6
[&Valves]
[->GATE_VLV]
[FLANGED]^C^CInsert flg_vlv \;;\
[WELDED]^C^CInsert wld_vlv \;;\
[<-SCREWED]^C^CInsert scd_vlv \;;\
```

Cascading menus can have menus cascading from them up to 10 levels. There must be a return symbol, left arrow/hyphen "<-", for each cascade symbol, as shown below:

```
[&Valves]
[->GATE_VLV]
[->FLANGED]
[STD]
[HVY]
[<-XTRHVY]
[->WELDED]
[SOCKET]
[<-<-BEVEL]
```

Metacharacters can be combined as in the following example of a bitmap, named GV, grayed out, and checkmarked:

```
!(^GV^
```

The Tool Bar

The Tool Bar is displayed at the top of the screen just below the menu bar. It is an enhancement of the traditional status line. In addition to displaying the current layer, the ortho/snap/paper space states, and the coordinates, you can customize the remaining spaces (called buttons). Up to 14 buttons may be displayed depending upon the graphics window size being displayed and the display resolution. This is in addition to the nonprogrammable layer/snap/coordinate spaces.

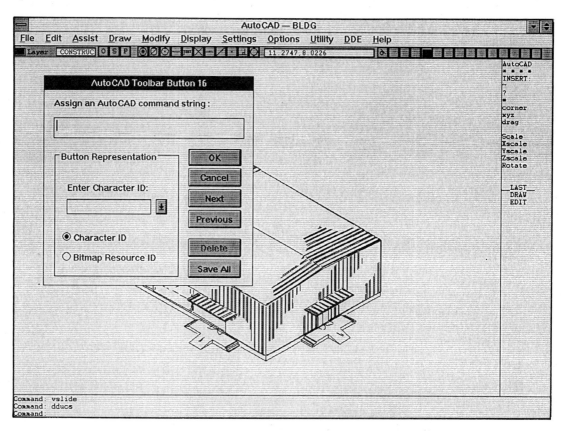

Figure 17-28 The Button Programming Dialogue Box

Button Programming A button can be customized by clicking with the right button of your mouse on the button you want to program. This in turn will pop up a dialogue box, as shown in Figure 17-28. The dialogue box has two different groups of options as explained as follows:

The first group of options is for assigning an AutoCAD command string. You can enter a single AutoCAD command, or a string of commands like a macro. For instance, you can program a button with the following string:

GRID .5 SNAP .25 LINE

When the button is selected the Grid will be set to .5, Snap to .25, and the LINE command will be executed. You may even include special characters in the command string. Following are the control character strings that can be used in the command string.

\n	forces a new line
\t	tab key
\3	is the same as Ctrl + C
\nnn (n's are numbers)	character's decimal number

The second group of options is for Button Representation. The button can be represented by a Character ID or Bitmap Icon. Click on the radio button of the

Character ID if you want a letter to appear on the Tool Bar button. By default, the first letter of the command string will appear on the button. If you want to specify a different letter, then select the letter from the combo box under Enter Resource ID. Instead of a letter, if you want to display an icon, then click on the radio button of the Bitmap Resource ID. Then select the appropriate icon from the combo box under Enter Resource ID. The bitmaps shown in the combo box are stored in files named tbar32.dll, tbar24.dll, and tbar16.dll. You can create your own bitmap icons to display on Tool Bar buttons.

The Next and Previous options will allow you to change to the next or previous programmable buttons, respectively.

The Delete option will delete the current definition shown in the edit box for the current programmable button.

The Save All option saves all the current definitions of the programmable buttons in the Tool Bar.

> **NOTE:** If you do not save the settings, your customized buttons only appear during your current AutoCAD session.

Select **OK** to keep the changes and close the dialogue box. Press Cancel to disregard the changes and close the dialogue box.

The following dialogue box will be displayed:

> The AutoCAD for Windows Installation and Performance Guide lists additional programming support. It includes topics as follows:
>
> Cursor Displays
> Keyboard Buffer Management
> Editing the acad.ini initiation file
> Creating bitmaps
> Using Visual Basic (for creating floating icon menus)
> Dynamic Data Exchange programs
> ADS for Windows
> Using Microsoft C with AutoCAD for Windows
> Using Borland C++ with AutoCAD for Windows
> Using Microsoft QuickC with AutoCAD for Windows
> Windows, ADS and C Programming
> DDE AutoLISP Functions

APPENDIX A

Hardware and Software Introduction

Appendix A

Figure A-1 Compaq 386 Deskpro.
(Reprinted with permission of Compaq Computer Corporation. All rights reserved.)

The configuration of your system is a combination of the hardware and software you have assembled to create your system. There are countless PC configurations available on the market. The goal for a new computer user should be to assemble a PC workstation that will not block future software and hardware upgrades. This section lists the essential hardware required to run AutoCAD 386 (Release 11).

AutoCAD 386 configuration requirements for a personal computer CADD workstation include the following:

1. IBM compatible, 386SX, IBM PS/2 models 70, 80, or a true 386 compatible. The 80486 is supported as well, since it is 80386 compatible.

2. Math Coprocessor 80387: (On 80486, the coprocessor is an integral part of the chip.) You should note that an 80486SX may not have the required math coprocessor.

829

3. Memory: Minimum of two megabytes of random access memory (RAM). One megabyte contains the 640K of conventional memory. At least four megabytes are recommended — the more the better.

4. Drives: A hard disk with at least 40 megabyte capacity and a 1.2 megabyte, 5 1/4-inch floppy drive or a 720K or 1.44MB, 3 1/2-inch floppy drive.

5. Video display and adapter.

6. MS-DOS or PC-DOS Operating System: Version 3.3 or later.

7. Input Devices: Digitizing tablet or mouse.

8. Plotters and Printers.

PERSONAL COMPUTER

AutoCAD supports 386 compatible computers. The 386 computers come in various classes with differing processor speeds, including the following:

1. 386SX (speeds 16MHz through 25 MHz)
2. 386DX (speeds 16MHz through 33MHz)
3. 486 (speeds 25MHz through 50MHz)

Select the one that best suits your workload. If you are planning to do large drawings then it is worthwhile buying a 486 (33MHz or 50MHz speeds). If you are not sure if AutoCAD is for you, or if you cannot spend a lot on a CAD workstation, then select a 386SX-based computer. Prices for 386SX (16MHz) and 486 (33MHz) stations with 4MB of RAM range from under $2000 to $3500 depending on the manufacturer. This does not include software and peripherals such as plotters and laser printers.

The central processing unit (CPU) is the heart of your personal computer. The job of the CPU is to process the interaction of instructions and data involved with your PC, and it is responsible for the majority of the work. The CPU coordinates the data from the "input" devices (keyboard, digitizer, etc.) and generates the appropriate data through the output devices (monitor, plotters).

The central processing unit is controlled by the operating system software. Equally important is the PC memory. While the operating system is responsible for processing all the data involved with your PC, the memory provides storage for program instructions and data until it is ready to be processed.

Math Coprocessor

AutoCAD requires a math coprocessor chip. This chip plugs into a socket reserved for this chip in the central processing unit. This chip increases the speed of the central processing unit's computations dramatically. Tests indicate that the performance improvement that results from this addition to the central processing unit justifies the comparatively low cost.

Memory

To run AutoCAD, your computer must be equipped with at least 2MB of RAM. Random access means that the operating system has direct access to the data it needs. The storage locations can be filled (written to) and refilled (written over) as the CPU processes data. Yet it is important to remember that RAM is temporary memory. The data is stored as long as the CPU has power. Once the electrical power is turned off, the data is erased from the storage locations. The second type of computer memory is Read-Only Memory (ROM). Read-only memory is used to store data required by the CPU to perform processing functions. The information can be "read" by the CPU programs and carried out. However, new data cannot be written to ROM. It is not lost when the power is turned off.

Drives

As we have discussed, data that is input to your personal computer is present in RAM for the length of time that your computer has power. To make future retrieval possible, data must be stored on some form of magnetic media. The two types of magnetic media storage devices we will discuss are hard disks and floppy disks.

Both hard disks and floppy disks are examples of direct access storage devices. Through them the central processing unit is able to go directly to the stored data regardless of the location on the magnetic media. The central processing unit uses electronic read/write heads to create and read magnetic fields on a specially coated disk.

Hard Disks The hard disk is the primary data storage device of your personal computer. The hard disk read/write heads are sealed units to protect against dust contamination. Sealing the units allows the read/write heads to fly just above the disk surface yielding greater density and access rates. The hard disk accesses data at a range from 16 milliseconds to 80 milliseconds. High performance is 30 milliseconds or faster, while 80 milliseconds is considered slow.

AutoCAD may be run with a 20-megabyte hard disk, but a larger capacity is advised. In choosing a powerful personal computer, you will obtain a faster response time and the ability to work with many large program files and data files.

Floppy Disks Floppy disks are commonly available in low density and high density and in 5 1/4" and 3 1/2" sizes. Low-density 5 1/4" floppy disks are capable of storing 360K (kilobytes) of data and 3 1/2" low-density diskettes can store 720K of information. The high-density 5 1/4" floppy disks have a data storage capacity of 1.2MB (megabytes), while the 3 1/2" high-density diskettes can store 1.4MB of information. An advantage to using floppy disks is that they are removable and easily transportable. They can be used to transfer program and data files from one computer to another. For those reasons, floppy disks are the standard means of software and data distribution. While floppy disks operate approximately 20 times slower than hard drives, they are most valuable when used to "back up" data located on the hard disk.

Video Display and Adapter

As with any graphics program for PC CADD systems, AutoCAD requires a video adapter capable of displaying graphics information. A video adapter is a printed circuit board which plugs into the central processing unit and generates signals to drive a monitor. When mounted in place, a socket (known as a port) will be accessible on the exterior of the computer for plugging in the monitor. AutoCAD supports a number of display options, ranging from low-priced monochrome set-ups to high resolution color units. Some of the video display controllers can be used in combination to give a two-screen display.

Resolution is the degree of graphic detail the board can provide. Both the monochrome and the color screen resolution are measured by the number of horizontal and vertical dots, called picture elements (or pixels), that the screen can display.

In selecting your graphics adapter board, you should be aware that general prices increase with the number of colors and resolution. Since the monitor must match the graphics board resolution and output specifications, the monitor price will increase or decrease proportionally, depending upon the graphics board you choose.

The Operating System

The operating system is an extremely elaborate program, and without it, none of your other programs will work. The operating system directs all the internal workings of the CPU by performing these important functions:

1. Governs the stream of data to and from the central processing unit and all other hardware associated with the computer system.
2. Defines the commands and directs the arithmetic/logic section to perform any calculations that are required.
3. Interacts with the random access memory to access instructions of the programs stored there.
4. Provides the utility to format your disk storage.
5. Provides the utility to read and write to the disk drives.
6. Gives you the ability to control and manage your data files through the system commands.
7. Provides the utility to keep and see the directory of your data files.
8. Allows you to check the amount of free space available for data storage.

The arithmetic/logic section is the area of the central processing unit that performs all the calculations and comparisons necessary in processing data. Both the operating system and the arithmetic section store data in temporary storage sections called registers.

The registers perform as part of the CPU main memory. While the main memory serves as a holding and storing place for data, it is also where application programs are stored when being used. The main memory of a PC is a random access memory.

Input Devices

AutoCAD supports several input device configurations. Data may be entered through the keyboard, the mouse, or a digitizing tablet with a cursor.

Keyboard The keyboard is one of the primary input methods. It can be used to enter commands and responses.

The arrow keys on the numeric keypad can be used to move the graphic cross-hair. The cross-hair may be moved to the right or left of the screen by using the 4 or 6 keys. It may be moved up or down with the 2 or 8 keys. When this method of manipulating the screen cross-hair is used, the speed of the cursor movement can be controlled by the PgUp or PgDn keys on your keyboard.

Mouse The mouse is used with the keyboard as a tracking device to move the cross-hair on the screen. This method is fast and far surpasses the keyboard for positioning the screen cross-hair.

The mouse is equipped with two or more buttons. The left button is the pick button, and the other buttons can be programmed to perform any of the AutoCAD commands.

Digitizer The digitizer is another means of input supported by AutoCAD. It is composed of the tablet and the puck.

Appendix A

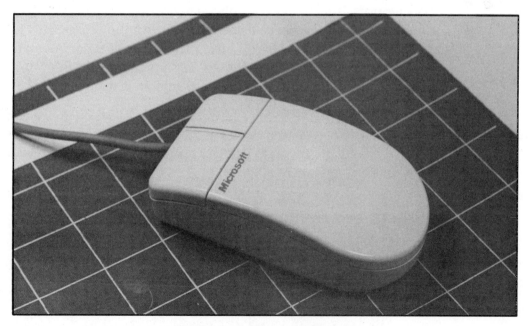

Figure A-2 Microsoft Mouse.
(Photo by Mary Beth Ray)

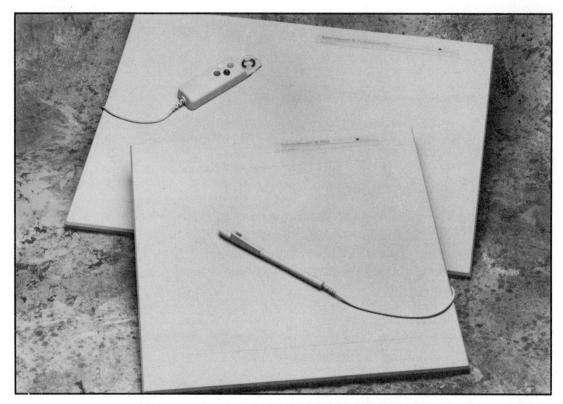

Figure A-3 Summagraphics Digitizer and Cursor.
(Courtesy of Summagraphics Corporation.)

The digitizing tablet is a flat, sensitized electromechanical device that can recognize the location of the tablet cursor. The tablet cursor moves over the surface of the digitizing tablet causing a corresponding movement of the screen cursor.

Another use of the digitizing tablet is to overlay a tablet menu, configured to enter commands when they are selected by placing the cross-hairs of the puck at the corresponding digitizer coordinates. This process automates any AutoCAD command options that are represented on the menu, and eliminates the use of the keyboard except to enter an occasional command value.

The tablet cursor (puck) may have from four to 16 buttons. Except for the first button, the current menu can be programmed to cause the remaining buttons to perform any of the regular AutoCAD commands. The first button is always the "pick" button.

Plotters and Printers

AutoCAD supports several types of output devices for producing hard copies of drawings. The three most common devices are the electrostatic plotter, pen plotter, and the dot matrix printer.

Electrostatic Plotter The electrostatic plotters produce an electrostatic charge on the drawing paper and deposit electrosensitive ink on the charged paper to create a hard copy of the drawing. They are much faster than other large plotting

Figure A–4 CalComp Electrostatic Plotter.
(Photo courtesy of CalComp Inc.)

Figure A–5 CalComp Pen Plotter.
(Photo courtesy of CalComp Inc.)

devices. The resolution of the output, which is measured in dots per inch (dpi), may range from a low-quality (200 dpi) product to a high-quality, state-of-the-art (1200 dpi) product.

To use an electrostatic plotter, your station will require a vector to raster conversion software. (Consult the manufacturer for more information.) The price of a good electrostatic plotter begins around $20,000, and such plotters are becoming increasingly popular with those who are upgrading to multiple workstations.

Pen Plotters Pen plotters convert digital computer signals into analog signals to draw continuous lines. The drawing pen is driven by vector commands that correspond to the X and Y coordinates on the drawing paper. Drawing media may vary between mylar, vellum, and bond. The pens used in such plotters also vary in size and quality, thus affecting the drawing resolution.

Pen plotters come in all shapes and sizes, and over the years pen plotters have improved in the areas of speed, accuracy, and price. The pen plotter is an established favorite for those who demand clear line and shape definition. Although prices vary on the different types of pen plotters, it is possible to get a good desktop pen plotter in the area of $1000 to $2000. Contact your dealer to find out if a particular model is supported.

Dot Matrix Printers Through third-party software, AutoCAD supports the ability to generate a hard copy of your drawing with a dot matrix printer. The hard copy may be produced by a simple graphics screen dump or a more involved output conversion program.

Figure A-6 AutoPlotter™ XP is a trademark of Japan Digital Laboratory Co., Ltd.

Dot matrix printers provide an inexpensive means for printing. They are generally used to provide rough draft hard copies for graphics and text data. They are an excellent and cost-effective way to produce check plots.

Dot matrix printers form characters and graphics by striking a wire-studded printhead against a printing ribbon onto standard paper. The average printer forms a 9 × 9 pin dot matrix. Clarity and higher resolution occur when the number of pin heads is increased. Most major manufacturers offer 24 pin models that cost an average of $400.

Laser Printers Laser printers are the newest printing device on the CADD market. They deliver a low-cost, medium- to high-resolution hard copy that can be driven from a personal computer. Laser printers boast resolutions from 300 dpi to 1200 dpi and printing speeds of about 8–12 pages per minute (ppm).

As with any raster device, laser printers require a vector-to-raster conversion to generate most graphics. AutoCAD can plot design files on laser printers that support the postscript graphic output language. The cost of laser printers ranges from $2000 to $12,000, yet the increase in resolution makes the price a good investment for many serious CADD users.

Configuring AutoCAD

Installing and configuring your system is a vital part of getting AutoCAD to function properly. Autodesk covers this portion with great detail and accuracy in the *Installation and Performance Guide* provided with your software.

Installing AutoCAD on your system by use of the INSTALL command will create several directories and subdirectories on your system. Below is a list of these directories and the general files found in them.

\acad	AutoCAD executable and support files
\acad\sample	Sample AutoCAD drawings and AutoLISP programs
\acad\source	Standard menu file and shape files
\acad\igesfont	IGES symbols and text fonts and shape files
\acad\ads	Library for ADS, and sample ADS programs
\acad\api	Library for API and API include files
\api\sample	Sample API source code and sample API programs

APPENDIX

B DOS and File Handling

Most AutoCAD users soon become acquainted with certain computer files and learn the DOS commands necessary to perform some operations on these files. Some of the more important DOS commands, such as DIR, COPY, ERASE, RENAME, etc., are made convenient through AutoCAD's Main Menu item 6 called File Utilities. Users may also access DOS directly while in the Drawing Editor.

DOS (DISK OPERATING SYSTEM)

It is possible that a drafter might create a drawing, save, and plot it without ever putting it on a floppy disk or tape. This would be rare indeed, unless the drawing or the time it took to create it were of so little value that its loss (perhaps due to a hard disk crash) could be ignored. It is a rare AutoCAD user who does not save work periodically on a floppy disk or tape during and at the end of the session.

Some DOS commands are easier to use while not in the AutoCAD Editor or at AutoCAD's Main Menu. For example, to copy a file while in AutoCAD, you must type in the filename for the source and then the filename for the target directory. Copying one or two files in this fashion is not a great inconvenience. Copying more than just a few files, though, might become tedious.

Some recommendations for easier file handling will be offered during the following sections. Some of the DOS-related features, commands, and terms that are useful to the operator are listed as follows:

COPY	RENAME
CHDIR or CD	ERASE
MKDIR or MD	FORMAT
DIRECTORY or DIR	The symbol \
DRIVE	The symbol *
FILE	The symbol :
DISKETTE	The symbol .
PATH	The symbol ..

Disk(ette)

Floppy disks are the media on which software is stored. The software is in the form of files. There are some things about the storage of data on diskettes, such as sectors, partitions, binary sequences, hexadecimals, etc., that are not necessary to learn in order to be able to use sophisticated and powerful CAD graphics programs. Once properly formatted, a diskette is simply addressed by the name of the drive in which it is inserted.

Usually, floppy disk drives are labeled drive A and (if there is a second floppy drive) drive B. Important uses of the floppy disk are:

1. Safe backup storage of files.
2. Transfer of files from one computer to another.
3. Temporary repository of files in the floppy drive for support or editing without copying them onto the fixed disk.

Fixed disks, like floppy disks, store software in the form of files. Like their name says, they are fixed and not removable for the purpose of transferring files to another computer. Their main advantage is in their large capacity, being that of hundreds of diskettes. Fixed drives are usually labelled drive C and (if a second fixed drive is installed) drive D. The fixed drive is where the main AutoCAD program files are stored. Because of the risk of fixed disk failure (beyond recoverability of files), all important files on a fixed disk should also be stored on floppy disks or backup tapes. These backup files differ from the files that are sometimes created by programs automatically and have the file extension of .BAK. Backup files that are copied to floppy disks for the purpose of safekeeping usually have the same name and file extension as the file they back up.

Files

File specifications (or filespec) include the drive label, the filename and an optional extension. The directory path is sometimes included when accessing a file. The drive label and directory path do not always have to be included, as will be explained later.

A file contains data and is stored under a particular filename. The filename may also include an extension. The data may be a simple two-line batch file, a 10-page letter, or a large encrypted and compiled executable program like AutoCAD's ACAD.EXE file or one of your larger drawing files with the file extension of .DWG. When DOS commands operate on a file, they usually operate on the whole file as a unit. Programs like AutoCAD, line editors, word processors, and data base manipulators (which are all program files themselves) create or open data files, edit, and close them. Being able to create files and knowing how and when to address them are skills necessary to do advanced file editing and manipulating. One application, for example, is if you wish to do programming in AutoLISP.

DRIVES AND DIRECTORIES

Drives and directories are established for the purpose of storing files. The combination of a floppy drive and a fixed drive is like a warehouse with a railroad loading dock attached. DOS is the warehouse manager and, when properly instructed, does the following:.

1. DOS handles the files into and out of storage.
2. DOS will take you to a program file that can operate on a data file. (Reading, editing, and printing are all done by using a program file.)
3. DOS will then take you to that data file and open it for you to read, edit, or print a copy of the file.
4. DOS will close the file when you are through and take you to another set of program and data files.

The main warehouse is the fixed drive. You may have the manager (DOS) store all the files in the open space commonly known as the root directory. But when enough files start to fill the root directory, it becomes unwieldly. Just listing all the files causes the screen to fill and scroll. It is difficult to locate and identify particular files. Therefore, DOS can create storerooms in the warehouse called subdirectories. This conveniently allows you to store a group of related files apart from other groups of files. A subdirectory may even have its own subsubdirectories, like storerooms within the storerooms in the warehouse.

It is advisable to keep the root directory (the area of the warehouse outside of all storerooms) as free as possible. Only the needed DOS command files and batch files (to be explained later) should be stored in the root directory. All other data and program files should be stored in subdirectories created especially for them. It is also advisable to use short names for the subdirectories. They will have to be typed in from the keyboard as part of the path to files. Keep them as short as possible and still have them identifiable. If you have created a directory named AutoLISP, you will be surprised how quickly you will get tired of typing in "AutoLISP," or even "LISP" (if you have given the directory one of those names), every time you type in the path to your file. You will soon get used to remembering that "AL" or just "L" is the name of the directory that your files are stored in. However, if most of your file manipulations are done with the help of a utility program such as Norton Utilities, PCTOOLS, or XTREE, then longer, more recognizable directory names will probably be advantageous.

The floppy drive is like a railroad loading dock. The floppy disk inserted in the drive is like a railroad car parked at the loading dock. It is accessible through the label for the drive it is in.

It is possible, though not as commonly done as on the fixed drive, to create subdirectories on the floppy disk while it is parked in the floppy drive. These subdirectories are like storerooms and rooms in the main warehouse. They stay with that diskette and when it leaves the dock (the floppy drive) the subdirectories go with it. A new car (floppy diskette) brings its own rooms (subdirectories) with it if they have been created previously by DOS.

As an experienced AutoCAD operator you will soon learn your way around drives and directories in order to get to appropriate files. The most common arrangement is to have the computer start up (boot up) with the floppy drive door open.

Appendix B

The computer, after memory check, looks at drive A (floppy) first, finds it inaccessible, redirects itself to the fixed drive, looking for the disk operating system on a file called COMMAND.COM. Then, when the boot up is complete, you are automatically logged onto the fixed drive (usually labeled "C") and a prompt appears which includes the "C>". Failure to keep the A drive (floppy) open during boot up will cause a message to appear regarding a "nonsystem disk..." (unless the A drive contains a diskette with the COMMAND.COM file on it). If that were the case, a prompt would appear having "A>" in it, indicating that you were logged onto the A drive. It would be your current drive until the time you invoked the DOS command to change drives.

Should the "nonsystem disk..." message appear, simply open the floppy drive door and press any key. The redirection to drive C should proceed without further problems.

Changing Drives

To change from one drive to another simply enter the new drive letter followed by a colon. For example, while on drive A the prompt reads:

    A>

After typing in the "C:" the prompt reads:

    A>C:

After pressing ⏎, the prompt reads:

    C>

You are now logged onto drive C. It is your current drive. Reversing the above: C>A: produces A> and logs you back on drive A, the floppy drive.

Logging Onto a Drive and Directory

The importance of being logged onto a particular drive and directory depends on the type of file you are operating with. As mentioned before, some files just contain data to be operated upon by other programs. These data files are letters, drawings, and lists of items such as a phone list or bill of materials. Other files are, of course, the programs themselves.

If you decide to delve into customizing AutoCAD, one of the first files you become involved with is the MENU file (whose EXTENSION is .MNU). It is an excellent example of a file that while being created or edited is a data file, but when completed becomes a program file. The student should note with care which drive and directory he/she is currently logged onto and which drive and subdirectory the program and data files are on at the time a command is invoked. It is possible that four different locations (drives and directories) could be involved at the same time during one command.

As mentioned previously, diskettes and fixed disks are addressed through their drive label. To access or operate on a file stored on a floppy disk in drive A (and drive A is not the current drive) the user must prefix the file specification with "A:." For example:

C>**TYPE A:MYNEW.LSP**

In order for the DOS command called TYPE to operate on the file called MYNEW.LSP, you must address MYNEW.LSP through its drive label followed by a colon if you are not logged onto drive A. If you are logged onto drive A you may address the file without using the drive label prefix as follows:

A:>**TYPE MYNEW.LSP**

Three things must be taken into consideration concerning drives when operating on files.

1. **Current Drive** — You need to know which drive you are presently logged onto.
2. **Source and Target Drives** — You need to know the drive(s) where the source file and the target are. For instance, in using the DOS COPY command, the source is where the file is stored before the command is used and the target is where the new copy of the file will reside.
3. **Internal or External DOS Command** — It is advisable to study the list of the particular DOS commands you will be using in order to know if they are internal or external commands. For example, the DOS commands COPY and TYPE are internal commands. They reside within the COMMAND.COM program file and can be invoked from any directory while logged on any drive because COMMAND.COM was loaded into RAM when the machine was booted up.

First the Rule! (Path Makes an Exception)

The DOS command PRINT is an external command. It requires access to the program file called PRINT.COM. In versions of DOS prior to 3.0, it can only be invoked when the directory that it is stored on is the current directory of its drive. The commands with the extension of .COM, .EXE, and .BAT are accessed in a similar manner.

In DOS version 3.0, accessing files on drives other than the current one can be done in an easier fashion than before. If the computer environment has previously been set up with a path to the .COM, .EXE, or .BAT files, then they can be invoked from directory other than their own. For example, PRINT.COM is on the directory named DOSX. When the computer is booted up, enter the following:

PATH=\DOSX

Then while in the ACAD directory you may simply enter:

PRINT MYNEW.MNU

and DOS will go to the DOSX subdirectory and use the PRINT command to print the file on the ACAD directory named MYNEW.MNU.

The "PATH=" entry is best included in the AUTOEXEC.BAT file.

Appendix B

By studying carefully and understanding the following examples, the novice can apply the same approach to other file handling procedures and programs, including his/her own custom programs that involve file handling. Even the moderately experienced DOS user can get into some procedural habits that might be improved upon.

Example No. 1

> Objective: *Print the file named MYNEW.LSP*
> Current drive: **A**
> Current directory: *Root directory (of drive A)*
> Drive where MYNEW.LSP is stored: **C**
> Directory where MYNEW.LSP is stored: **\LISP**
> Drive where PRINT.COM is stored: **C**
> Directory where PRINT.COM is stored: **\DOS**

Entering the following will work under one condition:

> A>**C:PRINT C:\LISP\MYNEW.LSP**

Even though the path to the file is correct, the path to the DOS command PRINT will work only if, when you changed from drive C, the current directory on drive C was \DOS (in older versions of DOS) or the PATH= \DOS\ has been entered previously. Otherwise, if you had been in the root directory or in the \LISP directory when you left drive C (by entering **A:** to get to drive A), then the path "C:" to PRINT.COM would not work.

Example No. 2

> Objective: *Print the file named MYNEW.LSP*
> Current drive: **C**   *changed from Example No. 1*
> Current directory: **\LISP**   *changed from Example No. 1*
> Drive where MYNEW.LSP is stored: **C**
> Directory where MYNEW.LSP is stored: **\LISP**
> Drive where PRINT.COM is stored: **C**
> Directory where PRINT.COM is stored: **\DOS**

Entry No.1

> C>**CD\DOS**

This logs you onto the DOS directory where the program file called PRINT.COM is stored. It is an external DOS command.

Entry No. 2

> C>**PRINT \LISP\MYNEW.LSP**

This will work now.

Review Files may be accessed through their paths no matter which drive and directory you are logged onto. The drive specifier and/or directory path may be omitted when you are logged onto the same drive and/or directory as the file you are accessing.

Internal DOS commands may be invoked from any drive and directory. But not at all times. While a program is running, DOS may or may not be accessible, depending on the program. As mentioned before, AutoCAD allows you to access DOS while editing a drawing by entering **Shell** for all commands and **SH** for just internal DOS commands. AutoCAD's Main Menu for file utilities also uses DOS commands, but this is indirect access. You must follow the procedures according to AutoCAD's prompts.

Using external DOS commands requires one of three things. One option is to be logged on the same directory as the DOS program file for that command. Another option is if you are on another drive, then the drive on which the DOS command program file is stored must have as its current directory the one on which the DOS program file is stored (this applies to older versions of DOS with or without the PATH= entry). The third option is to have entered a "PATH=" command so that DOS will seek out the .COM, .EXE, or .BAT file from any directory.

The Exceptional Path

The following example is a method of using external DOS commands from a directory other that the one on which they are stored. This shows how to set up a path to their directory. Care must be taken in doing this. If the computer environment has already had a path set up to include other directories, then arbitrarily using the DOS command called PATH might nullify the other preset paths. It is best to include the path to external DOS commands with the path to other necessary directories in the PATH command in the AUTOEXEC.BAT file as mentioned previously. An example would be as follows:

Objective: *Provide access to files in the ACADDWG directory, certain digitizer files in the DIGI directory, and to the external DOS commands in the DOSX directory.*

Context: **PATH=C:\ACADDWG;\DIGI;\DOSX;**

Because the DOS command PATH is an internal command, the above can be entered from any directory or drive.

CAUTION!
In using the above setting, it should be noted that duplicate filenames in different directories might cause a problem. Under the circumstances this is not likely, but if a drawing were named PRINT.DWG, then trying to use the DOS command named PRINT from some other directory, DOSX might try to access the PRINT.DWG file instead of the PRINT.COM file. Because of the different extensions, this may not happen, but extension differences may not prevent DOS from trying to use a wrong file in other cases. When DOS looks for a file by the path route, it looks in the directories in the order that they are placed after the PATH command. In the above example, the ACADDWG directory will be searched first, the DIGI second, and the DOSX last.

Appendix B

DIRECTORY COMMANDS

While logged onto the root directory of drive C, the prompt should show only the "C>" or "C:\>" without any subdirectory name displayed. It would be advisable to type in **CD** to be sure that you are on the root directory. Depending on the boot up parameters for the prompt, it is possible for you to be logged on a subdirectory and not have it show in the prompt area. Under certain prompt parameter settings, if you were logged onto the subdirectory named "ACAD" on drive C, the prompt might display "C:\ACAD>".

Making Directories

You may use the MKDIR or MD command to create a new directory as a branch of any directory, including the root directory. A subdirectory called MENU is created as follows:

    C:\>MD\MENU

This creates a subdirectory to the root directory. This only creates the subdirectory, and does not log you onto it. Another command is used for that purpose.

> **NOTE:** Note the use of the "\" (backslash) for specifying a directory. Any time you are logged onto a directory other than the root directory or the one whose path you wish to specify, you must prefix the name of the target directory with the \ symbol. The root directory is the "NO NAME" directory, therefore when specifying a path to it from some other directory, you must use the \ symbol without a directory name.

For simplicity, from here on, directories and subdirectories will primarily be referred to as just directories. The distinction between directories and subdirectories is primarily technical and not critical as long as one learns the correct path to any file.

Searching Directories

It is useful to be able to display on the screen a list of all the files that are stored on a directory. This is accomplished using the DOS command called DIRECTORY or DIR. This command will display the files and also any directories created as a part of the particular directory you are searching. A search of the root directory can be entered as follows:

    C:\>DIR

The following might be displayed:

```
Volume in drive C has no label
Directory of C:\
COMMAND     COM          23456       1-23-88
DOS                      <DIR>       1-23-88
AUTOEXEC    BAT            128       2-13-88
ACAD        BAT             28       3-21-88
ACAD                     <DIR>       3-21-88
PIPESTAR                 <DIR>       4-12-88
SIDEKICK                 <DIR>       4-30-88
```

After having used the MD\MENU command, the DIR command would display:

```
C:\> DIR
   Volume in drive C has no label
   Directory of C:\
COMMAND     COM          23456       1-23-88
DOS                      <DIR>       1-23-88
AUTOEXEC    BAT            128       2-13-88
ACAD        BAT             28       3-21-88
ACAD                     <DIR>       3-21-88
PIPESTAR                 <DIR>       4-12-88
SIDEKICK                 <DIR>       4-30-88
MENU                     <DIR>       (the current date)
```

An additional convenience of the DIR command is to be able to list the files across the screen in a wide fashion. This is done by adding a "/W" to the DIR command:

```
C:\>DIR/W
```

The display would be as follows:

```
C> DIR
   Volume in drive C has no label
   Directory of C:\
COMMAND COM      [DOS]        AUTOEXEC BAT        ACAD BAT
[PIPESTAR]       [SIDEKICK]   [MENU]              [ACAD]
```

The sizes and dates of files are not displayed when the "/W" parameter is added to the DIR command. Another handy feature is the "/P" either with or without the "/W" following the DIR command. "/P" causes the scrolling to pause each time the screen is filled with a display of the list of files and directories. Of course, it is only needed when the list is larger than the screen can display.

When a directory has been created there are two unnamed hidden files created at the same time. Their presence is indicated by the "." and the ".." symbols displayed when the DIR command is used. These are of no special concern to the average operator. An effort to delete them, however, might play havoc with DOS so they are best left alone.

Changing Directories

Logging onto another directory on the same drive is done by using the DOS command called CHDIR or CD. It requires the "\" (backslash) prefix in the following manner:

C:\>CD\MENU

This will log you onto the directory called MENU. In the later version of DOS, logging onto (or accessing) another directory from the root directory can be done without the backslash as follows:

C:\>CD MENU

Getting Back to the Root Directory

Because the root directory has no name, enter the following:

C>CD

This will return you to the root directory.

If the prompt parameter "PG" (which causes the current directory with the ">" following it to be included in the prompt area) is in effect, the display will read:

C:\MENU>

Drive and Directory Specifiers

It is possible (but not advisable at this time) to create a subdirectory inside the MENU directory. It may be done in three different ways depending upon which is the current drive and directory. This example is for the purpose of illustrating the use of the (:) symbol for the drive specifier and the (\) symbol for the directory specifier.

Example No. 3

> Objective: *Create a subdirectory named LISPMENU to the directory named MENU which is itself a subdirectory of the root directory of drive C.*
> Current drive: **A** *same as Example No. 1*
> Current directory: *(Root of A) same as Example No. 1*

Enter the following:

A>MD C:\MENU\LISPMENU

Example No. 4

> Objective: *Same as Example No. 3*
> Current drive: **C** *changed from Example No. 3*
> Current directory: *(Root of C) changed from Example No. 3*

Enter the following:

C>MD \MENU\LISPMENU

RENAMING FILES

An example of operating on a file with DOS while in the root directory is to RENAME a file. Each time a drawing is called into the AutoCAD Editor, it creates a backup file of the drawing before any changes are made. For example, you have previously created and ENDed a drawing named "XMPL." It is saved as a file with the name XMPL.DWG. At the begining of any subsequent editing session, AutoCAD will create a temporary file named XMPL.BAK. Should you SAVE or END during the subsequent editing session, XMPL.BAK becomes a permanent file. If you had QUIT the editing session without saving during the session, the XMPL.BAK file would have been abandoned. Each time you SAVE during the session, the drawing in its current status will be poised to replace the previous .BAK file. It will actually be kept as a third file in a temporary state, ready to take the place of the .BAK file. So before you use the SAVE command, be sure that you will not want to go back to the drawing in the status it was in when re-editing began.

There is a way to get back to the drawing in its status one SAVE prior to the last SAVE or END command. This requires renaming the .BAK file. AutoCAD drawings must, of course, have the extension of .DWG in order to edit them. So if you wish to use the XMPL.BAK file as a drawing, you must change the extension from .BAK to .DWG. But, there already exists a file named XMPL.DWG. DOS will not let you name or rename a file when one already exists with the same name ON THE SAME DRIVE AND DIRECTORY. Therefore, when renaming the .BAK file, you must also change the filename to something unique on that directory.

Example No. 5

Current drive: **C**
Current directory: **\DRAWINGS**
Drive where XMPL.BAK is stored: **C**
Directory where XMPL.BAK is stored: **\DRAWINGS**
Existing XMPL.DWG is on same path as XMPL.BAK

A suggested sequence would be as follows:

C>**RENAME XMPL.BAK XMPL2.DWG**

The above entry suggests two things you have just studied. One, you are logged onto the same drive and directory that XMPL.BAK is stored on. Two, RENAME must be an internal DOS command. The only way to RENAME the XMPL.BAK file XMPL.DWG is to first delete the existing XMPL.DWG file from the current directory.

Another thing is suggested by the sequence. That is, there is no existing file named XMPL2.DWG on the current directory. If the drawing in its latest status were in such bad shape as to not be worth saving, then deleting it and renaming the .BAK with the same filename is one way to keep the same drawing name.

Note in the following section on using the DOS command named COPY on files, the caution about losing an existing file on a directory. DOS prevents this in the use of the RENAME command.

Examples of using the RENAME command from other locations are as follows:

Example No. 6

> Current drive: **C**
> Current directory: *Root directory*
> Drive where XMPL.BAK is stored: **C**
> Directory where XMPL.BAK is stored: **\DRAWINGS**
> Existing XMPL.DWG is on same path as XMPL.BAK

A suggested sequence would be as follows:

> C>**RENAME \DRAWINGS\XMPL.BAK XMPL2.DWG**

Note that the path is only given to the file's old name. It is not necessary to prefix the new name with the drive and directory specifiers. You can send a copy of a file to another location and change the name at the same time in the COPY command. The RENAME command does not leave a copy of the file under its old name as the COPY command does.

Another sequence would be required if the file were in a subdirectory of another directory.

Example No. 7

> Current drive: **A**
> Current directory: *Root directory*
> Drive where XMPL.BAK is stored: **C**
> Directory where XMPL.BAK is stored: **\ACAD\DRAWINGS**

(Note that \DRAWINGS\ is a subdirectory of \ACAD\)

A suggested sequence would be as follows:

> A>**RENAME C:\ACAD\DRAWINGS\XMPL.BAK XMPL2.DWG**

As you can see, having to specify drives and directories in the path to a file can influence two things in using DOS commands:

1. If many file operations are required, try to keep required directory specifying to a minimum by either changing to the directory of the file or by limiting the depth of subdirectories.
2. Keep directory names as short as possible.

FORMATTING THE DISK

Before you can write information onto a new disk, you must prepare the diskette so that you can store information. This can be done by a program called FORMAT.COM. The formatting program is located on your DOS directory. You only need to format a disk once. Log into the directory that has the FORMAT program or, if you have a path for the directory that has the FORMAT program, then you can type the command at any DOS prompt.

Example No. 8

Current drive: **C**
Current directory: *Root directory*
Drive where FORMAT.COM is stored: **C:**
Disk to be formatted is in drive A

A suggested sequence would be as follows:

C:>**format a:**

The following message will appear:

Insert new diskette for drive A:
and strike ENTER when ready

Insert a new diskette and press ⏎. You will see the message:

Formatting...

After a while the following message appears:

Format complete
Format another (Y/N):

If you want to format another disk, take out the newly formatted disk and replace it with another new disk. Then press **Y** and ⏎. If you do not want to format another disk, press **N** and ⏎ to terminate the program. Remember, you only have to format a disk once, even if you erase the information on it.

> **NOTE:** To format a low-density diskette (360KB), you have to add switch /4 to the format command as shown below:
>
> C:>**format a:/4**

COPYING FILES

It is sometimes necessary to copy files from one location to another. Unlike the RENAME command this involves different drives and/or directories. The only case where a file can be copied to its same drive and directory is if the name is changed in the process. This would produce two identical files with different names.

One occasion to copy a file would be if you created a custom menu on a directory containing a word processor, and wished to transfer it to the ACAD directory for use in AutoCAD. This is not the most efficient way to write and test programs, but it does illustrate the DOS command called COPY.

Example No. 9

Objective: *Copy the file named TRIAL.MNU from the directory called WRDPRCSR to the directory called ACAD*
Current drive: **C**
Current directory: Root directory

A suggested sequence would be as follows:

C>**COPY\WRDPRCSR\TRIAL.MNU \ACAD\TRIAL.MNU**

Example No. 10

Objective: *Same as Example No. 11*
Current drive: **C**
Current directory:**\WRDPRCSR**

A suggested sequence would be as follows:

C>**COPY TRIAL.MNU \ACAD\TRIAL.MNU**

Example No. 11

Objective: *Same as Example No. 11*
Current drive: **C**
Current directory: **\ACAD**

A suggested sequence would be as follows:

C>**COPY \WRDPRCSR\TRIAL.MNU**

Note the permissible omission of the target altogether.

Copying Between Drives

Another common need for copying files is between floppy drives and fixed drives. This also facilitates transferring files from one computer station to another.

Example No. 12

Objective: *Copy the file named TRIAL.MNU from a floppy disk in drive A to the ACAD directory on the fixed drive.*
Current drive: **C**
Current directory: *Root directory*

A suggested sequence would be as follows:

C>**COPY A:TRIAL.MNU \ACAD\TRIAL.MNU**

Example No. 13

Objective: *Same as Example No. 14*
Current drive: **A**
Current directory: *Root directory*

A suggested sequence would be as follows:

A>**COPY TRIAL.MNU C:\ACAD\TRIAL.MNU**

Example No. 14

Objective: *Same as Example No. 14*
Current drive: **C**
Current directory: **ACAD**

A suggested sequence would be as follows:

C>**COPY A:TRIAL.MN**

Example No. 15 (Use of the global symbol "*")

Objective: *Copy all files with the file extension of .MNU from drive A to the ACAD directory on drive C.*
Current drive: **C**
Current directory: **ACAD**

A suggested sequence would be as follows:

C>**COPY A:*.MNU**

Example No. 16 (Use of the global symbol "*")

Objective: *Copy all files on drive A to the ACAD directory on drive C.*
Current drive: **C**
Current directory: **ACAD**

A suggested sequence would be as follows:

C>**COPY A:*.***

As you can see, like in programming, DOS commands can be made easier with a little planning.

DELETE A FILE OR GROUP OF FILES

The storage space on a disk is limited and all of it may eventually be occupied by files. Therefore, it is sometimes necessary to delete files you no longer need. The built-in command ERASE and its shorter form DEL can delete a single file or a group of files. Both commands do exactly the same thing and work the same way. You can use whichever command you prefer.

Example No. 17

Current drive: **C**
Current directory: *Root directory*
Drive where XMPL.BAK is stored: **C**
Directory where XMPL.BAK is stored: **\ACAD\DRAWINGS**

(Note that \DRAWINGS\ is a subdirectory of \ACAD\)

A suggested sequence would be as follows to delete the file XMPL.BAK:

A:\>**ERASE C:\ACAD\DRAWINGS\XMPL.BAK**

Example No. 18

Current drive: **C**
Current directory: *Root directory*
Objective: *Delete all the files with extension .BAK in drive A.*

A suggested sequence would be as follows to delete the files:

C:\>**ERASE A:*.BAK**

Example No. 19

Current drive: **C**
Current directory: **c:\DWG**
Objective: *Delete all the files in the directory DWG.*

A suggested sequence would be as follows to delete the files:

C:\DWG>ERASE *.*

The following message will appear:

Are you sure (Y/N)?

You must answer **Y** if you want DOS to continue. Otherwise, the operation is terminated without further action.

DOS REFERENCE BOOKS

A variety of books are available that discuss the MS DOS operating system. It is suggested that you read any one of the available books for detailed information about the operating system and system management.

APPENDIX

C

Quick Reference of Key-In Commands

COMMANDS

Command (Aliases)	Explanation	Options	Screen Menu	Pull-Down Menu
Aperture	Regulates the size of the object snap target box.	Select (1-50 pixels) to increase or reduce size of box.	SETTINGS	
Arc (A)	Draws an arc of any size.	A Included angle. C Center point. D Starting direction. E Endpoint. L Length of chord. R Radius. S Start point. ⏎ Continues arc from endpoint of line or arc.	DRAW	Draw
Area	Calculates the area of a polygon, pline, or a circle.	A Sets add mode. S Sets subtract mode. E Calculates area of the circle or pline selected.	INQUIRY	Utility
Array	Copies selected objects in circular or rectangular pattern.	P Polar (circular) arrays about a center point. R Rectangular arrays objects in horizontal rows and vertical columns.	EDIT	Modify
Attdef	Creates an Attribute Definition that assigns (tags) textual information to a Block.	I Regulates visibility. C Regulates constant/variable mode. V Regulates verify mode. P Regulates preset mode.	BLOCKS & DRAW	
Attdisp	Regulates the visibility of Attributes in the drawing.	ON Makes all Attribute tags visible. OFF Makes all Attributes invisible. N Normal visibility set individually.	DISPLAY	
Attedit	Permits the editing of Attributes.		EDIT	
Attext	Extracts Attribute information from a drawing.	C CDG comma-delimited format. D DXF format. S SDF format. E Select entities.	UTILITY	

(Reprinted with permission from Autodesk Inc.)

Command (Aliases)	Explanation	Options	Screen Menu	Pull-Down Menu
Audit	Performs drawing integrity check while in the Drawing Editor.	Y Fixes errors encountered. N Reports, but does not fix errors.	UTILITY	
Axis	Creates a ruler line of tick marks on the display.	ON Turns Axis on. OFF Turns Axis off. S Sets tick marks to Snap value. A Sets aspect to allow for different X,Y.	SETTINGS	
Base	Defines the origin point for insertion of one drawing into another.		BLOCKS	
Blipmode	Turns blip markers on and off.		SETTINGS	
Block	Makes a compound object from a group of entities.	? Lists names of defined Blocks.	BLOCKS	
Break	Breaks out (erases) part of an entity or splits it into parts.	F Allows you to reselect the first point again.	EDIT	Modify
Cancel Ctrl + C	Cancels the current command.		****	Assist
Chamfer	Makes a chamfer at the intersection of two lines.	D Sets chamfer distance. P Chamfers all intersections of a pline figure.	EDIT	Modify
Change	Makes changes in the location, size, orientation, and other properties of selected objects. This command is very helpful for editing text.	P Changes properties of objects. C Color LA Layer LT Linetype F Thickness	EDIT	
Chprop	Makes changes in the properties of selected entities.	C Color LA Layer LT Linetype T Thickness	EDIT	
Circle (C)	Draws a circle of any size. Default is center point and radius.	2P Two endpoints on diameter. 3P Three points on circle. D Enters circle diameter. TTR Tangent, Tangent, Radius	DRAW	Draw
Color 1. Red 2. Yellow 3. Green 4. Cyan 5. Blue 6. Magenta 7. White	Sets color for entities by name or number. Also sets color to be by Block or layer.	number Sets color by number. name Sets a color by name. BYBLOCK Retains color of Block. BYLAYER Uses color of layer.	SETTINGS	
Copy (CP)	Makes one or more copies of selected objects.	M Makes more than one copy of the selected object.	EDIT	Modify
Dblist	Makes a listing of every entity in the drawing data base.		INQUIRY	
Ddatte	Edits Attributes via a dialogue box.		EDIT	
Dedit	Edits text and Attributes via a dialogue box.		EDIT	

Command (Aliases)	Explanation	Options	Screen Menu	Pull-Down Menu
'Ddemodes	Sets current layer, linetype, elevation, and text style via a dialogue box.		SETTINGS	
'Ddlmodes	Sets layer properties via a dialogue box.		LAYER:	
'Ddrmodes	Allows drawing aids to be set via a dialogue box.		SETTINGS	
Dducs	Can adjust User Coordinate System via a dialogue box.		UCS:	
Delay	Sets timing for a sequence of commands used in a script file.			
Dim	Select dimensioning mode to allow dimensioning notations to be added to a drawing.		DIM:	Draw
Dim1	Resumes normal command mode after entering one dimension.		DIM:	
Dist	Determines distance between two points.		INQUIRY	Utility
Divide	Places markers along selected entities, dividing them into a specified number of parts.	B Sets a specified Block as a marker.	EDIT	Modify
Doughnut	Draws a solid circle or a ring with a specified inside and outside diameter.		DRAW	Draw
Dragmode	Allows control of the dynamic specification (dragging) feature for all appropriate commands.	ON Honors drag requests when applicable. OFF Ignores drag requests.	SETTINGS	
Dtext	Enters text on the display as it is typed in.	See Text command for options.	DRAW	Draw
Dview (DV)	Defines parallel or visual perspective views dynamically.	CA Selects the camera angle relative to the target. CL Sets front and back clipping planes. D Sets camera-to-target distance, turns on perspective. H Removes hidden lines on the selection set. OFF Turns perspective off. PA Pans drawing across the screen. PO Specifies the camera and target points. TA Rotates the target point about the camera. TW Twists the view around your line of sight. U Undoes a Dview subcommand. X Exits the Dview command. Z Zooms in/out, or sets lens length.	DISPLAY	Display

Command (Aliases)	Explanation	Options	Screen Menu	Pull-Down Menu
Dxbin	Inserts specially coded binary files into a drawing.		UTILITY	
Dxfin	Loads a drawing interchange file.		UTILITY	
Dxfout	Writes a drawing interchange file.	B Writes binary DXF file. E Outputs selected entities only.	UTILITY	
Edgesurf	Constructs a 3D Polygon mesh approximating a Coons surface patch (a bicubic surface interpolated between four adjoining edges).		SURFACES	
Elev	Sets elevation and extrusion thickness for entities to be drawn in 3D drawings.		SETTINGS	
Ellipse	Draws ellipses using any of several methods.	C Selects center point. R Selects rotation rather than second Axis. I Draws isometric circle in current isoplane.	DRAW	Draw
End	Exits the Drawing Editor after saving the updated drawing.		UTILITY	File
Erase (E)	Deletes entities from the drawing.		EDIT	Modify
Explode	Changes a Block or Polyline back into its original entities.		EDIT	
Extend	Extends a line, arc, or Polyline to meet another object. Selected to be the boundary edge.	U Undoes last extension.	EDIT	Modify
Files	Performs disk file utility tasks.		UTILITY	File
Fill	Determines if solids, traces, and wide Polylines are automatically filled.	ON Solids, traces and wide Polylines filled. OFF Solids, traces, and wide Polylines outlined.		
Fillet	Constructs an arc of specified radius between two lines, arcs, or circles.	P Fillets an entire Polyline. Sets fillet radius. R Sets fillet radius.	EDIT	Modify
Filmroll	Generates a file for rendering by Auto-Shade.		ASHADE	
Graphscr F1 Key	Flips to the graphics display on single-screen systems. Used in command scripts and menus.			
Grid F7 Key On Off toggle	Displays a Grid of dots, at desired spacing, on the screen.	ON Turns Grid on. OFF Turns Grid off. S Locks Grid spacing to Snap resolution. A Sets Grid aspect (differing X-Y spacings). number Sets Grid spacing (0=use Snap spacing). number X Sets spacing to multiple of Snap spacing.	SETTINGS	Settings

Command (Aliases)	Explanation	Options	Screen Menu	Pull-Down Menu
Handles	Assigns a unique, permanent number to each entity in a drawing.	ON Assigns handles to all entities and sets system variable HANDLES to 1. DESTROY Discards all entity handles.	SETTINGS	
Hatch	Creates cross-hatching and pattern-filling.	name Uses hatch pattern name from library file. U Uses simple user-defined hatch pattern. ? Lists selected names of available hatch patterns. NAME and U can be followed by a comma and a hatch style from the following list: I Ignores internal structure. N Normal style: turns hatch lines off and on when internal structure is encountered. O Hatches outermost portion only.	DRAW	Draw
"Help or '?	Displays a list of valid commands and data entry options or obtains help for a specific command or prompt.	To get a set of Help modes use Ctrl + C and F1 for flip screen.	**** INQUIRY	Assist
Hide	Regenerates a 3D visualization with hidden lines removed.			Display
Id	Displays the coordinates of a point selected on the drawing.		INQUIRY	Utility
Igesin	Loads an IGES interchange file.		UTILITY	
Igesout	Writes an IGES interchange file.		UTILITY	
Insert	Inserts a copy of a block or Wblock complete drawing into the current drawing.	fname Loads fname as Block. fname=f Creates Block fname from file f. *name Retains individual part entities. C (as reply to X scale prompt) Specifies scale via two points.	BLOCKS & DRAW	Draw
		(Corner specification of scale) XYZ (as reply to X scale prompt) Readies Insert for X,Y, and Z scales. - Displays a File Dialogue box. ? Lists names of defined Blocks.	BLOCKS & DRAW	Draw
Isoplane Ctrl + E	Changes the location of the isometric cross-hairs to left, right and top plane.	L Left plane. R Right plane. T Top plane. (Return) Toggle to next plane.		

Command (Aliases)	Explanation	Options	Screen Menu	Pull-Down Menu
Layer (LA)	Allows for creation of drawing layers and assigning color and linetype properties.	C Sets layers to color selected. F Freezes layers. L Sets specified layers to linetype. M Makes a layer the current layer, creating it if necessary. N Creates new layers. ON Turns on layers. OFF Turns off layers. S Sets current layer to existing layer. T Thaws layers. ? Lists specified layers and their associated colors, linetypes, and visibility.	LAYER:	Settings
Limits	Sets up the drawing size.	2 points Sets lower left/upper right drawing limits. ON Enables limits checking. OFF Disables limits checking.	SETTINGS	Utility
Line (L)	Draws straight lines.	(Return)(as reply to "From point:") Starts at end of previous line or arc. C (as reply to "To point:") Closes polygon. U (as reply to "To point:") Undoes segment.	DRAW	Draw
Linetype	Defines, loads, and sets the linetype.	? Lists a linetype library. C Creates a linetype definition. L Loads a linetype definition. S Sets current entity linetype. Set suboptions: name Sets entity linetype name. BYBLOCK Sets floating entity linetype. BYLAYER Uses layer's linetype for entities. ? Lists specified loaded linetypes.	SETTINGS	Utility
List	Provides data base information for objects that are selected.		INQUIRY	Utility
Load	Loads a file of user-defined shapes to be used with the Shape command.	? Lists the names of loaded Shape files.		
Ltscale	Regulates the scale factor to be applied to all linetypes within the drawing.		SETTINGS	
Measure	Inserts markers at measured distances along a selected object.	B Uses specified Block as marker.	EDIT	Modify
Menu	Loads a menu into the menu areas (screen, pull-down, tablet, and button).		UTILITY	

Command (Aliases)	Explanation	Options	Screen Menu	Pull-Down Menu
Minsert	Inserts multiple copies of a Block in a rectangular array.	fname Loads fname and forms a rectangular array of the resulting Block. fname=f Creates Block fname from file f and forms a rectangular array. ? Lists names of defined Blocks. C (as reply to X scale prompt) Specifies scale via two points (Corner specification of scale). XYZ (as reply to X scale prompt) Readies Mini-sert for X,Y, and Z scales. ~ Displays a File dialogue box.	BLOCKS & DRAW	
Mirror	Reflects selected entities about a user-specified Axis, vertical, horizontal or inclined.		EDIT	Modify
Move (M)	Moves selected entities to another location in the drawing.		EDIT	Modify
Mslide	Creates a slide of what is displayed on the screen.		UTILITY	
Mspace	Switches to Model Space from Paper Space.		MVIEW	
Multiple	Allows the next command to repeat until canceled.			
Mview	Sets up and controls viewports.	ON Turns selected viewport(s) on. Causes model to be regenerated in the selected viewport(s). OFF Turns selected viewport(s) off. Causes model to not be displayed in the selected viewport(s). Hideplot Causes hidden lines to be removed in selected viewport(s) during Paper Space plotting. Fit Creates a single viewport to fit the current Paper Space view. 2 Creates two viewports in specified area or fit to the current Paper Space view. 4 Creates four equal viewports in specified area or fit to the current Paper Space view. Restore Translates viewport configurations saved with the Vports command into individual viewport entities in Paper Space. <point> Creates a new viewport within the area specified by two points.	MVIEW & DISPLAY	Display

Command (Aliases)	Explanation	Options	Screen Menu	Pull-Down Menu
Offset	Reproduces curves or lines parallel to the one selected.	number Specifies offset distance. T Through: allows specification of a point through which the offset curve is to pass.	DRAW & EDIT	Modify
Oops	Recalls last set of entities previously erased.			Modify
Ortho F-8 Function Key	Restricts cursor to vertical or horizontal use.	ON Forces cursor to horizontal or vertical use. OFF Does not constrain cursor movement.		Settings
Osnap	Allows for selection of precise points on existing objects.	CEN Center of arc or circle. END Closest endpoint of arc or line. INS Insertion point of Text/ Block/Shape. INT Intersection of line/arc/circle. MID Midpoint of arc or line. NEA Nearest point of arc/circle/ line/point. NOD Node (point) NON None (off) PER Perpendicular to arc/line/circle. QUA Quadrant point of arc or circle. QUI Quick mode (first find, not closest). TAN Tangent to arc or circle.	**** & SETTINGS	Assist
'Pan (P)	Moves the display window.		DISPLAY	Display
Pedit (2D)	Allows from first point selected to second point selected.	C Closes to start point. D Decurves, or returns a spline curve to its control frame. F Fits curve to Polyline. J Joins to Polyline. O Opens a closed Polyline. S Uses the Polyline vertices as the frame for a spline curve (type set by SPLINETYPE). U Undoes one editing operation. W Sets uniform width for Polyline. X Exits Pedit command. E Edits vertices. B Sets first vertex for Break. G Go (performs Break or Straighten operation). I Inserts new vertex after current one. M Moves current vertex. N Makes next vertex current. P Makes previous vertex current.	EDIT	Modify

Command (Aliases)	Explanation	Options	Screen Menu	Pull-Down Menu
		R Regenerates the Polyline. S Sets first vertex for Straighten. T Sets tangent direction for current vertex. W Sets new width for following segment. X Exits vertex editing, or cancels Break/Straighten.		
Pedit (3D)	Allows editing of 3D polylines.	C Closes to start point. D Decurves, or returns a spline curve to its control frame. O Opens a closed Polyline. S Uses the Polyline vertices as the frame for a spline curve (type set by SPLINETYPE). U Undoes one editing operation. X Exits Pedit command. E Edits vertices. During vertex editing: B Sets first vertex for Break. B Go (performs Break or Straighten operation). I Inserts new vertex after current one. M Moves current vertex. N Makes next vertex current. P Makes previous vertex current. R Regenerates the Polyline. S Sets first vertex for Straighten. X Exits vertex editing, or cancels Break/Straighten.		
Pedit (Mesh)	Allows editing of 3D polygon meshes.	D Desmooth-restores original mesh. M Opens (or closes) the mesh in the M direction. N Opens (or closes) the mesh in the N direction. S Fits a smooth surface as defined by SURFTYPE. U Undoes one editing operation. X Exits Pedit command. E Edits Mesh vertices. D Moves down to previous vertex in M direction. L Moves left to previous vertex in N direction. M Repositions the marked vertex. N Moves to next vertex. P Moves to previous vertex. R Moves right to next vertex in N direction. RE Redisplays the polygon mesh. U Moves up to next vertex in M direction. X Exits vertex editing.		

Command (Aliases)	Explanation	Options	Screen Menu	Pull-Down Menu
Pface	Creates a 3D mesh of arbitrary complexity and surface characteristics.		SURFACES	
Plan	Puts the display in plan view (Vpoint 0,0,1) relative to either the current UCS, a specified UCS, or the WCS.	C Establishes a plan view of the current UCS. U Establishes a plan view of the specified UCS. W Establishes a plan view of the WCS.	DISPLAY	Display
Pline	Draws 2D Polylines.	H Sets new half-width. U Undoes previous segment. W Sets new line width. ⏎ Exits Pline command. C Closes with straight segment. L Segment length (continues previous segment). A Switches to arc mode.	DRAW	Draw
Pline (PL)		In arc mode: A Included angle. CE Center point. CL Closes with arc segment. D Starting direction. L Chord length, or switches to line mode. R Radius. S Second point of three-point arc.		
Plot	Plots a drawing on a pen plotter.		PLOT	File
Point	Draws single points on the drawing.		DRAW	Draw
Polygon	Creates regular polygons with the specified number of sides indicated.	E Specifies polygon by showing one edge. C Circumscribes around circle.	DRAW	Draw
Prplot	Plots a drawing on a printer plotter.		PLOT	File
Pspace (PS)	Switches to Paper Space.		MVIEW	
Purge	Removes unused Blocks, text styles, layers, linetypes, and dimension styles from the drawing. Must be the first command entered in the Drawing Editor.	A Purges all unused named objects. B Purges unused Blocks. D Purges unused dimstyles. LA Purges unused layers. LT Purges unused linetypes. SH Purges unused shape files. ST Purges unused text styles.	UTILITY	
Qtext	Replaces text with block.	ON Quick text mode on. OFF Quick text mode off.	SETTINGS	
Quit	Exits the Drawing Editor and returns to the AutoCAD Main Menu, discarding any changes to the drawing.		UTILITY	File
Redefine	Restores a built-in command deleted by Undefine.			

Command (Aliases)	Explanation	Options	Screen Menu	Pull-Down Menu
Redo	Reverses the previous command if it was U or Undo.		****	Utility
'Redraw (R)	Refreshes or cleans up the current viewport.		**** DISPLAY	Display
'Redrawall	Redraws all viewports.		DISPLAY	
Regen	Regenerates the current viewport.		DISPLAY	
Regenall	Regenerates all viewports.		DISPLAY	
Regenauto	Controls automatic regeneration performed by other commands.	ON Allows automatic regens. OFF Prevents automatic regens.	DISPLAY	
Rename	Changes the names associated with text styles, layers, linetypes, Blocks, views, UCSs, viewport configurations, and dimension styles.	B Renames Block. D Renames dimension style. LA Renames layer. LT Renames linetype. S Renames text style. U Renames UCS VI Renames view. VP Renames viewport configuration.	UTILITY & UCS:	
'Resume	Resumes an interrupted command script.		UTILITY/ SCRIPT	
Revsurf	Creates a 3D polygon mesh approximating a surface of revolution, by rotating a curve around a selected Axis.		SURFACES	
Rotate	Rotates existing objects to the angle selected.	R Rotates with respect to reference angles.	EDIT	Modify
Rscript	Restarts a command script from the beginning.		UTILITY/ SCRIPT	
Rulesurf	Creates a 3D polygon mesh approximating a ruled surface between two curves.		SURFACES	
Save	Updates the current drawing file without exiting the Drawing Editor.		SAVE:	File
Scale	Changes the size of existing objects to selected scale factor.	R Resizes with respect to reference size.	EDIT	Modify
Script	Executes a command script.		UTILITY	
Select	Groups objects into a selection set for use in subsequent commands.		EDIT	
'Setvar	Allows you to display or change the value of system variables.	? Lists specified system variables.	**** & SETTINGS	Settings
Sh	Allows access to internal operating system commands.		UTILITY/ EXTERNAL	
Shade	Shades model in the current viewport.		DISPLAY	Display

Appendix C

Command (Aliases)	Explanation	Options	Screen Menu	Pull-Down Menu
Shape	Draws predefined shapes.	? Lists available Shape names.	DRAW	
Shell	Allows access to other programs while running AutoCAD.		UTILITY/ EXTERNAL	
Sketch	Allows freehand sketching.	C Connect: restarts sketch at endpoint. E Erases (backs up over) temporary lines. P Raises/lowers sketching pen. Q Discards temporary lines, remains in Sketch. X Records temporary lines, exits Sketch. Draws line to current point.	DRAW	
Snap F-9 Function Key	Allows for precision alignment of points.	number Sets snap resolution. ON Aligns designated points. OFF Does not align designated points. A Sets aspect (differing X-Y spacing). R Rotates Snap Grid. S Selects style, standard or isometric.	SETTINGS	Settings
Solid	Creates filled-in polygons if fill is ON.		DRAW	
Status	Displays drawing setup.		INQUIRY	Utility
Stretch	Allows you to move a portion of a drawing while retaining connections to other parts of the drawing.		EDIT	Modify
Style	Sets up named text styles, with various combinations of font, mirroring, obliquing, and horizontal scaling.	? Lists specified currently defined text styles.	SETTINGS	
Tablet	Allows for configuration of a tablet menu or digitizing of an existing drawing.	ON Turns tablet mode on. OFF Turns tablet mode off. CAL Calibrates tablet for use in the current space.	SETTINGS	
Tabsurf	Creates a polygon mesh approximating a general tabulated surface defined by a path and a direction vector.		SURFACES	
Text	Enters text on the drawing.	J Prompts for justification options. S Lists or selects text style. A Aligns text between two points, with style-specified width factor; AutoCAD computes approriate height. C Centers text horizontally. F Fits text between two points, with specified height; AutoCAD computes an appropriate width factor. M Centers text horizontally and vertically.	DRAW	

Command (Aliases)	Explanation	Options	Screen Menu	Pull-Down Menu
		R Right-justifies text.		
		BL Bottom Left.		
		BC Bottom Center.		
		BR Bottom Right.		
		ML Middle Left.		
		MC Middle Center.		
		MR Middle Right.		
		TL Top Left.		
		TC Top Center.		
		TR Top Right.		
'Textscr F1 Function Key	Flips to the text display on single-screen systems. Used in command scripts and menus.			
Time	Indicates total elapsed time for each drawing.	D Displays current times. ON Starts user elapsed timer. OFF Stops user elapsed timer. R Resets user elapsed timer.	INQUIRY	
Trace	Creates solid lines of specified width.		DRAW	
Trim	Deletes portions of selected entities that cross a selected boundary edge.	U Undoes last trim operation.	EDIT	Modify
U	Reverses the effect of the previous command.		****	Utility
UCS	Defines or modifies the current User Coordinate System.	D Deletes one or more saved coordinate systems. E Sets a UCS with the same extrusion direction as that of the selected entity. O Shifts the origin of the current coordinate system. P Restores the previous UCS. R Restores a previously saved UCS. S Saves the current UCS. V Establishes a new UCS whose Z Axis is parallel to the current viewing direction. W Sets the current UCS equal to the WCS. X Rotates the current UCS around the X Axis. Y Rotates the current UCS around the Y Axis. Z Rotates the current UCS around the Z Axis. ZA Defines a UCS using an origin point and a point on the positive portion of the Z Axis. 3 Defines a UCS using an origin point, a point on the positive portion of the X Axis, and a point on the positive Y-portion of the X plane. ? Lists specified saved coordinate systems.	UCS: & SETTINGS	Settings

Appendix C

Command (Aliases)	Explanation	Options	Screen Menu	Pull-Down Menu
Ucsicon	Controls visibility and placement of the UCS icon, which indicates the origin and orientation of the current UCS. The options normally affect only the current viewport.	A Changes settings in all active viewports. N Displays the icon at the lower-left corner of the viewport. OR Displays the icon at the origin of the current UCS if possible. ON Enables the coordinate system icon.	SETTINGS	Settings
Undefine	Deletes the definition of a built-in AutoCAD command.			
Undo	Reverses the effect of multiple commands, and provides control over the Undo facility.	number Undoes the number most recent commands A Auto: controls treatment of menu items as Undo groups. B Back: undoes back to previous Undo mark. C Control: enables/disables the Undo mark. E End: terminates an Undo group. G Group: begins sequence to be treated as one command. M Mark: places marker in Undo file (for back).	EDIT	Utility
Units	Selects coordinate and angle display formats and precision.		SETTINGS	
'View	Saves the current graphics display and space as a named view, or restores a saved view and space to the display.	D Deletes named view. R Restores named view to screen. S Saves current display as named view. W Saves specified window as named view. ? Lists specified named views.	DISPLAY	
Viewports or Vports	Divides the AutoCAD graphics display into multiple viewports, each of which can contain a different view of the current drawing.	D Deletes a saved viewport configuration. J Joins (merges) two viewports. R Restores a saved viewport configuration. S Saves the current viewport configuration. S1 Displays a single viewport filling the entire graphics area. 2 Divides the current viewport into viewports. 3 Divides the current viewport into three viewports. 4 Divides the current viewport into four viewports. ? Lists the current and saved viewport configurations.		

Command (Aliases)	Explanation	Options	Screen Menu	Pull-Down Menu
Viewres	Adjusts the precision and speed of of circle and arc drawing on the monitor.		DISPLAY	
Vplayer	Sets viewport visibility for new and existing layers.	**?** Lists layers frozen in a selected viewport. **Freeze** Freezes specified layers in selected viewport(s). **Thaw** Thaws specified layers in selected viewport(s). **Reset** Resets specified layers to their default visibility. **Newfz** Creates new layers that are frozen in all viewports. **Vpvisdfit** Sets the default viewport visibility for existing layers.	MVIEW	
Vpoint	Selects the viewpoint for a 3D visualization.	**R** Selects viewpoint via two rotation angles. **(Return)** Selects viewpoint via compass and axes tripod. **x,y,z** Specifies viewpoint.	DISPLAY	Display
Vslide	Displays a previously created slide file.	**file** Views slide. ***file** Preloads next Vslide you will view.	UTILITY/ SLIDES	
Wblock	Creates a Block as a separate drawing.	**name** Writes specified Block Definition. **=** Block name same as file name. ***** Writes entire drawing. **(Return)** Writes selected objects.	BLOCKS	
Xbind	Permanently adds a selected subset of an Xref's dependent symbols to your drawing.	**Block** Adds a Block. **Dimstyle** Adds a dimstyle. **Layer** Adds a layer. **Ltype** Adds a linetype. **Style** Adds a style.	SCREEN/ BLOCKS	Draw
Xref	Allows you to work with other AutoCAD drawings without adding them permanently to your drawing and without altering their contents.	**Attach** Attaches a new Xref or inserts a copy of an Xref that you have already attached. **Bind** Makes an Xref a permanent part of your drawing. **Detach** Removes an Xref from your drawing. **Path** Allows you to view and edit the filename AutoCAD uses when loading a particular Xref.	BLOCKS	Draw

Appendix C

Command (Aliases)	Explanation	Options	Screen Menu	Pull-Down Menu
		Reload Updates one or more Xrefs at any time, without leaving and re-entering the Drawing Editor. ? Lists Xrefs in your drawing and the drawing associated with each one.		
'Zoom (Z)	Increases or reduces the display area of a drawing.	number Multiplier from original scale. numberX Multiplier from current scale. number XP Scale relative to Paper Space. A All C Center D Dynamic Pan Zoom E Extents ("drawing uses") L Lower left corner P Previous V Virtual screen maximum W Window	DISPLAY	Display
3Dface	Draws 3D plane sections.	I Makes the following edge invisible.	DRAW & SURFACE	Draw
3Dmesh	Defines a 3D polygon mesh (by specifying its size in terms of M and N) and the location of each vertex in the mesh.		SURFACES	
3Dpoly	Creates a 3D Polyline.	C Closes the Polyline back to the first point. U Undoes (deletes) the last segment entered. (Return) Exits 3Dpoly command.	SURFACES	Draw

DIMENSIONING COMMANDS

Command	Explanation
Aligned	Aligns dimension parallel with objects.
Angular	Draws an arc to show the angle between two nonparallel lines or three specified points.
Baseline	Continues a linear dimension from the baseline (first extension line) of the previous or selected dimension.
Center	Draws a circle/arc center mark or center lines.
Continue	Continues a linear dimension from the second extension line of the previous dimension.
Diameter	Dimensions the diameter of a circle or arc.
Exit	Returns to the normal Drawing Editor command mode.
Hometext	Restores the text of an associate dimension to its default (home) location if you have moved it.
Leader	Draws a line with an arrowhead placement of dimension text.
Newtext	Replaces the text of existing associative dimensions.
Oblique	Adjusts obliquing angle of a linear associative dimension's extension lines.
Ordinate	Creates ordinate point associative dimensions.
Override	Overrides a subset of the dimension variable settings associated with selected dimension entities.
Radius	Dimensions the radius of a circle or arc, with an optional center mark or center lines.
Redraw	Redraws the entire display, erasing any marker blips that were present (just like the normal REDRAW command).
Restore	Restores a specified dimension style by name or selection.
Rotate	Generates a linear dimension with the dimension line drawn at a specified angle.
Save	Saves a group of dimension variables as a named dimension style.
Status	Displays all dimensioning variables and their current values.
Style	Switches to a new text style.
Tedit	Allows repositioning and rotation of text items in an associative dimension without affecting other dimension subentities.
Trotate	Allows specification of a rotation angle for the text items of several associative dimensions at one time.

Command	Explanation
Undo	Undoes any changes made by the most recent dimensioning command.
Update	Updates existing associative dimension entities to use the current settings of the dimension variables, the current text style, and the current Units settings.
Variables	Lists the settings of dimension variables associated with a particular dimension style.
Vertical	Generates a linear dimension with a vertical dimension line.

DIMENSIONING VARIABLES

Name	Description	Type	Default
DIMALT	Alternate Units.	Switch	Off
DIMALTD	Alternate Units Decimal Places.	Integer	2
DIMALTF	Alternate Units Scale Factor.	Scale	25.4
DIMAPOST	Alternate Units Text Suffix.	String	None
DIMASO	Associative Dimensioning.	Switch	On
DIMASZ	Arrow Size.	Distance	0.18
DIMBLK	Arrow Block.	String	None
DIMBLK1	Separate Arrow Block 1.	String	None
DIMBLK2	Separate Arrow Block 2.	String	None
DIMCEN	Center Mark Size.	Distance	0.09
DIMCLRD	Dimension Line Color.	Color number	BYBLOCK
DIMCLRE	Extension Line Color.	Color number	BYBLOCK
DIMCLRT	Dimension Text Color.	Color number	BYBLOCK
DIMDLE	Dimension Line Extension.	Distance	0.0
DIMDLI	Dimension Line Increment.	Distance	0.38
DIMEXE	Extension Line Extension.	Distance	0.18
DIMEXO	Extension Line Offset.	Distance	0.0625
DIMGAP	Dimension Line Gap.	Distance	0.09
DIMLFAC	Length Factor.	Scale	1.0
DIMLIM	Limits Dimensioning.	Switch	Off
DIMPOST	Dimension Text Suffix.	String	None
DIMRND	Rounding Value.	Scaled distance	0.0
DIMSAH	Separate Arrow Blocks.	Switch	Off
DIMSCALE	Dimension Feature Scale Factor.	Switch	1.0
DIMSE1	Suppress Extension Line 1.	Switch	Off
DIMSE2	Suppress Extension Line 2.	Switch	Off
DIMSHO	Show Dragged Dimension.	Switch	On
DIMSOXD	Suppress Outside Dimension Lines.	Switch	Off
DIMSTYLE	Dimension Style.	Name	*UNNAMED
DIMTAD	Text Above Dimension Line	Switch	Off

Name	Description	Type	Default
DIMTFAC	Tolerance Text Scale Factor.	Scale	1.0
DIMTIH	Text Inside Horizontal.	Switch	On
DIMTIX	Text Inside Extension Lines.	Switch	Off
DIMTM	Minus Tolerance Value.	Scaled distance	0.0
DIMTP	Plus Tolerance Value.	Scaled distance	0.0
DIMTOFL	Text Outside, Force Line Inside.	Switch	Off
DIMTOH	Text Outside Horizontal.	Switch	On
DIMTOL	Tolerance Dimensioning.	Switch	Off
DIMTSZ	Tick Size.	Distance	0.0
DIMTVP	Text Vertical Position.	Scale	0.0
DIMTXT	Text Size.	Distance	0.18
DIMZIN	Zero Suppression.	Integer	0

APPENDIX
D

AutoCAD Menus

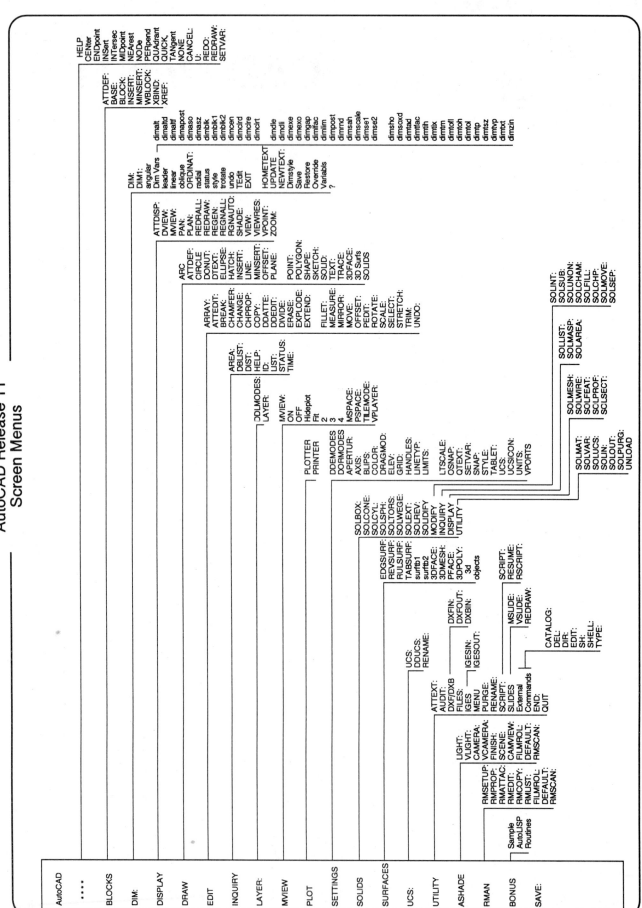

AutoCAD Release 11
Screen Menus

Appendix D

AutoCAD® Release 11
Pull-Down Menus

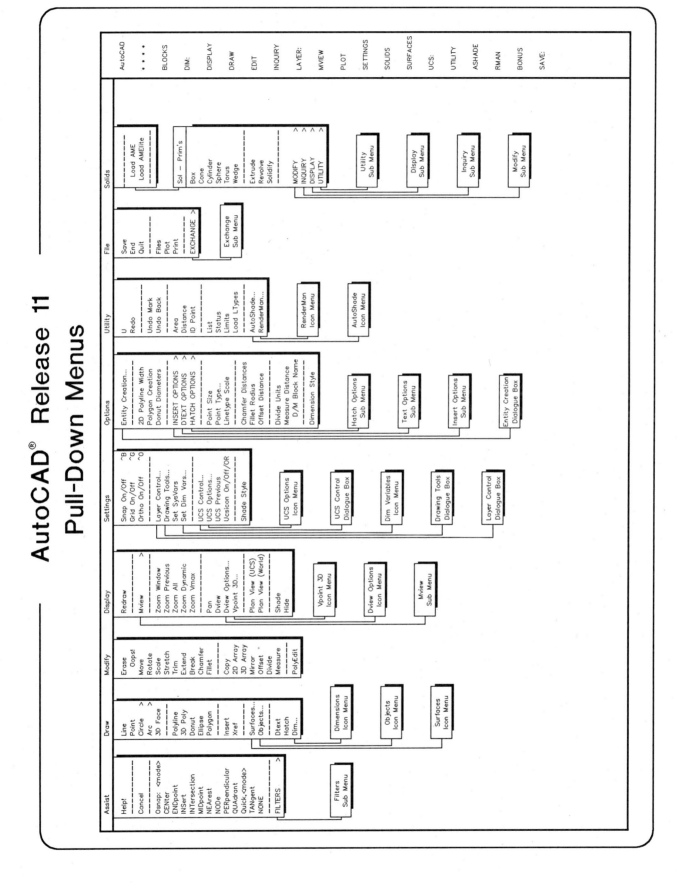

APPENDIX

File Utility Menu

The FILES command allows you to access files without leaving the AutoCAD Drawing Editor. Using this command you are able to list a disk directory, delete, copy, rename, and unlock files. If you are at the Main Menu you can use these same functions through the File Utility Menu, selection number 6 on the Main Menu.

Main Menu

0. Exit AutoCAD
1. Begin a NEW drawing
2. Edit an EXISTING drawing
3. Plot a drawing
4. Printer Plot a drawing
5. Configure AutoCAD
6. File Utilities
7. Compile shape/font description file
8. Convert old drawing file
9. Recover damaged drawing

Enter selection: **6**

File Utility Menu

0. Exit File Utility Menu
1. List Drawing files
2. List user specified files
3. Delete files
4. Rename files
5. Copy file
6. Unlock file

Enter selection (0 to 6) <0>:

Listing Drawing Filenames

Selection 1 allows you to list the AutoCAD drawing files (.DWG) in a directory. The prompt requests you to:

Enter directory path:

Appendix E

You will need to enter the directory prefix, or press ⏎ to indicate the current directory. After listing the drawing files you are returned to the File Utility Menu. Again, you will see the prompt:

Enter selection (0 to 6) <0>:

Listing User-Specified Files

Selection 2 allows you to search for any specific filename. The prompt requests you to:

Enter file search specification:

You can include a directory path as in \drawing\house.bak. A listing of files created or used by AutoCAD is shown below. You may list a single file or, by using the wild card characters, a list of files.

FILE EXTENSION	EXPLANATION
.adt	Audit report file
.bak	Drawing backup file
.bkn	Emergency backup file
.cfg	Configuration file
.dwg	Drawing file
.dxb	Binary drawing interchange file
.dxf	Drawing interchange file
.dxx	Attribute extract file
.flm	Filmroll file (for AutoShade)
.hlp	Help file
.hdx	Help index file
.igs	IGES interchange file
.lin	Linetype library file
.lsp	AutoLISP program library file
.lst	Printer plot output file
.mat	Materials file
.mnu	Menu file
.mnx	Compiled menu file
.msg	Message file
.old	Original version of converted drawing
.pat	Hatch pattern library file
.pgp	Program parameters file
.plt	Plot output file
.prp	ADI printer plotter output file
.pwd	Login file
.scr	Command script file
.shp	Shape/font definition source file
.slb	Slide library file
.sld	Slide file
.txt	Attribute extract file
.unt	Units file
.xlg	External references log file

After completing the file search you will be returned to the File Utility Menu and prompted:

Enter selection (0 to 6) <0>:

Deleting Files

When you select number 3 (Delete files) you will be prompted:

Enter file deletion specification:

You may list an individual file to delete, or by using the wild card characters, a list of files. After indicating the file to delete AutoCAD prompts:

Delete filename.ext? <N>

To delete this file press **Y** and ⏎. If you do not want to delete this file, simply press ⏎ to accept the default in <N> for no.

After completing the file deletion you will be returned to the File Utility Menu and prompted:

Enter selection (0 to 6) <0>:

Renaming Files

Selection number 4 allows you to rename a file. When you select Rename files you are prompted:

Enter current filename: *enter filename.extension*
Enter new filename: *enter the new filename.extension*

For example, if you lose the drawing you are currently working in (HOUSE.DWG), but you had saved it a few minutes earlier, you can rename the backup file and proceed to finish the drawing. An example of this appear as follows:

Enter current filename: **house.bak**
Enter new filename: **house.dwg**

After completing the file renaming you will be returned to the File Utility Menu and prompted:

Enter selection (0 to 6) <0>:

Copying Files

Selection number 5 allows you to make a copy of an existing file. When you select Copy file, you are prompted:

Enter name of source file: **house.dwg**
Enter name or destination file: **A: house.dwg**

This would copy the file to the A drive.

After completing the file copy you would be returned to the File Utility Menu and prompted:

Enter selection (0 to 6) <0>:

Unlocking Files

Selection number 6 allows you to unlock a file or a group of files if you use a wild card. When you select Unlock file you are prompted as follows:

Enter locked file(s) specification: *enter the filename and extension*

If you were unlocking the file HOUSE.DWG, the prompt would appear as follows:

The file: house.dwg was locked by *name of person who locked the file including the time and date it was locked*
Do you still wish to unlock it? <Y> ⏎
Lock was successfully removed.
1 files unlocked.
Press RETURN to continue:

You will again see the prompt:

Enter selection(0 to 6)<0>: **0**

This selection takes you back to the Main Menu.

APPENDIX

Error Messages

The most common error messages you are likely to see when using AutoCAD are the result of invalid input. The following are some of the messages you will see while working in the Drawing Editor:

Invalid input
Point or option keyword required
Requires numeric distance or two points.
Invalid

The above messages appear if you enter wrong information. In most cases, the prompt for the required input is repeated, and you can try again.

Disk Full Handling

When there is insufficient disk space on the drive containing the drawing file, AutoCAD displays the following message:

<Disk almost full>

If you see the above message, you have three choices:

1. End or Quit the drawing immediately.
2. Use the FILES command and delete some of the unwanted files from the drive that contains the drawing file.
3. Try changing the option under the UNDO command to None and it will free up some space in your drive.

Disaster Handling

AutoCAD updates the drawing data base after each command that adds, deletes, or changes anything in the drawing. The drawing data base is thus always up-to-date when the user begins a new command. If, for some reason, AutoCAD encounters a problem during execution of a command and cannot continue, one of the following messages is displayed:

Internal error *(followed by lot of numbers)*

or

Fatal error

Usually, an additional short message is displayed giving an error code. Following this, AutoCAD displays:

> AutoCAD cannot continue, but any changes to your drawing made up to the start of the last command can be saved. Do you want to save your changes? <Y>

If you answer **Y** or hit ⏎, AutoCAD writes the drawing data base to disk before exiting. If this operation is successful, the following message will appear:

> Drawing file successfully saved

If AutoCAD terminates with an internal error or fatal error, it tries to record diagnostic information concerning the error in the file ACAD.ERR. When reporting problems to Autodesk, the user should always include a printout of this file.

AutoCAD identifies drawing files saved after a Drawing Editor crash. The Drawing Editor refuses to edit such files until they are loaded with Main Menu task number 9 (Recover damaged drawing). Refer to Appendix G for additional information about recovery of a damaged drawing.

APPENDIX

G Recovery of Damaged Drawings

Task 9 of the Main Menu allows the user to recover a damaged drawing. Once the name has been given, the procedure is automatic, and the drawing is loaded. Block definitions, text fonts, linetypes, etc. are checked for invalid information (resulting from hardware problems, power surge, user error, software bug, etc.). Warning messages are displayed from the recovery and audit procedure to help the user in validation and correction. The output from the audit is also written to a log file. It puts this report file in the same directory as the current drawing, using the current drawing's name with the file extension .ADT.

Unfortunately, there are cases when the drawing is so badly damaged or corrupted that the drawing recovery will not be successful.

You can also use the AUDIT command while you are in the Drawing Editor, as a diagnostic tool in examining a drawing to determine if it is valid, and optionally to correct errors. For every error detected, AutoCAD recommends action to correct it. It also generates a report and places it in the current directory under the current drawing's name with the file extension .ADT. To invoke the command, type **AUDIT** at the "Command:" prompt:

Command: **audit**
Fix any errors detected? <N>:

By answering **Y**, AutoCAD reports the number of errors, gives a detailed description of the errors and recommendations for fixing the errors. If you answer **N**, then AutoCAD will report the errors, but will not fix them at the same time.

APPENDIX

H

System Variables

This is a complete listing of the AutoCAD system variables. Each variable has an associated type: integer, real, point, or text string. These variables can be examined and changed (unless read-only) by means of the SETVAR command and AutoLISP's (getvar and setvar) functions. Many of the system variables are saved across editing sessions; as indicated in the table, some are saved in the drawing itself, while others are saved in the AutoCAD general configuration file, ACAD.CFG.

Variable	Default Setting	Type	Saved in	Explanation
ACADPREFIX	" "	String	Read Only	The directory path, if any specified by the ACAD environment variable, with path separators appended if necessary (read-only).
ACADVER	"Z.0.9A"	String	11c2	This is the AutoCAD version number, which can only have values like "11" or "11a" (read-only). Note that this differs from the DXF file $ACADVER header variable, which contains the drawing data base level number.
AFLAGS	0	Integer		Attribute flags bit-code for ATTDEF command (sum of the following): 1 = Invisible 2 = Constant 4 = Verify 8 = Preset
ANGBASE	0	Real	Drawing	Angle 0 direction (with respect to the current UCS).
ANGDIR	0	Drawing	Drawing	1 = clockwise angles, 0 = counterclockwise (with respect to the current UCS).
APERTURE	3	Integer	Config	Object Snap target height, in pixels (default value = 10).
AREA	0.0000	Real		True area computed by Area, List, or Dblist (read-only).
ATTDIA	0	Integer	Drawing	1 causes the INSERT command to use a dialogue box for entry of attribute values; 0 to issue prompts.
ATTMODE	1	Integer	Drawing	Attribute display mode (0 = off, 1 = normal, 2 = 0).

(Reprinted with permission from Autodesk Inc.)   887

Appendix H

Variable	Default Setting	Type	Saved in	Explanation
ATTREQ	1	Integer	Drawing	0 assumes defaults for the values of all attributes during Insert of Blocks; 1 enables prompts (or dialogue box) for Attribute values, as selected by ATTDIA.
AUNITS	0	Integer	Drawing	Angular units mode (0 = decimal degrees, 1 = degrees/minutes/seconds, 2 = grads, 3 = radians, 4 = surveyor's units).
AUPREC	0	Integer	Drawing	Angular units decimal places.
AXISMODE	0	Integer	Drawing	Axis display on if 1, off if 0.
AXISUNIT	0.0000 0.0000	2D point	Drawing	Axis spacing, X and Y.
BACKZ	0.0000	Real	Drawing	Back clipping plane offset for the current viewport, in drawing units. Meaningful only if the back clipping bit in VIEWMODE is on. The distance of the back clipping plane from the camera point can be found by subtracting BACKZ from the camera-to-target distance (read-only).
BLIPMODE	1	Integer	Drawing	Marker blips on if 1, off is 0.
CDATE	199112 02:1354 1096	Real		Calendar date/time (read-only)
CECOLOR	"BY-LAYER" 0.0000	String	Drawing	Current entity color (read-only).
CELTYPE		String	Drawing	Current entity linetype (read-only).
CHAMFERA		Real	Drawing	First chamfer distance.
CHAMFERB	0.0000	Real	Drawing	Second chamfer distance.
CLAYER	"0"	String	Drawing	Current layer (read-only).
CMDECHO	1	Integer		When the AutoLISP (command) function is used, prompts and input are echoed if this variable is 1, but not if it is 0.
COORDS	0	Integer	Drawing	If 0, coordinate display is updated on point picks only. If 1, display of absolute coordinates is continuously updated. If 2, distance and angle from last point are displayed when a distance or angle is requested.
CVPORT	2	Integer	Drawing	The identification number of the current viewport.
DATE	24485 93.579 59931	Real		Julian date/time (read-only)
DISTANCE	0.0000	Real		Distance computed by DIST command (read-only).

Variable	Default Setting	Type	Saved in	Explanation
DRAGMODE	2	Integer	Drawing	0 = no dragging, 1 = on if requested, 2 = auto.
DRAGP1	10	Integer	Config	Regen-drag input sampling rate; (default value = 10).
DRAGP2	25	Integer	Config	Fast-drag input sampling rate; (default value = 25).
DWGNAME	"ACAD"	String		Drawing name as entered by the user. If the user-specified a drive/directory prefix, it is included as well (read-only).
DWGPREFIX	"C:/ ACADII\"	String		Drive/directory prefix for drawing (read-only).
ELEVATION	0.0000	Real	Drawing	Current 3D elevation, relative to the current UCS for the current space.
ERRNO		Integer		Code for errors caused by on-line programs such as AutoLISP and ADS applications (see ADS Programmer's Reference Manual).
EXPERT	0	Integer		Controls the issuance of certain "are you sure?" prompts, as indicated next.

EXPERT (continued):

0 = Issues all prompts normally.
1 = Suppresses "About to regen, proceed?" and "Really want to turn the current layer off?"
2 = Suppresses the preceding prompts and Block's "Block already defined. Redefine it?" and Save/Wblock's "A drawing with this name already exists. Overwrite it?"
3 = Suppresses the preceding prompts and those issued by linetype if you try to load a linetype that is already loaded or create a new linetype in a file that already defines it.
4 = Suppresses the preceding prompts and those issued by "Ucs Save" and "Vports Save" if the name you supply already exists.
5 = Suppresses the preceding prompts and those issued by "Dim Save" and "Dim Override" if the dimension style name you supply already exists (the entries are redefined).

When a prompt is suppressed, EXPERT, the operation in question, is performed as though you had responded **Y** to the prompt. In the future, values greater than 5 may be used to suppress additional safety prompts. The setting of EXPERT can affect scripts, menu macros, AutoLISP, and the command functions. The default value is 0.

Variable	Default Setting	Type	Saved in	Explanation
EXTMAX	-1.0000 E+120, -1.000 E+20, -1.0000 E+20	3D point	Drawing	Upper right drawing uses extents. Expands outward as new objects are drawn; shrinks only by ZOOM All or ZOOM Extents. Reported in World coordinates for the current space (read-only).

Variable	Default Setting	Type	Saved in	Explanation
EXTMIN	1.0000	3D point	Drawing	Lower left drawing uses extents. Expands outward as new objects are drawn; shrinks only by ZOOM All or ZOOM Extents. Reported in World coordinates for the current space (read-only).
FILEDIA	1	Integer	Config	1 = Use file dialogue boxes if possible; 0 = do not use file dialogue boxes unless requested via ~ (tilde).
FILLETRAD	0.0000	Real	Drawing	Fillet radius.
FILLMODE	1	Integer	Drawing	Fill mode on if 1, off if 0.
FRONTZ	0.0000	Real	Drawing	Front clipping plane offset for the current viewport, in drawing units. Meaningful only if the front clipping bit in VIEWMODE is On and the Front clip not at eye bit is also ON. The distance of the front clipping bit from the camera point can be found by subtracting FRONTZ from the camera-to-target distance (read-only).
GRIDMORE	0	Integer	Drawing	1 = Grid on for current viewport, X and Y.
GRIDUNIT	0.0000, 0.0000	2D point	Drawing	Grid spacing for current viewport, X and Y.
HANDLES	0	Integer	Drawing	If 0, entity handles are disabled, if 1, handles are on (read-only).
HIGHLIGHT	1	Integer		Object selection highlighting on if 1, off if 0.
INSBASE	0.0000, 0.0000, 0.0000 0.0000, 0.0000, 0.0000	3D point	Drawing	Insertion base point (set by BASE command) expressed in UCS coordinates for the current space.
LASTANGLE	0	Real		The end angle of the last arc entered, relative to the XY plane of the current UCS for the current space (read-only).
LASTPOINT	0.0000, 0.0000, 0.0000	3D point		The last point entered, expressed in UCS coordinates for the current space. Referenced by @ during keyboard entry.
LENSLENGTH	50.0000	Real	Drawing	Length of the lens (in millimeters) used in perspective viewing, for current viewport (read-only).
LIMCHECK	0	Integer	Drawing	Limits checking for the current space. On if 1, off if 0.
LIMMAX	12,000, 9,000	2D point	Drawing	Upper right drawing limits for the current space, expressed in World coordinates.
LIMMIN	0.0000, 0.0000	2D point	Drawing	Lower-left drawing limits for the current space, expressed in World coordinates.
LTSCALE	1,000	Real	Drawing	Linear units mode (1 = scientific, 2 = decimal, 3 = engineering, 4 = architectural, 5 = fractional).

Variable	Default Setting	Type	Saved in	Explanation
LUNITS	2	Integer	Drawing	Linear units decimal places or denominator.
MAXACTVP	16	Integer		Maximum number of viewports to regenerate at one time (read-only).
MAXSORT	200	Integer	Config	Maximum number of symbol/file names to be sorted by listing commands. If the total number of items exceeds this number, then none of the items are sorted (dflt. val=200).
MENUECHO	0	Integer		Menu echo/prompt control bits (sum of the following): 1 = Suppresses echo of menu items (^P in a menu item toggles echoing). 2 = Suppresses printing of system prompts during menu. 4 = Disables ^P toggle of menu echoing. The default value is 0 (all menu items and style prompts are displayed).
MENUNAME	"Acad"	Integer		The name of the currently loaded menu file. Includes a drive/path prefix if you entered it (read-only).
MIRRTEXT	1	Integer	Drawing	Mirror reflects text if nonzero, retains text direction if 0.
ORTHOMODE	0	Integer	Drawing	Ortho mode on if 1, off if 0.
OSMODE	0	Integer	Drawing	Object Snap modes bit-code (sum of the following): 1 = Endpoint 2 = Midpoint 4 = Center 8 = Node 16 = Quadrant 32 = Intersection 64 = Insertion 128 = Perpendicular 256 = Tangent 512 = Nearest 1024 = Quick
PDMODE	0	Integer	Drawing	Point entity display mode.
PDSIZE	0.0000	Real	Drawing	Point entity display size.
PERIMETER	0.0000	Real		Perimeter computed by Area, List, or Dblist (read-only).
PFACEMAX	4	Integer		Maximum number of vertices per face (read-only).
PICKBOX	3	Integer	Config	Object selection target height, in pixels.
POPUPS	1	Integer		1 if the currently configured display driver supports dialogue boxes, the menu bar, pull-down menus, and icon menus. 0 if these Advanced User Interface features are not available (read-only).

Variable	Default Setting	Type	Saved in	Explanation
QTEXTMODE	0	Integer	Drawing	Quick text mode on if 1, off if 0.
REGENMODE	1	Integer	Drawing	Regenauto on if 1, off if 0.
SCREENSIZE	573. 0000, 573. 0000, 415. 0000	2D point		Current viewpoint size in pixels, X and Y (read-only).
SHADEDGE	3	Integer	Drawing	0 = faces shaded, edges not highlighted. 1 = faces shaded, edges drawn in background color. 2 = faces not filled, edges in entity color. 3 = faces in entity color, edges in background color.
SHADEDIF	70	Integer	Drawing	Ratio of ambient to diffuse light (in percent of ambient light).
SKETCHINC	0.1000	Real	Drawing	Sketch record increment.
SKPOLY	0	Integer	Drawing	Sketch generates lines if 0, Polylines if 1.
SNAPANG	0	Real	Drawing	Snap/Grid rotation angle (UCS-relative) for the current viewport.
SNAPBASE	0.0000, 0.0000	2D point	Drawing	Snap/Grid origin point for the current viewport (in UCS XY coordinates).
SNAPISOPAIR	0	Integer	Drawing	Current isometric plane (0 = left, 1 = top, 2 = right) for the current viewport.
SNAPMODE	0	Integer	Drawing	1 = Snap on for current viewport; 0 = Snap off.
SNAPSTYL	0	Integer	Drawing	Snap style for current viewport (0 = standard, 1 = isometric).
SNAPUNIT	1.0000, 1.0000	2D point	Drawing	Snap spacing for current viewport, X and Y.
SPLFRAME	0	Integer	Drawing	If = 1: - the control polygon for spline fit Polylines is to be displayed. - only the defining mesh of a surface fit polygon mesh is displayed (the fit surface is not displayed). - invisible edges of 3D faces are displayed.
SPLFRAME	0	Integer	Drawing	If = 0: - does not display the control polygon for spline fit Polylines. - displays the fit surface of a polygon mesh, not the defining mesh. - does not display the invisible edges of 3D faces.
SPLINESEGS	8	Integer	Drawing	The number of line segments to be generated for each spline patch.

Variable	Default Setting	Type	Saved in	Explanation
SPLINETYPE	6	Integer	Drawing	Type of spline curve to be generated by Pedit Spline. The valid values are: 5 = quadratic B-spline 6 = cubic B-spline
SURFTAB1	6	Integer	Drawing	Number of tabulations to be generated for Rulesurf and Tabsurf. Also mesh density in the M direction for Resurf and Edgesurf.
SURFTAB2	6	Integer	Drawing	Mesh density in the N direction for Revsurf and Edgesurf.
SURFTYPE	6	Integer	Drawing	Type of surface fitting to be performed by Pedit Smooth. The valid values are: 5 = quadratic B-spline surface 6 = cubic B-spline surface 8 = Bezier surface
SURFU	6	Integer	Drawing	Surface density in the M direction.
SURFV	6	Integer	Drawing	Surface density in the N direction.
TARGET	0.0000, 0.0000, 0.0000	3D point	Drawing	Location (in UCS coordinates) of the target (look-at) point for the current viewport (read-only).
TDCREATE	244 8080. 5342 4653	Real	Drawing	Time and date of drawing creation (read-only)
TDINDWD	0.0027 8194	Real	Drawing	Total editing time (read-only)
TDUPDATE	244 8080. 5345 7246	Real	Drawing	Time and date of last update/save (read-only)
TDSURTIMER	0.0026 5475	Real	Drawing	User elapsed timer (read-only)
TEMPPREFIX	" "	String		This variable contains the directory name (if any) configured for placement of temporary files, with a path separator appended if necessary (read-only).
TEXTEVAL	0	Integer		If = 0, all responses to prompts for text strings and Attribute values are taken literally. If = 1, text starting with "(" or "!" is evaluated as an AutoLISP expression, as for nontextual input. Note: The DTEXT command takes all input literally, regardless of the setting of TEXTEVAL.
TEXTSIZE	0.2000	Real	Drawing	The default height for new text entities drawn with the current text style (meaningless if the style has a fixed height).
TEXTSTYLE	"STANDARD"	String	Drawing	This variable contains the name of the current text style (read-only).

Appendix H

Variable	Default Setting	Type	Saved in	Explanation
THICKNESS	0.0000	Real	Drawing	Current 3D thickness.
TILEMODE	1	Integer	Drawing	1 = Release 10 compatibility mode (uses Vports) 0 = Enables Paper Space and Viewport entities (uses MVIEW).
TRACEWID	0.0500	Real	Drawing	Default trace width.
UCSFOLLOW	0	Integer	Drawing	The setting of UCSFOLLOW is maintained separately for both spaces and can be accessed in either space, but the setting is ignored while in Paper Space (it is always treated as if set to 0).
UCSICON	0	Integer	Drawing	The coordinate system icon bit-code for the current viewport (sum of the following): 1 = On – icon display enabled 2 = Origin – if icon display is enabled, the icon floats to the UCS origin if possible.
UCSNAME	" "	String	Drawing	Name of the current coordinate system for the current space. Returns a null string if the current UCS is unnamed (read-only).
UCSORG	0.0000, 0.0000, 0.0000	3D point	Drawing	The origin point of the current coordinate system for the current space. This value is always returned in World coordinates (read-only).
UCSXDIR	1.0000, 0.0000, 0.0000	3D point	Drawing	The X direction of the current UCS for the current space (read-only).
UCSYDIR	0.0000, 1.0000, 0.0000	3D point	Drawing	The Y direction of the current UCS for the current space (read-only).
UNITMODE	0	Integer	Drawing	0 = Displays fractional, feet and inches, and surveyor's angles as previously. 1 = Displays fractional, feet and inches, and surveyor's angles in input format.
USERI1 - 5		Integer	Drawing	Five variables for storage and retrieval of real numbers. Intended for use by third-party developers.
USERR1 - 5		Real	Drawing	Five variables for storage and retrieval of real numbers. Intended for use by third-party developers.
VIEWCTR	6.2133, 4.5000 0.0000	3D point	Drawing	Center of view in current viewport, expressed in UCS coordinates (read-only).
VIEWDIR	0.0000, 0.0000, 1.0000	3D point	Drawing	The current viewport's viewing direction expressed in World coordinates. This describes the camera point as a 3D offset from the TARGET point (read-only).

Variable	Default Setting	Type	Saved in	Explanation
VIEWMODE	0	Integer	Drawing	Viewing mode bit-code for the current viewport (read-only). The value is the sum of the following: 1 = perspective view active 2 = front clipping on 4 = back clipping on 8 = UCS follow mode 16 = Front clip not at eye. If On, the front clip distance (FRONTZ) determines the front clipping plane. If Off, FRONZ is ignored and the front clipping is set to pass through the camera point (i.e., vectors behind the camera are not displayed). This flag is ignored if the front clipping bit (2) is off.
VIEWSIZE	9.000	Real	Drawing	Height of view in current viewport, expressed in drawing units (read-only).
VIEWTWIST	0	Real	Drawing	View twist angle for the current viewport (read-only).
VSMAX	12.4265, 9.0000, 0.0000	3D point		The upper right corner of the current viewport's virtual screen, expressed in UCS coordinates (read-only).
VSMIN	0.0000, 0.0000, 0.0000	3D point		The lower left corner of the current viewport's virtual screen, expressed in UCS coordinates (read-only).
WORDDUCS	1	Integer		If = 1, the current UCS is the same as the WCS. If = 0, it is not (read-only).
WORLDVIEW	1	Integer	Drawing	Dview and Vpoint command input is relative to the current UCS. If this variable is set to 1, the current UCS is changed to the WCS for the duration of a DVIEW or VPOINT command. Default value = 1.

APPENDIX

I

Hatch Patterns

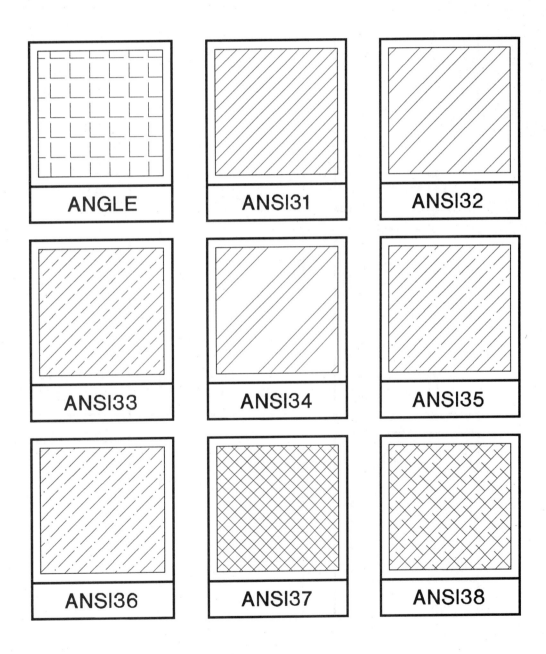

ANGLE	ANSI31	ANSI32
ANSI33	ANSI34	ANSI35
ANSI36	ANSI37	ANSI38

897

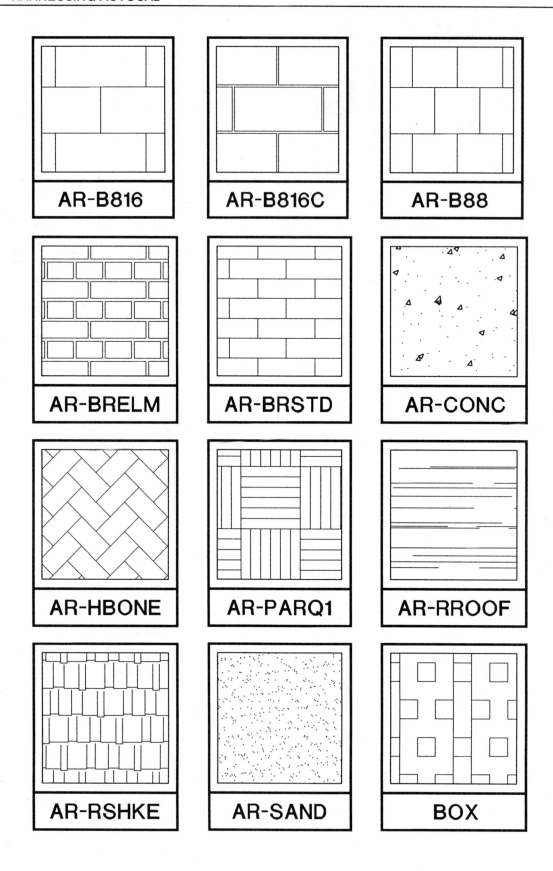

AR-B816

AR-B816C

AR-B88

AR-BRELM

AR-BRSTD

AR-CONC

AR-HBONE

AR-PARQ1

AR-RROOF

AR-RSHKE

AR-SAND

BOX

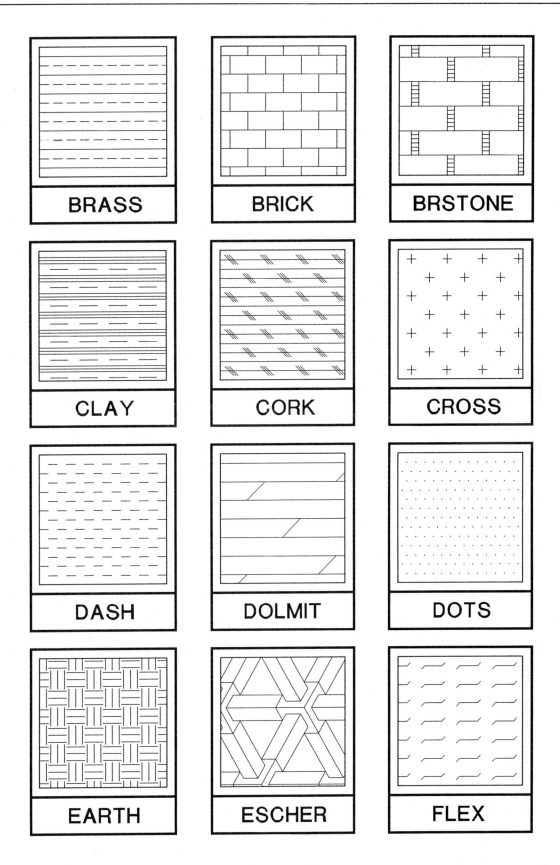

BRASS	BRICK	BRSTONE
CLAY	CORK	CROSS
DASH	DOLMIT	DOTS
EARTH	ESCHER	FLEX

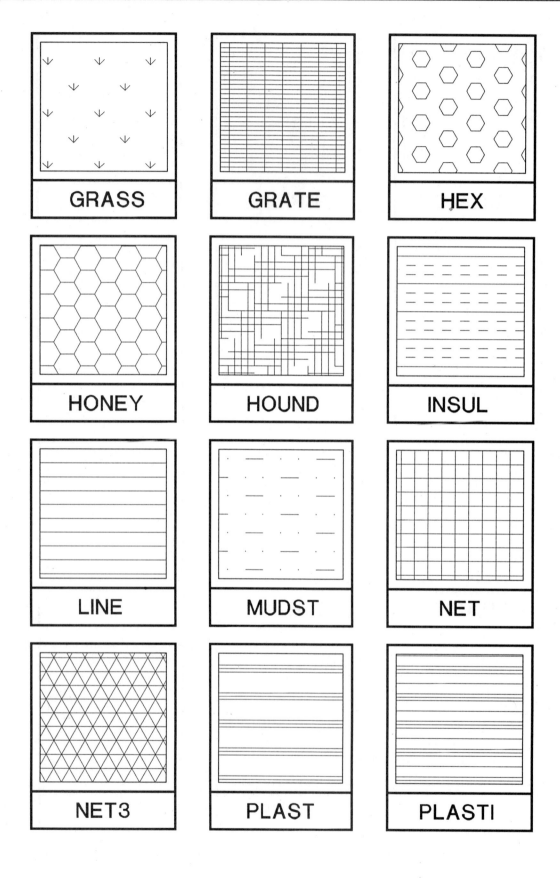

GRASS

GRATE

HEX

HONEY

HOUND

INSUL

LINE

MUDST

NET

NET3

PLAST

PLASTI

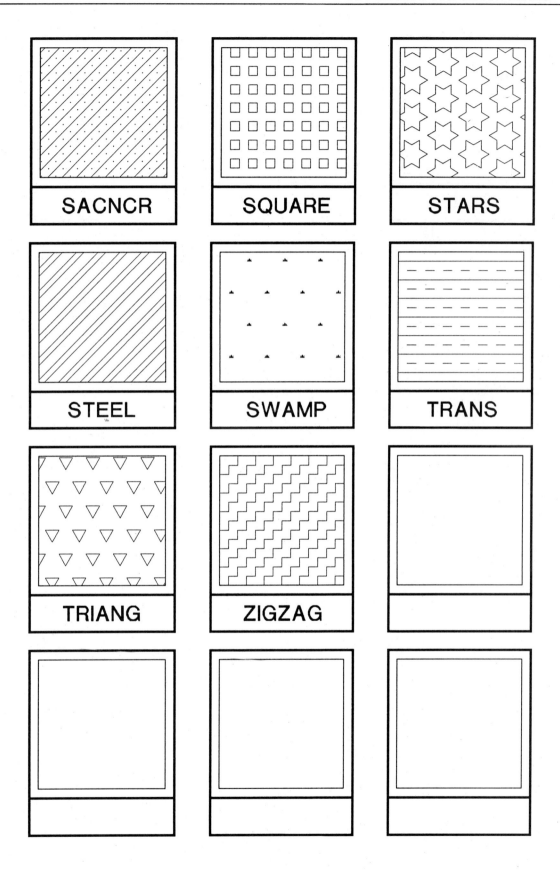

SACNCR

SQUARE

STARS

STEEL

SWAMP

TRANS

TRIANG

ZIGZAG

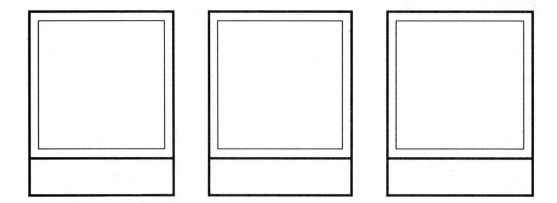

APPENDIX

J

Fonts

STANDARD TEXT FONTS

FAST FONTS

TXT   ABCDEFGHIJKLMNOPQRSTUVWXYZ 1234567890

MONOTXT   ABCDEFGHIJKLMNOPQRSTUVWXYZ 1234567890

SIMPLEX FONTS

ROMANS   ABCDEFGHIJKLMNOPQRSTUVWXYZ 1234567890

SCRIPTS   ABCDEFGHIJKLMNOPQRSTUVWXYZ 1234567890

GREEKS   ABXΔEΦΓHIϑKΛMNOΠΘΡΣΤΥΩΞΨZ 1234567890

DUPLEX FONTS

ROMAND   ABCDEFGHIJKLMNOPQRSTUVWXYZ 1234567890

COMPLEX FONTS

ROMANC   ABCDEFGHIJKLMNOPQRSTUVWXYZ 1234567890

ITALICC   ABCDEFGHIJKLMNOPQRSTUVWXYZ 1234567890

SCRIPTC   ABCDEFGHIJKLMNOPQRSTUVWXYZ 1234567890

GREEKC   ABXΔEΦΓHIϑKΛMNOΠΘΡΣΤΥΩΞΨZ 1234567890

TRIPLEX FONTS

ROMANT   ABCDEFGHIJKLMNOPQRSTUVWXYZ 1234567890

ITALICT   ABCDEFGHIJKLMNOPQRSTUVWXYZ 1234567890

STANDARD TEXT FONTS

GOTHIC FONTS

GOTHICE ABCDEFGHIJKLMNOPQRSTUVWXYZ 1234567890

GOTHICG ABCDEFGHIJKLMNOPQRSTUVWXYZ 1234567890

GOTHICI ABCDEFGHIJKLMNOPQRSTUVWXYZ 1234567890

SYMBOL FONTS

A B C D E F G H I J K L M N O P Q R S T U V W X Y Z
a b c d e f g h i j k l m n o p q r s t u v w x y z

SYASTRO

SYMAP

SYMATH

SYMETEO

SYMUSIC

APPENDIX

K

Linetypes

STANDARD LINETYPES

BORDER ────── ────── . ────── ────── . ────── . ──────
BORDER2 ────── ──── . ──── . ──── . ──── . ──── ──── .
BORDERX2 ──────── ──────── ──────── . ────────

CENTER ──────── ──── ──────── ──── ────────
CENTER2 ──── ─ ──── ──── ─ ──── ─ ──── ──── ─ ────
CENTERX2 ──────── ──── ──── ────────

DASHDOT ────── . ────── . ────── . ──────
DASHDOT2 ──── . ──── . ──── . ──── . ──── .
DASHDOTX2 ──────── . ──────── . ────────

DASHED ────── ────── ────── ────── ──────
DASHED2 ──── ──── ──── ──── ──── ──── ──── ──── ────
DASHEDX2 ──────── ──────── ──────── ────────

DIVIDE ────── . . ────── . . ────── . . ──────
DIVIDE2 ──── . . ──── . . ──── . . ──── . . ────
DIVIDEX2 ──────── . . ──────── . . ────────

DOT . . . .
DOT2 . . . .
DOTX2 . . . .

HIDDEN ── ── ── ── ── ── ── ── ── ── ── ── ── ──
HIDDEN2 ─
HIDDENX2 ──── ──── ──── . ──── ──── ──── ────

PHANTOM ────── ──── ── ── ────── ── ──
PHANTOM2 ──── ─ ─ ── ── ──── ── ── ────
PHANTOMX2 ──────── ──── ──── ────────

INDEX

Note: Entries to nontext material are in italics.